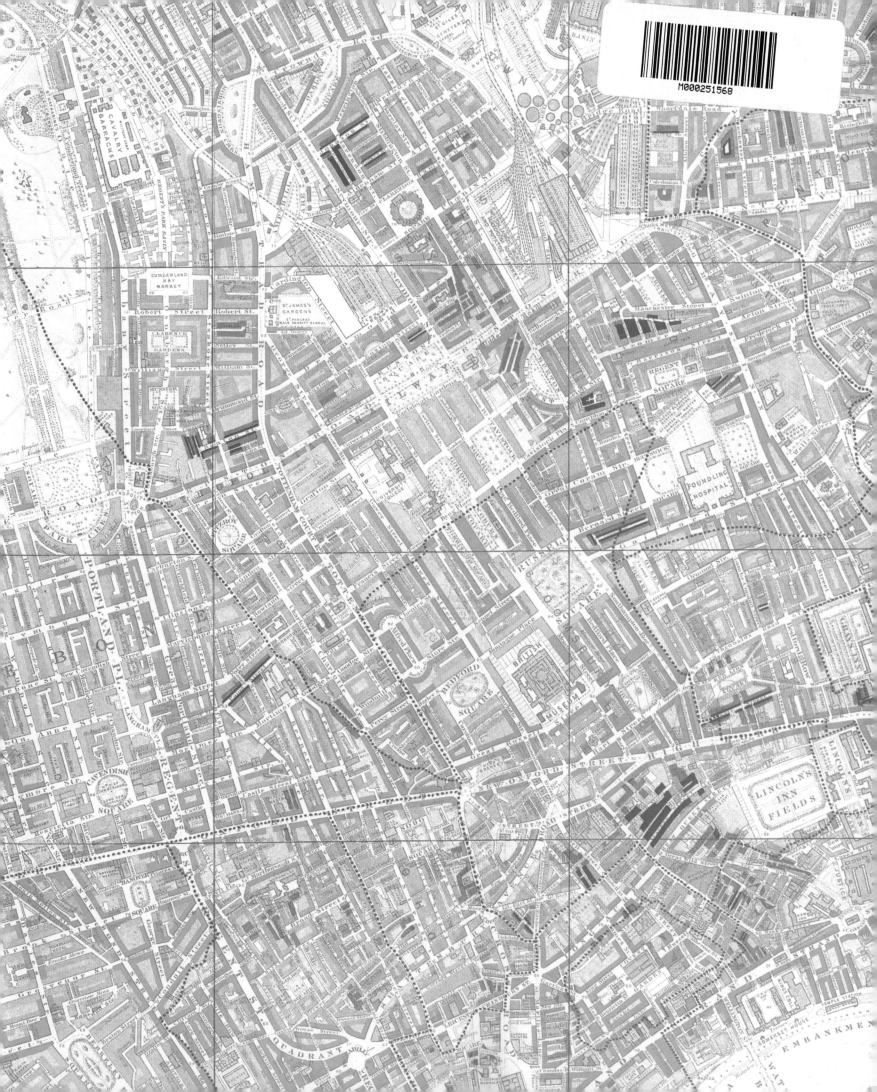

LOST LONDON
1870-1945

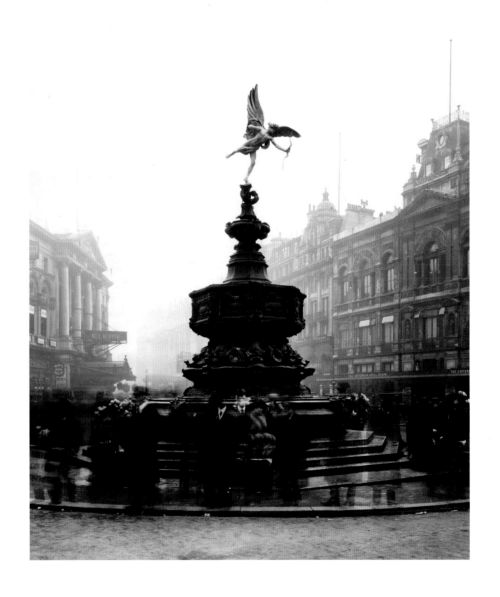

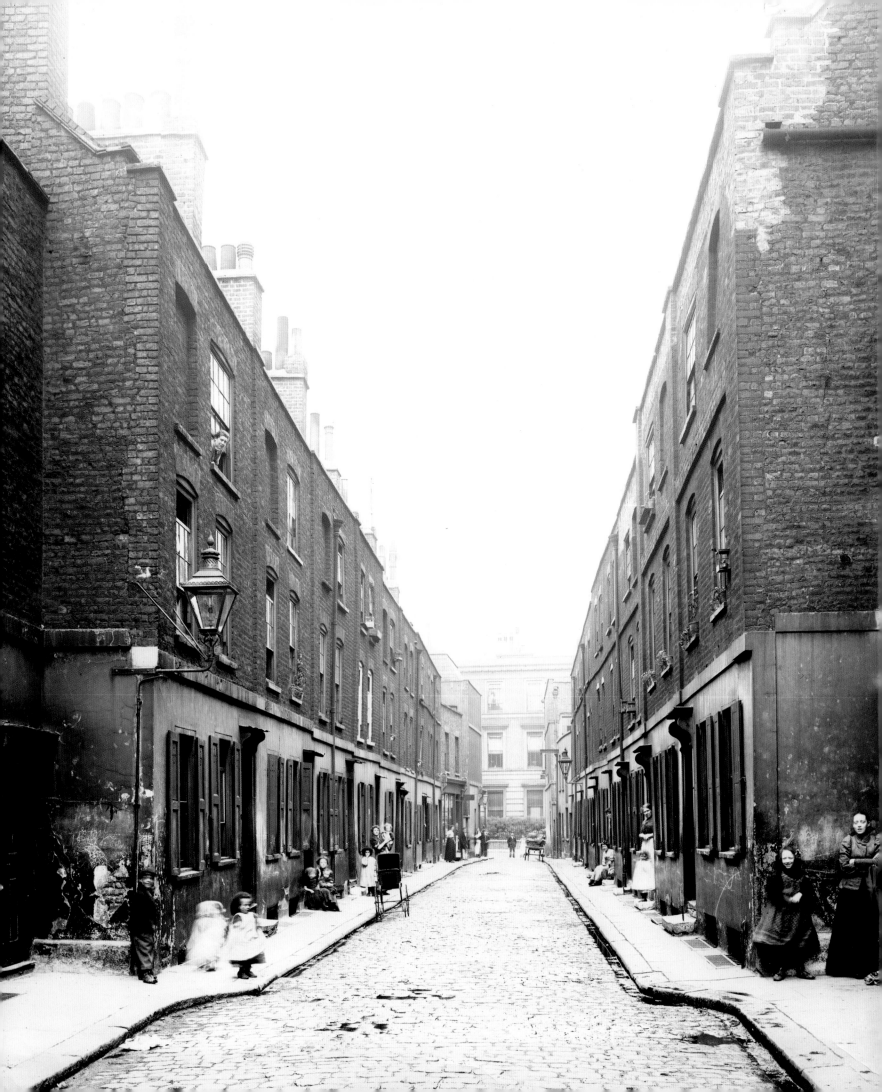

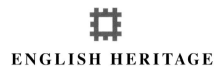

ENGLISH HERITAGE

LOST LONDON
1870-1945

Philip Davies

Foreword by
HRH The Duke of Gloucester

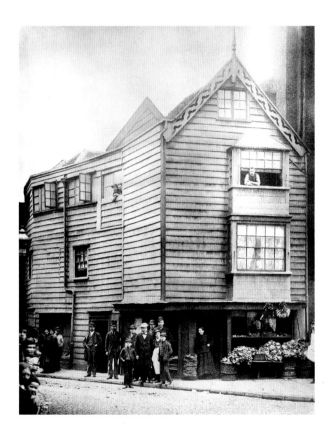

Trans
Atlantic
Press

This is a Transatlantic Press book
First published in 2009 by Transatlantic Press

38 Copthorne Road, Croxley Green

Hertfordshire, WD3 4AQ, UK.

© Transatlantic Press
Text copyright © Philip Davies
Photographs from English Heritage – see page 368

A catalogue record for this book is available from the British Library.

ISBN 978-0-9557949-8-8

Printed in China

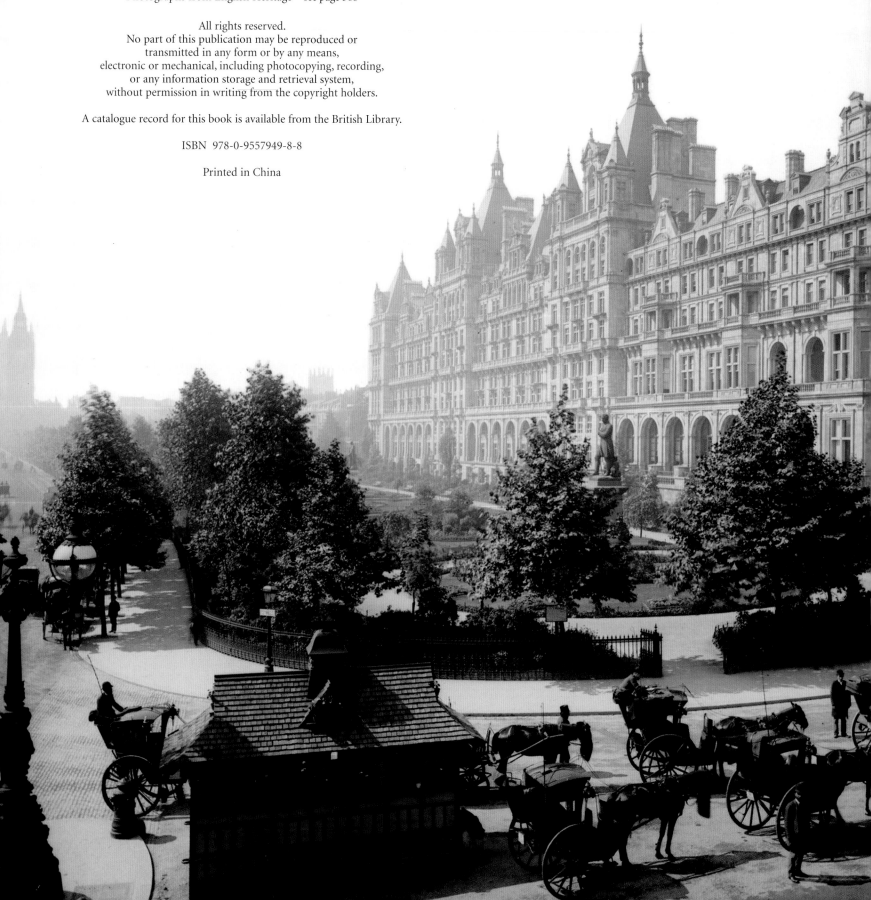

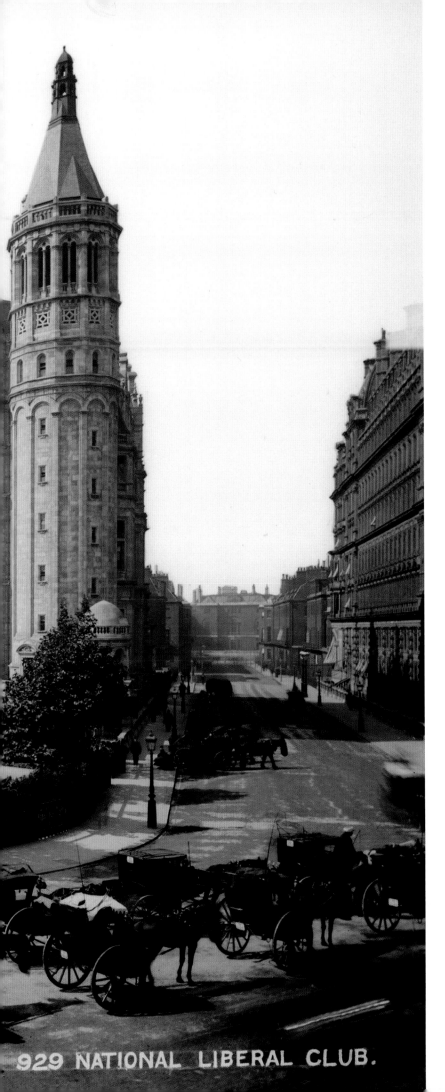

929 NATIONAL LIBERAL CLUB.

CONTENTS

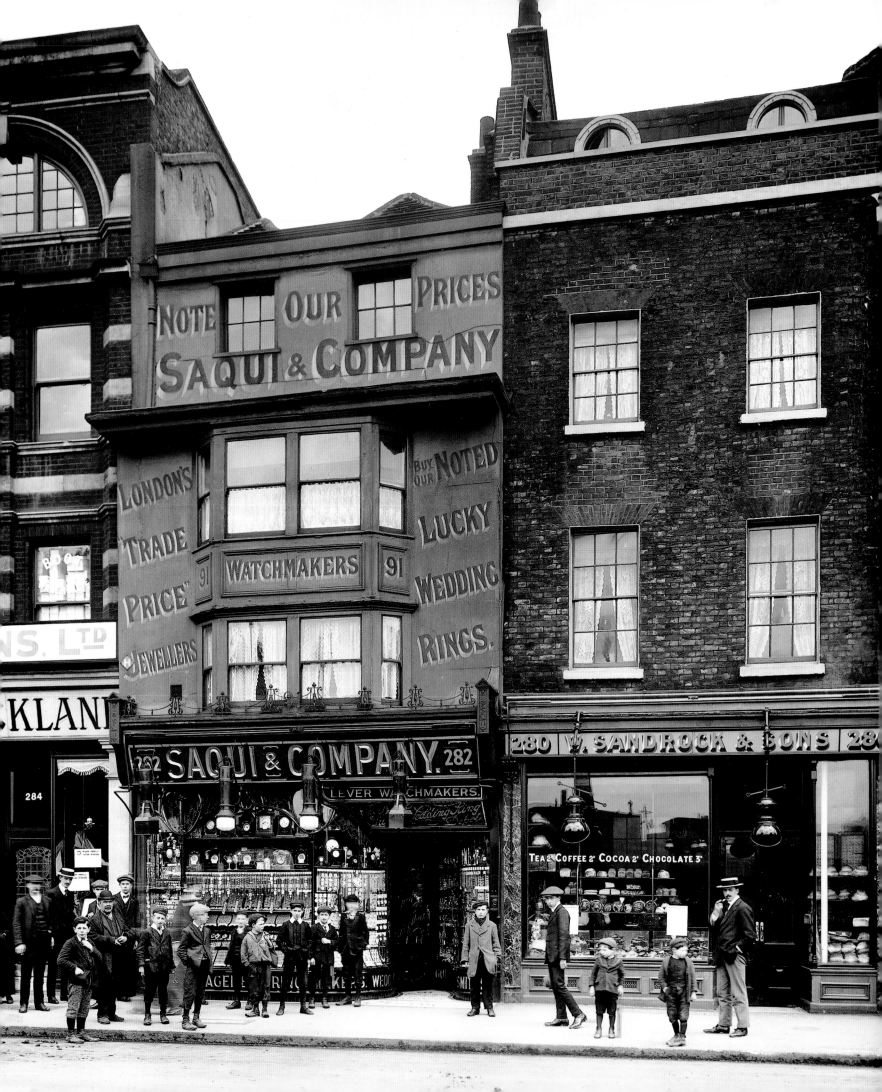

FOREWORD

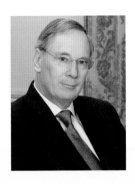

HRH The Duke of Gloucester

HRH The Duke of Gloucester KG GCVO

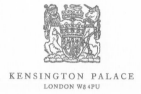

KENSINGTON PALACE
LONDON W8 4PU

London has been a vibrant and prosperous city for two thousand years and has always had the resources to build well. The consequence is large parts of the city have elegant, comfortable houses easily and effectively adapted to modern life. It wears its history well and is admired for its historic character.

As cities grow pressure is put on their older central buildings to adapt to new circumstances – over the centuries the consequence has been frequent re-development. To some, the new buildings represent prosperity and growth, to others these changes are a threat to their memories and a feeling that the history of their community is being buried by the oncoming new.

This book records some of the buildings which did not survive the process. The reader can judge whether the right decisions were taken about their replacement, although, of course, some of the destruction was a result of random Luftwaffe bombing.

Britain was at the forefront of 19th and 20th century technology, so it is not surprising that there is so much significant early photography. These photographs have been selected from an extensive archive held by English Heritage for the people of London. They record not only lost buildings, but also some survivors, with an expert commentary that reinforces our understanding of their past.

It is the task of English Heritage not only to preserve the best of our historic buildings, but also to demonstrate why they should be preserved and increase public understanding of their significance. This book does so magnificently. I hope many people will find insight not only about the buildings which have gone, but also the context of the historic buildings that we still enjoy today.

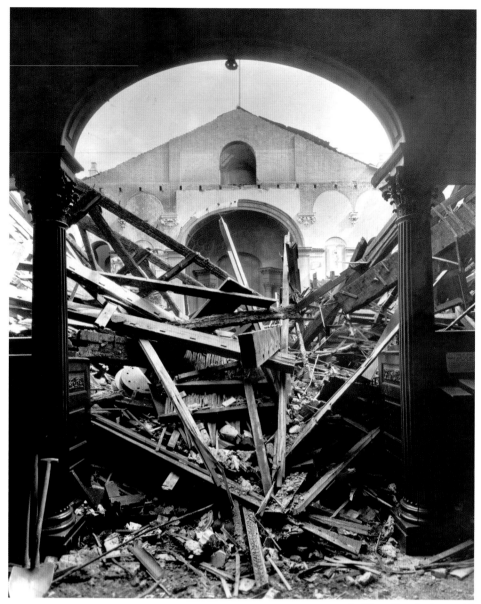

St Alfege Church, Greenwich

DEDICATION

For my parents, Hugh and Pearl, who were married as London burned on 7 September 1940, and for Rufus and Millie, who will witness the changes yet to come.

'In fine, we plead that the object of the work we have before us, is to make nobler and more humanely enjoyable the life of the great city whose existing record we seek to mark down; to preserve of it for her children and those yet to come whatever is best in her past and fairest in her present; to induce her municipalities to take the lead and to stimulate among her citizens that historic and social conscience which to all great communities is their most sacred possession'.

C R Ashbee
On behalf of the Committee for the Survey of London 1900

AUTHOR'S NOTE

The photographs in this book open windows on a vanished past; one which is tantalisingly familiar, but also hauntingly remote. Spanning a period of 75 years from the mid 1870s to 1945, they depict a world in transition – from the horse-drawn city of the late 19th century, through the inter-war years to the devastated streets and buildings of the wartime capital.

All the images are taken from the English Heritage archive of early London photographs inherited from the Greater London Council, and its predecessor, the London County Council. Most were taken as an historical record for the *Survey of London* as old buildings and streets were awaiting redevelopment. They have been selected to show the commonplace rather than the great set-pieces, though these are there too, but it is the commonplace which conveys so vividly the actual feel of London as it then was – the genius loci – that intangible spirit of place which resonates so evocatively across the decades. The selected photographs are a representative cross-section from the archive chosen to illustrate some of the major themes of the period, and organised in a loose geographical and chronological order to maintain a coherent narrative.

Old photographs have a truth and clarity to them which is lacking from architectural prints, drawings or paintings. Depicting people and places frozen in time, and at random moments of their existence, they convey a haunting message of mortality. As primary sources of historical evidence, they are by their very nature impartial, and bear witness to past places or events, undistorted by the interpretation of their creator. Unlike the artist, or draughtsman, ostensibly the camera never lies, so photographs provide a direct, tangible link to a long-distant past.

Captured here are the yards and alleys of Georgian and Victorian London at the dawn of the 20th century – the maze of streets around Drury Lane before the creation of Kingsway, Nash's Regent Street as it was being transformed into a monumental Imperial boulevard and the lost buildings and streets of Bankside, Bermondsey, Rotherhithe and Lambeth. As well as being important documents of social and topographical history, they are stunning images in their own right.

Each is a full plate photograph with a subtle patina of age, many suffused with rich sepia tones which convey remarkable levels of detail. The spectral figures of people and vehicles, which are the product of long exposure times, add to the haunting quality of the images. Figures stare at the camera, and, where they have moved, leave a ghostly trace on the plate. The arrival of the photographer seems to have been a notable event, particularly in the poorer districts, where neighbours assembled for poignant group portraits outside their houses. It is impossible not to speculate what happened to these people. What sort of lives did they lead? Who did they love? What were their hopes and dreams? How many were destined to die on the Western Front, or in the great influenza epidemic of 1920? So great have been the changes of the past century, yet they encompass but a single lifetime.

Perhaps most fascinating of all are the incidental details of everyday life – the chalk inscriptions on the alleyway walls, the clothes and hats, the advertisements, the horse-drawn vehicles and early motor cars; the shabbiness of wartime London and the extent of its devastation. Shopfronts with canvas apron blinds display myriad different wares, some of them startlingly familiar today. Entire buildings are covered in hand-painted signs, posters and enamel advertisements offering everything from patent medicines to ginger beer. Economic stability meant prices were constant, so the cost of goods and services was painted onto signboards, hoardings and shopfronts. Old wooden scaffolding and great baulks of raking timber shores can be seen propping up collapsing brick facades. The roofs of the houses are strung with telegraph poles and wires.

The street surfaces too vary – granite setts, wood block, rammed earth and tarmac punctuated by elegant street furniture – lamp columns, ornate bollards, street urinals, troughs and drinking fountains; and fire alarm pillars, which have now vanished completely, and, in the inter-war period, the first K2 telephone kiosks by Sir Giles Gilbert Scott, so successful that they became icons of British design. The innate sense of visual order which once characterised London seems a constant throughout. Even in the most unprepossessing areas, and during periods of major reconstruction, the footways and streets seem ordered and well-respected. The back alleys of Bankside and Stepney are paved with York stone and kept clean and free of municipal clutter.

In reviewing these photographs it is easy to lament the lost city of the past. There is no doubt that redevelopment and war fragmented London into a less interesting, less varied place, but the greatest change is perhaps the most intangible – the loss of the vibrant, spontaneous street life which once animated so many districts and which provided the human drama to which the buildings were but a backdrop.

Go where we may, rest where we will,
Eternal London haunts us still

Thomas Moore

INTRODUCTION

THE LOST CITY
Images of London 1870 – 1945

London was the first great metropolis of the industrial age. In 1800 it was a major European city of one million inhabitants. By 1911 it was the greatest city in the world – the first city of the British Empire with over seven million people – greater than the combined populations of Paris, Berlin, St Petersburg and Moscow. This phenomenal expansion was unique in Europe – both for the speed of its growth and the way in which it happened. Even today London remains unlike any other European city with its own distinctive form which is a direct result of its history.

London was never controlled by a single political or religious body able to guide the layout of its streets to one grand design. It was the largely-unplanned creation of a pluralist society driven by trade and commercial imperatives. In the aftermath of the Great Fire of 1666, the evanescent visions of Christopher Wren, Robert Hooke and John Evelyn evaporated like morning mist before the rising sun of commercial resurgence. London always was, and still remains, a city founded on commerce, flourishing today as a world centre for the trading of financial services.

London's expansion in the 18th and 19th centuries was driven by speculative development. Pragmatic contracts between wealthy landowners and opportunistic builders were regulated by the leasehold system; the former in search of long-term income, and the latter by the prospect of turning a quick profit.

Narrow timber-framed houses were the established building type in London before the Great Fire. The average twelve feet plot width was dictated by the maximum length of structural timber. A significant number of these houses survived the Fire well into the 20th century on the fringes of the City of London in Smithfield, Holborn, Aldgate and Borough, providing a very tangible link with the mediaeval past. Their distinctive gables and jettied upper storeys can be seen in the photographs, often heavily overlain by subsequent alterations. On the expiry of leases, it was quite common for such houses to be encased in brick, or given a polite facade, rather than completely redeveloped; many London houses, whilst ostensibly similar, embraced much older structures and interiors beneath – individual metaphors for the city as a whole.

In the wake of the Great Fire, various London Building Acts were passed – in 1667, 1707 and 1709 – specifying common standards of construction. Increasingly, brick replaced timber for external use which facilitated much greater external uniformity. The earliest surviving example of a row of matching London town houses can be found at Nos 52-55 Newington Green. Built in 1658, they pre-date the Fire, but in the reconstruction of London after 1666, the brick terrace became the established urban form creating a key component of what made London unique as a European city.

Nicholas Barbon (d 1698), a financier, builder and adventurer, refined the system of speculative leasehold development through which much of Georgian and Victorian London was built. Various builders undertook to construct small numbers of houses within a particular development, often overseen by the landowner or his agent. In order to ensure consistency, the row of uniformly-designed houses evolved and became fashionable. This form of housing was remarkably versatile, providing flexible accommodation for a whole variety of uses – houses, taverns, offices, shops and workshops – usually with a private rear yard, or garden. Short rows of terraced housing were built in central and inner London, but also as ribbon development in outlying areas along the main roads such as Mile End, Chiswick, Tottenham and Peckham.

Often minor variations in window heights or parapet levels marked the work of each builder, but the overall aspiration was greater uniformity. In the first half of the 18th century this trend towards understated regularity was reinforced by the Palladian revival. Carved doorcases and other elaborate sculptural enrichment were eschewed in favour of external sobriety and abstract qualities of proportion.

In 1774 the Building Acts were consolidated into a new London Building Act which specified different 'rates' of houses. This dictated the form and design of much of London for over a century and created the city which can be seen in these photographs. The floor area set the rate, which in turn determined the thickness of the principal walls. Like industrial products, a family of building types emerged – from the highest first rate house with a five bay frontage and a linked mews building to the modest fifth rate dwelling just one room deep.

Much of Georgian and early Victorian London owes its remarkable unity to the increasingly standardised approach to elevations drawn up by estate surveyors. This is why 18th and 19th century housing looks so similar in areas as diverse as Camberwell, Bloomsbury and Bow. The serial construction of whole neighbourhoods of planned streets and squares on the private landed estates of central and inner London was a process of continuous refinement, and it created a distinctive city completely unlike anything else in Europe. "*While the Continental architect considered it his task to make the fronts of the building as imaginative as possible, the English endeavoured to let them express what had to be said in the simplest and most concise way*".[1] Nevertheless, these plain, understated exteriors often concealed lavish interiors with elaborate ornamental plasterwork and joinery, such as the inside of 1 Bedford Square.

One of the unique characteristics of this city was, and still remains, the London square. Terraces of individual houses, each subordinated to the wider composition, were set around a communal garden area enclosed by railings for the private enjoyment of surrounding residents. By 1900 there were over 460 across the capital. As well as providing much needed oases of green space, they created a highly distinctive urban grain which imparted a unity to the city as a whole and linked the wealthiest with the poorest districts.

But there was another much more subtle reason for the remarkable cohesion of Georgian and early Victorian London, long since forgotten; a secret ingredient which conferred an innate harmony on the city, and which influenced everything from the layout of an entire neighbourhood to the size of a window pane – the Imperial system of measures.

Neighbourhoods were laid out by surveyors who used acres, furlongs, rods and chains – measurements which had been in common usage for marking out arable land since the 9th century. An acre was the length of a furlong (or furrow's length), 660ft, and its width was one chain, 66ft. For shorter lengths a perch, a pole or a rod were used. There were four rods to one chain. A London workman's house had a frontage of one rod or 16ft 6inches. In East London one chain corresponded to four house frontages, so entire districts were created based on endogenous proportional relationships. The builders used rules divided into feet and inches, or fathoms (the length of outstretched arms), which meant that the actual proportions deployed for the construction of public spaces, houses and their internal furnishings were derived directly from the human form, which accounts for their inherent unity. Covent Garden, for instance, was laid out as 6 x 5 chains and Belgrave Square as 10 x 10 chains, or 10 acres.

Thus the late Georgian/early Victorian city was infused by a common system of harmonious proportions from the layout of an entire area to the pattern of its paving. Much of the subsequent development of London saw the fragmentation of this unified whole – with the coming of the railways, road widening, metropolitan improvements and the construction of larger buildings on aggregated plots for a whole variety of new uses. Nevertheless a great deal of this urban backcloth still remains in areas like Islington, Bloomsbury, Hackney, Camberwell and Lambeth.

As London expanded relentlessly outwards from its bi-polar centres in the City of London and Westminster, it embraced and later subsumed older village cores and outlying areas, many of which retained rural and

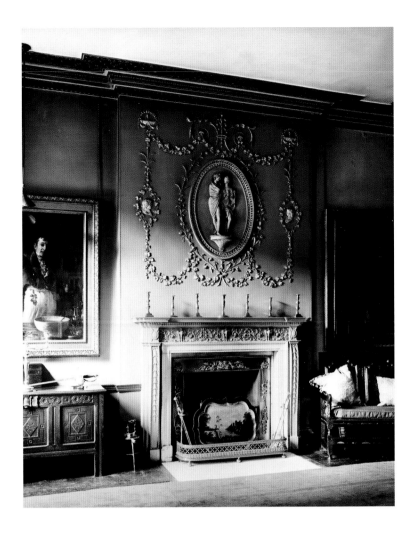

1 Bedford Square, Bloomsbury: 1 July 1913.
Ground floor rear room. The plain exterior of the London terrace house often concealed ornate, enriched interiors.

vernacular buildings. The astonishing pictures of Homestall Farm in Peckham Rye on page 283 depict a rural idyll, which remained well into the 20th century, whilst Rotherhithe, with its weatherboarded cottages (pp 264-267), had a greater affinity with the fishing villages of the Thames Estuary than the great maw of London.

Contrary to popular perceptions, timber remained common for smaller Georgian houses until well into the mid-18th century, particularly near the river where there was a ready supply of timber from the wharves and warehouses serving the Baltic and North American trade. Sometimes this was concealed behind brick facades, but often houses were fully weatherboarded. Rare today, many survived into the 20th century, as can be discerned in the photographs of Bermondsey, Rotherhithe, Lambeth and Limehouse. In these outlying areas, there was a creative intermingling of the urban tradition of 'polite' architecture with long-established rural vernacular traditions, which reached into town from the east along the river and from the surrounding Home Counties.

In the poorer areas, away from estate control, development pressures were intense as speculative builders vied to cram as many fifth rate dwellings into as small a space as possible. The result was the sort of housing which can be seen at Bankside on pages 256-258 and across many parts of the East End with families densely packed into tight networks of sunless courts and blind alleys, sharing communal privies with a single tap or pump providing (frequently contaminated) water for an entire parish. A handful of the more fortunate lived in charitable almshouses erected by City livery companies, or local parishes for the deserving poor, such as the Esther Hawes Almshouses in Bow on page 229.

In the mid-19th century urban life was a nightmare for the poorer classes. Until the "Sanitary Idea" promoted by reformers such as Edwin Chadwick and Southwood Smith began to make headway in the 1850s, the concept of environmental health was as alien to Victorian minds as the connection between dirt and disease. Cholera was thought to be a miasmatic vapour transmitted by foul air. Dustheaps and middens the size of four-storey houses attracted scavengers or 'bunters' who made a living from reclaiming anything of value. The largest, a huge dustheap at King's Cross, was the setting for Noddy Boffin's business in Dickens' *Our Mutual Friend*.

At Letts Wharf (seen on page 248 fifty years later), bands of women once stood up to their waists in filth, breathing foul air mixed with emissions of methane, sifting refuse for anything which might have a recyclable value. Oyster shells, for instance, were sold to builders for insulation between floors, and old shoes to manufacturers of Prussian blue dye.

Scrap merchants and dealers in second-hand paper, clothes, rags, metals and furniture were commonplace. Bartholomew Close and Cloth Fair specialised in second-hand rags and textiles (pp 48-49). Similar dealers can be seen in Sheffield Street (p 135) and Drury Court (p 121), whilst picturesque Holywell Street (p 117), was the centre of the capital's trade in second-hand books and pornography.

A very lucrative trade operated in architectural salvage. Harding-ham's in Petty France (p 299) was typical of many local outlets. As old buildings and areas were swept away, chimneypieces, doorcases, staircases and panelling were auctioned. At Savage Gardens (p 68) a single carved porch fetched £145, equivalent to £7,500 at current values. Sometimes particularly important pieces were salvaged and reused in new buildings on the site. At Whitehall Gardens entire rooms were dismantled from Pembroke House (p 173) and Cromwell House and installed in the new Air Ministry. When Dorchester House (p 302) was demolished in 1929 over 20,000 tons of material was dismantled and sold in just seven weeks, although the magnificent marble staircase which originally had cost over £30,000 fetched a mere £273, finally ending up in Dallas in 1965. Several of the best chimney pieces were acquired by the Walker Art Gallery in Liverpool and the Victoria & Albert Museum in London.

By 1900, after 50 years of metropolitan improvements and sanitary

Right: Poster advertising the sale of items from Savage Gardens. A lucrative trade operated in architectural salvage. High prices could be obtained for the best items.

reform some of the worst nuisances of the previous decades had been addressed, but poverty was still endemic and life expectancy much lower for the indigent poor. In 1850 in London the average life expectancy at birth was 38 compared with the national average of 41. By 1890 it had risen to 44 compared with 46 nationally, but these figures concealed terrible differentials. In 1900 a person in the West End had twice the life expectancy of a person in the East End. The average age at death in the West End was 55. In the East End it was 30.

Childhood mortality rates were even more shocking. In the West End 18% of children died before the age of 5; in the East End 55%. In some streets, Jack London noted *"out of every hundred children born in a year, fifty-five die before they are five years old"*. [2]

Rather than uniting London, the river was always a great divide. To pass over London Bridge was to cross a natural dividing line of peoples. South London, or London-over-the-Water as it was known, was an alien land. Subordinate to the Cities of London and Westminster, it was relatively isolated until the construction of new bridges in the early 19th century opened up new areas for development beyond the ancient centres of Borough and Lambeth. This was London's service area lined with a chaotic jumble of wharves, warehouses and noxious industries (pp 247-248); dark canyons separated by slit-like alleys leading to river stairs and jetties. Many, such as those in Shad Thames, Bermondsey and Rotherhithe, still survive converted into stylish loft apartments,

By Order of the PORT OF LONDON AUTHORITY.

CATALOGUE

OF THE ANTIQUE

Fixtures and Fittings

COMPRISING

"WREN" WOOD DOORWAYS,

Corinthian Portico, Doric and Ionic Doorways,

With 8 and 10-panel Doors and Original Door Furniture,

Early 18th Century Carved Staircases,

Original " Adam " and other Mantels,

Early 18th Century Mantels and Overdoors, Sculptured Marble Mantel, Old Iron Railings, &c.,

In the various Buildings in Trinity Square, Crutched Friars, Seething Lane and Savage Gardens, now about to be demolished in order to clear the site for the new Offices of the Port of London Authority,

Which will be Sold by Auction by Messrs.

FULLER, HORSEY, SONS & CASSELL

At No. 10, TRINITY SQUARE, E.C.,

On FRIDAY, JANUARY 31st, 1913,

At Twelve o'clock precisely.

May be viewed from 9 a.m. to 1 p.m. and from 2 to 4 p.m. by orders to be obtained of **Messrs. FULLER, HORSEY, SONS & CASSELL, 11, Billiter Square, London, E.C.; and 100, King Street, Manchester.**

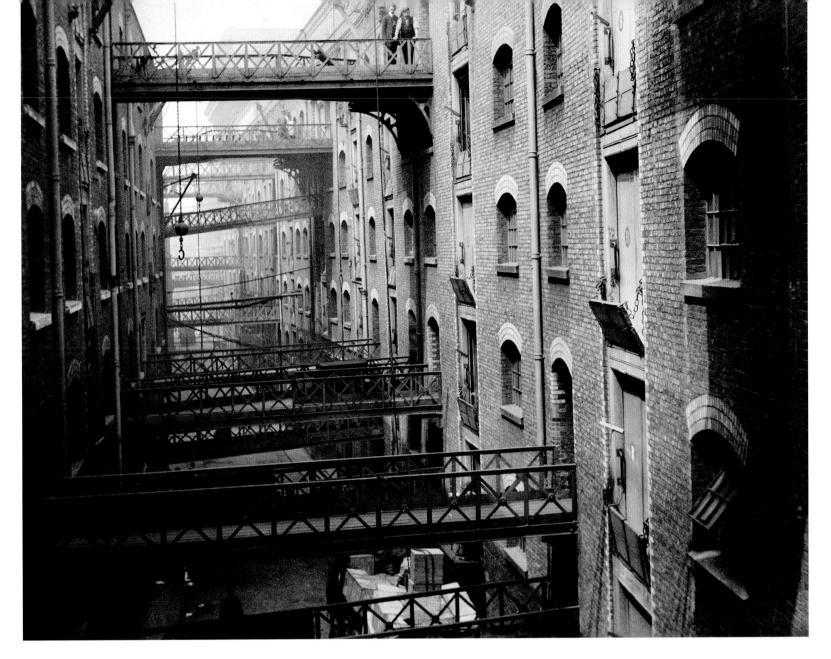

Shad Thames, c 1910.

Much of the river was lined by vertiginous warehouses creating dark canyons separated by slit-like alleys leading to ancient stairs, jetties and wharves. At Shad Thames a myriad of iron bridges spanned the street to allow goods to be moved across the walkways to warehouses inland.

demonstrating the innate versatility and sustainability of so much of London's historic fabric. Particular areas were distinguished by their smells. Bermondsey, for instance, was rank with the smell of leather tanning, breweries and vinegar vats.

The polycentric nature of London's urban villages and neighbourhoods gave rise to fierce tribal loyalties that persist to this day. Moving across the Euston Road from Somers Town to Bloomsbury was referred to as "*crossing the River Jordan*". Current teenage gang culture is simply the latest manifestation of such deep-seated territorial identity.

In 1902, Charles Booth completed his magisterial 17-volume work, *The Life and Labour of the People in London*, one of the most comprehensive surveys of the social stratification of the capital ever carried out.

Originally intended to disprove socialist claims that a quarter of Londoners lived in poverty, what it revealed was infinitely worse. The highest concentration of poverty in London – 68% – could be found south of the river in the area between Blackfriars and London Bridge, followed by Greenwich with 65%. The worst social conditions – both moral as well as physical – were directly linked to the actual plan and grain of a district. Where streets were cut short, so as not to go through an area, there was a tendency to the worst extremes of deprivation. He noted that "*immediately about St George's Church and on all sides of it lie nests of courts and alleys, yielding in places to improvements … but still harbouring an appalling amount of destitution not unmixed with crime, and in this respect maintaining only too well the historic character of the Borough*". [3]

This was London unexplored. He went on to add, "*These places are indicated very imperfectly on the map, as their narrowness and intricacy defies reproduction on any but the largest scale. Among these courts, close behind the church, was the Marshalsea prison, of which some part remains standing*". [4]

Typical of this maze of streets and blind alleys was the area around Bankside photographed in 1903 for clearance for a new Thames bridge (pp 256-258). Marshalsea Prison, where Dickens visited his own father and family in his formative years, and later the scene of *Little Dorrit*, can be seen just prior to its disposal and demolition (pp 254-255).

Maypole Alley and the tenements to the west of Borough High Street were notorious. In 1894 *The Standard* wrote of "*wretched remains of dingy structures connected with the main street by tunnel-shaped entries*".[5] Booth's inspector, George Duckworth, visited the worst spot in nearby Redcross Place on 17 May 1899 and noted: "*Notorious women's lodging house at the north-east end …. Hardly a whole pane of glass in any window of houses on the south side. A row of stables runs down the centre …. Stableyard used as dumping ground for house refuse and full of manure, bread, bones, rotting oranges, brickbats …. Women decoys at entrance to High Street … Many evil faces at the windows, but nothing happened. Police don't go down here unless they have to and never singly.*"[6]

The mark of poverty was stamped indelibly on both the people and the houses. It can be seen here in the faces of the people who bear mute testimony to lives of hard unremitting grind (pp 256-257). Booth noted that "*with the people it is the children who mark the greatest contrast, and then the women; the appearance of the men is less affected by poverty. With the houses it is … the windows and doors that tell the tale. The windows are cracked and patched, and are imperfectly screened by dirty and ragged blinds stretched across, or by falling curtains of the very commonest description … But more than all else, the brickwork round about each door carries the stamp of poverty. The surface of each brick by the rubbing of arms and shoulders takes a black polish.*"[7]

This stamp of poverty affected entire areas. Bird fanciers were to be found close to the poorest neighbourhoods. "*Fried fish, and still more stewed eel shops commonly mark the vicinity of great poverty, and a catsmeat shop is seldom far removed from it. The cats themselves may be taken as a last test. People are poor indeed whose cat looks starved.*"[8]

This bleak harsh world can be seen in these photographs. What is so remarkable is the persistence of poverty in the same areas over generations. In spite of the massive social changes of the past century, many of the areas of greatest deprivation in London remain the same as those identified by Booth over 100 years ago, which in turn reflect much older evils. It is not uncommon to find recurrent patterns of activity emerging, submerging and re-emerging over time in the same places – what Peter Ackroyd has described as "*chronological resonances*", which haunt the history of London.

Given this first-hand evidence, what is so striking in the photographs is the apparent cleanliness of the alleys, courts and streets of even the poorest quarters. This is in marked contrast to the buildings which, even when new, looked tired and shabby – encrusted with soot from the all-pervasive Newcastle coal which blew eastwards across the capital with the prevailing winds and rapidly coated everything in thick black grime. London was commonly referred to as The Smoke, whilst the ubiquitous

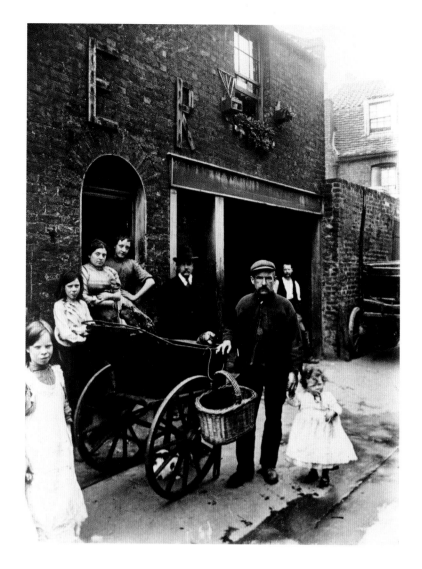

The cats' meat man, c 1902.

Once a familiar sight in the poorer districts of London, many a poor wife resorted to discarded meat or offal to feed her unsuspecting family. The house in the background is emblazoned with ER to celebrate the coronation of Edward VII.

use of coal fires generated the pea-souper fogs for which London was notorious, captured so vividly on page 163 at mid-day in Trafalgar Square in 1913.

Many foreign visitors were fascinated by the ethereal romanticism of such London 'particulars', as they were known. Whistler revealed London as a city of fugitive, mysterious beauty. Chiang Yee, a Chinese visitor devoted an entire chapter to fog in his book *The Silent Traveller in London*. He concluded: "*To be sure, a part of all human action should be hidden under a cover such as fog, so that it might be visible and invisible at once, and I think that is why London has a particular beauty, perhaps more than any other city in the world*".[9] *Punch* was less forgiving:

"You clothe the City in such gloom,
We scarce can see across the street,
You seem to penetrate each room,
And mix with everything I eat".[10]

Pea-soupers are now a thing of the past, eliminated by the Clean Air Act 1956, although environmental pollution still hangs over London in the equally-insidious form of photochemical smog.

In the 1890s Charles Booth calculated that more than 30% of Londoners – 1,800,000 – were living below the poverty line. Irregular earnings accounted for 68%, circumstances such as large families and illness 19%, and drunkenness and thriftlessness about 13%. A further 1,000,000 lived with just a week's wages between respectability and pauperism. 21% of the entire population were dependent on the parish for relief. 1 in 4 died on public charity, ie in the workhouse, hospital or lunatic asylum. During the golden age of Edwardian England, 939 people out of every 1,000 in Britain died in poverty.

In the late 1890s London's East End was referred to commonly as "*the city of dreadful night*", "*a modern Babylon*" inhabited by "*people of the abyss*", constantly teetering on the brink of riot or social breakdown. "*East London lay hidden from view behind a curtain on which were painted terrible pictures: starving children, suffering women, overworked men; horrors of drunkenness and vice; monsters and demons of inhumanity; giants of disease and despair.*"[11] This was the London stalked by Jack the Ripper – a maze of squalid streets and alleys where for many life was dominated entirely by the daily search for food and shelter.

Even for those in work life was precariously balanced. An outward image of respectability was crucial for survival, which is why even the poorest often pooled resources to share a bonnet or boots. Unpunctuality could mean dismissal, so those working unsocial hours often paid a knocker-up. Illness or accident could condemn a family to instant homelessness and destitution; one workman in eight was disabled for at least three to four weeks. Many industrial jobs were lethal. White-lead works were a living death sentence – the early sign of lead poisoning being a blue line along the gums which presaged an excruciating death from epileptic convulsions.

Many of the gaunt faces seen staring at the camera in these photographs in the slums of Whitechapel, Limehouse or Bankside lived just such a pitiful existence as sweated labour or industrial fodder. Harriet Walker, for example, was a young girl employed as an enamelled ware brusher where lead poisoning was common. Her father and brother were both out of employment. To support her family, she concealed her illness, walked six miles a day to and from work, earned seven or eight shillings a week, and died at seventeen.[12]

All too often the Victorian underclass was equated with moral laxity. These perceptions, fuelled by ignorance and prejudice, were a direct result of the size and complexity of London. Middle class residents lived in their own neighbourhoods in polite terraces, garden squares or suburbs, but casual workers were forced to live close to their places of work in the inner city ring of neighbourhoods, often in pre-Victorian houses which had descended into lodging houses, tenements and slums.

Living conditions for the poor were a shocking reproach to Edwardian England. Some of the worst slums in London could be found less than 500

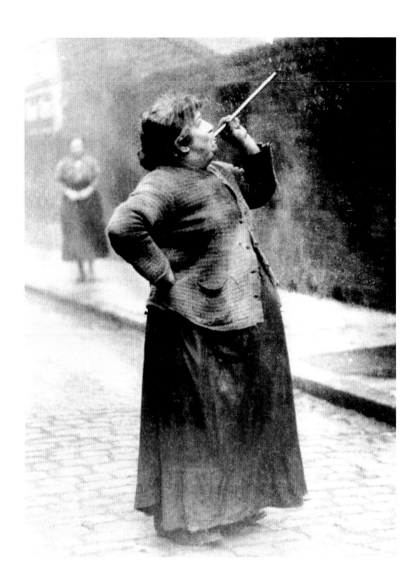

A knocker-up: Mrs Mary Smith of Brenton Street, Limehouse Fields, was paid sixpence a week to shoot dried peas at the windows of market workers who had to get up for work in the early hours of the morning.

yards from the gates of the Palace of Westminster in places like Parker Street (p 180) or Grubb Street in Pimlico (p 189). Weekly renting was the norm. 90% of the poor had no home they could call their own beyond the end of the week. Often rooms were occupied on a relay system with two or three tenants each occupying the same bed for 8 hours with the space underneath let on a similar basis. In one instance, in a room with a capacity of 1,000 cu ft, three adult women were found in a single bed with two more beneath it.

For malnourished, overcrowded families, the death of a child could be a merciful release. "*When a child dies … the body is laid out in the same room. And if they are very poor, it is kept for some time until they can bury it. During the day it lies on the bed, during the night, when the living take the bed, the dead occupies the table, from which in the morning, when the dead is put back in to the bed, they eat their breakfast. Sometimes the body is placed on the shelf which serves as a pantry for their food.*"[13]

300,000 people lived in one-room tenements and over 900,000 were housed in illegal lodging houses or doss houses. Lodging houses were

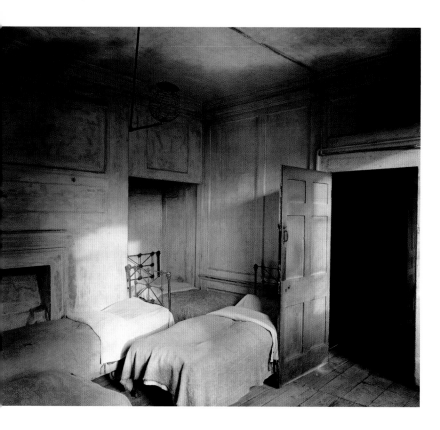

The Old Farm House, Southwark, was a respectable lodging-house, but it epitomised the conditions in which over 1.2 million Londoners were housed. Many illegal doss houses were rife with vermin and often little more than brothels.

regulated and inspected. Their owners were required to register their names and addresses, allow regular police inspections, cleanse the premises, limewash the walls and ceilings twice a year, and give immediate notice of the outbreak of infectious diseases. Such limewashed interiors can be seen clearly in the Old Farm House, Southwark (p 252-253) and at Bow Road (p 234). Both were respectable establishments.

William Henry Davies, the tramp-poet, recalled life at the Old Farm House: "*What a strange house was this, so full of quaint chambers*" One unusually clever man "*disappointed at his circumstances … would sit on his bed and try to throttle himself, night after night; and then would smother his face in his bedclothes and invariably end his mad fit by sobbing … I felt like standing to his side, before the outraged face of his Maker, so great was my pity for him.*"

Howard Goldsmid stayed at a less salubrious doss house nearby in a room shared with seven others and wrote: "*It was not, however, too dark to see the insects of one sort and another which were crawling over the beds in all directions*".[14] Parodying Thomas Hood, he recalled:

> "A monster there dwelt, whom I came to know
> By the name of the Cannibal Flea
> And the brute was possessed with no other thought
> Than to live – and to live on me"

"*As the night drew on the smell became intolerable … increased … by the effluvium proceeding from these necessary utensils … the contents of which were occasionally knocked over and slopped about the floor. It was horrible …*"[15] The image to the left vividly conveys just such a scene.

For many of the middle classes, the poorer districts of London were quite simply a foreign country where it was best not to go. For his book *People of the Abyss* the American writer Jack London resolved to visit London's East End in 1903. Such was the separation between the classes and between the East End and polite society that the police believed that he intended to commit some bizarre form of suicide. He sought advice from Thomas Cook & Son, who with ease and celerity would have transported him to Darkest Africa or innermost Tibet, but they were utterly unable to help him on the grounds that his enterprise was too 'unusual'.

What he discovered both fascinated and appalled him. On the evening of 20 August 1902 he accompanied two skilled men – a carter and a carpenter – in their search for a bed. They had not slept for three and five days respectively and, apart from crusts, had not eaten during the same periods. London noted that their eyes never left the pavement:

> "*From the slimy, spittle-drenched sidewalk, they were picking up bits of orange peel, apple skins and grape stems, and they were eating them. The pits of greengage plums they cracked between their teeth for the kernels inside. They picked up stray crumbs of bread the size of peas, apple cores … black and dirty …. and these things, these two men took into their mouths, and chewed them, and swallowed them … their guts a-reek with pavement offal … and this … in the heart of the greatest, wealthiest, and most powerful empire the world has ever seen.*"[16]

The destitute were often worse off. Unable to find a bed, churchyards and burial grounds provided outdoor dormitories for the homeless and sleepless. In 'Itchy Park' in the shadow of Christ Church, Spitalfields, Jack London: "*saw a sight I never wish to see again*".

At three o'clock in the afternoon,

> "*on the benches on either side arrayed a mass of miserable and distorted humanity, the sight of which would have impelled Doré to more diabolical flights of fancy than he ever succeeded in achieving. It was a welter of rags and filth, of all manner of loathsome skin diseases, open sores, bruises, grossness, indecency, leering monstrosities and bestial faces. A chill, raw, wind was blowing, and these creatures huddled there in their rags, sleeping for the most part, or trying to sleep. Here were a dozen women ranging in age from twenty years to seventy. Next, a babe, possibly of nine months, lying asleep, flat on the hard bench with neither pillow or covering, nor with anyone looking after it … Further on, a man, his clothing caked with gutter mud, asleep, with head in the lap of a woman, not more than twenty-five years old, and also asleep.*"[17]

Such scenes were commonplace in the poorer quarters of London as armies of men and women tramped the streets in search of work or a bed for the night in the workhouse casual wards. Women were acutely vulnerable. Prostitution was commonplace as women sought to find 4d for a night's lodgings; the origin of the sexual euphemism "a four-penny one". In many of the poorest areas there was little distinction between common lodging houses and brothels.

By 1900, thirty years after the opening of the first Barnardo orphanage in 1870, the scale of juvenile delinquency had begun to decline, but it was still commonplace for thousands of destitute children to sleep on the streets at night.

For the outcast poor, who lived on the streets, and the semi-criminal gangs of pickpockets who had exclusive rights to certain areas, there was an ancient custom of marking or inscribing walls or pavements with chalk marks to communicate to others working the areas in a comprehensible, but semi-secret code. Chalk markings can be seen in many of the photographs, mostly simple children's games.

For those who gaze at the past depicted in these photographs with wistful nostalgia, it is as well to remember the human misery and degradation which lay just beneath the surface. The poorest areas were also where new arrivals gravitated. London has always thrived by being an open, if not always tolerant city, and for centuries it was the major port of entry for immigrants seeking refuge from persecution in Europe and elsewhere. In the 1650s Cromwell had allowed persecuted Jews to return to London. Sephardic Jews settled in Whitechapel followed later by Ashkenazi Jews from central Europe. Located on the eastern edge of the city, they could operate without interference from the City Guilds and Livery companies.

With the Revocation of the Edict of Nantes in 1685, large numbers of Huguenots had fled to London from France. In the houses and garrets of the newly-completed terraces of Spitalfields and Bethnal Green, they set up a silk-weaving industry which continued well into the 20th century (p 57). Soho became known as "Little France" for the sheer number of craft workshops set up by émigré Huguenots. A surviving example can be seen in Archer Street on (p 211) where spinning was still active in 1896.

As London's population exploded in the 19th century, it attracted large numbers of economic migrants. Those from other English regions usually went into domestic service or worked as skilled artisans, but those from overseas took the worst jobs – in tailoring and shoemaking sweatshops, or as casual labourers. Of necessity, they congregated in some of the poorest districts of inner London.

By 1861 there were an estimated 178,000 Irish in London – 1 in 20 of all Londoners. Concentrated in the rookeries of St Giles (known as Little Dublin), Holborn and Southwark, they lived in appalling poverty. By 1900 Clare Market, Macklin Street, Drury Lane and its hinterland enjoyed a particularly unwholesome reputation. The streets and alleys swept away for the construction of Kingsway (pp 108-130) were typical of the crowded insanitary conditions into which the many were still crammed half a century later.

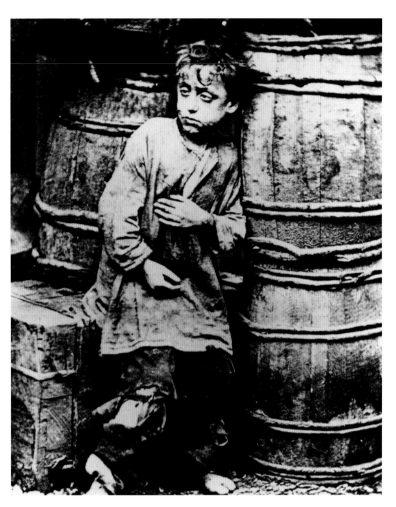

A typical street arab, c 1890. By the time of his death in 1905, Dr Barnardo had saved over 60,000 destitute children from appalling squalor, vice and degradation, and conditions for homeless children had been transformed.

The assassination of Czar Alexander II in 1881 triggered further mass Jewish immigration from Poland and Russia, as Jews fled westward from anti-Semitic pogroms. The scale and speed of this took the authorities by surprise, and was resented by many Jewish elders who had worked hard to assimilate older Jewish communities inconspicuously into London life. In the 1890s six ships a week arrived from the Baltic.

Fleeced by swindlers, thieves and muggers, many arrived off the boats in a totally wretched condition. Watching their arrival Beatrice Webb openly wept at the derision heaped on these poverty-stricken arrivals. "*In another ten minutes eighty of the hundred evacuees are dispersed in the back of slums of Whitechapel; in another few days the majority of these, robbed of the little they possess, are turned out of the lodgings destitute and friendless.*"[18]

For many new arrivals, London was a hard, unyielding place, but for those who made it, it offered both the freedom and the opportunity to build new lives. By 1914 there were over 140,000 Jews in London. Whitechapel became a Jewish 'ghetto' with shuls, mikvahs, libraries, soup kitchens, ritual slaughterhouses, bakeries and synagogues, established for the diverse immigrant Jewish communities from Eastern Europe. The Artillery Lane synagogue (p 358) was grander than most. Many who climbed from the

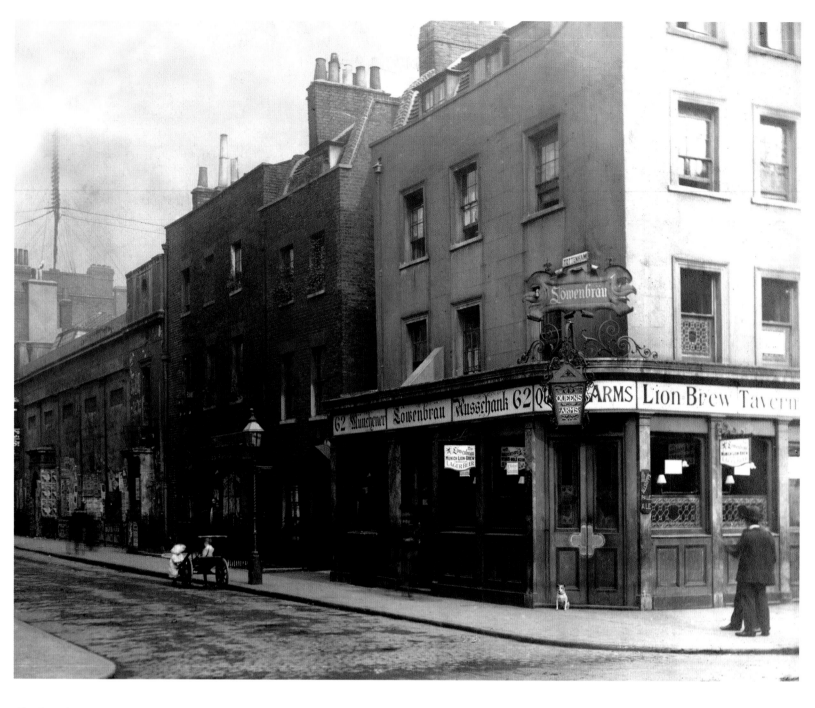

Charlotte Street, c 1890
For generations immigrant communities have left their mark on London's neighbourhoods. The Germans settled in Fitzrovia, until internment during the First World War. It is a measure of their impact that the Queen's Arms at the junction of Tottenham Street and Charlotte Street was covered with advertisements for German beers and lager.

abyss went on to prosper and played a prominent role in the clothing and tailoring trades, and in jewellery-making, commerce and finance.

Other ethnic groups formed enclaves in different neighbourhoods. From the 1850s groups of Italian urchins brought over from Italy as barrel organists and hurdy-gurdy men to work the streets of central London, settled in the foetid slums around Hatton Garden and Saffron Hill. Gradually these early colonists attracted others. By 1901 there were

over 10,000 working as skilled building craftsmen or opening cafes, delicatessens and ice cream parlours. St Peter's, Clerkenwell Green, built in 1863 and modelled on St Crisogono in Rome, was the first Catholic church to be built in Britain since the Reformation.

Elsewhere as pioneer immigrants became established they triggered chain reactions, drawing friends and families into newly-emerging colonies. In 1914 there were 30,000 Germans in London, many of whom were later interned. So many were clustered around Fitzrovia that Charlotte Street was known as "Charlottenstrasse".

Although constantly thought to be on the brink of social breakdown, the East End inferno never erupted. The greatest revolutionary influence came from the immigrant communities – the communists and anarchists who regarded the festering morass of the East End as fertile soil for world revolution.

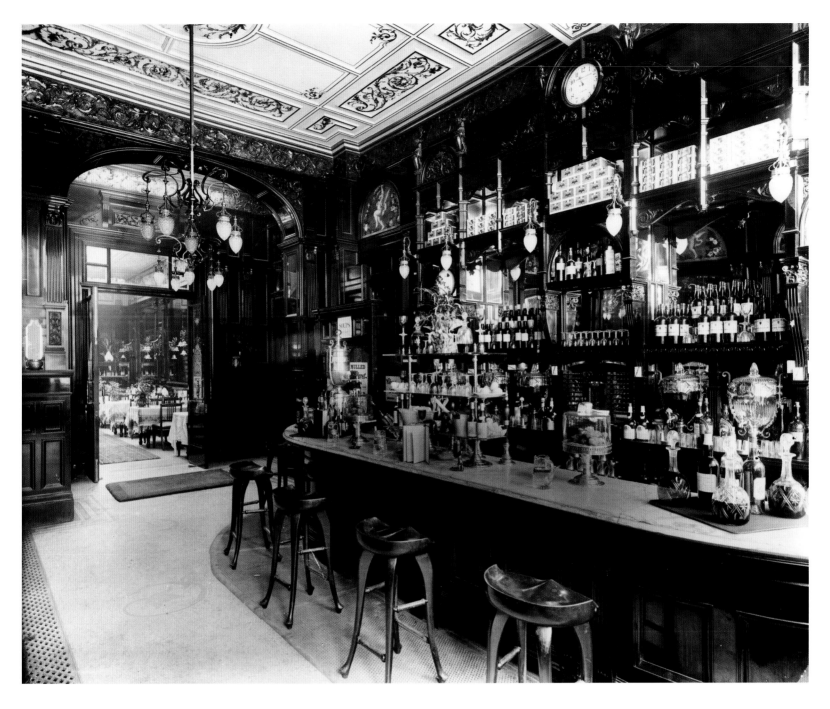

The Dover Castle, Westminster Bridge Road, Lambeth c 1890: a dazzling interior of painted glass and ornate plasterwork with mahogany panelling and bar fittings. For the poor the palatial interior of a London gin-palace was the grandest building many ever experienced.

In being an open city, London had a long tradition of embracing political exiles and radicals. It was the international arena for political and social debate and the creation of new ideologies. A generation earlier, in the mid-19th century, the Hungarian patriot Kossuth had arrived followed by Mazzini and Garibaldi, Marx and Engels, and later, Litvinov, Kropotkin, Trotsky, Lenin and Stalin. In the unprepossessing surroundings of a hall in Fulbourne Street, opposite the London Hospital, the Bolshevik party declared its supremacy at the 5th Congress of the Russian Social Democratic Labour Party, leading Peter Ackroyd to conclude that "*the East End can be considered one of the primary sites of world communism*".[19] In a nearby doss house, Tower House, Stalin and Litvinov shared adjoining cubicles. The very cosmopolitan nature of the East End with its broad ethnic diversity fuelled the development of international communism, as much as the municipal socialism which characterised the local politics of the area.

London's role as a great processing centre for immigrants remains today, fuelling its booming economy. Over 40% of Londoners are from ethnic minorities. Over 300 languages are spoken. One in twenty businesses is owned by an immigrant. In 1900 some of the streets of London's East End were more than 90% Jewish. Today few remain. The same streets are now 90% Bengali. Nowhere encapsulates the astonishing versatility of the East End better than the old Huguenot chapel in Brick

Lane. Built in 1743 for émigré French Protestants, in 1819 it became a Methodist chapel before it was converted into the Machzike Adass, or Great Synagogue in 1897 for the Jewish community. In 1976 it became the Jama Masjid serving the Bengali population of Spitalfields. *Plus ca change.*

There is no doubt at all that the growth of the early conservation movement was driven by a reaction against the massive scale of the changes that were transforming late 19th century London into a great imperial and commercial capital and at the wholesale destruction of old buildings that accompanied it. Successive waves of railway construction from 1836 onwards, compounded later by the underground railway, cut huge swathes through the metropolis. Increasingly, the repetitive terraces of the 18th and 19th century city that had once imparted such a remarkable unity to the capital were being scythed through by massive waves of reconstruction.

With the relentless expansion of London's population, major metropolitan improvements cut further swathes through some of London's most historic neighbourhoods. In the City of London, Cannon Street had been widened as early as the 1850s, but later improvements were even more radical. In the 1860s a whole series of new thoroughfares were driven through the Cities of London and Westminster. Queen Victoria Street radically altered the geometry and grain of the City of London, whilst in the 1860s the creation of Holborn Viaduct and Farringdon Street transformed the entire morphology of the area between the City of London and the poorer districts to the west around Hatton Garden, triggered by the colossal metropolitan market improvements at Smithfield, one of the greatest exercises of Victorian civic improvement ever seen in Britain – a massive, multi-layered complex of grand new market buildings designed by the City Surveyor, Sir Horace Jones, superimposed over a network of subterranean railways.

In 1860 Dickens' abiding impression of London had been one of unremitting shabbiness. He lamented:

"The shabbiness of our English capital, as compared with … almost any important town on the continent of Europe – I find very striking after an absence of any duration in foreign parts … In detail, one would say it can rarely fail to be a disappointing place of shabbiness to a stranger from any one of those places. There is nothing shabbier than Drury Lane, in Rome itself …. London is shabby by daylight and shabbier by gaslight … the mass of London people are shabby." [20]

In the early part of the 20th century the remarkable unity of the Georgian and Victorian city was castigated as remorselessly monotonous – *"one damned Georgian building after another".*

The dreary monotony of much of the East End was a common refrain of many contemporary observers – *"the long lines of low houses – two storeys always – or two storeys and a basement – of the same yellowish brick, all begrimed by the same smoke, every door knocker of the same pattern, every window-blind hung in the same way, and the same corner 'public' on either side, flaming in the hazy distance".*

For many the corner pub provided transient solace. In 1905 gin sold at $4\frac{1}{2}$d a quarter and beer at 1d for a half-pint. In poorer areas some pubs were little more than domestic buildings given over to the sale of alcohol (p 287) but others, like the opulent Leicester public house in the West End (p 214), were glittering palaces of cut-glass and polychromatic tiles, their seductive pleasures announced in the refulgent glow from myriad massive gas lanterns: beacons of light in a world of bleak horizons.

But for all the social deprivation, poverty and underprivilege, comments on East End life were all too often coloured by the superficial perception of outsiders. For those who actually lived in the poorer districts of London, stoical cheerfulness was the most commonly recognised quality epitomised by the Cockney with a ready wit and readiness to laugh.

In 1900 London was an extraordinary kaleidoscope of districts with a constantly shifting social geography as areas declined, prospered or were redeveloped with bewildering rapidity.

London was, and remains, a city of extremes. During 'la belle epoque' the West End was London's playground, a glittering, vibrant world of the demi-monde, which offered illimitable opportunities for pleasure for all classes. The primary focus of this was around Piccadilly Circus (pp 197-198), the centre of the Empire and hub of London's nightlife, where the new electric signs were regarded as one of the wonders of the age, and the theatres, music-halls and restaurants offered a seductive world of gaiety and glamour.

London's high society revolved around the London Season, and the rituals of its calendar, opening on the Friday nearest 1 May with the Royal Academy Summer Exhibition and ending in late July after Goodwood. In between were the Derby, Ascot, the Chelsea Flower Show, Wimbledon and Henley, punctuated by visits to the opera, ballet and theatre, culminating in Queen Charlotte's Ball where debutantes were presented at Court.

Some of the most lavish parties took place in the great aristocratic town houses of Mayfair – like Devonshire House, Chesterfield House and Dorchester House depicted on pages 300-304. Here the sons and daughters of the old landed families could be introduced socially to the new wealth of the rising industrial and commercial classes in a sort of exclusive upper-class mating ritual, the primary purpose of the soirees and balls being to provide young ladies with a respectable opportunity to find eligible young men.

This highly-structured social milieu with its finely-honed traditions of class and status was supported by a self-perpetuating, seasonal economy, which dictated much of the character of the West End.

"Fine meals reached the tables of the rich by courtesy of a complex chain of human labour made up of dealers and traders, groups of porters in the docks and markets, poorly paid Irish men and women who humped heavy baskets of vegetables on their heads from markets to shops, carters and shopkeepers, delivery boys and, finally, domestic servants." [21]

This seasonal service economy had widespread repercussions across

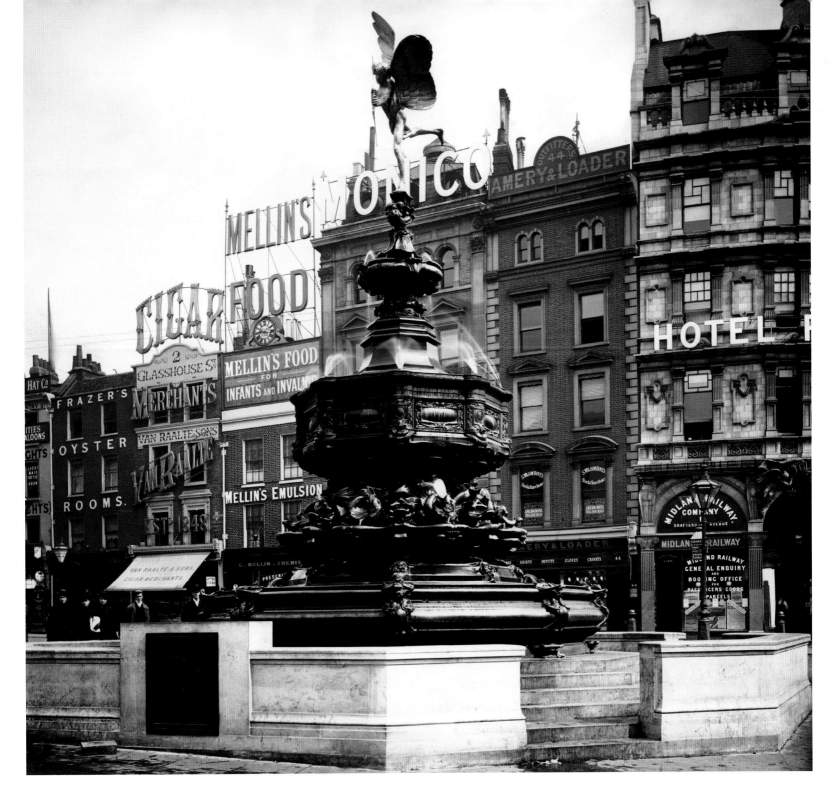

Piccadilly Circus, 1893: the symbolic centre of the British Empire: Alfred Gilbert's Angel of Christian Charity, was unveiled in 1893 as a memorial to the 7th Earl of Shaftesbury, the great philanthropist and social reformer. It rapidly became the haunt of flower-sellers, newspaper boys and London's louche nightlife.

central and west London. A huge dressmaking and clothing industry blossomed for a few months each year to cater for the demands of the Season. Over 20,000 young women were employed as casual seamstresses in the grand fashion houses and tailoring shops of the West End, and for furnishing the great houses of Mayfair, only to be put out of work afterwards. The two upholstery trimmers shown at work in Archer Street (p 211) in 1908 were typical of many. Further west in Kensal New Town poor Irish families living in single-storey hovels (p 273) provided a laundry service for the entire West End; there were so many that the entire area was christened Soap Suds Island.

The social elite lived within a tightly-defined geographical area bounded by Oxford Street, Regent Street, the Palace of Westminster and the South Kensington Museum in the west. The importance of a good address was paramount for anyone with aspirations to becoming part of Society, and estate agents specialised in the renting of large aristocratic town houses to the non-landed super-rich. William Waldorf Astor, for instance, rented Lansdowne House, and Sir Ernest Cassel, Brook House. In 1910 the Duchess of Norfolk was berated in *The Tatler* for not using the magnificent interior of Norfolk House (p 303) for entertainment during the Season. An invitation to Devonshire House (pp 304-305) was particularly highly sought-after as a mark of acceptance to the favoured few – the elite 7,000 or so around whom the Season revolved. There was a strict social hierarchy of addresses across Mayfair, Belgravia and the fringes of Bayswater around the park. A 14 bedroomed house in Grosvenor Place, for instance, cost around 800 guineas (the present equivalent of £46,000) to rent for the Season between May and the end of July.

The endless ritual of calls, teas, dinners and balls directly influenced the architecture and form of well-to-do houses – from the grandest with their entrance gates, lodge and drive to the quality of the door furniture on a London terrace house. Within, the drawing room, dining room and hall received pride of place, part of a domestic processional route that reflected the social status of the occupant. Occasionally artists, bohemians and those with more exotic tastes departed from convention. William Burges's Tower House, for instance (pp 274-275), was a romantic exercise in mediaeval revivalism.

London remained the largest port in the world – with the Thames and the Docks crammed with shipping (p 244). An entire quarter of streets north of the Tower was levelled to make way for the palatial new headquarters of the Port of London Authority, built to the designs of Sir Edwin Cooper in 1909. This workaday quarter of fine Georgian houses around Seething Lane can be seen on the eve of its destruction on pages 68-69. Elsewhere the London County Council's County Hall was commenced in the same year – an immense civic landmark designed by Ralph Knott, in grand classical style, which completely expunged the ramshackle riverside wharves and warehouses of the South Bank, and transformed the area opposite Whitehall.

The momentum of civic improvement continued remorselessly. Proposals for a major new road between Holborn and the Strand had been discussed for over 60 years before they came to fruition in 1905. They entailed the comprehensive redevelopment of a huge area, the eviction of over 3,700 people and the eradication of one of London's worst slums. Captured here are images of the 17th and 18th century streets around Drury Lane and Clare Market. These were recorded systematically as the entire neighbourhood was reconfigured for the formation of the great new commercial boulevards of Kingsway and Aldwych, which over the next twenty years were lined with majestic classical buildings reflecting the commercial might of the British Empire. In the process some of inner London's most historic areas were destroyed completely including Danes Inn, New Inn (p 110) and Cliffords Inn (pp 108-109). One of the most grievous losses was the clearance of Holywell Street and Wych Streets which were regarded as the most picturesque in London, and which contained one of the finest concentrations of pre-Fire houses in the capital. The south-west corner of the Lincoln's Inn Fields with its peculiar arched entrance (p 138) and historic Sardinia Chapel was another conspic-

uous casualty. Today, only the erroneously named Old Curiosity Shop, No. 13 Portsmouth Street (p 133) and a sole survivor – the White Horse public house in Clements Inn Passage – predate the Edwardian improvements.

Transport imperatives were also the driver for the construction of a new river crossing east of the City. The completion of Tower Bridge in 1894 (p 246) generated major changes on both banks for the new Tower Bridge Approach Road.

In the City and West End, large swathes of central London were reconstructed in grand Edwardian Beaux Arts style in a magnificent expression of civic pride and commercial and imperial self-confidence. In the City vast new citadels were raised for commerce, banking and insurance. The massive, forbidding hulk of Newgate Prison was demolished for the spectacular new Central Criminal Courts in 1903. Even the old Christ's Hospital (p 90-91), a City institution for over 300 years succumbed, when it was relocated to Horsham and its site redeveloped.

A set of photographs was taken on both sides of the river to record areas proposed for demolition for a new St Paul's Bridge, one of several potential improvements which failed to materialise. In Southwark the mean yards and courts of Bankside were swept away later in stages in a series of slum clearance measures, and the entire area was transformed with the completion of Bankside Power Station in 1963.

In Westminster, the government precinct around Whitehall was also being transfigured as offices of state in old 17th and 18th century town houses gave way to a magnificent new generation of government palaces. Depicted here is Whitehall on the cusp of change as the fashionable town houses of Great George Street, sitting cheek by jowl with some of the worst slums in London, were flattened for a gigantic new office building for the Board of Trade, Ministry of Health and Education Department (pp 176-181). Nearby, the once elegant mansions of Whitehall Gardens lie poised for destruction to make way for the vast new complex for the Air Ministry designed by Vincent Harris in 1914, but not commenced until 1939.

The very heart of ceremonial London was remodelled to reflect the Imperial zeitgeist. In 1912 Sir Aston Webb completed its reconfiguration with one of the finest examples of monumental axial planning London has ever seen. A great processional route was created from Trafalgar Square through Admiralty Arch (p 164) to a new rond-point at the Victoria Memorial and on to Hyde Park Corner. A year later the entire east front of Buckingham Palace was refaced to his designs in just three months (pp 170-171), replacing Edward Blore's lacklustre facade .

In the West End the motivation behind the creation of Charing Cross Road and Shaftesbury Avenue in the 1880s had been as much to do with slum clearance of the notorious rookeries of St Giles and Soho, as from the desire to improve public transport, but by the turn of the century massive new investment was being made in prestigious new facilities for the wealthy – hotels, clubs, and shops, using new techniques of steel and concrete-framed construction.

The Ritz Hotel, in Piccadilly, one of London's first steel-framed

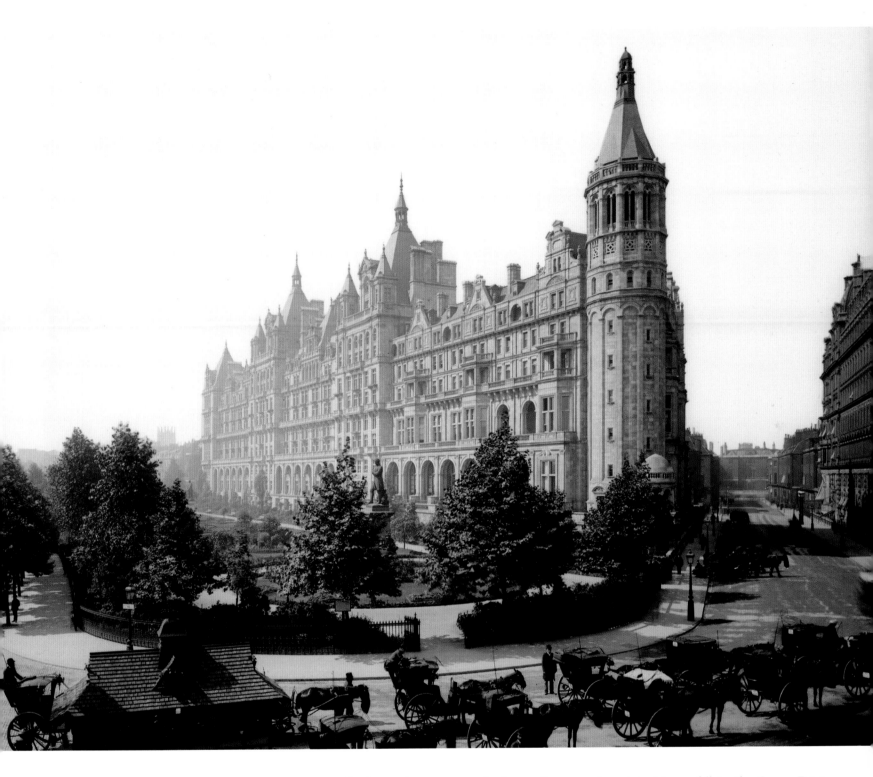

Imperial London: Westminster Embankment c 1895 with the newly-completed National Liberal Club to the right and Whitehall Court beyond and a cabmen's shelter with a line of hansoms in the foreground. The great departments of state were being transformed with palatial new offices which expressed the political and commercial might of the British Empire.

buildings, was completed in 1906 to the design of Mewès and Davis. Others followed, most notably the Piccadilly Hotel by Norman Shaw in 1904-08, which towered over Nash's tired old Regent Street terraces as the harbinger of things to come (p 200).

In Regent Street, as the original leases fell in, the Crown Estate triggered one of the greatest rebuilding projects ever seen in London. Progressively, block by block, Nash's decaying stucco terraces were replaced by huge new stone edifices in a variety of Edwardian classical styles, dwarfing the original buildings like a fleet of modern dreadnoughts amongst a squadron of sailing ships.

This great thrust of development continued south into St James's, where opulent new gentlemen's clubs replaced the mansions of the aristocracy. The spectacular new Royal Automobile Club displaced both Cumberland House and Buckingham House in 1911. To the north in Oxford Street, a line of new department stores such as Waring and

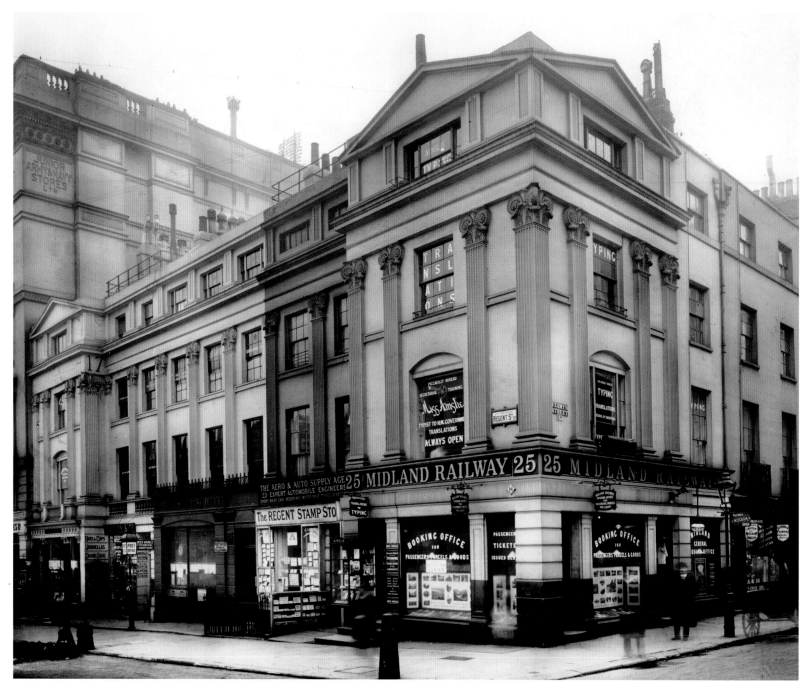

Regent Street c 1906: The reconstruction of Nash's Regent Street was one of the greatest redevelopments ever seen in London. Nos. 17-25 Regent Street, depicted here at the junction with Jermyn Street, boasted unusual Ammonite capitals.

Gillow (1901-05) and Selfridges (1907), anchored alongside revitalised stores like Marshall & Snelgrove and Bourne & Hollingsworth. In Knightsbridge, Harrods opened new premises in 1905 in a terracotta leviathan, which occupied an entire street block. The interior of Slater's shown on page 275 was typical of the great emporia of the period. In Holborn the opening of Gamages in 1904 sounded the death knell for a large number of old buildings including The Black Bull coaching inn depicted on (p 103). Next door, Waterhouse's extravagant red-brick Gothic fantasy for the Prudential Assurance Company (1899-1900) had already consigned the famous Old Bell coaching inn (p 100) to oblivion.

Partly because of the sheer scale of development and the relentless pace of change, London lay in the forefront of the movement to save historic buildings, and photographers were in the vanguard of those who were recording what was being lost.

As early as 1875 the Society for Photographing Relics of Old London was formed by a group of friends to record buildings that were threatened with demolition. Over an eleven year period they recorded and published over 120 images of mostly 17th and 18th century buildings which were being demolished in the name of progress. Negatives were made by Alfred and John Bool of Pimlico, and prints were then produced by Henry Dixon & Son of Albany Street, which were distributed amongst subscribers from 1875 onwards.

Photography was not easy in London. Henry Dixon recorded how he had to obtain a photograph in a crowded street by removing a wheel from

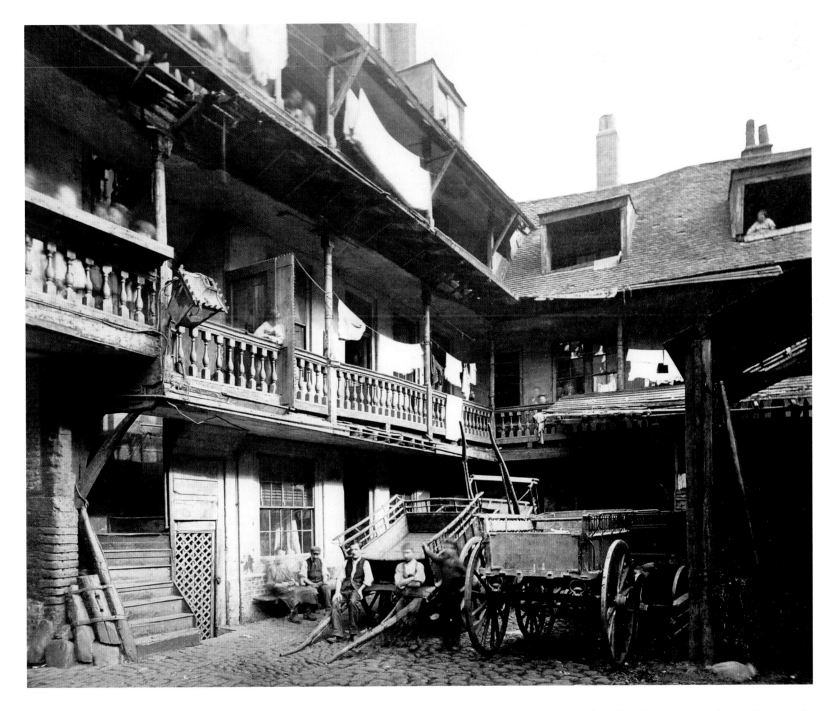

Oxford Arms, Warwick Lane, 1875.
View of the ramshackle galleried courtyard of The Oxford Arms. Its demolition in 1878 was a landmark in the development of the conservation movement and triggered the formation of the Society for the Protection of Ancient Buildings a year later.

a wagon, and while his assistant pretended to mend it, he photographed his subject from under the canvas. *The Times* soon commented on "*their beauty of chiaroscuro*", which over 130 years later has improved with age. The Society also lobbied owners to prevent the destruction of buildings they considered worthy of preservation. Many of these were the old ramshackle timber-framed and gabled houses of mediaeval and 17th century London. A significant number were coaching inns, which had survived on the fringes of the City and central London.

The trigger for the formation of the Society was the impending demolition of The Oxford Arms, a wonderfully evocative 17th century remnant which lay in Warwick Lane in the shadow of St Paul's Cathedral (above and p 97). When it finally succumbed in 1878, its loss galvanised public opinion, and it became a landmark in the development of the early conservation movement.

By the 1890s only a handful of coaching inns survived. Some of the last can be seen on pages 100-103. Most had a common form and plan – a simple domestic street frontage with an arched or gated entrance that led through to galleried yards and stabling beyond. By the time they were recorded in these photographs, virtually all had long since ceased to function for their original purpose. From the mid-19th century they had been rendered obsolete by the railways; most were simply used for storage and stabling.

Just a year after the demolition of The Oxford Arms, William Morris founded the Society for the Protection of Ancient Buildings (SPAB) "*to keep watch on old monuments*" and "*to protect against all 'restoration' that means more than keeping out wind and weather*". In the early days this was much more to do with the need to curb the vandalism of architects engaged in the wholesale reconstruction and conjectural restoration of historic buildings, particularly churches, than from any great appetite for campaigning against demolition,

As the pace of change quickened, the preservation of historic buildings began to be seen as a popular cause for the educated middle-classes, and as an integral part of the emerging interest in town planning and philanthropy. In 1889 The London Topographical Society was formed. In 1893-95 Octavia Hill, Robert Hunter and Canon Hardwicke Rawnsley, a keen amateur photographer, founded the National Trust for Places of Historic Interest and Natural Beauty, which drew together interest in protecting landscapes with enthusiasm for preserving historic buildings. It attracted 250 members in its first year. Initially the Trust worked with private companies to help keep historic buildings in use. The restoration of Staple Inn by the Prudential Assurance Company under the watchful eye of the SPAB was an early success.

Growing public unease at both the scale and pace of change was expressed both in the press and in parliamentary committees, but in 1893 the demolition of the finest building in East London – the old Royal Palace at Bromley-by-Bow for an LCC Board School provoked widespread comment. In exasperation at the unthinking and unplanned destruction of so much of London's architectural heritage, a group of private individuals came together to form the London Survey Committee with the primary aim of recording buildings before they were destroyed. C R Ashbee was appointed editor, and in 1900 the first volume was published recording the parish of Bromley-by-Bow.

Ashbee fulminated against the loss of the palace, which could have been saved as a museum, "*the nucleus there of one of the most beautiful collections in London … in short, the epitome of the life of a London parish preserved in a most exquisite setting, and of the utmost value for its beauty and its living interest to the young citizens who are bred in what is now a disgraced slum*". He went on to complain "*sometimes one is apt to ask whether their historic conscience is entirely lost to the citizens of London, so swift, so complete, so apparently needless – and alas so ignorant – is often the destruction of the records of the past*".[22]

In the introduction to the first volume of the Survey of London a demand was made for a committee to be appointed "*representative of all the bodies in London who are engaged upon work dealing with the historical remains of London*" and calling for "*every case of impending destruction to be openly considered, and the results of its deliberations forwarded to the London County Council with a view of action being taken thereon*".[23]

The work of the London Survey Committee was hugely important for the growth of the conservation movement. Increasingly, preservation was identified with progressive planning and utilitarian ideals rather than just whimsical antiquarianism. The preservation of historic buildings, parks and open spaces was seen as an integral part of a wider social idealism – the provision of the proper amenities of life for a great city and for adequate housing for the poor; a concept taken up and given substance in the Utopian visions which underpinned the new Garden Suburbs, which were being built on the fringes of London at Brentham, Hampstead, Ealing and elsewhere.

The Survey Committee soon worked in close partnership with the LCC. Subsequently it was absorbed into the LCC, and much later it became the GLC Historic Buildings Committee. With the abolition of the GLC in 1984, the old GLC Historic Buildings Division and its Historic Buildings Committee were united with the newly-formed English Heritage. The London Advisory Committee of English Heritage continues this valuable role today. Over 100 years since its creation, it still provides advice on all major development affecting London's historic environment.

As a result of the work of the SPAB and the London Survey Committee, there was growing interest in positive intervention to save individual buildings and monuments. The Ancient Monuments Act 1882, which listed 29 nationally-significant ancient monuments, had established the principle of state intervention and the whole idea of maintaining historic buildings through the public purse. In 1893 the LCC established an important precedent by acquiring the York Water Gate in Embankment Gardens under the London Open Spaces Act. Other acquisitions soon followed. Five years later the LCC was vested with the power to purchase or contribute towards expenditure on the preservation of buildings and places of architectural or historic interest. It acted immediately to acquire a rare timber-framed survival at No.17 Fleet Street, once the Chancery of the Duchy of Cornwall, and also the 18th century Sir Robert Geffrye's Almshouses in Shoreditch, now the Geffrye Museum.

In 1901 the LCC took over from the Royal Society of Arts the scheme for marking the houses of eminent figures with plaques, some of which can be seen in the photographs. The first LCC plaque to Lord Macaulay at Holly Lodge, Campden Hill, followed shortly after, and 20 years later the distinctive glazed Doulton blue plaque was adopted as the standard.

In some cases parts of important early buildings were salvaged and re-erected for their antiquarian interest. The most notable example of this was the dismantling of Crosby Hall, Bishopsgate in 1909-10, a great 15th century City merchant's house. The Great Hall was reconstructed at Chelsea Embankment under the supervision of the architect Walter Godfrey. It is illustrated prior to its removal on pages 74-75. Sir Paul Pindar's house, also in Bishopsgate, had set an earlier precedent in 1890 when the elaborately-carved oak frontage was dismantled and re-erected as an exhibit in the Victoria & Albert Museum.
Another seminal case which demonstrated the inadequacy of public attempts to save some of London's finest houses was the debacle over No. 75 Dean Street. The new Ancient Monuments Act 1913 had specifically allowed that buildings in private ownership could be put on the list of ancient monuments. Provisions were made for a list to be drawn up and

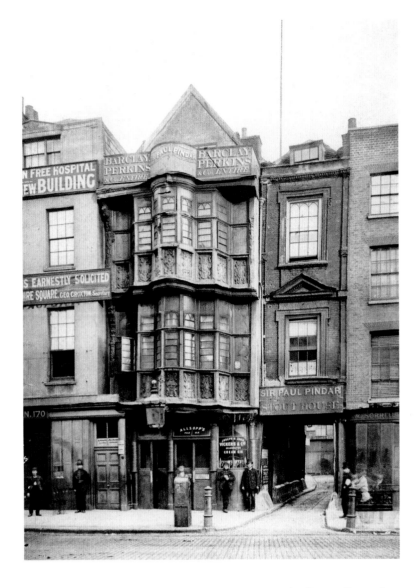

View of Sir Paul Pindar's house, Bishopsgate, c 1885. The dismantling and re-erection of the famous frontage of this 16th century merchant's house was an indication of growing antiquarian interest in London's vanishing past.

for owners to be informed, after which they were required to give one month's notice of any proposals to alter or demolish the building, at which point the Commissioners for Works Council could decide whether to make a preservation order, which was then subject to ratification by parliament. The house, part of a short terrace built in 1713 by Thomas Richmond, boasted a fine staircase enriched with murals that were thought to be the work of Sir James Thornhill, or William Hogarth (p 209). The owner planned to sell the house for demolition and to give the best features to the Victoria & Albert Museum.

Unfortunately the Act was flawed. It made no provision for financial compensation to the owner, which outraged public opinion. The owner appealed successfully to the House of Lords and, after various abortive attempts to find an authority or organisation prepared to take it on, the house was eventually demolished in 1919. The staircase and some of the panelled rooms were salvaged, eventually ending up in the Art Institute of Chicago.

The National Trust Act 1907 reincorporated the organisation as a statutory body for the express purpose of preserving interesting and beautiful places for the nation and to hold places inalienably. In parallel, town planning pioneers like Patrick Geddes began to argue for the importance of saving historic districts as part of town plans overseen by local councils, as was the case in Europe – the birth of the modern system of area-based conservation. In 1912 the London Society was founded to lobby for the preservation of historic buildings.

From 1900 to 1914 London underwent a public transport revolution that facilitated the development of outlying areas into new residential suburbs. The electrification of the railways and tramways, and the development of the deep tube and bus network precipitated major population shifts. In the 10 years from 1901 over 55,000 people, 12% of the population, migrated from inner London, most to the new suburbs. Journeys on public transport virtually doubled over the same period from 142 to 250 per head of population.

Some of the physical impacts of these profound changes can be seen in these photographs – the arrival of tramlines, the progressive replacement of horse-drawn vehicles by motor cars, the redevelopment of outlying villas, like Carnwath House in Fulham (p 276) and the Well Hall estate in Eltham (p 330) for new suburban housing estates. In Hammersmith, many of the old west London coaching inns were swept away, or

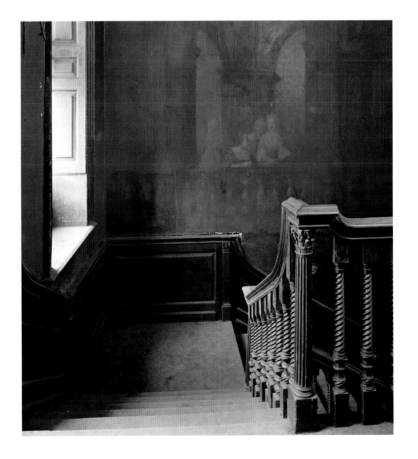

No. 75 Dean Street, Soho, 1912. The painted hall and staircase. Its demolition in 1919 exposed fundamental flaws in the legislation designed to protect important historic buildings and ancient monuments.

rebuilt, as outlying areas developed into vibrant new town centres (pp 278-279).

Traffic too was changing. The world's first traffic light with green and red gas powered signals had been installed in Bridge Street by the Palace of Westminster as early as 1868. Motorised taxis first appeared in 1903 and motor buses a year later. By 1911 most of the open-topped old horse buses were obsolete. With the outbreak of war in 1914 horses were requisitioned, spelling the death-knell for surviving hansoms and growlers. The very sound of the city changed as pneumatic tyres reduced the roar of iron-rimmed wheels and hooves on granite setts. Tarred wood blocks and tarmac were introduced to reduce noise and improve comfort.

While many suburbs like Pinner, Blackheath, Hampstead or Carshalton grew around older village cores, some like Muswell Hill, or Golders Green, were crafted as new places entirely from scratch – and remarkably successfully too. In 1907 the Charing Cross, Euston and Hampstead tube railway opened. Within five years a completely new town centre of elegant neo-Georgian and Arts & Crafts terraces and shops was created at Golders Green – as the centrepiece of a whole new suburban community. Many of these new outlying suburbs were sophisticated exercises in placemaking which make current attempts to create sustainable new communities risible by comparison.

With the outbreak of the First World War, shortages of both labour and supplies torpedoed many of London's Edwardian "grands projets". The reconstruction of Regent Street, Kingsway and County Hall ground to a halt, together with most new house building when in 1916 all new building was proscribed under the Defence of the Realm Act.

In the period following the First World War, rising land values, population growth and the demands of the car generated intense commercial pressures for new development and further waves of metropolitan improvements. The pre-war momentum for new buildings for a new age re-emerged with even greater vigour as department stores, cinemas, commercial buildings, government offices and blocks of flats transformed the face of the capital (pp 294-296).

By 1927 the population of London had reached 7,800,000, an increase of 20% in just 25 years fuelled by the expansion of the public transport network. The first bus stops arrived in the 1920s and buses with roofs were introduced in 1925. The extension of a sophisticated network of buses and electric tramways facilitated the development of new outlying areas like East Sheen, Wimbledon, Kingston and Teddington, whilst the radical expansion of the underground and surface railways generated unprecedented opportunities for further suburban growth. In 1921 Dagenham, for example, was a struggling parish on the eastern fringe of London with a population of less than 10,000. In six years it had grown into a town of 50,000 with 'homes fit for heroes' to live in.

Swollen by high post-war birth rates and suburban expansion London's population continued to grow – from 7.5 million to 8.7 million by 1939. For some, the relentless expansion of London into the greatest city in the world was a source of immense national pride. In 1927 Harold Clunn, an enthusiastic chronicler of changing London, launched into patriotic hyperbole:

"May our beloved London, the largest city and the capital of the greatest Empire the world has ever seen, upon which the sun never sets, remain for all time as long as mankind dominates the earth a worthy record of that long and prosperous history of the great British community, and a monument to progress". [24]

Others were not quite so sanguine about the pace and scale of change. In the 1920s the rebuilding of Regent Street, which had been interrupted by the war, was resumed. With rising land values, property developers moved into parts of Westminster and the West End acquiring whole groups of domestic buildings to build much larger residential blocks of serviced flats which dwarfed their neighbours. The acquisition of High Row on the north side of Knightsbridge (p 308) was typical of this trend, although hit by the recession and then the war, it was not fully redeveloped until 1956.

In the inter-war years the height, massing and bulk of central London underwent a step-change. Many were apoplectic at the changes. Having celebrated London as *The Unique City*, the Dane, Steen Eiler Rasmussen castigated the introduction of continental experiments and ideas, which he believed were unsuited to London's character, particularly the replacement of conventional London streets with large estates of flats for public housing.

"London, the capital of English civilisation, has caught the infection of Continental experiments which are at variance with the whole character and tendency of the city. The foolish mistakes of other countries are imported everywhere, and at the end of a few years, all cities will be equally ugly and equally devoid of individuality." [25]

He was not alone in his concern. Anger at the loss of so much of London's heritage increasingly galvanised public opinion.

Seven years after the Phillimore Report in 1919, proposals were advanced for the demolition of nineteen historic City churches to make way for commercial offices, but the ensuing public outcry forced a climbdown and virtually all were saved. Carlton House Terrace was threatened and only reprieved after vigorous public protest, but elsewhere some of London's most important historic buildings succumbed.

The Adelphi (p 152), built by the Adam Brothers between 1768-74, and one of London's grandest compositions, was demolished in 1936. But perhaps most shocking was the loss of so many of the great West End mansions, and, in particular, the aristocratic houses of Mayfair. Here rising land values and the high running costs for houses, which were occupied for only a few months of the year during the Season, offered tempting opportunities for both impoverished peers and speculative developers. In 1924 Devonshire House (pp 304-305) was demolished for a huge block of flats and American-style car showrooms. In 1929 Dorchester House, the grandest private house in London (p 302), was felled to make way for the

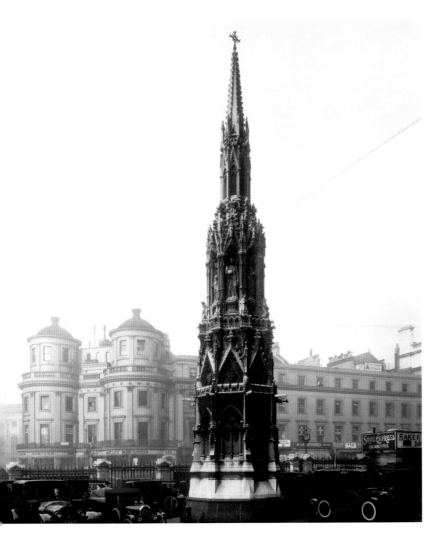

Charing Cross, 1932. Seen here surrounded by cars, a replica of the original mediaeval Eleanor Cross, designed by E M Barry with sculpture by Thomas Earp, was erected on the forecourt of Charing Cross station in 1863. The original, which stood at the end of Whitehall, was pulled down in 1647, and the site later occupied by Le Sueur's famous equestrian statue of Charles I.

sumptuous new Dorchester Hotel in a swanky new moderne style by William Curtis Green. In 1934 Lansdowne House in Berkeley Square was truncated for road improvements. A year later Norfolk House (p 303), one of London's last great mansions was condemned, and Chesterfield House (p 300), soon followed in 1937.

However, alongside the accelerating pace of change, a number of important legislative changes were made. In 1924 the Royal Fine Art Commission was established to advise on matters of artistic importance including the demolition of historic buildings, and, increasingly, it exerted a benign influence on emerging development proposals.

Relentless exploitation of land led to the unity of a number of West End squares such as Portman, Berkeley and Grosvenor Squares, being compromised by overscaled blocks of offices and flats and, in Bloomsbury, by the huge bulk of the Senate House of the University of London, part of a much larger scheme to redevelop the heart of the entire district. But it was not just the buildings that were at risk from misguided development. It was the London square itself.

As early as 1900, under pressure from the Metropolitan Public Gardens Association, the LCC began to acquire the gardens of a number of East End squares to safeguard them from development. In 1904 Edwardes Square in fashionable Kensington was threatened. The resulting public furore triggered direct statutory intervention. Two years later the gardens of 64 London squares, where the freeholders were prepared to waive their development rights, were protected by parliament.

But the battle was by no means won. Rocketing land values and intense development pressures meant that any unprotected open space was regarded as fair game by unscrupulous developers. Endsleigh Gardens on the south side of Euston Road was lost – destroying the carefully composed relationship between Bloomsbury, Euston station and its famous Arch (p 290). Further north, the loss of the enclosed gardens of Mornington Crescent for the giant Carreras factory was the last straw. Following a Royal Commission on London Squares in 1928, three years later one of London's most enlightened pieces of legislation was passed. The London Squares Preservation Act 1931 gave statutory protection to 461 squares and other enclosed spaces. At a stroke many of London's most important open spaces were saved for posterity.

A year later the Town & Country Planning Act 1932 empowered local authorities to make Preservation Orders on important buildings, subject to compensating the owners, but perhaps the most significant consequence of the Act was that the LCC undertook the listing of major buildings in London, so that it could intervene directly when the need arose.

The rising tide of public concern at the demolition of some of London's finest Georgian buildings came to a head in 1937 with the foundation of the Georgian Group, initially as a subsidiary of the SPAB, and later as an independent organisation.

Inter-war residential development was shaped by powerful centrifugal forces. Between 1921 and 1938 almost 200,000 people were displaced from central and inner London by slum clearance projects and Council housing programmes. Most never returned to their old neighbourhoods as large blocks of Council flats replaced the terraced houses, yards and alleys of Victorian London, dispersing many old communities in a Cockney diaspora. Waves of successive migration pushed people out from the centre into the inner ring, which, in turn, eroded the cohesion of middle-class communities, who moved out to the suburbs. Charles Booth had noted this ripple effect as early as 1903:

"Everyone I have consulted mentioned this centrifugal tendency of the better-off, and almost all have complained that, in consequence, their district is going down".[26]

Once fashionable middle-class areas like Stoke Newington, Highbury, Hammersmith, Camberwell and Paddington were occupied by those displaced from poorer areas and their once-comfortable houses descended into multiple occupation.

In 1929 a New Survey of London Life and Labour was commissioned. Over the next six years a team from the London School of Economics reviewed Booth's findings 40 years on. It precipitated a widespread public

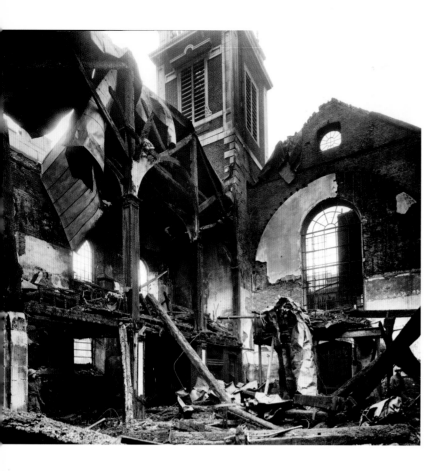

St Andrew-by-the-Wardrobe, 29 February 1941
The devastation of war: the burnt-out interior showing sheet lead hanging
from the aisle roofs. Just under half of the City's churches were damaged or
destroyed by wartime bombing.

debate about the true nature of the poverty threshold and, with the advent of better food and new commodities, what should and should not be regarded as genuine essentials. Nonetheless, by the 1930s the sort of poverty which had so appalled Beatrice Webb, Jack London and their contemporaries had declined dramatically. Both life expectancy and living standards had improved substantially.

At the other end of the social spectrum, in the period following the First World War, the rituals of the Season were re-established, but with less of the suffocating rigidity which had characterised fin-de-siècle society. The liberating effect of charity and war work, and the increasing ability of respectable women to meet outside the confines of their own homes in literary societies, cafes, tea rooms and even on public transport, generated new aspirations, which in turn fuelled demands for female suffrage. A new emphasis on entertainment and leisure epitomised by the flapper were symbols of much greater social mobility. In a number of the photographs of the inter-war period confident young women can be seen acting independently at Tower Hill, for example on page 316, or reclining in the front seat of the automobile in Soho on page 297: new women for a new age.

By 1939 the population of Greater London was 8.2 million – well ahead of New York with 6.93 million. It was not just the largest city in the

world, it was its largest port handling twice the tonnage of Liverpool. It was the seat of government, the monarchy and the judiciary. It was the cosmopolitan capital of the British Empire at the moment of its greatest extent. It financed half the world's trade, while the volume of its manufacturing output exceeded that of any of the great industrial conurbations of the Midlands and the North. It was the focal point of its road and rail network, and its primary cultural centre with many of the leading museums and galleries of the world containing world-famous collections. London was the pre-eminent world city, the dynamo that powered Britain and widely acknowledged to be the finest city in the world. But with one-fifth of Britain's population concentrated into just 610 sq miles, by 1939 London was also a shockingly vulnerable target.

Only twice in the past 1,000 years has London suffered catastrophic damage – in the Great Fire of 1666 when virtually the entire City of London was levelled, and again during the Second World War when one in six of its buildings was damaged or destroyed by enemy action. So traumatic were the six years of war that they formed the defining period of the 20th century: "*For everyone life would henceforth be divided into 'before the war' and 'after the war'*".[27]

Today it is difficult to comprehend the scale of wartime destruction. In one night alone, on Sunday, 29 December 1940, the City of London lost about a third of its entire floorspace. The ensuing fire, which could be seen 30 miles away, leapt the river and ignited a line of warehouses on the south bank between London Bridge and Tower Bridge. Almost every building between Moorgate and Aldersgate Street was obliterated, including the ancient maze of streets and alleys around Paternoster Row in the shadow of St Paul's (pp 92-93). Over 6 million books burned in the flames. Tragically, old buildings were the most vulnerable. While modern steel-framed buildings withstood high explosives and fire relatively well, older masonry structures simply collapsed.

With their large expanses of roof and deep gutters, churches suffered particularly badly from incendiary bombs. Twenty of the City's forty-seven churches were damaged or destroyed in the Blitz. But for London as a whole the most destructive night of the entire war was on 10-11 May 1941 when over 100,000 incendiaries were dropped all over London by the light of the full moon. The Palace of Westminster, Inns of Court, Royal Courts of Justice and Tower of London were all hit. In just one night 1,436 people were killed and 12,000 rendered homeless. Depicted here are just a handful of London's historic churches which were gutted by fire, the heat often so intense that the stonework delaminated and shattered. At St Clement Danes the damage was so devastating that the distraught rector died soon after of shock. But the Blitz gave birth to its own inspiring stories, not least the miraculous, symbolic survival of St Paul's, depicted in Herbert Mason's famous picture of the cathedral rising serenely above the surrounding devastation, and the touching story of Faith, the church cat which endured the inferno at St Augustine, Watling Street (p 344).

Each district had its own story to tell but Holborn had the highest per capita casualty rate. George Edinger, a Bencher of Gray's Inn, described the devasting damage to Grays Inn and Holborn, its picturesque historic buildings, courts and alleys ravaged by bombing and fire:

"*Until the outbreak of the second World War ... for the whole mile I would be enclosed by the unbroken sequence of late seventeenth and early eighteenth century buildings whose bland facades of mellow brick made up what was, to my mind, the most gracious harmony of town architecture in any capital ... I cannot do that now. The phenomenon that was my Georgian mile is swallowed up in dust and rubble. It was not the greatest tragedy among the lost treasures of Western Europe. But it was something unique.*"[28]

By the end of the war the level of damage was truly shocking, 50,000 houses destroyed or irreparable in inner London alone, and over 60,000 in outer London. An additional 290,000 houses suffered serious damage and a further 2 million or more slight damage. The extent of this destruction can be glimpsed in these photographs, of which a disproportionate number are of City churches, but that is a reflection of the nature of the archive, which concentrated on recording damage to London's great architectural set pieces.

To the modern eye, the level of destruction seems hard to comprehend and the loss of such priceless cultural assets almost inconceivable. Just look at the burnt-out ruins of St Bride's, Fleet Street (p 350), or St Giles, Cripplegate (p 348): 400 years of history destroyed in minutes. Few of London's historic buildings escaped unscathed in the war. Many were lost forever.

The overwhelming impression of wartime London is one of unmitigated shabbiness – (p 357) weed-strewn bomb sites; drab buildings patched up with corrugated iron and cheap fletton brick; bomb-scarred houses with broken windows, and gap-toothed terraces propped up by raking shores of timber. This extraordinary, desolate townscape of a tired and broken city seems as distant today as Victorian London. Although by 1947 most of London's damaged houses had been rendered habitable again, it was literally decades before London shook off its wartime shabbiness and years of decline to re-emerge as a reinvigorated world city – a phoenix arising from the ashes.

Partly in response to the extent of devastation, and partly as a result of campaigning by enlightened individuals and societies, public concern to conserve what remained gathered momentum as the threat of post-war comprehensive redevelopment reared its head. Following interim legislation in 1944, the Town & Country Planning Act 1947 introduced a national system for the listing of buildings. It allowed the Minister to serve a Building Preservation Order on a building and laid the foundation for the current system of statutory protection, although it was not until 1971 that proposals for the demolition or alteration of Listed buildings required specific prior consent from the local authority. In 1967 the Civic Amenities Act, pioneered by Duncan Sandys, introduced the concept of conservation areas which enabled local Councils to begin to manage change more sensitively on an area-wide basis.

In Britain a whole series of factors determined the form and pattern of post-war reconstruction – not least radical idealism coupled with an

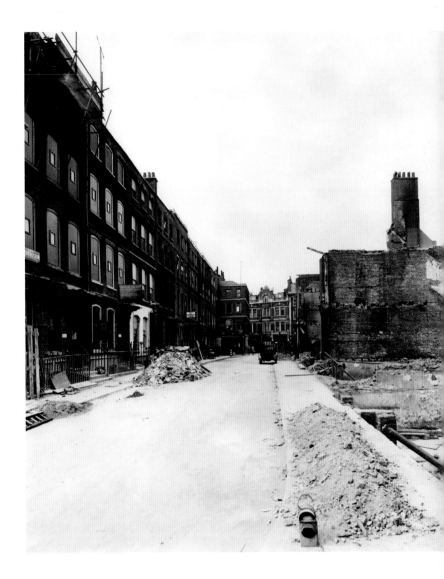

Featherstone Buildings, Holborn, 9 May 1941: typical of the once unbroken sequence of mellow Georgian buildings so admired by George Edinger. Holborn suffered the highest per capita casualty rate from bombing in London.

unprecedented opportunity to create a socially-engineered New Jerusalem. With the exception of major landmark buildings, in the headlong rush to embrace the future there was little appetite for retaining the past. Whole streets of perfectly serviceable, but damaged, houses like Swedenborg Square (p 356), were left to rot by speculative developers, or abandoned by local authorities determined to build a fairer and more socially just society. In many parts of inner London and the East End the opportunity was seized to clear large areas of insanitary and sub-standard housing in a concerted effort to improve social conditions. As a result even greater damage was inflicted on historic areas which had survived the Luftwaffe through comprehensive redevelopment, particularly in the poorer areas of inner and east London – at King Square, Finsbury (p 352), for instance, or Bromley-by-Bow, which was virtually wiped off the map by an unholy alliance of comprehensive redevelopment and massive new highway engineering. The demolition of Columbia Market (pp 354-355) was a grievous blow not just to the architectural heritage of the East End, but to

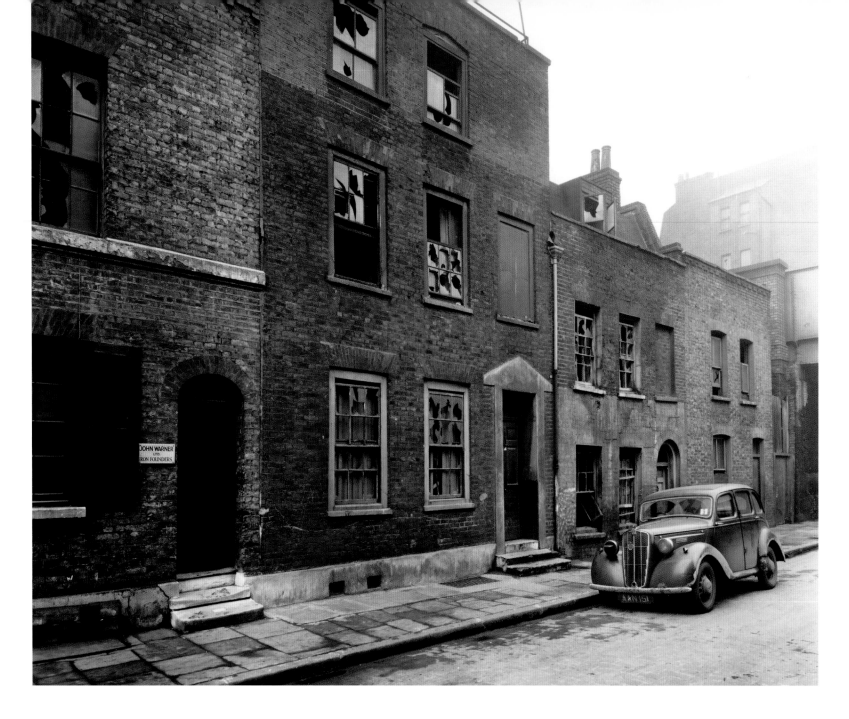

Stepney Causeway, 10 February 1943: a tired and broken city. To modern eyes the extent of wartime damage is truly shocking.

London as a whole. Although redundant, had it survived another 10 years, the rising tide of interest in conservation and the creative reuse of old buildings surely would have secured its future.

However, in pluralist Britain, there were some who stood against the tide of comprehensive redevelopment in favour of a more delicate form of urban surgery and place-making. Many of the great architectural set-pieces such as Buckingham Palace and the Palace of Westminster were repaired with painstaking authenticity. The landed estates of the West End which exercised freehold control – the Crown, Grosvenor, Portman, Bedford and Howard de Walden, for instance, took a much longer and more enlightened view of their stewardship. By and large they carefully stitched back the damaged fabric of their buildings and streets to their pre-war appearance. Elsewhere at New End Square, Hampstead (p 334), for example, many private owners simply chose to rebuild what had been lost.

Twelve of the ruined Wren churches in the City of London were reconstructed with sensitivity by some of the least appreciated architects of their day including Godfrey Allen, the Surveyor of St Paul's Cathedral. But just as many were lost forever. St John's Horsleydown (p 361), St John's, Red Lion Square (p 341) and St Mary's Whitechapel (p 359), for example, were never to rise again.

Many of the most attractive and historic areas of London owe their survival to similar enlightened decisions to repair, restore and rebuild the fabric of what was lost in the war. It is instructive to compare how well they have worn compared with areas like Paternoster Square, where the decision was taken to rebuild to a radical new layout and design, which failed within 30 years. Some of London's most historic and colourful thoroughfares, such as High Holborn, were ruined by post-war architecture of staggering mediocrity.

Today it is possible to walk from the Embankment through Inner and Middle Temple, past Street's magnificent Law Courts, through Lincoln's Inn, across High Holborn to Gray's Inn and beyond into Bloomsbury and still appreciate the qualities which so captivated George Edinger and his pre-war contemporaries. The primary reason for this was the unfashionable approach adopted by the privately-owned Inns in insisting upon recreating the qualities which made a place special – based on a deep understanding that the importance of the place transcended the sum of its component parts. This was achieved in the face of intense opposition by local authorities, and of scorn from the modernist architectural establishment of the day, who strongly favoured the Paternoster approach, sweeping the past away in favour of comprehensive redevelopment. Yet with the benefit of hindsight who was more progressive in their approach to placemaking?

In 1938 Rasmussen had recognised the intrinsic qualities that made London special in his lament at "*the infection of Continental experiments*". Reviewing his prophecy that traditional London would be ruined, he wrote 40 years later:

"*My prophecy has come true so far as London is concerned. It has been spoiled by a number of meaningless skyscrapers; the streets are covered with myriad private cars at the same time as public transport has decayed; buildings with flats have replaced the typical London houses in the depopulated East End. But this is not the bitter end, rather the beginning of a new era.*"[29]

Thirty years on again, London is the economic powerhouse that drives Britain. If London were a country, it would rank within the top 15 world economies with a GVA of £217.5 billion, greater than that of Russia or Saudi Arabia. Together with New York and Tokyo, London is one of three pre-eminent world cities, and arguably it can still lay claim to being the greatest.

Reviewing the photographs in this book, it is impossible not to be transfixed by images of a century of change. Fascinating though they are, it would be wrong to wallow in nostalgia for the buildings and areas which have vanished. Whilst the loss of many noble landmarks like the Adelphi, Devonshire House, the Euston Arch, or Columbia Market reflected a deep-seated cultural failure to appreciate good architecture and was wholly avoidable, the redevelopment of other buildings was an inevitable consequence of demands for better housing, improved transport and the transmutation of London into a modern world city. Sometimes even better buildings replaced those which had been lost – the great palazzi of the City of London for example.

What underpins the narrative of this book is the gradual growth of the conservation movement over the last century as a dynamic force for progressive change, and the evolution of a planning system which now enables decision-makers to make consciously informed decisions about managing change based on a proper understanding of the value and significance of a building or a place. The days when fine buildings could be demolished wastefully at random are being consigned to history. Britain now leads the world in the sophistication of its mechanisms for managing change to its historic environment.

One of the reasons London has become so successful is that as a result of public pressure a much better balance has been struck between continuity and change which, in turn, has enhanced its attraction to overseas investors and visitors. The long and noble battle of national and local societies, pressure groups, public and pundits to save historic buildings and areas from unthinking destruction and institutional philistinism largely has been won. People care passionately about the places where they live as much as individual buildings. Increasingly, historic buildings are seen as an asset, not a constraint on progress. They command a premium in the open market, and, at a time when it is imperative to reduce carbon emissions, it is recognised that the creative reuse of old buildings is inherently sustainable, reutilising the embodied energy they contain. Routinely warehouses, tenements, factories and other old buildings are being adapted, converted and reused by developers who have realised, at last, that history sells. The way to the New Jerusalem lies in the imaginative recycling of the old satanic mills.

But just as we have made huge strides forward in valuing the historic environment, we seem to have lost the art of placemaking which seemed so effortless 100 years ago. Where is the vision which created the garden suburbs or new towns? Where is the social idealism? What has happened to the art of town planning?

In 1900 C R Ashbee wrote:

"*We Londoners flatter ourselves that with the more enlightened municipal government which we enjoy we now take more thought for the well-being of the community … But are we not deceiving ourselves? Is any attempt made now to layout a suburban estate such as was once the Bedford Estate in Bloomsbury, or the Tredegar Estate in Bow?*"[30]

A century later we are infinitely richer, but with a handful of exceptions, no nearer to building successful places. We struggle to emulate the achievements of our grandfathers.

Nevertheless, after two world wars and massive economic, social and technological change, London remains one of the world's great cities; a vast brooding immensity pulsating with energy and life – timeless, immutable and serenely beautiful. The challenge is to ensure that it remains so.

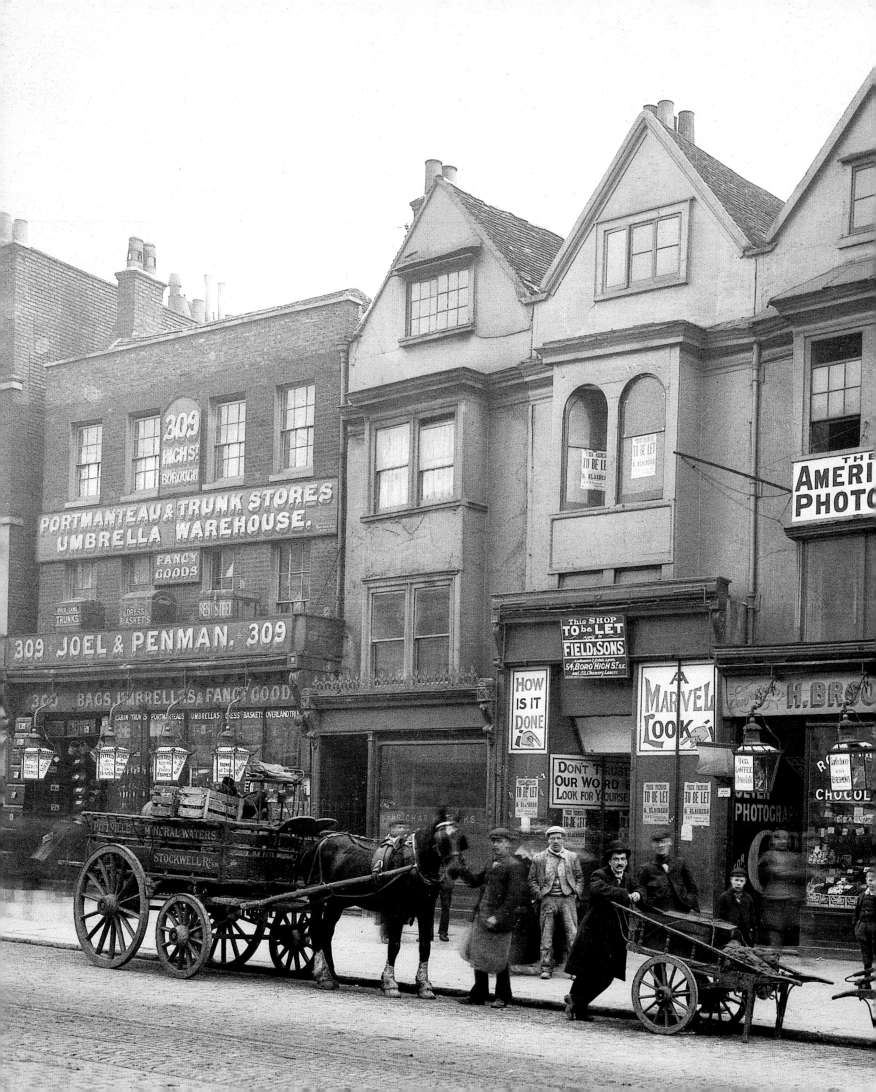

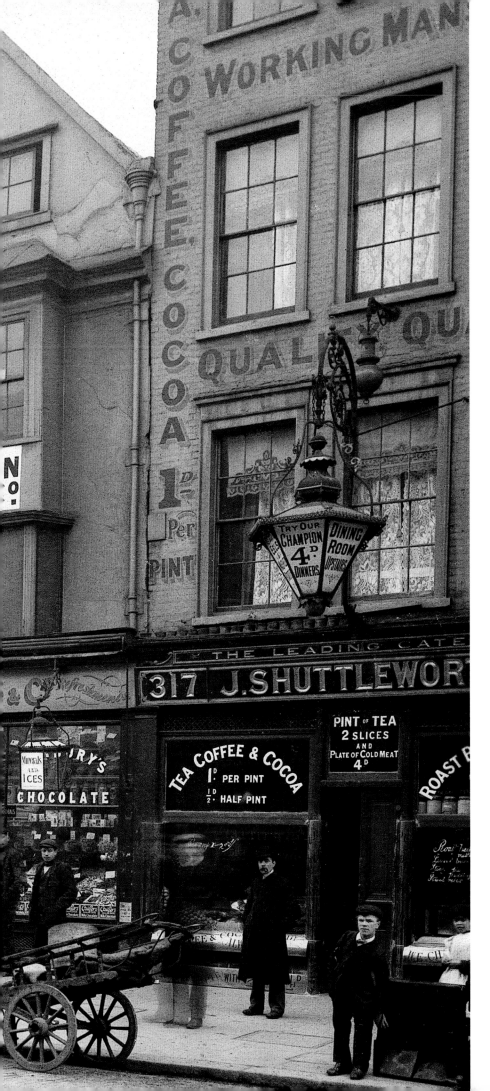

LOST
LONDON
1870-1945

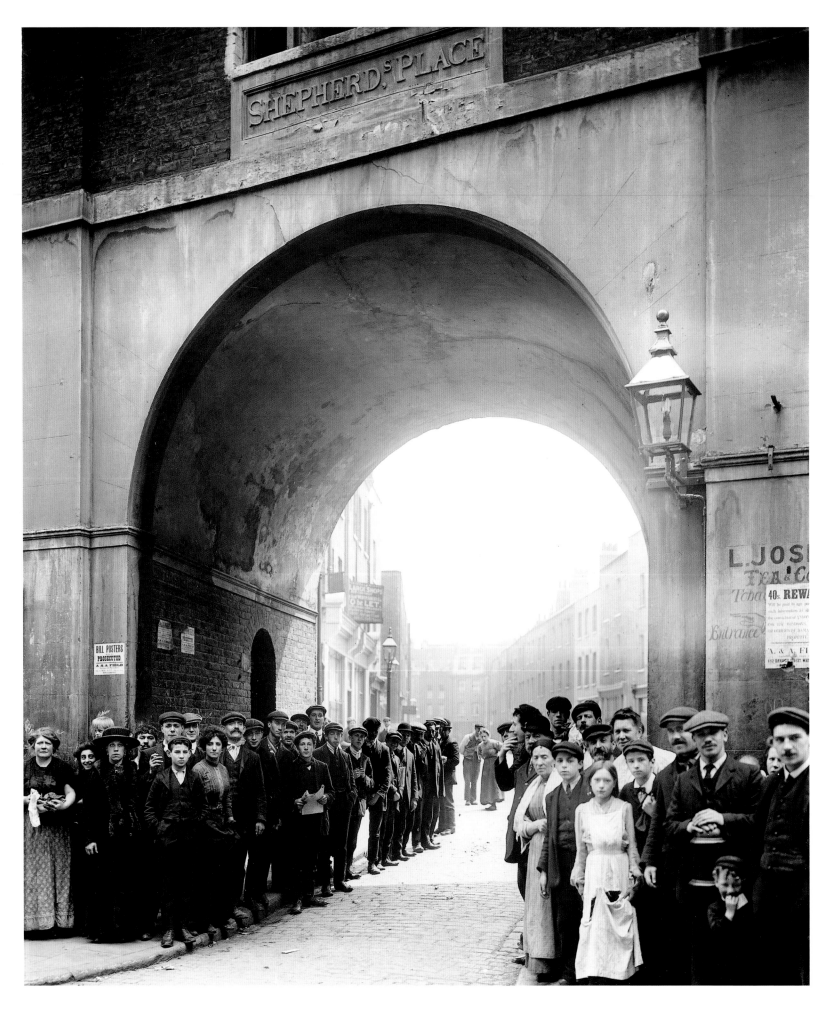

CHAPTER ONE

URBAN PENUMBRA
The City fringe

The loosely-defined arc of inner London from Clerkenwell and Smithfield in the north-west to Spitalfields and Minories in the south-east is referred to commonly as the City Fringe.

Clustered around St John's Gate and the old Priory Church of St John of Jerusalem, Clerkenwell is depicted on the cusp of change as ancient streets of 17th and 18th century domestic buildings were giving way to new light industrial and commercial premises. At a time when scant regard was given to architectural conservation, the preservation of St John's Church is an indication of the growing awareness of the importance of retaining London's architectural treasures.

To the south, Smithfield, or Smoothfield, was a large expanse of marshy land on the edge of the City used for mediaeval tournaments and, before Tyburn, as a place of execution. It was here in 1305 that Sir William Wallace was hanged, drawn and quartered, and where in 1557 the Protestant martyrs were burned under the Marian persecution. The famous cattle market was established in 1638, but in 1855 the sale and slaughter of live animals moved to Caledonian Market. A huge new meat market served by underground railways was erected to the designs of the City Surveyor, Sir Horace Jones.

Cloth Fair takes its name from an important cloth market, St Bartholomew's Fair, its tolls supporting the adjacent Priory and hospital. Held for three days from the eve of St Bartholomew on 24 August, it was opened by the Lord Mayor cutting a piece of cloth – the origin of the cutting of a ribbon to open buildings or events. The Fair had its own court – the Court of Pie Powder – which had jurisdiction over commercial complaints, weights and measures, and theft. It was notorious for immorality, crime and public disorder. "Knavery is here in perfection, dextrous cutpurses and pickpockets", wrote a French visitor in 1698. In a concerted effort to clean up the area it was abolished when the cattle market moved in 1855. The eponymous Cloth Fair can be seen here – a remarkable series of mediaeval, timber-framed houses which survived well into the 20th century, many of which were still in use by dealers in second-hand clothes and rags.

Further east the great merchant houses of Georgian Spitalfields are portrayed clinging to vestiges of their original elegance, even though by 1900 many had fallen into multiple occupation as cheap lodging houses. Hit by cheap French imports, silk weaving had virtually collapsed by 1860 generating massive hardship and an economic vacuum filled by mass immigration from Eastern Europe. By 1900 only a handful of weavers remained in Bethnal Green.

Opposite: Shepherd's Place Archway and Tenter Street, Spitalfields, 10 May 1909
Shepherd's Place archway (1810) with Tenter Street beyond. The houses on the old Tenter Ground estate were mean and closely-packed with little space at the rear. Chronic poverty was endemic, the main access to the estate was through this single archway from White's Row. What happened to these people?

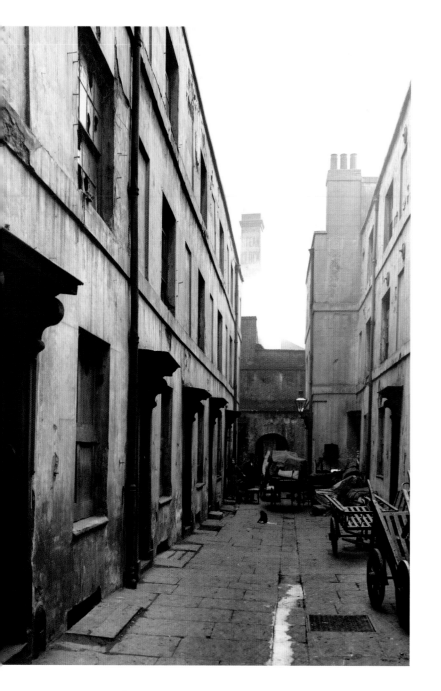 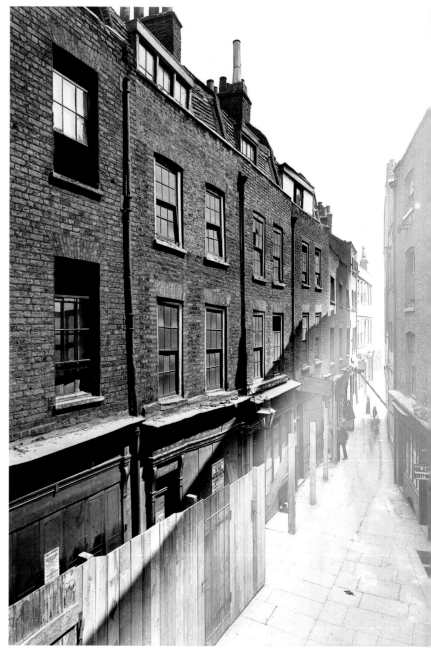

A working neighbourhood

CLERKENWELL

**Above left: Bishops Court, Aylesbury Street, Clerkenwell,
28 October 1904**

A typical inner city courtyard development built in 1726-28, and probably always intended for multiple occupation. The chimney in the background carries a sign for John Smith & Son, Steam Clock Factory. Smith's manufactured the clock tower which still stands at the junction of City Road and Goswell Road.

Above right: Jerusalem Passage (east side), Clerkenwell, 8 June 1906

Showing early 18th century houses prior to demolition. This was a rough and dangerous area with high levels of infant mortality.

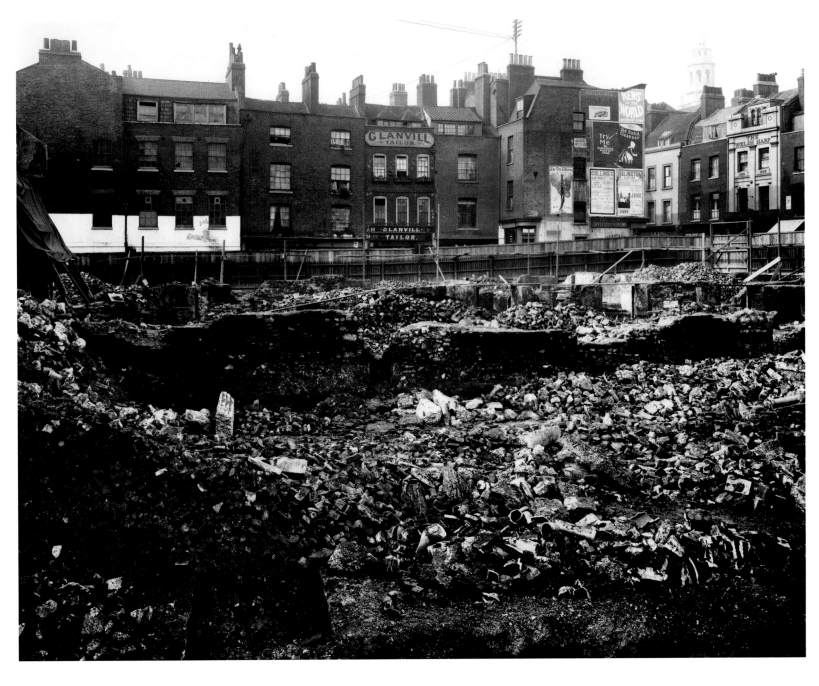

Above: Aylesbury Place, Clerkenwell, 19 October 1912

The houses on the east side of Jerusalem Passage have been cleared revealing the remains of the mediaeval Hall of the Priory of St John of Jerusalem in the foreground. The houses in the background on the west side of Jerusalem Passage still remain.

Right: 36, 37 and 38 Clerkenwell Close at the junction with Scotswood Street, 19 October 1909

The street layout still remains with the setted road surface surviving beneath later tarmac.

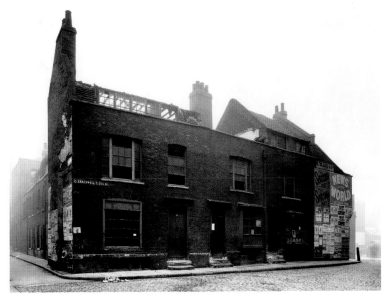

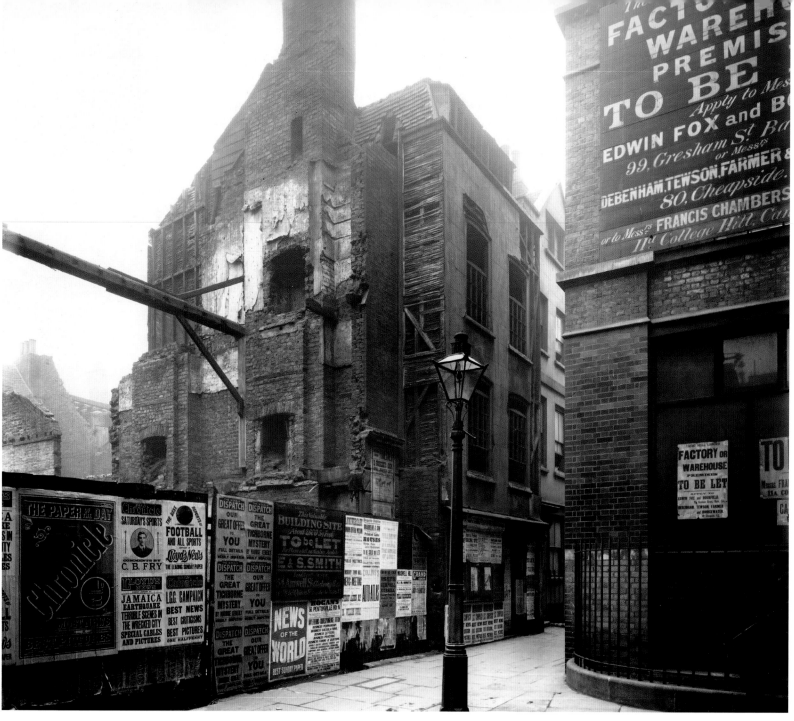

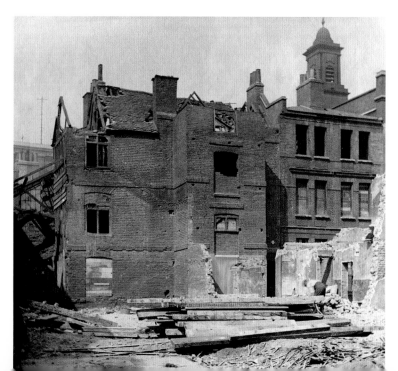

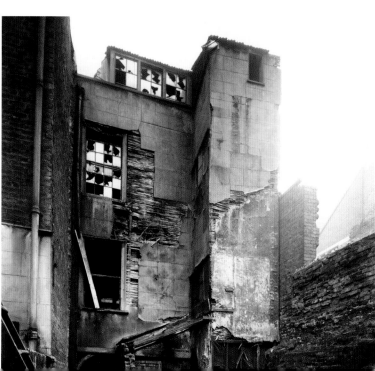

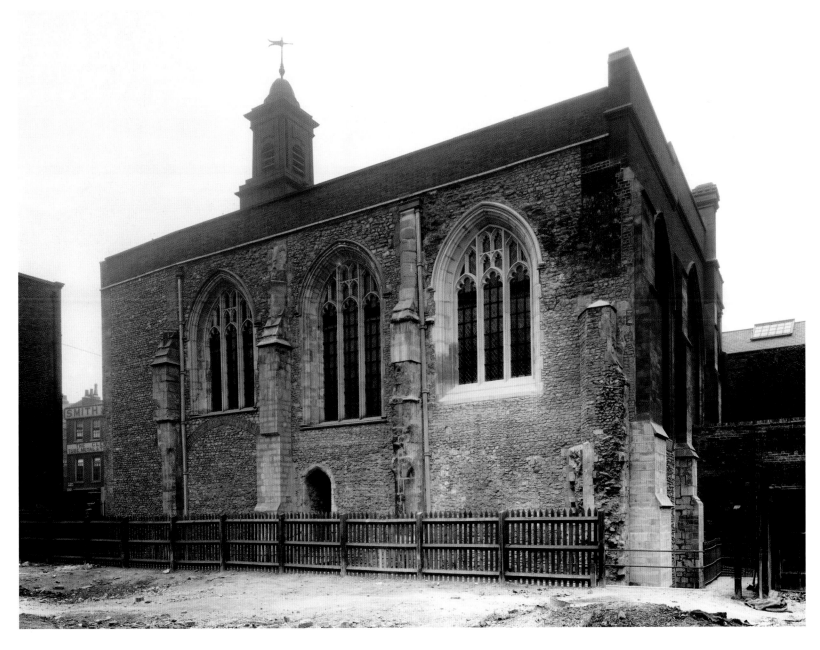

Fragments of an ancient priory

Opposite top: 11 St John's Square, 30 January 1907

In this oblique view the earlier 17th century building can be seen clearly behind the skin of the later front facade. The posters are of particular interest. The *Weekly Dispatch* leads with the "The Great Tichborne Mystery" and *Lloyds News* with "The Jamaica Earthquake" for its Sunday edition on 20 January.

Opposite bottom left: St John's Church, May 1904

Photograph taken from the site of the Horse & Groom public house showing the clearance of buildings around the Grand Priory Church, the cupola of which can be seen to the right.

Opposite bottom right: 11 St John's Square, 30 January 1907

Rear elevation showing earlier timber studwork and lath and plaster beneath the external skin.

Above: St John's Church, south side, 19 August 1908

The Grand Priory Church of the Order of St John of Jerusalem after the clearance of surrounding buildings.

The Priory was founded in 1140 as the English headquarters of the Knights Hospitallers: a military order of knights dedicated to the care of the sick. The original 12th century crypt survives beneath the church, which is still in use today, a fragment of the original Priory complex which once extended across the entire centre of Clerkenwell.

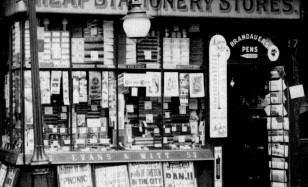

EVANS & WITT

STATIONERS & BOOKBINDERS.

BOOKSELLERS & TOBACCONISTS.

71ᴬ G. BURRELL 71ᴬ
DEALER IN PICKLED TONGUES, SWEETBREADS &ᶜ

SMOKE WILL'S "OLD FLAKE" CIGARETTES.

CHEAP STATIONERY STORES.

BRANDAUER'S PENS

BOILED BEEF   THE BEST BOIL

57ᴬ

D

PRIORY CHURCH
OF
S. BARTHOLOMEW
The GREAT

SERVICES

EVANS & WITT   57

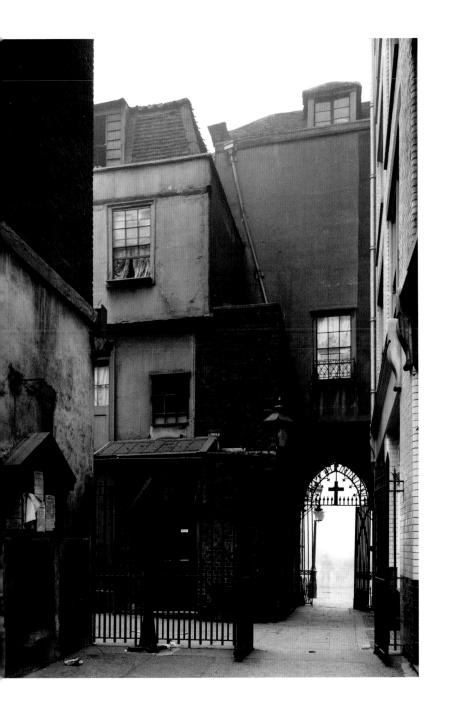

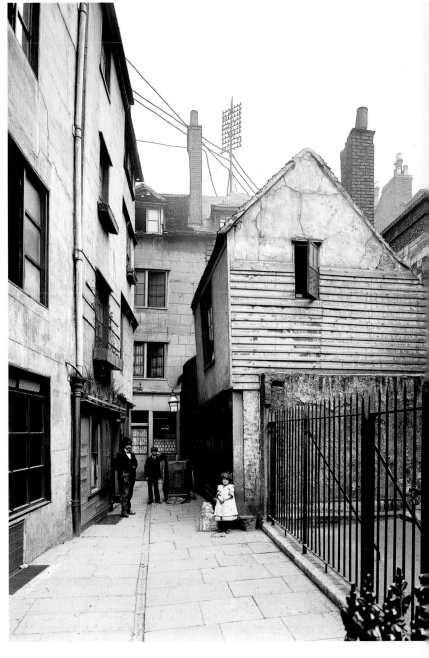

SMITHFIELD

Opposite: Gatehouse to the Church of St Bartholomew the Great, Smithfield, 18 November 1908

St Bartholomew the Great, built by Rahere in 1123, is London's oldest parish church. This polite Georgian facade was destroyed in a Zeppelin raid in 1916 revealing the original 16th century timber-framed frontage behind. It was restored in the 1920s.

Above left: Rear elevation of the gatehouse to St Bartholomew the Great, 18 November 1908

The entrance passage to the church.

Above right: Cloth Fair, Smithfield, 16 May 1904

"*Here are narrow walled lanes, where two persons can pass one another with difficulty … The explorer may thread covered passages from which he can note details of domestic life passing within easy ken. That houses built so closely, and of such inflammable material, should have survived to the present day seems little short of marvellous.*" (William Dixon)

The view from Schoolden Street depicting a small 17th century dwelling against the walls of St Bartholomew's church.

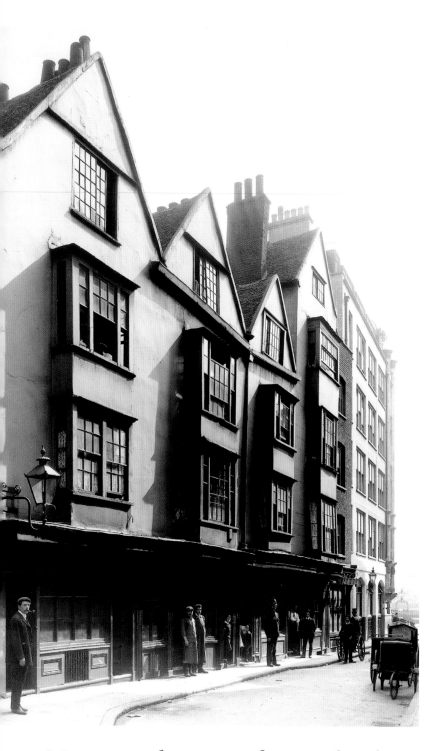

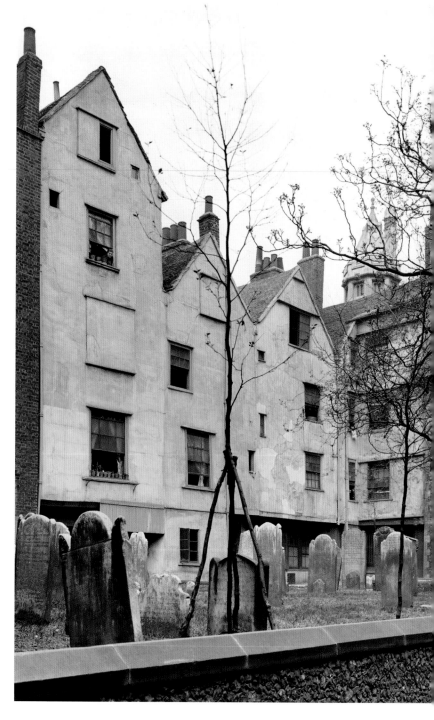

Narrow lanes of crooked, overhanging houses...

Above left: Cloth Fair, Smithfield, 27 July 1908

A fine group of 17th century timber-framed houses between the north door of St Bartholomew's Church and West Smithfield prior to demolition.

Above right: Rear elevation of the houses above from the churchyard of St Bartholomew the Great, 16 May 1904

Opposite: The Old Dick Whittington Inn, Cloth Fair, 16 May 1904

"It was pleasant … to sit through winter's amethystine dusk and watch the fire and its play of shadows … sportive, fantastic shadows, which hovered and darted, and sometimes made a long arm as if to snatch the very tankard out of one's hand." (R Thurston Hopkins 1927)

Allegedly the oldest inn in London, the Old Dick Whittington was demolished in 1916. Two carved wooden satyrs of 1550 from its corner posts are in the Museum of London.

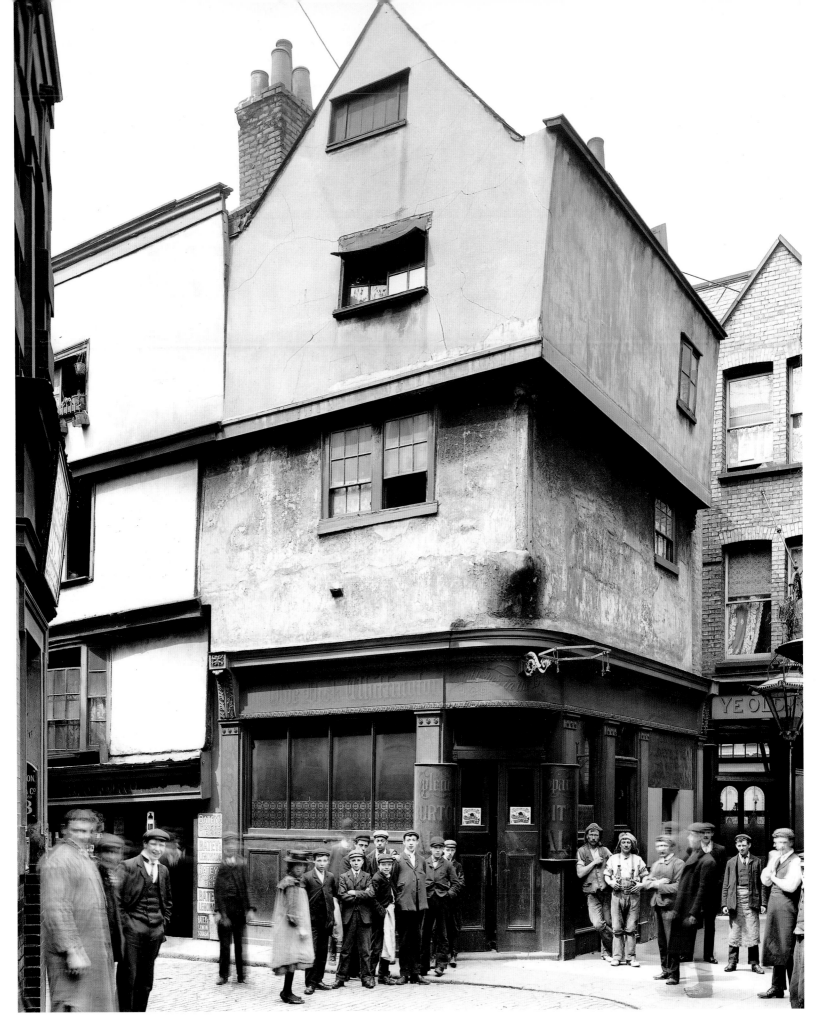

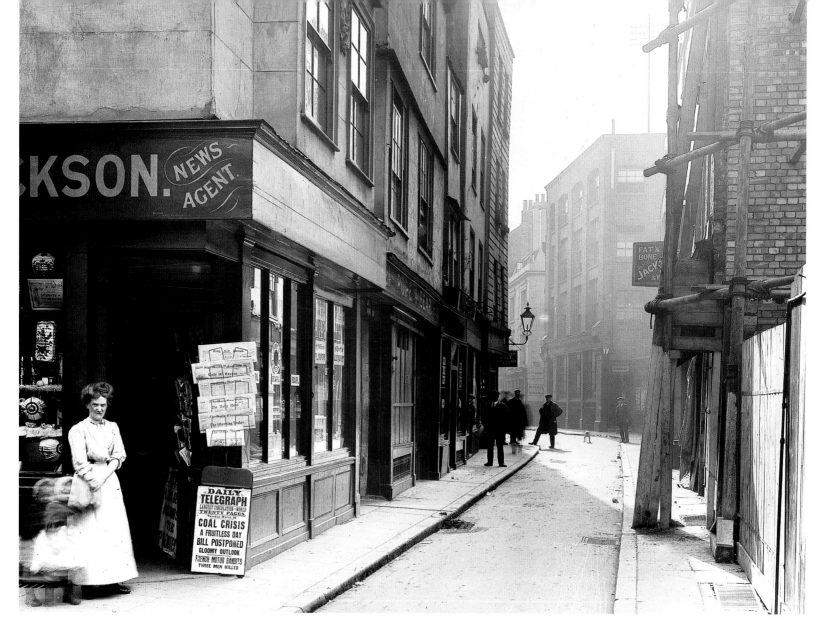

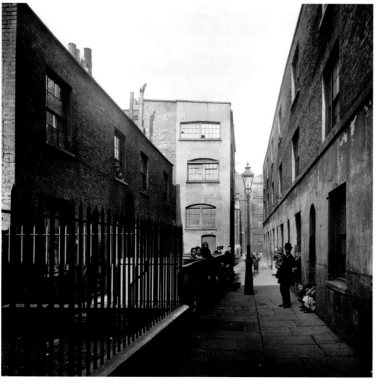

Above: 20 Cloth Fair and entrance to Red Lion Passage looking west, 26 March 1912

Note the patriotic paper lanterns for sale in the shop window and the sign for the Fat and Bone merchant on the extreme right. The newspaper placard features French Motor Bandits. Three Killed. Wooden scaffolding was common at this time.

Left: Cockerills Buildings, Red Lion Passage, Cloth Fair, 26 March 1912

View looking east. The buttress of St Bartholomew's Church can be glimpsed in the middle distance.

Opposite: Bartholomew Close, 1906

Weatherboarded timber-framed house with a grocer's shop on the ground floor. The arrival of the photographer was an occasion of considerable local curiosity. Hats were a mark of respectability; note the variety of headgear – top hats, bowlers and cloth caps are worn by men and boys of all ages.

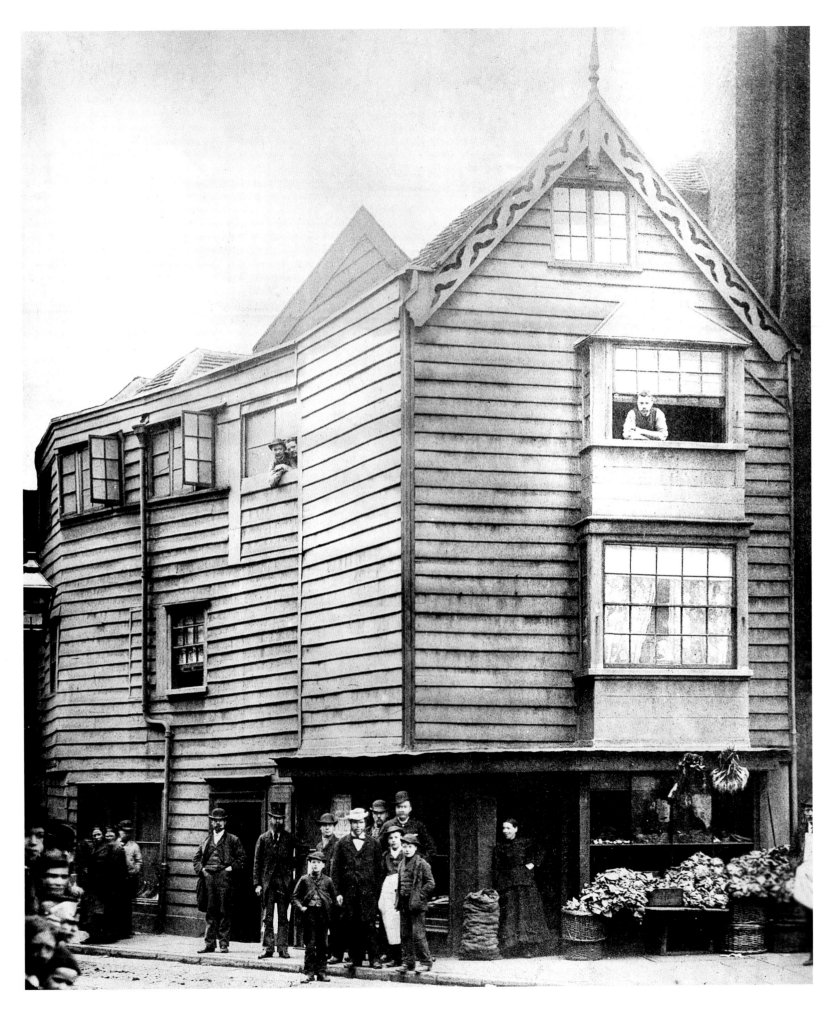

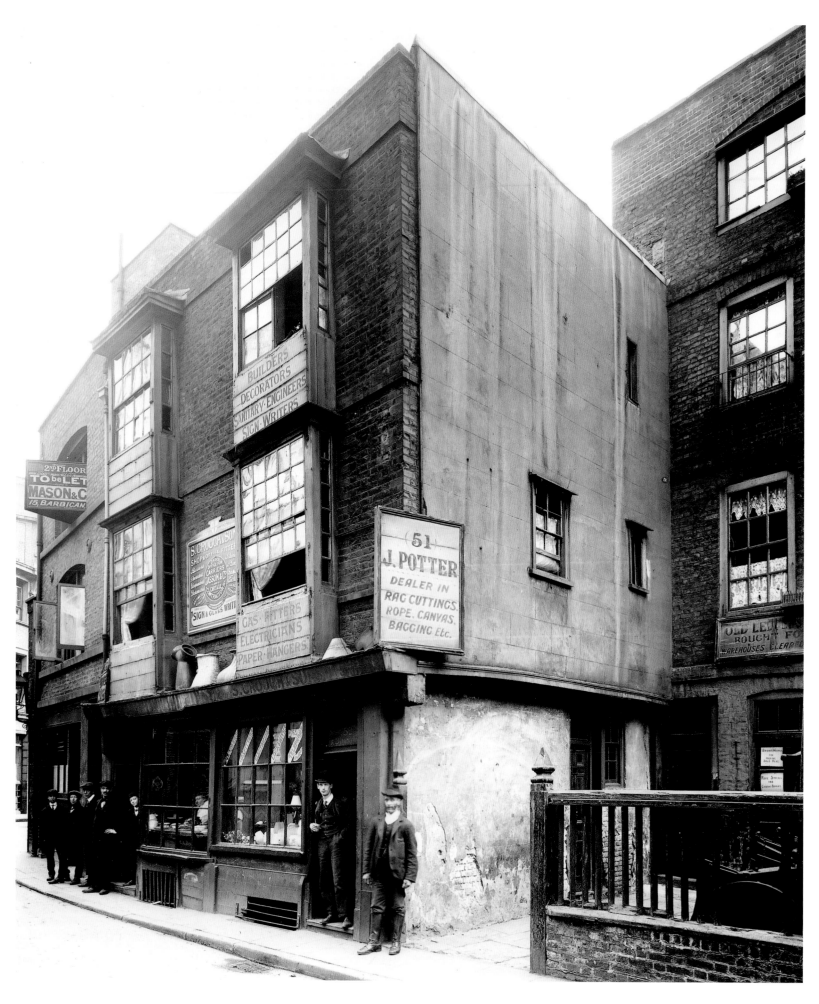

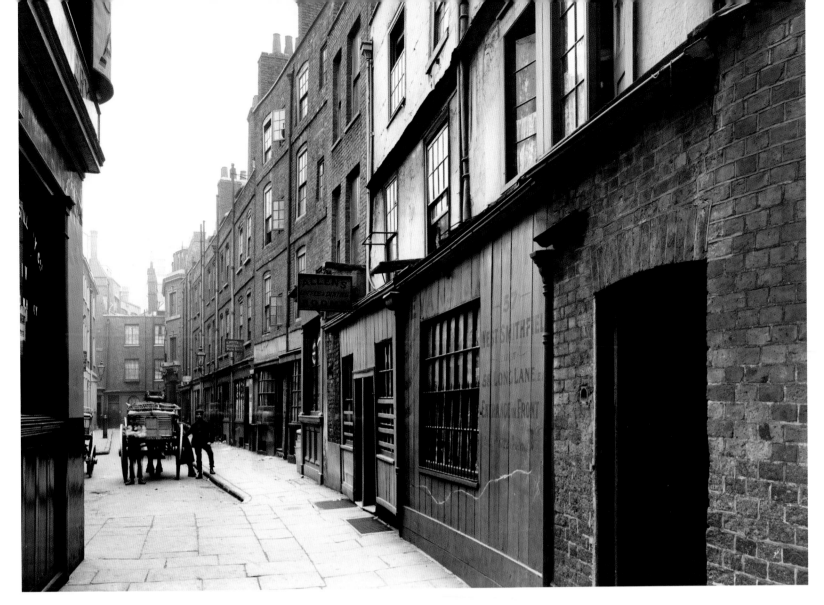

Time-worn houses

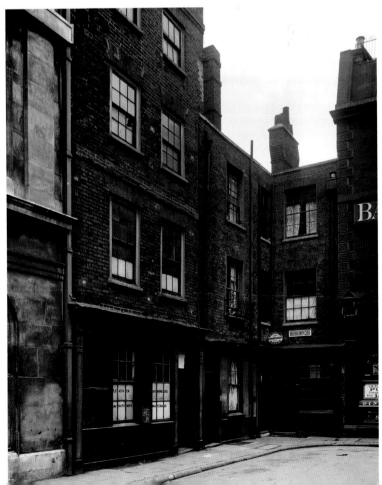

Opposite: 51-54 Bartholomew Close, Smithfield, 7 October 1909

The premises of S Crouch & Son, Shop and Office Fitters, general builders and signwriters. No. 51 is occupied by J Potter, a dealer in second-hand cloth and paper, a trade once common in the area. The front wall with the cart behind retains its original wooden posts and railings. The original thick-section glazing bars to the windows are typical early 18th century details.

Above: 78-80 Bartholomew Close, 7 October 1909

View looking north towards the entrance to St Bartholomew's Church with early 18th century houses to the right.

Right: Nos 73-80 Bartholomew Close, 7 October 1909

View looking south with the stone frontage of Butchers' Hall to the extreme left.

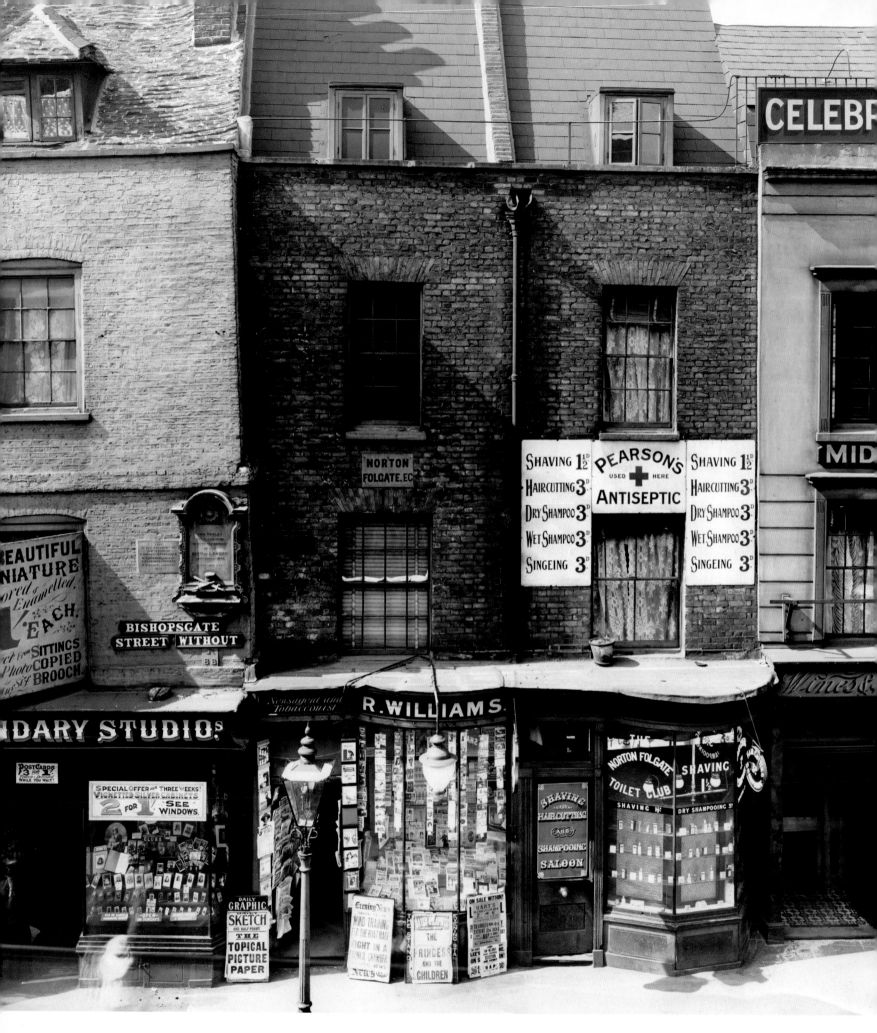

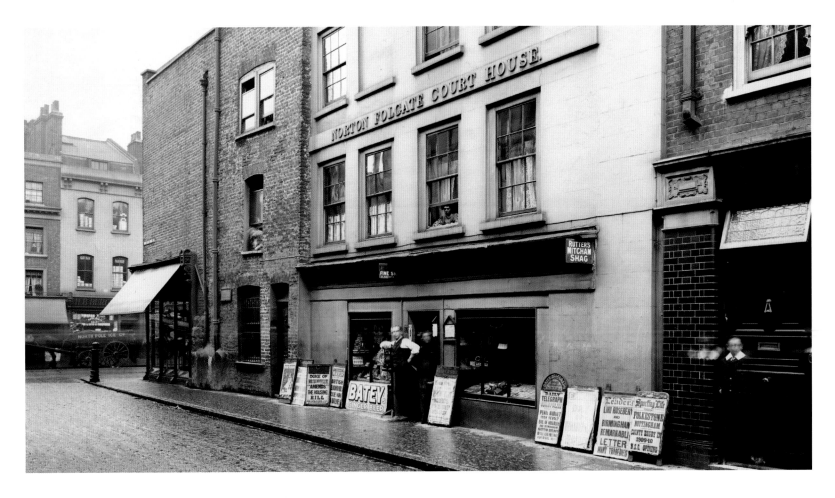

Ancient city boundary

Opposite: 39-40 Norton Folgate, Spitalfields, 25 March 1909

Norton Folgate at Bishopsgate Street Without – the boundary between Shoreditch and the City of London. The elaborate stone boundary plaque is dated 1846. The photographic studio on the extreme left offers coloured or enamelled miniatures for 1/-. The hairdressers is the home of the Norton Folgate Toilet Club. p52 shows the wider view immediately to the south.

Above: Norton Folgate Court House, Folgate Street, 6 October 1909

This late 17th century building became the court house for the manor and liberty of Norton Folgate in 1744. An upper room was used for the court house, and a lower room as a watch house until the abolition of the liberty and its incorporation into the Borough of Stepney in 1900. On the extreme left, beside the corner shop and downpipes, is a fragment of mediaeval stonework alleged to be the remains of St Mary Spital Priory.

Right: 10-11 Norton Folgate, 25 March 1909

The Golden Eagle was a dispensing chemist founded in 1750 with a delightful double-bowed shop front of about 1780, a railed stall board and brass cill bands engraved with the names of the store – Peter Jones. The traditional apothecaries' jars can be seen in the left-hand window. No. 10 was occupied continuously by lead and glass merchants from 1809 until the 20th century.

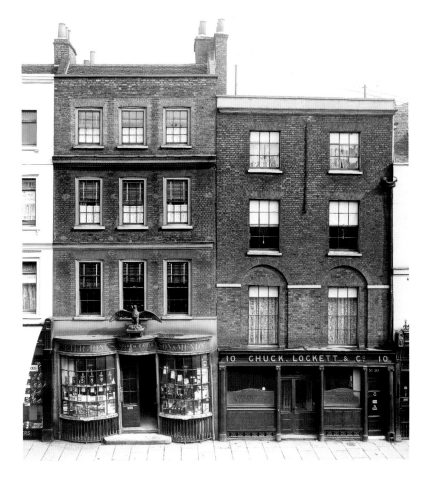

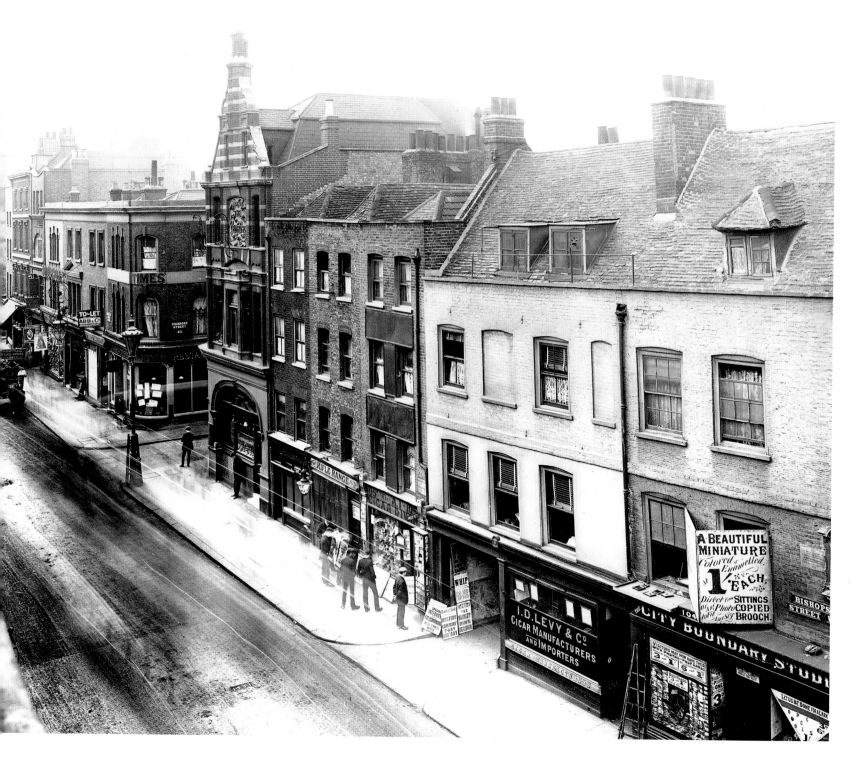

By the Bishop's Gate

Above: Bishopsgate Street Without looking south from boundary with Norton Folgate, October 1909

Even on the edge of the City of London, the original mediaeval house plots persist filled by 18th and 19th century buildings of a domestic scale and character. Such areas of the City fringe serviced the daily needs of the great temples of commerce further south in the heart of the City.

Note the "Al Cigar Diwan" and adjacent "Rifle Range". The same photographic studio can be seen on p 50.

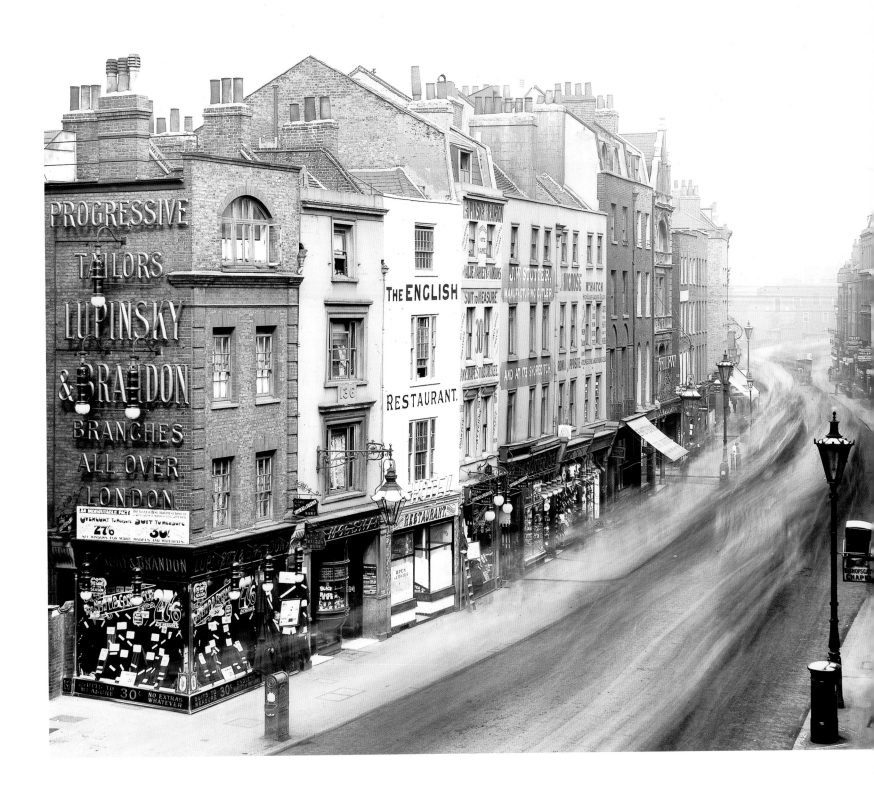

**Above: Bishopsgate Street (west side) looking north to Norton Folgate,
7 October 1909**

A typical street scene on the City fringe at the beginning of the 20th
century. The shops boast elaborate gas lanterns and signs; street orderly
bins of the type shown in the foreground are still in widespread use in the
City of London.

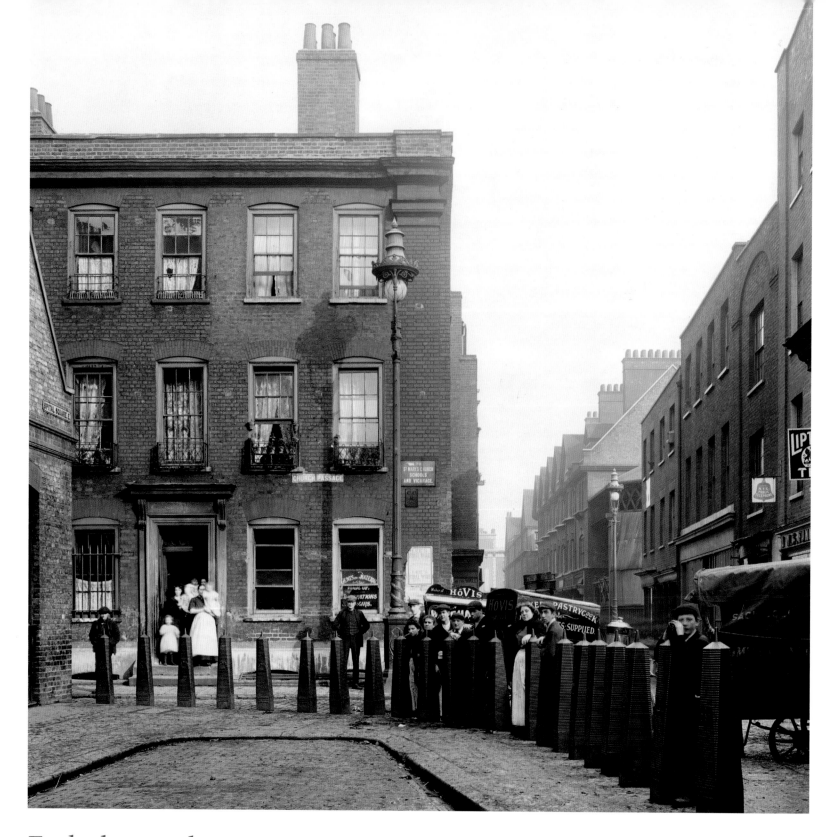

Faded grandeur

SPITALFIELDS

Above: St Mary's Passage and Lamb Street from Spital Square, October 1909

No. 1 St Mary's Passage was a large, double-fronted merchant's house built in 1733 by Samuel Worrall, a local carpenter. Giant Doric pilasters frame the frontage. By the mid-19th century it had become a police station, although by the time of this photograph it was in use as a workshop and lodging house.

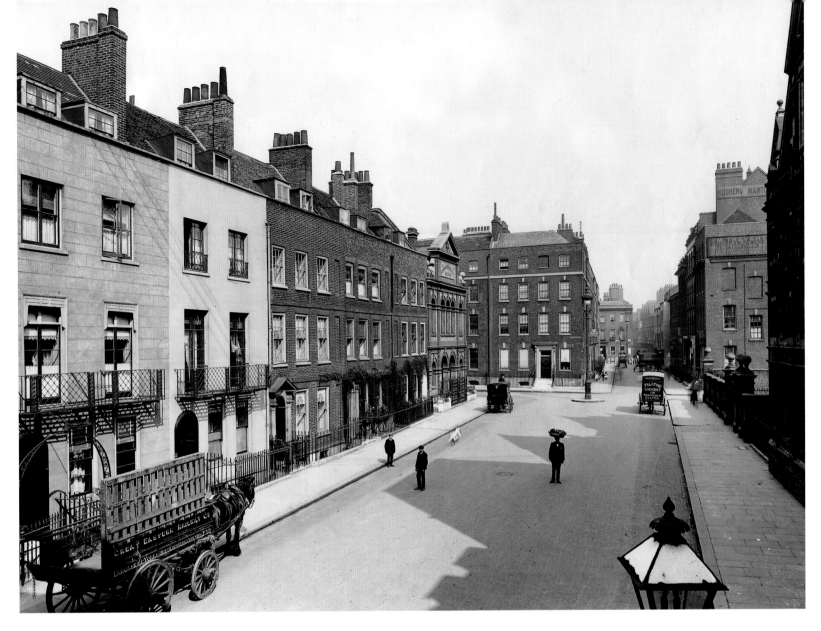

Above: Spital Square looking towards No. 22 with St Mary's Passage beyond, 3 May 1909

Nos. 5-9 Spital Square (left) were built as a terrace c 1704. Nos. 5 and 6 were remodelled during the Regency with faux stone-coursed stucco, wrought iron balustrades and an elaborate iron lamp overthrow to No. 5. Beyond is the German Synagogue (1858) in a heavy classical style. The cleanliness of the street, the absence of clutter and the innate sense of visual order are particularly notable.

Right: Spital Square looking towards Folgate Street, October 1909

No. 15 Spital Square to the left was a substantial five-bay wide merchant's house of 1724 of a type once common in Spitalfields. Nos. 11-14 were demolished in the 1930s for the Co-operative Wholesale Society Fruit Warehouse. No. 15 survived until 1952. No. 17 (1725) to the right, and 19-21 Folgate Street (1723) in the left background, still exist.

Only 30 years ago Spitalfields was threatened with wholesale destruction. Today it is regarded as one of the finest concentrations of early Georgian town houses in Britain. To lose buildings of such quality now would be unthinkable.

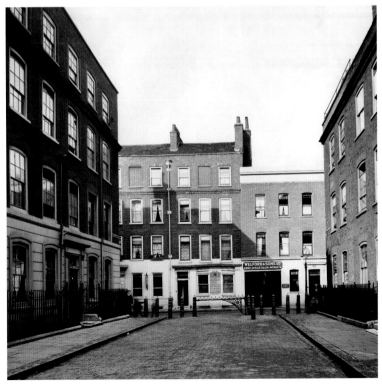

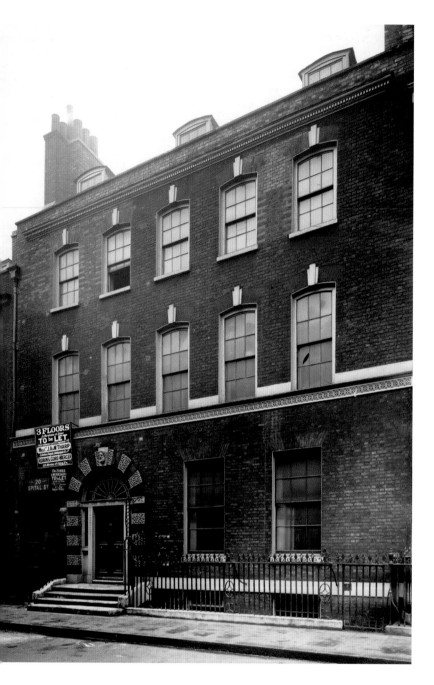

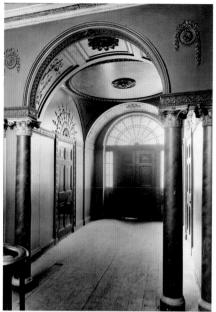

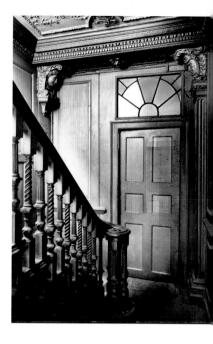

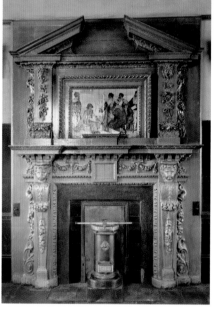

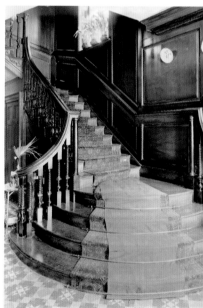

Above & top centre: 20 Spital Square, c 1900

Grand five-bay houses of this type were erected for prosperous merchants, bankers, brewers and weavers. Built in 1732, the house was remodelled extensively around 1790 when the basement and ground floors were refronted. The arch-headed doorway with its leaded fanlight and Coade stone mask and dressings were fashionable later alterations. The guilloche frieze and wrought iron railings also date from this period. The house still survives.

The superb entrance hall (c 1790) with its screen of Corinthian columns and delicate neo-classical plasterwork.

Typical early Georgian interiors of Spital Square

Top right: 25 Spital Square, 22 April 1909

The remarkable entrance hall (1733) with alternating fluted and twisted balusters to the staircase. Masked consoles carry the cornice with richly-detailed rococo plasterwork above.

Above centre: 30 Spital Square, 6 November 1908

Ground floor room: this spectacular carved chimneypiece (c 1739) was one of four which were salvaged and sold when No. 30 and its neighbours were demolished in 1922.

Above right: 22 Spital Square, 4 May 1909

Entrance hall and staircase (c 1733) with splayed steps, twisted balusters and raised and fielded panelling.

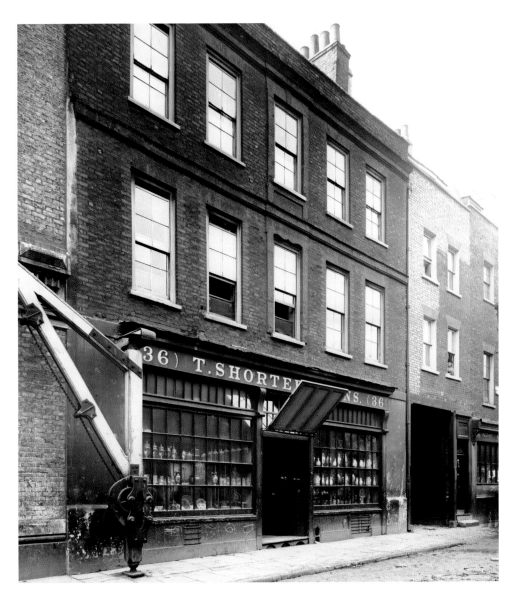

Silk weavers

Left: 36 Crispin Street, 25 March 1909

An elegant Spitalfields mansion (c 1713) with a subtle carved ogee shape cut into the brickwork over the central bay. A French Huguenot chapel once stood at the rear. The shop, which was added around 1800, was occupied by a glass and china merchant until its demolition in the 1920s.

Below right: 42 Alma Road, Bethnal Green, 24 May 1909

The weavers' houses of Bethnal Green were highly distinctive, often only one room deep, with irregular fenestration patterns and long horizontal weavers' lights. Good light was crucial for the delicate art of silk weaving and colour matching, but by 1909 silk weaving was in sharp decline.

The revolving drums of the spreading out machine can be seen in operation.

Below left: 42 Alma Road, 24 May 1909

The front half of the same room showing spreading out machinery and hand looms.

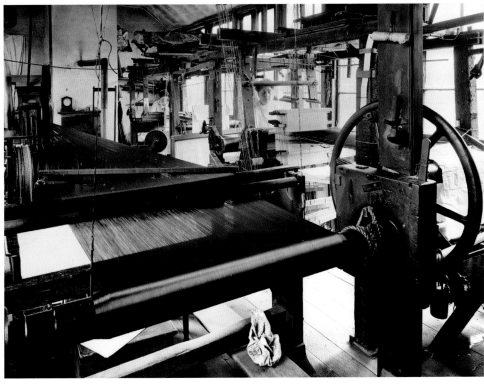

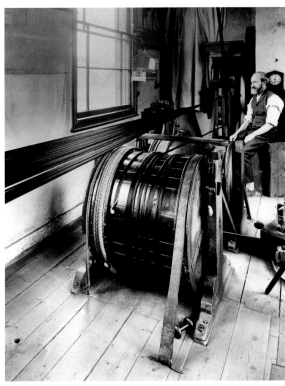

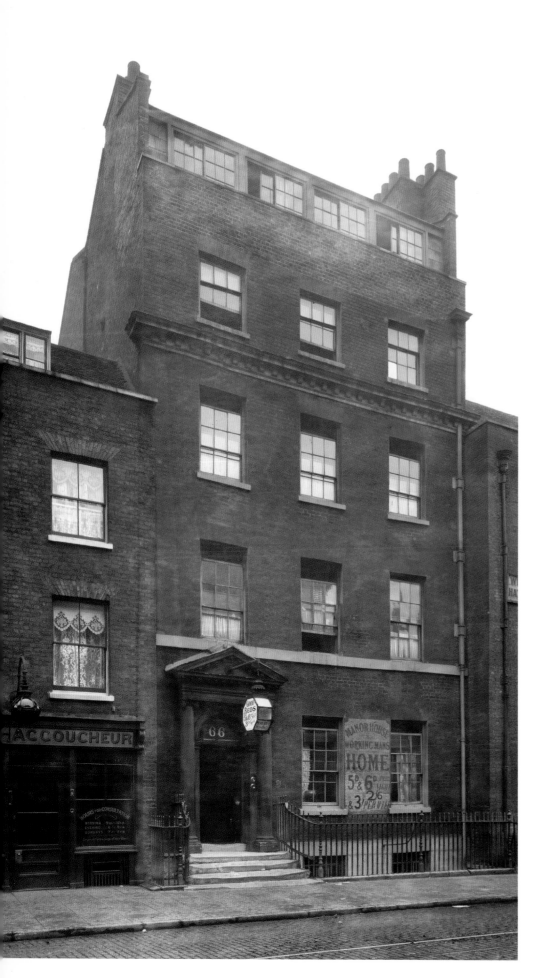

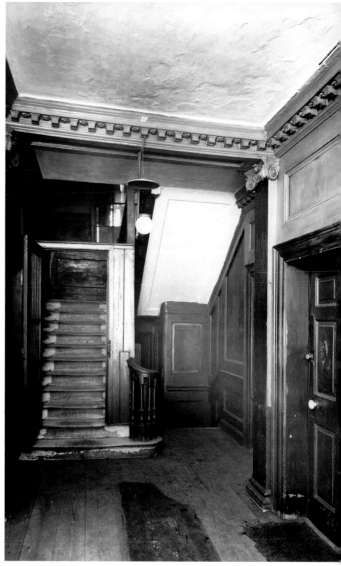

Cheap lodgings

Left: 66 Leman Street, Whitechapel, 8 February 1910
Manor House Working Man's Home: a once grand 18th century merchant's house in use as a common lodging house for the working man. Rooms varied from 5d to 6d a night or 2/6d or 3/- per week. The house still survives. The "Surgeon-Accoucheur" to the left, marked by a distinctive red globe lantern, offered medical care and midwifery to those who could afford it.

Above: 62 Leman Street, 8 February 1910
The fine 18th century panelled entrance hall and staircase fallen on hard times.

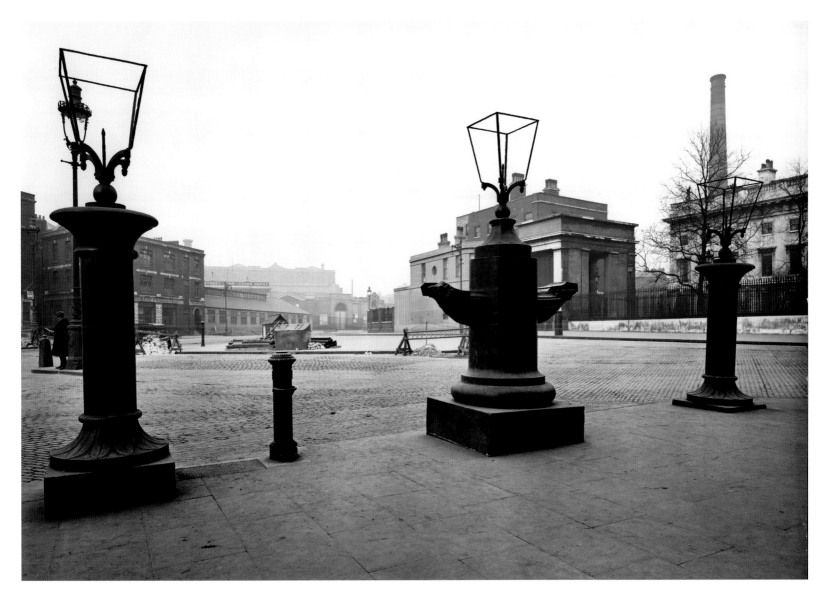

Mint by the Tower

Above: St Katherine's Dock House, Tower, c 1910

Superb cast iron ornamental lamp standards on the forecourt of St Katherine's Dock House, which was destroyed in the Blitz in 1940. The former Royal Mint building, designed by James Johnson and built by Sir Robert Smirke 1807-12, can be seen clearly to the right. In the middle distance is the GNR Goods Depot. Note the complete absence of road traffic.

Right: 1-2 Little Prescot Street, 14 December 1906

Little Prescot Street shortly before clearance in 1907 for the widening and extension of Mansell Street to meet Tower Bridge Approach. O'Connell's Coffee and Dining Rooms in the background catered for carmen serving the surrounding goods depots. A rasher and two eggs could be had for 4d.

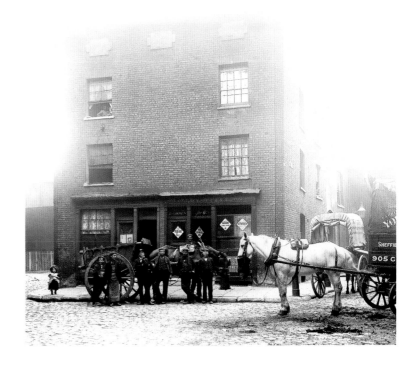

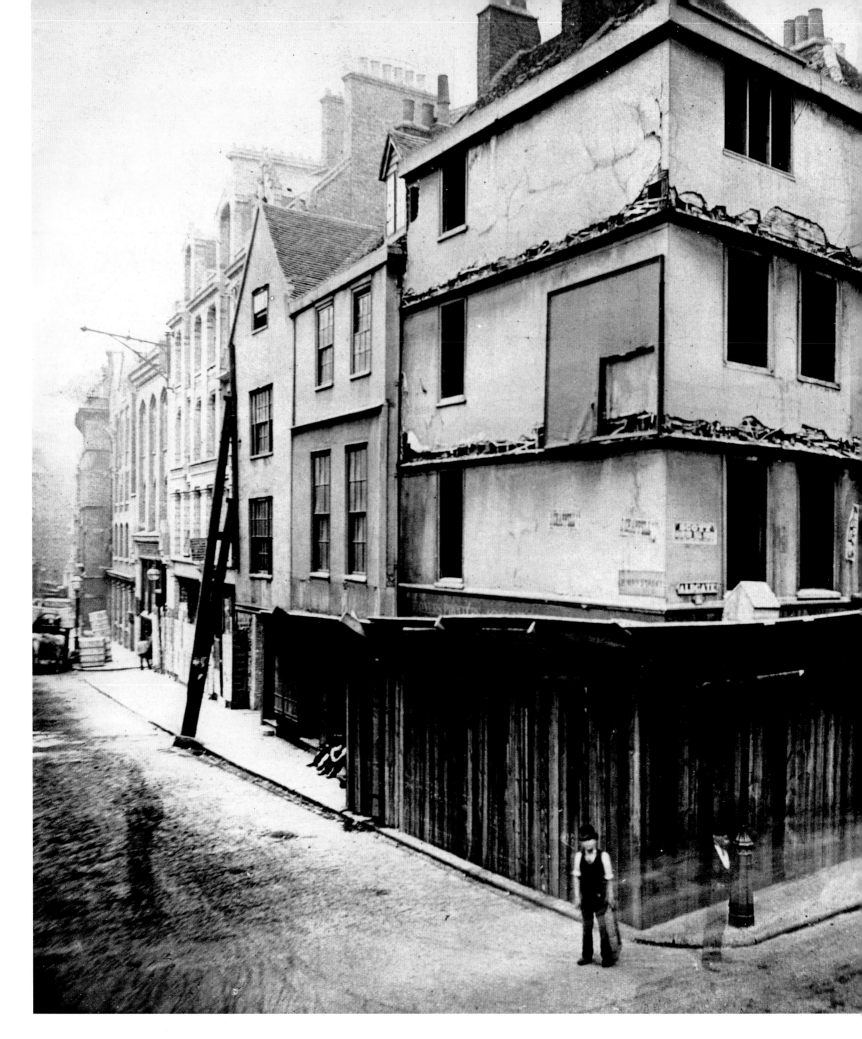

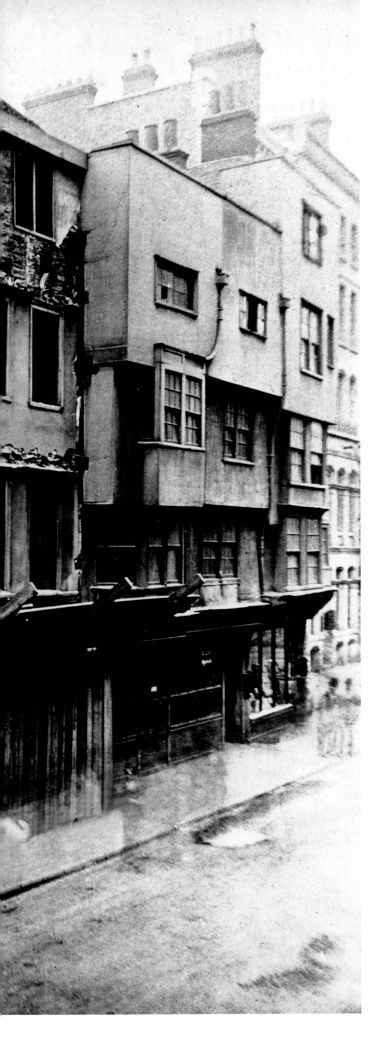

CHAPTER TWO

ENGINE OF COMMERCE

The City of London

The City of London is shown on the cusp of change. The old Roman and mediaeval grain of the City is still very apparent in the maze of narrow lanes and alleys, whilst groups of domestic buildings of all periods conferred a great sense of history until the Second World War. Numerous old, timber pre-Fire houses could be found on the edges of the City around Aldgate, Fleet Street and Cloth Fair, and many streets were still punctuated by later, brick, Georgian town houses, once occupied by City merchants, but later converted to commercial use or offices.

In 1851 the resident population of the City had been 129,000, many of whom were shopkeepers, tailors, craftsmen and artisans. A large amount of manufacturing still took place over the shop and in small factories and workshops, but by 1901 the population had shrunk to just 27,000. Many small traders and craftsmen migrated to the City fringe, or to new, purpose-built commercial premises. Increasingly the characteristic domestic scale and form of the City underwent a step change. By 1905 four-fifths of the entire City had been rebuilt in the previous 50 years, doubling the amount of available floorspace for the banks, insurance companies, shipping agents and brokers that financed half the world's trade. Entire street blocks were felled for gigantic new temples of commerce as older residential buildings gave way to monumental palaces which overtly expressed British commercial pre-eminence. The City's residential population was replaced by armies of office workers, who commuted daily via the great railway termini and on the underground and, later, the deep tube.

Whilst the livery halls of the wealthy City guilds held their own and prospered alongside dozens of pre-Fire and Wren churches, other great City institutions succumbed. Christ's Hospital moved out in 1902 hard on the heels of Charterhouse School, which had relocated to Godalming in 1874. Newgate Prison was cleared in the same year to make way for the Central Criminal Courts, and Smirke's elegant General Post Office was rendered redundant by a huge new Post Office on the site of Christ's Hospital.

Corner of Jewry Street & Aldgate, c 1906
This superb group of 17th century timber-framed houses stood at the junction of Jewry Street and Aldgate. Photographed for their antiquarian interest by the London Stereoscopic and Photographic Society, the images were annotated by hand with the names of the premises. The lath and plaster finishes and timber studwork are exposed clearly on the corner house.

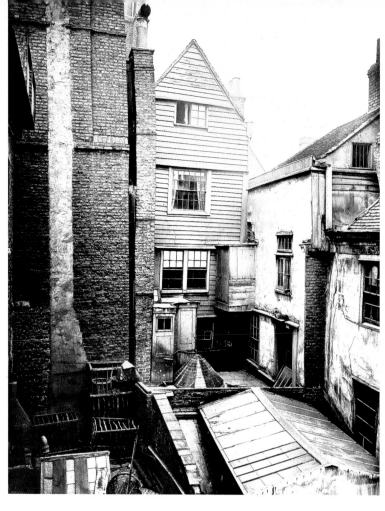

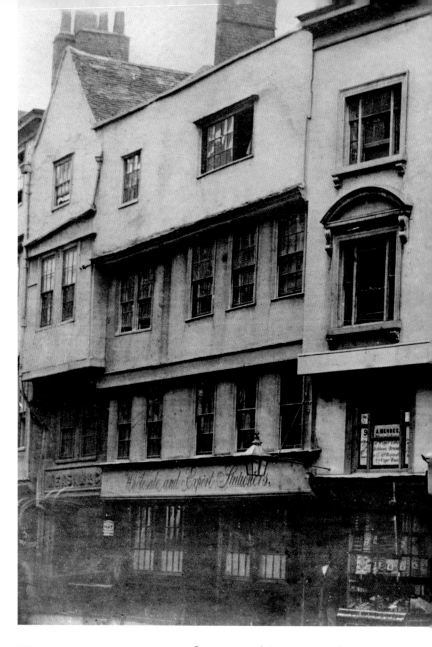

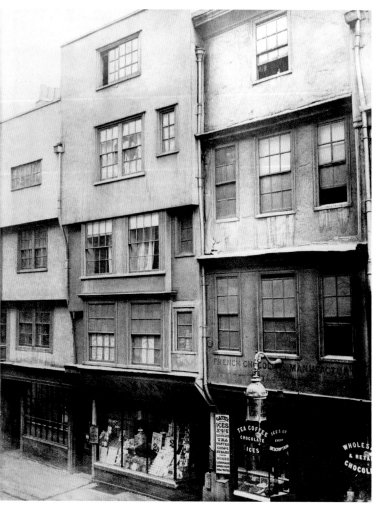

Fragments of mediaeval London

ALDGATE

Above left: Jewry Street, c 1904
Rear elevation of 17th century buildings and outbuildings taken from a collection of Notes on Aldgate Ward 1904 by Richard Kemp. The gabled rear elevation belongs to the third house from the corner in the far photograph on page 60.

Above right: View of Aldgate towards junction of Jewry Street, c 1904
17th century timber-framed houses with jettied upper floors over shops and business premises.

Left: Aldgate, c 1904
Jettied timber frontages

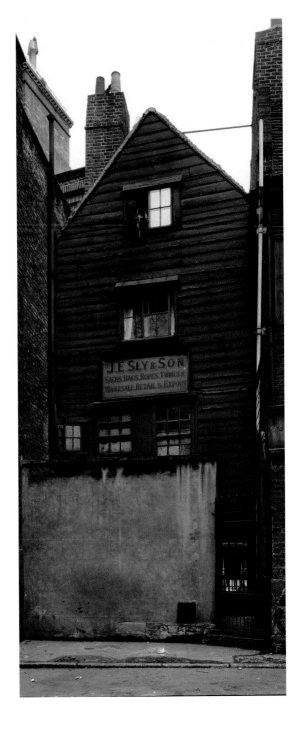

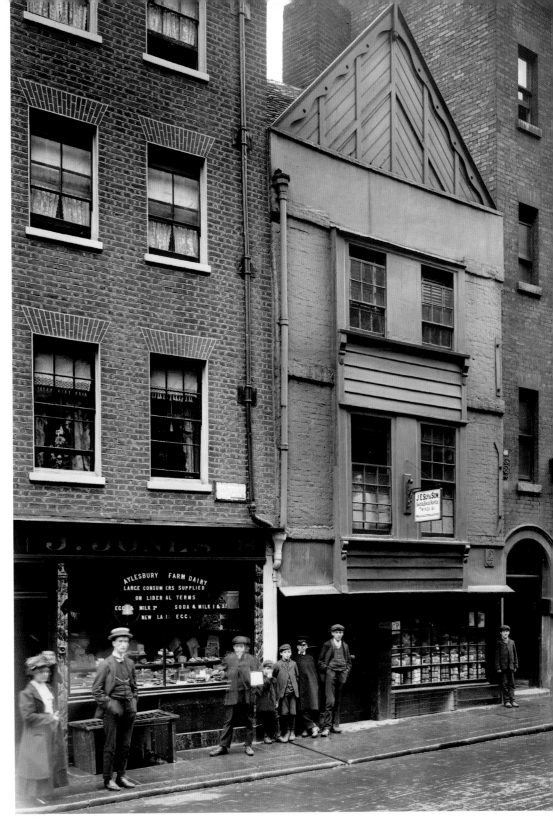

Above right: 7 Jewry Street, Aldgate, 20 August 1909

No. 7 Jewry Street was built in 1650. It survived both the Great Fire and the Blitz, which destroyed the buildings on either side, before succumbing to a fire in 1946. The old clay tile roof can be seen behind the Victorian gable. J E Sly & Son, a well-known firm of rope, sack and bag manufacturers, occupied the house from the early 19th century. The figure in the first floor window is probably one of the Sly family.

Above left: 7 Jewry Street, 14 October 1912

Rear elevation showing the weatherboarded gable with horizontal sliding sashes to the first and second floors.

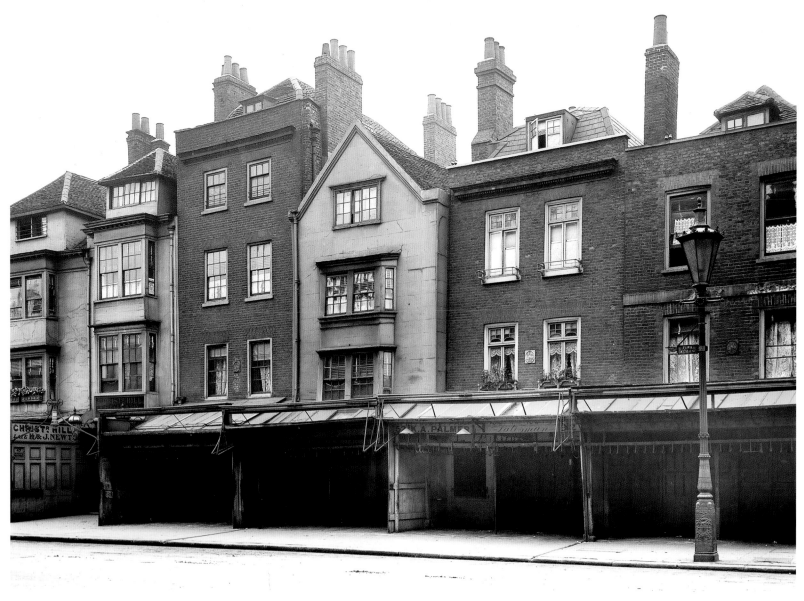

Hidden antiquity

Above: 47-52 Aldgate High Street, 27 September 1908
Christopher Hill's wine shop is now the Hoop and Grapes public house, which has 13th century cellars and a listening tube to the bars overhead to allow the landlord to eavesdrop on conversations. Two ancient carved oak posts flank the entrance. It is one of the oldest taverns in London.

Right: 48-50 Aldgate, 27 September 1908
The butchers and eel shops which occupied this group of buildings provided produce to nearby City restaurants.

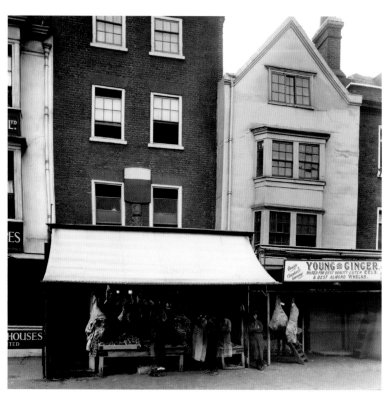

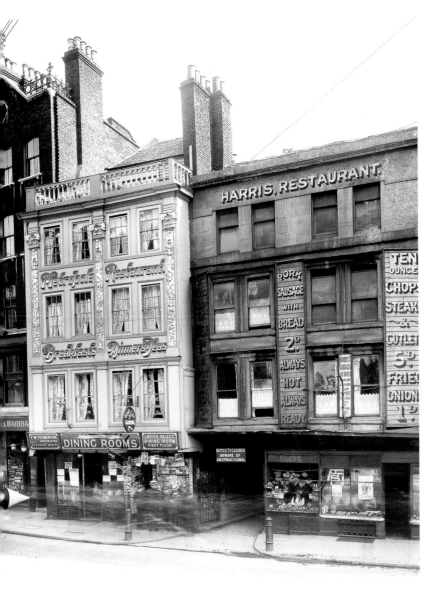

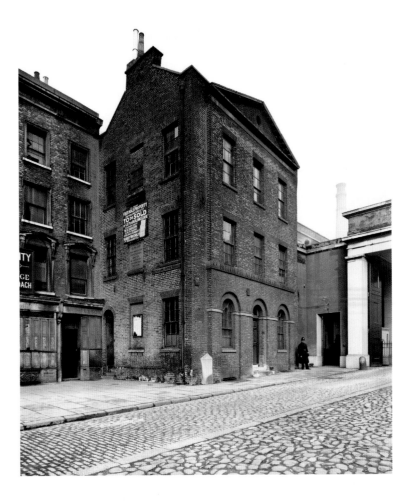

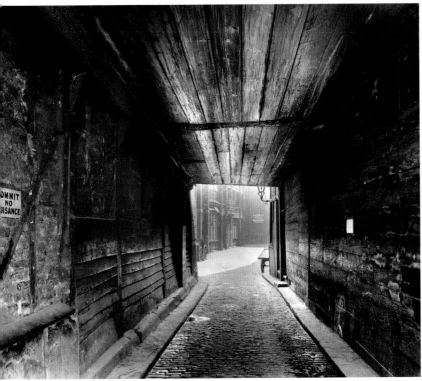

Above left: 4-7 Aldgate, 30 August 1909

The Metropole Restaurant occupied part of the old Saracens Head Inn, a fine 17th century coaching inn with timber-framing overlain with elaborate carved Corinthian pilasters, which on demolition were salvaged by the Guildhall Museum. Note the Select Ladies Dining Room on the first floor at no extra charge. Behind the timber balustraded parapet is a roof terrace with a recessed weatherboarded garret and clay tile roof. Harris's Restaurant clearly catered for a different clientele. Beside the bunches of bananas in the window of Levy's shop is the entrance to Saracens Head Yard.

Above right: St Botolph Aldgate Charity School, c 1907

The Charity School, built in 1793, was demolished for the Tower Bridge Approach road improvements. The gate lodge to the Royal Mint can be seen to the right. Note the superb street surfaces with randomly-laid cobbles in the foreground, the setted carriageway and York stone footway beyond.

Left: Saracens Head Yard, Aldgate, 30 August 1908

The Saracens Head Inn, founded in 1681, once offered a daily coach service to East Anglia. Cary's List of 1817 advised that the coach to Yarmouth started at 5pm each afternoon and arrived at 1.30pm the following day. By 1908 only the timber-framed and boarded entrance and a redundant booking office in the yard, survived.

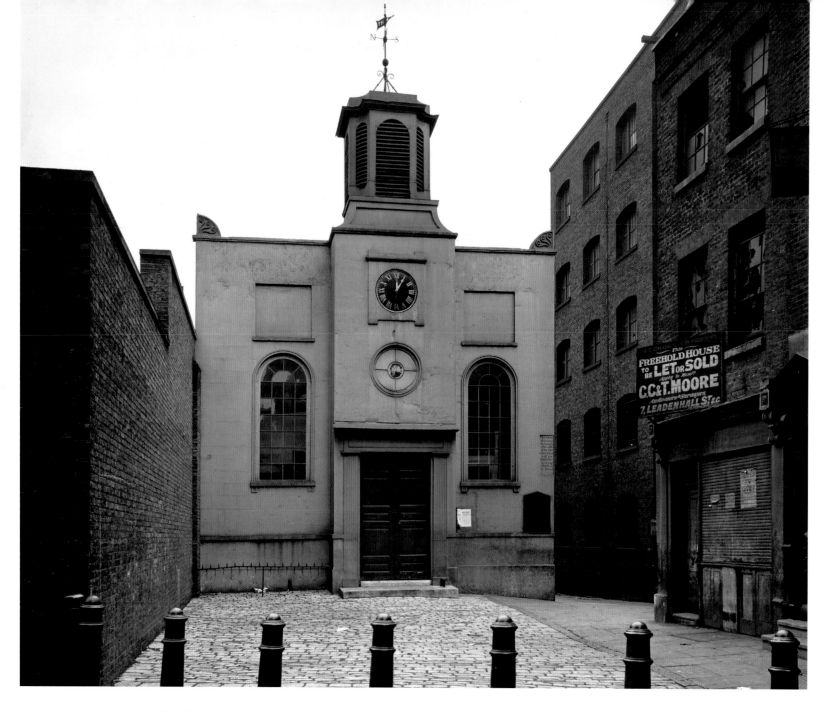

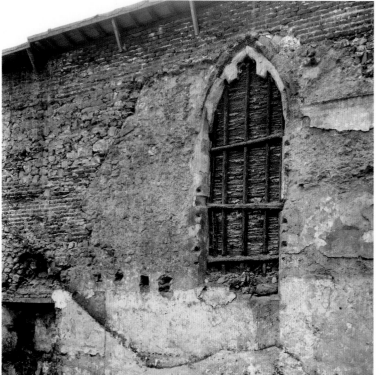

Above: Holy Trinity Minories, 14 October 1913

The Abbey of Graces of the Blessed Virgin was founded in 1293 for Minorite or Franciscan nuns. After the Dissolution, it was adapted for use as a parish church and later rebuilt in a severe Georgian style in 1706. The church was destroyed by enemy action in 1940.

Left: Holy Trinity Minories, 27 August 1904

Part of the original fabric was retained in the Georgian rebuilding. This late 13th century arched window was exposed following the clearance of buildings adjoining the north wall.

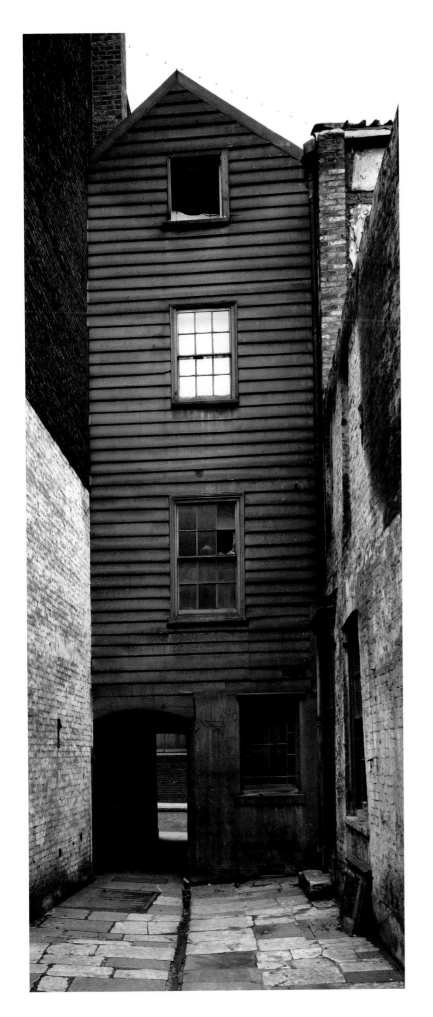

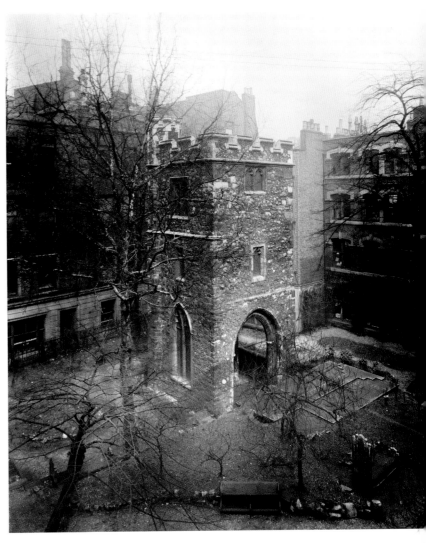

TOWER

Left: Three Crown Court, Minories, 14 October 1913
Typical alley and courtyard; a mediaeval form which once characterised much of the City of London and its fringes.

Above: All Hallows Staining, Star Alley, 25 March 1909
All Hallows Staining was demolished in 1870 except for the 15th century western tower which survives dwarfed by a modern office building. On the south side of the church is a small mid-12th century crypt with moulded ribs and zig-zag decoration re-erected from underneath Lambe's chapel in Markwell Street.

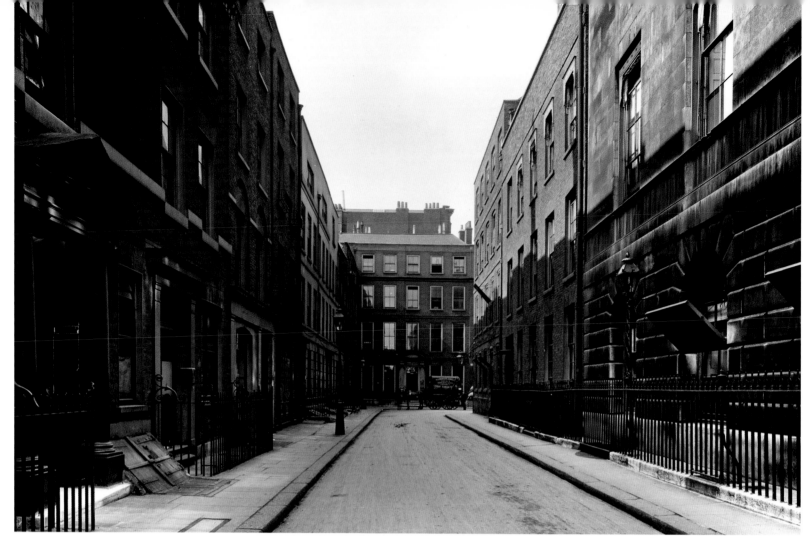

On the cusp of change

The erection of a palatial new headquarters for the Port of London Authority to the designs of Sir Edwin Cooper necessitated the clearance of a huge block of Georgian properties to the north and east of Trinity Square. This was typical of much of the development in the City of London at this time as older domestic-scaled buildings gave way to sumptuous new monumental buildings.

Above: Savage Gardens, Tower, 20 June 1913
View looking north from Trinity Square with the side of Trinity House to the right.

Right: 6, 7 & 8 Savage Gardens, 16 December 1912
Gabled rear elevations of late 17th century houses.

Opposite: Catherine Court, 25 January 1913
Catherine Court was a narrow court of early Georgian houses between Seething Lane and Trinity Square enclosed at each end by wrought iron gates. The plaque is dated 1725. The poster on the wall advertises the sale of antique fixtures and fittings from the houses (see p 12). The fine carved Corinthian porch to the double-fronted house on the right was sold for £145, the equivalent of £7,500 today.

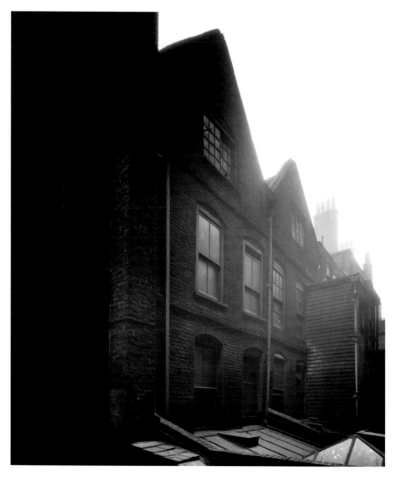

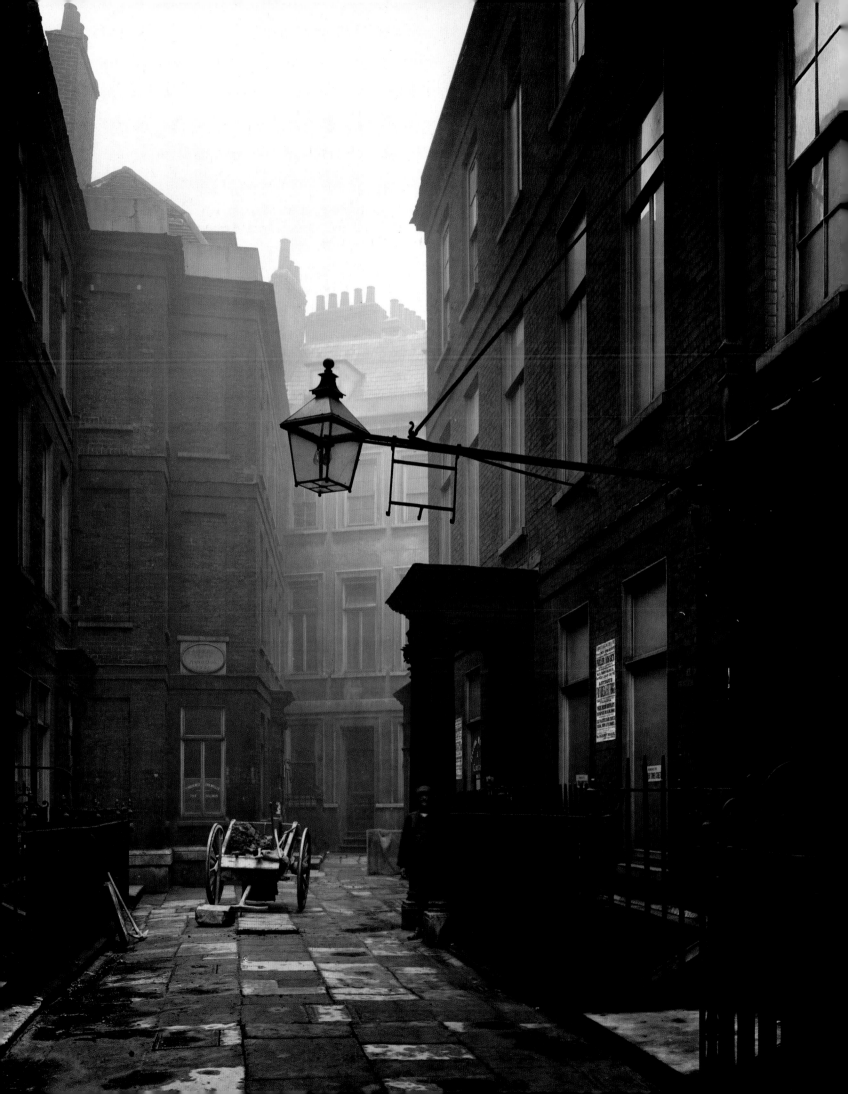

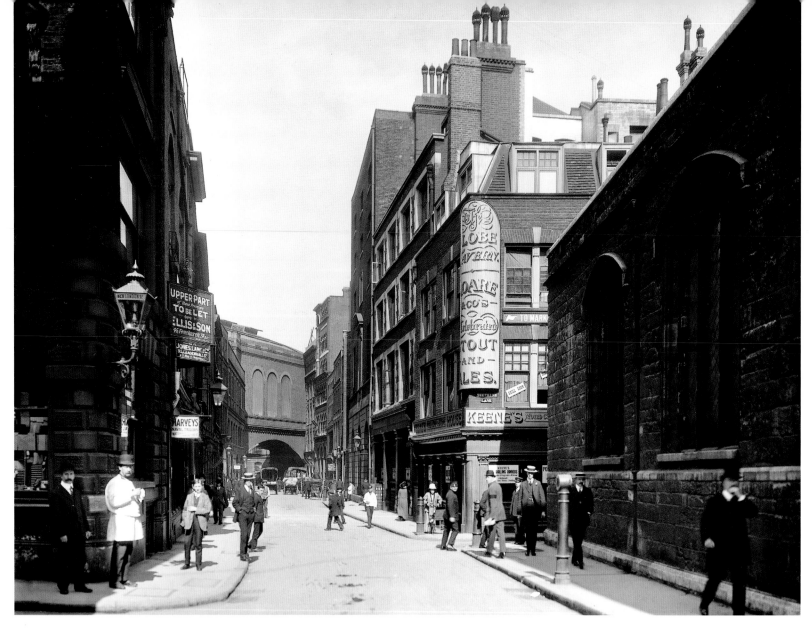

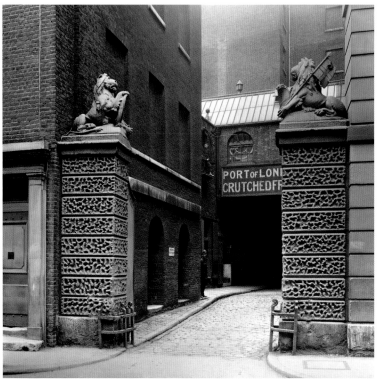

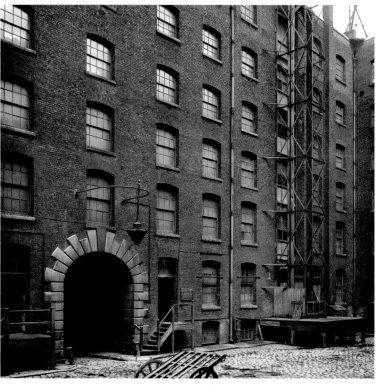

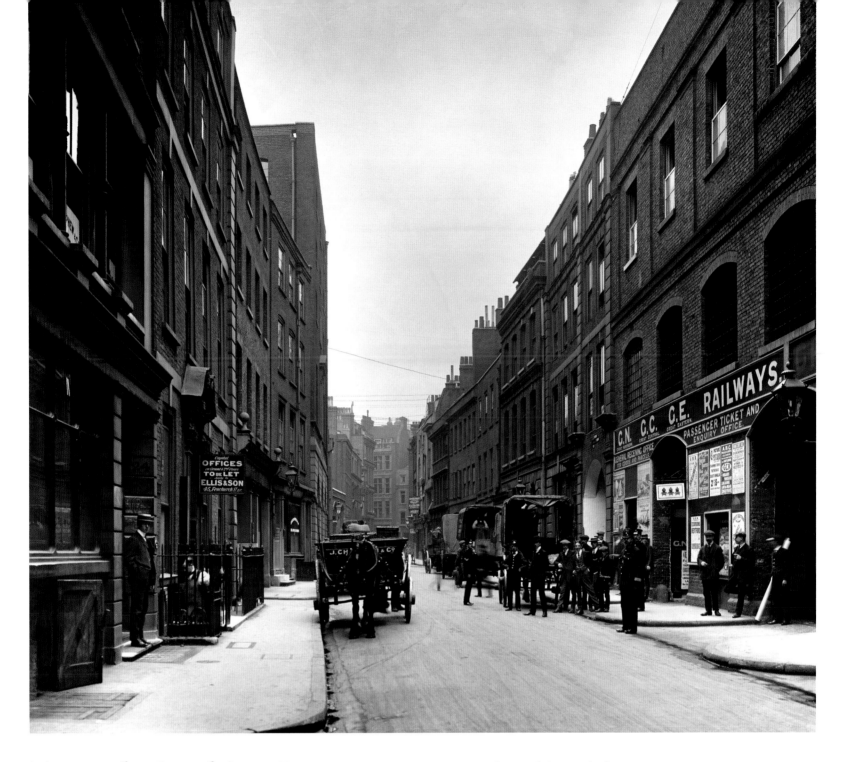

Towards Seething Lane

Opposite top: Crutched Friars, 20 June 1912

View along Crutched Friars from New London Street looking east towards the end of Fenchurch Street station. To the right is the side of St Olave's, Hart Street, the model for "St Ghastly, Grim" in Dickens' *The Uncommercial Traveller* with Seething Lane beyond. On the pavement is a cast-iron fire alarm pillar, once a common item of street furniture, now entirely vanished.

Opposite bottom left: Crutched Friars, 20 June 1912

Entrance gateway to PLA warehouses from Crutched Friars with vermiculated stone pillars crowned by the City arms. Iron guards have been installed to protect the base of the piers. A policeman stands guard discreetly with a warehouseman above next to the iron hoist.

Opposite bottom right: Crutched Friars, 10 February 1913

Port of London Authority warehouses showing the south elevation of the inner quadrangle and entrance archway.

Above: Crutched Friars, 20 June 1912

View looking west to Hart Street and Mark Lane from beneath the arch to Fenchurch Street railway station with railway offices to the right.

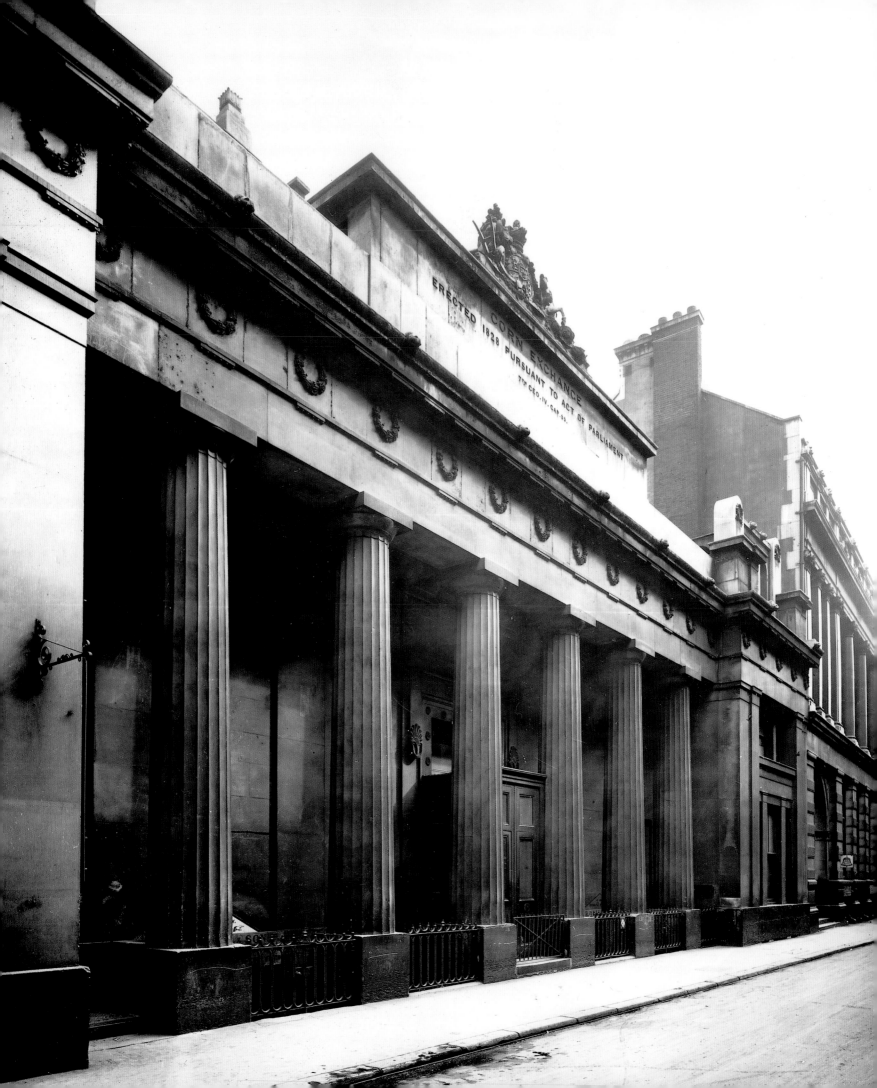

Trade and wealth

Opposite: Corn Exchange, Mark Lane, c 1908

The Corn Exchange was erected in 1828 with a handsome arcade of fluted Greek Doric columns to the front surmounted by the royal arms. Factors, farmers, seedgrowers and millers gathered here to trade in grain. However, with the arrival of the motor car, and the disappearance of the horse from London, trade declined. By 1928 it was losing £90,000 per annum. It was demolished three years later.

Right top: 33-35 Mark Lane, 7 March 1910

The spectacular Baroque entrance doorcase and hood carved by Grinling Gibbons and adorned with cherubs and garlands of flowers around a central cartouche. Known as the Spanish Ambassador's House, and built around 1680, the house was set back off Mark Lane and approached through an arched entrance. It too was enriched with elaborate carved details by Gibbons, which were acquired by the Victoria & Albert Museum when the street frontage was demolished in 1884.

Below left: 33-35 Mark Lane, 7 March 1910

A superb staircase of c 1710 with richly carved balusters of varying patterns. The twisted corner newel post boasts an intricately carved base and Corinthian capital.

Below right: 33-35 Mark Lane, 7 March 1910

The entrance hall: beautifully carved entrance screen and cornice. Part of a lead statue, which once stood in the garden, can be seen behind the door.

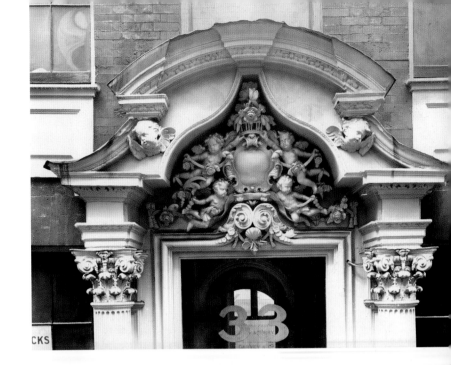

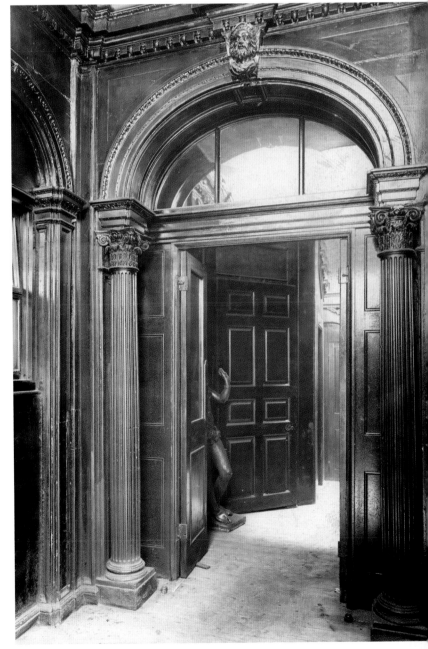

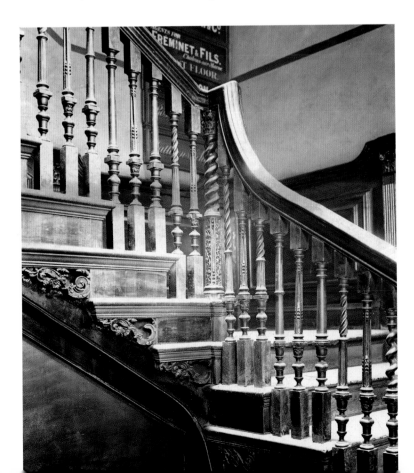

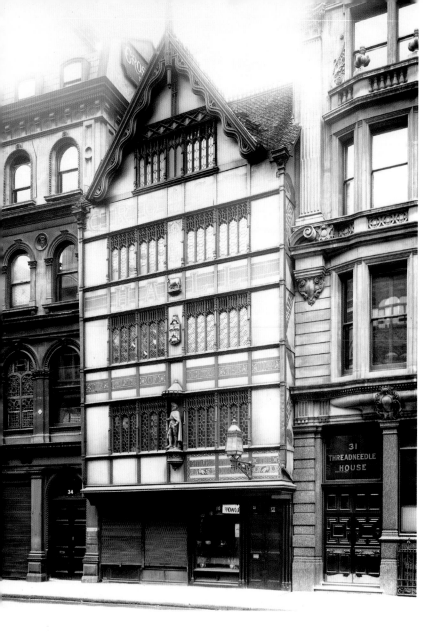

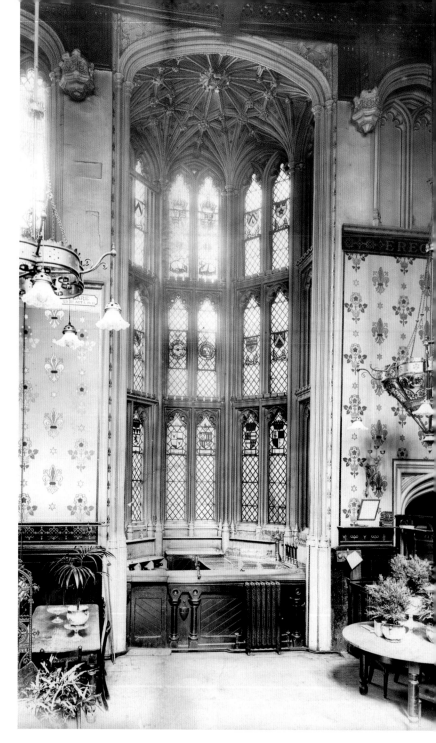

A merchant's palace

BISHOPSGATE

Crosby Hall, Bishopsgate

One of the great private merchant's houses of mediaeval London, Crosby Hall was built between 1466-1475 for Sir John Crosby, whose tomb (1476) lies in the nearby Church of St Helen, Bishopsgate. In 1909 the great hall was dismantled and re-erected at Danvers Street, Chelsea Embankment under the supervision of Walter Godfrey for the British Federation of University of Women. In 1993 the Chelsea site was sold and the hall reverted to its original purpose as part of a magnificent neo-Tudor private residence for a City trader.

Above left: Crosby Hall, 8 June 1907

The elaborate gabled frontage to Bishopsgate advertising The Palace of Richard III. Richard of Gloucester lived here at the time of the murder of the princes in the Tower.

Above right: Crosby Hall, 8 June 1907

The mediaeval bay window enriched with armorial stained glass. From 1868 the hall was used as banqueting rooms. The base of the bay window is a bar.

Opposite: Crosby Hall, 8 June 1907

The magnificent 15th century carved oak roof and central lantern. The City arms and stencilled decoration are 19th century details. The frieze beneath the windows reads "For Good Digestion Wait on Appetite".

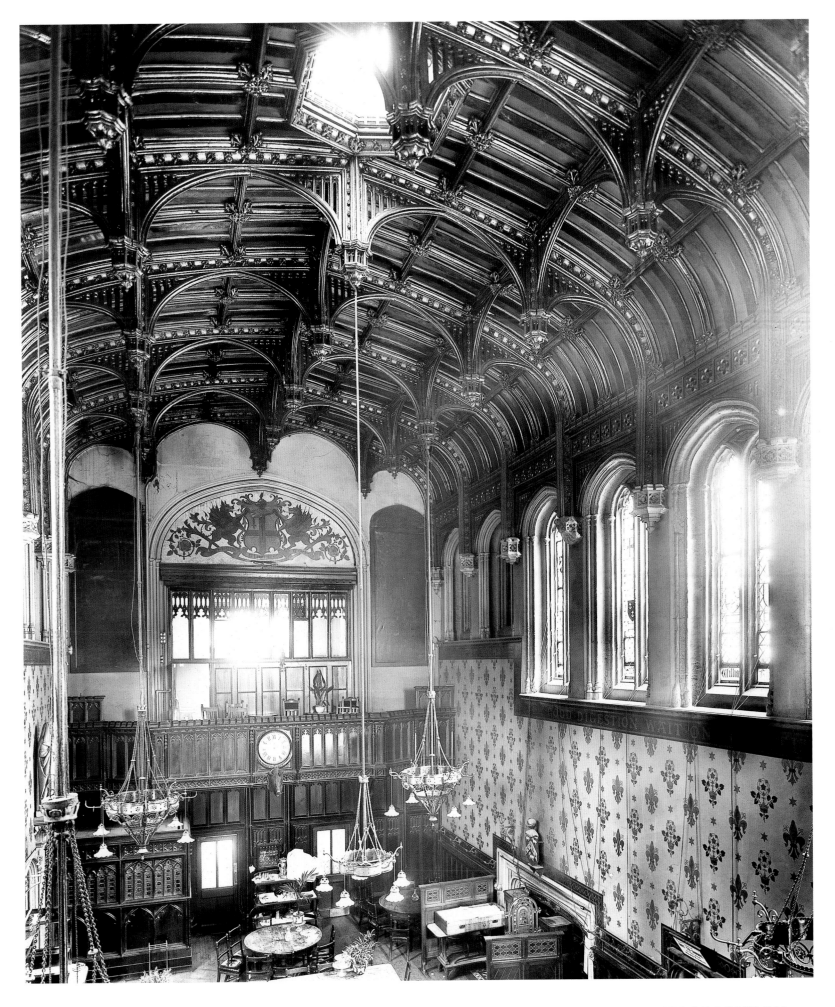

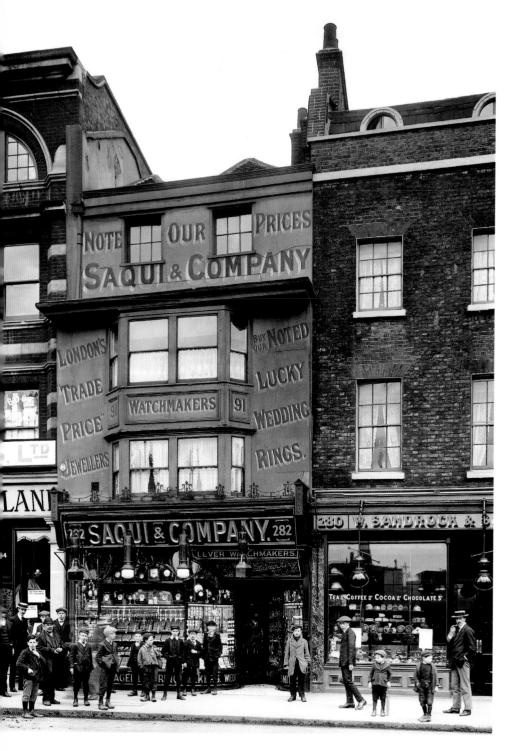

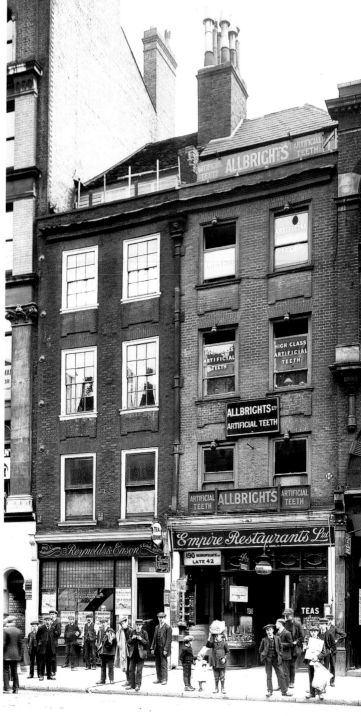

Bustling Bishopsgate

Above left: 280-282 Bishopsgate, August 1912
Elaborate gilt and glass fascias were commonplace at this time. Saqui and Company is embellished with an ornate Art Nouveau shopfront, a curved glass entrance and mahogany display cases. The building above is a timber-framed 17th century house with a double-hipped clay tiled roof.

Above right: 190 and 192 Bishopsgate, 22 August 1912
A fine pair of early 18th century town houses in mixed use. The floors over the Empire Restaurant are given over to a dental surgery advertising Allbrights Artificial Teeth. The small girl in the foreground appears to be wearing a high-crowned paper hat.

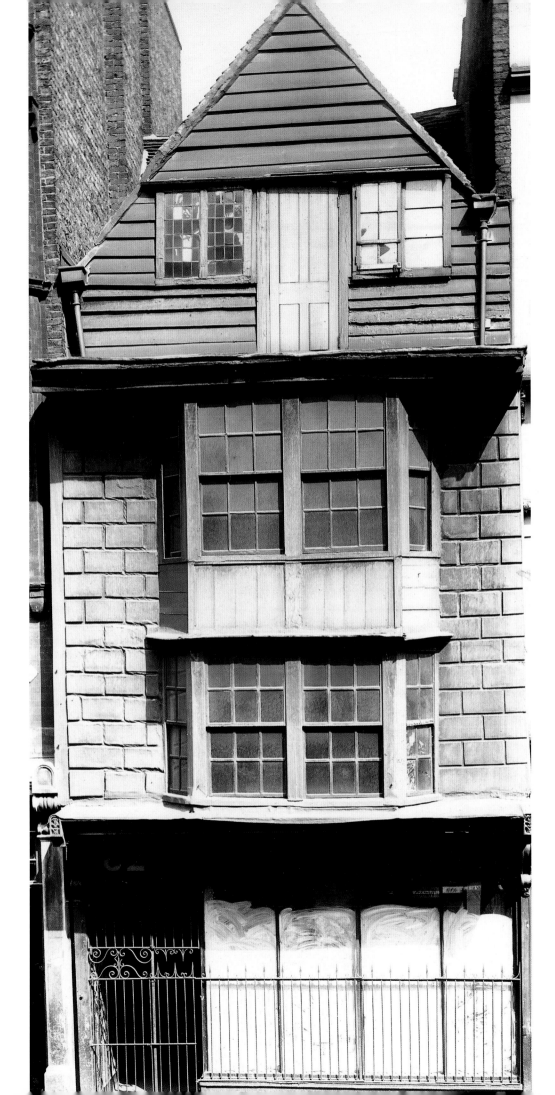

Left: Ye Olde Adam & Eve Inn,
264 Bishopsgate, 1907
A fine timber-framed 17th century inn of a type
once common in the City with a simulated
rusticated stone facade and canted central bay.
The weatherboarded gable retains one of its
original 17th century leaded casements.

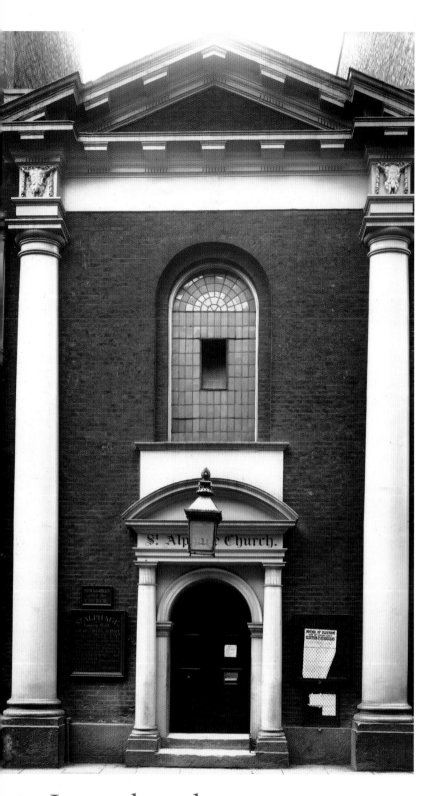

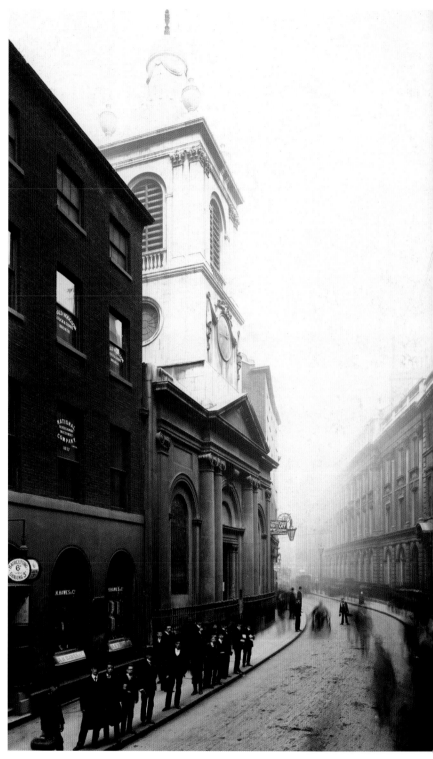

Lost churches

Above left: Church of St Alphage, London Wall, c 1907
This austere, monumental elevation of 1777 was remodelled in Gothic style in 1913, but the church was substantially destroyed in the Second World War. Only the remains of the 14th century tower of St Alphage, once part of the Chapel of the Priory of Elsyng Spital, survive.

Above right: Church of St Peter-le-Poer, Old Broad Street, c 1905
First mentioned in 1181, the church was rebuilt by the architect Jesse Gibson in 1792. In 1907 the parish was united with St Michael, Cornhill, and the church demolished for road widening. The pulpit, font and panelling were relocated to St Peter-le-Poer, Friern Barnet, which was built with the proceeds of the sale of the City site.

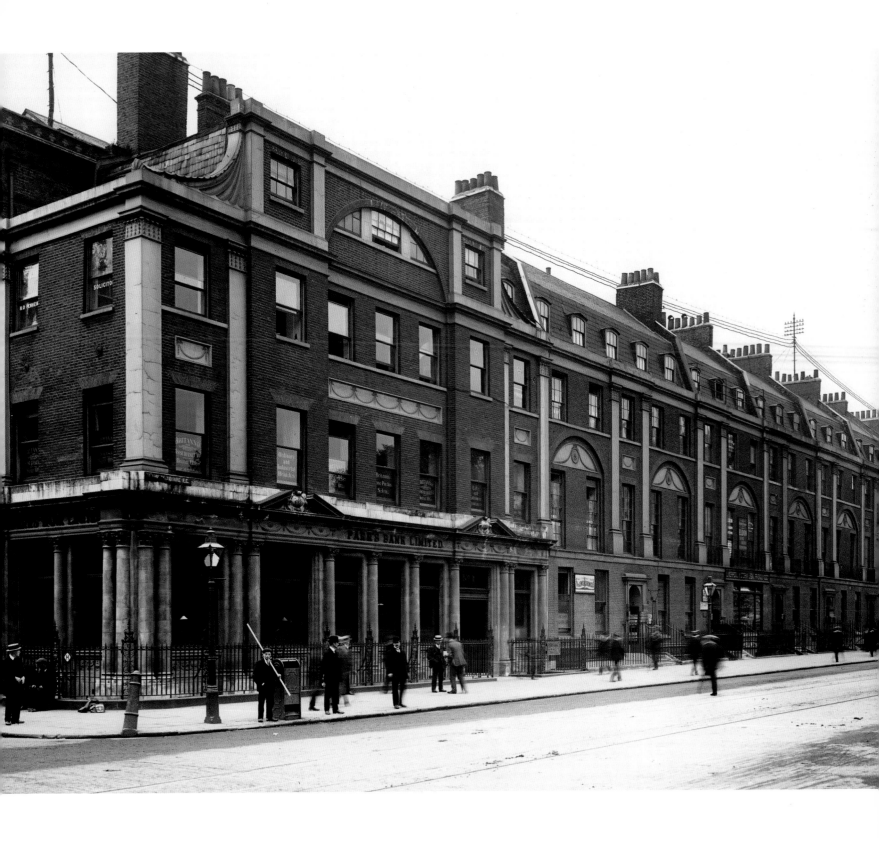

Above: 1-9 Finsbury Square, 2 September 1910

Although officially part of the Borough of Finsbury, and subsequently Islington, commercially Finsbury Square has been an important location for City businesses for generations given its proximity to Broad Street and Liverpool Street stations. This elegant symmetrical terrace designed in 1777 by James Peacock, the assistant to George Dance the Younger, stood on the west side backing onto the grounds of Honourable Artillery Company. Virtually the entire terrace was destroyed by enemy action in the Second World War.

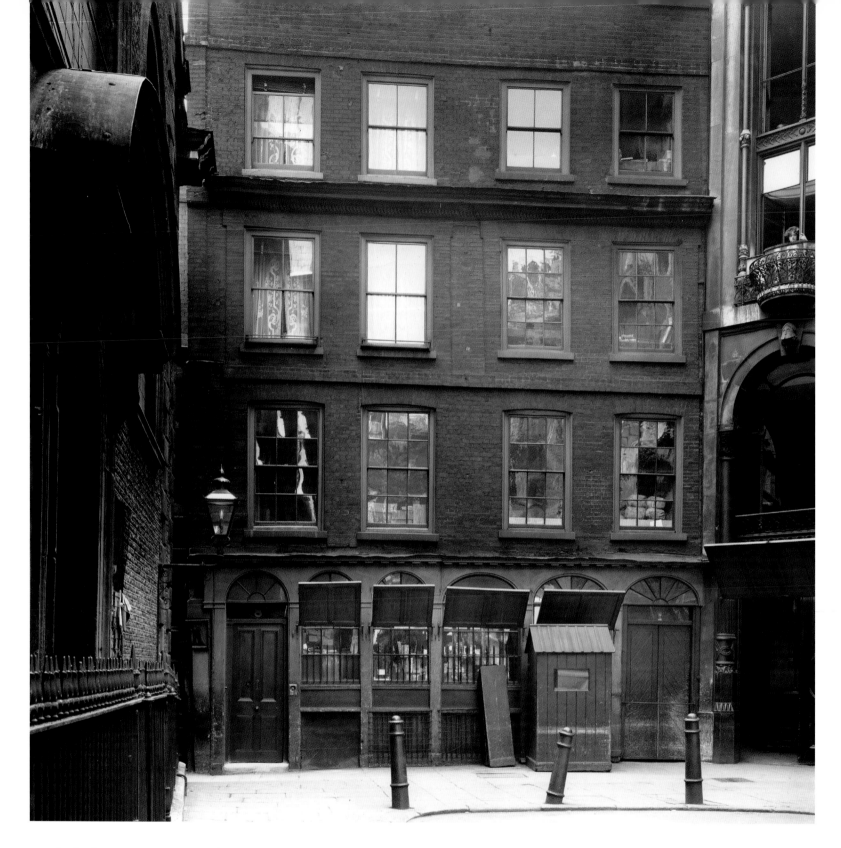

Old houses of the City

ST PAUL'S

Above: 8 Bow Churchyard, Cheapside, 30 August 1908
This splendid old 17th century house stood next to St Mary-le-Bow, Cheapside. Beneath the soft rubbed brick cornice the first and second floor windows are framed within eared brick panels. A curious young woman can be seen peering through the second floor window of the warehouse to the right.

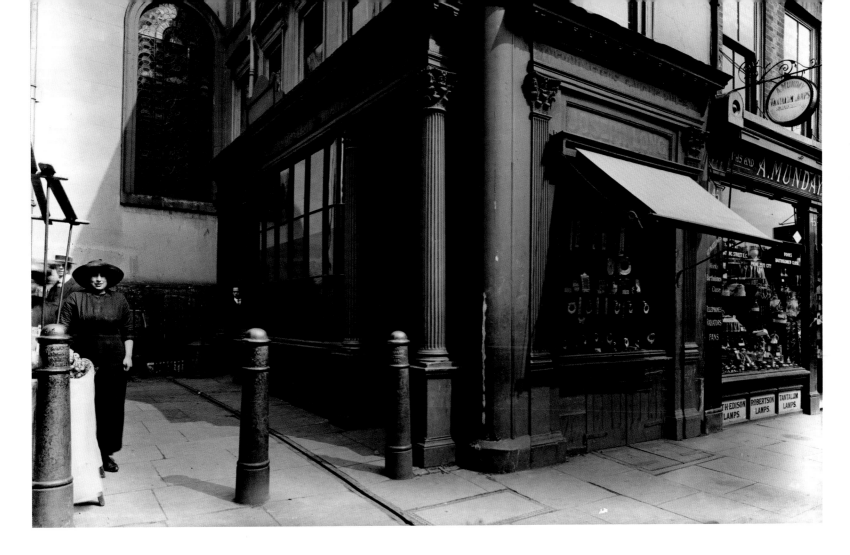

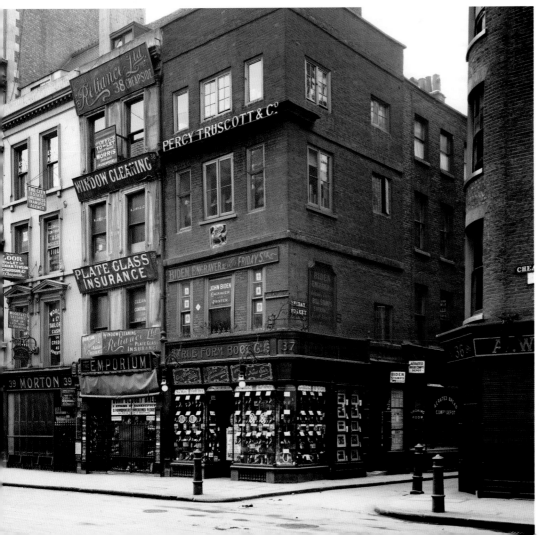

Above: 43 Eastcheap, 22 August 1912
This evocative corner of the old City with its elegant early 19th century shop windows still survives remarkably unchanged. The house, which once formed part of a group of 17th century merchants' houses, abuts the side of Wren's St Margaret Pattens Church of 1684-87.

Left: 37 Cheapside, 27 September 1908
Built in 1667-68, and still with its original casement windows, this was the earliest surviving example of a house erected immediately after the Great Fire. Beneath the second floor window is a carved tablet depicting The Chained Swan, the name of the tavern which once occupied the building.

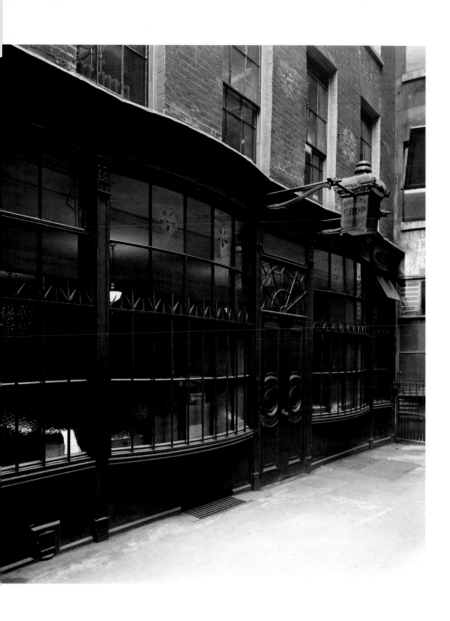

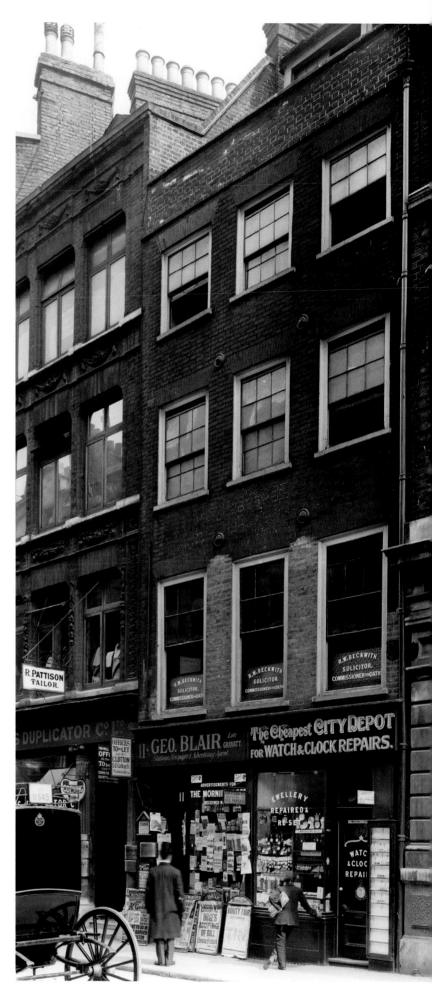

Above: 1 Change Alley, Cornhill c 1910

In the early 18th century Change Alley was used as an open bourse frequented by speculators. It was the focus of the South Sea Bubble. Baker's Coffee and Chop House with its elegant twin-bowed frontage was typical of the small coffee houses where early City trading started. The London Missionary Society was founded here, after a particularly lavish meal, by eight non-conformist ministers on 4 November 1748.

Right: 11 King Street, 23 March 1912

Small City retailers trading from the ground floor of an early Georgian house with a City cab in the foreground. The poster behind the cab for the *Amateur Gardener* offers advice on *What to do in your garden at Easter.*

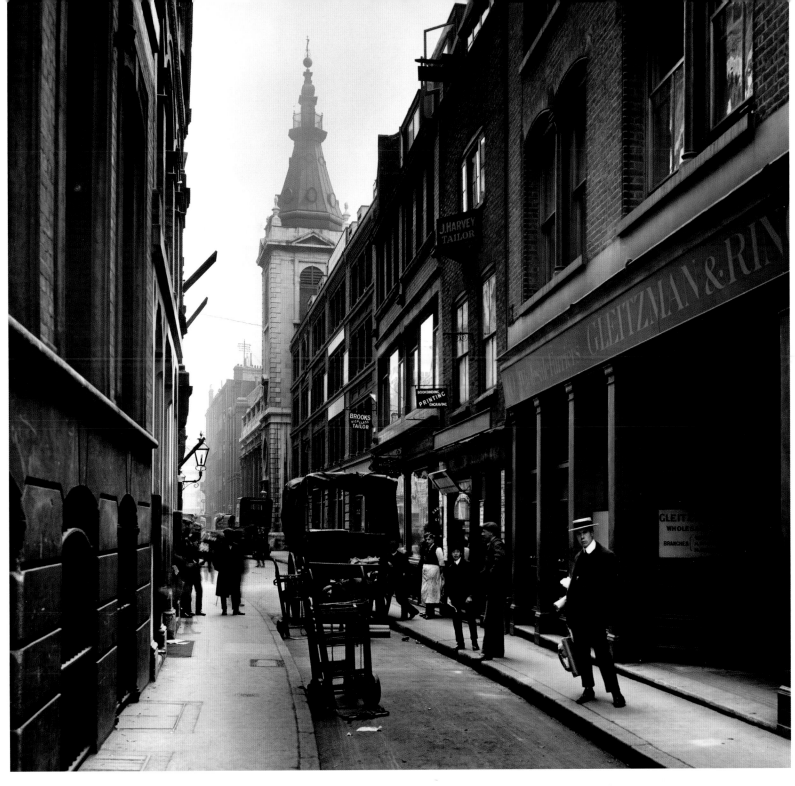

Above: Knightrider Street, 16 May 1912
General view of Knightrider Street showing the Church of
St Nicholas Cole Abbey.

Right: Sermon Lane, Knightrider Street, c 1912
18th century Ward school figures which once adorned the
school entrance.

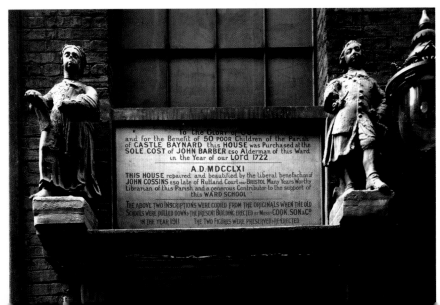

Haunted riverside stairs

THE RIVER

Below left: All Hallows-the-Less, Upper Thames Street, c1910
Once Upper Thames Street had eight churches. Today not one remains. This powerful rusticated arched gateway provided access to the graveyard. Inset into the churchyard railings is a pair of Victorian pillar boxes offering eight to ten collections a day.

Below right: Trig Lane, 16 May 1912
View south to the river from Upper Thames Street with Trig Lane Stairs and the chimneys of Bankside in the distance. Countless narrow canyon-like alleys running down to the river and lined with warehouses were a highly distinctive feature of Upper Thames Street until its complete remodelling in the 1960s.

Bottom left: 80 Upper Thames Street, 12 May 1908
The old 18th century gateway to the former Joiners Hall salvaged and reused at the rear of a warehouse.

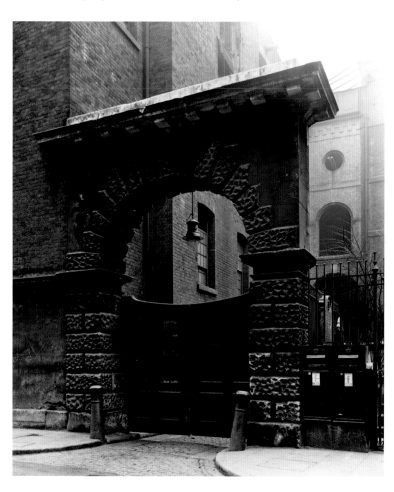

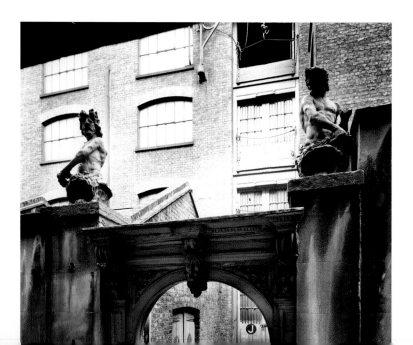

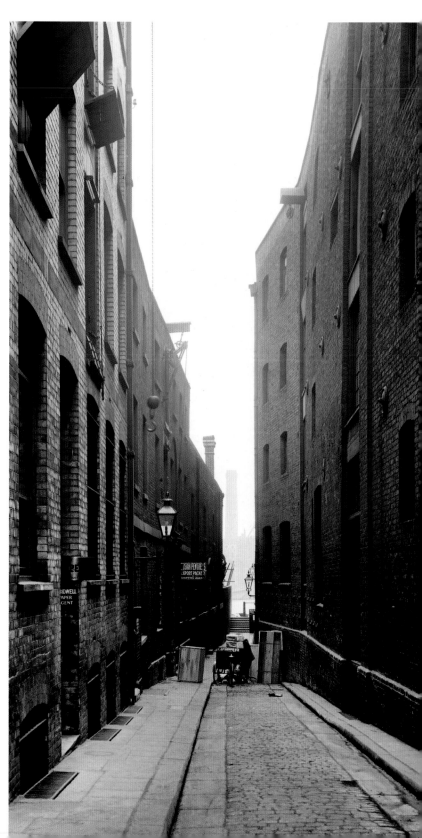

BILLINGSGATE

Until 1835 and the construction of King William Street, Fish Street Hill was the main approach to London Bridge.

Below: 26-27 Fish Street Hill, Billingsgate, c 1913
Ramshackle 18th century houses supported by raking shores. No. 26 carries a royal crest over the shopfront. Evans's Stores provided sundries for fishmongers at nearby Billingsgate Fishmarket.

Right: 18-19 Fish Street Hill, Billingsgate, c 1913
The produce suggests a general store catering for the particular working needs of the Billingsgate Fishmarket with baskets for porters.

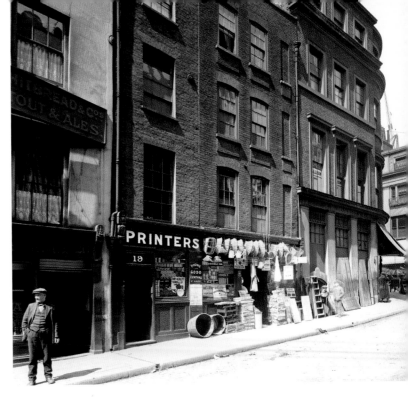

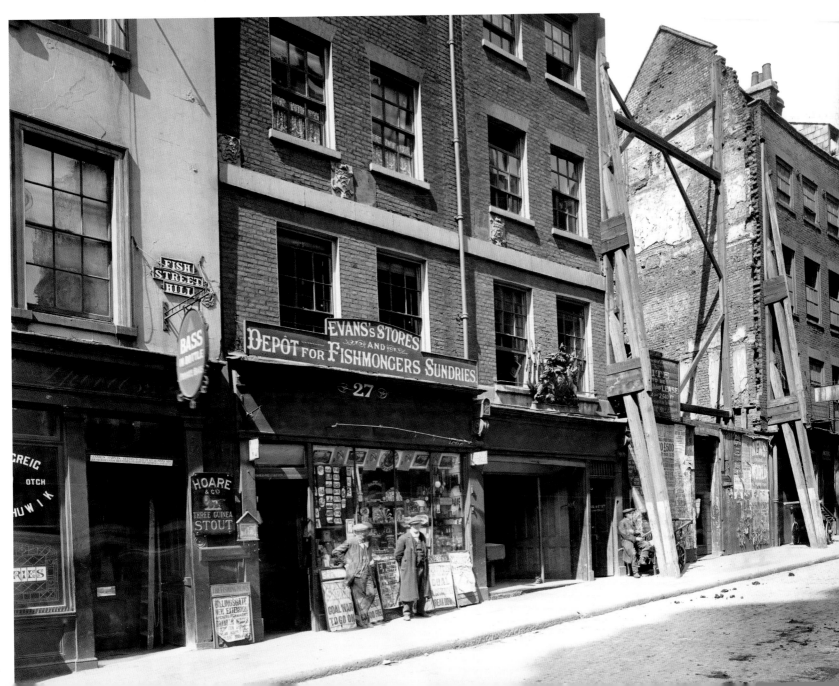

ST PAUL'S

General Post Office, St Martin's-Le-Grand, 26 July 1911
Designed by Sir Robert Smirke and opened in 1829, the General Post Office was
one of the most elegant buildings in London with a grand Greek Revival
frontage. A new GPO building was opened on the site of Christ's Hospital in
King Edward Street immediately to the west in the same year, and Smirke's
landmark demolished.

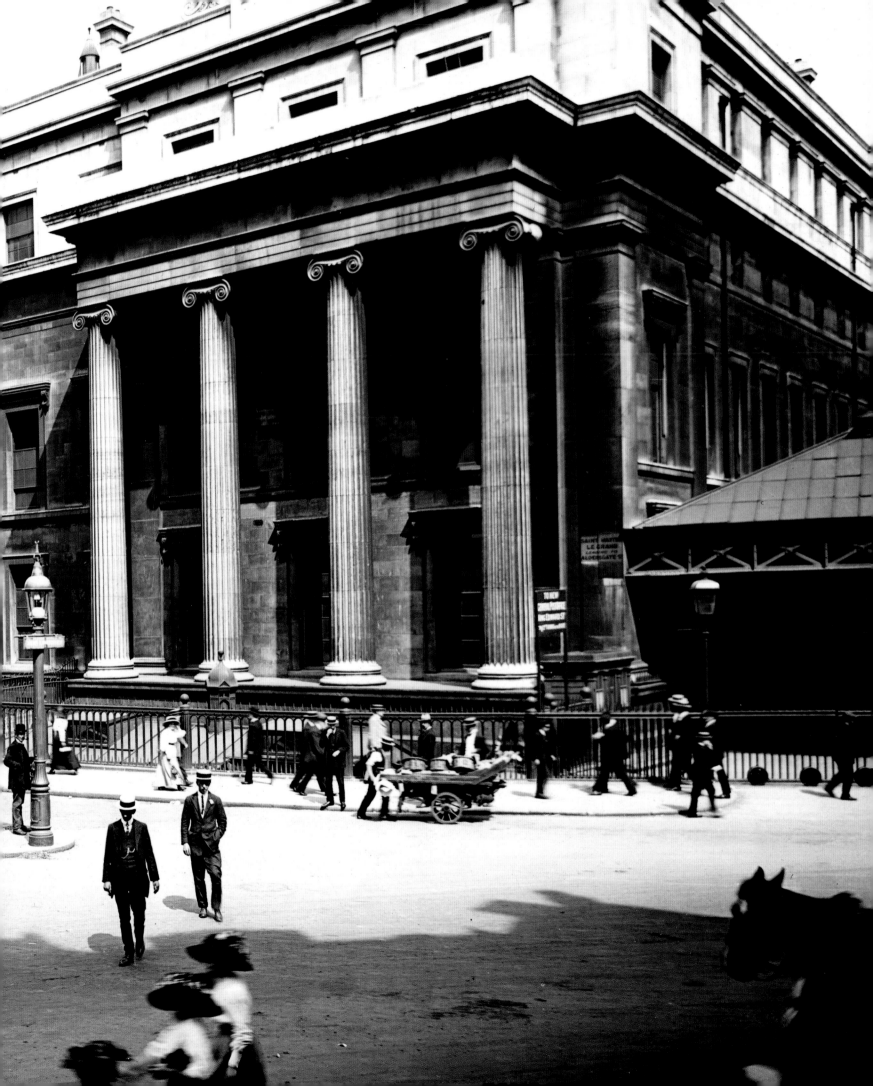

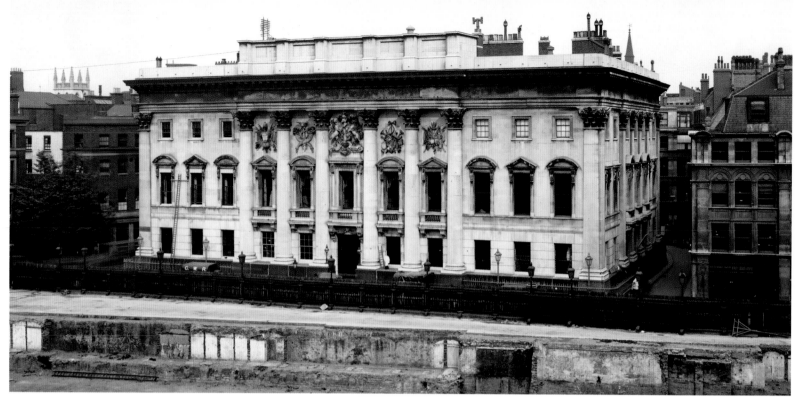

Bastions of wealth

Above: Goldsmiths' Company Hall, Foster Lane, 1913

The Goldsmiths' Company received its Charter in 1327 and in the 17th century it pioneered the use of promissory notes, the foundation of modern banking. The Hall, which still survives, was designed by Philip Hardwick between 1829-35 in a handsome Baroque style. The facade to Foster Lane is exposed in this view following the demolition of Smirke's General Post Office. The interior has a Roman altar to Diana discovered during the construction of the Hall in 1830, a chimneypiece from Canons Park reputedly by Roubiliac, and 17th century panelling, relocated from East Acton Manor House in 1912, along with a fine collection of plate.

Right: Ironmongers' Company Hall, Fenchurch Street, 26 April 1912

The old Ironmongers' Hall, founded in 1457 and rebuilt in 1748 around a courtyard, was considered the most impressive livery hall of its time. Unfortunately, it was bombed during a Zeppelin raid on 7 July 1917 and later demolished, after which the Company relocated to a site near Aldersgate Street.

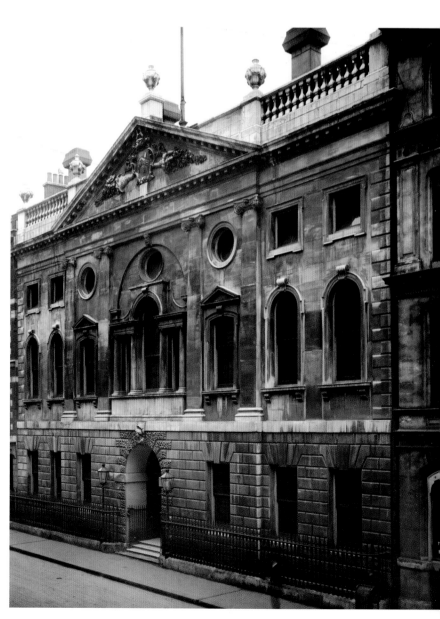

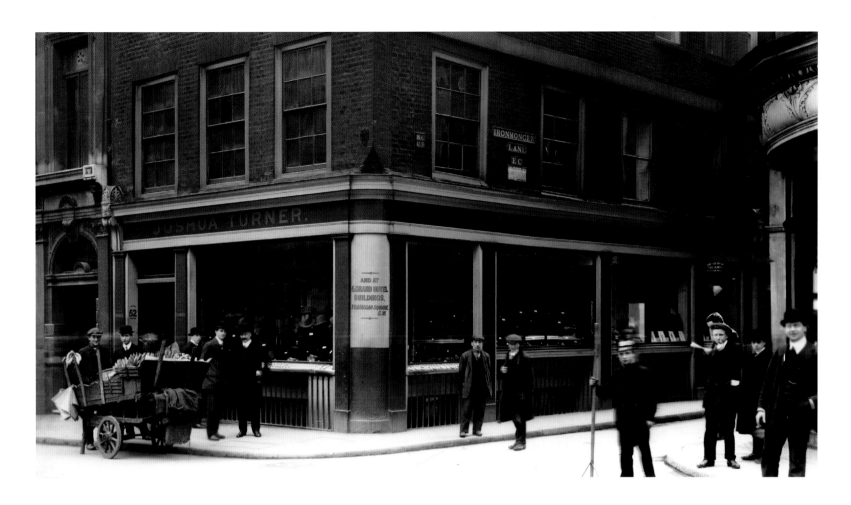

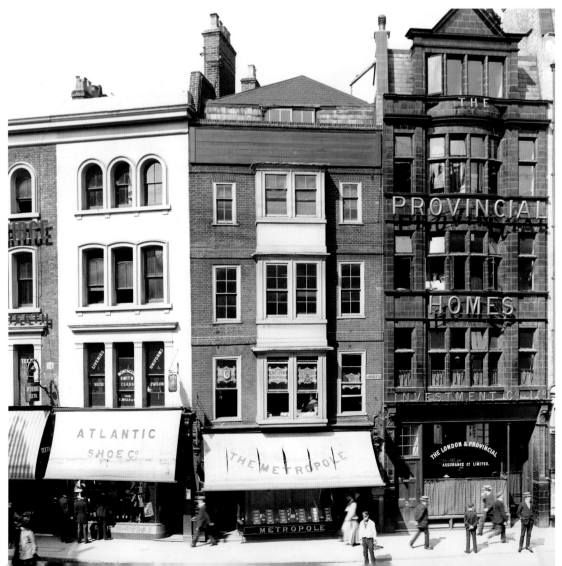

Above: 52 Gresham Street, 23 March 1912
Early 18th century house at the junction with Ironmonger Lane.

Left: 72 Leadenhall Street,
30 August 1909
The north side towards the eastern end. The Metropole building appears to be an altered 17th century house with a central timber bay. The curious slashes in the shop blind are probably to prevent water collecting as run-off from the bay above.

THE CITY OF LONDON 89

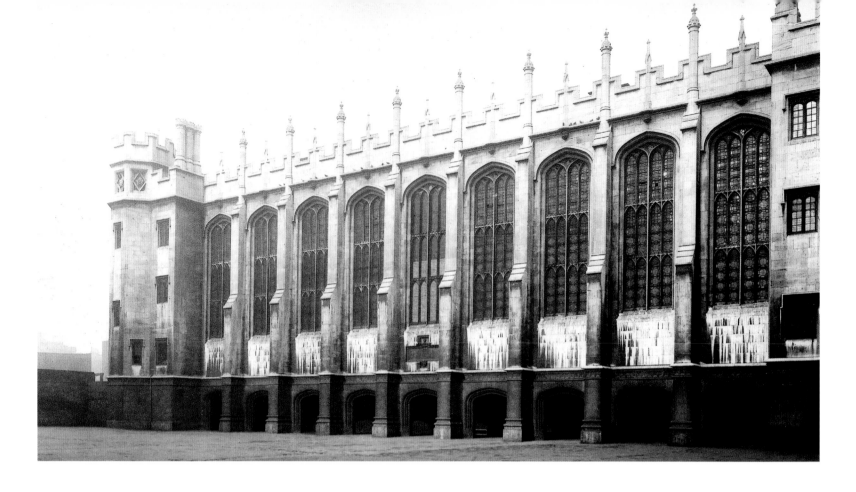

Christ's Hospital, c 1906

Christ's Hospital was founded in 1552 on the site of the old Greyfriars Monastery and later rebuilt by Wren after the Great Fire incorporating the old Greyfriars cloisters. The Bluecoat school occupied a large area behind St Bartholomew Hospital between Giltspur Street and King Edward Street. In 1890 a Royal Commission recommended its removal from London and twelve years later it moved to Horsham. Samuel Taylor Coleridge, Leigh Hunt and Charles Lamb were all Bluecoat boys, Lamb recalling in later years how runaways were incarcerated in tiny dungeons and subjected to systematic chastisement.

In spite of public indignation and strong opposition from the National Trust and the Society for the Protection of Ancient Buildings, the entire site was sold to the Post Office and levelled.

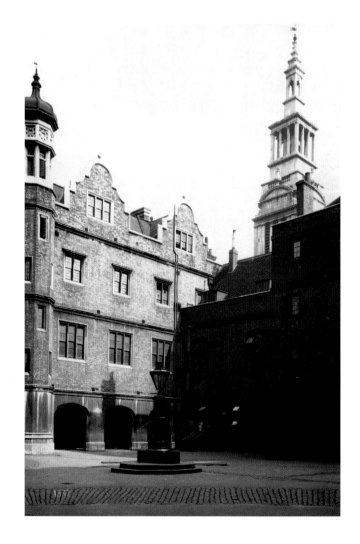

Above: Modelled on the chapel of King's College Cambridge, the main hall was designed by John Shaw Snr in 1825 in a romantic Tudor style. After Westminster Hall, the roof span was thought to be the largest in London without intermediate support. The hall was famous for its rats, which, attracted by the fragments of food, foraged about after dark in their hundreds.

It was a matter of pride for an "Old Blue" to catch them by hand, traps being considered cowardly.

Opposite: Part of the 17th century complex designed by Wren after the Great Fire with a fine carriageway of limestone setts.

Right: The late Tudor style gabled range designed by John Shaw with Christ Church, Newgate Street beyond. To the right is part of Wren's earlier work for the hospital.

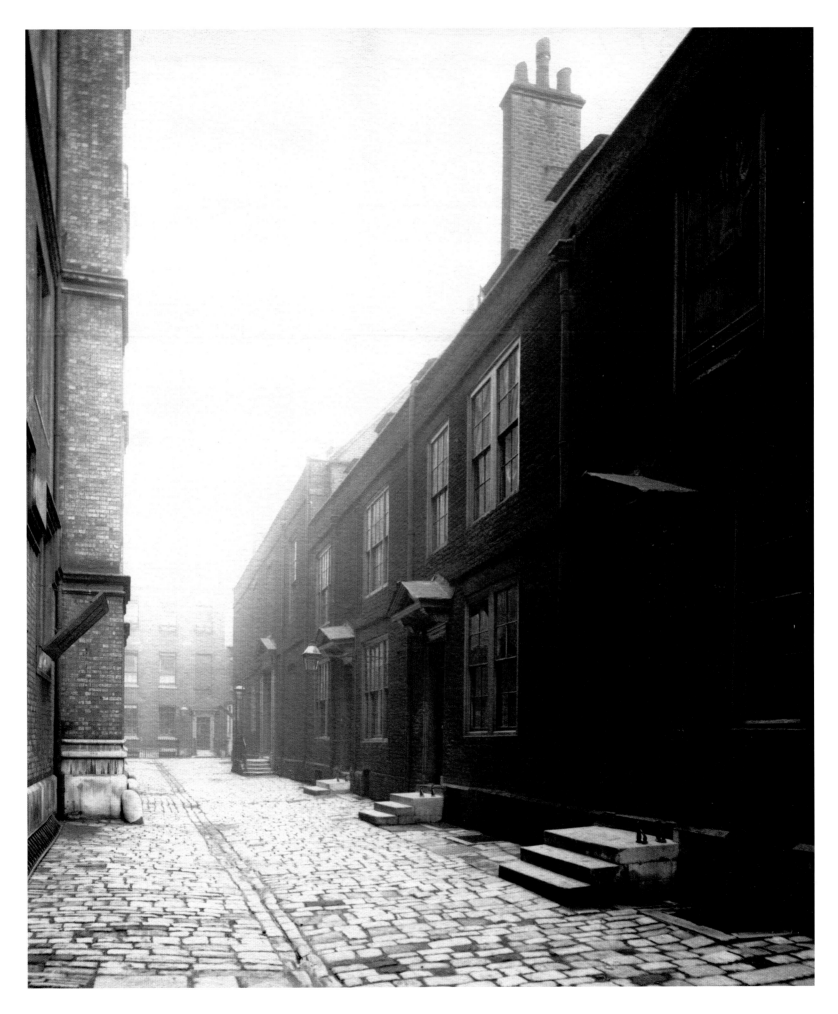

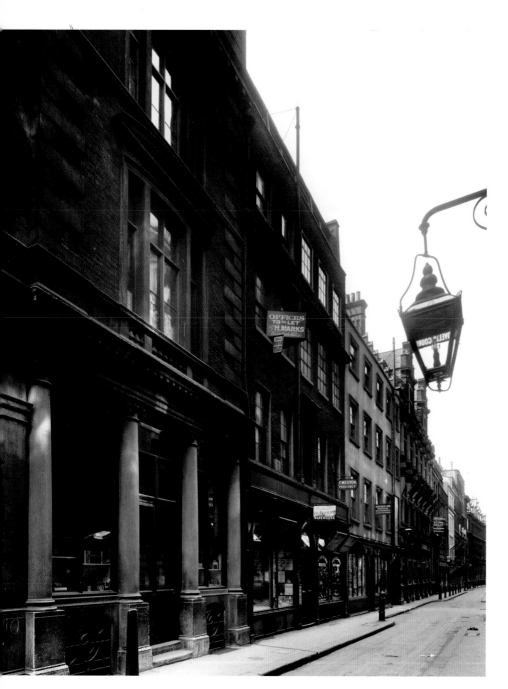

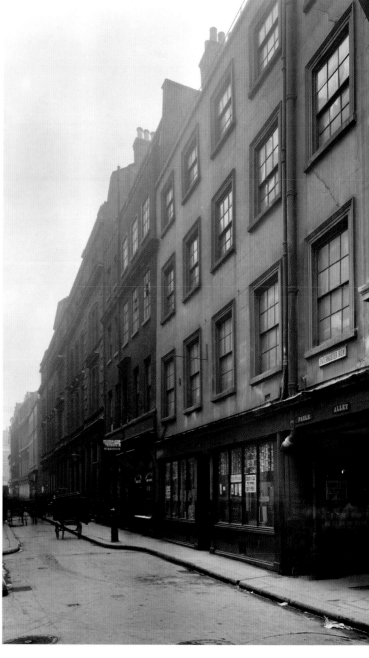

London's library

Paternoster Row

To the north of St Paul's Churchyard was one of the great centres of the English book trade. Stationers and text writers sold religious and educational books as well as paternosters and graces, hence the name. By the early 18th century the book trade prevailed, supplanting mercers, silk and lace merchants and tire-men who sold "*top knots and other dressings for the female head*". "*By degrees … learning ousted vanity, chattering died in to studious silence, and the despots of literature ruled supreme.*" The entire district was destroyed by enemy action on the night of 29 December 1940 along with six million books.

Above left: 51-52 Paternoster Row, 26 March 1912
View looking east showing the entrance to Paul's Alley. The London Bible Warehouse is on the right.

Above right: 53-54 Paternoster Row looking west, 17 August 1908
The bookshops for which the area was renowned. The London Bible Warehouse trading from a fine 18th century house continued a tradition of ecclesiastical publishing which originated in the shadow of St Paul's in the Middle Ages.

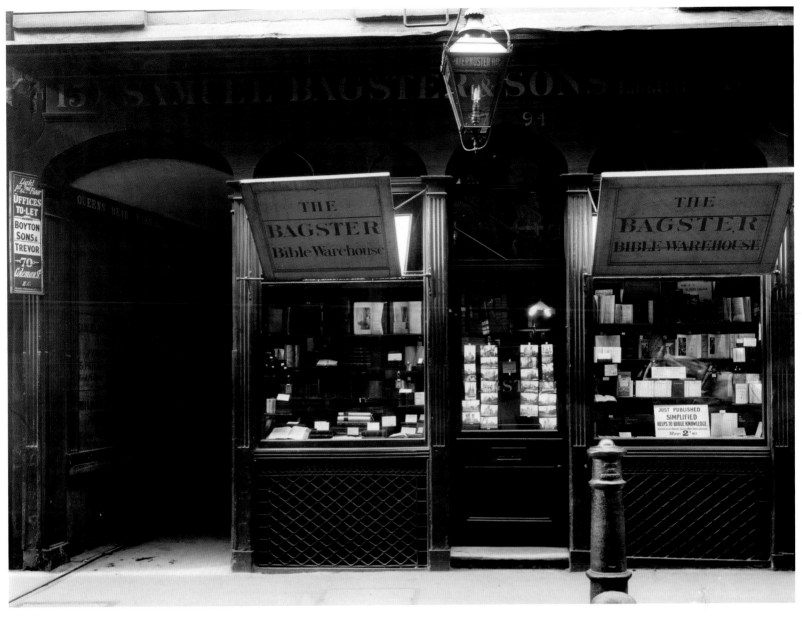

Above: 15 Paternoster Row, 18 August 1908

Samuel Bagster's Bible Warehouse with angled mirrors to each bay; a beautifully-detailed 18th century shopfront with a side entrance to Queen's Head Passage. Gas lanterns carry the street name and mark the entrances to side alleys.

Right: 47 Paternoster Row, 17 August 1908

A fine late 17th century house that was typical of many in the area. The angled boards on the fronts of many of the houses are mirrors to reflect light into the windows above – once a common feature of the narrow alleyways of the City.

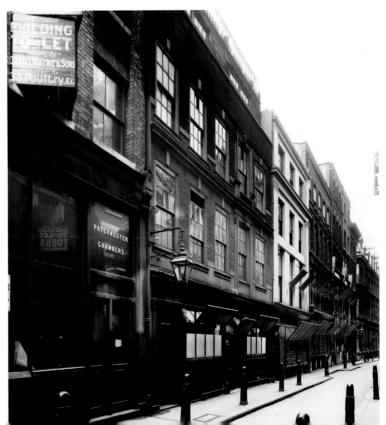

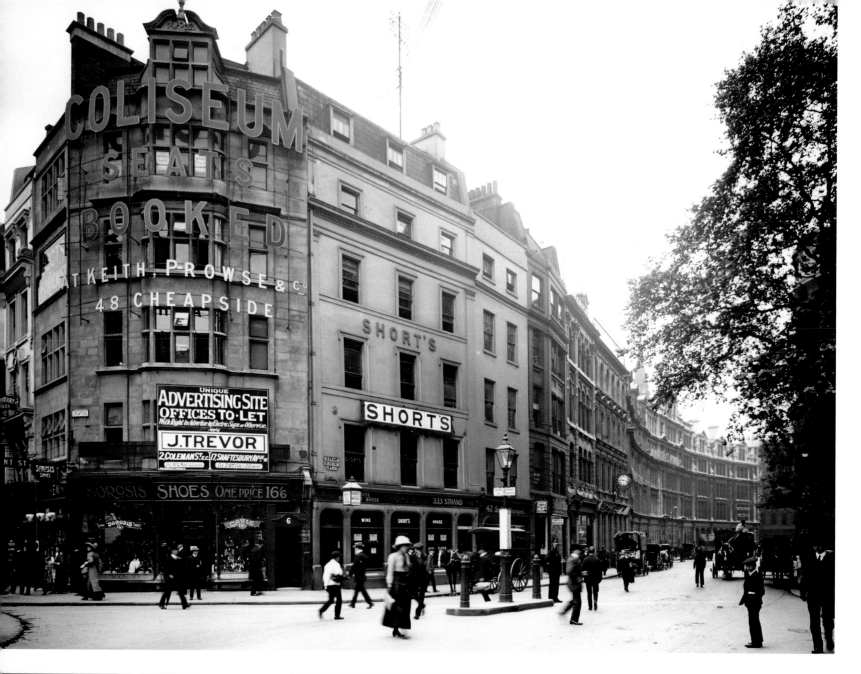

Hub of commerce

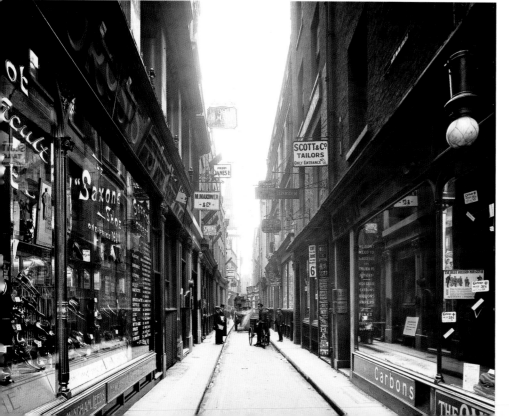

Above: St Paul's Churchyard, 21 June 1912
East elevation from No. 7 Cheapside to Watling Street. View looking south towards the spire of St Augustine's Church. The east end of St Paul's Cathedral can be glimpsed to the right. Sorosis Shoes has a fine sinuous Art Nouveau shopfront and lettering.

Left: Old Change, 16 May 1912
View south showing the intimate scale of the street. The carriageway is only wide enough for a single vehicle. To the left is Sorosis Shoe Shop. The spire of St Augustine's church is in the distance.

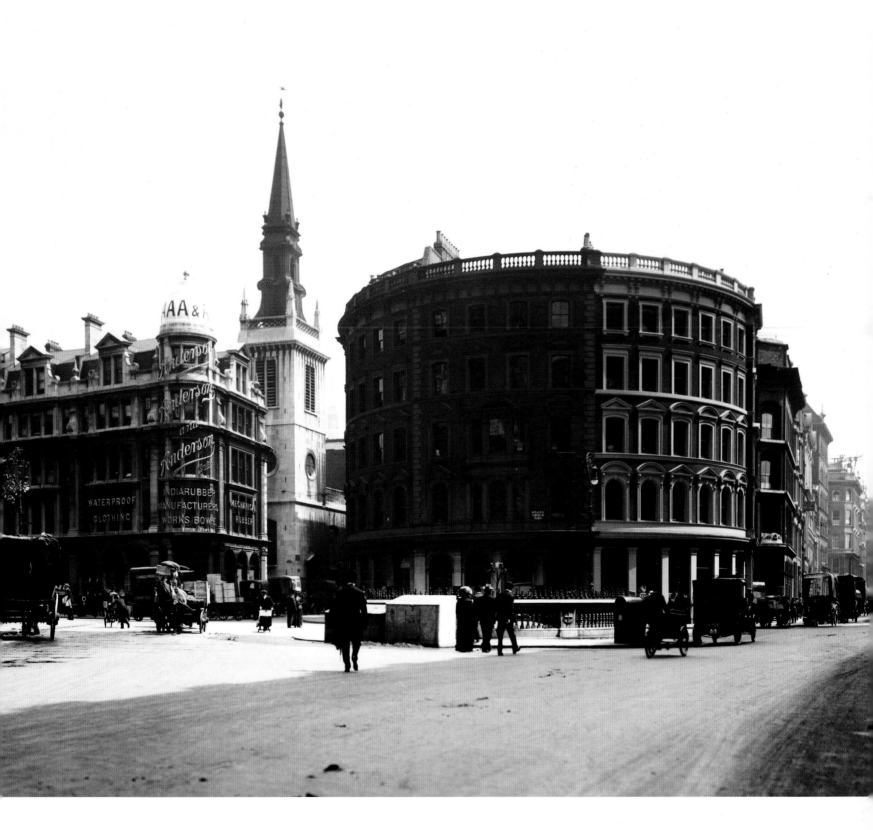

Above: Junction of Old Change and Watling Street

The south-east corner of St Paul's Churchyard viewed from the west with
Cannon Street to the right and an elegant semi-circular block of Italianate
offices in the foreground. The entire area was earmarked for clearance for
St Paul's Bridge, a new Thames crossing, which was eventually abandoned.
St Augustine Church (1680-83 by Wren) was destroyed in the Second
World War, but rebuilt around surviving remnants as part of St Paul's
Choir School.

Horse-drawn cacophony

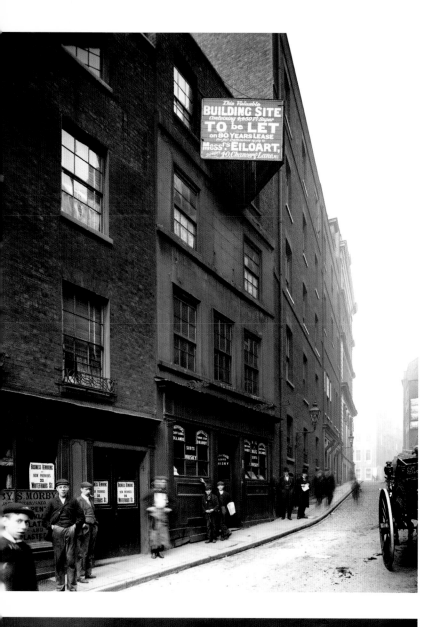

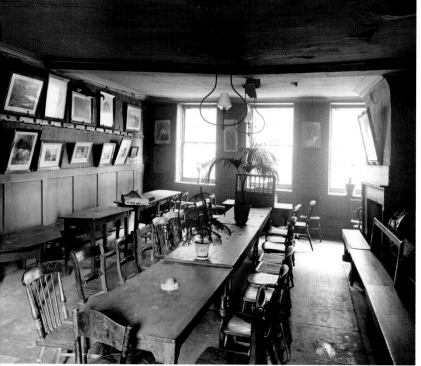

Left: The Old Blue Last public house, Dorset Street, 3 November 1904
An early Georgian facade and later ground floor frontage with applied lettering to the windows advertising popular brands of spirits.

Bottom left: *"Unlike the Paris cafe, which delights in the free sunshine of the boulevard, and displays its harmless revellers to the passers-by, the London tavern aims at cosiness, quiet and privacy".* (*Old and New London*, 1897)

A typical working man's public house interior. The first floor Club Room with gas lighting, plainly-detailed panelling and original chimney-piece with eared architraves.

Opposite top: Ludgate Hill, c 1905
View looking south towards Ludgate Circus showing the railway bridge and signal gantries of the London, Chatham and Dover railway erected in 1865 in the face of public protest – "*a miracle of clumsy and stubborn ugliness*". To the right marked by a lavish array of barometer clocks is J W Benson, Steam Factory for Watches and Clocks. The elaborate coats of arms boast patronage by the ruling houses of Greece, Prussia, Russia and Siam with Queen Victoria's royal arms over the centre.

Opposite below: Oxford Arms, Warwick Lane, 1875
"*Despite the confusion, the dirt and the decay, he who stands in the yard of this ancient inn may get an excellent idea of what it was like in the days of its prosperity when not only travellers in coach or saddle rode into or out of the yard, but poor players and mountebanks set up their stage for the entertainment of spectators who hung over the galleries or looked on from their rooms.*" (*The Athenaeum*: 20 May 1876)

The Oxford Arms, one of London's most famous coaching inns, was situated at the end of a short lane leading out of the west side of Warwick Lane and was bounded to the west by the old City Wall. Rebuilt after the Great Fire, its first proprietor, Edward Bartlet, had "*a Hearse with all things convenient to carry a Corps to any part of England*". Its demolition in 1878 became a landmark in the development of the movement to preserve historic buildings.

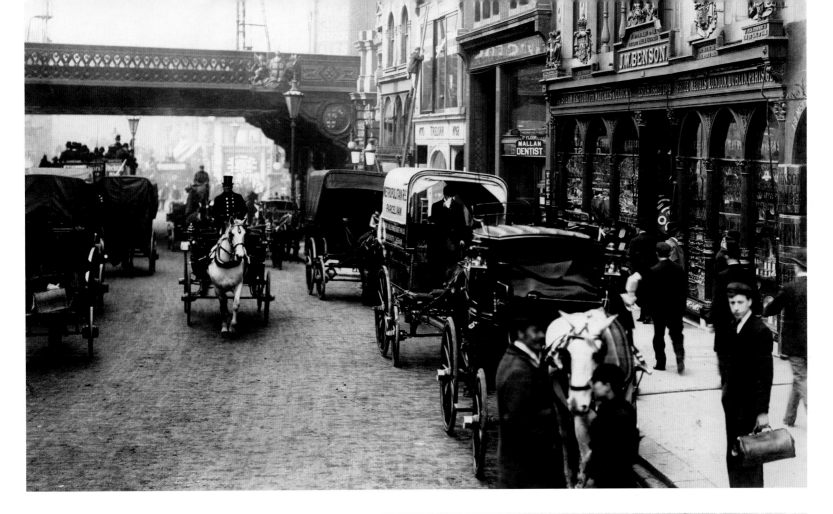

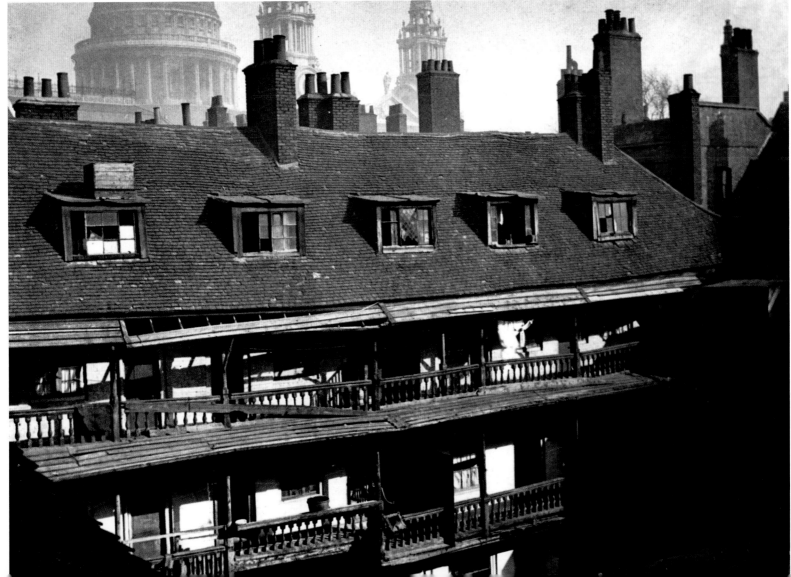

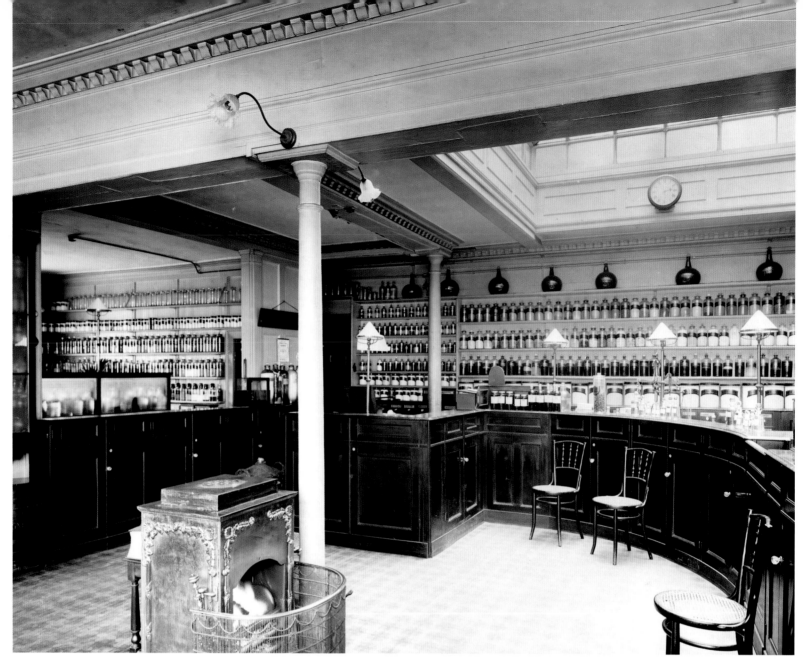

Guild of Apothecaries

BLACKFRIARS

Above: Apothecaries Hall, Blackfriars Lane, 16 November 1911
Apothecaries Hall dates from 1684 and was altered in 1779. The main buildings are of 1669-71 arranged around a central courtyard, parts of which rest on the mediaeval stone walls of the old Blackfriars monastery. The Pharmacy (shown here) is lined with traditional gilt and glass chemists' jars.

Right: View of the Still Room. Although the livery hall was the grand formal function room of the guild, medicines and pharmaceutical products were also prepared here for public use.

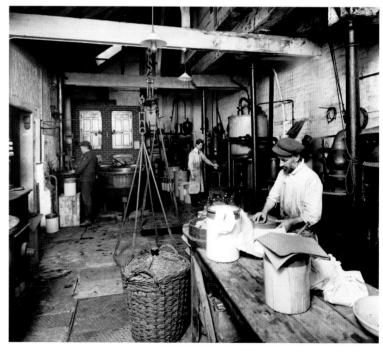

The fourth estate

FLEET STREET

Right: 109 Fleet Street, 24 March 1909
This extraordinary picture shows a much-altered 18th century house with later sgraffito decoration to the facade subsumed within a grand new Baroque building. It was not uncommon for individual owners to refuse to sell, and to frustrate wider redevelopment schemes. Note the pediment and entablatures awaiting completion hanging over the attic windows of the house beneath.

Below: 71-76 Fleet Street, 28 March 1912
A group of 18th and 19th century buildings in multiple use as newspaper offices, workshops, engravers and hairdressers, prior to clearance for street improvements. Signwriting and advertisement boards across the facades of buildings were commonplace until the introduction of controls over advertisements.

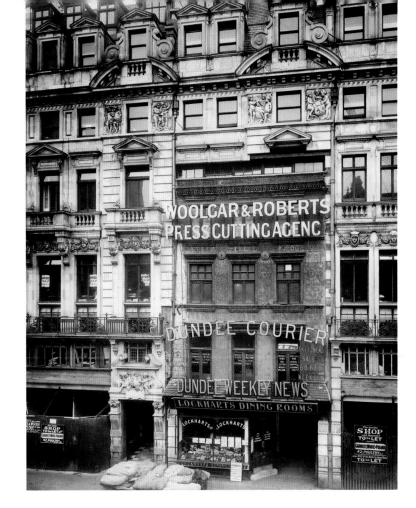

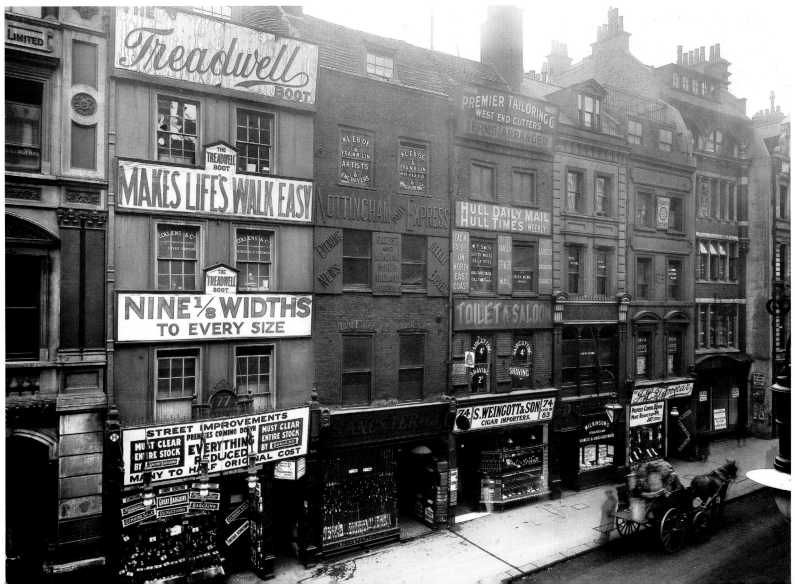

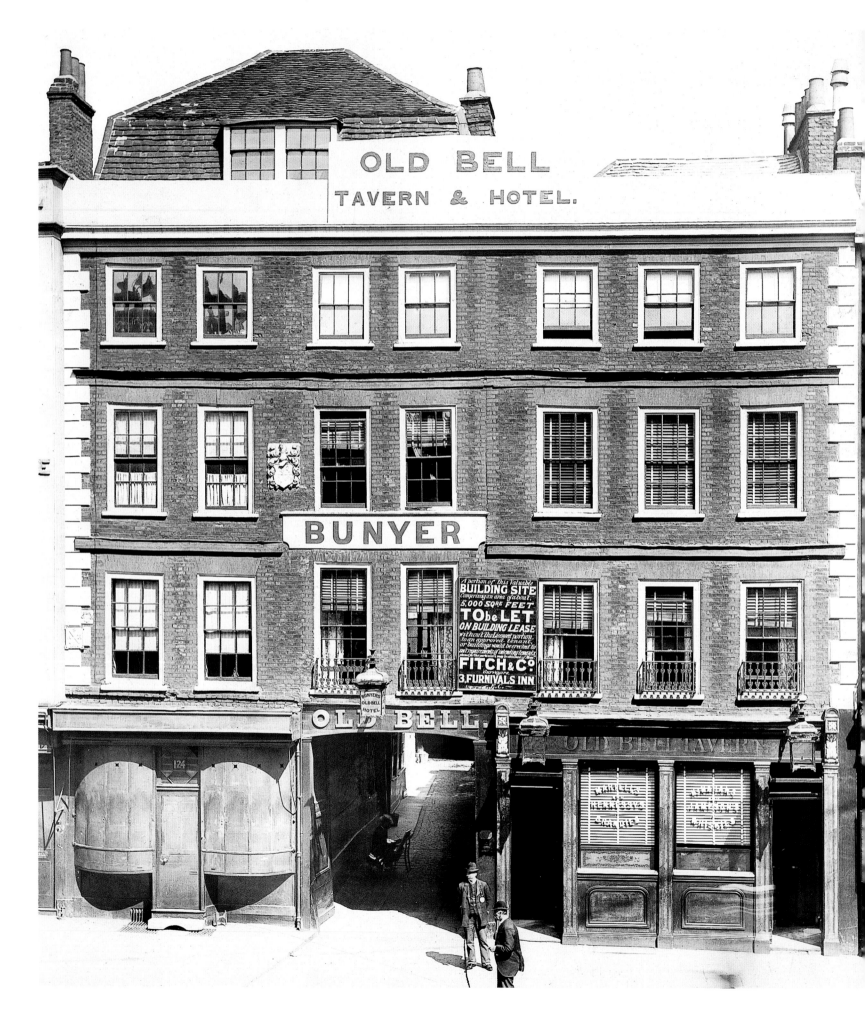

CHAPTER THREE

BETWEEN TWO CITIES

Holborn and Strand

For centuries the Strand and Holborn-High Holborn were the principal historic routes westwards from the City of London to Westminster, but even after the removal of Temple Bar in 1878, congestion was severe. North-south movement was even worse with traffic confined to Chancery Lane or Drury Lane, or consigned to a convoluted maze of ancient streets between the two.

Planned for decades, the new Holborn to Strand road was the first and largest of the metropolitan improvements carried out by the newly-formed London County Council. The sheer scale of the project was immense – the most extensive clearance project undertaken in London since the Great Fire. Many of the images captured here were taken to record the neighbourhood on the eve of its destruction.

As well as eliminating traffic bottlenecks, the aim was to sweep away one of London's worst slums which lay between Drury Lane and Clare Market; a hotbed of criminal activity. A grand new Imperial boulevard – Kingsway – was created. This was linked to a massive sweeping crescent at its south end – Aldwych - beneath which ran a tunnel to accommodate the LCC's new electric trams. Gradually over 20 years the vacant plots were developed to a consistent design with elegant stone classical buildings housing offices, hotels, theatres and banks with space for new institutions, like the BBC at Bush House, and for the great halls of Empire, like Australia and India House.

The collateral damage was extensive. Whilst few mourned the loss of the squalid, if characterful, alleys off the Strand, or the infamous rookery around Clare Market, there was widespread dismay at the clearance of Holywell Street and Wych Street, which were regarded as amongst the most picturesque places in London; atmospheric rows of timber-framed buildings overhanging narrow streets imbued with a deep sense of antiquity. However, the enlightened decision to retain both St Mary-le-Strand and St Clement Danes was praised by contemporaries: evidence of growing concessions towards public interest in conservation. Some of London's most ancient Inns of Court fell victim too – Clements Inn, Danes Inn and New Inn were all swept away, and Clifford's Inn followed soon after.

Further north the last of the old coaching inns, like the Old Bell and the Black Bull in Holborn, were photographed on the brink of oblivion – rendered redundant by the railways and omnibuses of a new age, as motorised transport displaced the horse. In Bloomsbury the old Foundling Hospital at Corams Fields was still the focal point of the neighbourhood, but its days were numbered.

Westward along the Strand, change was more incremental as rows of older houses on individual domestic plots surrendered to much larger commercial buildings. The vast 1,000 room Hotel Cecil was one of the largest in the world when it opened in 1896 and the harbinger of things to come. Soon, Exeter Hall, that great bastion of radicalism, Cockerell's wonderful neo-classical Westminster Insurance offices, and, just to the south, the iconic Adelphi, were all to fall prey to a new generation of buildings designed to meet the needs of a new century.

Opposite: The Old Bell Tavern and Hotel, Holborn, c 1897
The frontage of The Old Bell dated from 1720, but the galleried portion at the rear where Shakespeare is alleged to have conducted one of his plays was built in 1521. Dickens and Thackeray were regulars.

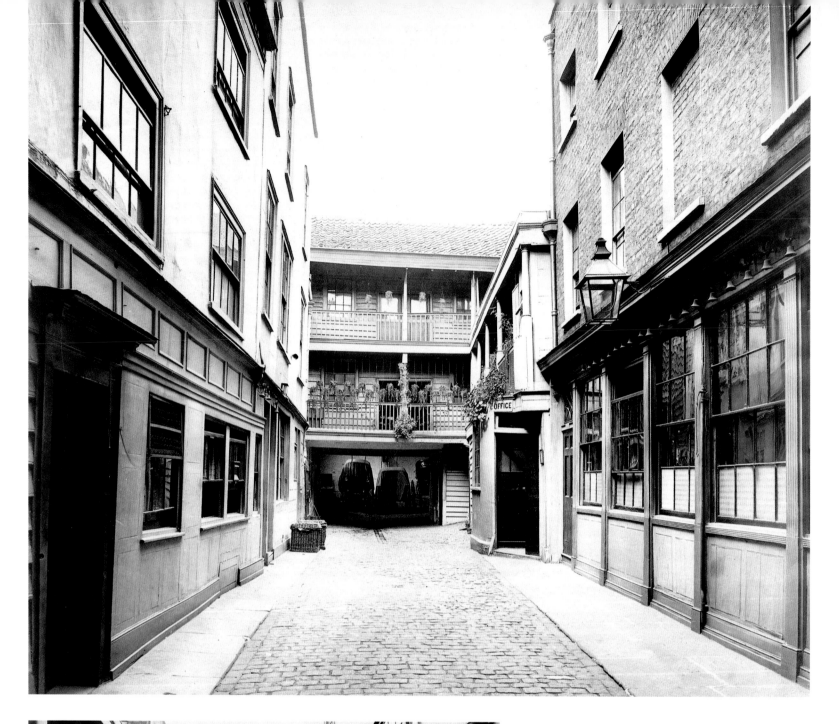

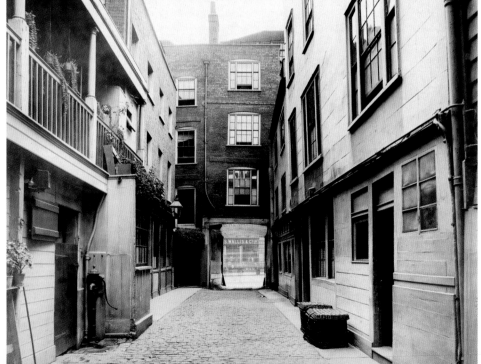

HOLBORN

The Old Bell Tavern and Hotel, Holborn, c 1897

Above: "*Passing through the ponderous wooden gates that have hung there for 300 years, visitors' attention is attracted by a row of bells for summoning chambermaids, boots, ostlers etc.*"

Left: Looking back along the yard, the curious little niche to the left of the window over the entrance contained a small painted figure of Napoleon. Quite why, no-one ever knew.

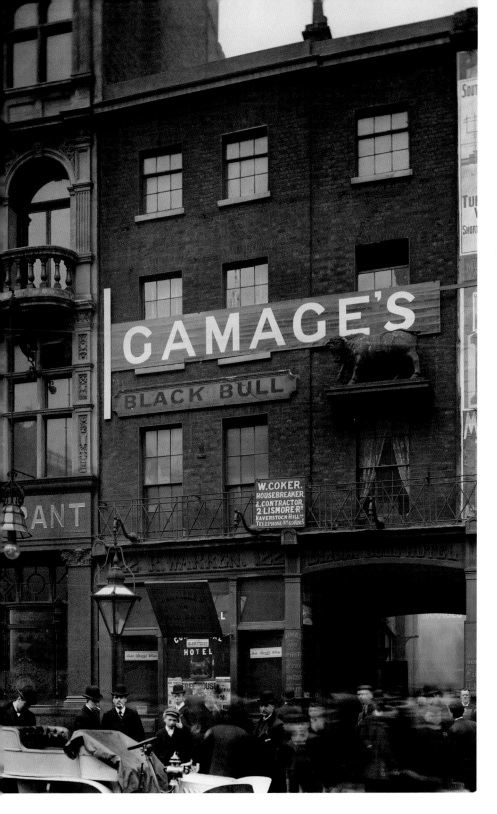

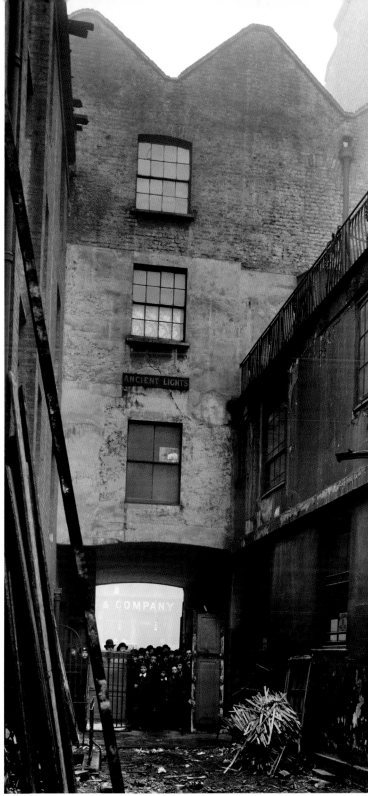

Coaching inns on the road to Tyburn

Above left: The Black Bull Inn, Holborn, 8 April 1904

"Many a mournful procession passed its doors … coming up the 'Heavy Hill' on its way from Newgate or the Tower to the gallows at Tyburn."

Situated next to The Old Bell, the Black Bull was another well-known coaching inn. It was here that Sarah Gamp and Betsey Prig nursed Mr Lewsome in Dickens' *Martin Chuzzlewit*. The figure of the bull over the main entrance was modelled for William Lockwood, the inventor of Portland cement. On demolition for the new Gamages Department store, it was relocated to the offices of Sir William Bull MP in King Street, Hammersmith.

Above right: In its last years the galleries at the rear were converted into tenements for the poor.

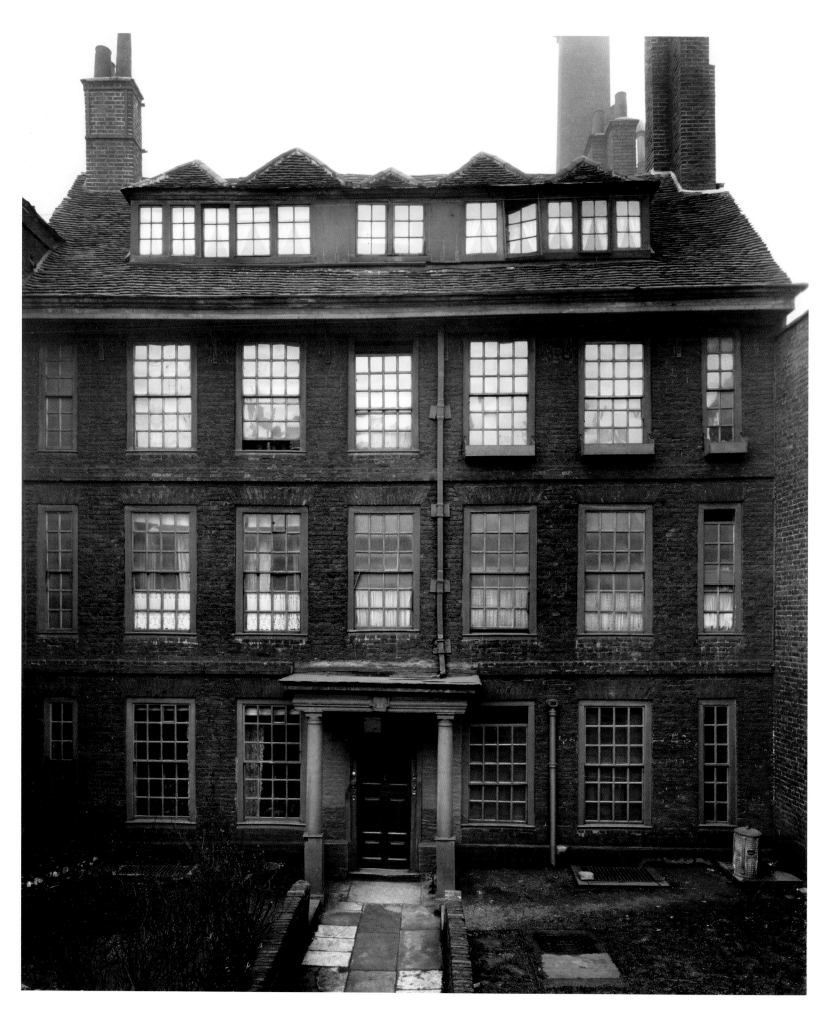

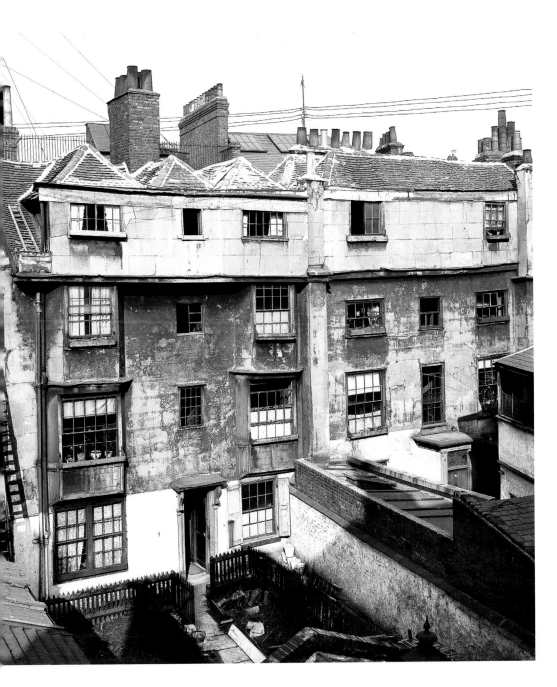

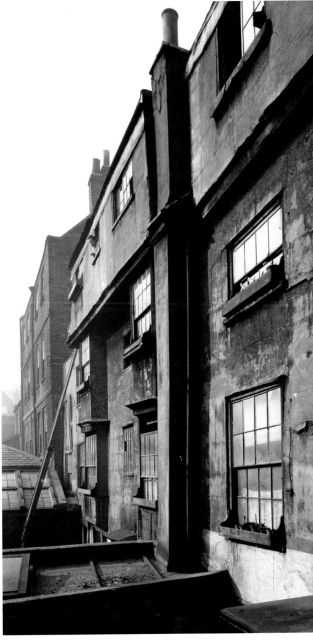

Ramshackle survivors of the Great Fire

Opposite: 10 Nevill's Court, 16 March 1910

Nevill's Court was a small alley off the east side of Fetter Lane. This superb late 17th century merchant's house was the town house of the Nevills until 1744 when it was acquired as the mission house of the Society of Moravians, or United Brethren. At the time of its demolition in 1910, even though it had been divided into suites of rooms, its magnificent panelled interiors survived. The adjacent Moravian chapel was attacked during the Gordon Riots of 1780 in the mistaken belief it was Catholic.

Above left: Nos. 13a-15 Nevill's Court, 16 March 1910

This remarkable group of 17th century, pre-Fire houses on the north side of the court had small courtyard gardens enclosed by wooden palings. Keir Hardie lived for several years at No. 14. Christabel Pankhurst was another notable resident.

Above right: Nos. 13a-15 Nevill's Court, 16 March 1910

Oblique view of the front elevations of the buildings which were in use as lodging houses, before their demolition in 1912. The remainder of Nevill's Court was swept away in 1929 to create a new road from Shoe Lane to Chancery Lane.

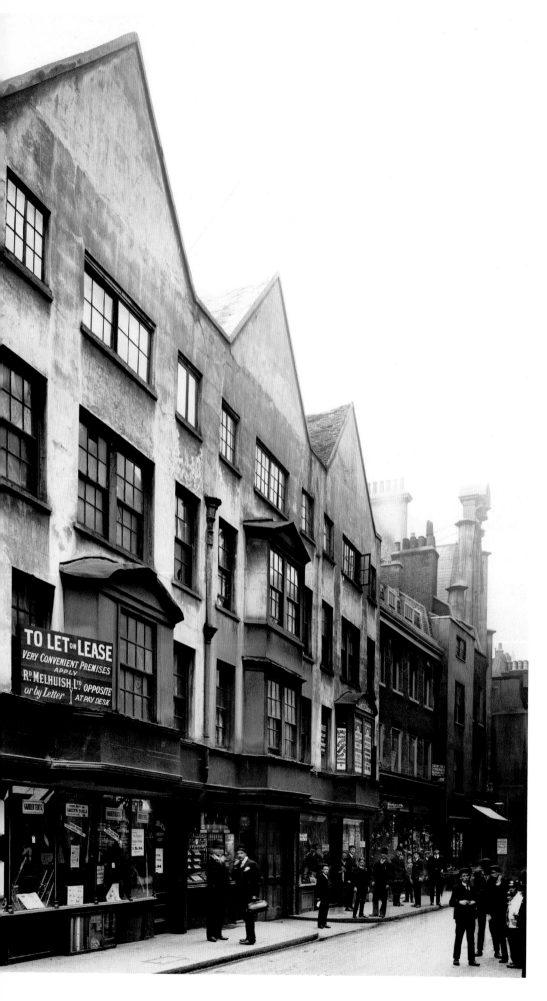

Left: 85-87 Fetter Lane, 21 July 1908
A surviving group of 17th century, timber-framed houses at the north end of Chancery Lane. The gabled building in the background, a fine Edwardian Art Nouveau composition by the architects Treadwell and Martin, still remains.

Below: Quality Court, Chancery Lane, c 1910
Early 18th century houses. View looking south-west. Quality Court remains, lined with later buildings, including a fine Edwardian interpretation of an 18th century merchant's house.

Opposite: The Rolls Chapel, Chancery Lane, c 1895
The Rolls Chapel was occupied by the Keeper of the Rolls of Chancery and used as a repository of records as well as a place of worship. The 16th century chapel was demolished in 1895 for an extension of the Public Record Office, which can be seen in the distance. A fragment of an arch of the original chapel can be found embedded in the back wall of the former Public Record Office, which is now used by King's College, London.

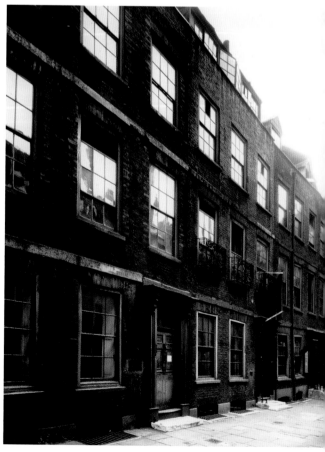

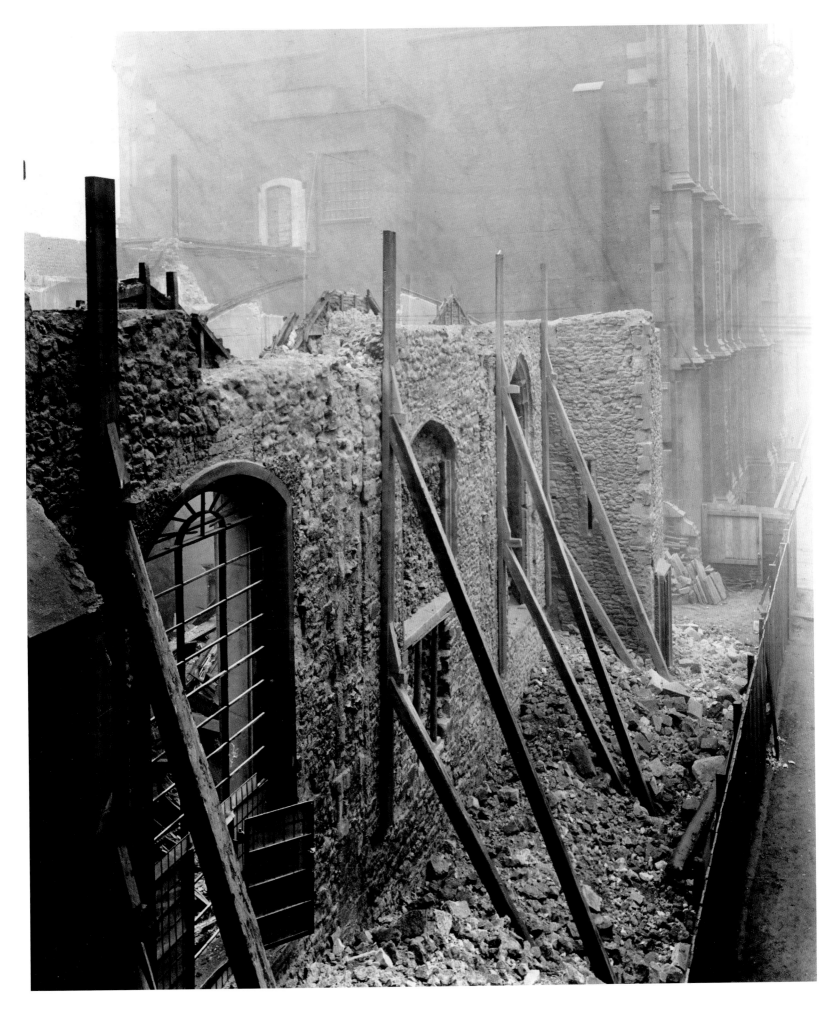

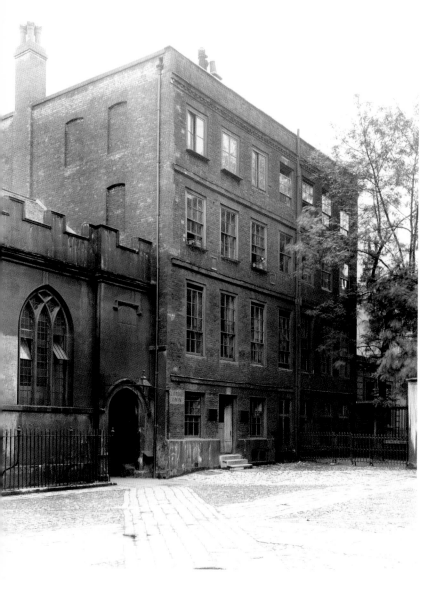

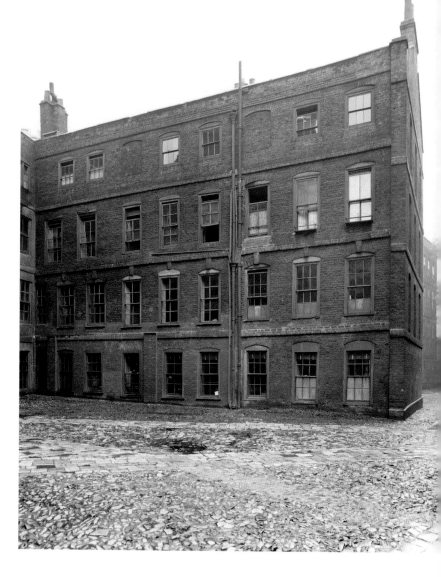

Legal precincts

CHANCERY LANE

Clifford's Inn, 1903
Named after Robert de Clifford, who was granted the property by Edward II, an independent Inn was established by law students in 1345 and affiliated to the Inner Temple. The entire Inn was sold in 1903, when these photographs were taken, but it remained occupied until its demolition in 1935. Only the gateway survives.

Above left: Early 18th century lawyers' chambers and the western end of the hall, built in 1767. The original hall escaped the Great Fire. The Judges of the Great Fire Court met there in 1670 to resolve rebuilding disputes between landlords and tenants.

Above right: 10, 12 & 13 Clifford's Inn, 1903
View showing the passageway through to Serjeants Inn, Chancery Lane and the beautifully textured courtyard surface in natural stone.

Opposite: View of 1-9 Clifford's Inn
The elegant young woman is probably the secretary of the South American Missionary Society, which occupied the first floor of this range, which was built in 1682. Note the huge York stone slabs, cobbles and limestone setts to the courtyard.

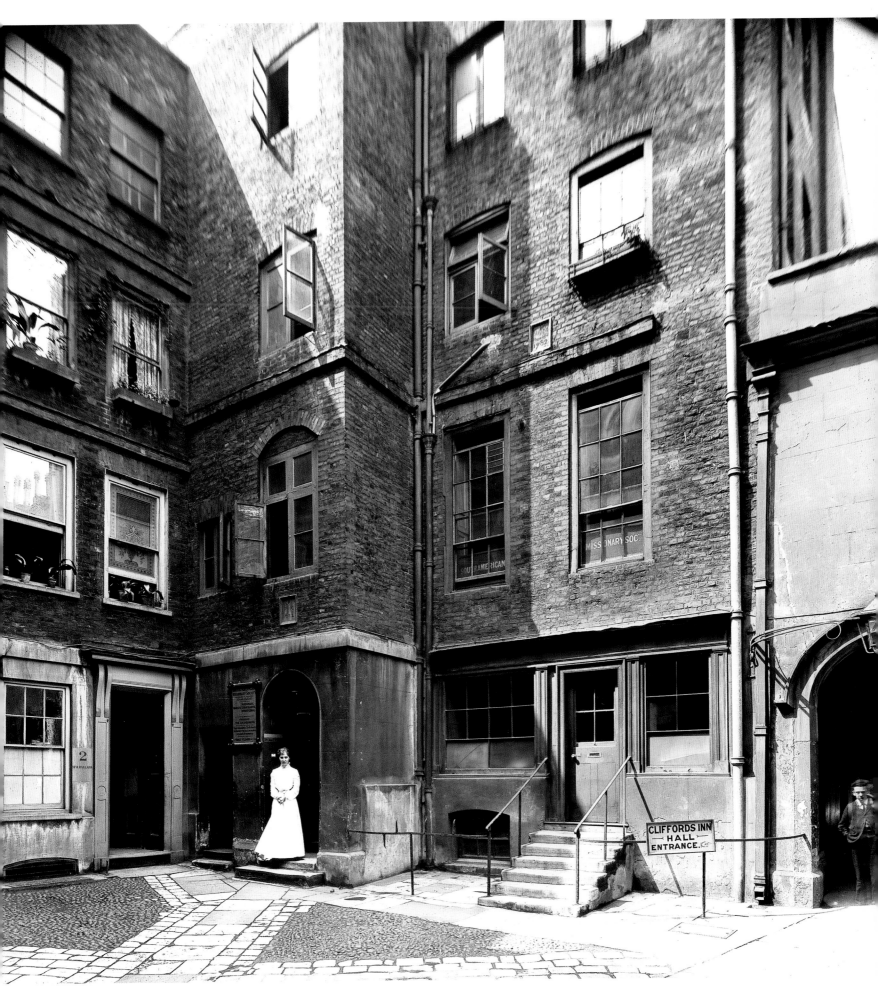

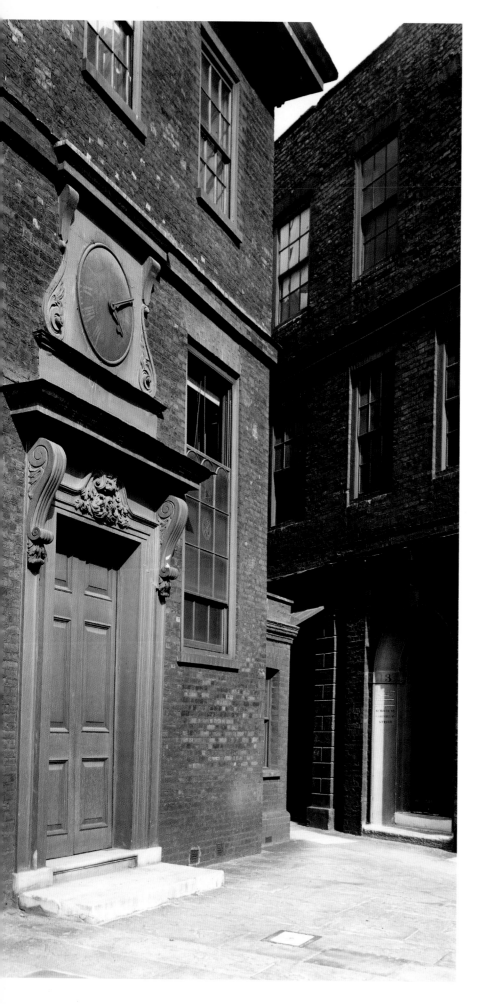

STRAND

New Inn, 1906

Founded in a converted tavern around 1460, New Inn lay north-west of St Clement Danes Church behind Wych Street, and was affiliated to the Middle Temple. In the 19th century membership declined and the entire Inn was acquired by the LCC in 1909 for the Holborn-Strand improvement scheme.

Left: Benchers Hall, c 1906

View of the entrance

Below: Benchers Hall, c 1906

The richly-modelled 17th century ceiling

Opposite: New Inn Passage, 11 June 1906

View along New Inn Passage from Houghton Street. To the left is a Girls' Infants School, which explains the large numbers of children around the entrance to the corner shop.

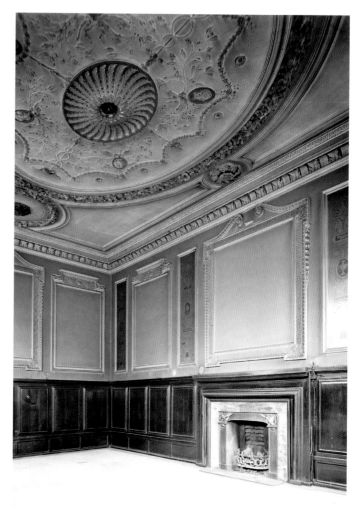

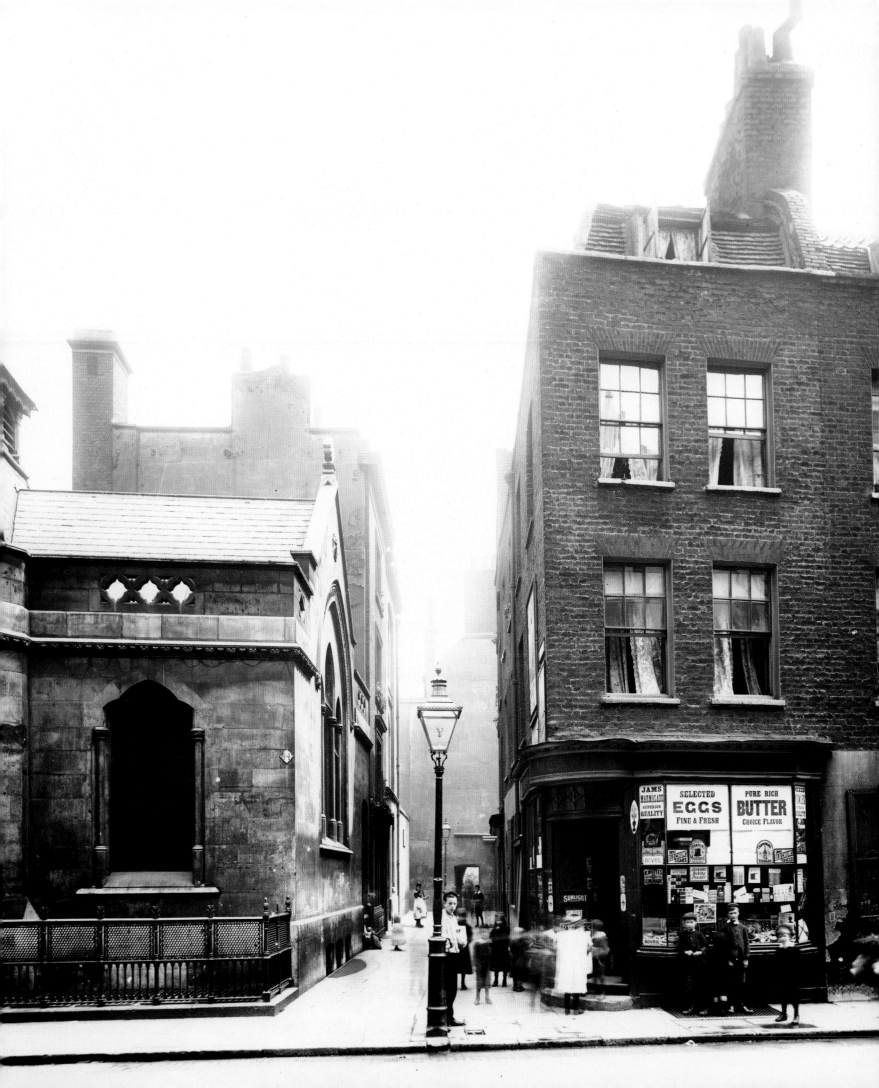

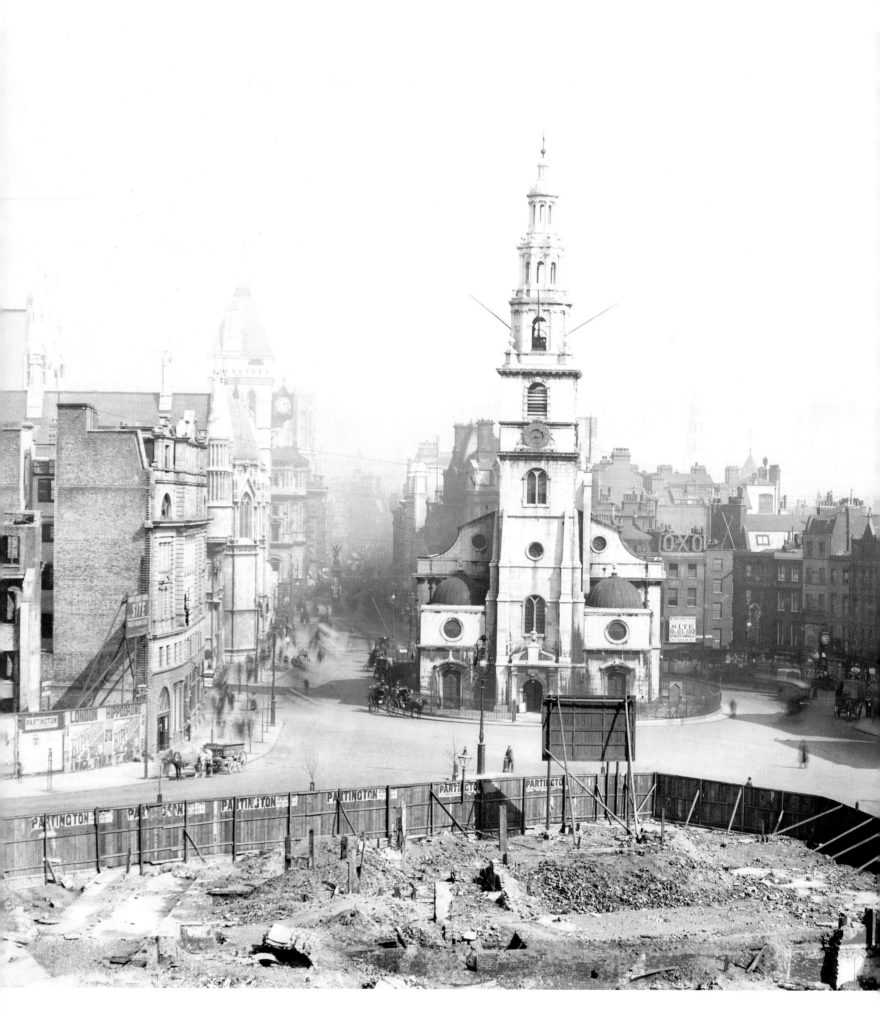

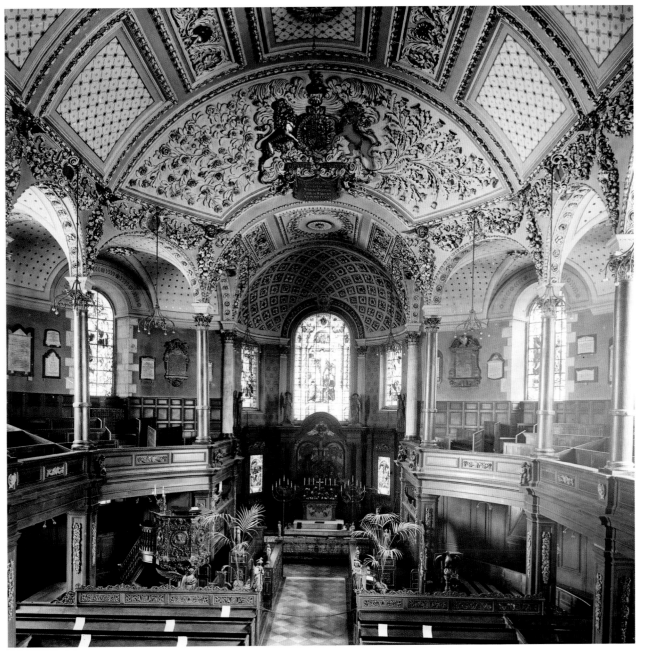

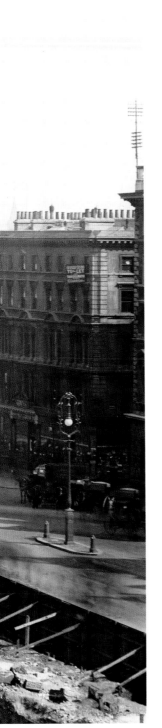

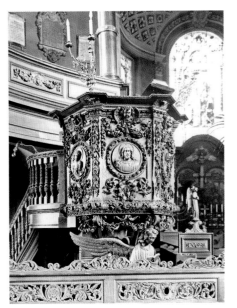

Most extensive clearance

St Clement Danes Church

Opposite: 12 July 1906: View looking east from Newcastle Street showing the clearance of buildings by the LCC for the Holborn-Strand improvement scheme. The site in the foreground is now occupied by Australia House. The steeple of St Bride's, Fleet Street and the ethereal outline of St Paul's can be seen shimmering in the background haze.

Above: 22 July 1905, the spectacular nave and apse showing Wren's lavish original plasterwork. The church was gutted by fire in 1941 and restored in 1955-58 by Anthony Lloyd.

Left: 22 July 1905, the magnificent original 17th century carved oak pulpit.

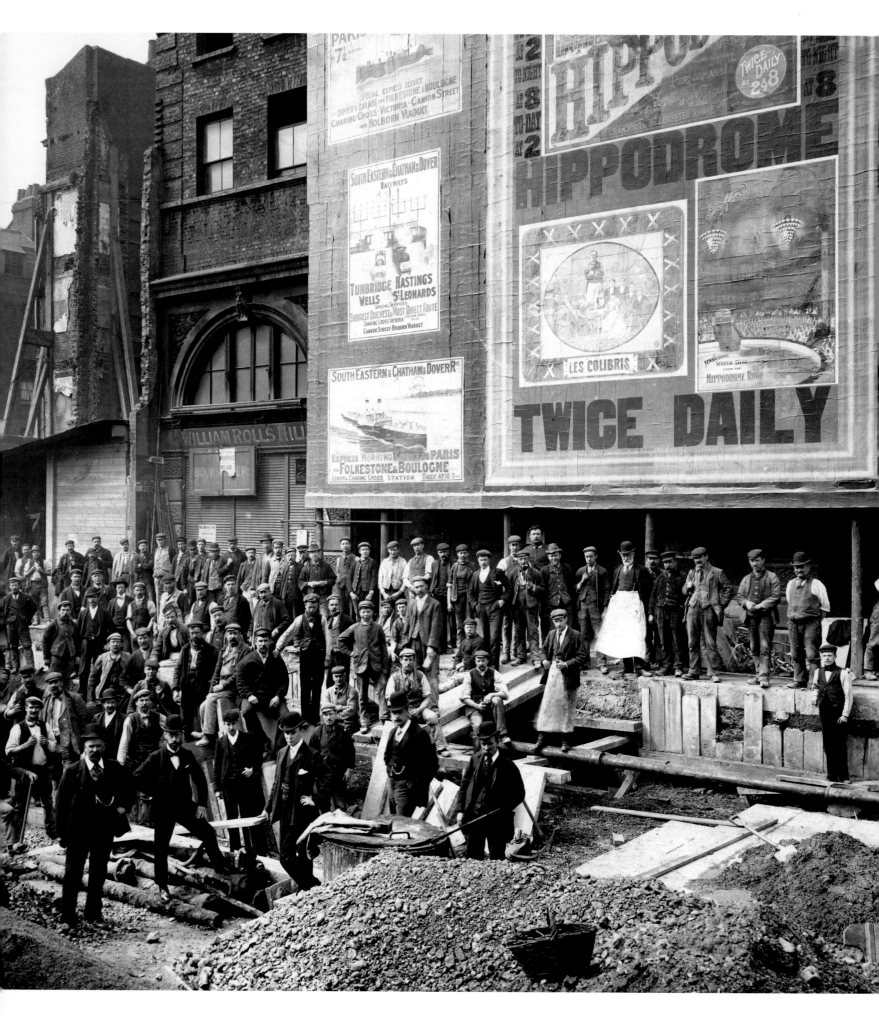

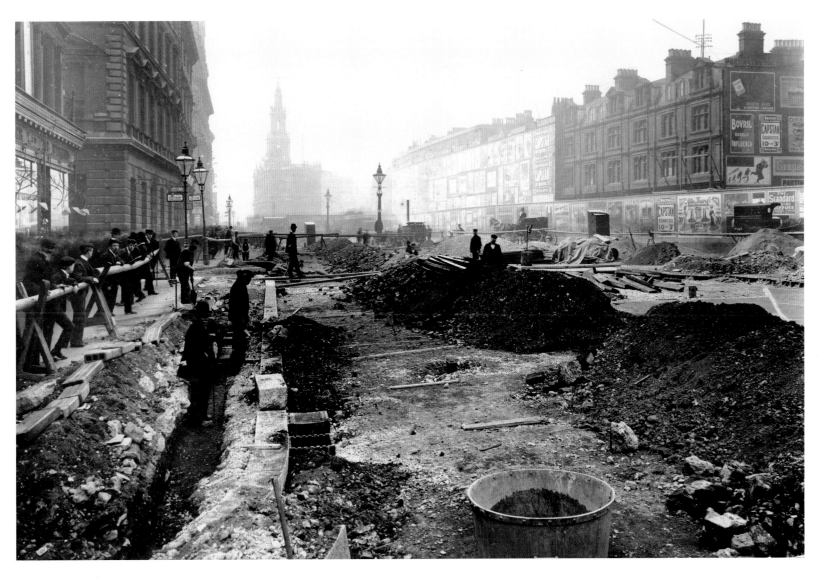

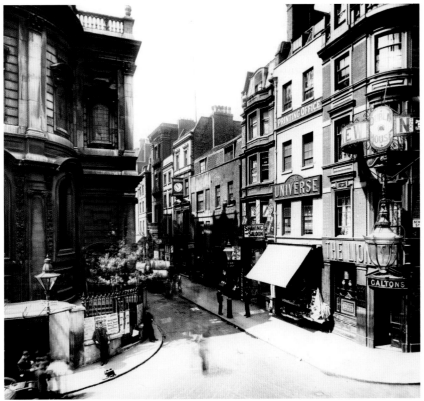

The dignity of labour

Opposite: Strand – north side, c 1902
Demolition of buildings for the Holborn-Strand improvements. The photograph is carefully posed with the professionals – the surveyors and clerks of works – to the fore. The topmost advertisement on the hoarding behind offers a special express service to Paris in $7^1/_2$ hours.

Above: Strand, 14 April 1902
View from the south side looking west towards St Mary-le-Strand Church.

Left: Strand, 22 May 1901
The east end of St Mary-le-Strand at the junction with Newcastle Street. The cart in the background is delivering large rolls of newspaper. Note the shoeshine boy on the corner and the colossal iron and glass lantern to the public house.

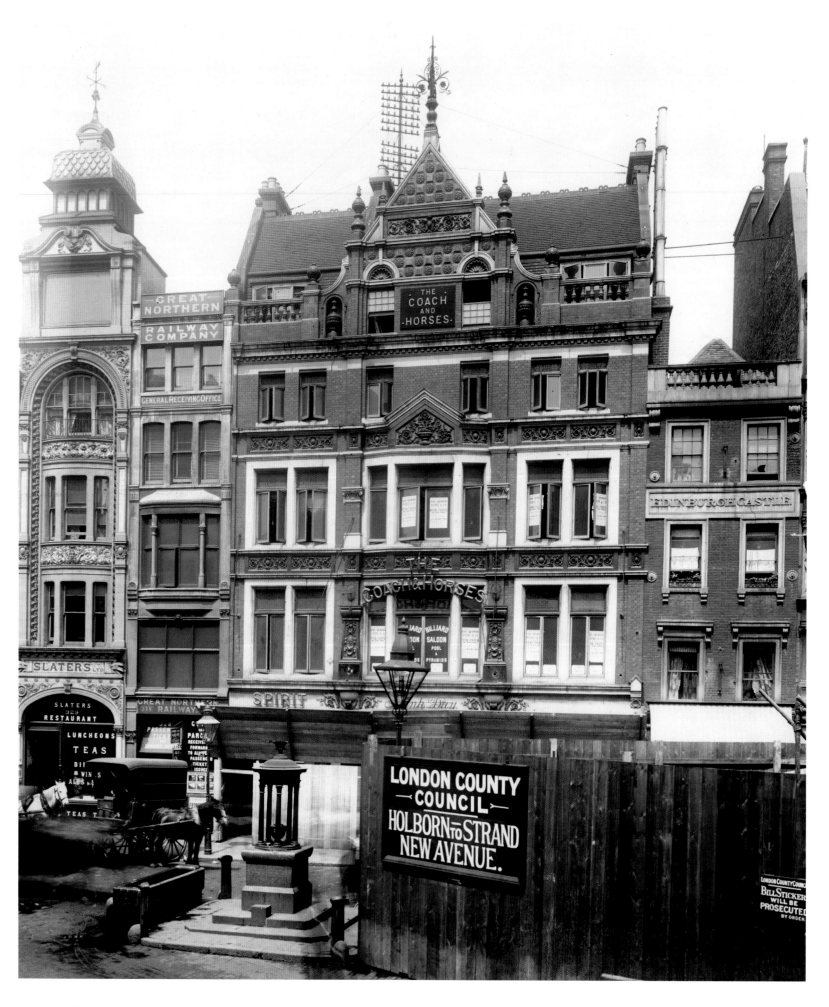

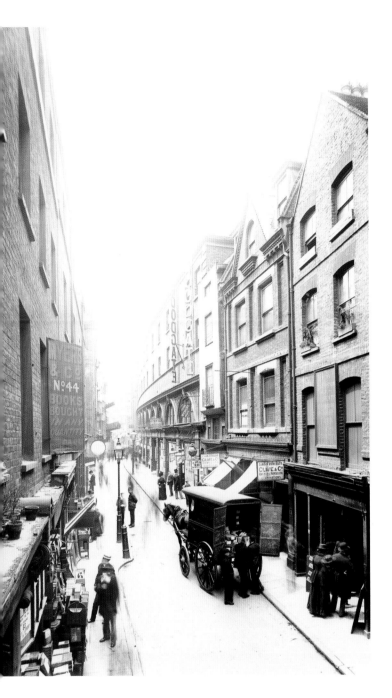

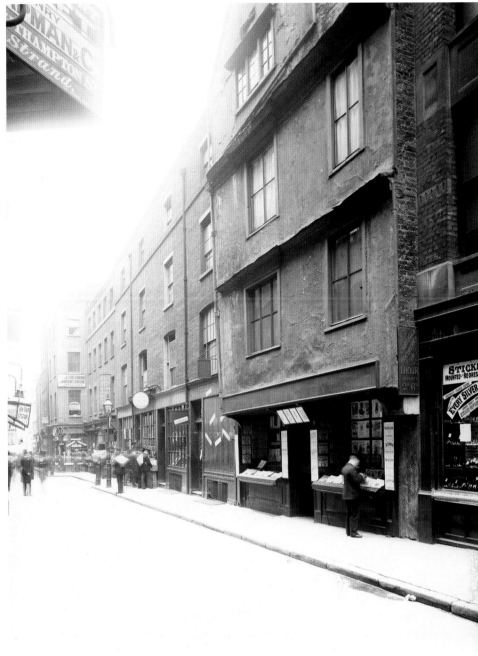

Sink of iniquity

Opposite: 321-320 Strand, 11 June 1906
The north side of the Strand outside the west end of St Mary-le-Strand. The elegant cast iron drinking fountain was re-erected at Wimbledon Common.

Above left: Holywell Street, 11 June 1906
"*Holywell Street was a wretched narrow lane … It was insanitary, physically as well as morally; at one time … it was the sink of iniquity; indecent literature and prints were always to be got there, and it took police many prosecutions to purify it … An attempt was made to change the name of the street into Booksellers Row, but the foul odour of Holywell Street still clung to it.*" (*Old Time Aldwych*: 1903).

The view looking west with demolition proceeding in the far distance.

Above right: Holywell Street, 11 June 1906
In spite of its notorious reputation for pornography, and its constriction of traffic along the Strand, Holywell Street was a place of immense character. The view looking east with a fine old timber-framed house to the right.

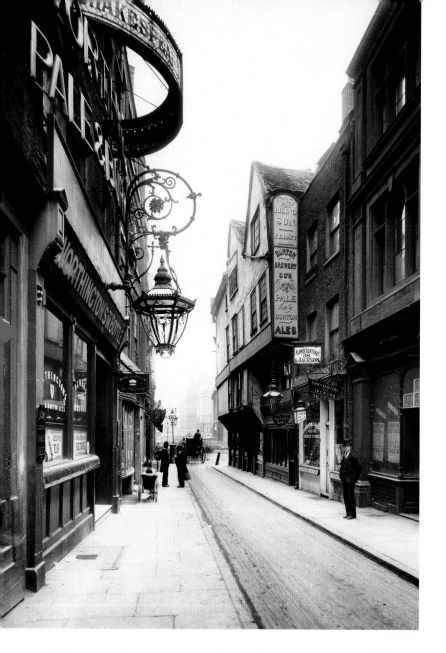

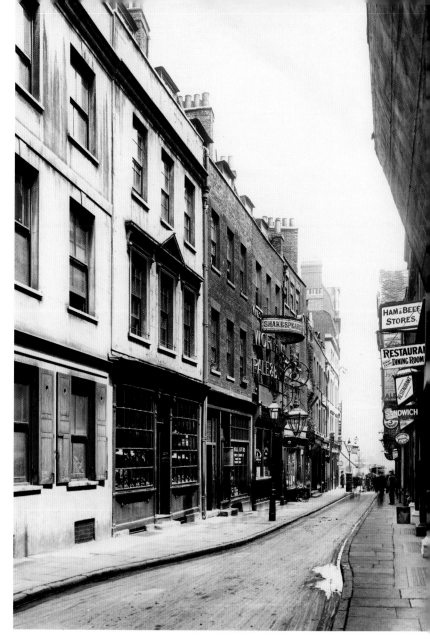

Quoting, quipping, quaffing

Wych Street was considered by many to be the most picturesque street in London and, for its size, it had the largest number of old houses, including many 17th century survivals.

Above left: Wych Street, 21 June 1901
View of the east end with the north side of St Clement Danes Church in the distance.

The Rising Sun was a fine Elizabethan tavern, at the junction with Holywell Street. In the bar was a glass case containing a bone of Sir Thomas Armstrong who was hanged, drawn and quartered without trial for suspicion of involvement in the Rye House Plot, 1683. One of his quarters was fixed over Temple Bar. Dislodged in a high wind, it was brought to the pub as "*everlasting testimony to the lawlessness of the law*".

Above right: North side of Wych Street looking east, 11 June 1906
The Shakespeare Head boasts a magnificent cut glass ornamental gas

lantern typical of the period. Martin Lemon, the editor of *Punch* was once the proprietor. It was also the meeting place of 'The Owls' – "*a little quoting, quipping, quaffing club*". Note the elegant Georgian shopfront to the left with bracketed, canted bays.

Opposite: 38-48 Wych Street, 5 July 1901
"*There still remains some picturesque old patchwork buildings in and around Wych Street, Holywell Street and Drury Lane. Their picturesqueness largely relies on the varied and uncertain angles of tottering timbers, and the promiscuous arrangement of windows which protrude and overhang the little shops … Staircases lead to dingy rooms with hilly floors and blackened beams, running at all angles, drooping and groaning under the mingled weight of years and heavy tread*" (*Pall Mall Gazette*: 17 October 1889).

This well-known group of Jacobean survivors stood on the south side of Wych Street, but were swept away for the Holborn-Strand scheme.

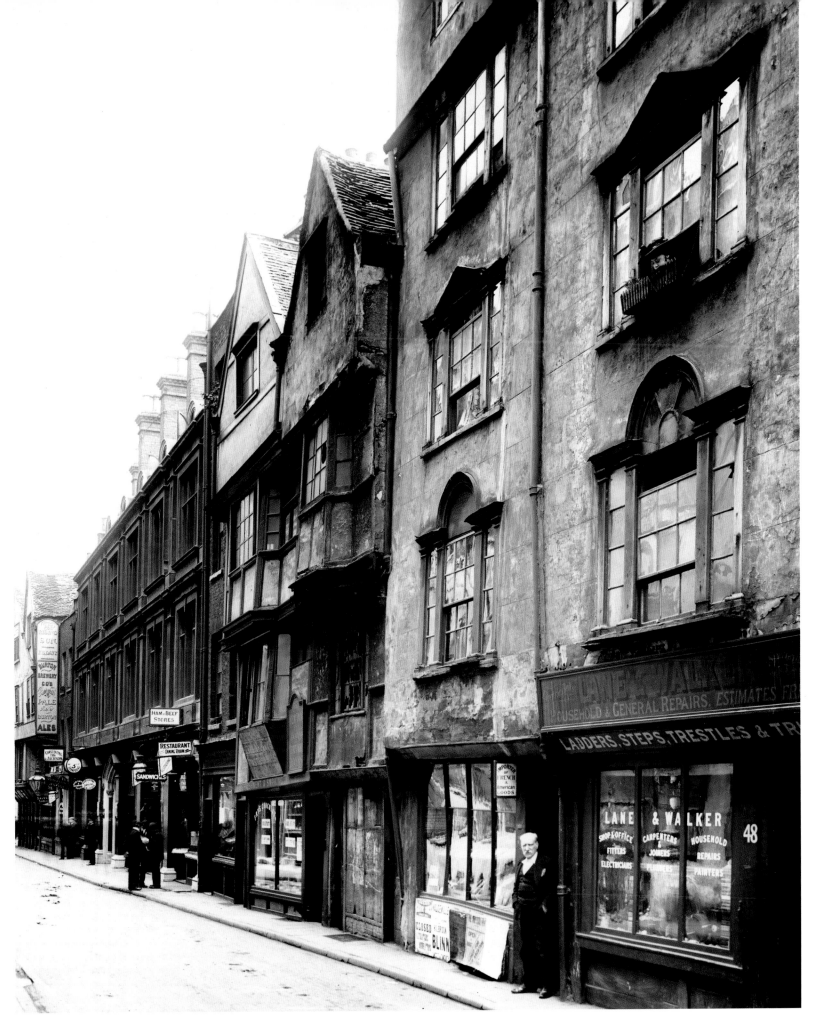

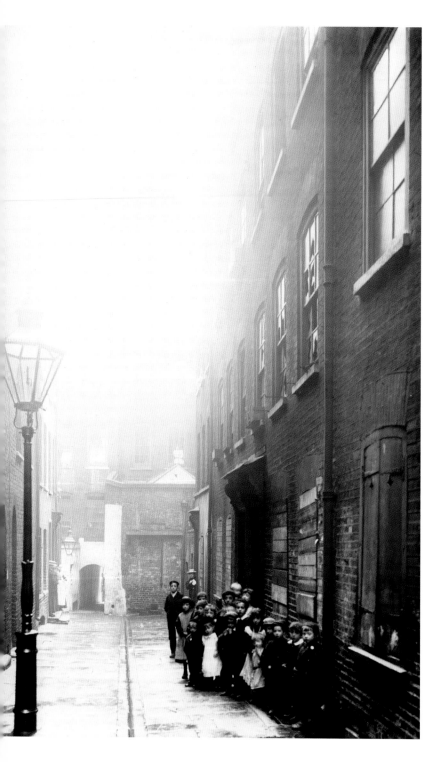

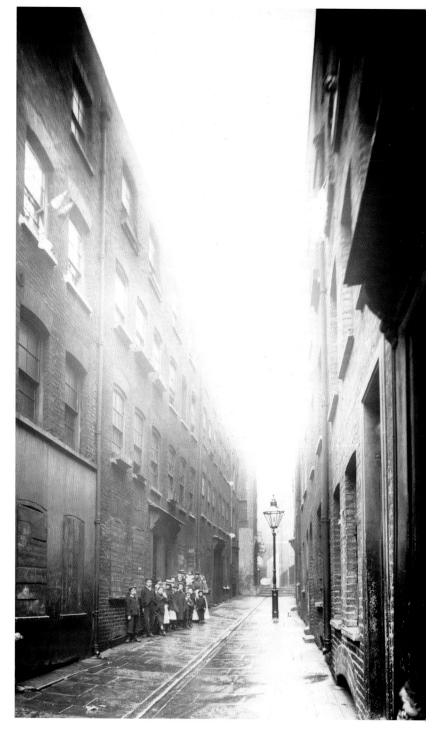

The bitter cry of outcast London

Above left: Helmet Court, 11 June 1906

For centuries, the north side of the Strand was characterised by a whole series of narrow, mediaeval passages and courts, a handful of which can still be found towards the west end. Helmet Court stood just to the north and west of Somerset House. The narrow whitewashed entrance to the Strand can be seen in the distance. Poverty is etched into the faces of the children in the foreground – a poignant scene all too common in the courts and alleys of inner and central London.

Above right: Angel Court, c 1906

Angel Court was a narrow alley lined with 18th century dwellings which ran into Eagle Court.

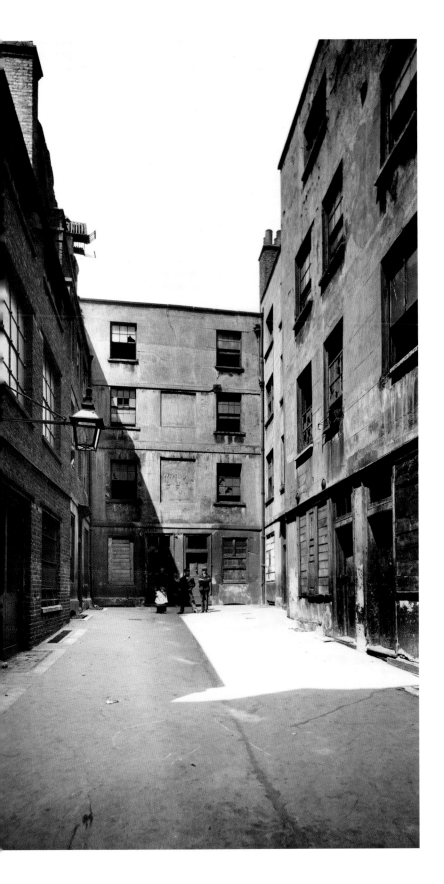

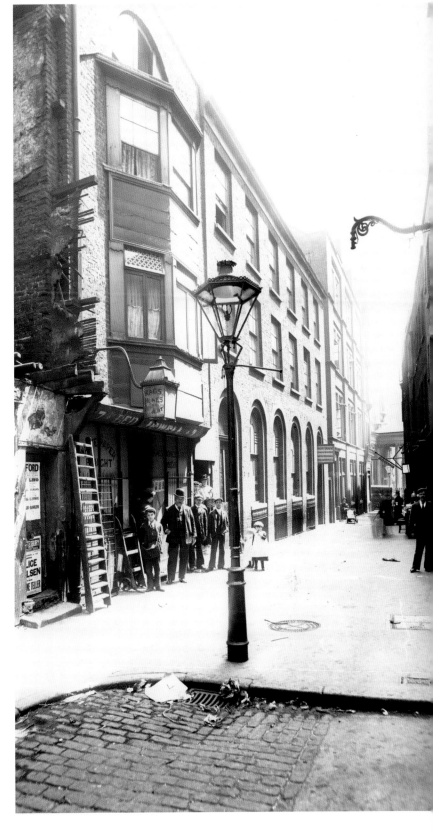

Above left: Windsor Court, 22 April 1901
Windsor Court was typical of the foetid courts and alleys of mean dwellings which provided shelter to some of London's most deprived people.

Above right: Drury Court, 11 June 1906
Drury Court linked Drury Lane with the Strand. The portico of St Mary-le-Strand can be seen in the distance. To the left, is Ben Jewell, a Rags, Bones and Fat merchant. The gap site next door shows the truncated timbers and laths of a timber-framed house.

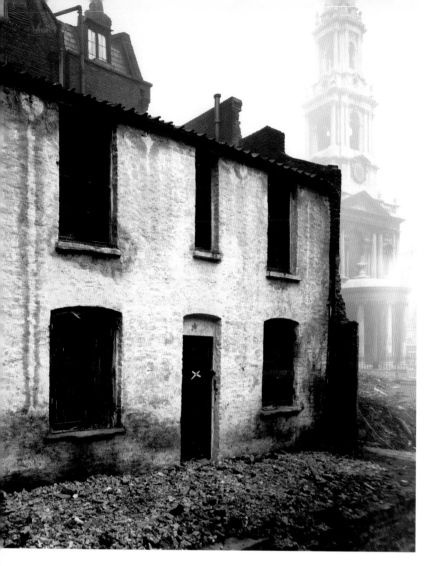

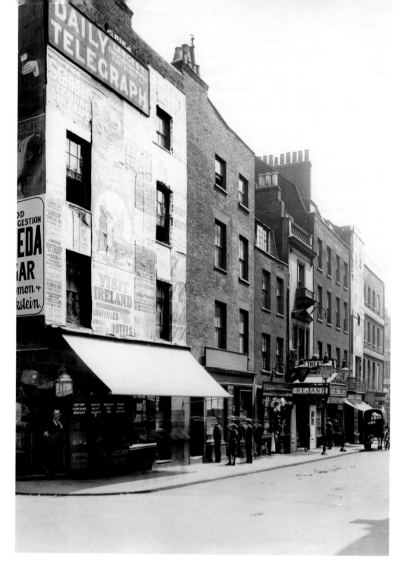

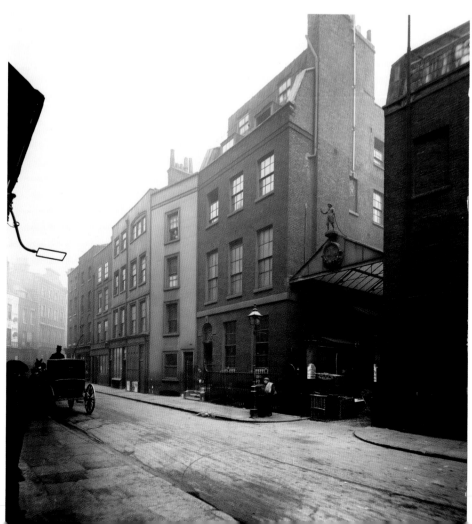

Above left: Denham Court, 11 June 1906
Beneath the atmospheric shadow of St Mary-le-Strand was some of London's meanest housing.

Above right: Newcastle Street, 11 June 1906
The east side of Newcastle Street between Wych Street and the Strand. The area was renowned for its dealers in second-hand furniture, bedding and old clothes. The Globe Theatre, which held 1500 people, had its pit and stage underground, the dress circle and boxes being level with Newcastle Street. Another entrance in Wych Street provided access to the gallery and royal box.

Right: The east side looking north with the entrance to Dent and Hellyer, lead works, marked by a lead figure above the glazed canopy.

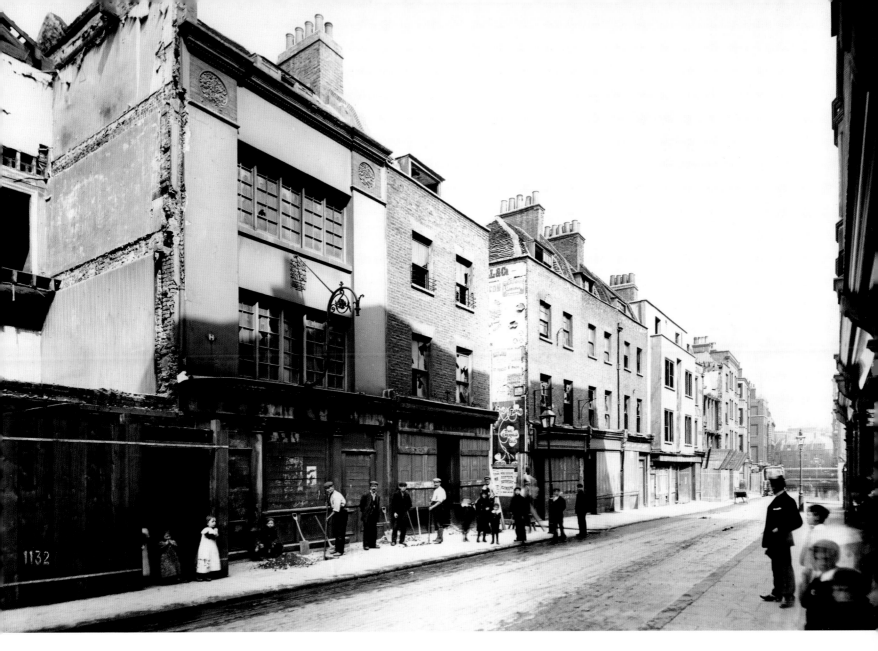

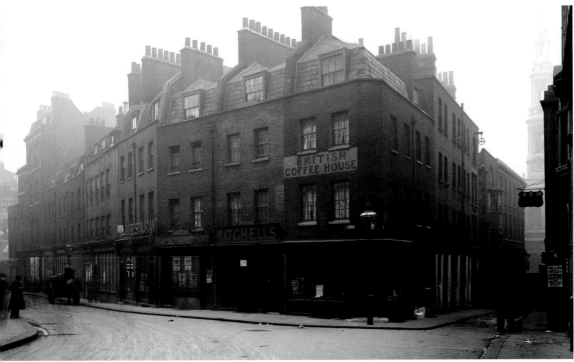

Above: Drury Lane, 11 June 1906
The north side of Drury Lane looking east towards Wych Street in the distance. The narrow entrance to Harford Place can be seen marked by posters. The tiny children in the foreground show the single entrance to Nags Head Court, which is still in occupation even though the street frontage has been demolished.

Left: The junction of Drury Lane and Wych Street with Drury Court off to the right and St Mary-le-Strand beyond.

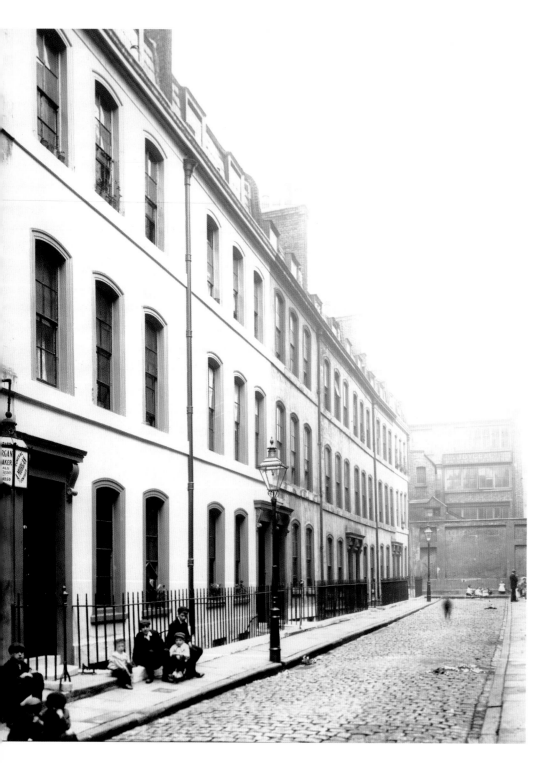

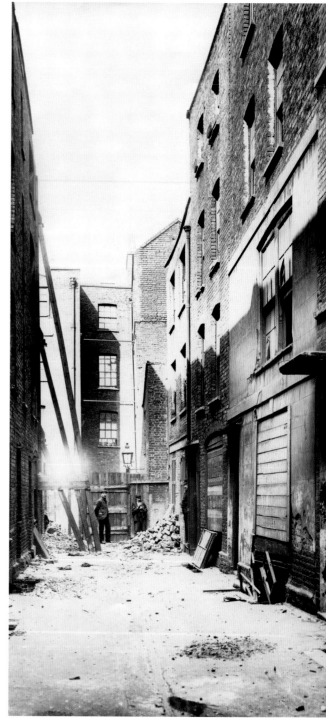

A dilapidated rookery

Above right: Feathers Court, 11 June 1906
View looking north-east towards the entrance which has been boarded over during demolition works.

Above left: Craven Buildings, 11 June 1906
Craven Buildings were erected in 1723 on part of the grounds of Craven House. At the end of the street was once a fresco of the Earl of Craven in armour, which was plastered over around 1813, but the panelled wall can be seen clearly in the distance. The undertaker's lantern on the extreme left advertises 'Funerals to Suit all Classes'.

Opposite: 8-11 Houghton Street, 5 August 1906
The hat shop at No. 9 advertises Gentlemen's Hats Polished for Sixpence. To the right, the jars over the shop fascia denote a hardware dealer selling oil for domestic use. The carriageway in the foreground is being relaid with a tarred wood block surface by 'The Improved Wood Pavement Company'. Wood blocks generated less noise than granite setts.

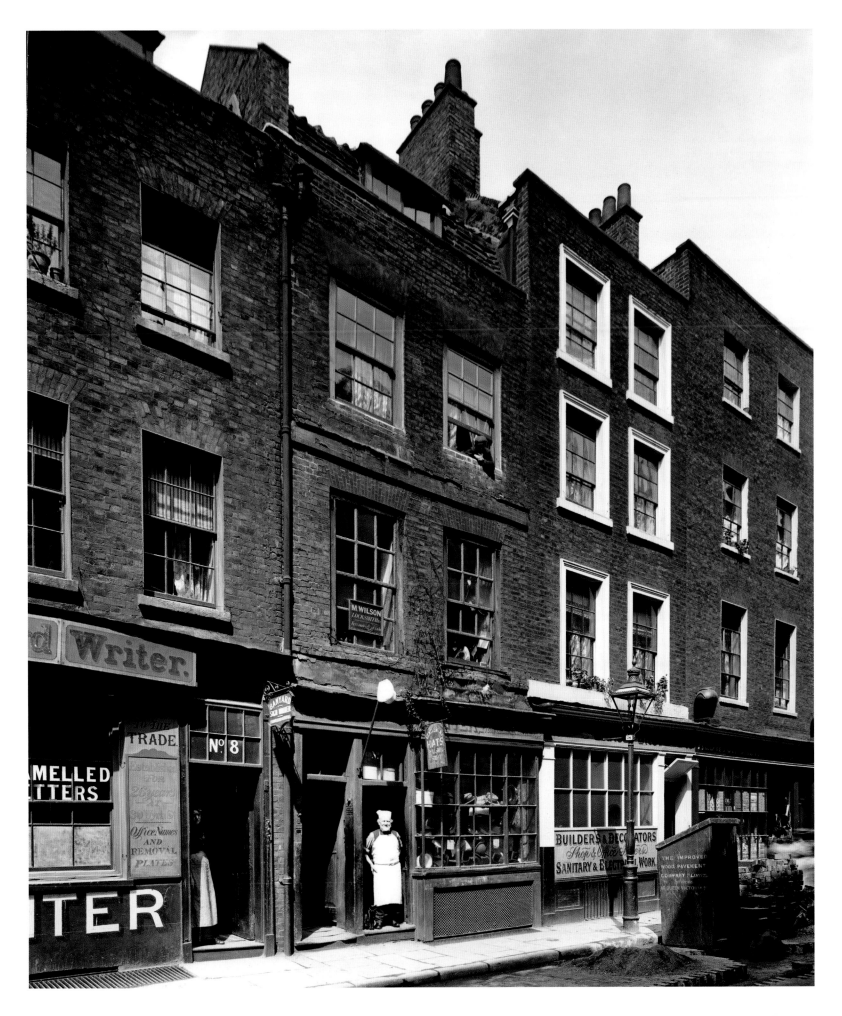

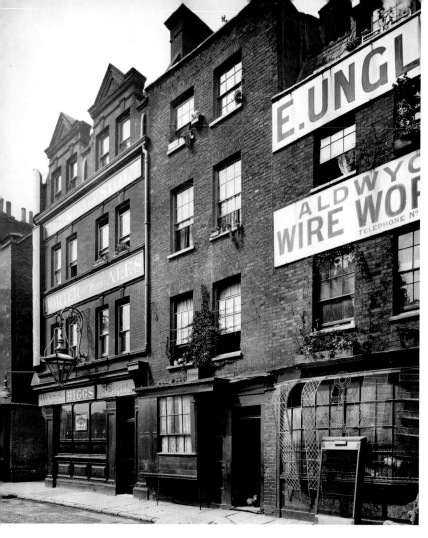

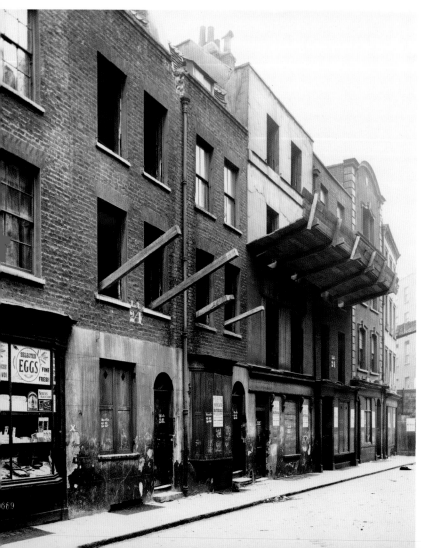

Left: 4-6 Houghton Street, 21 May 1906

To the left is the entrance to Clare Passage. The Aldwych Wire Works has a fine Georgian shopfront with an ornamental wire anchor hanging from the front. A pair of cats haunt the entrance next door.

Below left: 21-26 Houghton Street, 11 June 1906

View looking south to the junction with Newcastle Street showing demolition in progress. The shop on the extreme left offers 'Cupids Whispers' and 'Select Old Charms Tobacco' in the window alongside 'Selected Fine Fresh Eggs'.

Below right: 3 Houghton Street, c 1906

The late 19th century was the heyday of ornamental signwriting before the advent of neon. H. West occupied this fine bowed shopfront with decorative Ionic columns to the entrance and fluted Greek pilasters to the window. To the right is the narrow entrance to Clare Passage.

Opposite: 1 Clare Market, 21 May 1906

Clare Market was notorious as "*one of those filthy, dilapidated rookeries that clung desperately to a sordid existence amid a changing environment*". It was well-known for its prize-fighters and as a hotbed of criminal activity, but "*a sort of romantic aura attached to the locality … from the old world air permeating the surrounding houses*". (*Old Time Aldwych*, 1903).

The junction of Houghton Street and Clare Market. One of the oil jars over No. 11 Houghton Street can be glimpsed to the left.

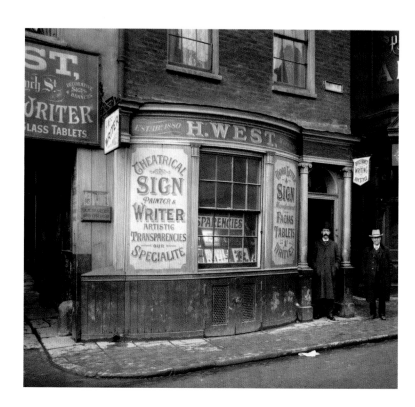

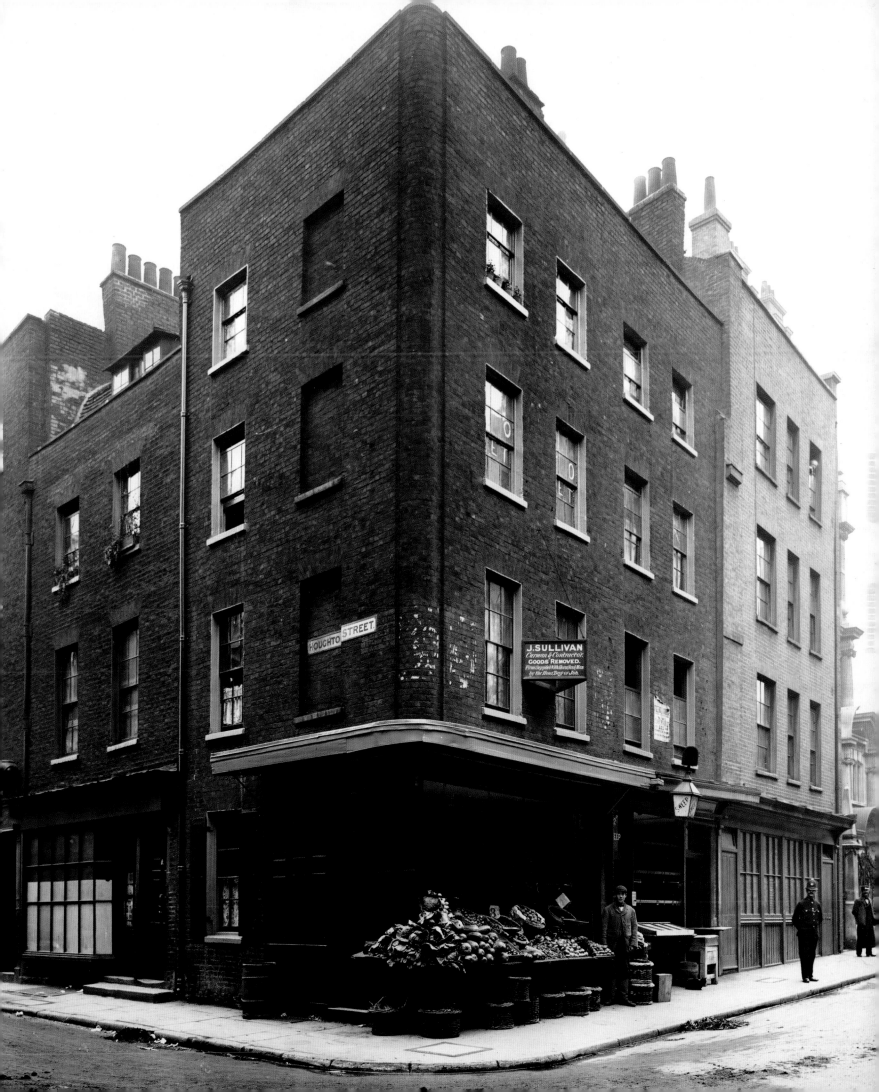

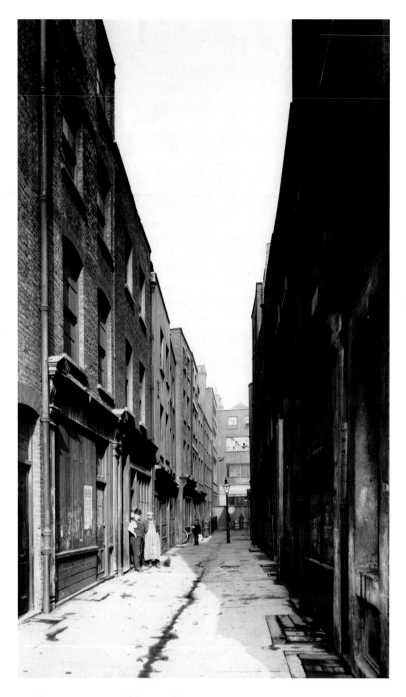

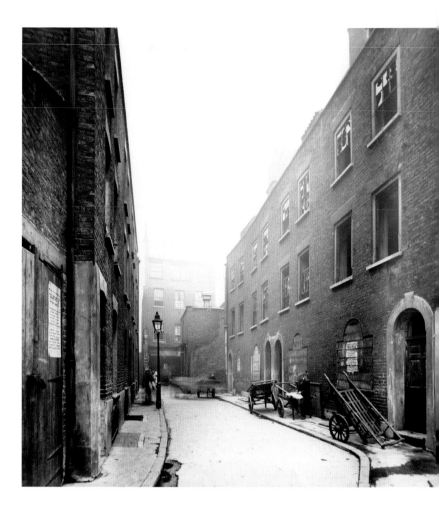

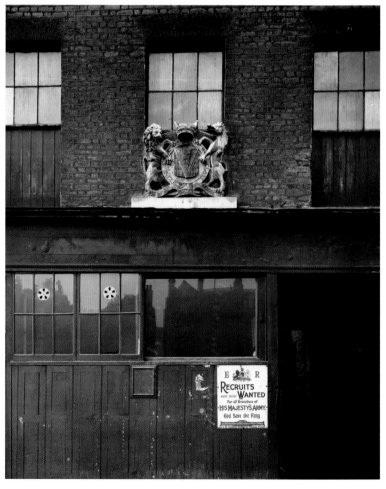

The Earl's domain

Above left: Clare Court, 11 June 1906
Clare Court, off Drury Lane was typical of the insanitary alleys and courts which gave the area its insalubrious reputation.

Above right: Harford Place, 11 June 1906
An early 18th century terrace in Harford Place, off Drury Lane just prior to demolition.

Right: 8 Clare Street, 4 April 1903
The sculptured arms dated 1665 are those of Gilbert Holles, Earl of Clare who had a house here in the mid-17th century, and subsequently laid out the area. Poor districts were a popular source of recruits for the army.

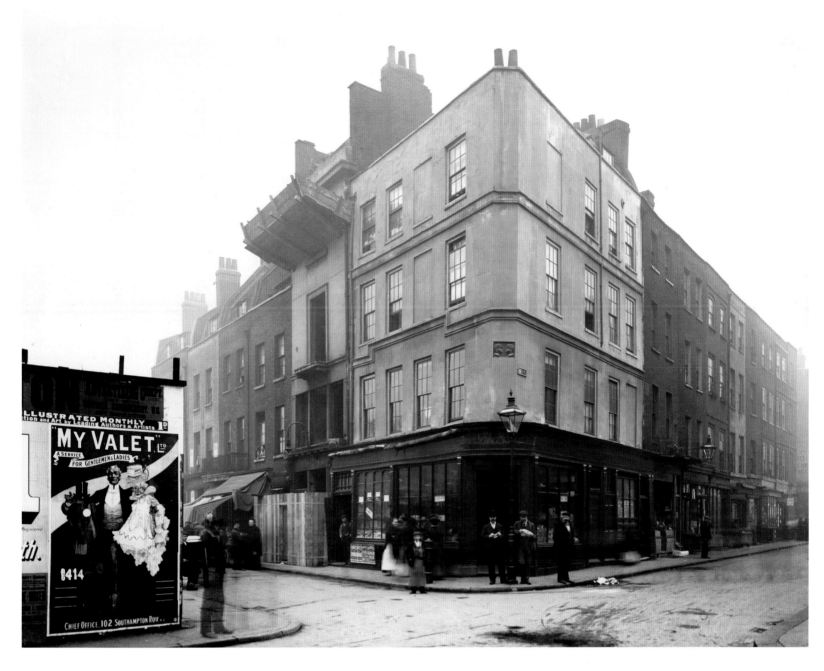

Above: Vere Street, 11 June 1906

This early 18th century corner building was formerly The Blackmoor public house, which gave its name to Blackmoor Street, a continuation of Clare Street. The plaque on the splayed corner depicts two negroes' heads, the initials S.W.M. and the date 1715.

Right: Blackmoor Street, 9 October 1902

Blackmoor Street was a narrow thoroughfare linking Drury Lane with Clare Street. A side entrance to Clare Court can be seen to the left. The beehive above the shop to the right was popular with wax chandlers, but also used as a trade sign by drapers and hosiers.

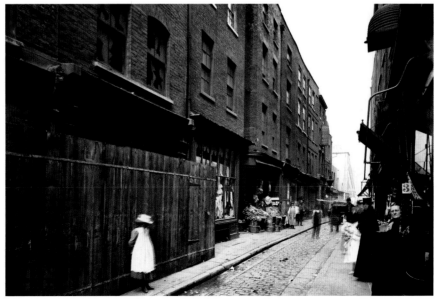

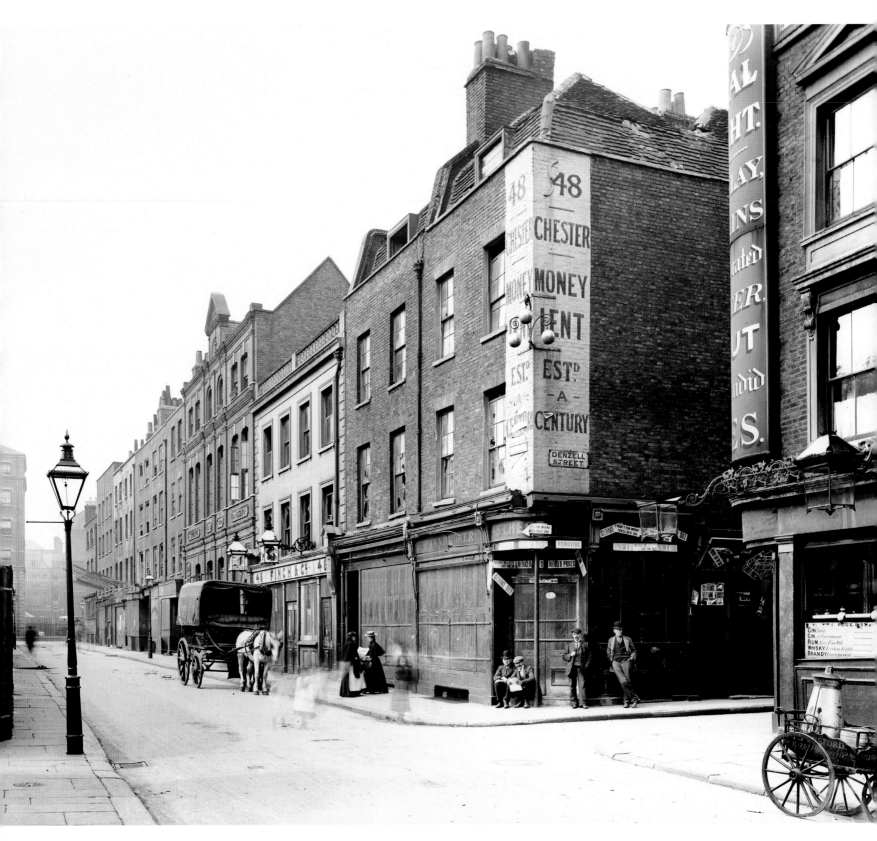

Clinging to a sordid existence

Above: Denzell Street, c 1906

The junction of Denzell Street and Stanhope Street. The pub advertises a glass of gin for 4d. Opposite lies the pawnbrokers, which has relocated prior to demolition. Beyond Finch & Co on the right is the mixed Parochial School.

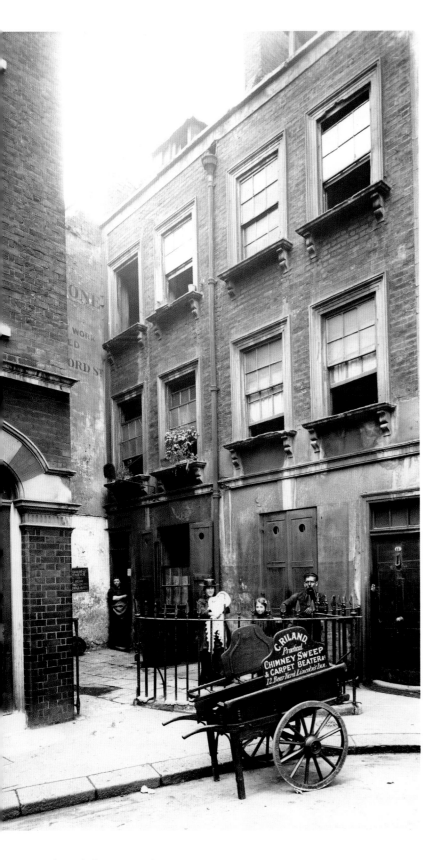

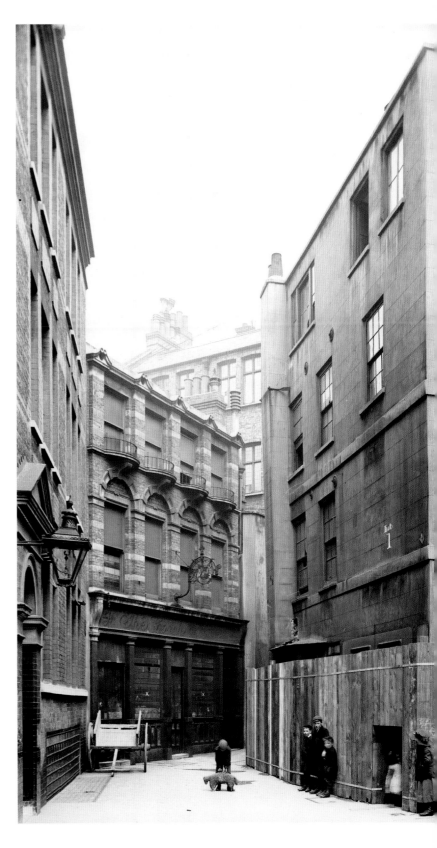

Above left: Bear Yard, 11 June 1906

The Riland family, chimney sweep and carpet beater, outside their home at 12 Bear Yard.

Above right: Bear Yard, c 1906

In 1850 Bear Yard was a slaughterhouse. Over 300-400 sheep and 50-60 bullocks were butchered here weekly. The yard was filthy, occupied by tallow-makers, cowkeepers, slaughtermen, tripe-boilers and stables. The last closed in 1889 when the yard was taken over by other trades.

The child in the foreground appears to be removing a stone sheep, a symbol of its former use.

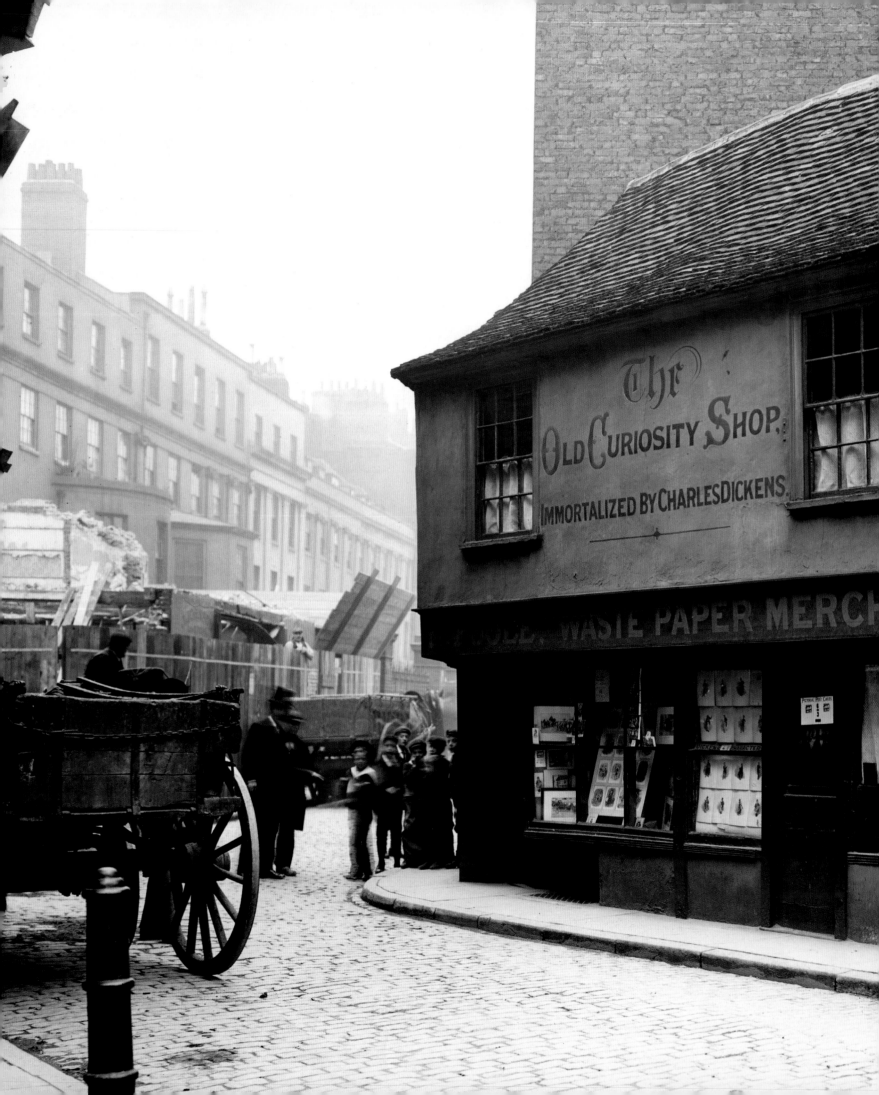

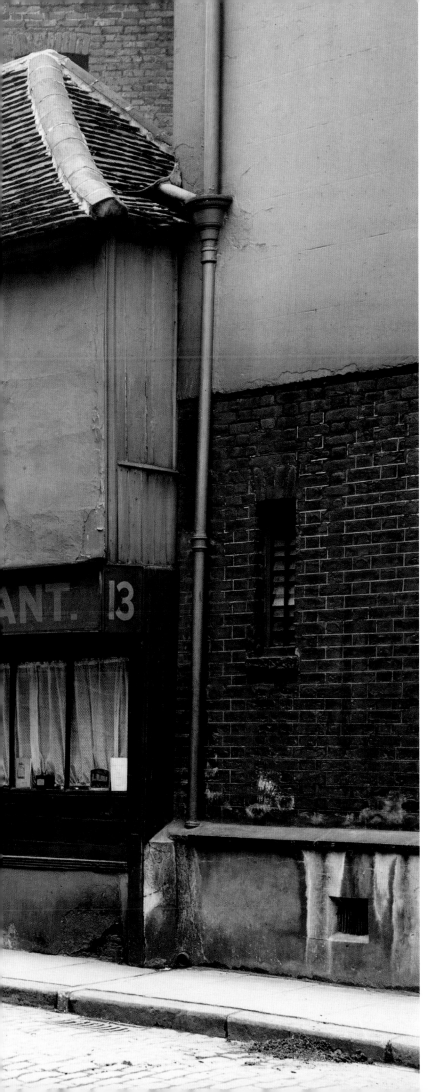

A Dickensian fake

LINCOLN'S INN FIELDS

13 Portsmouth Street, 5 May 1904

A truly remarkable survival of a modest 16th century house, which escaped demolition during the development of the area in the 18th century, and again with the Holborn-Strand improvements of the early 20th century. Its claim to be Dickens' 'Old Curiosity Shop' is entirely spurious, the name having been painted on the front to attract business to a dealer in books, paintings and old china in 1868.

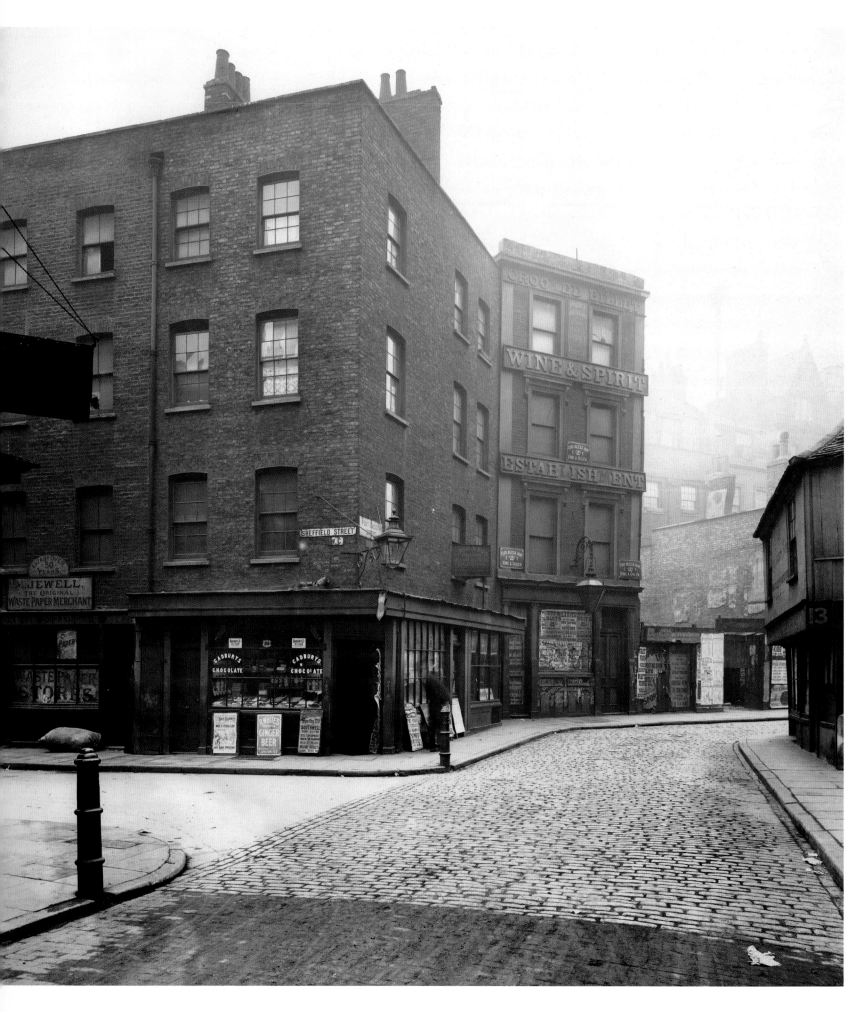

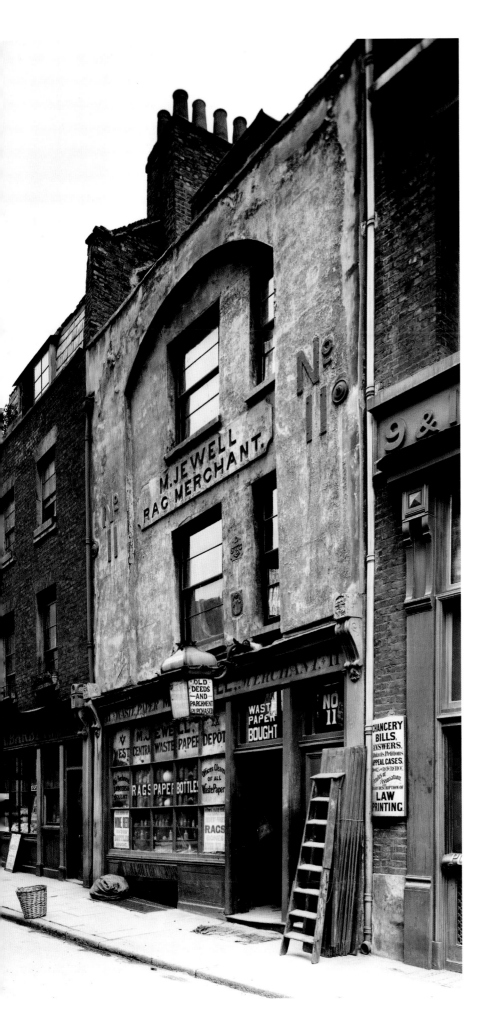

Opposite: Portsmouth Street, 1904
The junction of Sheffield Street and Portsmouth Street with the so-called 'Old Curiosity Shop' to the right.

Left: 11 Sheffield Street, 3 May 1904
The dilapidated premises of M. Jewell, Waste Paper and Bottle merchants. The plaque on the front wall is a parish marker of St Clement Danes.

Below: 2 Portsmouth Street, 27 April 1904
The evocative interior of No. 2 Portsmouth Street, believed to have been designed by Inigo Jones, showing the panelled staircase compartment.

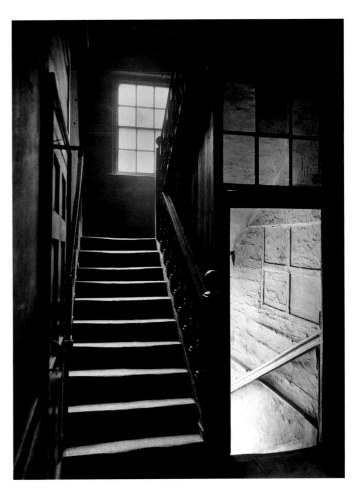

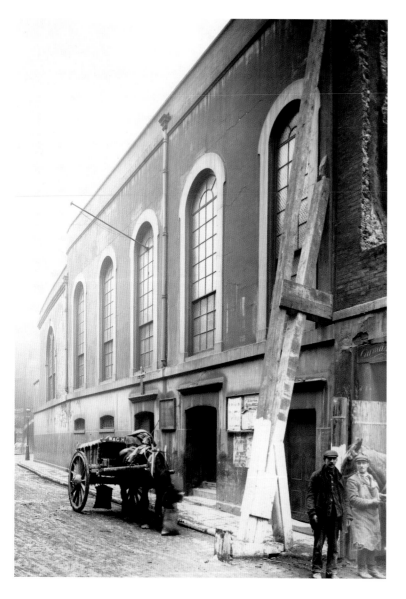

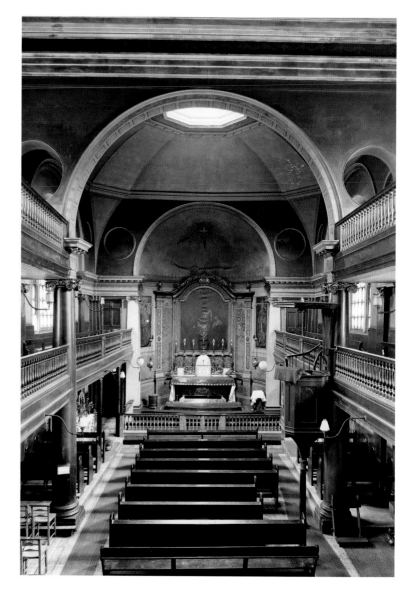

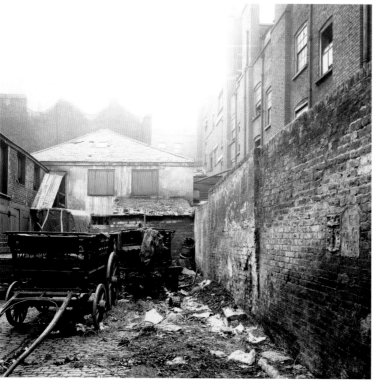

Above left: Sardinia Chapel, Sardinia Street, c 1905
The Roman Catholic chapel of S.S. Anselm and Cecilia was the oldest Catholic place of worship in London. As an attached chapel to the Portuguese, and later Sardinian embassy, it was immune from laws prohibiting Catholic worship. Rebuilt in 1759 at the expense of the King of Sardinia, it was damaged again in the Gordon riots of 1780, before succumbing in 1909 to the Holborn-Strand improvements.

Above right: Sardinia Chapel, 17 June 1904
The chapel interior was divided into two parts by a semi-circular chancel arch carried on two Ionic columns with two tiers of galleries. In 1793 Fanny Burney, the writer and diarist, married the French émigré General D'Arblay here.

Left: Chapel Yard, 11 June 1906
Chapel Yard stood behind the Sardinia Chapel. The stone plaques on the wall mark the boundary between the parishes of St Clement Danes and St Giles in the Fields, which is dated 1787.

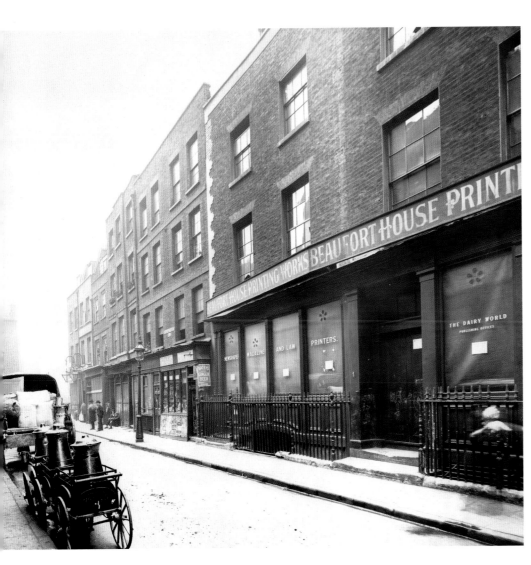

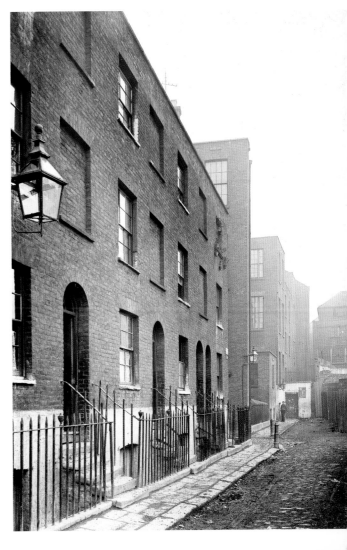

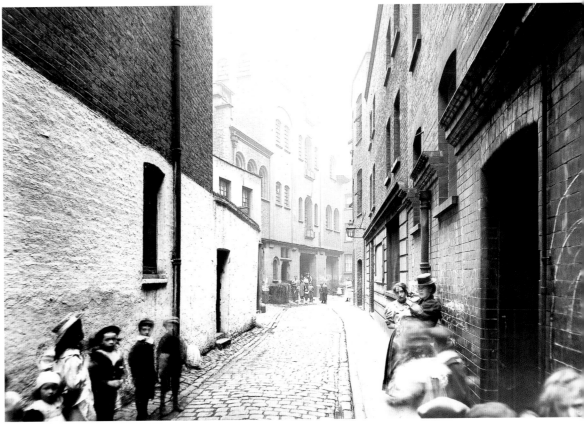

Above left: Sardinia Street, 11 June 1906
View looking east, showing milk delivery cart in the foreground.

Above right: Sardinia Place, c 1906
The mud-choked street at the northern end of Sardinia Place.

Right: Sardinia Place, 11 June 1906
View looking north into Sardinia Place with warehouses beyond.

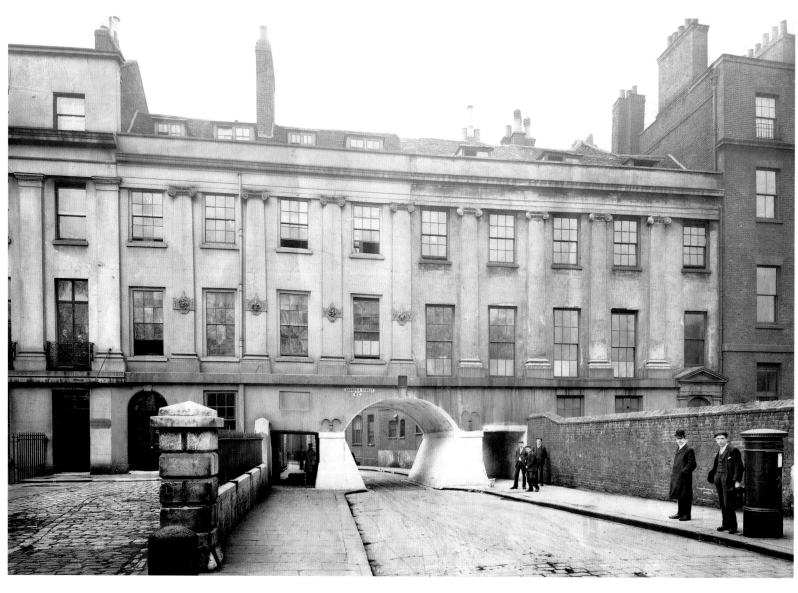

54-55 Lincoln's Inn Fields, 21 May 1906

Above: Lincoln's Inn Fields, London's largest square, was laid out in the 1630s. This splendid pair of houses, erected by David Murray in 1640, are alleged to be by Inigo Jones. The pilasters to No. 54 were decorated with roses, fleur-de-lys and torches of Hymen to commemorate the marriage of Charles I and Henrietta Maria in 1625. Over the peculiar central arch were two stone tablets inscribed 'Duke Street 1648'. No. 54 was the house of the Sardinian ambassador. At the rear of the ground floor was a link to the Chapel behind to provide direct access into the ambassador's personal pew in the gallery.

Right: The rear elevation and closet wing showing the curious arched entrance to Lincoln's Inn Fields. In 1688 the mob attacked the rear of the house and chapel during anti-Catholic riots. The arrow points to a small window over the passageway which lit a secret closet where the Catholic priests are said to have hidden during the Gordon Riots in 1780. The houses were demolished in 1912.

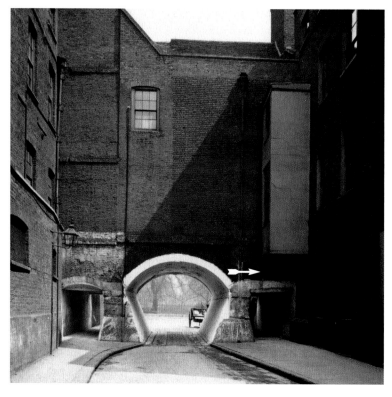

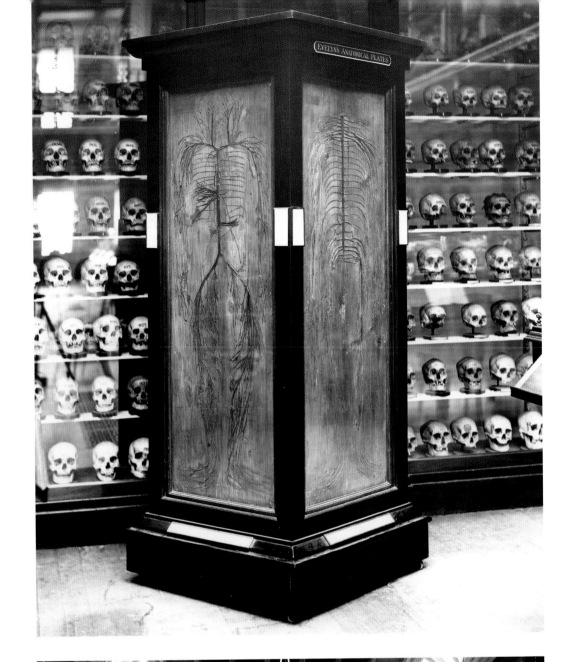

Anatomy at Lincoln's Inn

Left above: Royal College of Surgeons, 39-43 Lincoln's Inn Fields, 1 March 1911
John Evelyn's Anatomical Tables were prepared in Padua in 1640 by Giovanni Leoni, and later presented to the Royal Society by Evelyn in 1667. After a period at the British Museum, they were sold to the Royal College of Surgeons in 1809. The tables, which are the oldest anatomical preparations in Europe show the nerves, arteries and veins drawn out of several human bodies pasted on to wooden boards. They remain a centrepiece of the Hunterian Museum within the College.

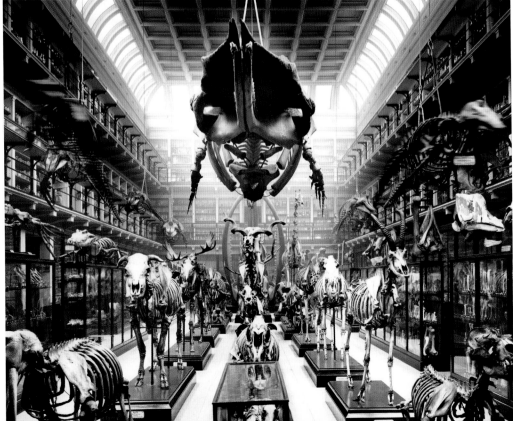

Left below: Royal College of Surgeons, 15 February 1911
The Museum Gallery No. 5 designed by Sir Charles Barry and completed in 1855 with an astonishing display of animal skeletons. On the night of 10/11 May 1941 two thirds of the entire collection was destroyed by bombing and the ensuing fire, fuelled by thousands of alcohol-filled specimen jars, which were scattered in the street. Bemused local children spoke of dead babies in jars strewn across the area.

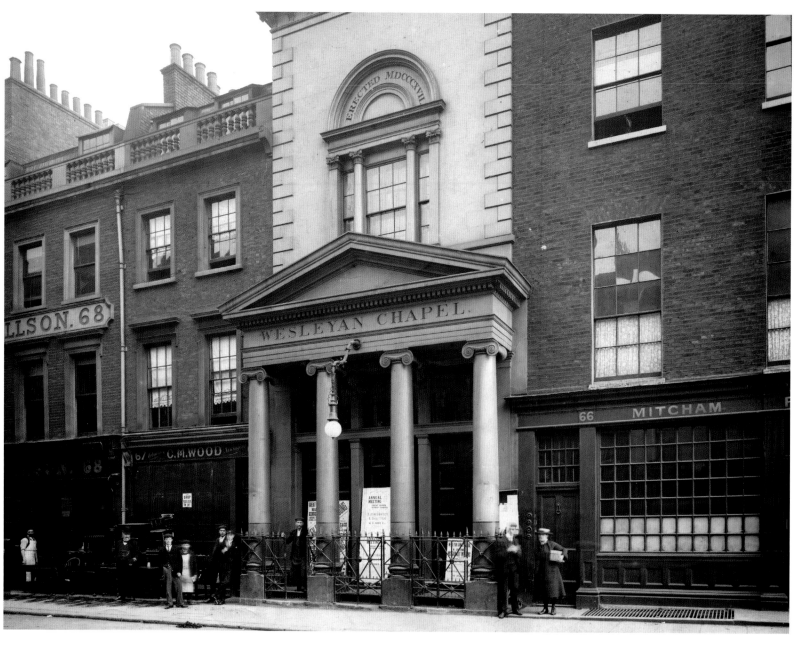

HOLBORN

Above: Wesleyan Chapel, Great Queen Street, 22 May 1906
Opened in 1817, the elegant Ionic portico of Welsh stone was added in 1840 beneath the fine tripartite north window. The chapel was demolished in 1910.

Right: Burial vaults in the crypt of the Wesleyan Chapel, 23 May 1906

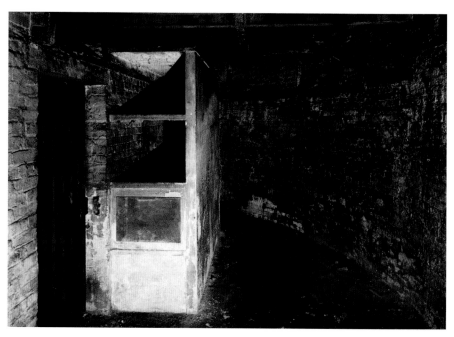

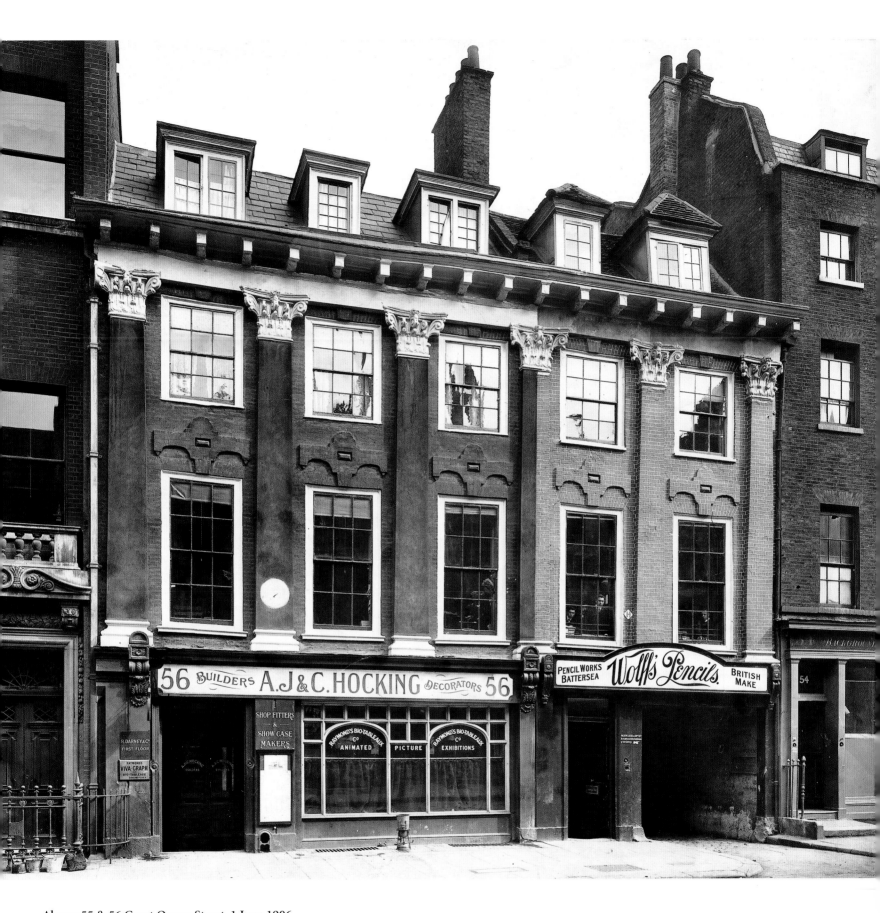

Above: 55 & 56 Great Queen Street, 1 June 1906

This half of a splendid town house erected in 1638 stood on the south side of Great Queen Street, and is attributed to John Webb, a pupil of Inigo Jones. First occupied by the Earl of St Albans, and later, briefly, by Sir Thomas Fairfax, it was acquired in 1684 by Lord Belasyse, by which time it had already been subdivided. The LCC plaque commemorates James Boswell, the biographer of Dr Johnson, who lived here until 1788. The two right hand bays have been tuck-pointed. The buildings were demolished for the new Freemasons Hall in 1927.

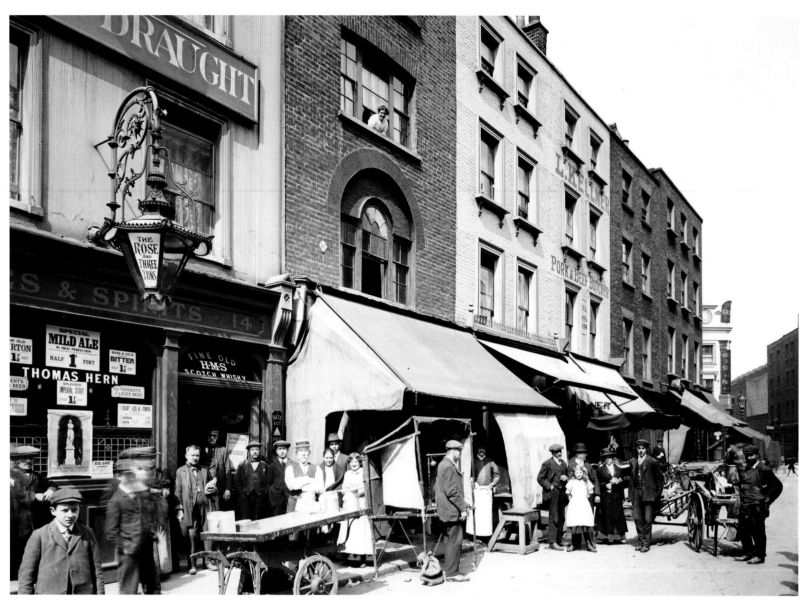

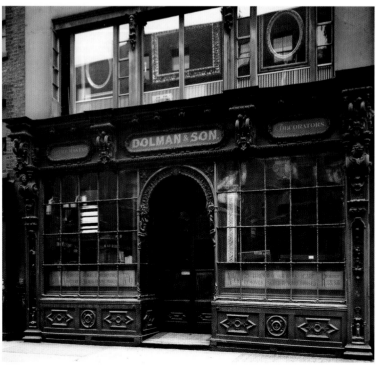

ST GILES

Above: Earlham Street, Seven Dials, c 1905
View of the north side of Earlham Street looking east with Seven Dials in the background showing the spontaneous street life which has been lost from so many parts of London.

Left: 6 New Compton Street, St Giles, c 1905
Dolman & Son were carvers and frame makers which might account for this spectacular Jacobean-style frontage with its intricately-carved glazing bars and riot of ornamental detail. Its provenance is a mystery.

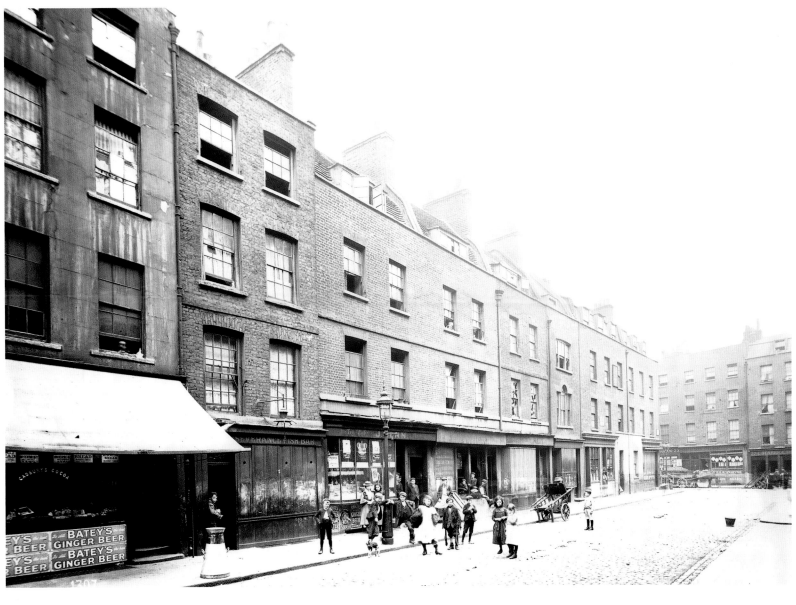

HOLBORN

Above: Great Wild Street, Holborn, 11 June 1906
View looking south towards Sardinia Street. The young boy in the centre is holding two animal bones. Note the milk churn by the kerb.

Right: Little Queen Street, 11 June 1906
Little Queen Street was swept away for the creation of Kingsway. To the extreme left is the side of the famous Holborn Restaurant.

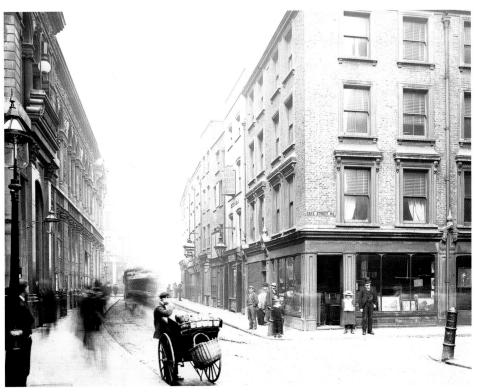

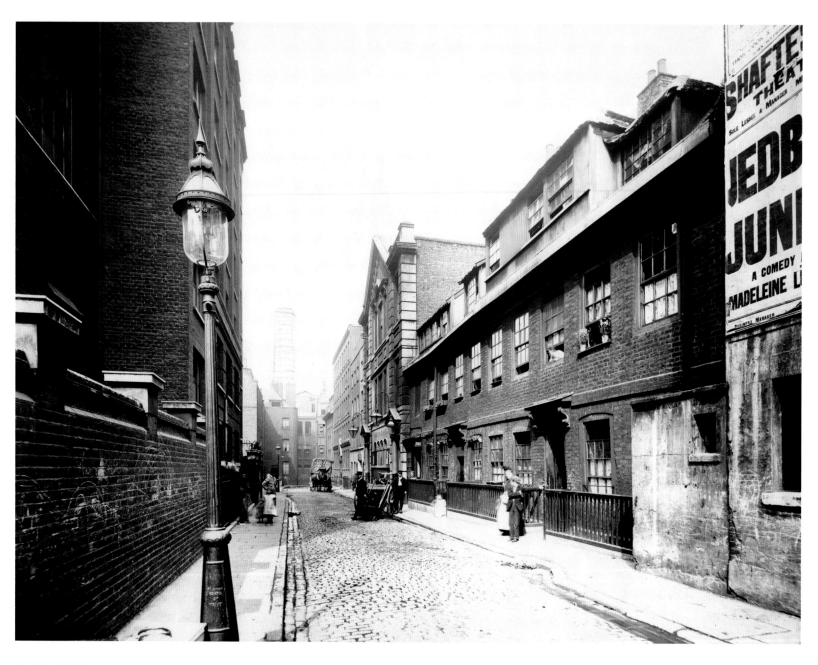

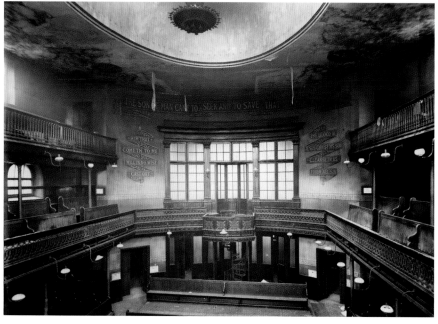

Above: Little Wild Street, Holborn, 11 June 1906
View looking north-east towards Sardinia Place. To the right is a remarkable group of original houses erected about 1690 with box gutters and timber balustrading to the front areas. Beyond is the Baptist Chapel and Mission Hall.

Left: Little Wild Street, 11 June 1906
Interior of the Baptist Chapel and Mission Hall with a ventilating gasolier suspended from the ceiling.

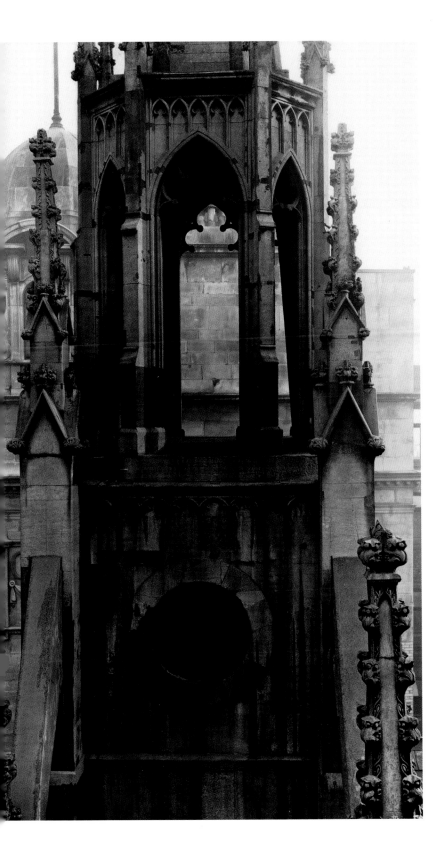

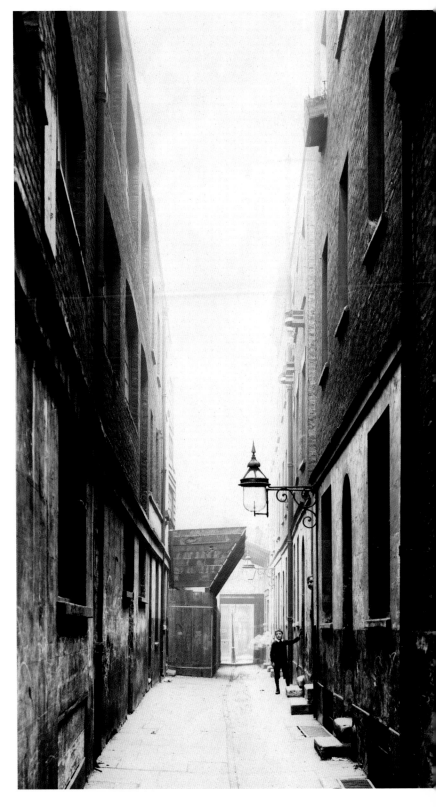

Above left: Holy Trinity, Kingsway, 17 January 1908
The crocketted finials, steeple and spire of Holy Trinity, Kingsway. In 1910 it was demolished and replaced by a classical composition designed by Belcher and Joass in keeping with the emerging Beaux Arts grandeur of Kingsway. In the background is the flank of the newly-completed Craven House.

Above right: Twyford Buildings, 11 June 1906
Twyford Buildings was a narrow alley linking Gate Street with Little Queen Street. Demolished to make way for Kingsway, the name was retained for a new pedestrian alley on the site alongside the new Church of S.S. Anselm and Cecilia.

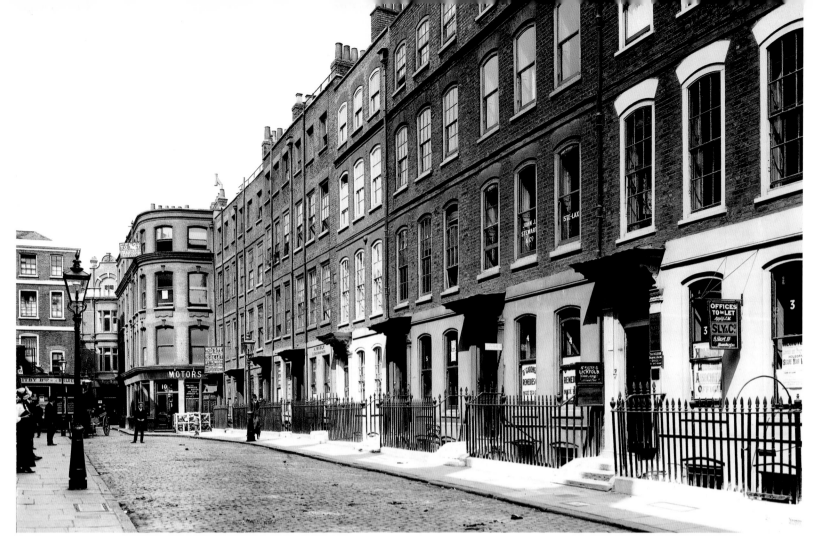

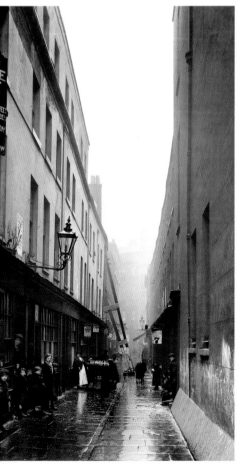

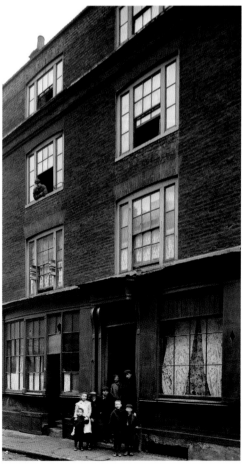

**Above: Featherstone Buildings, Holborn,
17 August 1908**

Featherstone Buildings was a fine composition of two early 18th century terraces between High Holborn and Bedford Street. It was badly damaged by bombing and later demolished for post-war offices. Similar houses survive in Great James Street to the north of Theobalds Road. View of east side looking north.

**Below left: Lamb's Conduit Passage, Holborn,
23 March 1912**

View looking west along Lamb's Conduit Passage from the north-east corner of Red Lion Square. The corner building to the left of the picture was a mixed infants' school which accounts for the large numbers of children gathered outside in the rain. Conway Hall now occupies the north side of the passage.

**Below right: 9 Eagle Street, Holborn,
8 April 1904**

An early 18th century house with a refined pair of bowed shopfronts in use as a cheap lodging house. The boxes on the mullions to the first floor window are bird cages.

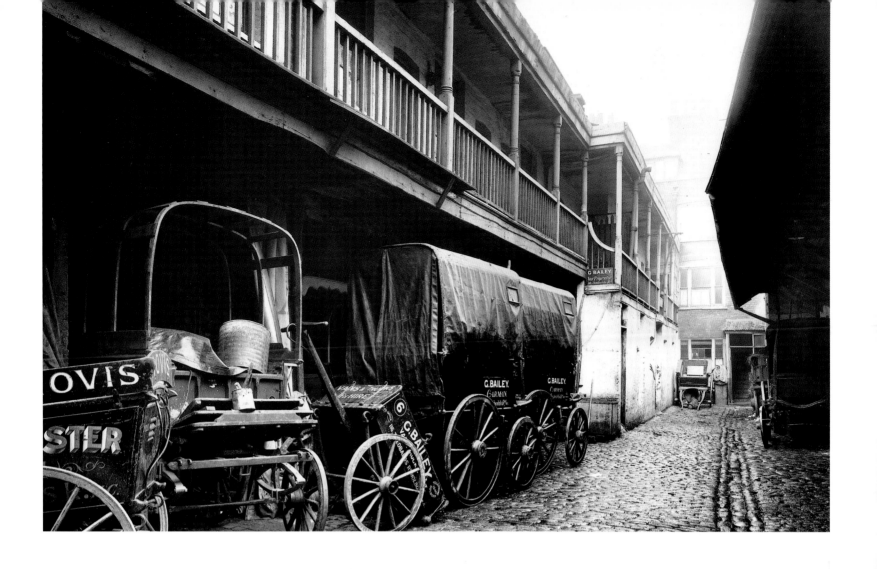

**Above: 116-117 Theobald's Road, Holborn,
19 December 1910**
The last of the Holborn coaching inns showing the
galleried courtyard to the rear with Bailey's covered
vans in the foreground.

**Right: 8-16 Boswell Street, Holborn,
23 March 1912**
A wonderfully atmospheric view of the gables and
chimney stacks at the rear of early 18th century
houses in Boswell Street, formerly Devonshire
Street, probably taken from Bedford Court.

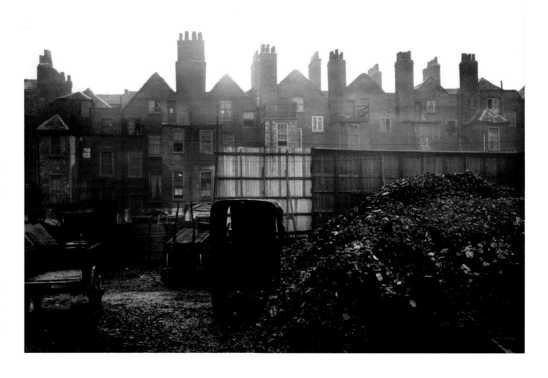

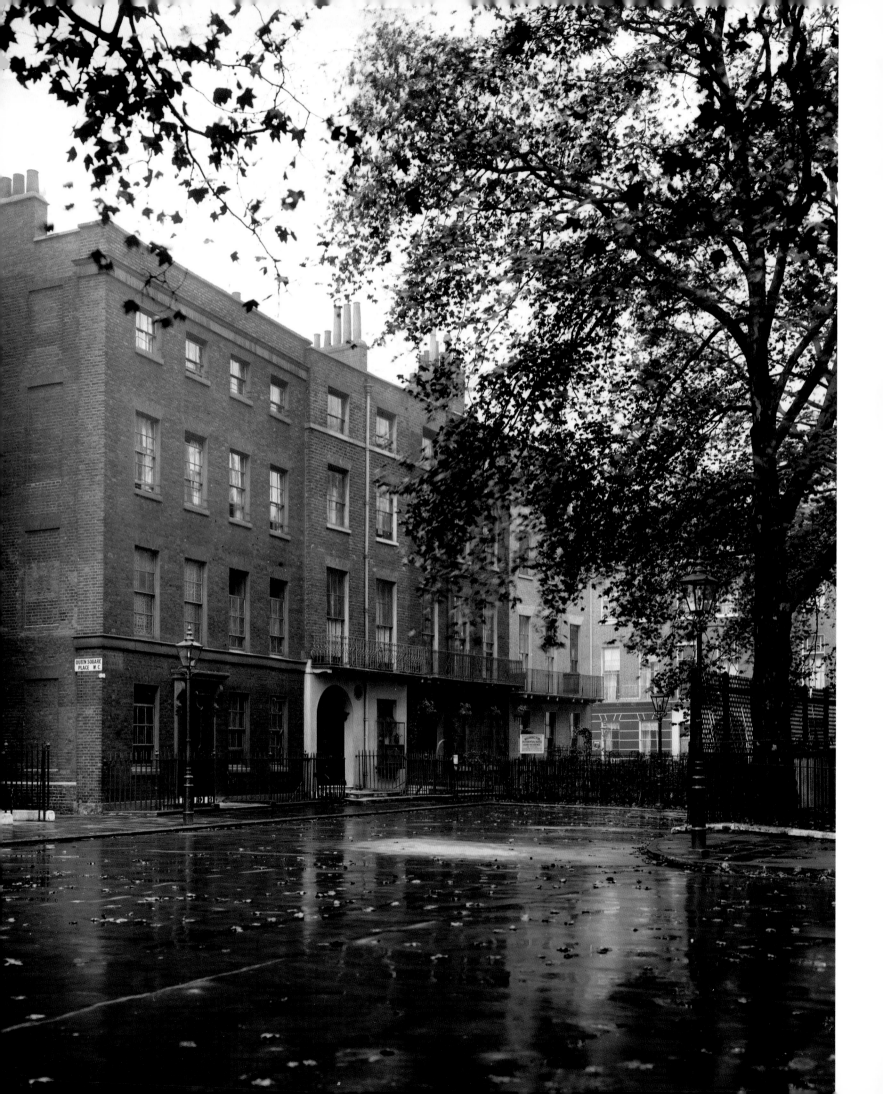

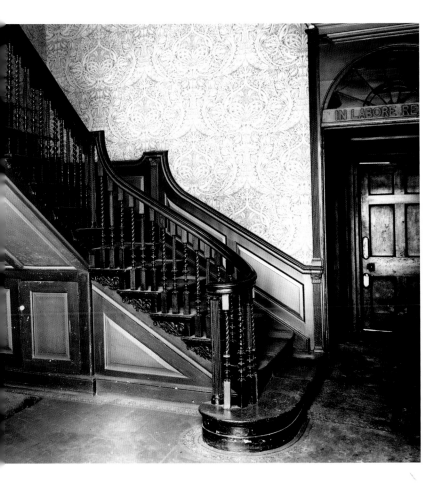

Underground well

Opposite & left: 20 Queen Square, Holborn, 19 October 1910
This spacious mid-18th century mansion in the north-west corner of the
square was occupied by Louisa Twining, the philanthropist and poor law
reformer and used as a refuge for the elderly and chronic epileptics. It was
later the home of Thomas Henry Wyatt, President of the RIBA. At the time
of its demolition for a hotel extension in 1960, it was in use as the Imperial
Ladies Turkish Baths.

Top left The superbly carved oak staircase with fluted newels, turned and
twisted balusters and panelled soffit: Georgian craftsmanship at its finest.

**Below left: The Devil's or Chimney Conduit, 20 Queen Square,
24 November 1910**
Beneath a trapdoor in the garden a flight of steps led to an underground
passage that ran to a mediaeval well which once supplied water to Christ's
Hospital in the City. On the stonework of the passage were ancient graffiti
including several dates 1411, 1640 and 1642. In this remarkable picture
the water can be seen in full spate at the base of the steps. The conduit was
demolished in 1911-13, but the stones were re-erected by the Metropolitan Water Board at their offices in Rosebery Avenue.

Below right: View along the subterranean passage showing the entrance to
the conduit head and base of stairway.

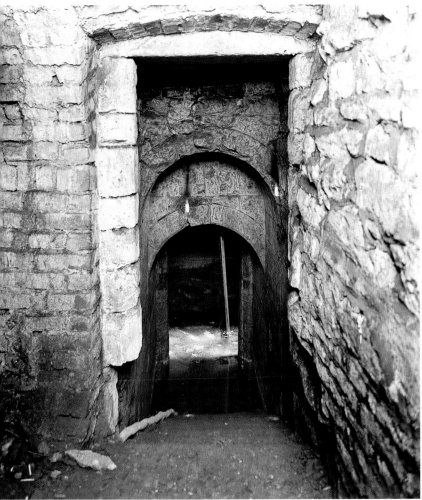

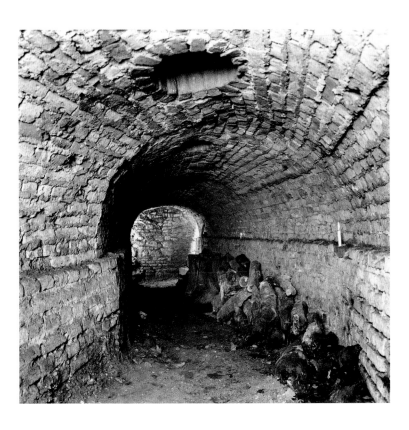

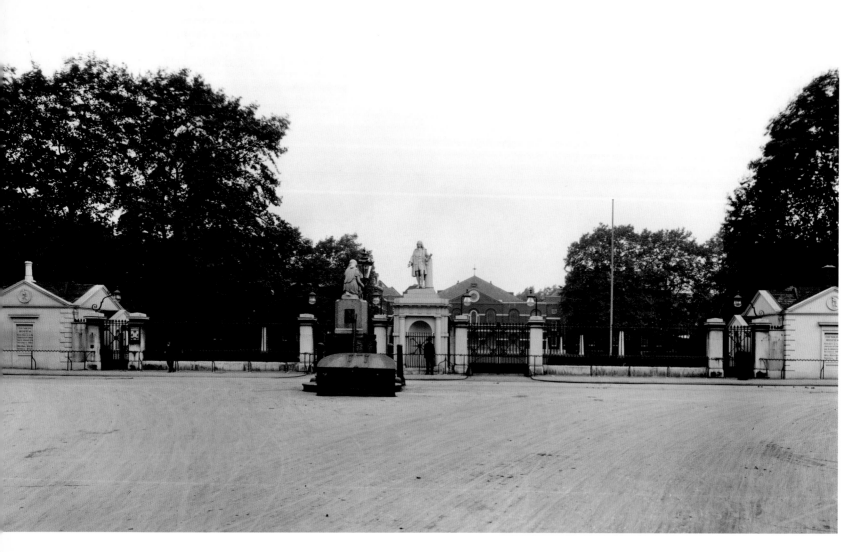

Refuge for children

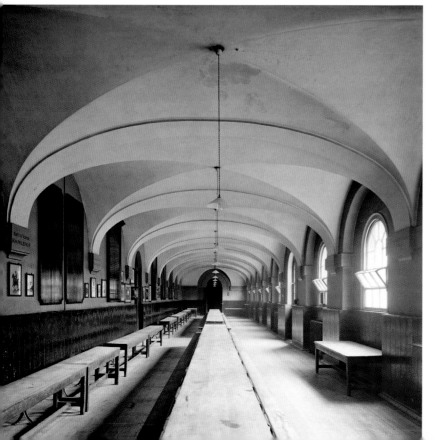

The Foundling Hospital, Guilford Street, Holborn, c 1912

Above: The Foundling Hospital was established in 1742 by Captain Thomas Coram whose statue can be seen above the central stone niche. In the early days, abandoned babies were left here for the hospital to take in as foundlings, but due to the sheer level of demand a ballot system was introduced. The plainly-detailed buildings behind the entrance screen and lodges were laid out between 1745-53 by Theodore Jacobsen. Hogarth and Handel were both governors.

Left: The austere, vaulted Boys Dining Room with bench seating.

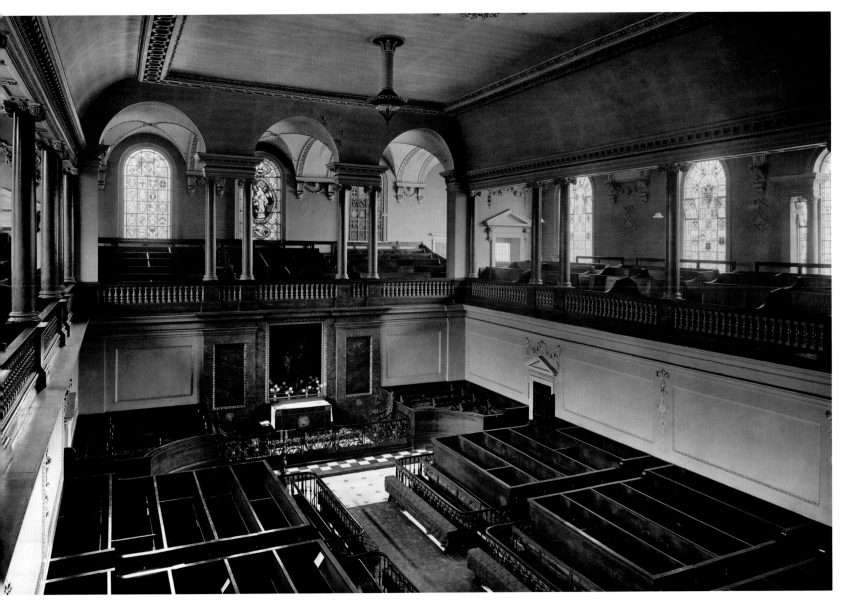

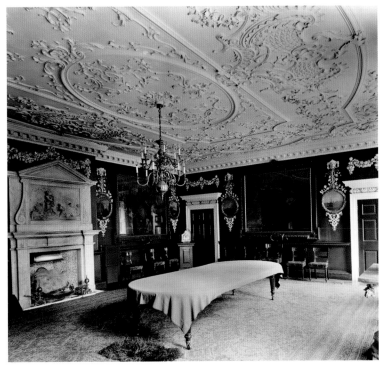

Above: The splendid chapel was renowned for its organ which Handel gave to the hospital and on which he played several performances of *Messiah* raising over £7,000 in funds. The chapel became fashionable, attracting many eminent figures, including Dickens who lived nearby in Doughty Street. The font, pulpit and organ were relocated to the chapel of the new hospital at Berkhamsted in 1926.

Right: The Court Room, with its splendid rococo ceiling by William Wilton, was a repository for some of the finest mid-18th century art in London. The relief panel over the fireplace by Rysbrack depicted charity children gainfully employed in husbandry and navigation. On demolition in 1937, many of the original contents and fittings were salvaged and relocated in a new neo-Georgian building for the Thomas Coram Foundation including the Court Room, chimneypieces and a massive oak staircase from the former Boys' Wing.

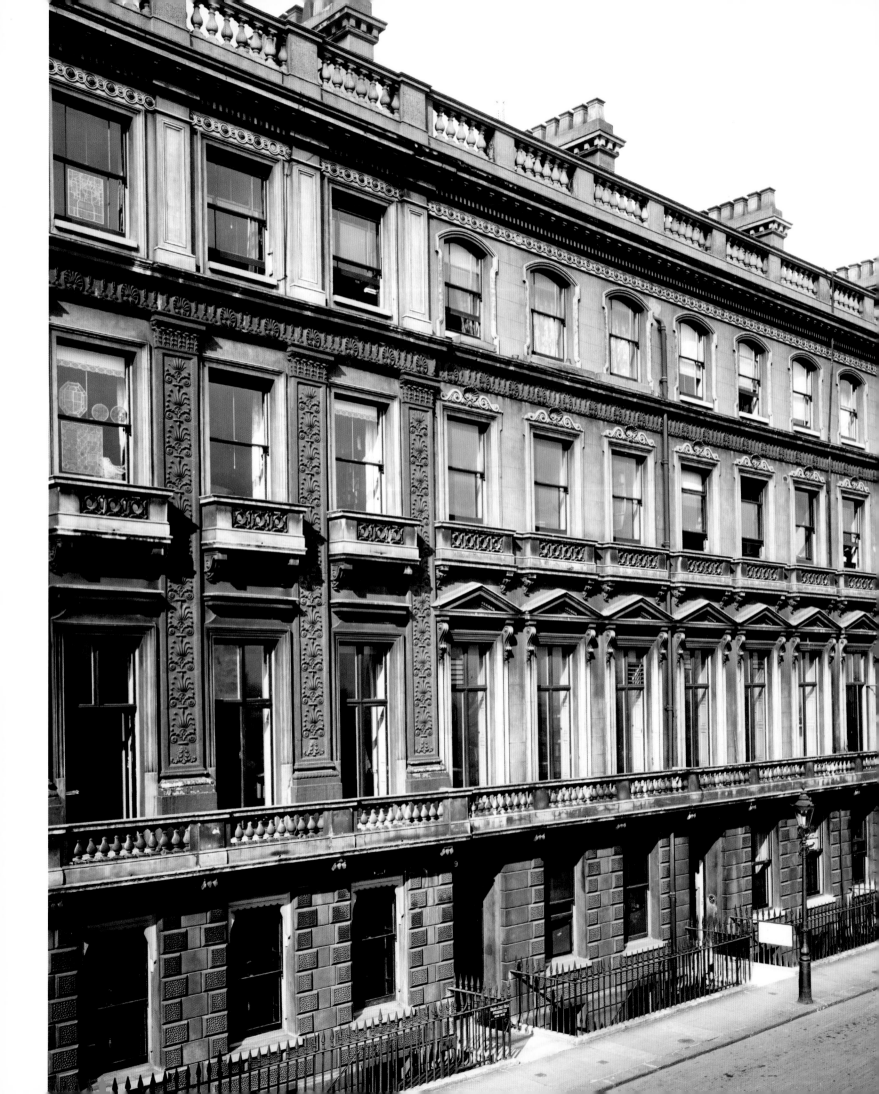

Lost riverside masterpiece

STRAND

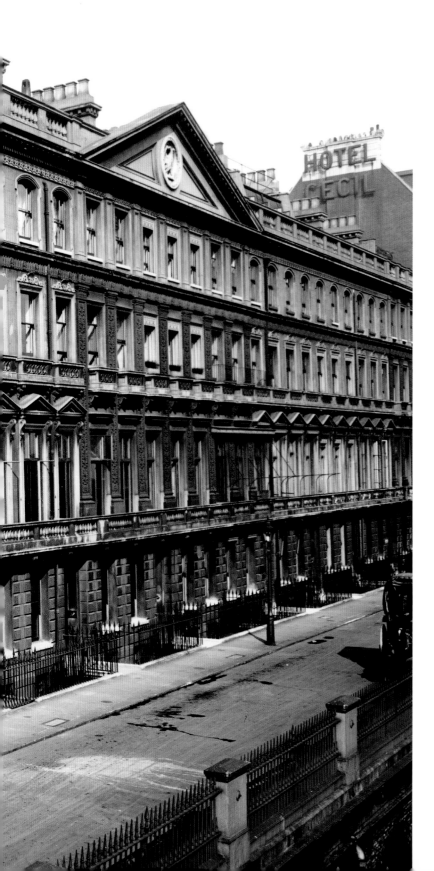

Left: Adelphi Terrace, 6 March 1913
The Adelphi, developed by the Adam brothers between 1768-74, involved building high over the Thames foreshore on a vast complex of subterranean arches to the level of the Strand. The scheme covered several streets to the south of the Strand, and was saved from bankruptcy by a parliamentary lottery.

Adelphi Terrace was the centrepiece, but its relationship to the river was transformed by the construction of the Victoria Embankment in 1864-70. Two years later the terrace was rendered and vulgarised and a central pediment added. The Adelphi was demolished amid great public outcry in 1936.

Below: The brick arches beneath the Adelphi were a Piranesian world of vaulted cobbled streets lit by shafts of light from portholes above. A small part of this atmospheric complex still survives off York Buildings beneath the later Adelphi development.

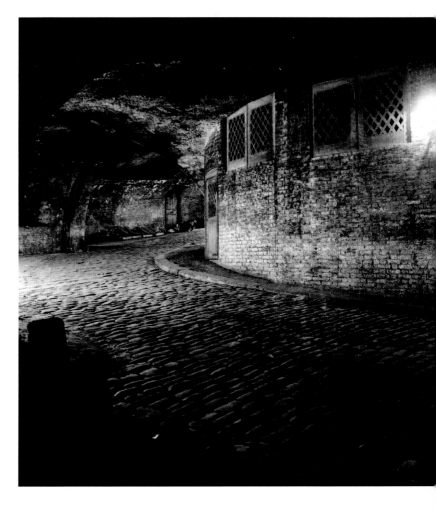

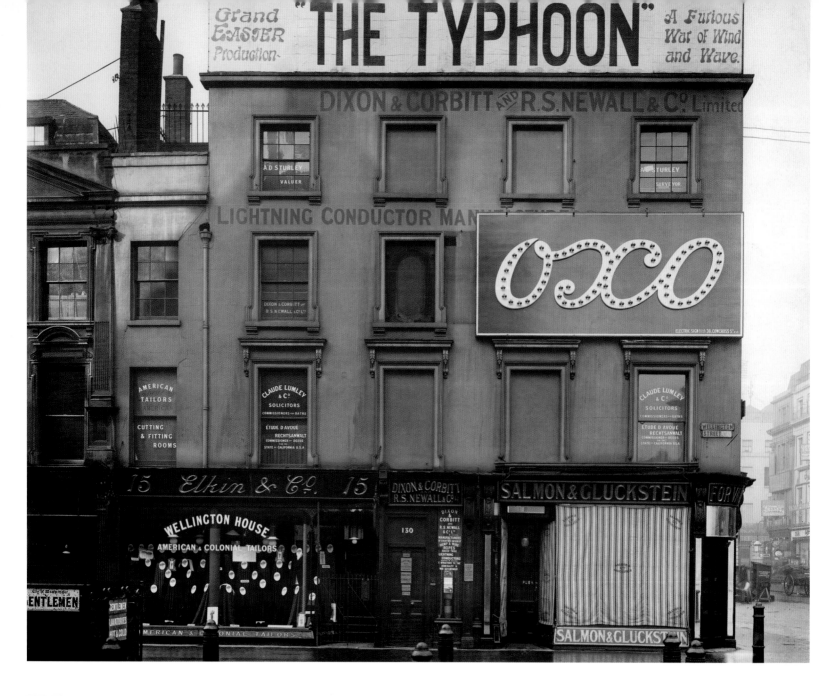

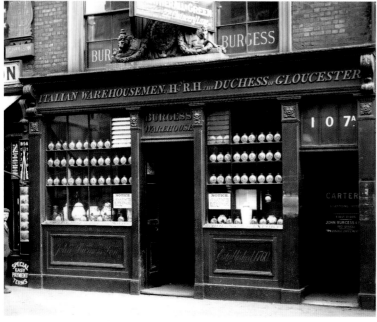

Above: 130 Strand, 22 April 1907

This fascinating photograph shows the development of commercial advertising in the early 20th century. The ground floor shopfronts follow the conventional late 19th century form with gilt and glass fascias and stall risers with applied lettering to the shop windows and floors above. The entire attic storey is covered by a painted signboard for *The Typhoon*, a production at the London Hippodrome, which boasted an arena that sank into a massive 100,000 gallon water tank for aquatic spectacles. The large Oxo sign heralds the arrival of electric advertisements which took little account of the architectural details of the buildings to which they were affixed.

Left: 107A Strand, 24 July 1908

The elegant frontage of John Burgess & Son with the royal warrant over the entrance.

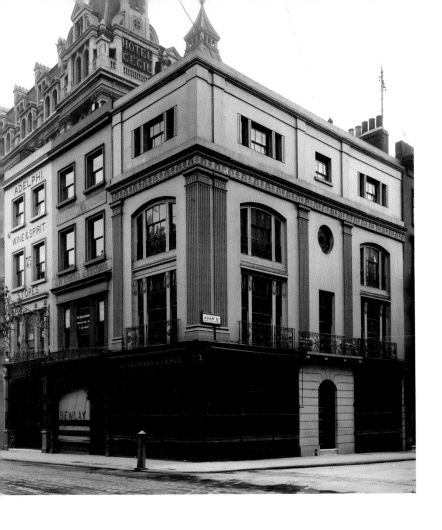

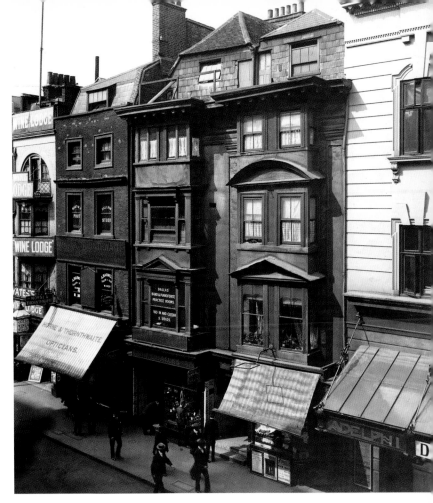

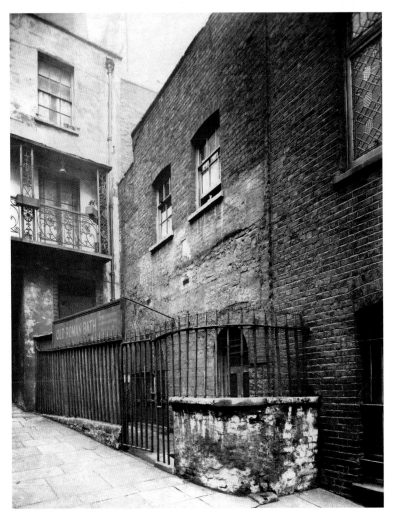

Above left: 73 Strand, 30 August 1908

In order to complete the Adelphi scheme, Adam Street was cut through to the Strand. No. 73 was completed to Robert Adam's design in the 1770s. After a disastrous fire in 1822, it was rebuilt to the same design. The elaborate ornamental ironwork to the Adelphi Wine and Spirit Stores was fashionable in the late 19th century. Beyond lies the massive Hotel Cecil.

Above right: 413-415 Strand, 1914

This fine pair of 17th century houses situated next to the Adelphi Theatre with three storey projecting timber bays were typical of many which survived in the Strand until the early 20th century.

Right: Old Roman Bath, 5 Strand Lane, 12 January 1906

Situated well below street level, this long-standing London curiosity comprises a brick vaulted plunge bath measuring 13ft x 6ft. First referred to as "*a fine antique bath*" in 1784, later Charles Dickens bathed here, referring to it in *David Copperfield*. The spring feeding the bath still flows. In the background is the old parish watch house, built to prevent body-snatching from the nearby churchyard of St Clement Danes. The scene remains remarkably unchanged.

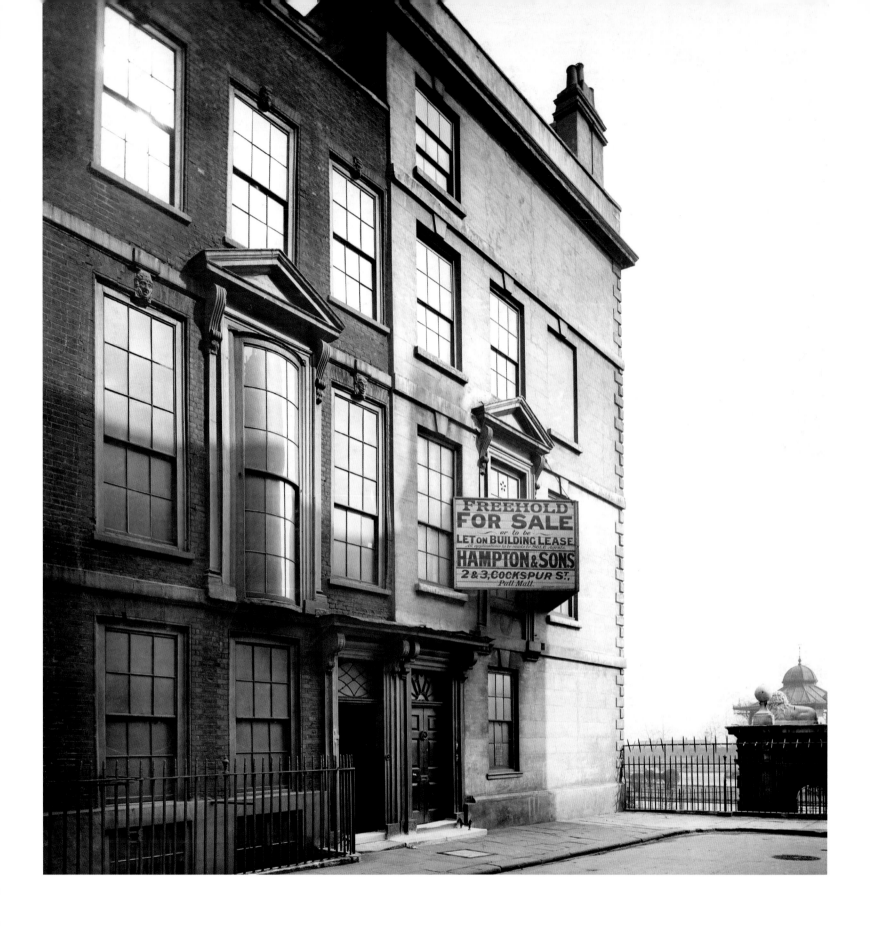

Above: 15 & 16 Buckingham Street, c 1905

These late 17th century houses at the south end of Buckingham Street stood beside the old York Water Gate which can be seen to the right of the picture. Used as the Prize Office from 1704-10, and later by the Institute of Civil Engineers, No. 15 was the residence of the architect William Burges between 1875-81. When it was pulled down in 1906, two ceilings and various fixtures were relocated to the new building on the site. No. 16 has a fine shallow bow window and carved masks to the window arches.

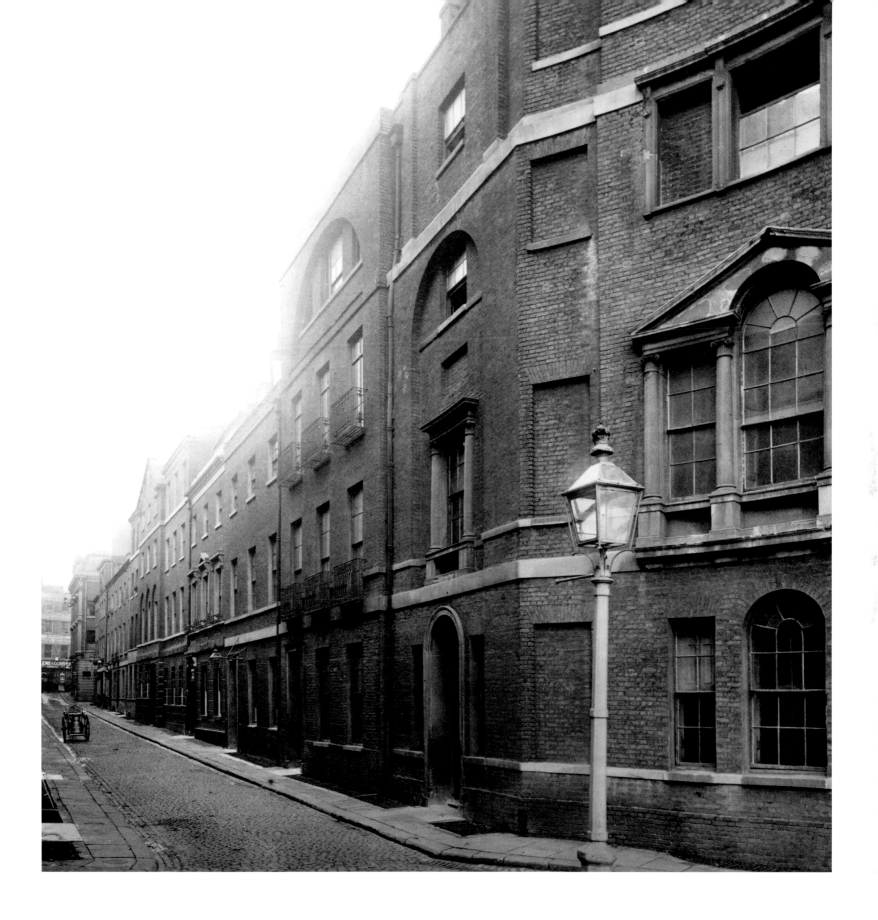

Above: Salisbury Street, c 1890

Salisbury Street was rebuilt as a single architectural composition in 1783 by the architect James Paine, flaring out into a shallow curve at the southern end. Too narrow and too steep ever to be fashionable, it was sold in 1888 and pulled down shortly after for the Hotel Cecil, which in turn was replaced by Shellmex House in 1930.

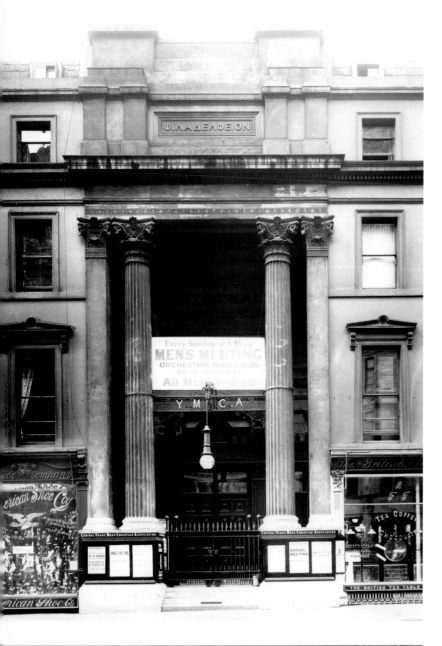

Great institutions

Left top: Exeter Hall, Strand, 27 April 1907

A great London institution and centre of radical religious activity, Exeter Hall was erected in 1831 to the designs of J P Gandy-Deering in a refined Greek style. Gandy-Deering perfected his knowledge of Greek architecture in Greece in 1811-13, which accounts for the close resemblance of the Corinthian capitals to the Choragic Monument of Lysicrates in Athens, one of which was salvaged for use by the Brixton School of Building on its demolition in 1907. The Greek inscription reads '*Philadelpheion*' meaning Loving Brethren. "*From this Hall was struck the death-blow of slavery, of state lotteries, of capital punishment, and many other gigantic evils.*" (F M Holmes, 1881)

Left below: Exeter Hall, Strand, 27 April 1907

Exeter Hall was the centre of the anti-slavery campaign and a bastion of radicalism. Many famous speeches and meetings were made within its walls. In June 1840 the Prince Consort made his first public appearance in England here. Livingstone, Stanley, Brougham, Shaftesbury, Clarkson and Wilberforce all "took the chair" at Exeter Hall. In 1880 it was taken over by the YMCA, after which it was remodelled and enlarged. It was demolished in 1907 to make way for the Strand Palace Hotel. The organ was sold and relocated to Ipswich public hall.

Opposite: 429 Strand, c 1905

Designed by C R Cockerell in 1831-32 as the Westminster Insurance Offices, No. 429 was a powerful, but refined exercise in neo-classicism with elegant figures paired over the first floor window arches and simple iron balconies punctuating the facades. It was demolished in 1906 for the British Medical Association, later Rhodesia House. To the right marked by a timber owl and flamboyant Art Nouveau fascia is Aitchison's Optical Works.

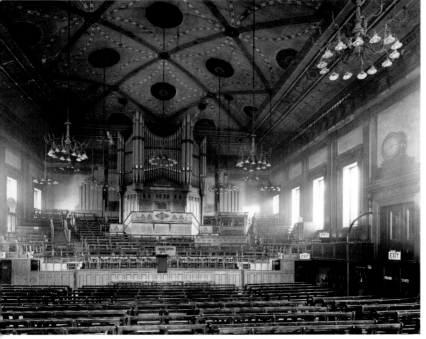

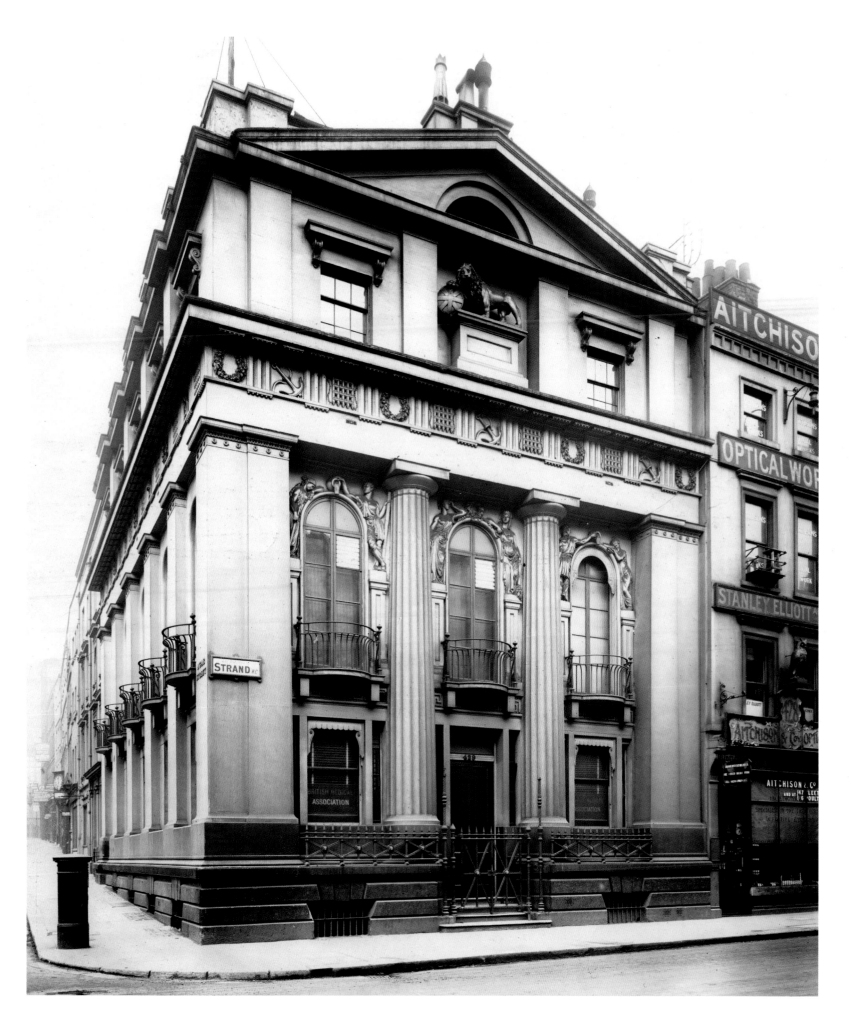

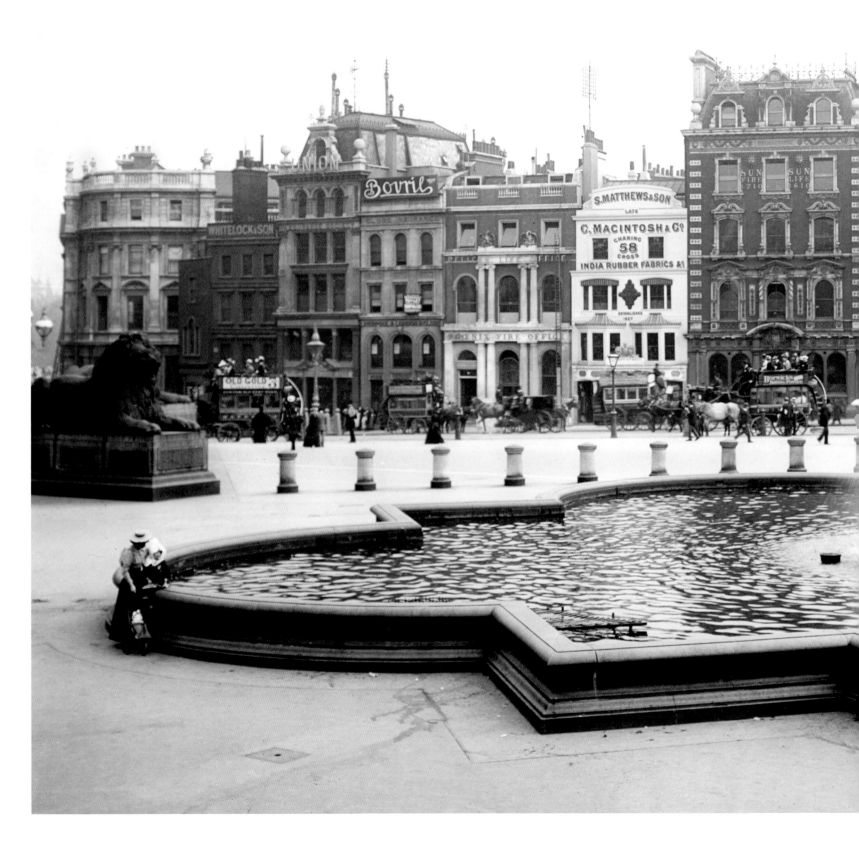

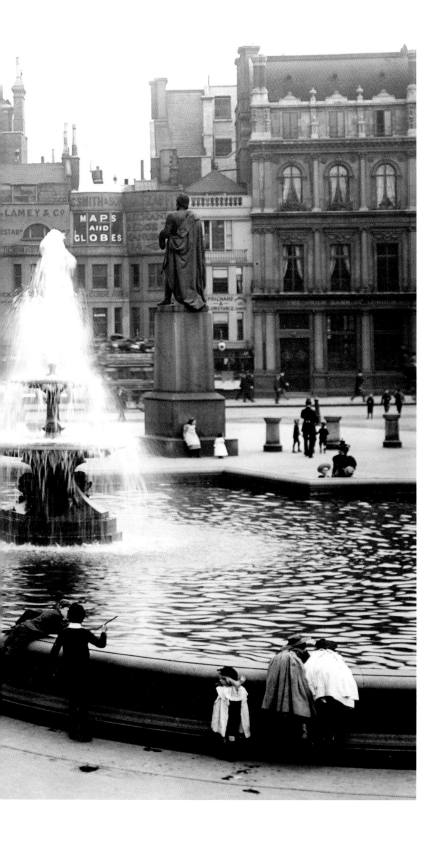

CHAPTER FOUR

IMPERIAL CAPITAL
Westminster and the West End

Westminster was united by its very diversity. At its heart lay the government precinct with the great offices of state, many of which were moving out of the old aristocratic mansions into imposing new purpose-built edifices fit for modern government.

The ceremonial heart of London too was changing. Trafalgar Square is clearly recognisable, but its relationship with the Mall was transformed with the construction of Admiralty Arch and Aston Webb's remodelling of The Mall into an Imperial processional route culminating in the refaced frontage of Buckingham Palace.

Nash's Regent Street was poised to undergo complete reconstruction which took over 20 years to complete, whilst to the south the old aristocratic houses of Pall Mall were giving way to the opulent new gentlemen's clubhouses of St James's.

In sharp contrast, poverty was endemic in many areas. Some of the worst slums in London lay within a stone's throw of the Palace of Westminster, and to the west in Millbank.

At the heart of the West End amongst the glittering new shops, department stores, hotels and restaurants of Edwardian London, Soho retained its cosmopolitan character and raffish reputation.

Trafalgar Square, 31 July 1896
Panoramic view from the National Gallery looking south with the statue of General Sir Charles Napier to the right. In the background is a group of horse-drawn omnibuses.

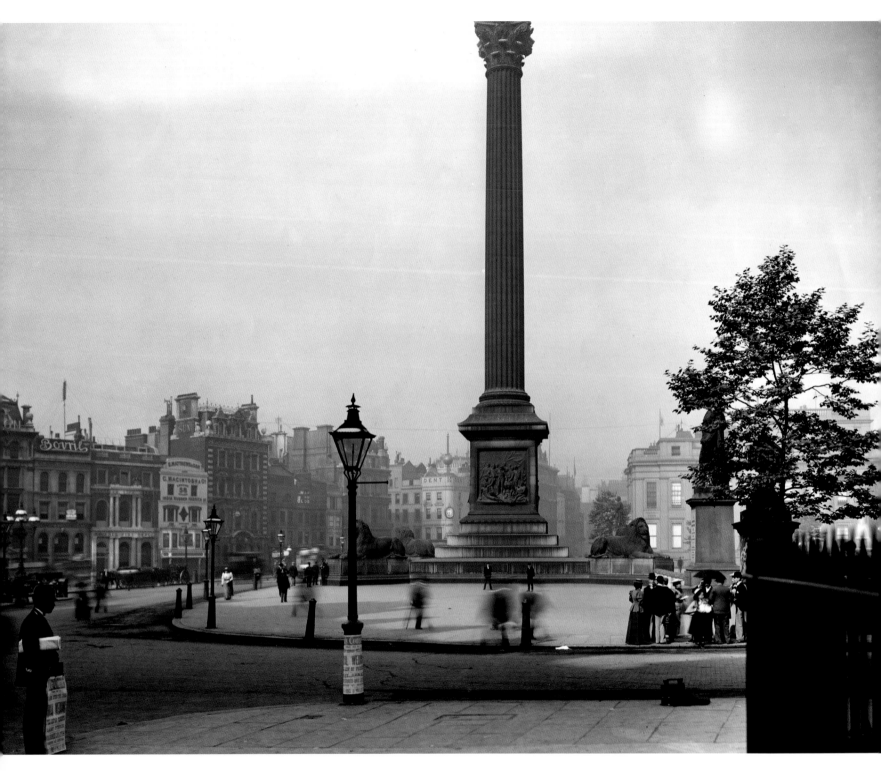

Heroes of the British Empire

CHARING CROSS

Above: Trafalgar Square, 31 July 1896

Early morning view taken at 8.30am looking west from outside the Post Office on the corner of Morley's Hotel on the east side of the square. Note the shoeshine equipment at the pavement's edge. Behind the genteel group to the right is the statue of Major General Sir Henry Havelock, the hero of the relief of Lucknow, erected by public subscription in 1861. Such was the esteem in which he was held that on his death from exhaustion, the lights of all the ships in New York Harbour were dimmed on news of his passing. The posters announce the marriage between Prince Charles of Denmark and Princess Maud of Wales in the private chapel at Buckingham Palace on 22 July.

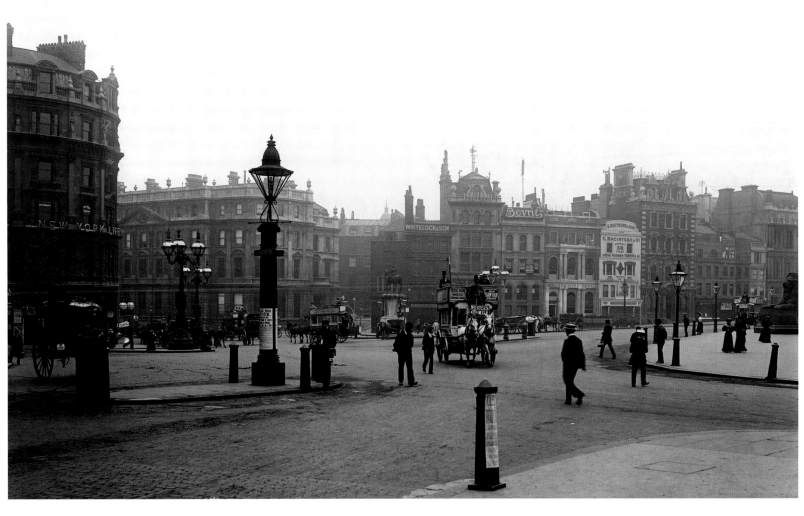

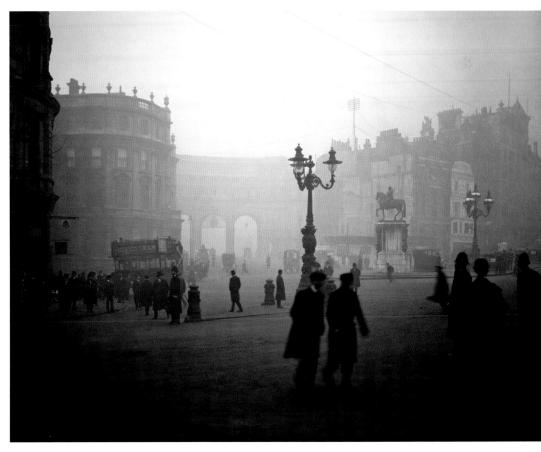

Above: Trafalgar Square, 31 July 1896
Panoramic view of Charing Cross. Le Sueur's famous statue of Charles I can be seen in the middle distance. Beyond the horse-drawn omnibus are the buildings at Charing Cross, soon to be removed for the creation of Mall Approach and Admiralty Arch.

Right: Trafalgar Square, 14 February 1913
A pea-souper; photographed at 12.05pm looking towards the newly-completed Admiralty Arch in the distance. To the right, the houses in Charing Cross are being demolished for the new Mall Approach. London was renowned for its dense winter fogs – the product of the universal use of coal fires in houses and offices.

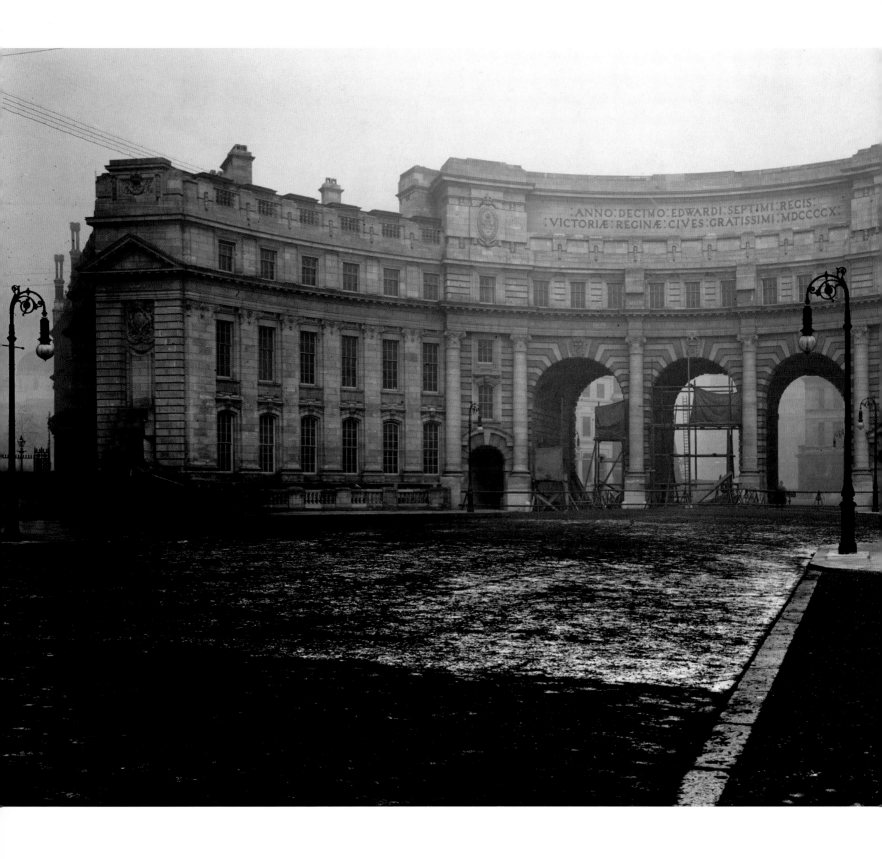

Above: Admiralty Arch, Mall Approach, 21 November 1910
Admiralty Arch in the process of completion. Sir Aston Webb's remodelling of the Mall, Buckingham Palace and the completion of the Queen Victoria Memorial was one of the finest examples of grand axial planning in Europe, transforming the old ceremonial heart of London into a magnificent new Imperial capital.

Opposite top: Morley's Hotel, Trafalgar Square
Morley's Hotel, on the east side of Trafalgar Square, was built in 1831with a handsome Ionic centrepiece and ends. Beneath the semi-circular bay at the junction with the Strand was the Charing Cross Post Office.

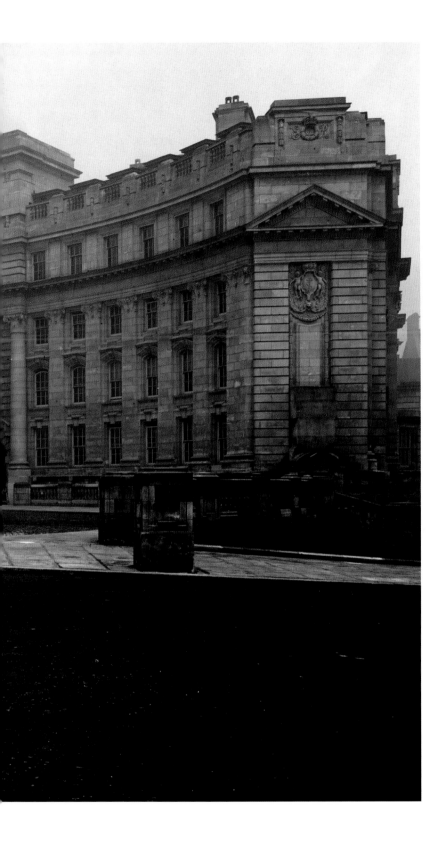

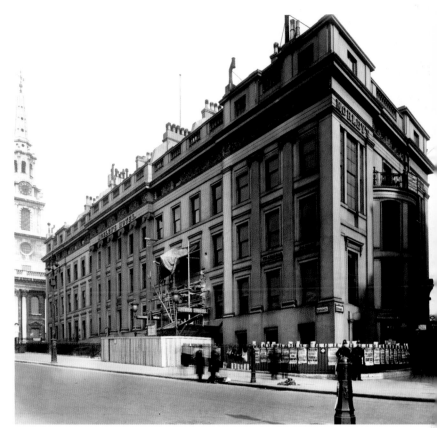

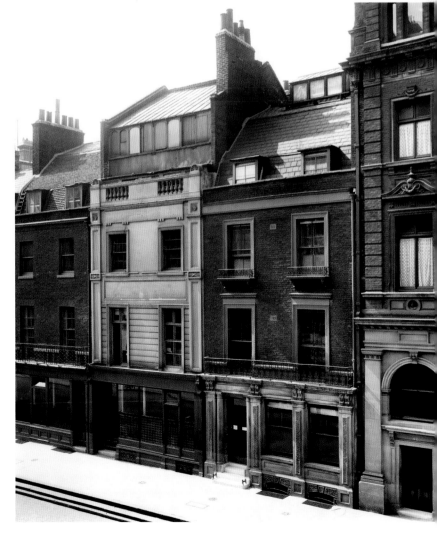

Right: 37-41 Charing Cross, 3 September 1910

Nos. 37 and 38 to the left, built by James Lambe in 1758-59, retain their original shopfronts. The entrance to Buckingham Court lies beyond with wooden bracing over the passageway. No. 39-41 are of a similar date. No. 40 was the home of Sir James Nicholl McAdam, the 'macadamiser' of roads. No. 41 was part of the Salopian Coffee House, and the residence of Thomas Telford, the great engineer, for over 21 years.

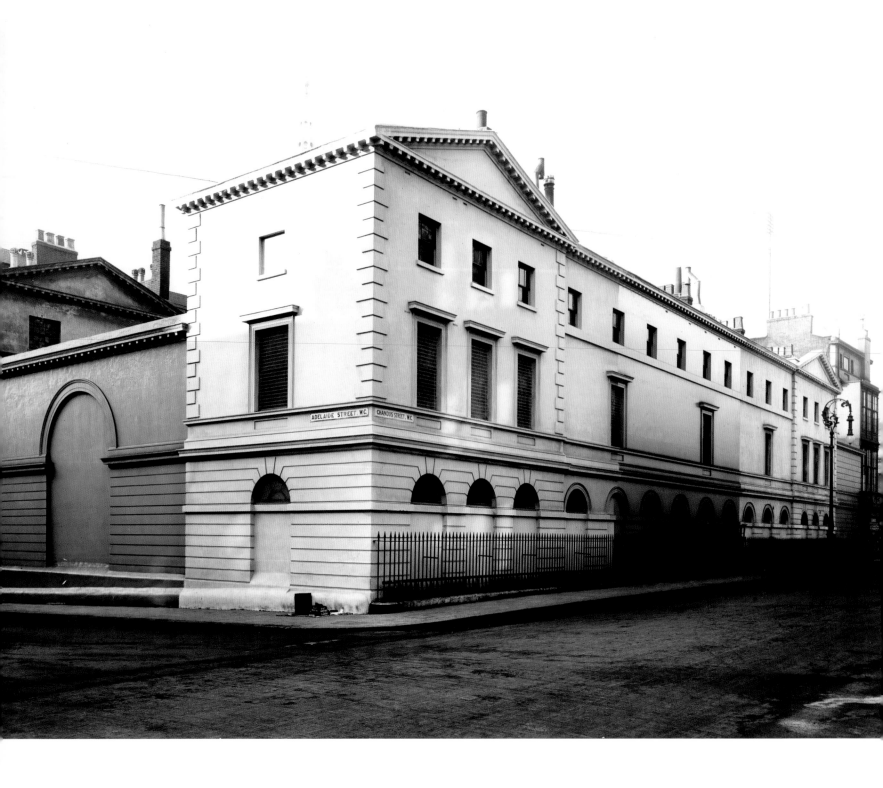

Metropolitan splendour

Above: Chandos Street, 18 October 1906
This palatial stable block stood at the junction with Adelaide Street. The first floor window openings are filled with ventilating grilles. To the right is a new electric arc street lamp enriched with elaborately detailed ironwork.

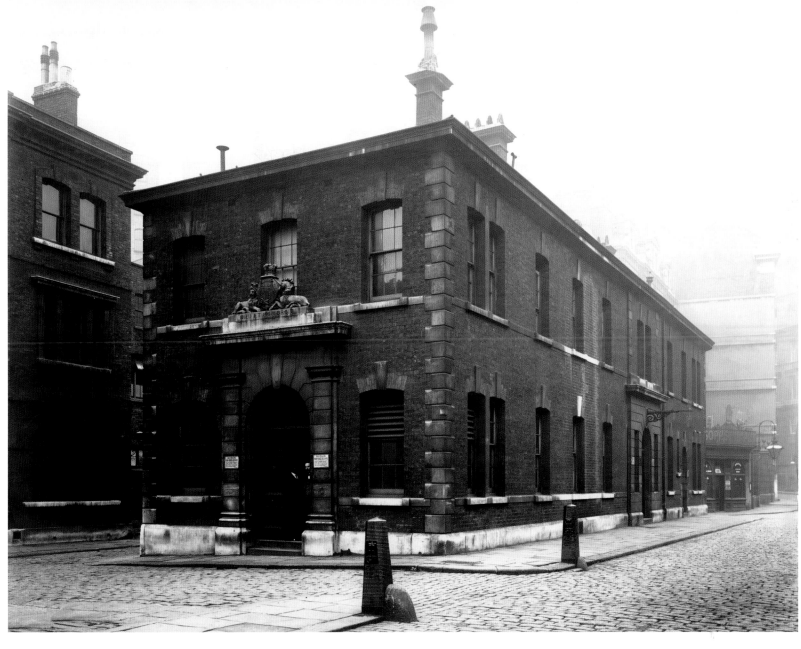

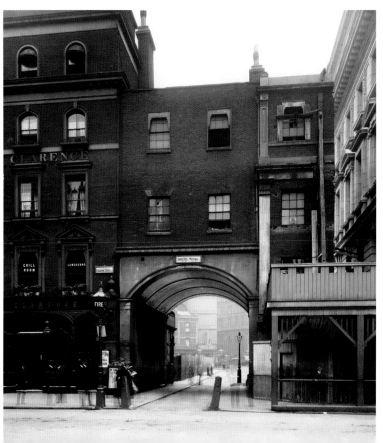

Above: Great Scotland Yard, 3 November 1906
A police station was established here in 1829. It became the Metropolitan Police headquarters until 1891 when it relocated to New Scotland Yard.

Right: 1 Whitehall, 27 September 1909
1 Whitehall was designed by Robert Adam and completed in 1772 as a gateway to Great Scotland Yard. In 1818 the gateway was raised and the frontage remodelled to provide improved access. It was demolished in 1909.

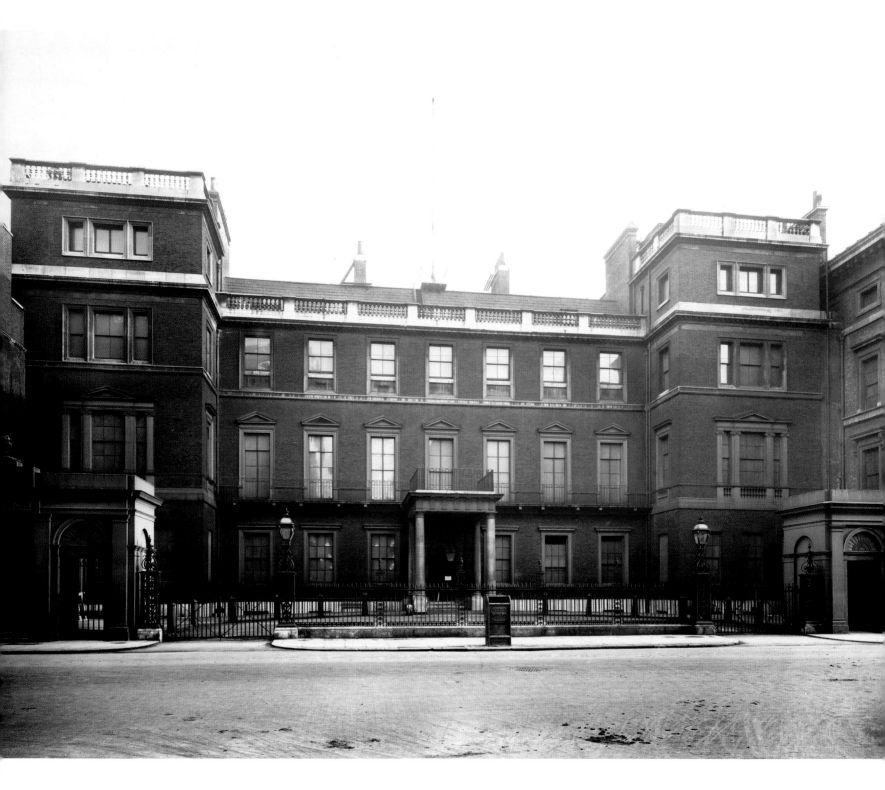

Old aristocratic mansions

ST JAMES'S

Above: Cumberland House, Pall Mall, c 1907

In 1760 the Duke of York, the younger brother of George III purchased a group of houses on the south side of Pall Mall, and commissioned Matthew Brettingham Snr to design a substantial new town house. On his death in 1767, it passed to the Duke of Cumberland who enlarged the courtyard and built the projecting wings, including the two gate lodges by Robert Adam. In 1806 it passed to the Boards of Ordnance, later the War Office, which occupied it until it was pulled down in stages for the Royal Automobile Club between 1906-12.

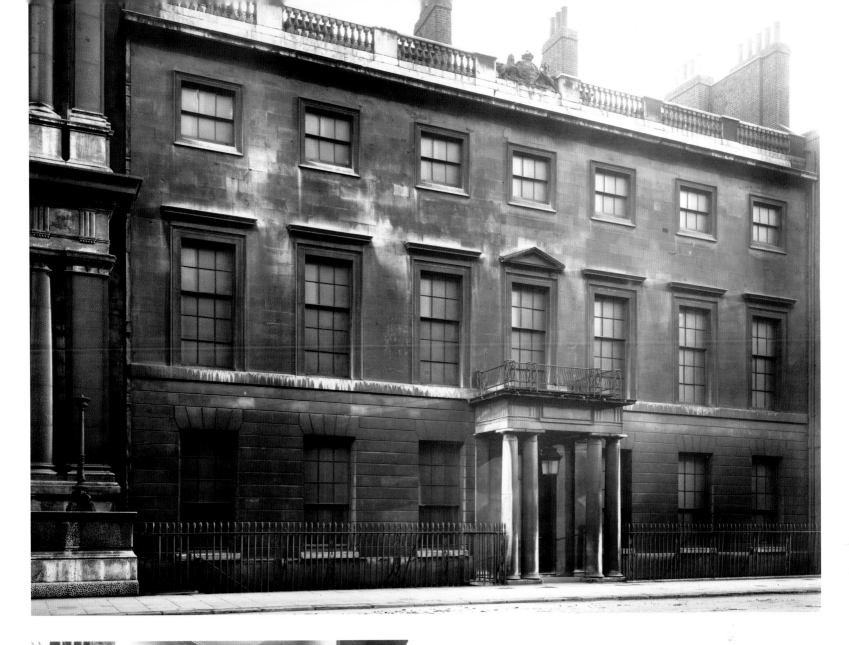

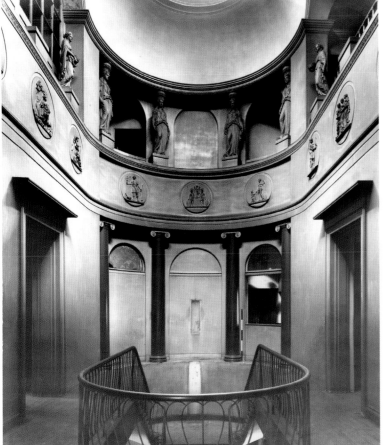

Above: Buckingham House, Pall Mall, c 1906

Buckingham House was the residence of the first Marquis of Buckingham, whose Coade stone coat of arms crowned the parapet. He inherited his uncle's house in Pall Mall in 1779, and commissioned Sir John Soane to rebuild it. In 1855 it was acquired by the War Office, which continued to occupy it until 1906. Two years later it was demolished to make way for the Royal Automobile Club. Some of the chimneypieces were saved and reused in the new War Office building in Whitehall.

Left: Buckingham House, Pall Mall, c 1906

Soane's magnificent staircase compartment. In the apsidal ends were four Coade stone caryatids copied from the Erechtheum in Athens. The original colour scheme would have been striking – blue-grey walls, marbled columns with bronzed capitals and bases to the Ionic columns.

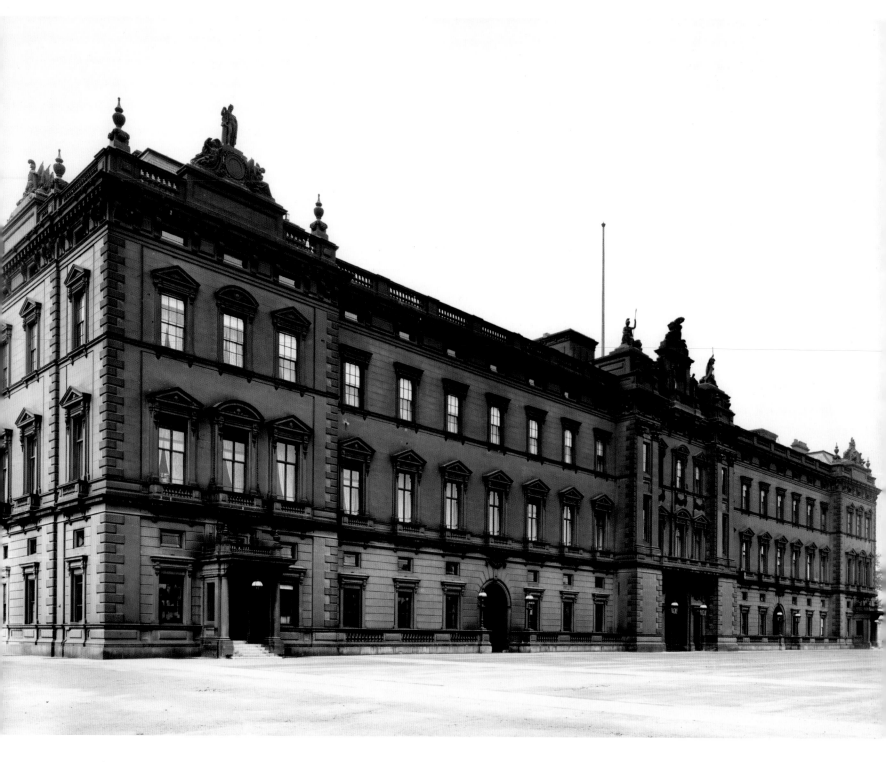

Fit for a king

Above: Buckingham Palace, 2 August 1913

The east front of Buckingham Palace, built by Edward Blore between 1846-50, showing the centre and end pavilions enriched with allegorical sculpture and the much-criticised over-ornate centrepiece. Excoriated at the time for its ponderous design, it was refaced in 1913 by Sir Aston Webb in Louis XVI style to complement the Beaux-Arts replanning of the Mall and the Imperial iconography around the Queen Victoria Memorial.

Opposite top: Buckingham Palace, 9 October 1913

The re-facing of the palace was completed in just three months. In this view the stonework is virtually complete. Commonly derided as insipid and bland, in fact, it was a vast improvement over the earlier Blore facade and complemented Admiralty Arch, and the grand Imperial planning of the Mall.

Opposite below: Buckingham Palace, 2 August 1913

View of Blore's east front just prior to its refacing by Sir Aston Webb. The rond-pont of piers and gates surrounding the Queen Victoria Memorial is complete, but work has not started yet on the palace. To the left are the Australia Gates.

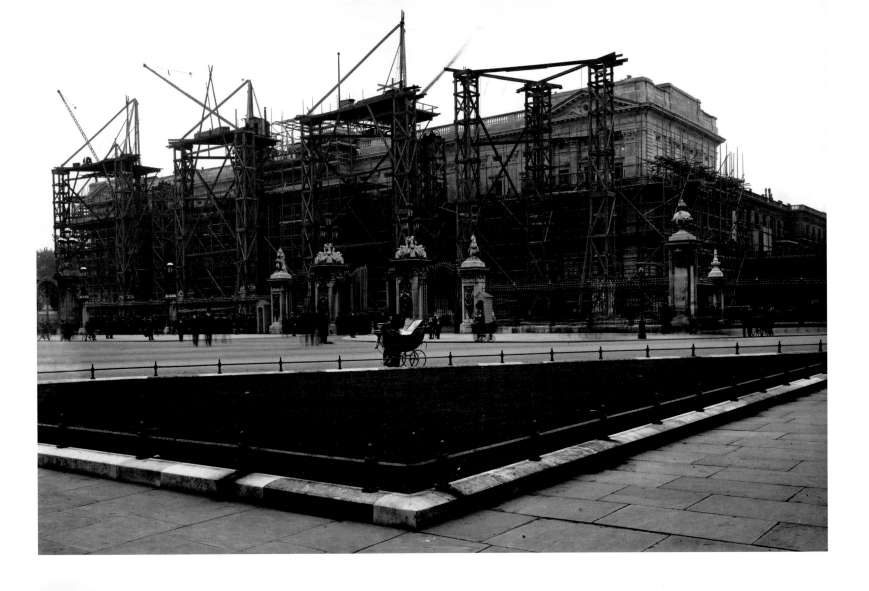

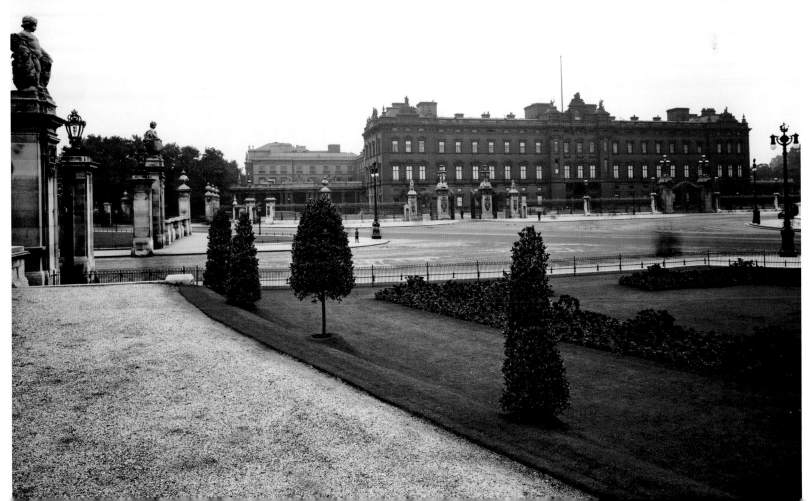

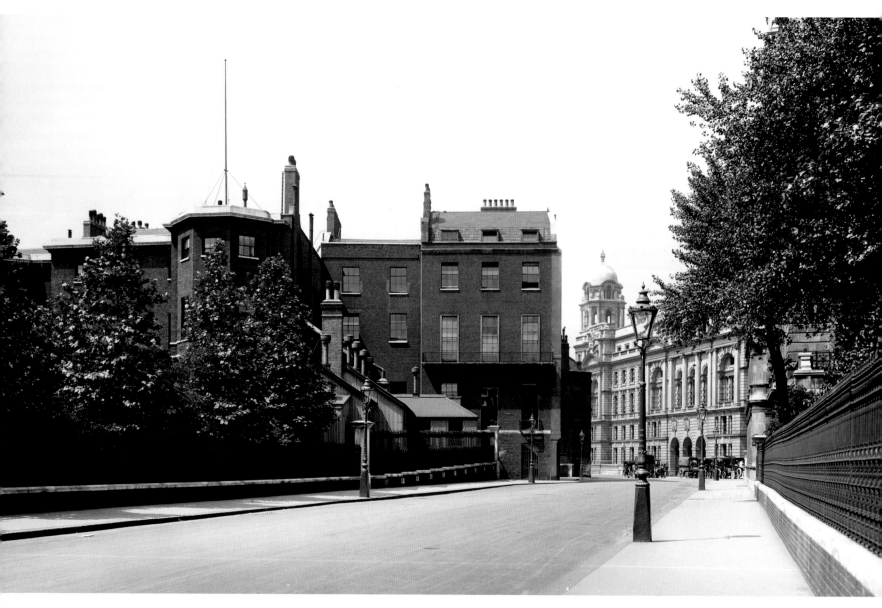

Offices of state

WHITEHALL

Above: Horseguards Avenue, Whitehall, 10 June 1912
This view from Horseguards Avenue towards the rear of Whitehall
Gardens shows the Old War Office in the distance. The end house, No. 1
Horseguards Avenue, was built by Michael Angelo Taylor, the son of the
architect Sir Robert Taylor, a prominent Whig MP and campaigner for
improved paving and lighting. The canted bay to the rear of Pembroke
House can be seen to the left.

Right: 2 Whitehall Gardens, 22 May 1912
2 Whitehall Gardens was used by the Cabinet Office and the Committee
of Imperial Defence.
  The first floor rear room was treated in a French rococo style with oil
paintings of rural scenes painted by E J Parris in 1841.

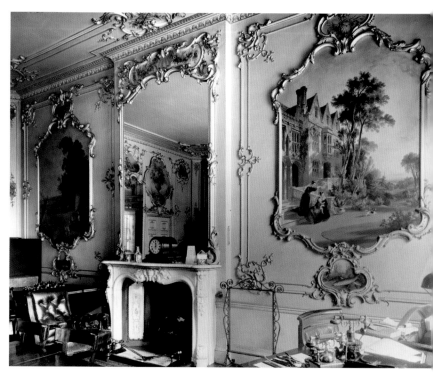

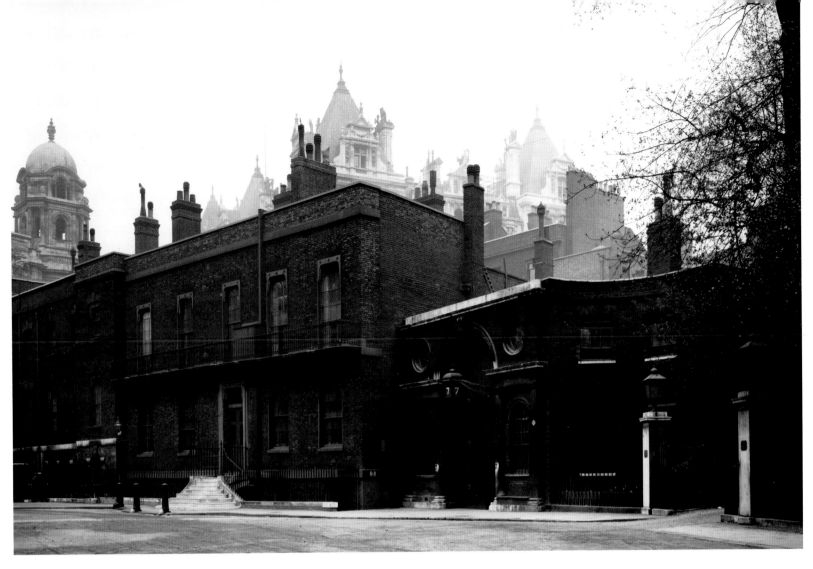

Above: Whitehall Gardens, 1 May 1912

Whitehall Gardens, formerly Privy Gardens, lay at the rear of the Banqueting House and was lined with fashionable mansions which, until the formation of the Victoria Embankment, had gardens and lawns sloping down to the Thames.

Malmesbury House to the left of the picture was built in the 1720s and once faced the rear of the Banqueting House. From 1834-61 it was the house of James Howard, 3rd Earl of Malmesbury, Foreign Secretary and later Leader of the House of Lords. The Ionic entrance screen adjacent is the entrance lodge to Pembroke House, one of the first Palladian villas, built in 1724 and later altered by Sir William Chambers in 1757. Whitehall Gardens was levelled in 1936 for a huge new building for the Air Ministry and Board of Trade, now the Ministry of Defence.

Right: Pembroke House, 7 Whitehall Gardens, 23 September 1912

Pembroke House was renowned for its exquisite plasterwork by William Parfitt to designs by Sir William Chambers. This view shows Room 24 on the first floor with its superb spider's web ceiling with an entwining vine encircled by a large rope of fruit and flowers. Room 24 and three others from Pembroke House were reassembled in the new Ministry building.

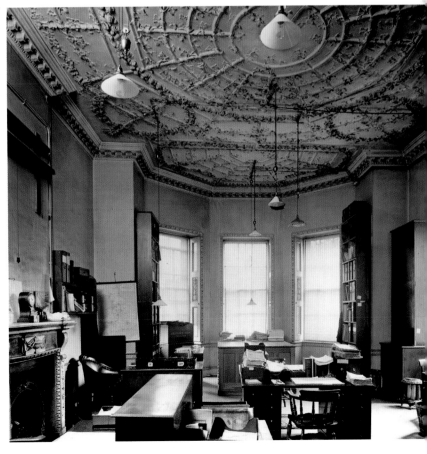

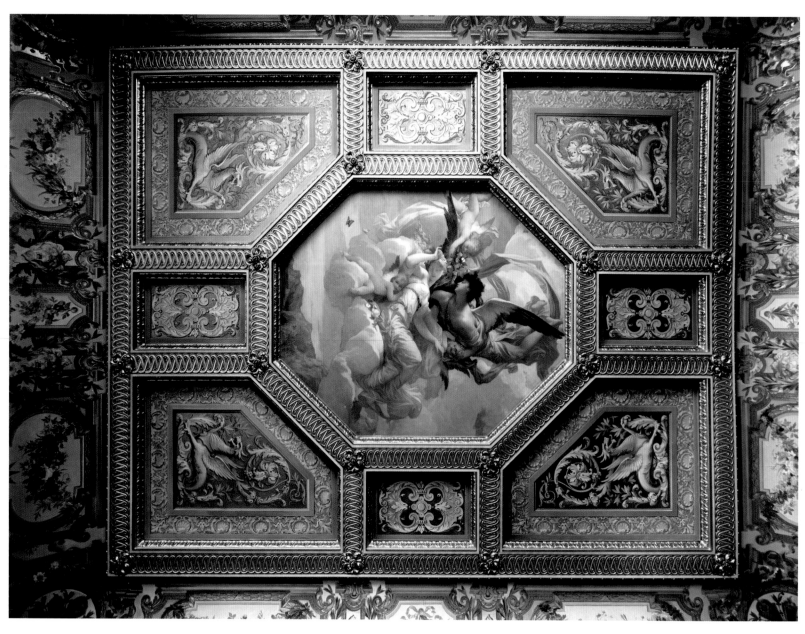

Montagu House, Whitehall Gardens, c 1910

Montagu House was a palatial French Renaissance style residence with steeply pitched French mansard roofs designed by William Burn in 1859-62 for the Dukes of Buccleuch. Ironically, from 1917 it was taken over and used as offices by the Ministry of Labour.

Above: View of the ceiling over a first floor rear room, later used by the Parliamentary Secretary.

Right: View of carved chimneypiece in a first floor rear room.

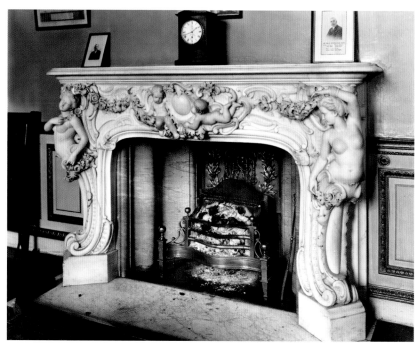

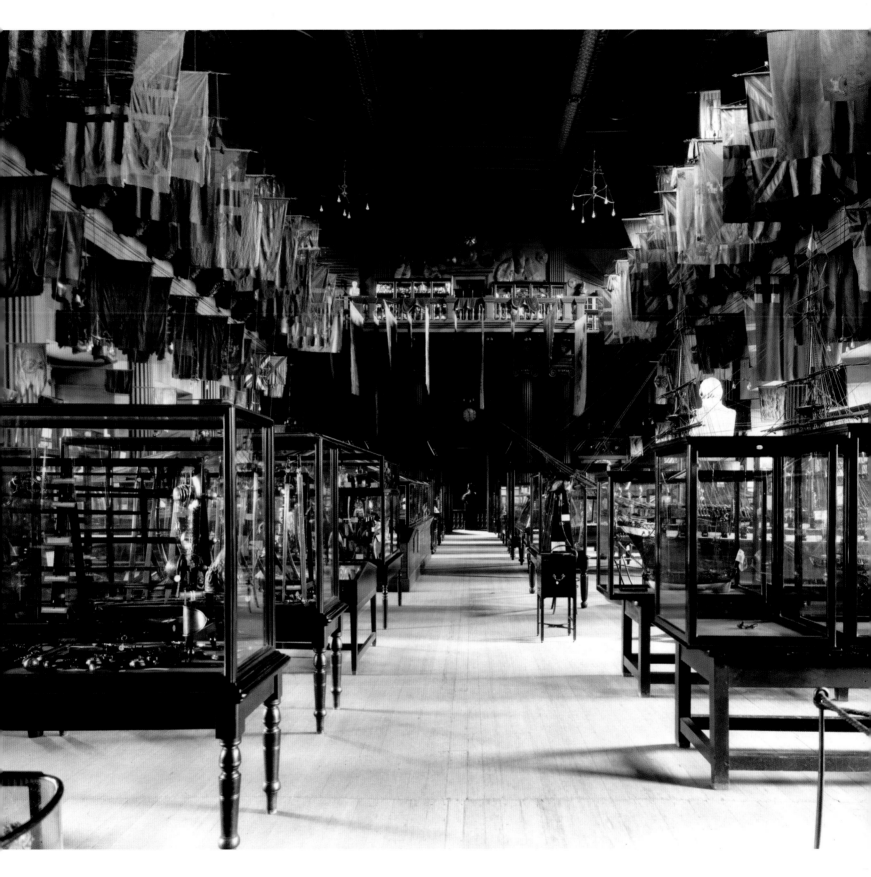

Above: Banqueting House, Whitehall c 1910

For a long period Inigo Jones' great Banqueting House was used as a military chapel before it reopened as a Royal Chapel in 1837, but in 1890 it was taken over as a museum for the Royal United Services Institute. Exhibits included regimental flags, arms, trophies and model ships.

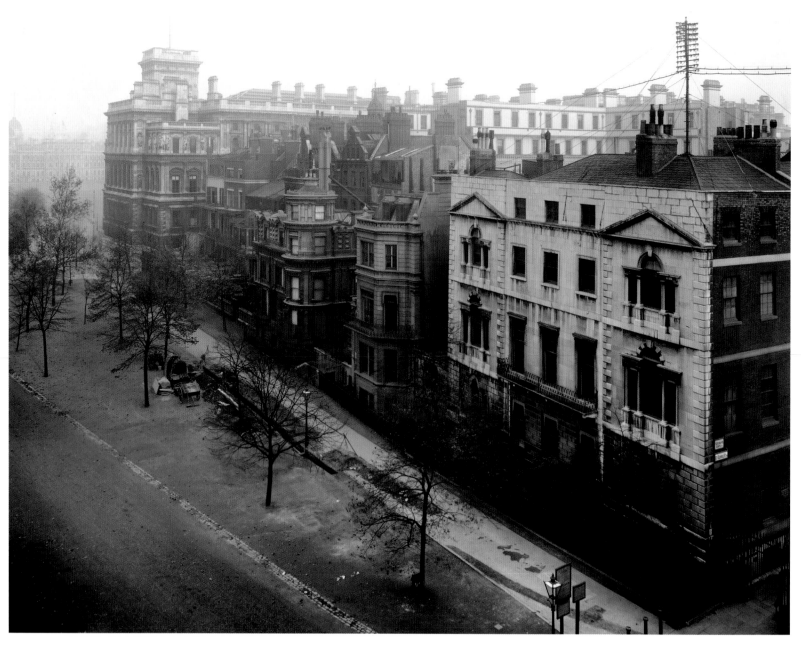

Civic improvements

Above: Storeys Gate, c 1905

Storeys Gate with St James's Park to the left and the Foreign Office beyond. Judge Jeffreys Steps, seen clearly in the centre of the picture, were permitted by James II to allow the infamous judge private access to the royal park. The end house was faced in Portland stone to provide a polite facade to the park. The architect is not known, but when the entire block was levelled in 1910, the facade was dismantled and re-erected at Horseguards as the rear elevation to the Old Paymaster-General's Office.

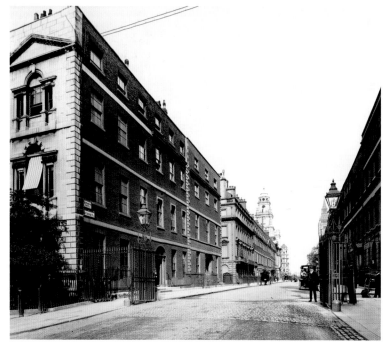

Left: Great George Street, c 1905

The north side of Great George Street comprised a handsome group of first-rate Georgian houses occupied by government offices and professional institutions. The whole street block was demolished for New Government Offices designed by J W Brydon between 1899-1915 in a confident neo-Baroque style to express British commercial and Imperial might.

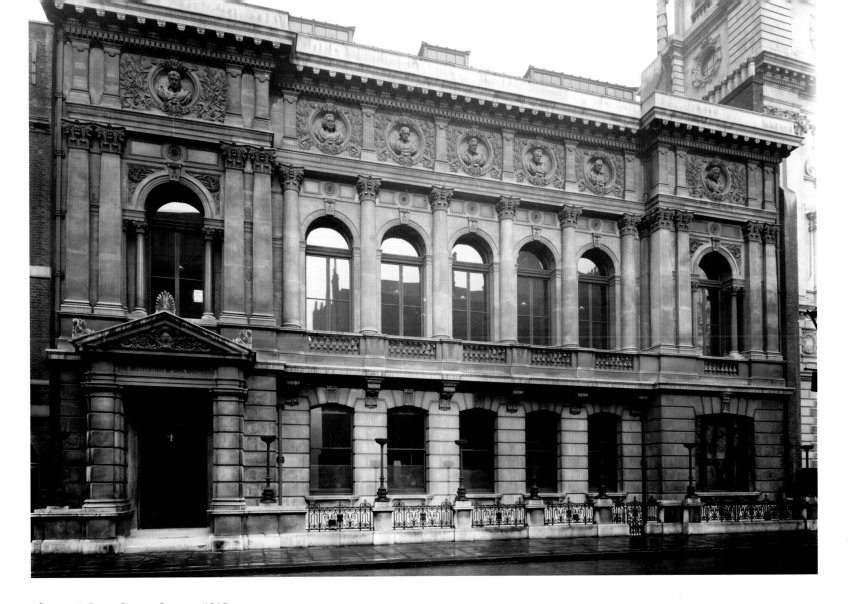

Above: 12 Great George Street, c 1910

The Institution of Civil Engineers was designed by Charles Barry Jnr in 1895-96 but, in spite of its grandeur, only 14 years later the whole street block was pulled down for New Government Offices. The Institution relocated into a new building opposite by James Miller of Glasgow. Panelling and pilasters were salvaged and reused in the library of the new building, together with painted glass by A W Moore & Sons depicting vignettes of bridges, and other great engineering structures.

Right: 37 Great George Street, 13 January 1910
Vaulted hall and staircase compartment.

Below: 12 Great George Street, 11 July 1910
Detail of the central panel of the chimneypiece from the Tribunal of Appeal Office.

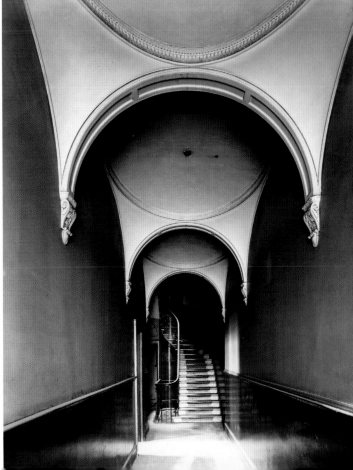

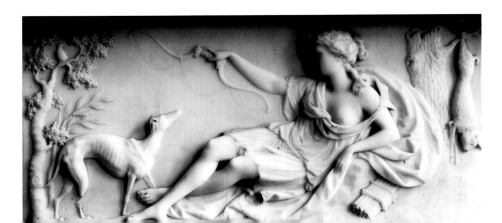

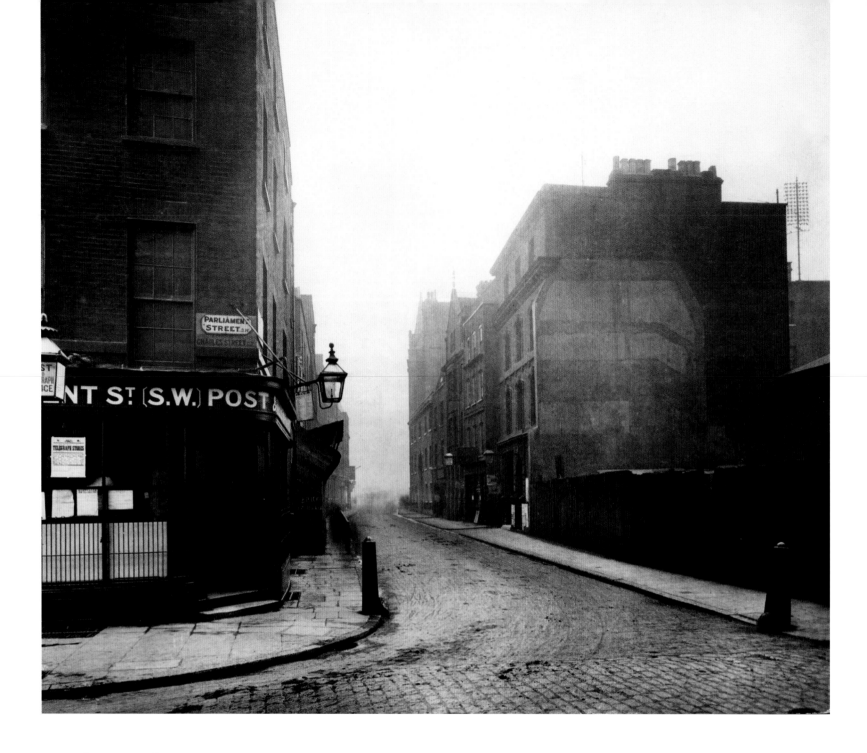

Colonial missions

Above: Parliament Street, c 1909

Parliament Street Post Office at the junction with King Street looking south to Parliament Square. To the right of the picture clearance has started for the New Government Offices.

Opposite top: Parliament Street, 1909

View from the east side of Whitehall looking south towards Parliament Square. To the extreme right is the corner of the Foreign Office on what is now the junction with King Charles Street.

Opposite bottom left: Delahay Street, c 1910

View of Delahay Street at the junction with Charles Street. To the immediate right, out of the picture, is Clive Steps. Delahay Street was a centre of colonial missionary activity, including the Society for The Propagation of the Gospel, the Colonial Bishopric Fund, the Ladies' Association for Promoting Female Education in India and the Universities' Mission to Central Africa.

Opposite bottom right: 6 Delahay Street, 13 January 1910

The closet wing and rear; the old clay tile roofs and flush-framed sash windows are typical of a London town house c 1700.

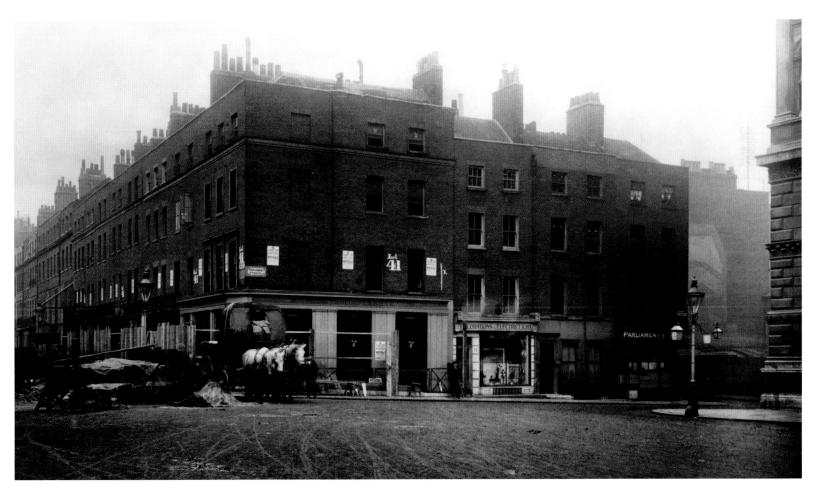

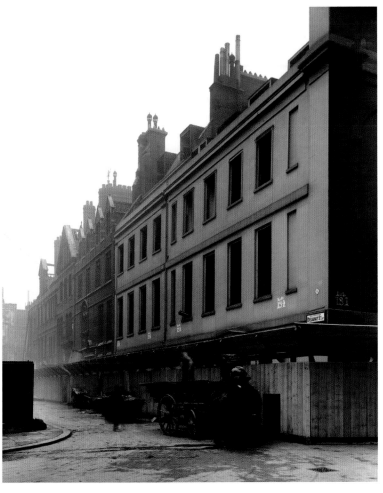

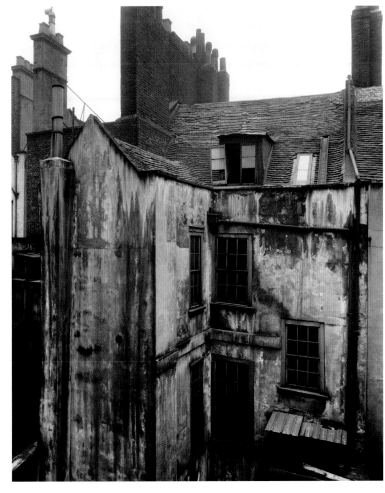

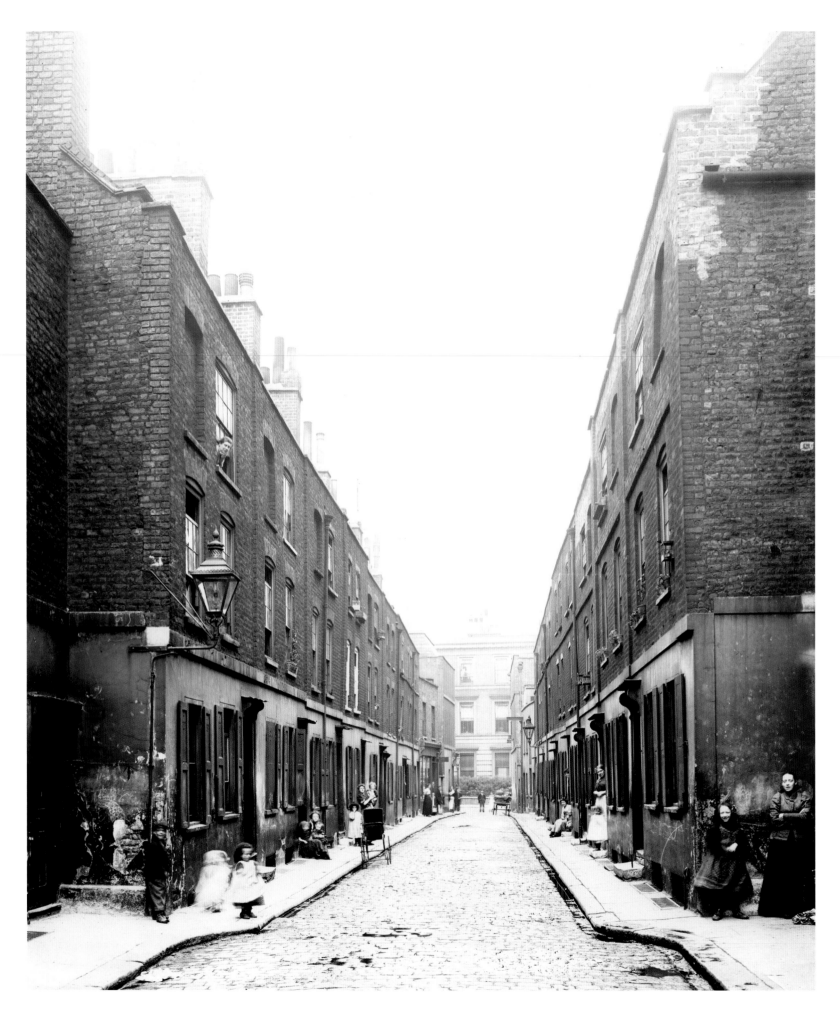

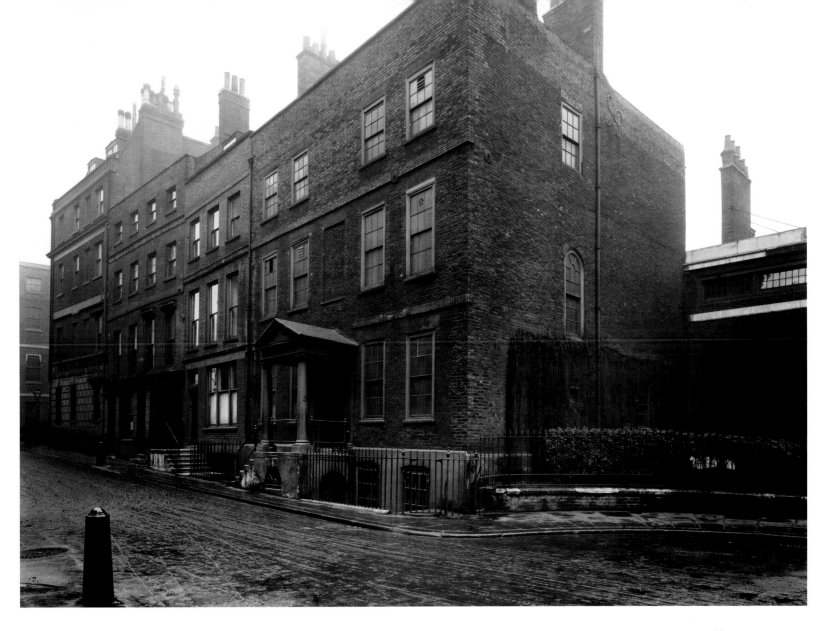

In the shadow of Parliament

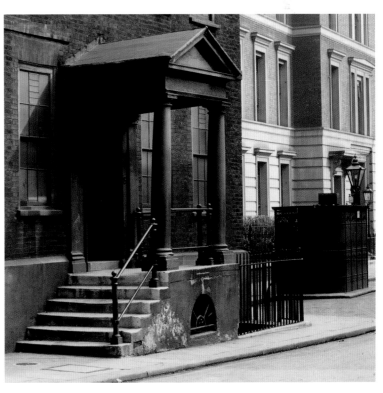

Opposite: Parker Street, c 1905

View east along Parker Street towards Princes Street. The heart of old Westminster was notorious for its chronic poverty. Within 300 yards of the gates of the Palace of Westminster, Parker Street was typical of the squalor which was a standing rebuke to the national conscience until well into the 20th century. By 1905 these early 18th century terraces had fallen into use as cheap lodging houses.

Above: Princes Street, c 1909

Princes Street looking north to the junction with Great George Street. The handsome five bay house with the raised projecting, pedimented porch is of c 1720. The entrance to Princes Mews can be seen just beyond.

Right: Princes Street, 31 August 1909

View looking south towards the rear of the Westminster Hospital. Beyond the porch is a cast iron street urinal. Of the two now remaining in London, only one is still in use.

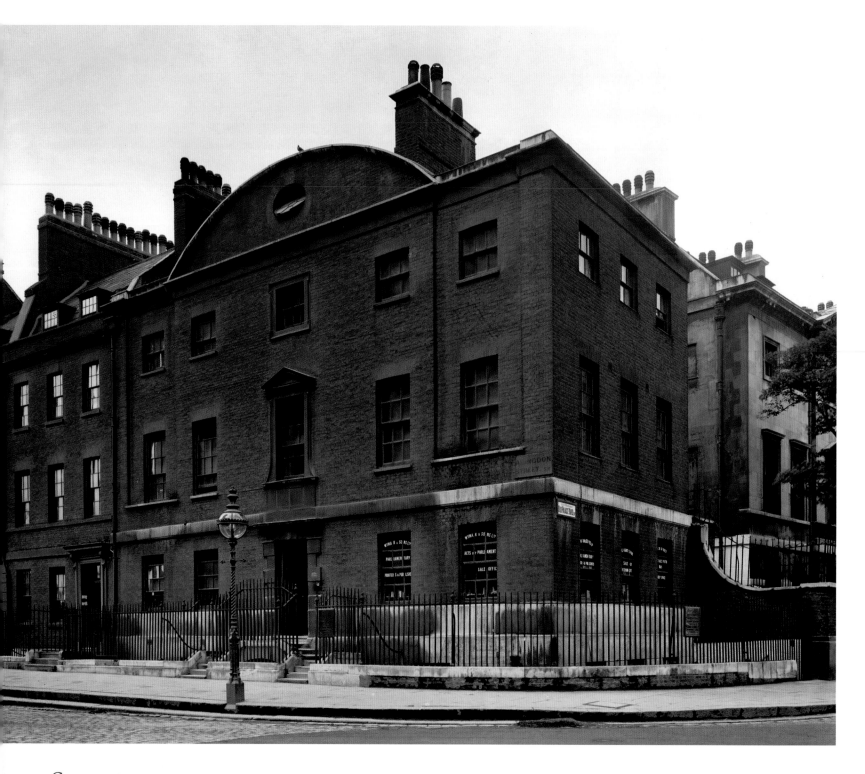

Sanctuary

WESTMINSTER

Above: 32 Abingdon Street, 20 August 1910
32 Abingdon Street stood at the corner with Old Palace Yard. Designed in 1723 in the style of William Kent, it was an exceptionally handsome town house in an austere Palladian style.

Opposite: Westminster Hospital, Broad Sanctuary, c 1910
Westminster Hospital stood opposite the Abbey and opened for patients in 1834. It was designed by W and H W Inwood between 1831-34 in a Tudor Gothic style and extended in the later 19th century. Originally it had room for over 100 patients, but only two baths, and drained into a cesspool. The hospital moved to Horseferry Road in 1939, but the building survived until 1951. The Queen Elizabeth II Conference Centre was built on the site between 1981-86.

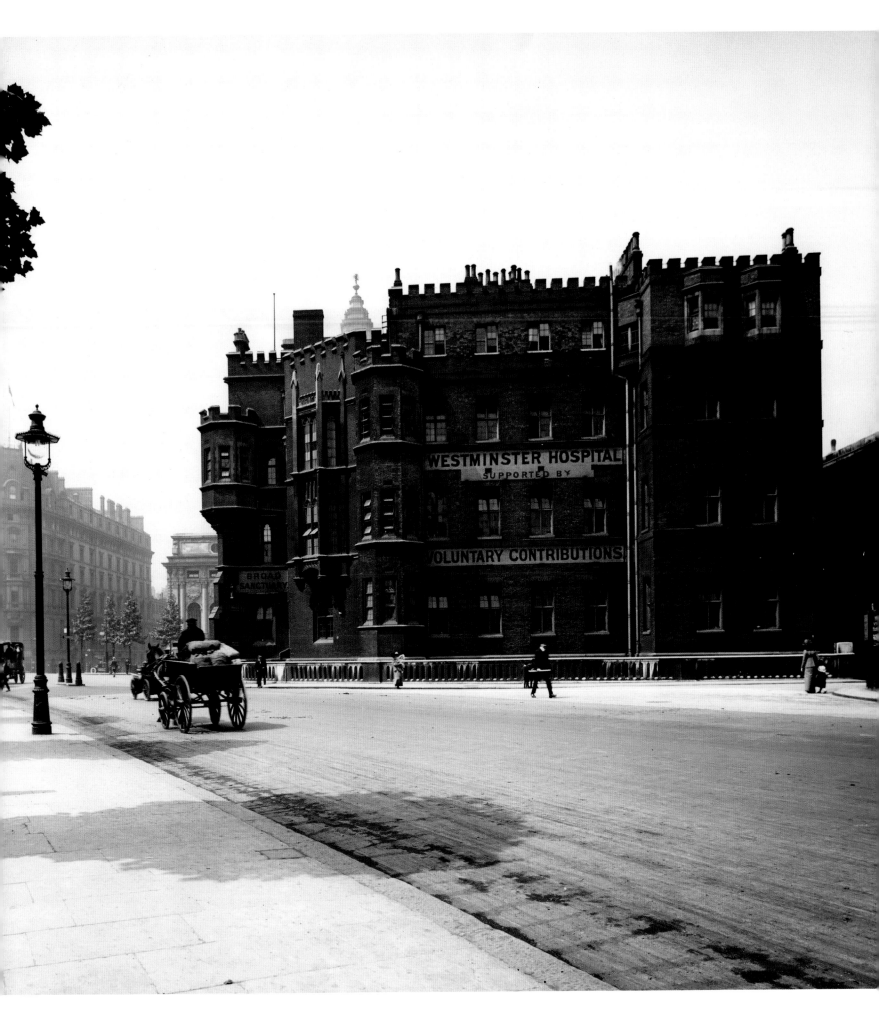

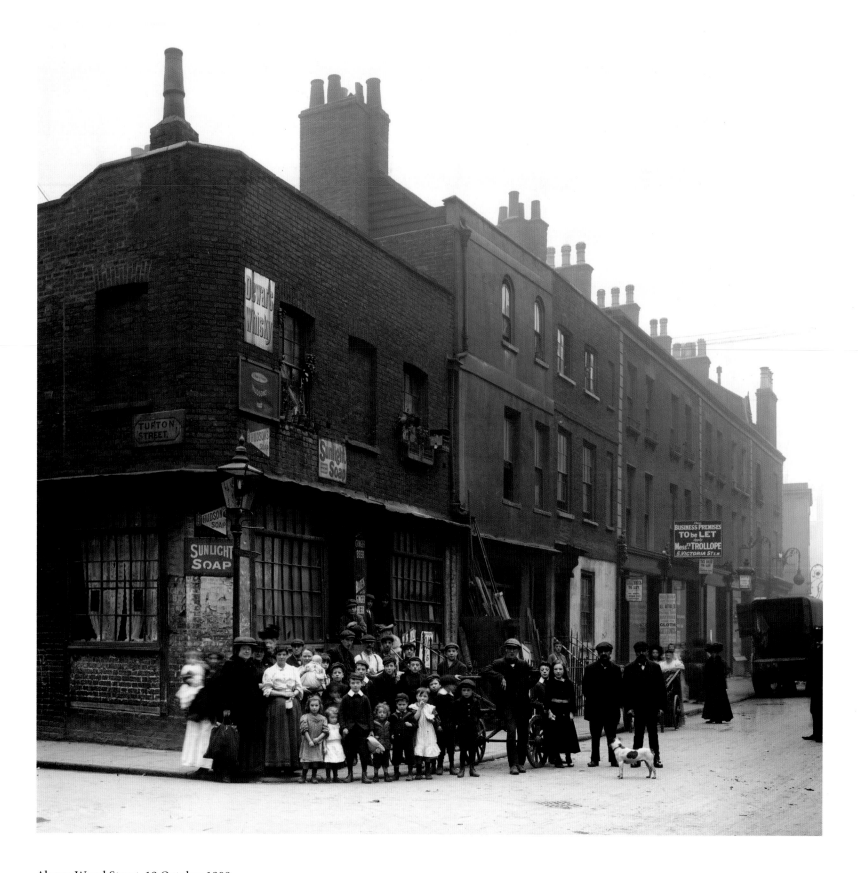

Above: Wood Street, 19 October 1909

The south-west corner of Wood Street at the junction with Tufton Street looking west. All are well-shod and most have hats or caps which suggests a group of respectable working families rather than the indigent for which the area was notorious. The entire neighbourhood was redeveloped between 1900-39.

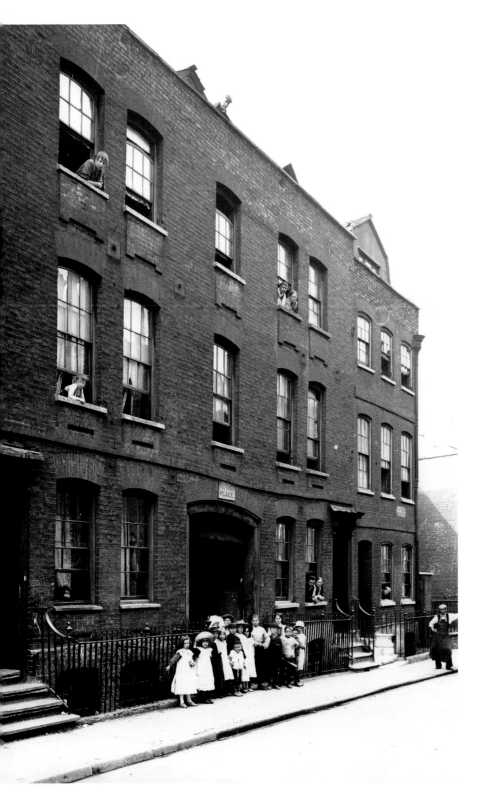

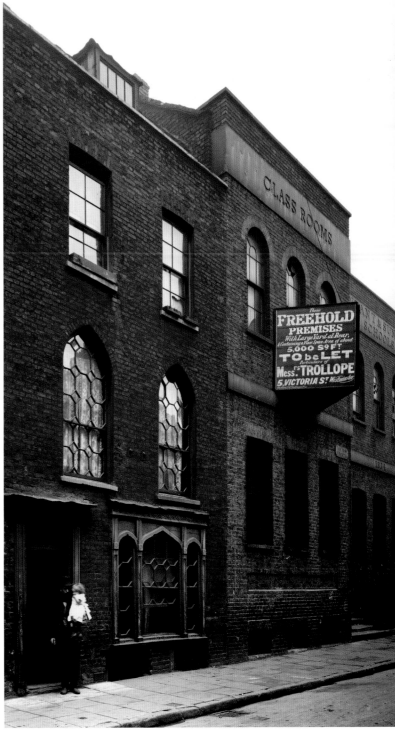

Above left: 38-40 Tufton Street, 21 May 1906

A once-handsome pair of early 18th century houses in use as lodging houses. The photographer appears to have attracted keen interest with faces at virtually every window.

Colonel Blood, who attempted to steal the Crown Jewels in 1671, is reputed to have retired to the previous house on the site with a royal pardon and a pension, fuelling suspicions that he had been acting on behalf of the King. The house was distinguished by a carved brick shield and coat of arms, but was demolished for the buildings seen here.

Above right: 49 Tufton Street, 19 October 1909

This remarkable building, next to the Infant and Sunday Schools of 1834, has pointed brick arches to the first floor windows filled with elaborate, octagonal tracery and a tripartite Gothic window to the ground floor, but a conventional second floor. Its provenance is a mystery.

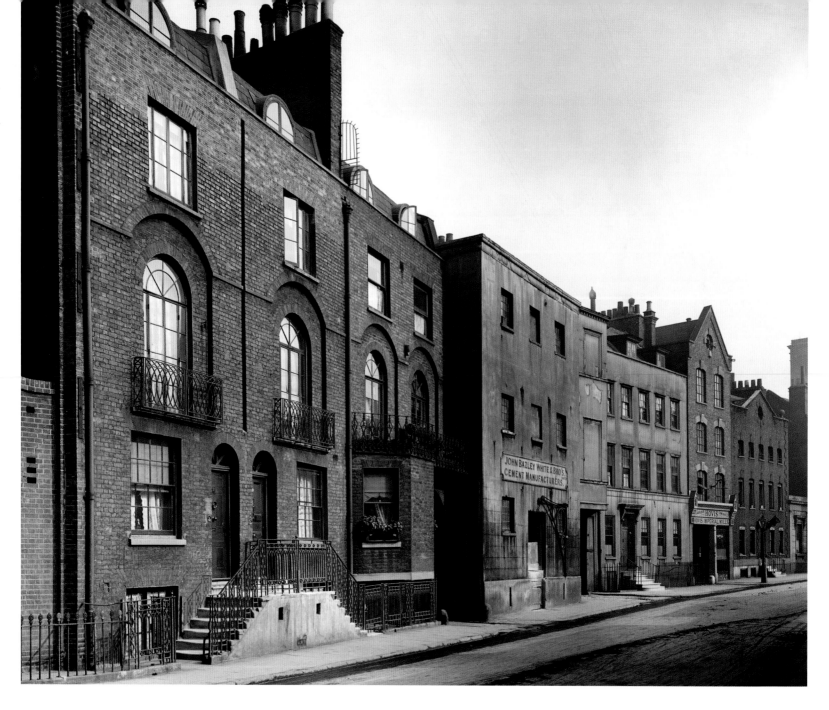

MILLBANK

Above: Nos. 17-25 Millbank Street, 11 April 1904
The east side of Millbank was a jumble of wharves, jetties, and industrial buildings. In the centre of the picture is John Bazley White & Bros, Cement Works with the Hovis Imperial Flour Mills beyond. In between are earlier 18th and 19th century houses. All were swept away for an extension of the Thames embankment and Victoria Tower Gardens under the Westminster Improvement Act 1900.

Right: 20-22 Millbank Street, 21 May 1906
Old printing press.

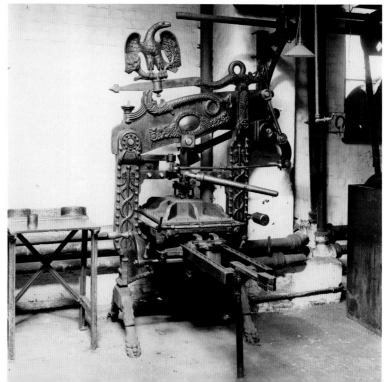

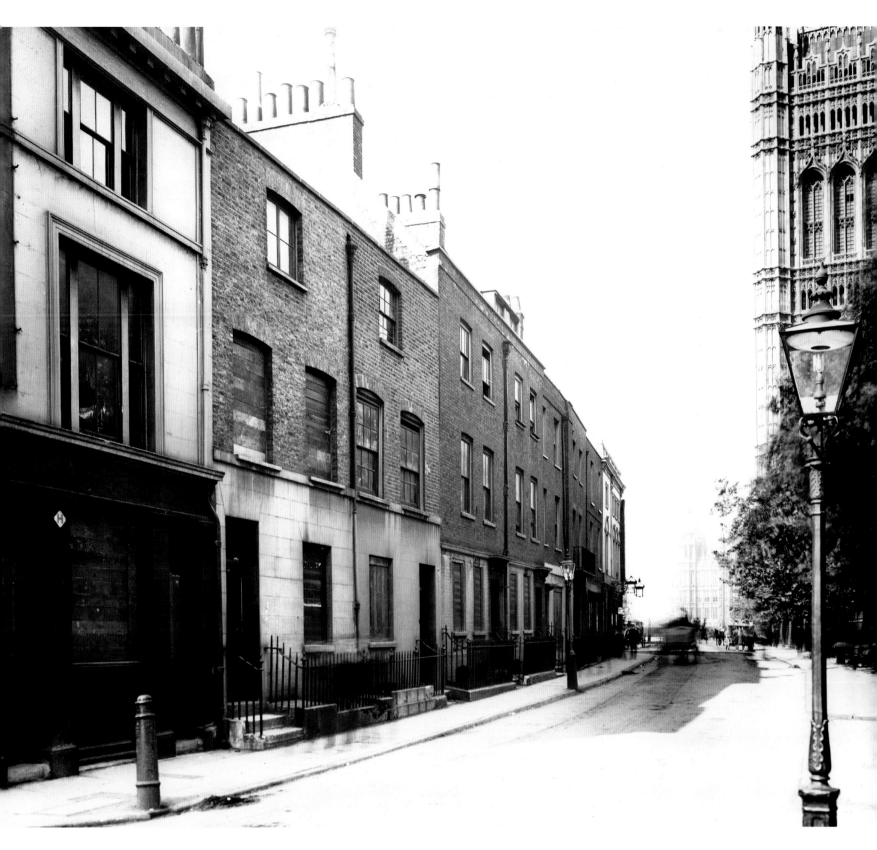

The Westminster improvements

Above: Millbank Street, 21 May 1906

The west side of Millbank Street looking north with the Victoria Tower of the Palace of Westminster to the right: the largest square tower in the world when built. The houses are boarded up pending demolition and road widening.

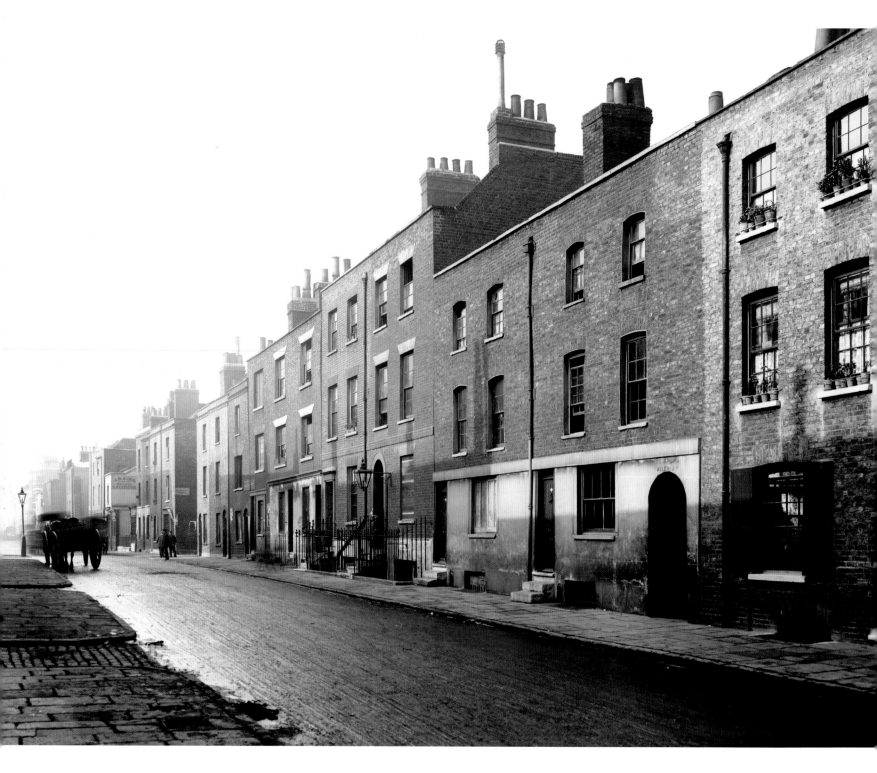

Above: Horseferry Road, 21 May 1906

The north side of Horseferry Road with the narrow entrance to Champions Alley to the right. Millbank was notorious for its poor housing plagued by damp and the perpetual threat of flooding from the Thames. On the night of 6 January 1928 fourteen people were drowned in the poorer areas next to the Thames when the river burst its banks. The Palace of Westminster was flooded and a section of the Embankment collapsed at Millbank.

Opposite top: Grubb Street, 21 May 1906

Grubb Street was characteristic of the grinding poverty of the Millbank area, which was rebuilt comprehensively from 1900-39. The entrance to York Buildings can be seen to the right.

Opposite below: York Buildings, 21 May 1906

Living conditions in parts of Westminster were as bad as parts of the East End. By 1906 this squalid series of hovels was no longer fit for human habitation and had been given over to the storage of costermongers' barrows. Life in foetid courts like these must have been unbearable with little light or air. Whitewashing was common to increase reflected light.

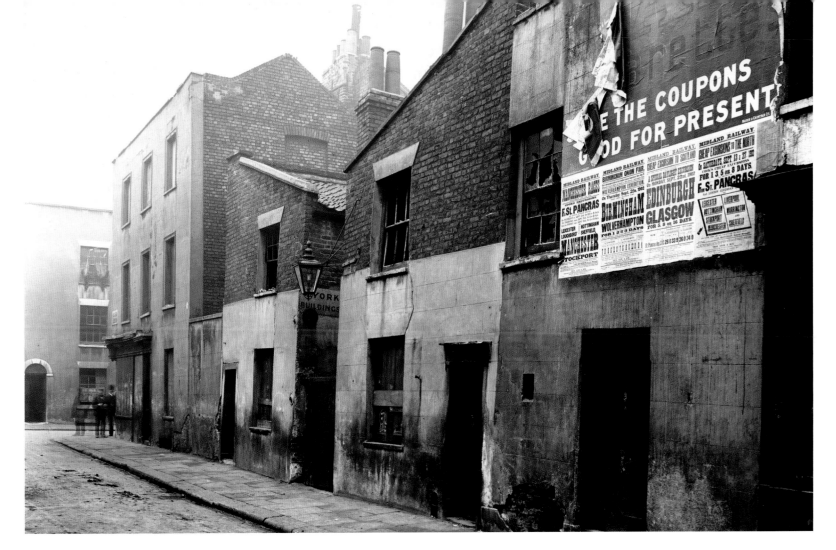

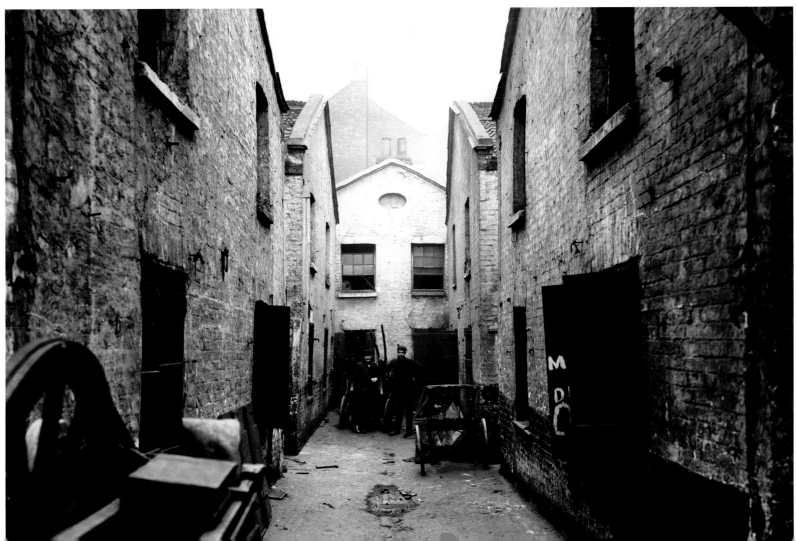

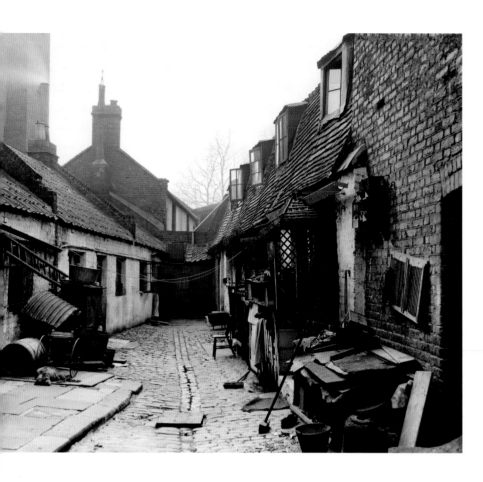

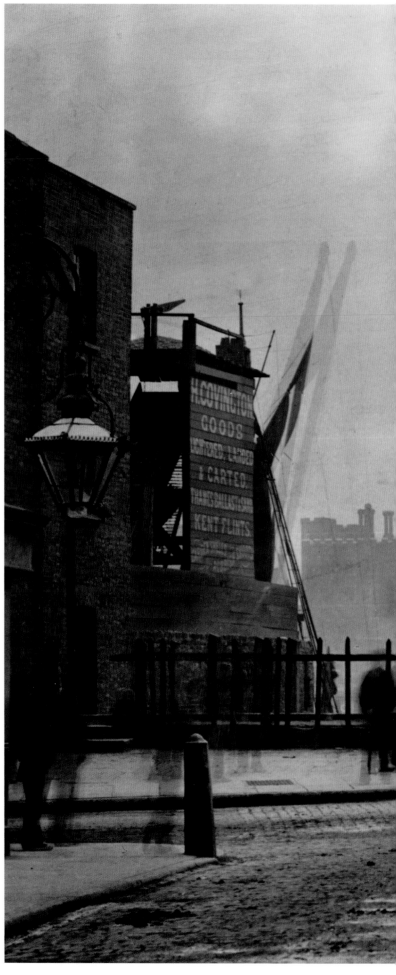

Above: Scotts Rents, Smith Square, c 1910

These mean little 18th century cottages stood in a small yard in the south-east corner of Smith Square, and originally were built as cheap rented dwellings, probably for unskilled workers. The dog to the left of the picture is chained to the wall.

Right: Lambeth Bridge, 8 June 1896

Old Lambeth Bridge looking south from Millbank. Lambeth Palace and St Mary's, Lambeth can be seen to the left in the distance. The old narrow lattice-stiffened suspension bridge by P W Barlow was never successful and suffered from severe corrosion. A new Lambeth Bridge was completed in 1932 upstream of the old by the LCC's engineer Sir George Humphreys. The buildings in the foreground were pulled down for ICI's Nobel House (1927-29) and Thames House (1929-30), by Sir Frank Baines, one of the last expressions of late Imperial classical planning.

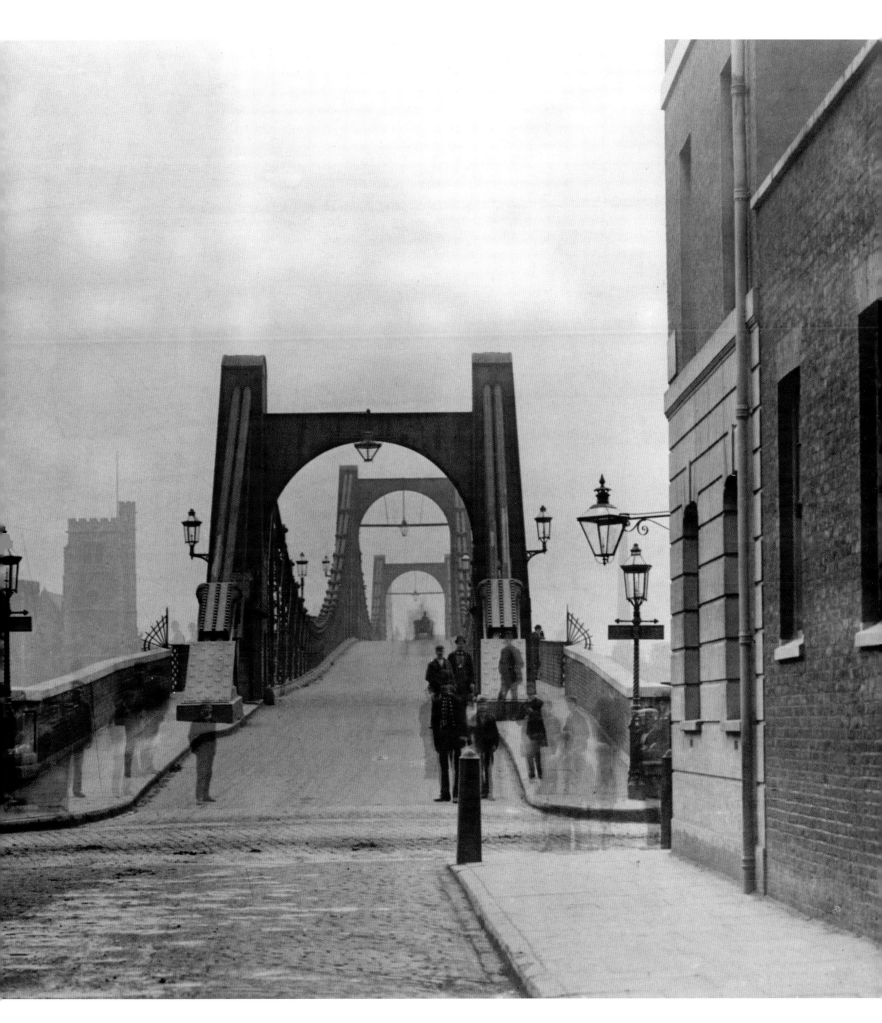

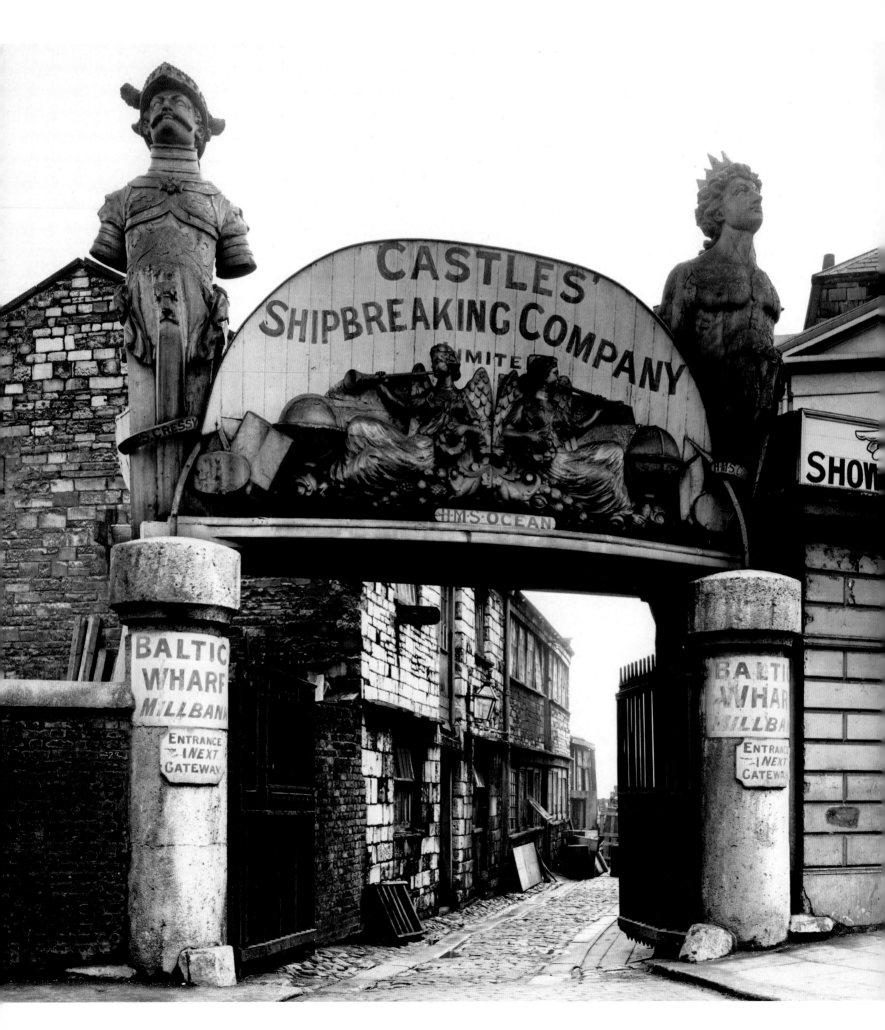

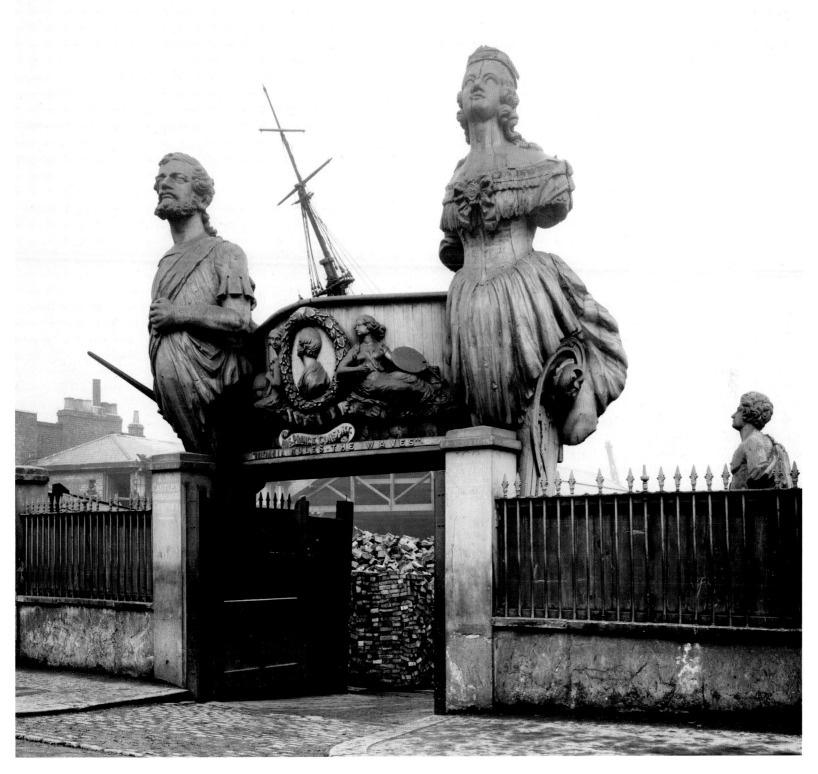

A Thameside curiosity

Opposite: Baltic Wharf, Millbank, 25 March 1909

Henry Castle & Son Shipbreakers Yard, with carved oak naval figureheads marking the south entrance. For many years these massive oak sentinels were a local landmark soaring high above the walls and gates of the yard. The carved arms over the gate are from HMS *Ocean* flanked by figureheads from HMS *Cressy* and HMS *Colossus*.

Above: Baltic Wharf, Millbank, 25 March 1909

The main entrance guarded by figureheads from HMS *Edinburgh* and HMS *Princess Royal* wth the legend "Britannia rules the waves" beneath. A ship's mast can be seen in the background. The yard was bombed in 1941 and its extraordinary collection of naval artefacts destroyed.

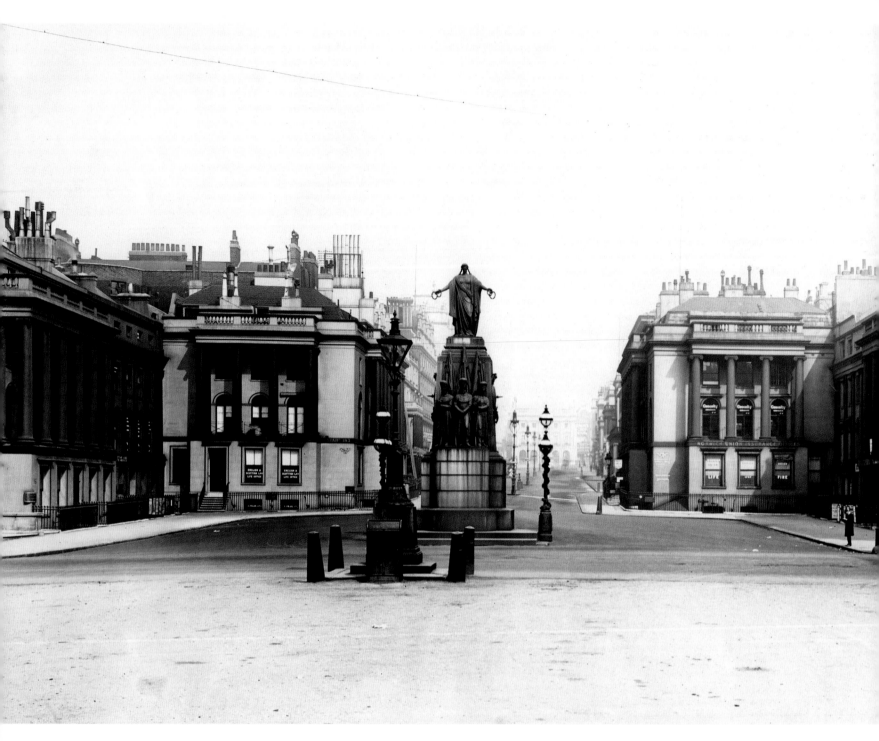

Regency elegance of Nash

Above: Waterloo Place, St James's, c 1907
A remarkable view of Waterloo Place looking north to Piccadilly Circus showing Nash's original buildings with the Guards Crimea Memorial in the foreground and a complete absence of traffic.

Opposite: 11 & 12 Waterloo Place, 9 September 1910
The west side of Waterloo Place at the junction with Charles Street showing a typical section of Nash's original composition. The columns were painted dark brown to simulate stone and contrast with the cream stucco.

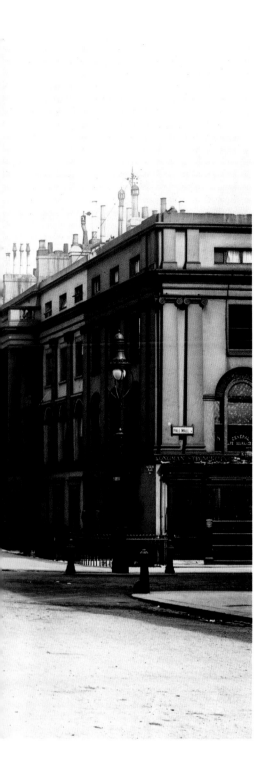

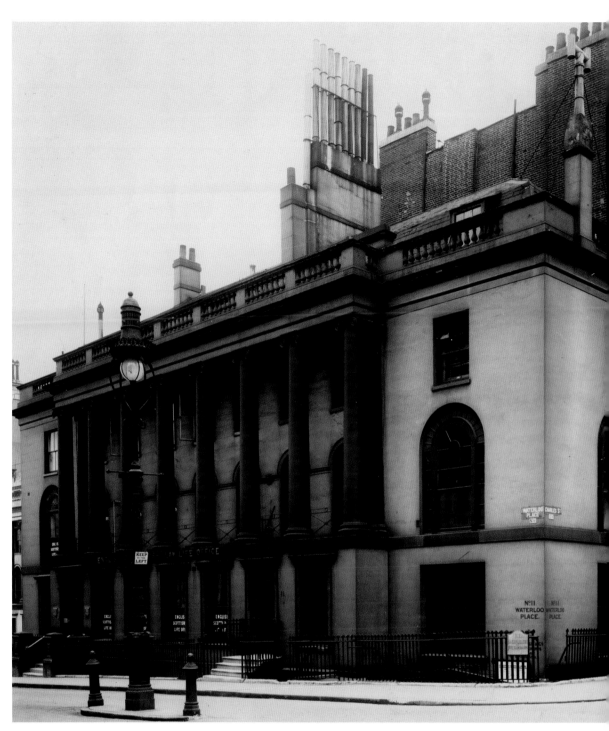

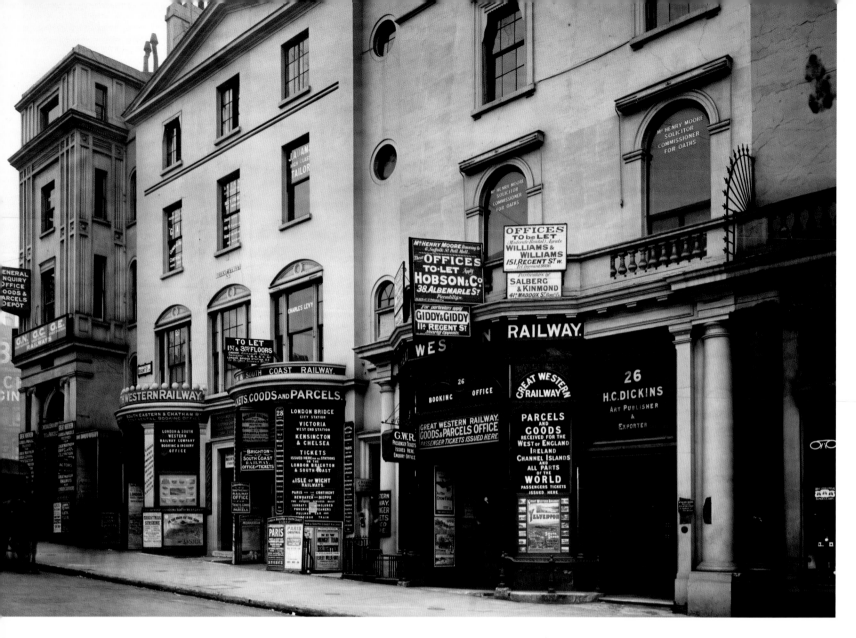

Angel of Christian charity

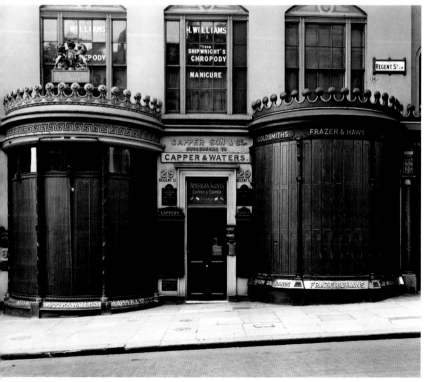

Above: 26-30 Regent Street, 23 November 1911
Railway booking offices on the east side of Regent Street close to the junction with Piccadilly Circus which can be glimpsed to the extreme left.

Left: 29 Regent Street, c 1910
Directly opposite the railway booking offices was this splendid pair of bowed shopfronts with coronets crowning the fascias and beautifully-detailed timber shutters.

Opposite: Shaftesbury Memorial Fountain, Piccadilly Circus, 1909
An atmospheric picture of the Shaftesbury Memorial Fountain (1886-93) by Alfred Gilbert with the winged figure of Eros above; the first use of aluminium on a large-scale English monument. It rapidly became a London icon and the focus for flower-sellers and newspaper boys.

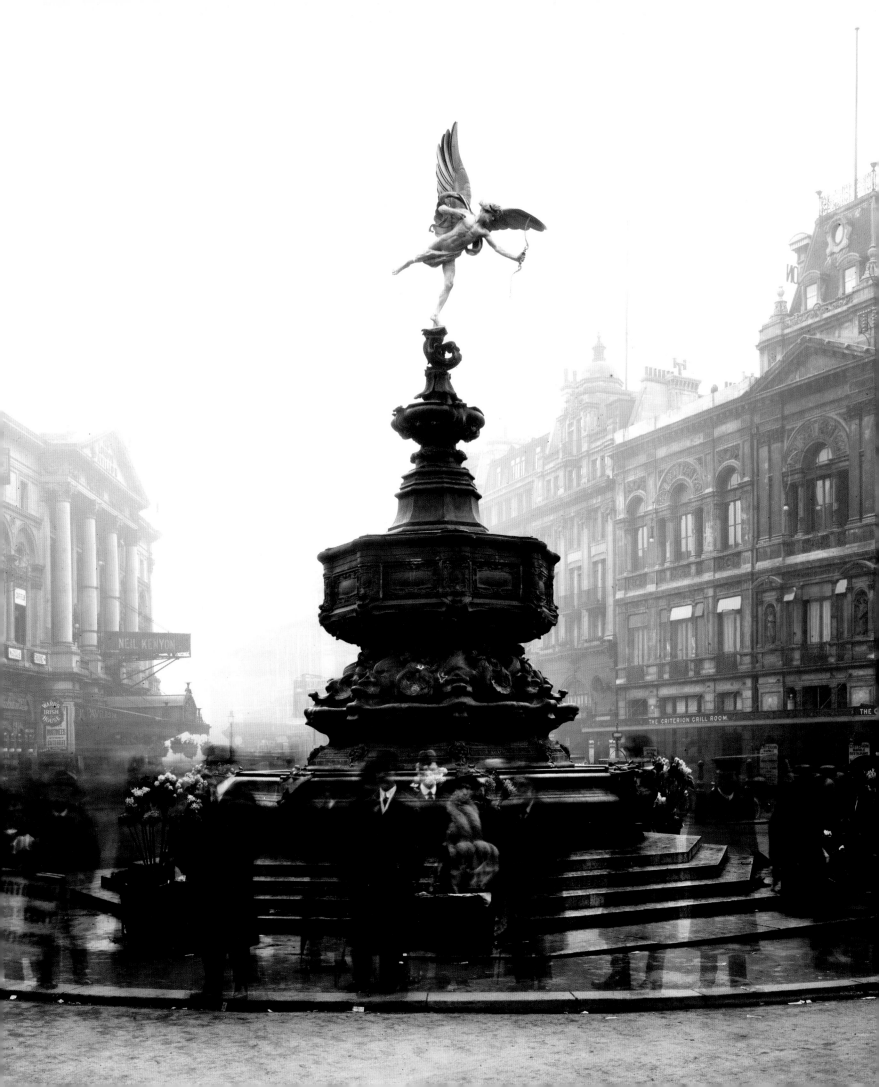

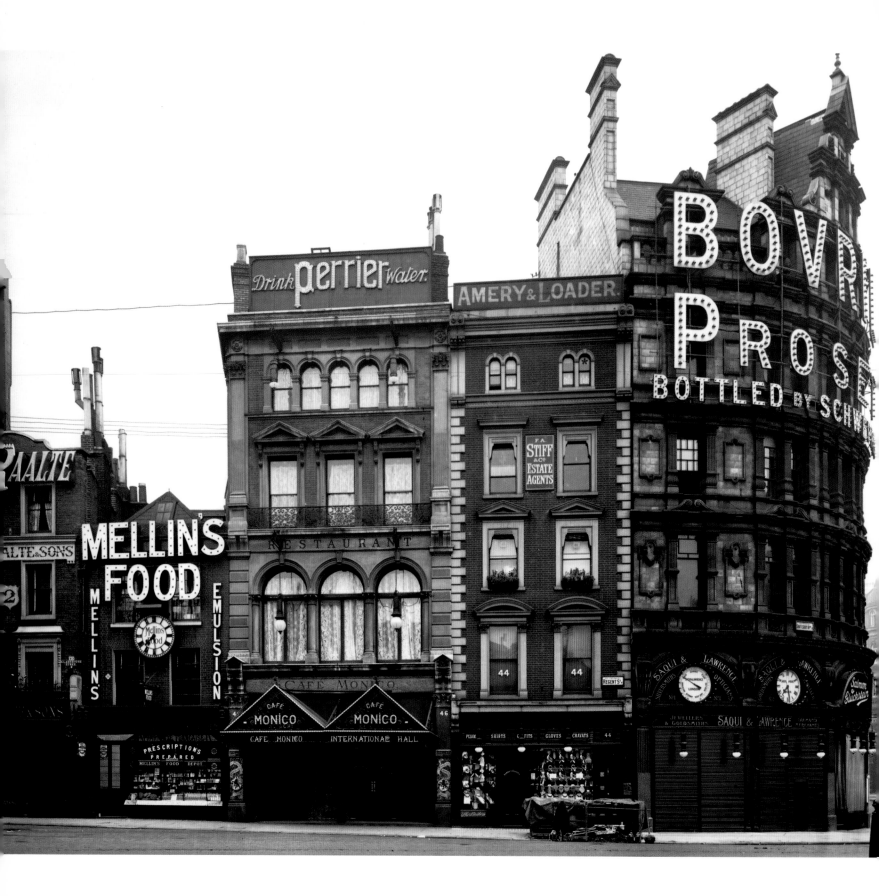

Above: 44-48 Regent Street, 1910

Elaborate advertising attached to prominent buildings was a hallmark of the Victorian city, but in the 1890s illuminated lettering began to be introduced. By 1910 it was well-established on the north-east corner of Piccadilly Circus in spite of attempts by the London County Council to resist it. The first illuminated sign above fascia level was probably Mellins Pharmacy at number 48, but it was almost certainly unauthorised. The Crown Estate Commissioners resisted similar displays on the Criterion, Swan & Edgar and other adjacent buildings under their control through strict covenants.

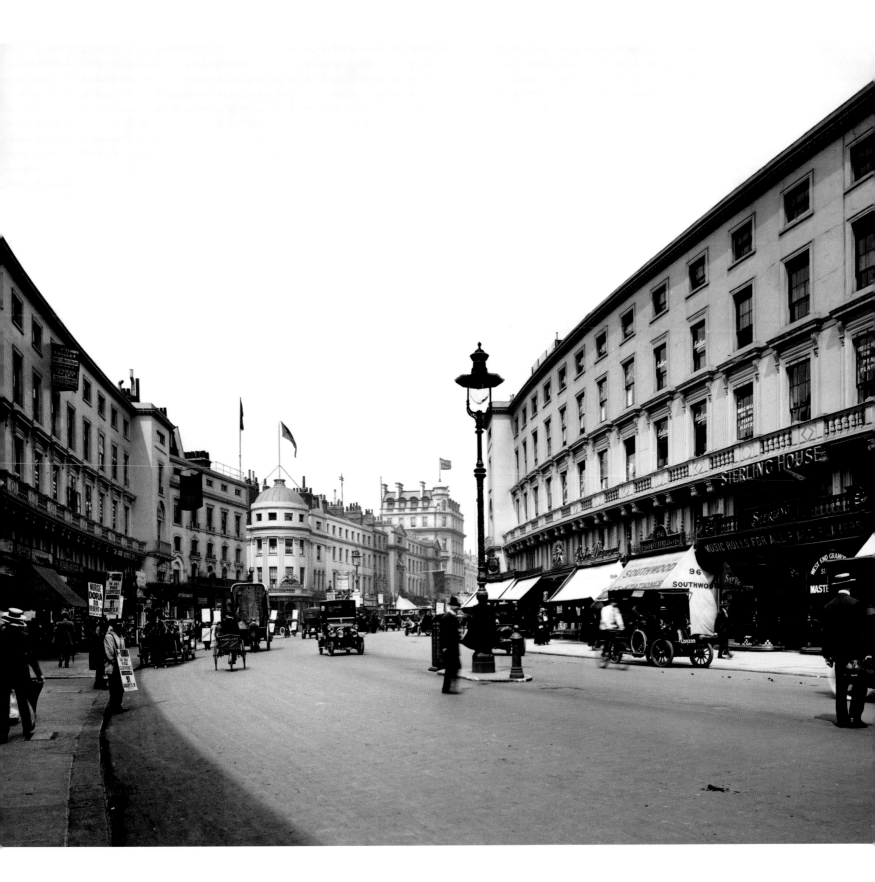

Above: Regent Street, c 1910

Only once has a great plan for London been conceived and completed. The great metropolitan improvements of the Regency created a whole new spine through the centre of the West End and triggered a wave of northward expansion. Built as a personal speculation by John Nash between 1818-19, originally the Quadrant had continuous Doric colonnades running in a great curve from the projecting pavilions which can be seen (above). These were removed in 1848 to improve daylight and discourage vice.

View showing the Quadrant in 1910 prior to reconstruction. In the distance is a new office building breaking Nash's carefully orchestrated parapet line.

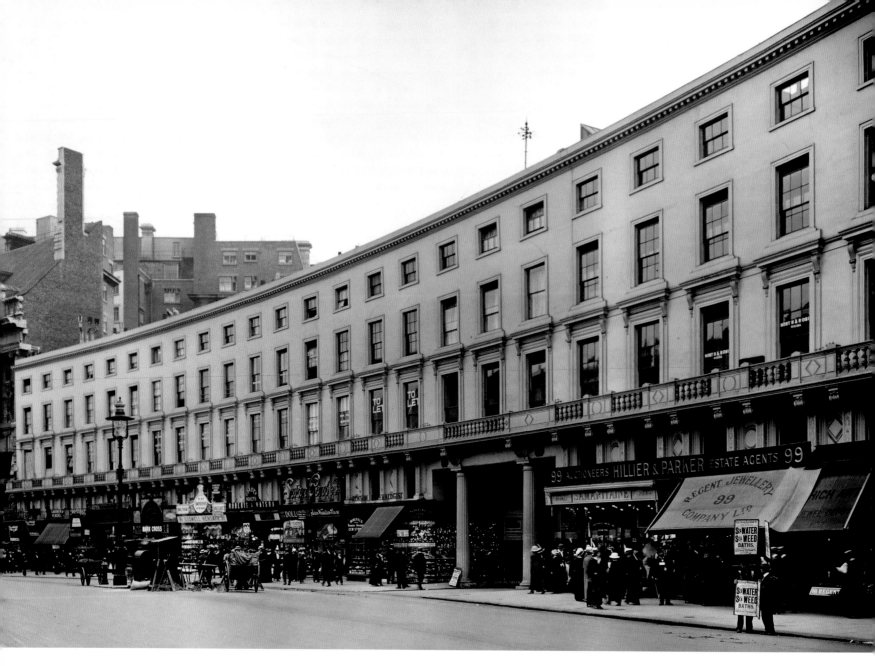

The outbreak of war

Above: 83-89 Regent Street, 4 August 1914

There is little evidence that this was taken on the day Britain declared war on Germany. Life appears to continue as normal with the sandwich-boards promoting seaweed baths in Great Portland Street. To the left is the abrupt end of Norman Shaw's Piccadilly Hotel which triggered the complete reconstruction of the remainder of Regent Street as the leases progressively expired.

Right: 153-167 Regent Street, 8 August 1912

View of the west side south of New Burlington Street showing the elaborate ironwork over Hudson Bay House, the International Fur Store, and a battery of royal warrants over shopfronts.

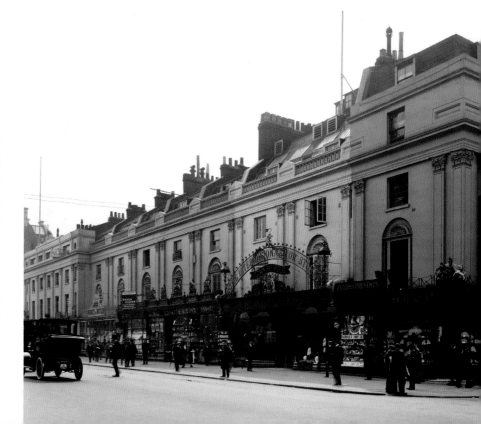

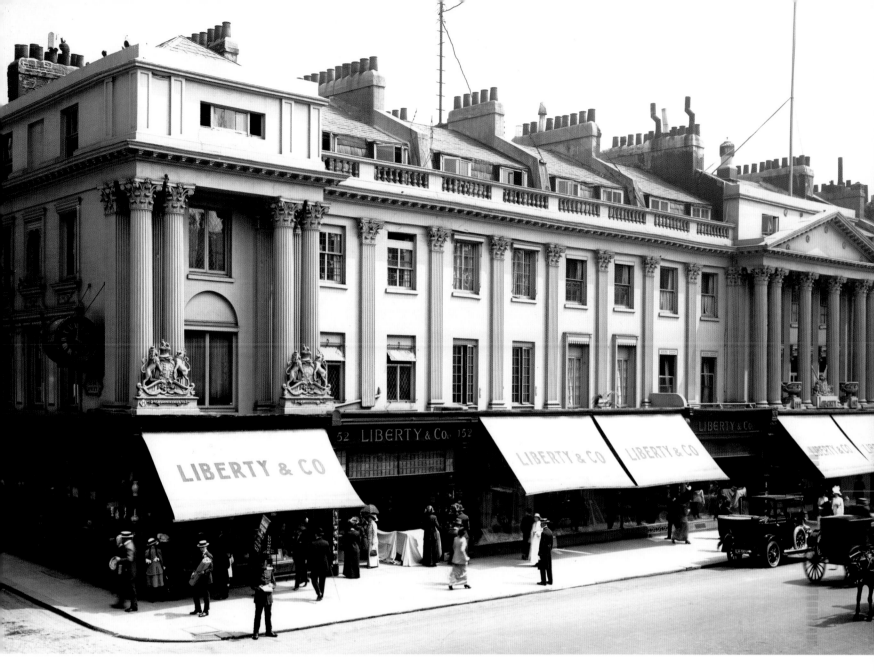

Above: 142-154 Regent Street, 1913
Originally Liberty's store stood on the east side of Regent Street south of the junction with Beak Street which can be seen to the left, before it relocated further north in the early 1920s.

Right: 169-191 Regent Street, 9 October 1913
View of the west side with New Burlington Street to the left and a newly-completed office building in the distance breaking Nash's symmetrical composition.

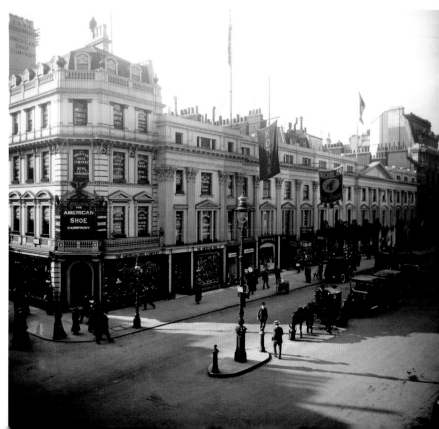

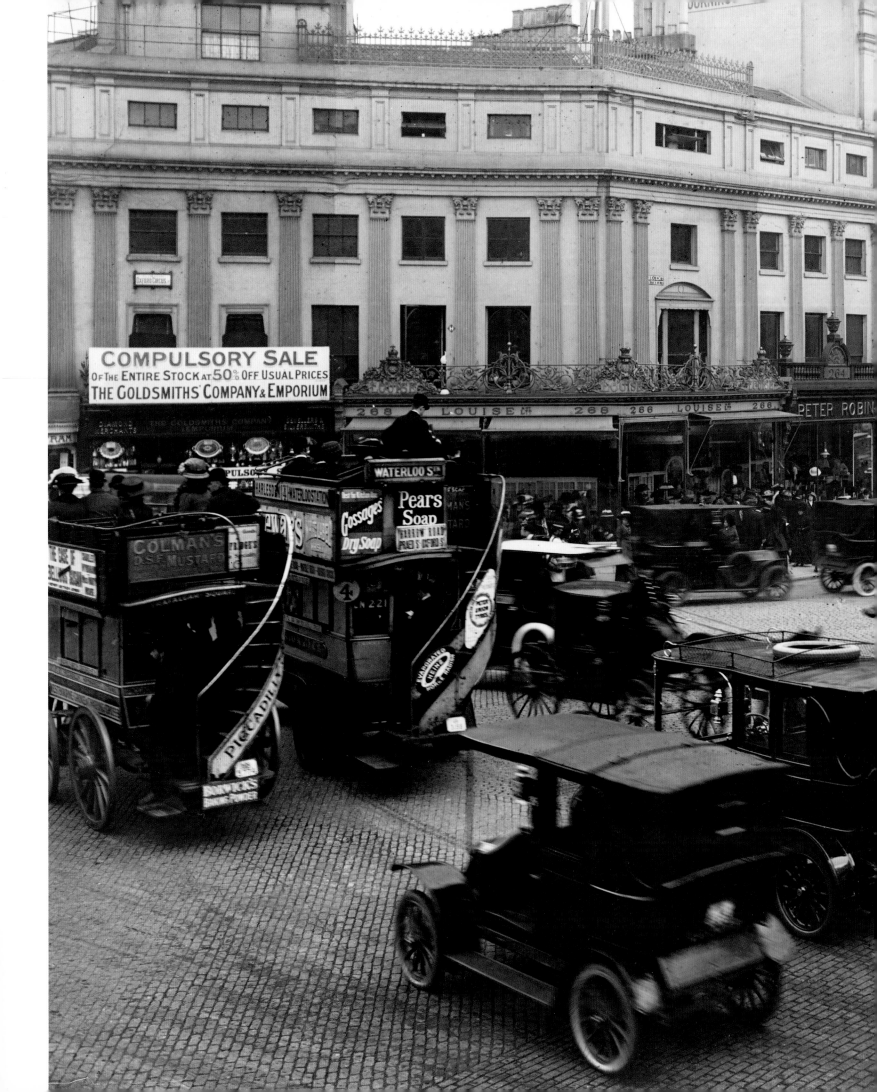

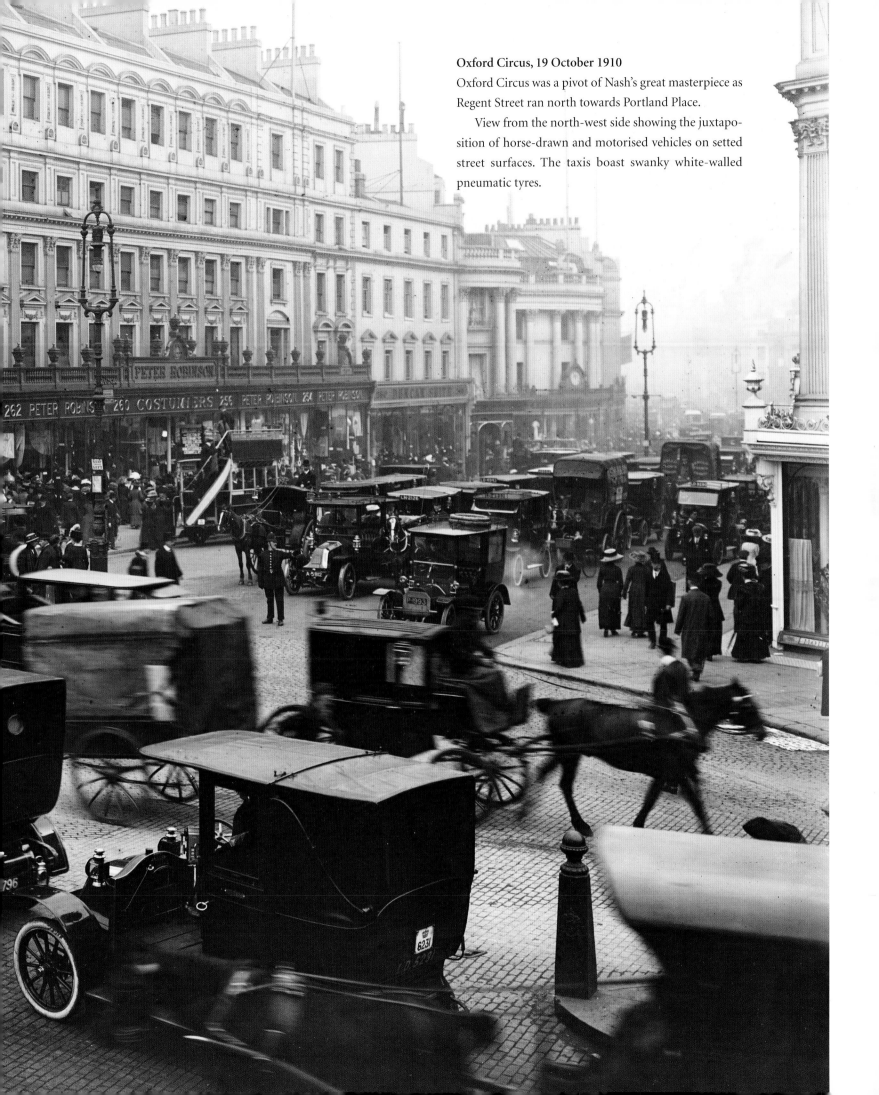

Oxford Circus, 19 October 1910
Oxford Circus was a pivot of Nash's great masterpiece as Regent Street ran north towards Portland Place.

View from the north-west side showing the juxtaposition of horse-drawn and motorised vehicles on setted street surfaces. The taxis boast swanky white-walled pneumatic tyres.

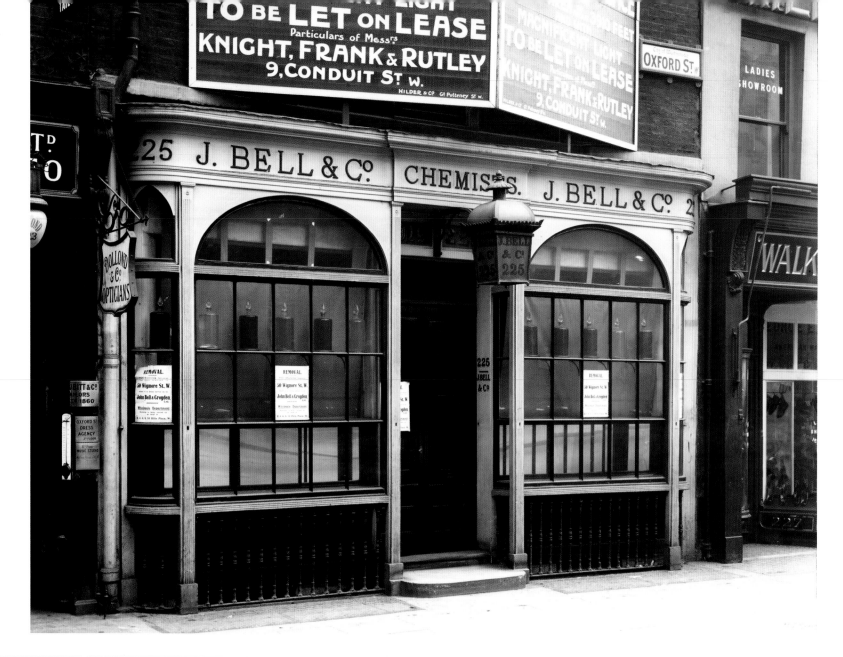

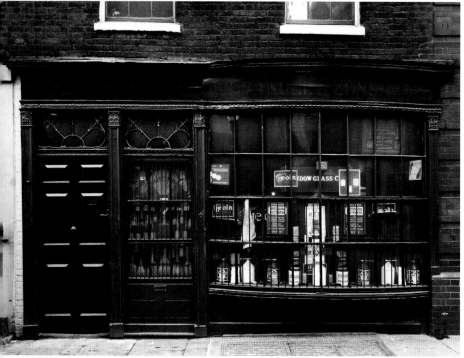

Above: 225 Oxford Street, 2 January 1908

John Bell & Co, traded from this delightful late 18th century shopfront for over a century before amalgamating with Croyden & Co, and relocating to Wigmore Street. The building was redeveloped in 1909 for the London Cinematograph Co, later the home of the Studio One and Studio Two cinemas.

MARYLEBONE

Left: 7 George Street, Marylebone Lane, c 1906

A fine late 18th century shopfront with leaded fanlights, a shallow curved window subdivided by glazing bars, and a raised and fielded panelled entrance door to the upper floors.

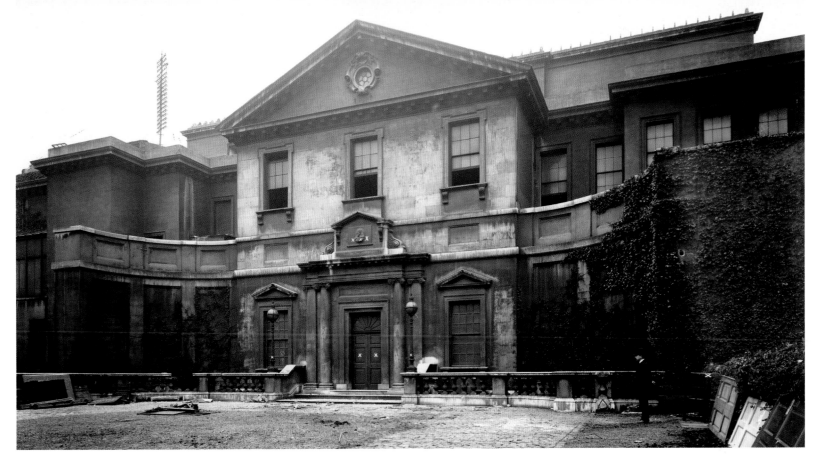

Lost at cards

Above: Harcourt House, Cavendish Square, 11 June 1906

Harcourt House, built by Lord Bingley in 1722-23 and designed by Thomas Archer, occupied the whole of the western side of Cavendish Square. Lost at cards by Lord Harcourt in 1825, it passed to the reclusive Duke of Portland who commissioned Thomas Cundy to rebuild the main frontage seen here. Regarded as "*a dull, heavy drowsy-looking house, which has about it an air of seclusion and privacy almost monastic*" (*Old and New London*), its seclusion was increased by high perimeter screen walls of cast iron and ground glass.

The medallion over the entrance is of Inigo Jones. The white crosses mark items for salvage.

Below left: First floor ceiling. The delicate painted plasterwork suggests a house that was far from dull and heavy inside.

Below right: The staircase and entrance hall in the process of stripping out and demolition.

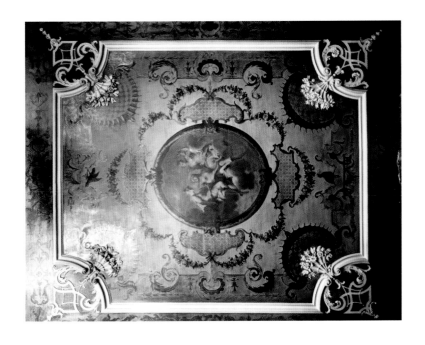

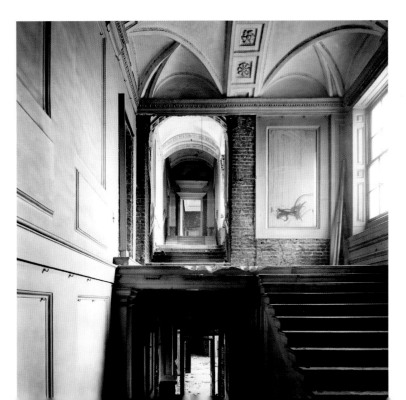

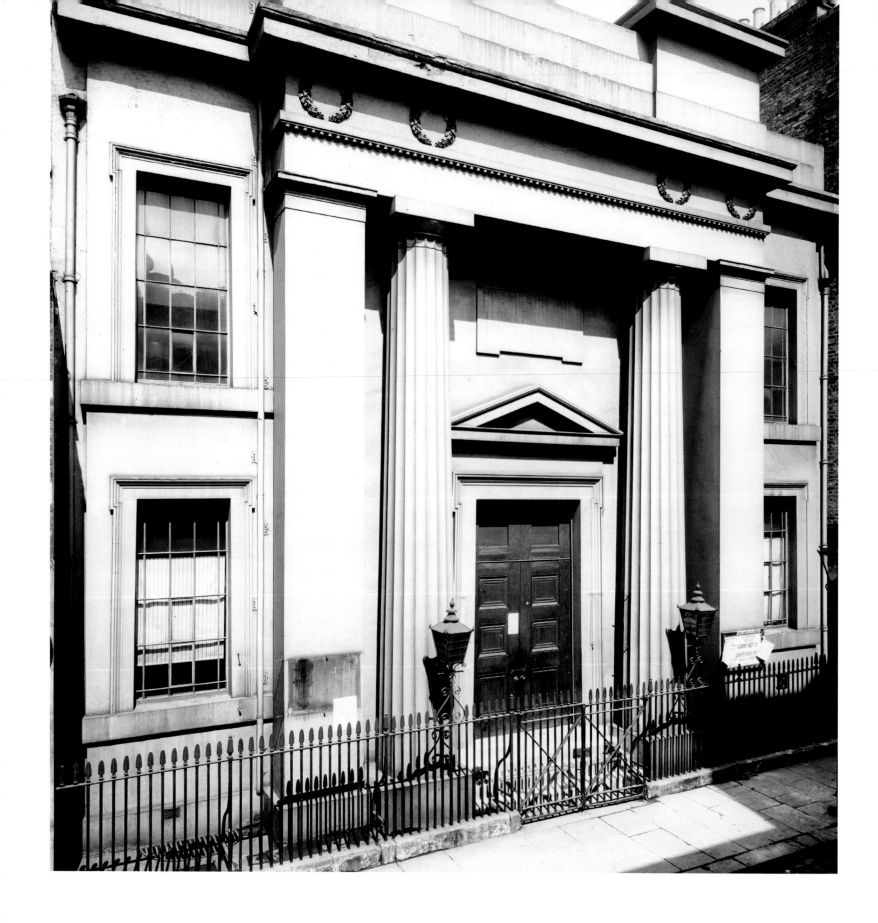

Above: Unitarian Chapel, Little Portland Street, 14 August 1909

The splendid Greek Doric frontage of the Little Portland Street Unitarian Chapel shortly before it was demolished to make way for a Masonic banqueting hall as an extension of Pagani's Restaurant. Dr Martineau, the charismatic preacher and philosophic champion of Theism, was pastor from 1857-69. Both George Eliot and Charles Dickens were among those who listened to his teachings here.

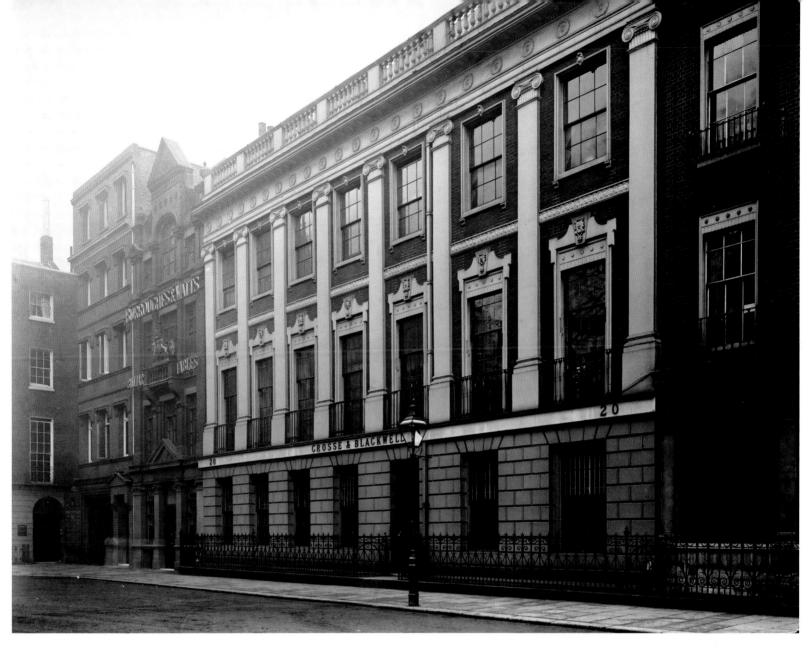

Bohemian streets & squares

SOHO

Above: Fauconberg House, 20 Soho Square, c 1908
Robert Adam remodelled an earlier 17th century house on the site for John Grant, a sugar planter from Grenada as a fashionable new London town house in the early 1770s. In 1858 it was taken over by Crosse & Blackwell, who owned the adjacent building, and used as offices and bottling rooms.

Right: View of the chimneypiece and ceiling in the Chief's Room at Crosse & Blackwell, 9 July 1908
It was redecorated in the mid-Victorian period in a lavish faux-mediaeval style, including this monumental chimneypiece. The ceiling was enriched with heraldic motifs and the arms of English Kings and nobles. On its demolition in 1924, Adam's original ceiling was discovered beneath.

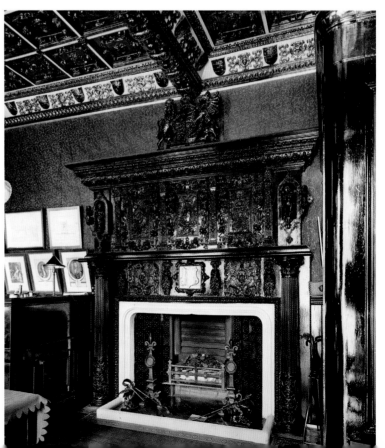

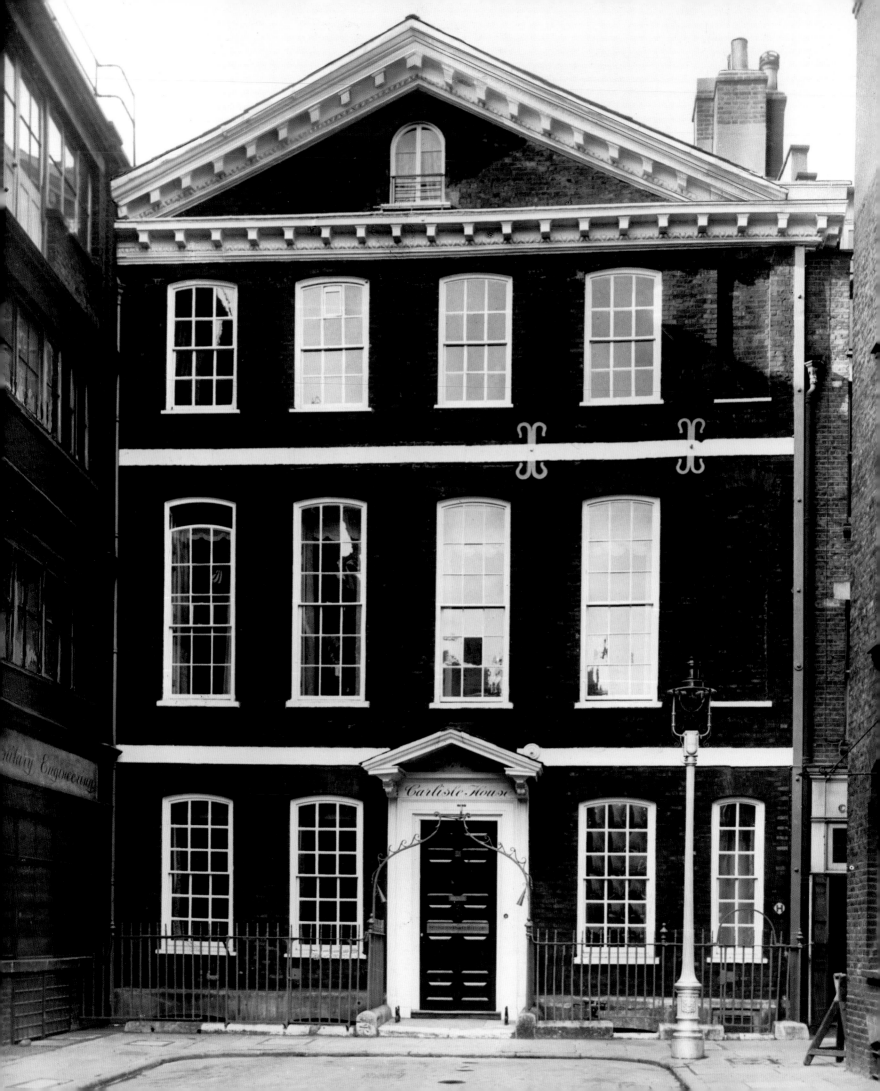

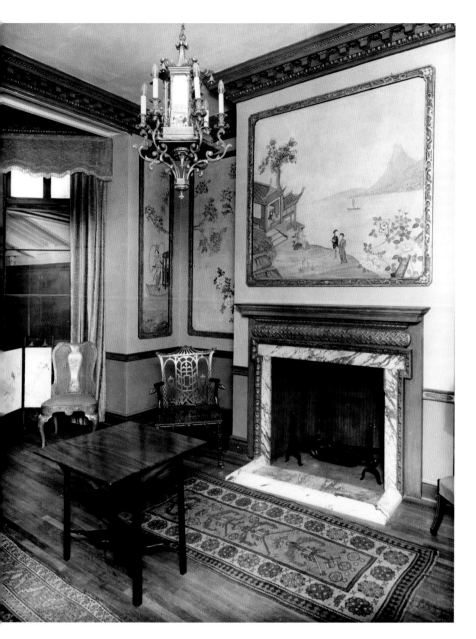

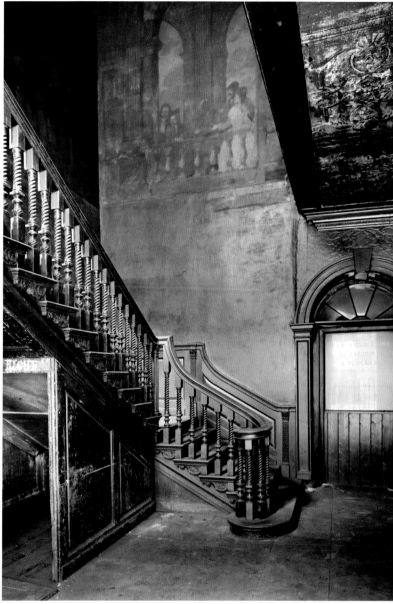

A school of manners

Opposite: Carlisle House, Carlisle Street, c 1910

Completed in 1687, Carlisle House was probably built by three speculative builders on the western edge of Soho Fields. From 1763 until the early 1780s it was the residence of Domenico Angelo, riding and fencing master to the Prince of Wales, and the most fashionable school of arms and manners in London. David Garrick, Thomas Sheridan, George Stubbs and Sir Joshua Reynolds were frequent visitors, after which it was subdivided as it became less fashionable. It was destroyed by enemy action on 11 May 1941.

Above left: The Chinese Room in the south-west corner of the house.

Above right: 75 Dean Street, 1 April 1912

The well-known painted staircase, falsely attributed to Sir James Thornhill, or his son-in-law, William Hogarth. The house was the subject of an unsuccessful battle to secure parliamentary confirmation of a Preservation Order under the Ancient Monuments Act 1913. After a two-day hearing in a select committee, the owners' petition was upheld. The house was demolished in 1923, but the staircase, hall and ground floor rooms were re-erected in the Art Institute of Chicago.

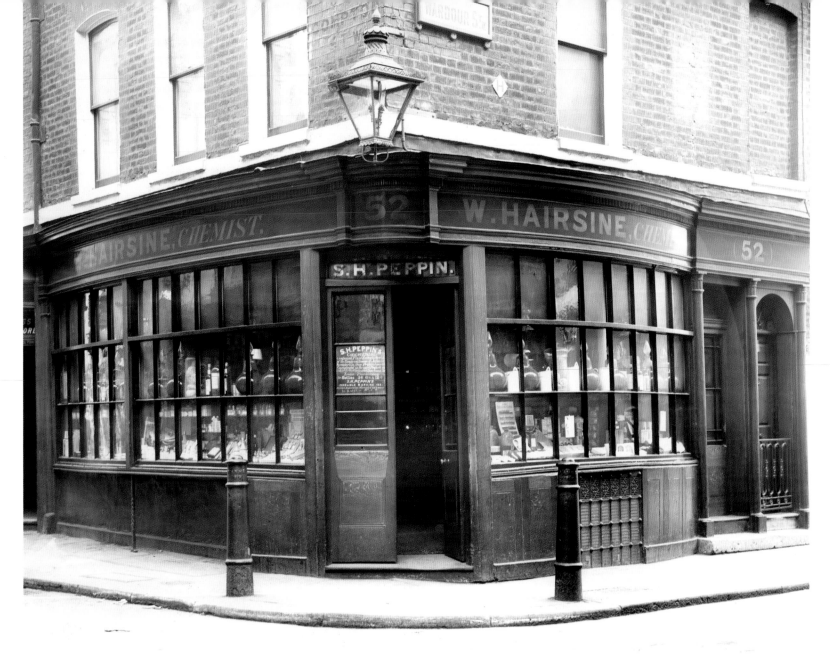

Above: 52 Wardour Street, c 1910
This elegant Regency shopfront with shallow bays to each frontage stood on the corner of Wardour Street and Old Compton Street until its demolition in the 1920s.

Right: 51-52 Frith Street, c 1905
Built in 1805 as two houses over a shop and manufactory, Nos. 51-52 Frith Street had elaborate rococo cast iron guard rails to the first floor windows over an imposing shopfront embellished with lions' heads and patterned fanlights.

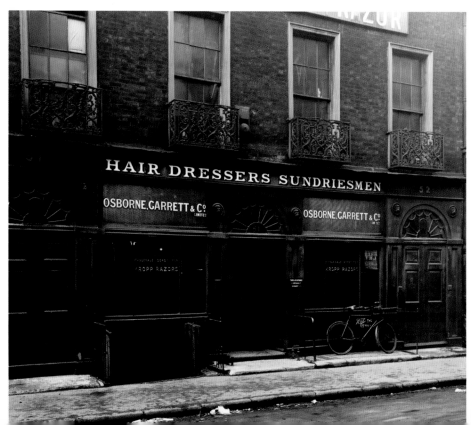

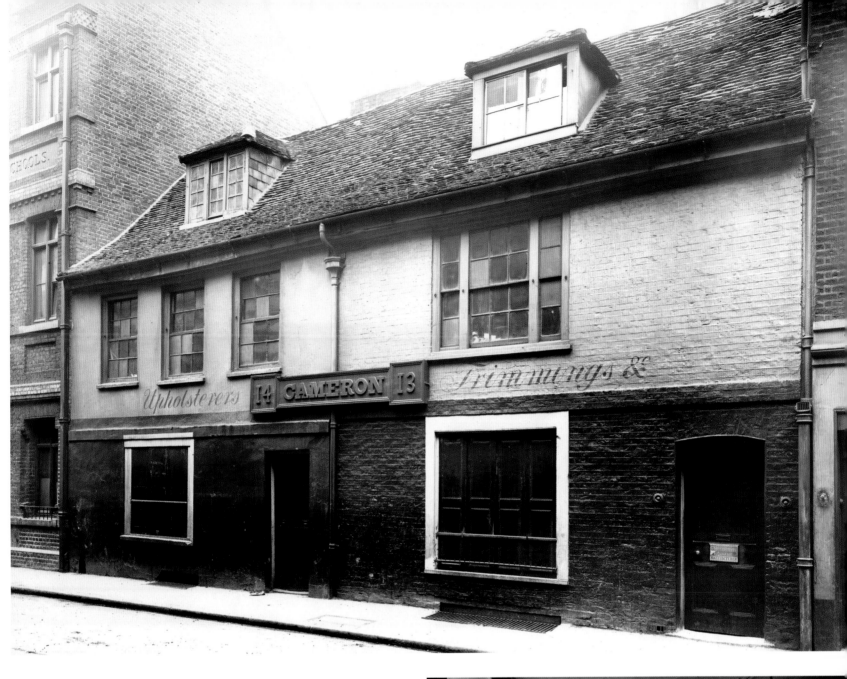

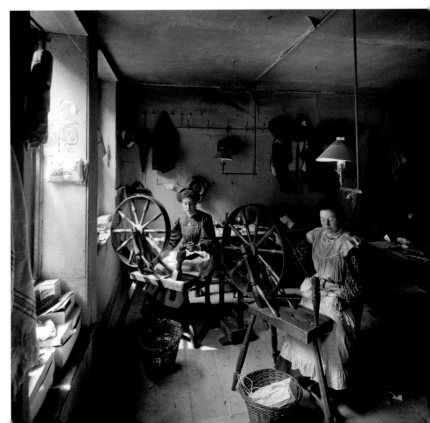

Above: 13 & 14 Archer Street, 15 March 1908

A remarkable survival of two modest artisans' cottages of 1700 with old clay tiled roofs broken by hipped dormer windows to light the garret. The buildings were demolished in 1912 to make way for new headquarters for the Orchestral Association.

Right: 13 & 14 Archer Street, 20 May 1908

The upper floors of many Soho houses were given over to workshops, often serving the larger West End stores, particularly the rag trade. In this case the two women are engaged in upholstery and trimming for the furniture trade.

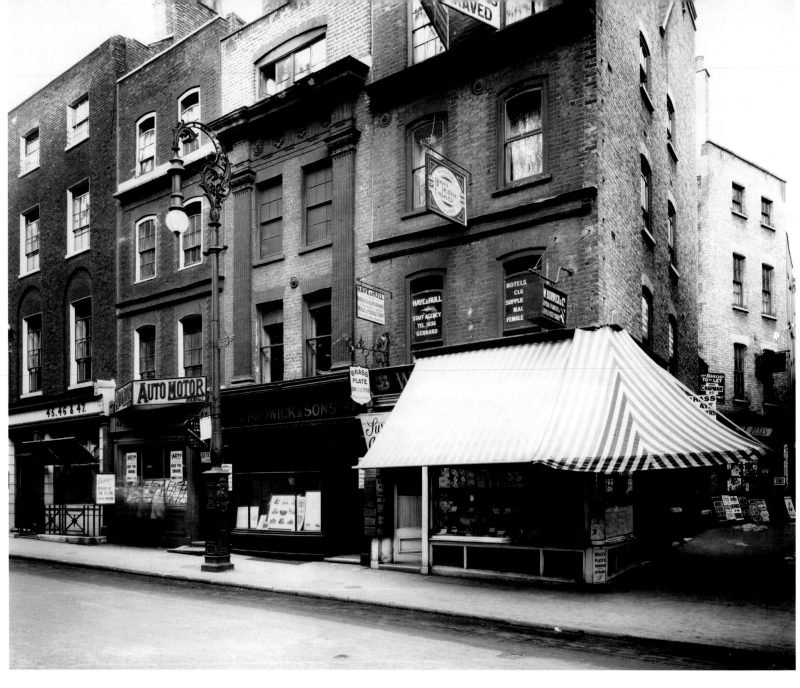

Above: 42, 43 & 44 St Martin's Lane, 22 September 1910

An interesting group of early 18th century houses on the east side built by Thomas Parton in 1739, together with May's Buildings which can be seen to the right. In the foreground is a characteristic St Martin's in the Fields lamp column with delicate Art Nouveau detail. They are still in widespread use.

Right: Coliseum, St Martin's Lane, c 1900

An eerily atmospheric view of the old vaults discovered under the site of the Coliseum prior to its construction in 1902–04.

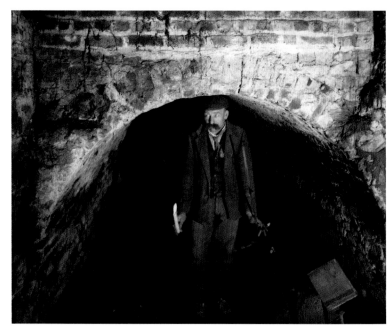

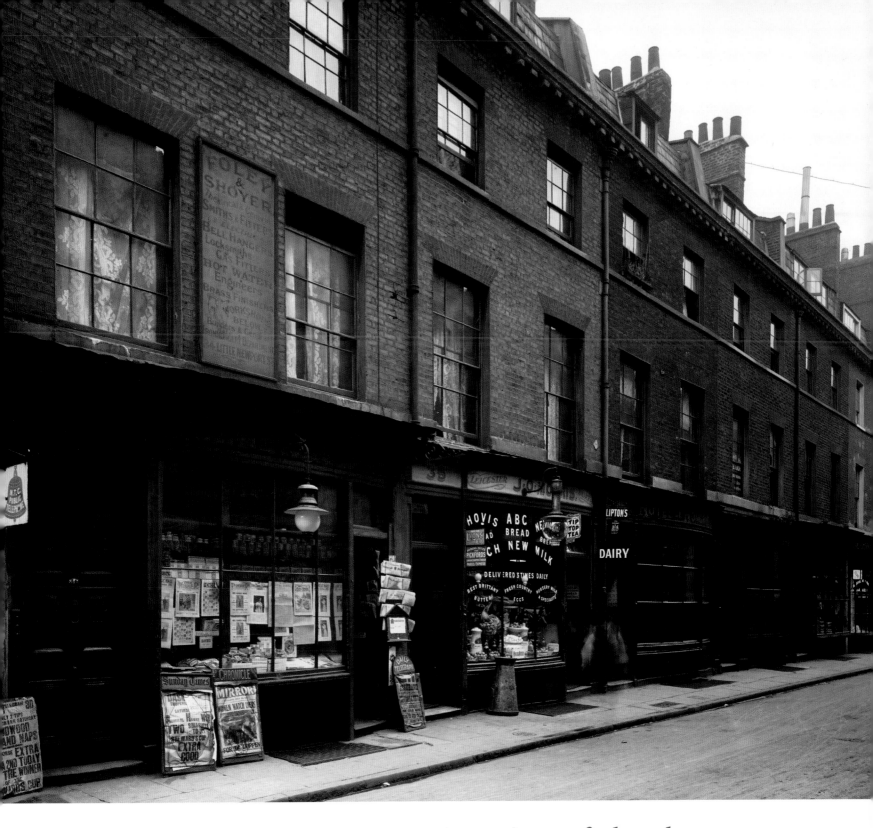

A nation of shopkeepers

Above: 34-39 Lisle Street, Soho, 26 July 1910

A fine terrace of late 18th century houses with a good run of contemporary shopfronts and a wealth of detail. The newsagents to the left has an enamel sign for the National Telephone Company to advertise a public telephone prior to the introduction of street kiosks. The placard for the *Mirror* leads with "Women watch for Dr Crippen". A similar terrace still survives on the north side now used by the Chinese community as shops and restaurants.

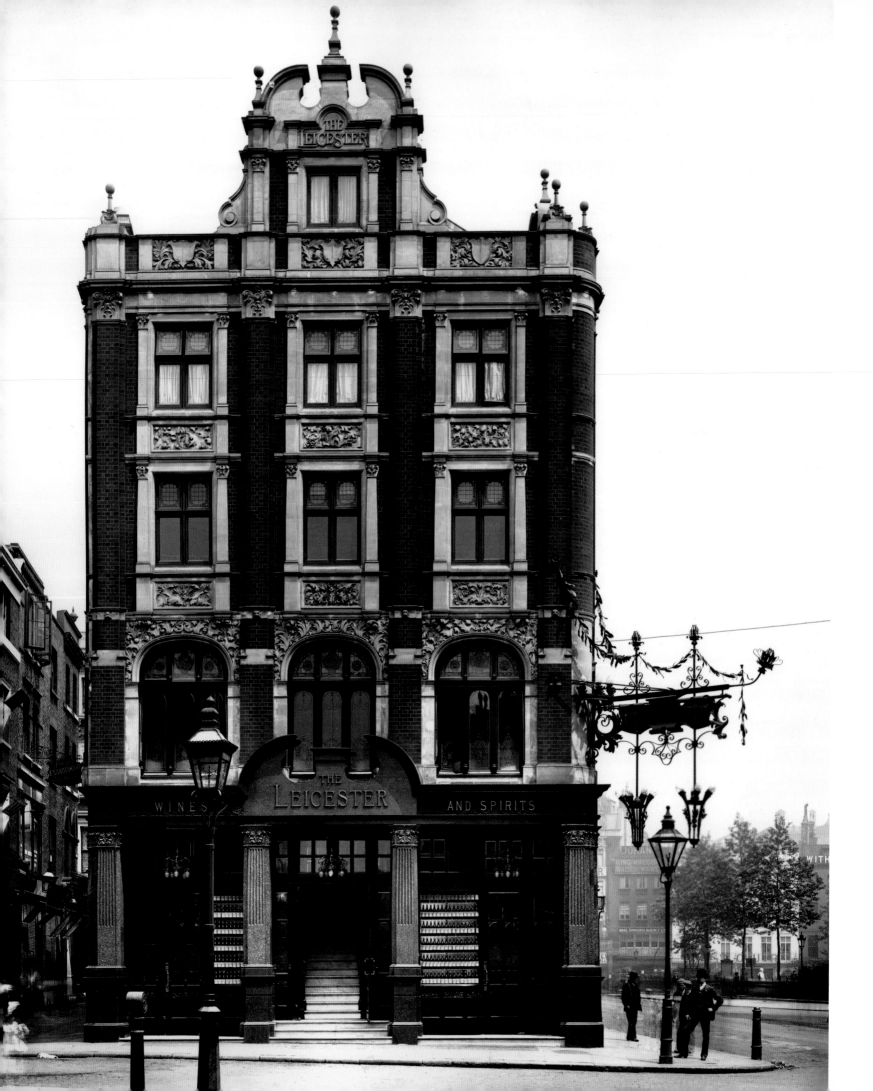

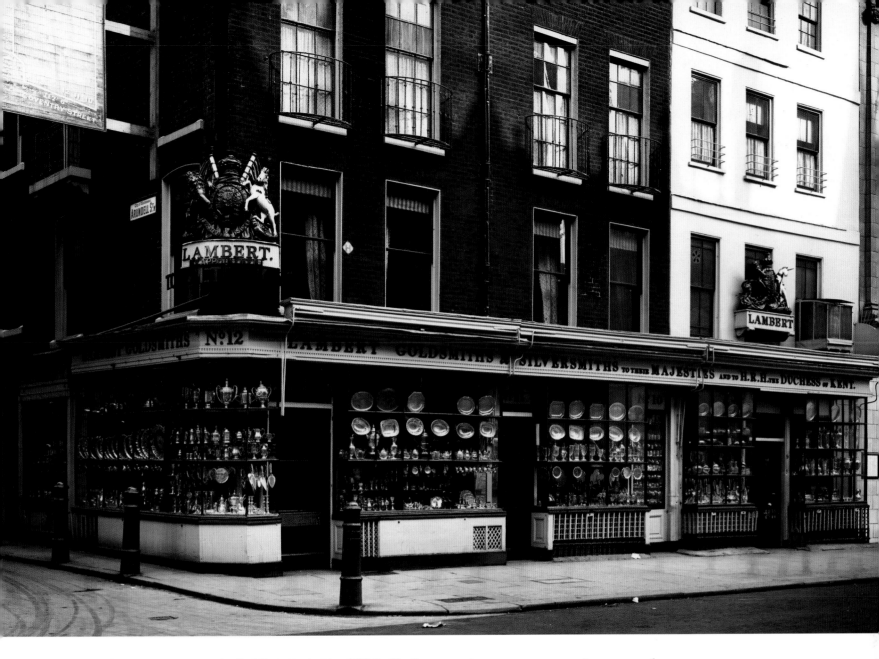

Ornate gin palace

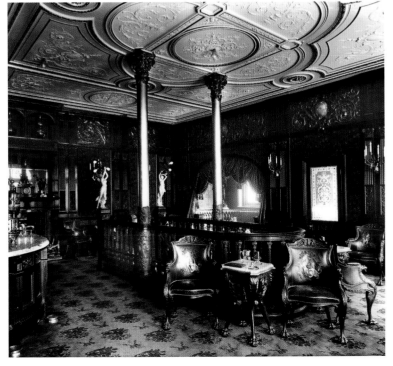

Opposite: The Leicester, Leicester Square, c 1905
The Leicester, on the corner of Wardour Street at the junction with Leicester Square, was renowned for its spectacular ornamental ironwork. A battery of angled mirrors can be seen in the passageway to the left to improve the daylighting.

Left: The opulent lounge bar on the first floor.

Above: 10-12 Coventry Street, 17 March 1914
Lambert's, gold and silversmiths, proudly displays the royal warrants over a fine range of early 19th century shopfronts. Nos. 10-12 were demolished in 1920 for an extension of the Lyons Corner House which obliterated Arundell Street.

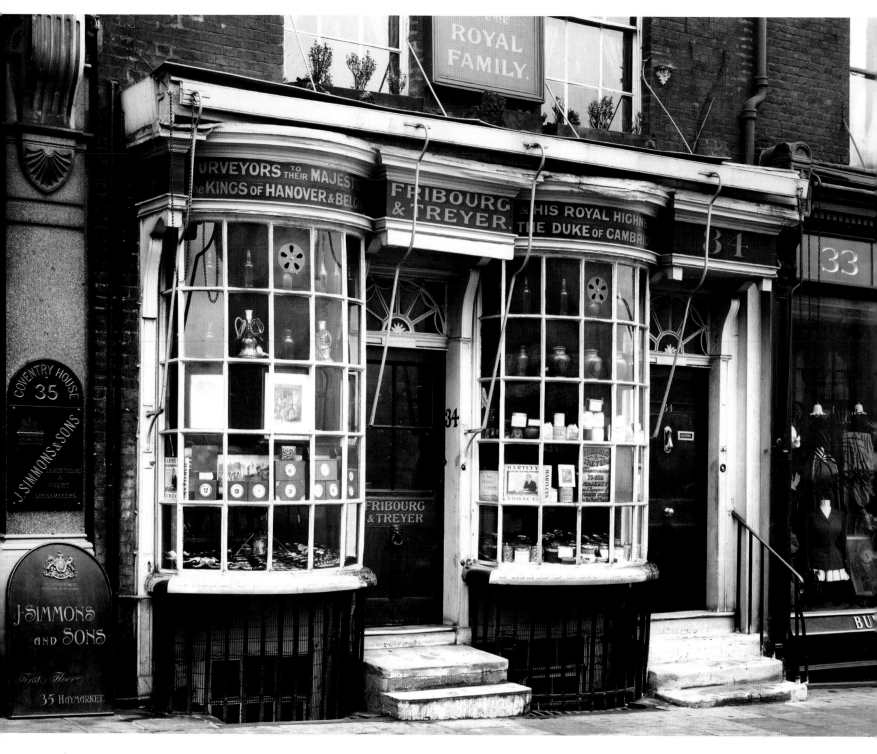

The royal tobacconist

ST JAMES'S

Above: 34 Haymarket, 7 December 1908

Fribourg and Treyer, purveyors of snuff and tobacco, began trading in 1751, but closed in 1977. The delightful bow-fronted shopfront, the oldest in London, with its separate side entrance to the upper floors and wrought iron grilles, still survives as a gift shop, but it has lost much of its original character.

Opposite top: View of the shop interior and fittings looking towards the street.

Opposite below: The delicate Adam period screen which divided the rear part of the shop from the front remains in situ in the new shop.

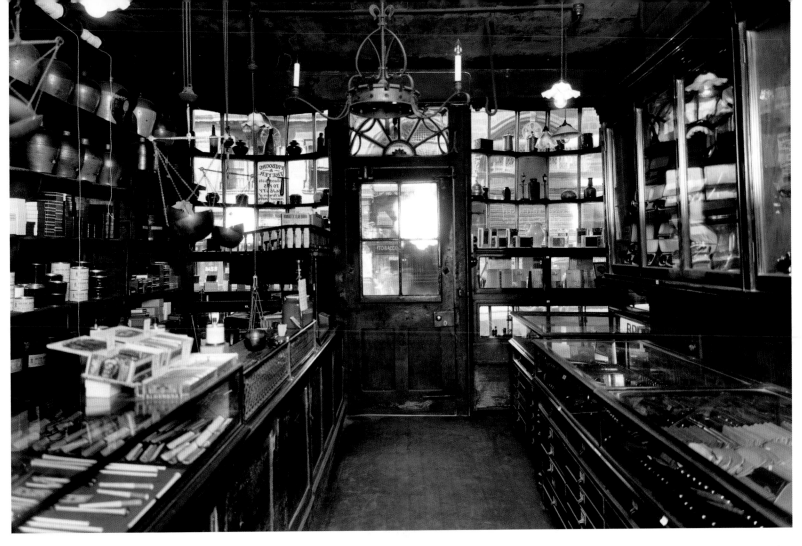

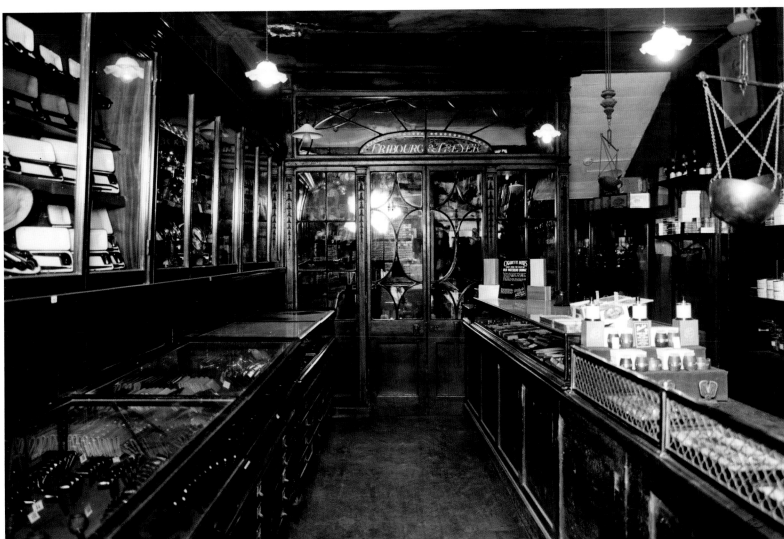

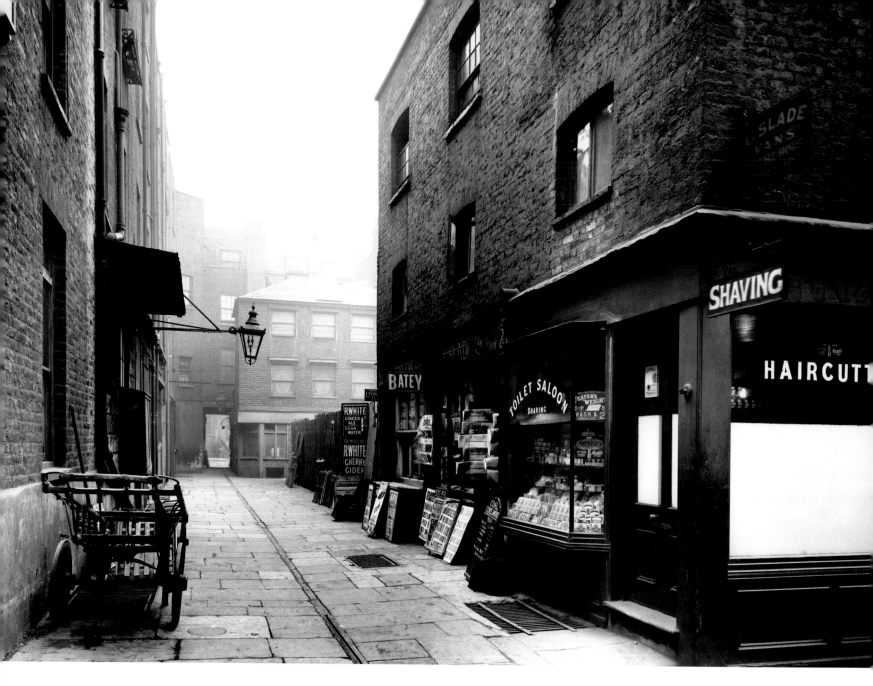

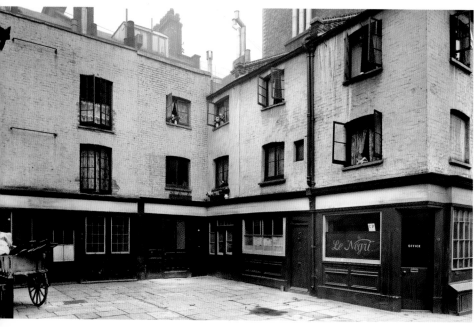

Above: St James's Market, Haymarket, 6 November 1908
St James's Market was built in 1663-66 to serve the newly-planned quarter around St James's Square. Rebuilt by Nash in 1817-18, the modest brick dwellings were levelled in 1916. The passageway in the distance led into the Haymarket.

Left: View of the south side of the market.

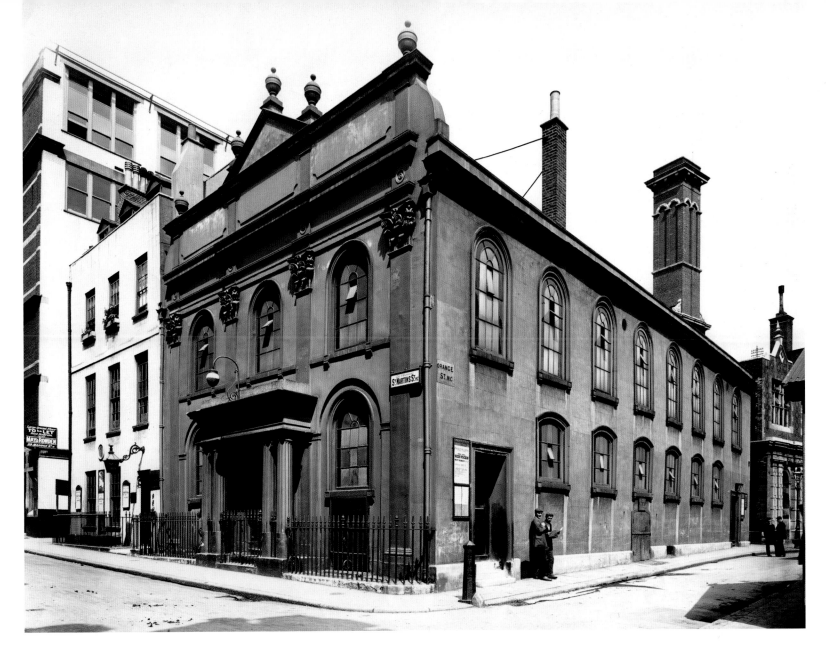

Above: Orange Street Congregational Chapel, St Martin's Street, 23 July 1906

Orange Street Chapel was used by the Huguenots from its foundation in 1693 until 1787 when it was taken over and converted into a Congregational chapel, which closed in 1917. A small replacement chapel was built in 1929 in Orange Street. The adjacent house was the home of Sir Isaac Newton from 1711 until his death in 1727. Fifty years later Fanny Burney lived there. Dr Johnson, David Garrick and Sir Joshua Reynolds were frequent visitors. The house and chapel were demolished in 1913 for Westminster Public Library.

MAYFAIR

Right: 9-11 Shepherd Market, Mayfair, 4 November 1911

Shepherd Market serviced the grander houses of Mayfair, but in 1911 it was an enclave of dingy, rundown streets surrounded by great wealth.

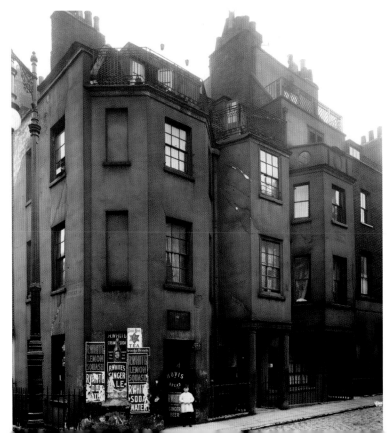

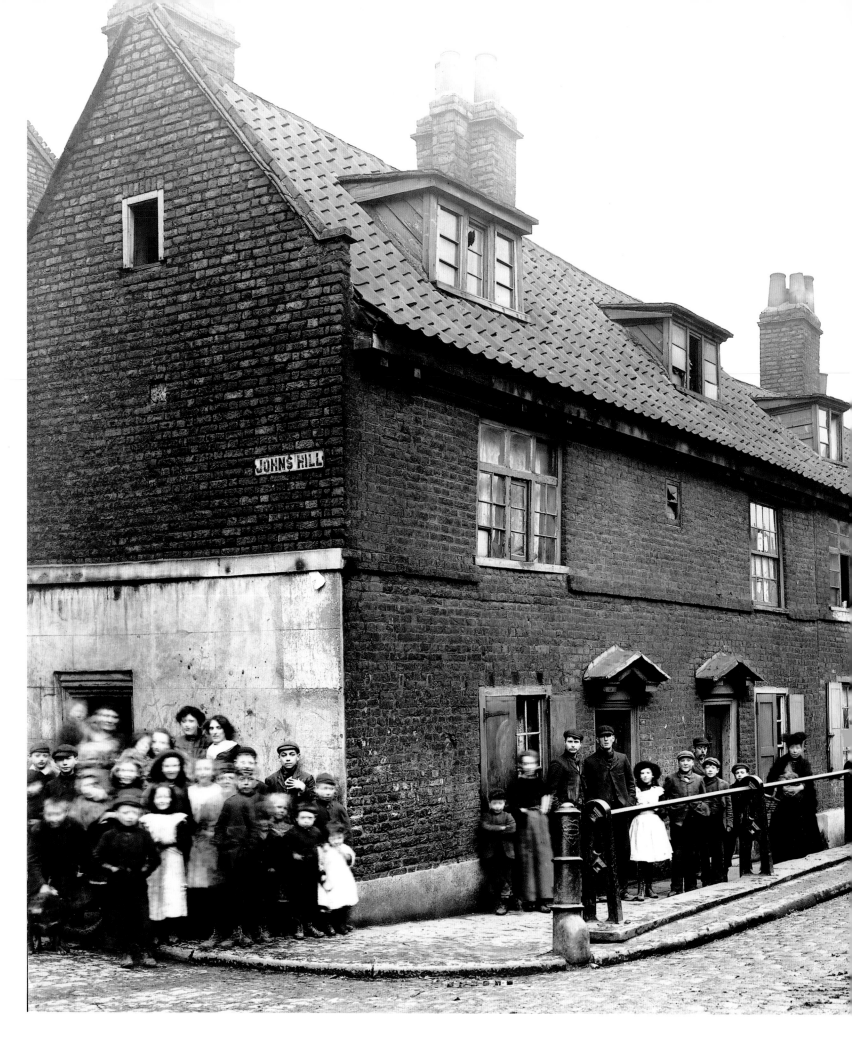

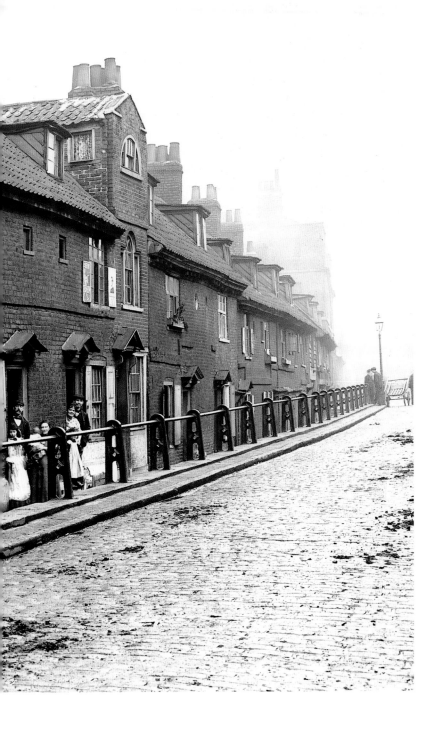

Pennington Street, December 1906

This long range of late 17th century dwellings stood directly opposite the enclosing wall and warehouses of London Dock. The poignant figures in the foreground were poor, but respectable. All are well-shod and most have hats or caps.

CHAPTER FIVE

CITY OF DREADFUL NIGHT

The East End

Cheek by jowl with the wealth of the City of London lay a completely different world – the East End: three square miles of densely-packed streets of terraced housing stretching east to the river Lea and shading imperceptibly northwards into the fringes of Hackney.

Over 1 million people from all corners of the earth were crammed into a labyrinth of streets, courts and alleys – a vast reservoir of cheap labour employed in casual work, sweated trades, or the Docks.

For the respectable poor home, was a rented room, or for the more fortunate, a house; for the less fortunate, a common lodging-house, the streets or the workhouse. It was a place of poverty, hardship, crime and degradation leavened only by an indomitable sense of humour and a deep-seated sense of community.

The river and the Docks continued to exert a powerful influence; the only escape from repetitive drudgery being the pub, which offered transient solace to those who could afford it; and for those who could, particularly for women, the risk of moral decline, many of whom descended from alcoholism to casual prostitution. The high population density supported a large number of small shops serving their local communities interspersed with workshops and small factories along the river and canals, or crowded into dingy backyards.

By 1900 some of the older trades, like silk weaving, were in sharp decline replaced by immigrants engaged in tailoring and the rag trade. Over 90% of the population of Stepney were immigrants or the children of immigrants, mainly East European Jews. Increasingly, radical improvements swept aside some of the worst slums, and the lives of many slowly improved, supported by charitable and philanthropic undertakings. The first Peabody block in London was in Commercial Street in 1864. Over 40 years later the LCC's Boundary Estate replaced the notorious slums around Old Nichol Street in Bethnal Green.

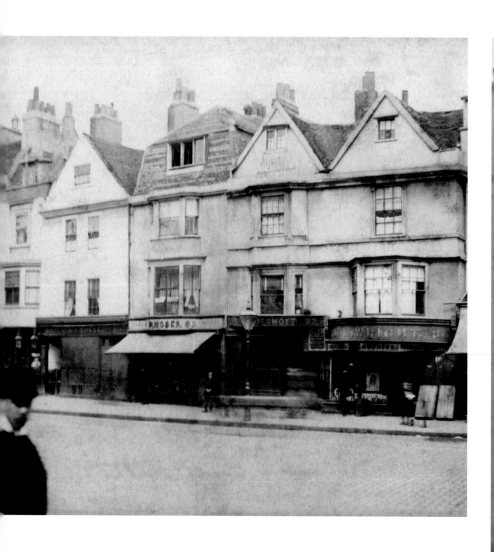

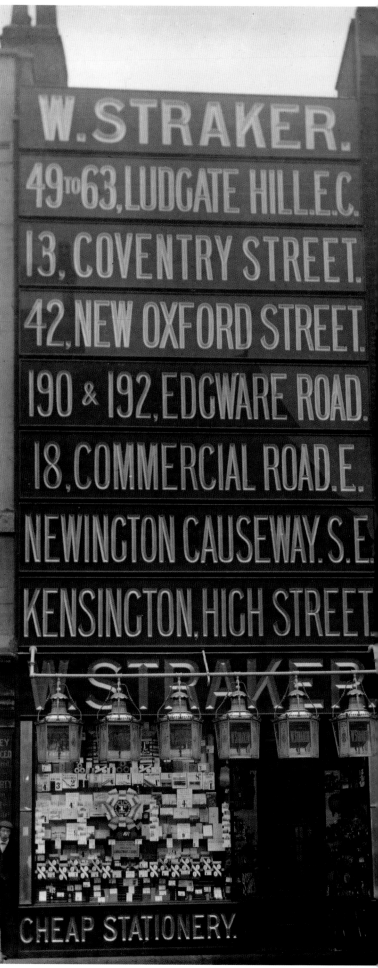

WHITECHAPEL

Above: 81-84 Whitechapel High Street, 1904
This interesting group of 17th century, timber-framed houses stood on the site of the Whitechapel Art Gallery and Library. To the left is The Angel public house, to the right, W Wright's photographic studio.

Right: 278 Whitechapel Road, 4 October 1899
Straker's stationers with a magnificent array of gas lanterns across the fascia. The entire upper floor is covered with incised gilded panels advertising other branches.

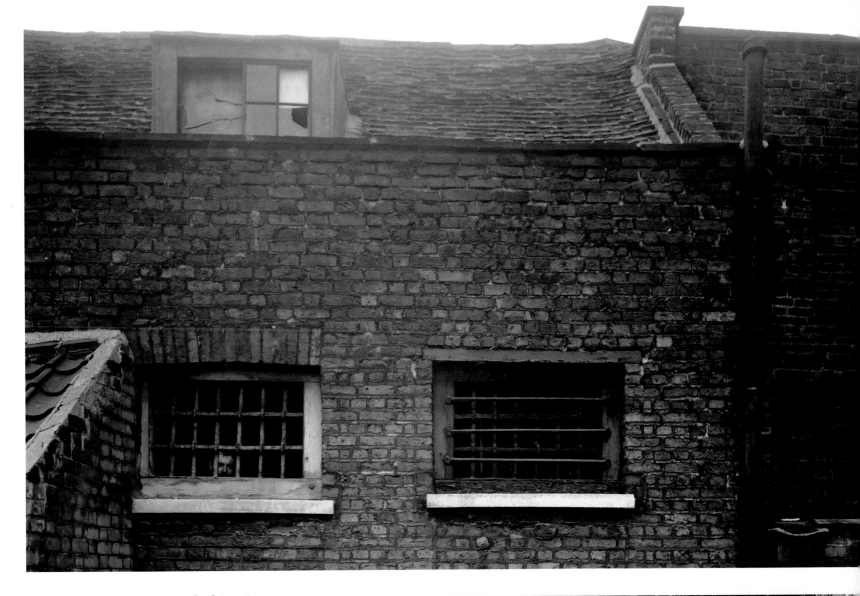

Passage to oblivion

STEPNEY

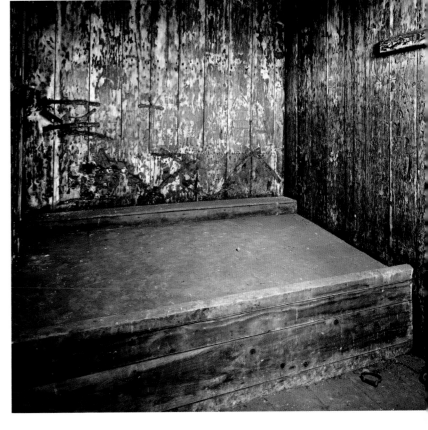

Above: The Old Court House, Wellclose Square, Stepney, 17 August 1911
The Old Court House on the south side of Wellclose Square was formerly
the High Court of the Liberties of the Tower behind which stood the oldest
cells in London outside the Tower.

A massive barred door with a peephole led to a winding stone staircase
and two cells in a rear building, each with an iron grating fitted with a
shutter. Beneath the cells an underground passage, guarded by a skeleton,
allegedly led to the Tower but may have been used to conduct prisoners
direct to old convict ships moored in the river.

Right: Nearly half of each cell was filled by a wooden bed. Attached to the
walls were rusty manacles and a stiff canvas strait-jacket with iron rings
which could be fastened to the chains. The wooden walls were covered
with designs and inscriptions, the earliest being 1698, with several to
Edward Ray dated 27 December 1753. On demolition, one of the cells was
salvaged for display at the London Museum.

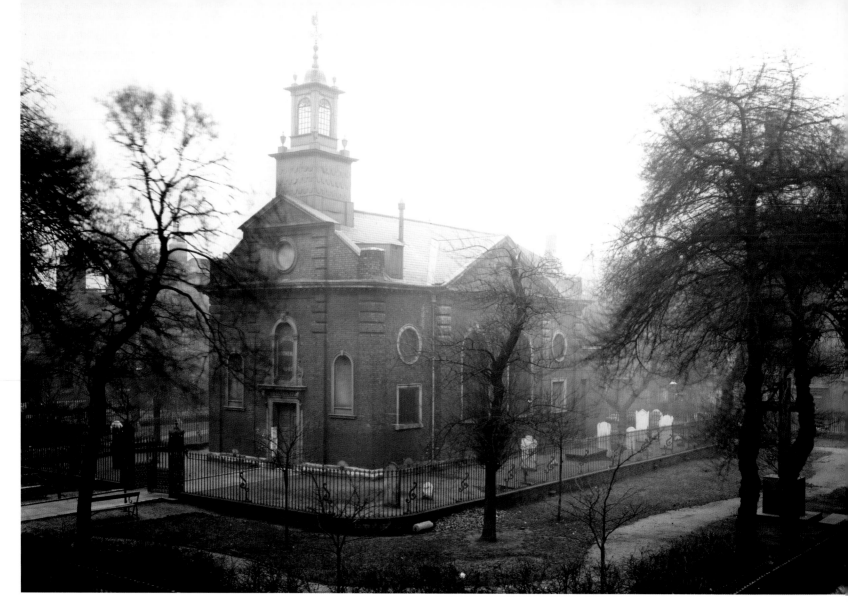

Church for seamen

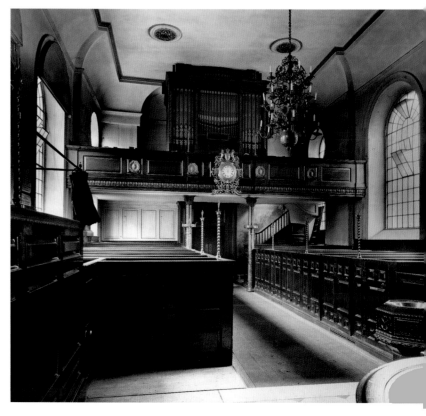

Above & right: Swedish Lutheran Church, Swedenborg Square, Stepney, 7 December 1908

Swedenborg Square (formerly Prince's Square) was occupied by naval families. At its centre was the Swedish Lutheran Church, opened in 1728. In 1772 the body of the mystic and philanthropist, Emanuel Swedenborg was interred in the crypt. In 1816 a Swedish captain *"whose sense of things outweighed his reverence for the remains of his great countryman, abstracted the cranium of Swedenborg with the aim of interring it in his own land"*. (*History of the Squares of London*: Chancellor). On the captain's death, it was returned.

Right: The interior, 2 June 1908, showing the organ loft and box pews.

The church was the focus of a protracted public appeal to save it and became a *cause-célèbre* of the early conservation movement. The appeal pleaded: *"It would be a thousand pities if this oasis in a centre of squalor were to be lost forever"*; but it was. The church was demolished in 1921, and Swedenborg's body was returned to his native land for reburial in Uppsala Cathedral.

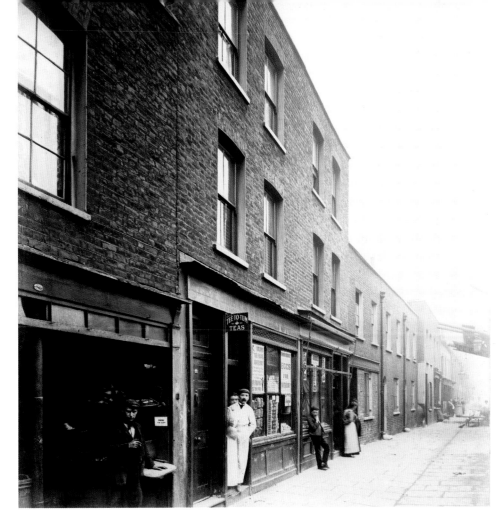

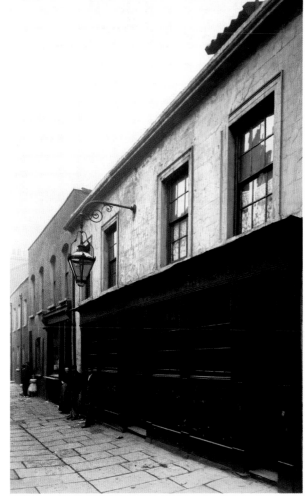

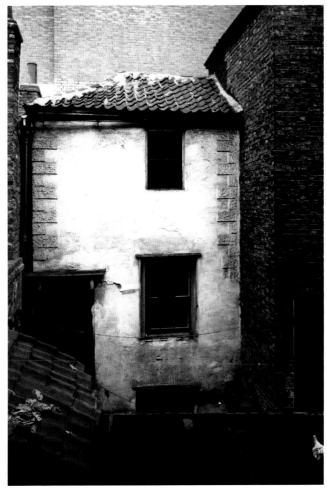

WAPPING

Above left: 70-80 Red Lion Street, Wapping, 10 October 1904

Red Lion Street was a long, narrow street which lay at the heart of old Wapping, pre-dating the construction of London Dock in 1805. The southern half, once known as Anchor and Hope Alley, was lined with mean lodging houses and small shops catering for the teeming population of the area. The poster on the grocer's shop reads *Solving the Fiscal Question? Our Food will cost you Less*, the sign of a community struggling to subsist.

Above right: 64 Red Lion Street, 10 October 1904

The Old George, a small rundown public house which offered transient solace to the dockers and working poor of the neighbourhood.

Right: 3 Hamburg Place, William Street, Shadwell, 9 November 1911

Shadwell was notorious for its densely-packed streets of squalid housing, much of which was cleared in the early 20th century for the King Edward VII Memorial Park. This extraordinary old house was a fragment of earlier 18th century development. The whitewash helped to reflect light into the gloomy back yards, but the crude vermiculated quoins, a feature of grander buildings, are peculiar.

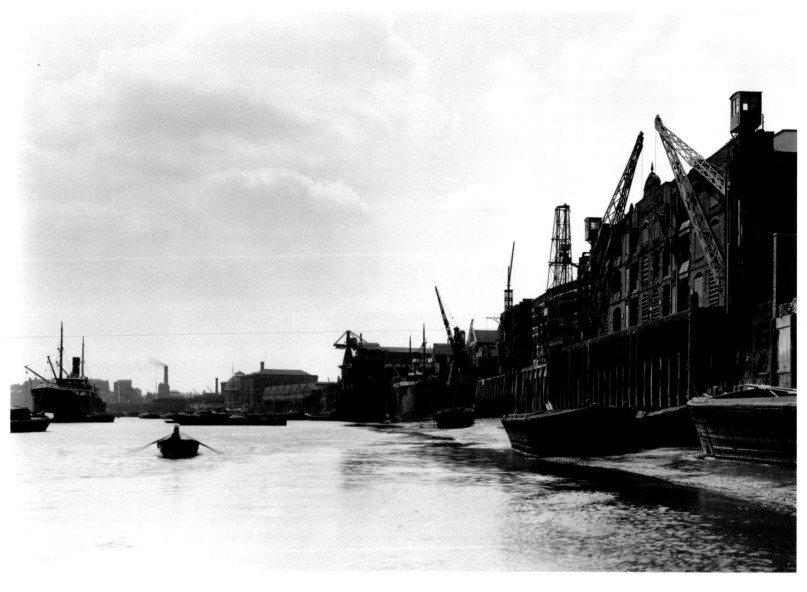

RATCLIFF

Above: Ratcliff Cross, c 1914
View of the river, wharves and warehouses looking east beyond Kerrier's Wharf from Ratcliff Cross.

Right: Ratcliff Cross Stairs, 4 February 1914
Once the Thames was approached through a myriad of stone causeways and stairs providing access between the warehouses to the river and its foreshore. Ratcliff Cross Stairs was typical. From here the great 16th century explorers embarked on their voyages to the Arctic and elsewhere.

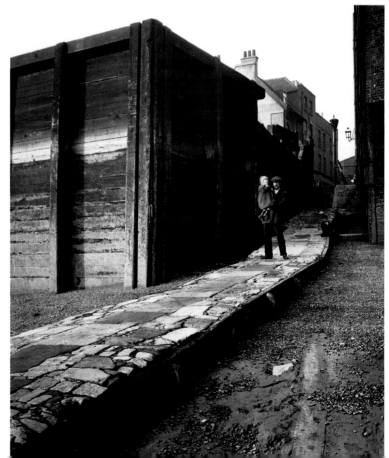

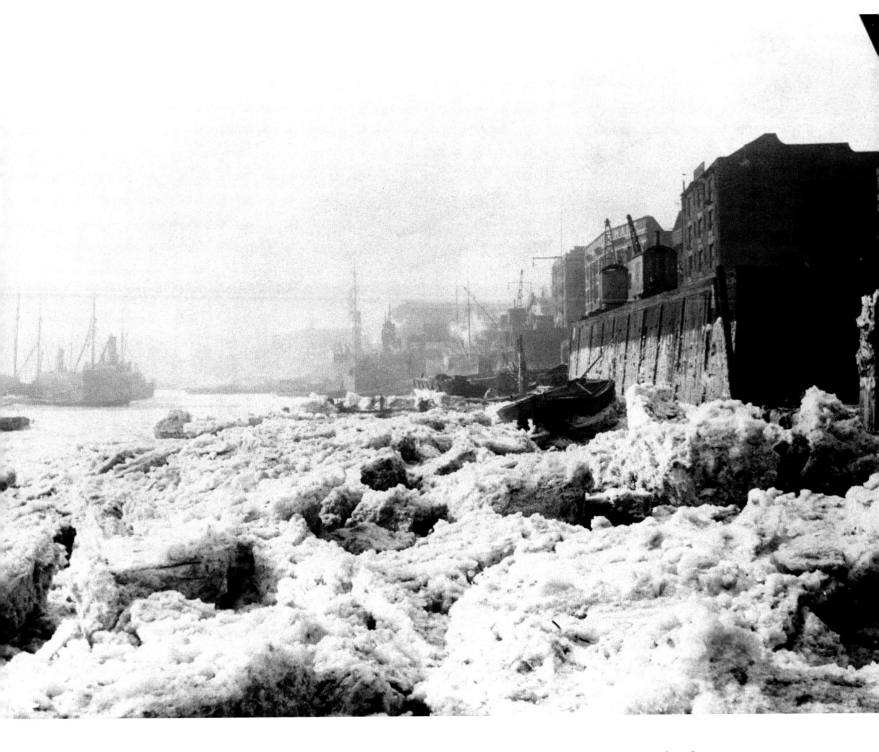

A wilderness of dirt, rags and hunger... a mud desert

Above: Ratcliff Cross, February 1895

The nineteen massive piers of old London Bridge impeded the flow of
the river so much that it was not uncommon for the Thames to freeze
over. Frost fairs were held on the ice. With the removal of the bridge
and its replacement by Rennie's elegant new five-arch span in 1831,
this became much rarer. This remarkable picture shows the great
freeze of February 1895.

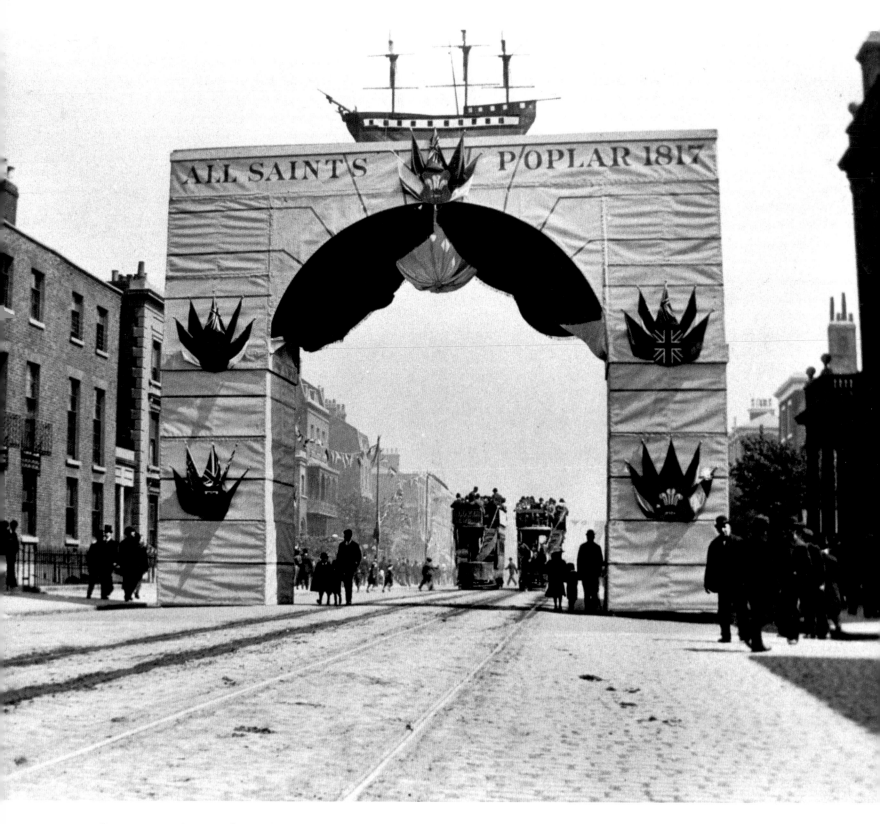

Pride in the docks

POPLAR

Above: East India Dock Road, Poplar, 1897
A commemorative arch raised to celebrate the 80th anniversary of All Saints parish. The arch is a replica of the West India Dock Gate, which was used as an emblem on the vestry mace in 1817. Street dressing for major royal or civic events was common at the time and popular in the East End.

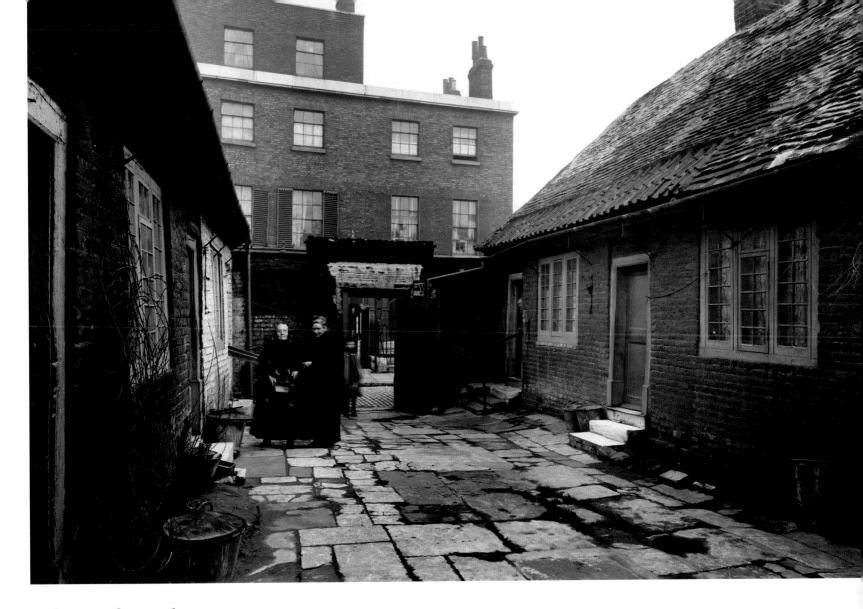

Alms for the poor

Above: Esther Hawes Almshouses, Bow Lane, Poplar, 25 January 1910
Charitable almshouses provided housing for certain categories of the deserving poor. Esther Hawes Almshouses were established in 1686 for six elderly Poplar women and comprised two brick ranges with tiled roofs, each house with a single room.

By the 1850s the almshouses were condemned as unfit for human habitation, but in the 1860s, some improvements were made. The original leaded lights were replaced with timber casements. After further repairs in the 1930s they were regarded as a bottleneck and in 1938 were sold to Poplar Council for clearance for road widening. Eventually, they were demolished in June 1953, 100 years after they were condemned.

Right: 131 Mile End Road, c 1910
The decaying attic. Note the discarded women's shoes beside the table.

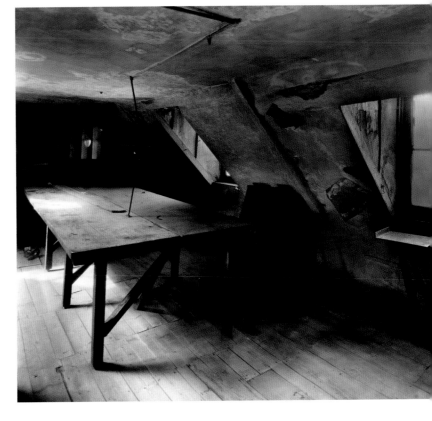

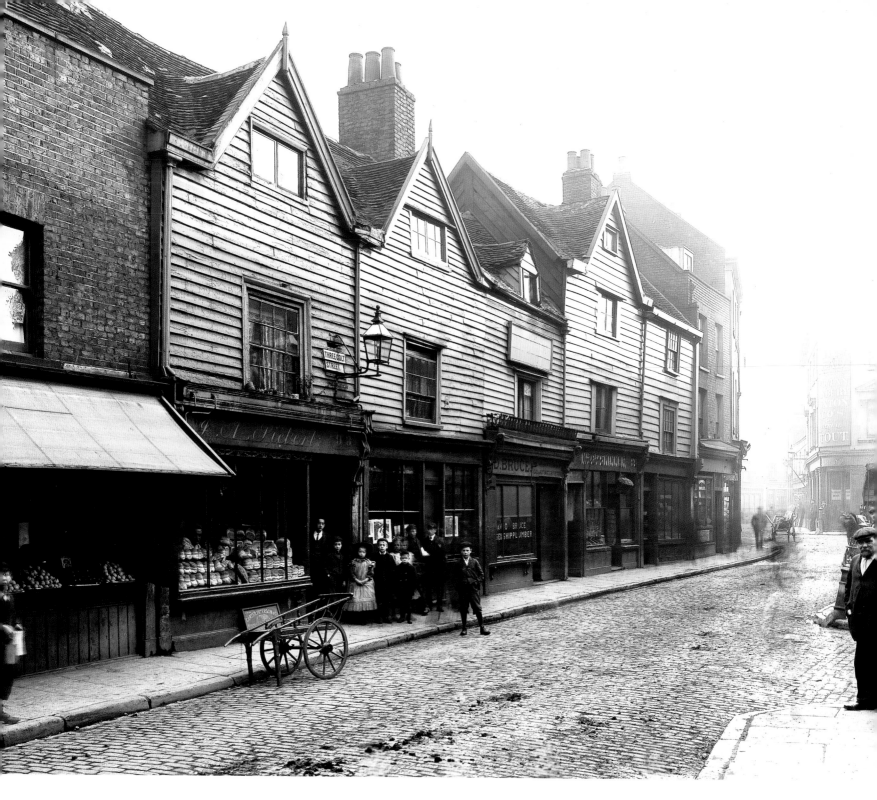

Ship chandlers and opium dens

LIMEHOUSE

In the 13th century lime burning began in kilns and oasts, known as "*lymostes*" at the mouth of an insanitary creek called the Black Ditch. By the mid-16th century the entire district was known as Limehouse. By the 1880s it was Chinatown, home to large numbers of Chinese and Lascar sailors and migrants, with an unsavoury reputation for illicit opium dens and Chinese criminal gangs in the area around Pennyfields.

Above: 93-101 Three Colt Street, c 1900
Textures of the past. This remarkable street scene epitomises London at the dawn of the 20th century with stone pavements, setted streets and small local shops in old vernacular buildings. Weatherboarded houses were once common in inner London, but today only a few fragments remain. Siebert's, with its queue of children outside a well-stocked shop window, was one of two German bakers in the street.

Below: 89-95 Ropemakers Fields, Limehouse, c 1900

The eastern end of Ropemakers Fields at its junction with Nightingale Lane. The left-hand pair of early 18th century houses have once-elegant Georgian shopfronts, No. 89 with an elegant double bow. George Morrow and Son was a scull and mast maker; James Barnett, next door, a ship chandler offering canvas, rope fend-offs, lamp glasses and oakum for both river and canal trade. Two of the three children have no shoes – a sign of abject poverty.

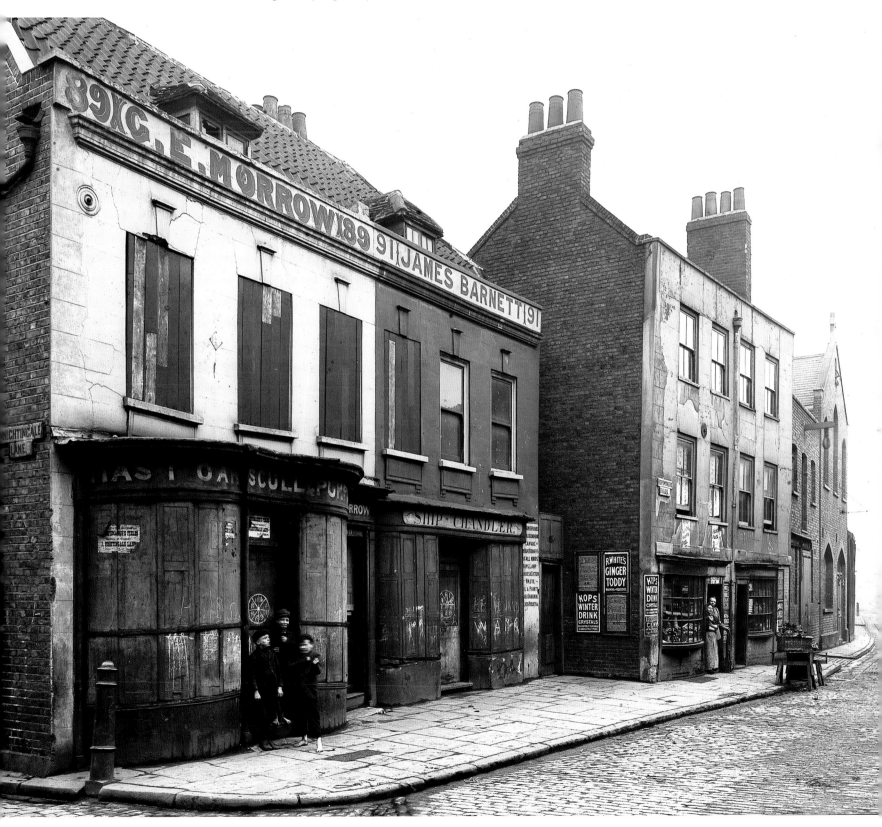

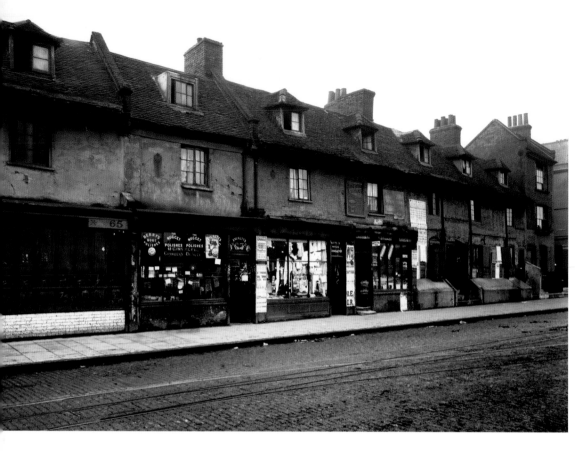

MILE END

Left: 65-79 Cambridge Road, Mile End, 14 November 1910
An interesting survival of a late 17th century terrace with tiled roofs and dormer windows. The right hand end has been divided into mean lodging houses with brick screen walls to the front steps.

Below: 168 Cambridge Road, 15 October 1903
A typical East End street scene with modest two-storey artisans' houses and shops, a setted street and tramlines. W T Maughan was a wholesale and retail confectioner operating from a small yard next to the store.

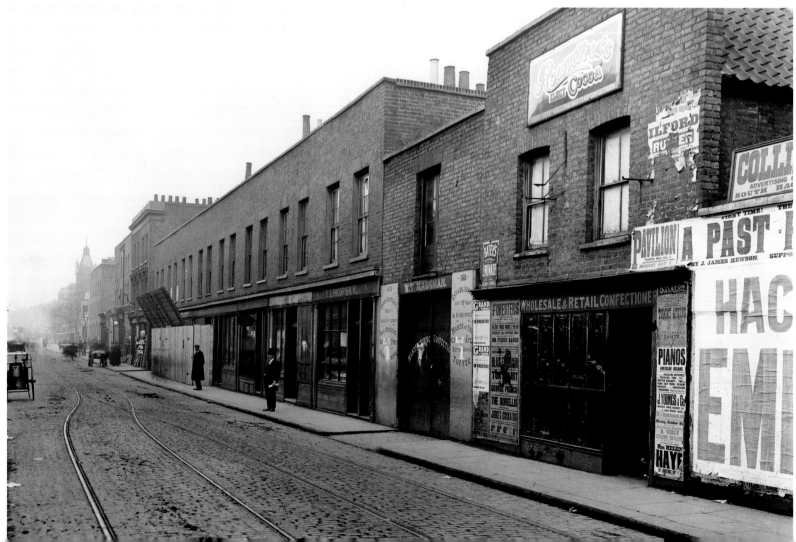

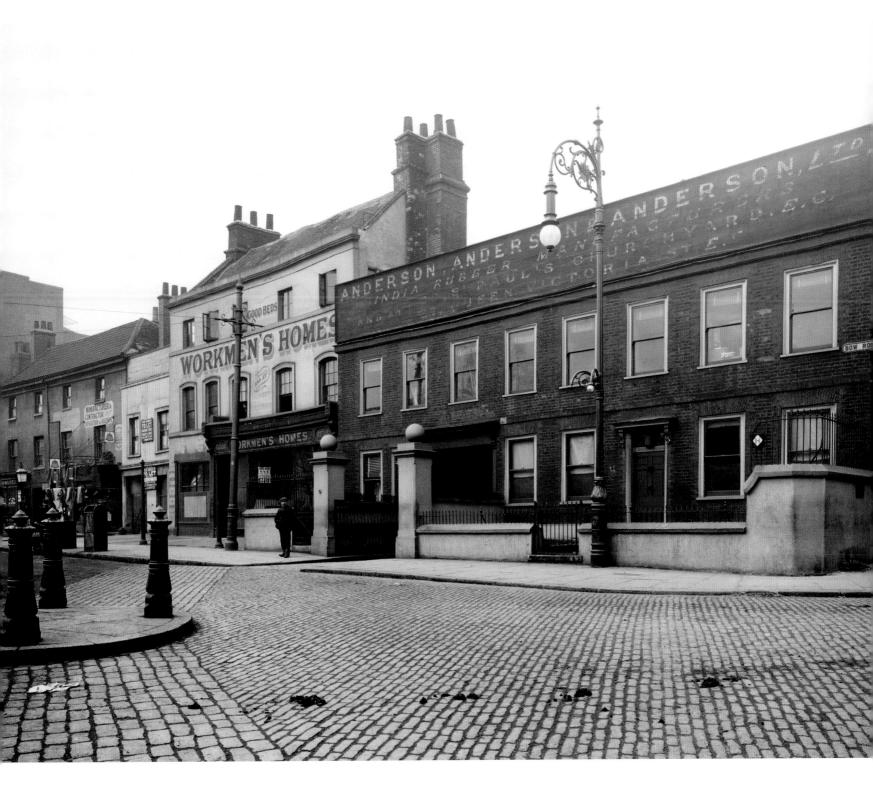

Lost lustre

BOW

Above: 215-223 Bow Road, Bow, 19 November 1909
A fine group of buildings of various periods just east of St Mary's Church.
The houses to the extreme left and right still stand, but the remainder have
been swept away, including the impressive, eight-bay Georgian facade to
Anderson's.

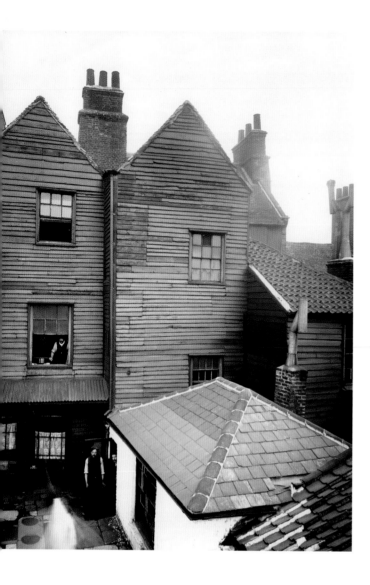

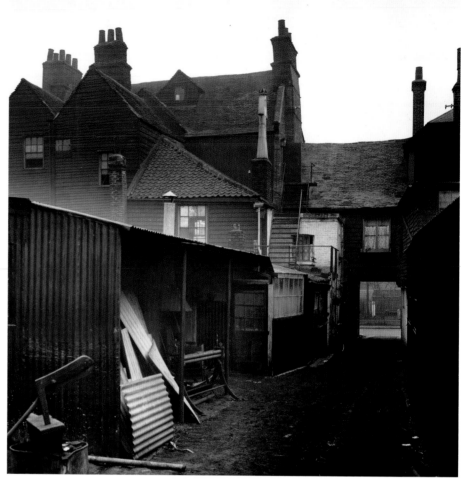

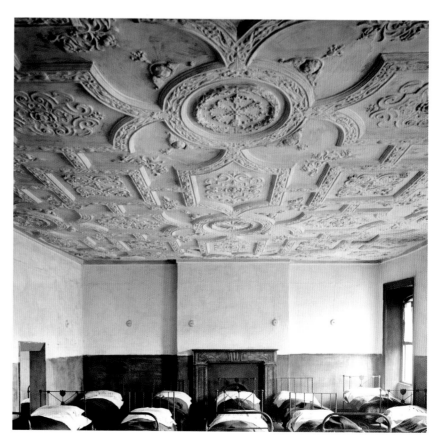

Above left: 215-217 Bow Road, 19 November 1909

The polite Georgian facade to Anderson's (see previous page) concealed a fascinating range of early 17th century vernacular buildings behind with weatherboarded gables and massive chimney stacks.

Above right: 215-217 Bow Road, 9 November 1905

A wonderfully evocative view of the rear of the buildings which are timber-framed. St Mary's churchyard can be seen beyond.

Right: 217 Bow Road, 9 November 1905

In the 17th century Bromley by Bow was a popular royal retreat. The Old Palace of Bromley, built in 1606 for James I, stood nearby, and this magnificent first-floor ceiling at No. 217 was of the same design as that in the north-west room of the palace. The house was believed to have been built for Lord Sheffield in 1612, but at the time of the photograph it had come down in the world and was being used as a dormitory by the Workmen's Home next door.

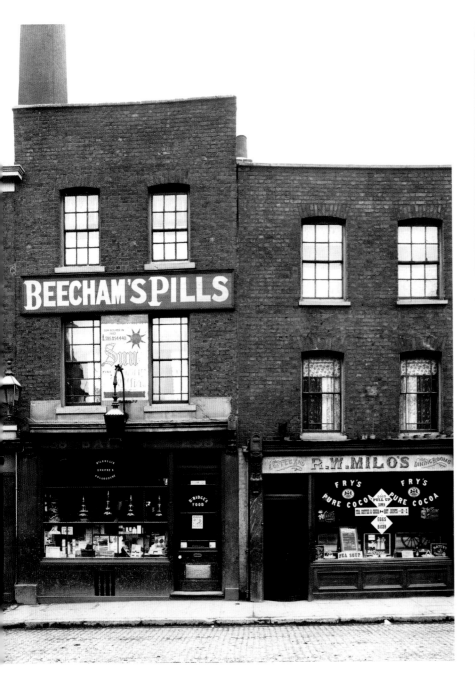

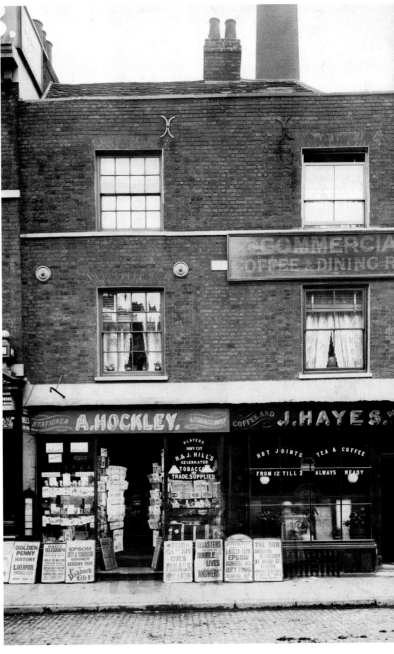

Teeming neighbourhoods with small shops

Above left: 236-238 Bow Road, 18 April 1899

The teeming neighbourhoods of high-density housing in the East End supported a huge number of local businesses and shops. Milo's Dining Rooms offered *a Good Pull Up for Carmen*, whilst Bailey's Chemist next door with a display of traditional apothecaries' jars in the window offered Dr Collis Brown's Chlorodyne.

Above right: 242A-244 Bow Road, 18 April 1899

Inner London as it was once. The old tiled roof suggests the refronting of an older building in the early 19th century. Note the Venetian blinds to the first floor windows. The placards outside Hockley's show a moment frozen in time, *The Golden Penny* offered a History of Liverpool Football Club; *The Sun*, "Shocking Discovery at Broad Street Station" to the right of which stands the ghostly trace of a young girl.

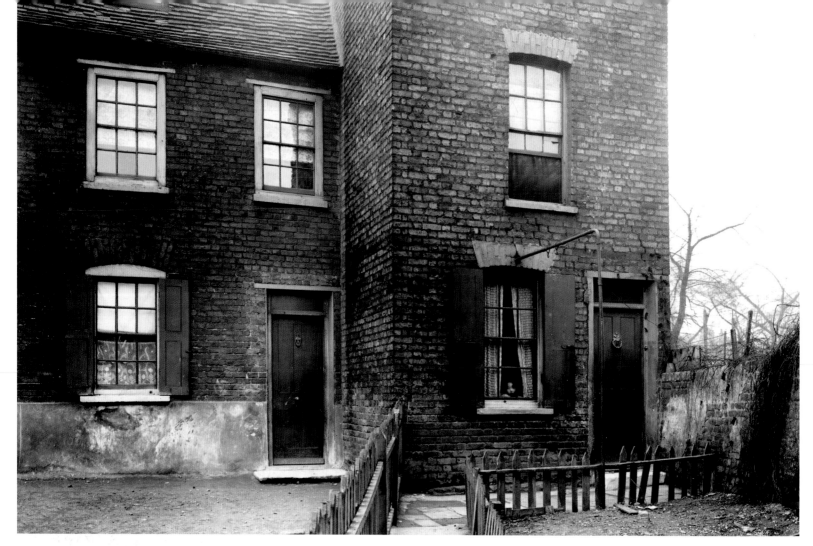

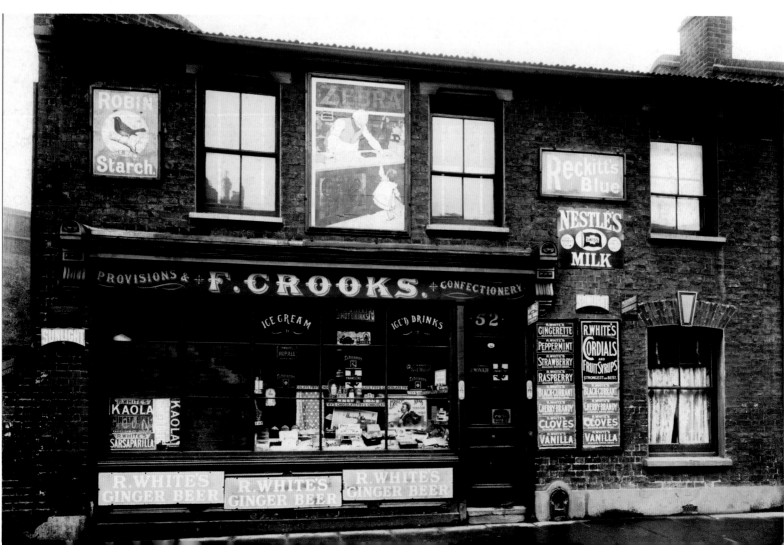

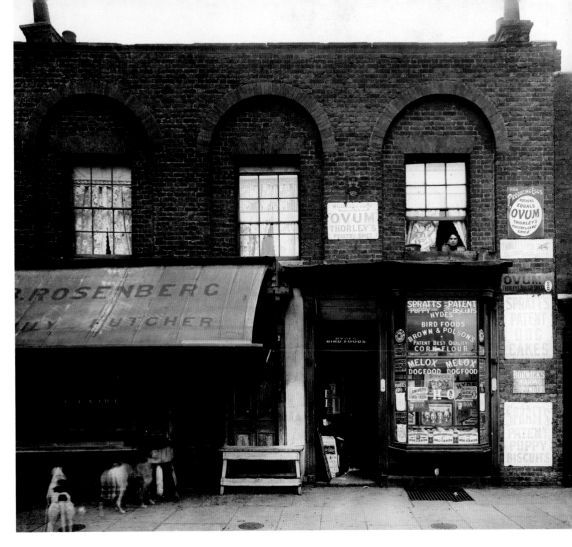

OLD FORD

Opposite top: 800 Old Ford Road, 29 March 1899
Old 18th century cottages. A child can be glimpsed in the ground floor window over which a gas pipe has been hacked crudely through the window arch.

Opposite below: 52 Dace Road, Old Ford 8 December 1904
F Crook's local corner shop with a splendid array of enamel advertisements promoting a whole range of products, most of which are familiar today.

HACKNEY

Right top: 75-77 Broadway, London Fields, 16 October 1906
The dogs seem more interested in Rosenberg's the family butcher rather than the dog food shop next door, which has a finely-detailed canted bay shopfront coruscated with colourful enamel advertisements.

Right below: 85 Broadway, London Fields, 16 October 1906
P J Ryan, tobacconists, with a fascinating amount of contemporary detail. The advertising lantern is angled to throw light onto the shop window which advertises Victory V gums and Fry's chocolate. The *Daily Mirror* announces a major mine disaster in Durham with 30 killed and 150 entombed. The poster above the neighbouring shop offers the entire street block for immediate redevelopment, but similar parts of Broadway still exist.

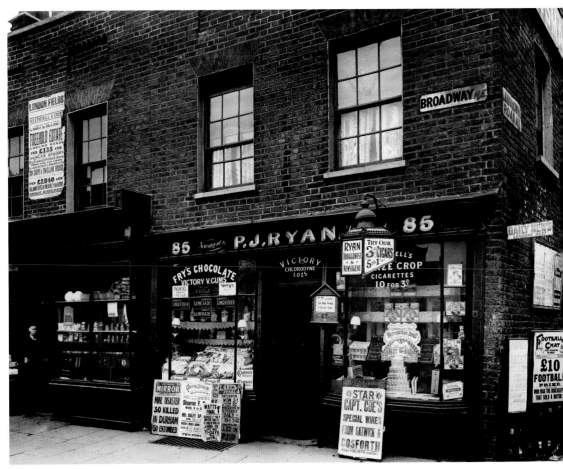

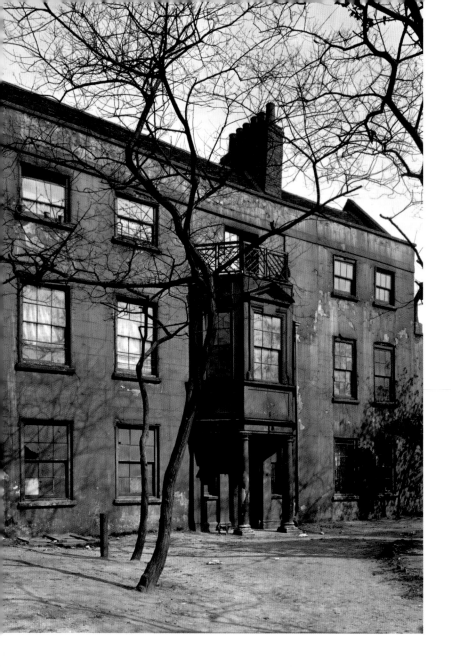

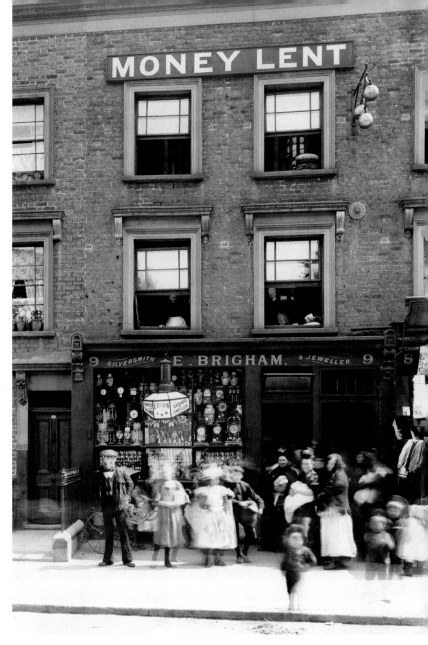

A lifeline in hard times

Above left: Grove House, 36 Chatham Place, Hackney, c 1912
Grove House was one of the larger houses built on the St Thomas's Hospital estate in the early 18th century. In 1783 it became an Academy for the Deaf & Dumb, one of its pupils being the illegitimate child of Charles James Fox. After a brief period as a clothing factory, it passed to the Hackney Progressive Club, after which it fell vacant. It was demolished in 1921.

Above right: 9 Gainsborough Road, Hackney Wick, 29 May 1909
Pawnbrokers were a common sight across London and their regular use a way of life in the East End. Edwin Brigham was typical, offering short-term loans against items of value. The window is crammed with clocks, vases, watches and silver, whilst the crowd milling outside shows that there was no shortage of business.

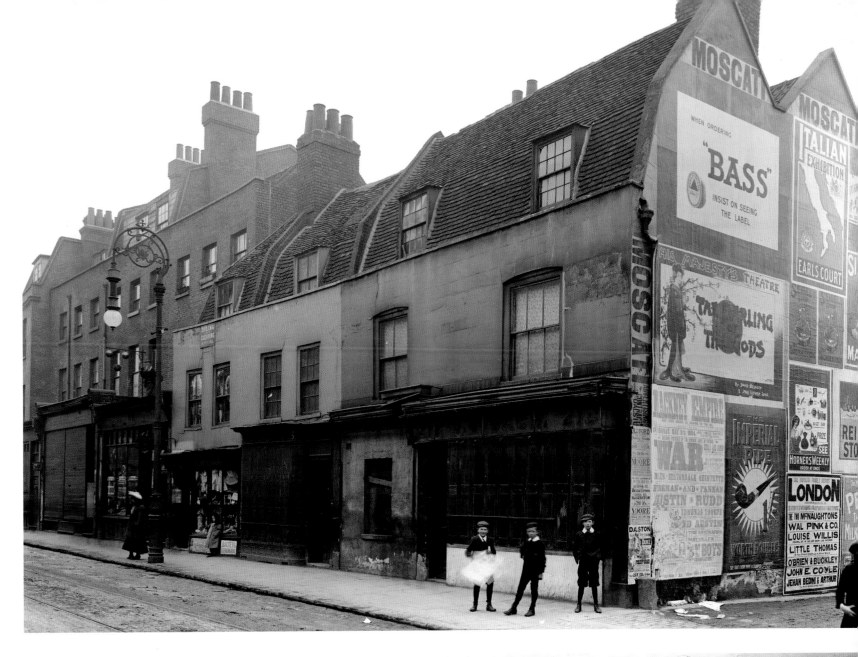

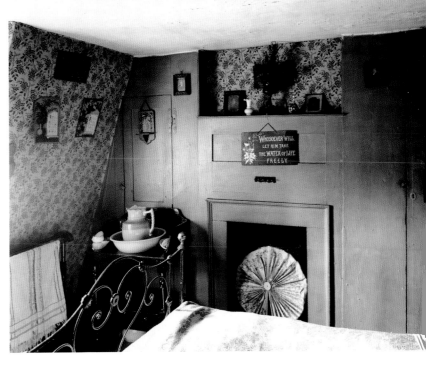

Above: 209-213 Mare Street, Hackney, 13 May 1904
A short terrace of early 18th century cottages with the gable end covered with contemporary posters. The children in the foreground in caps and high collars look particularly stylish.

Right: 209 Mare Street, 30 May 1904
A fascinating glimpse of the first floor rear room of No. 209 with typical early 18th century square-edged panelling, a plain chimneypiece, butterfly hinges to the china cupboard, and religious tracts on the walls.

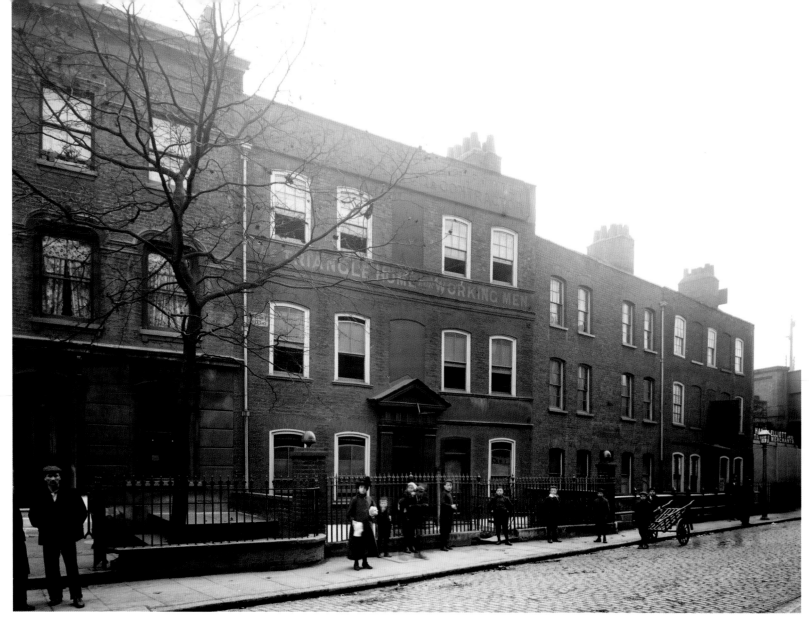

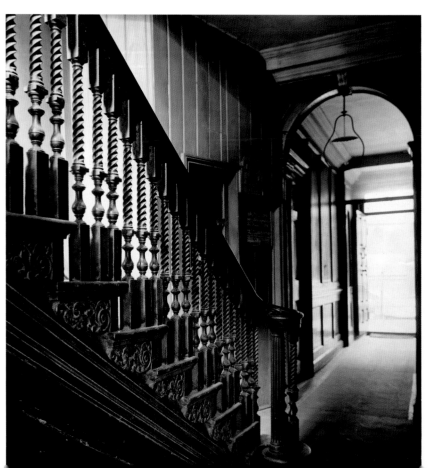

Above: 1-5 Westgate Street, Hackney, 28 October 1904
The large early Georgian house with the grand pedimented doorcase would have been occupied originally by a merchant of some substance. By the time of the photograph, it was in use as the Triangle Home for Working Men. It was commonplace for once genteel houses to be divided into rooms and lodgings as the social composition of districts changed, and fashionable society moved elsewhere.

Right: 1-5 Westgate Street, 28 October 1904
The entrance hall and staircase show a house of considerable refinement with elegant carved and twisted balusters to the original staircase and a fluted Doric newel post.

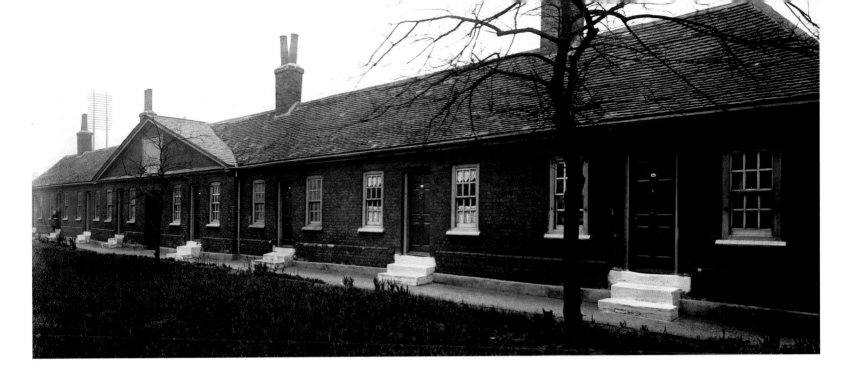

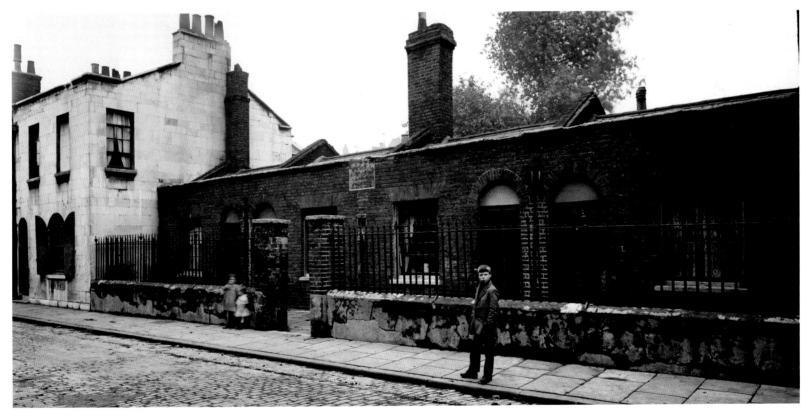

Housing the poor of the parish

SHOREDITCH

Top: Framework Knitters Almshouses, Kingsland Road, Shoreditch, 1907
The Framework Knitters, or Bourne's Almshouses, built in 1734 by the City Livery Company, lay just north of the Geffrye Almshouses in Kingsland Road, to which they bore a close resemblance. In 1907 the almsmen were moved out to Oadby in Leicestershire, and the buildings were swept away soon after for a new factory.

Above: Aldermanbury Almshouses, 52-60 Philip Street, c 1910
Local tradition alleged that the curious stone house to the left of the picture was built with stone from old London Bridge. This was probably true as a stone tablet inside the party wall stated it was built in 1817 by Mr Malcott, who also built Old Bridge House, 54 Streatham Hill (demolished 1928) utilising stone from the bridge, hence the name.

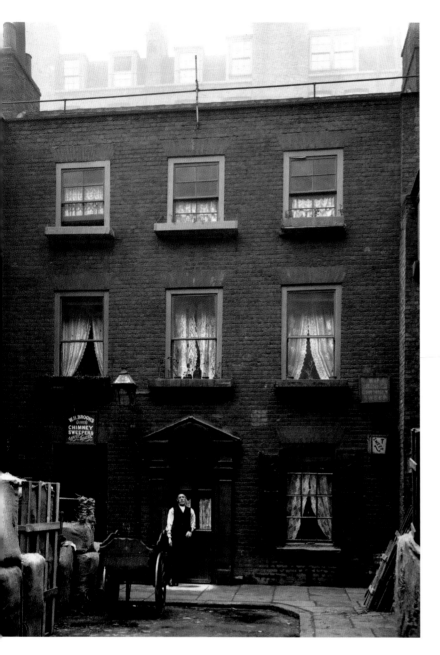

An eccentric city of
unexpected delights

Above left: Queen Square, Finsbury Avenue, Shoreditch, c 1905
Situated on the northern fringe of the City of London, Queen Square was
a narrow courtyard of early 18th century houses off Finsbury Avenue, close
to Broad Street Station. W H Brooks, a chimney sweeper and carpet beater,
poses outside the grand pedimented doorcase to the house, which has
fallen on hard times.

Above right: 11 Pitfield Street, c 1905
This ancient late 17th century house with a mixed pantile and clay tile
roof and timber eaves cornice was a hardware shop. The engaged oil jars
denote a dealer in oils. The shop window is stacked with Sunlight and
Lifebuoy soaps. The bakers to the left has a display of Peek Freans and
Huntley & Palmers biscuit boxes.

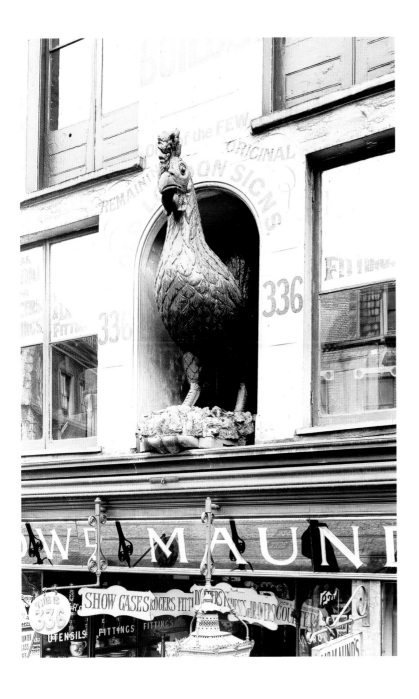

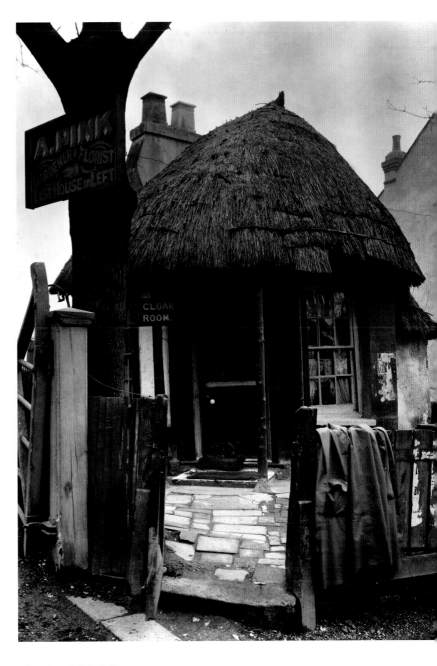

CLAPTON

Above left: 336 Old Street, Shoreditch, c 1910
This resplendent gilded cockerel, implausibly attributed to Grinling Gibbons, once adorned The Cock public house in Fleet Street, haunt of Pepys, Thackeray, Dickens and Tennyson, until 1887 when the building was demolished for the Bank of England Law Courts Branch. Tennyson wrote of it:

> The Cock was of a larger egg
> Than modern poultry drop,
> Stept forward on a firmer leg,
> And cramm'd a plumper crop

Edward Maund, a joiner and shopfitter, acquired the bird and gave it pride of place in a niche on the front of his premises in Old Street, where it became a local landmark.

Above right: Thatched Cottage, Spring Hill, Clapton, 26 February 1912
This quaint little thatched cottage was probably built on common land in the late 18th century. It was used as John Such's refreshment rooms next to Pink's Nurseries, until it was burnt out in 1919.

Pool of London, c 1914

Panoramic view of the Pool of London showing the river crowded with shipping. The tower of the Church of St Magnus the Martyr is in the centre of the picture with the Monument to the right. The vast mass of Cannon Street train shed obscures the view of St Paul's which can be seen in the haze on the horizon.

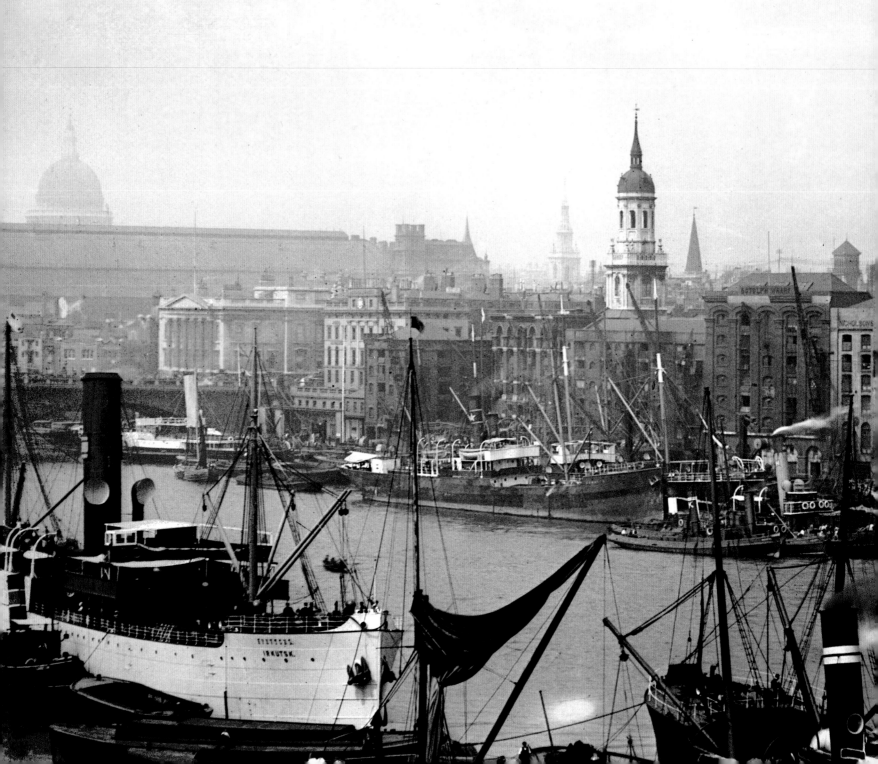

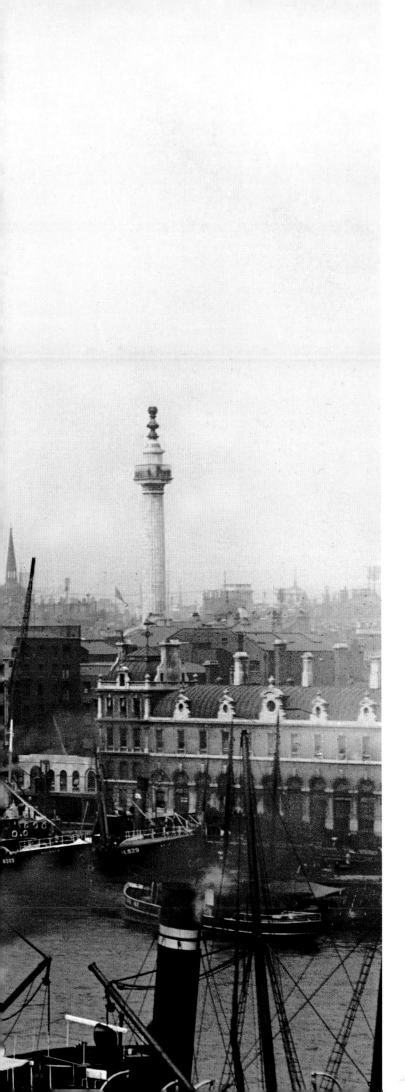

CHAPTER SIX

LONDON-OVER-THE-WATER

South London

South London was always the capital's backyard – a service area for the Cities of London and Westminster across the river. In the Middle Ages Southwark was London's red-light district, with theatres, inns, bull- and bear-baiting rings, but it was relatively isolated – hence the soubriquet "London-over-the-water" – and its administration confused. Its development was unlocked first by the construction of a series of new bridges – Vauxhall (1816), Waterloo (1817) and Southwark (1819) – which triggered major new road improvements, such as St George's Circus and Blackfriars Road, and later by the arrival of a congeries of railways.

In 1900 river-borne trade and industry dominated the northern edges in a huge arc along the Thames in a chaotic jumble of vertiginous warehouses, wharves, printing works, sawmills, factories and breweries. Many industries, like white lead works, were highly toxic, slowly poisoning the workforce. Noxious trades were widespread including bone-boiling, cat-gut making, fish-smoking and leather tanning. Large numbers of costermongers and street traders working from handcarts operated from here. Bankside was one of the principal sources of London's power with the old Phoenix Gas Works, an electricity generating station and the pumping station of the London Hydraulic Power Station all housed on the site later occupied by Bankside Power Station.

Borough High Street retained much of its mediaeval street plan and grain with dozens of narrow passages and alleys running off the main frontage interspersed with ancient coaching inns and an unwholesome reputation for poverty and crime. It was here that Charles Booth found the worst extremes of deprivation and squalor close to the old Marshalsea Prison.

As London expanded outward it absorbed many older, outlying settlements such as Clapham, Rotherhithe, Camberwell, Peckham and Greenwich. The new suburbs created were often rigorously socially stratified with subtle nuances of class and wealth ranging from the genteel through various gradations of the middle and working classes to slum districts full of cheap lodging-houses. The bewildering shifting dynamic of London's neighbourhoods oscillating between the fashionable and the downwardly mobile remains a constant feature of London's history which persists to this day.

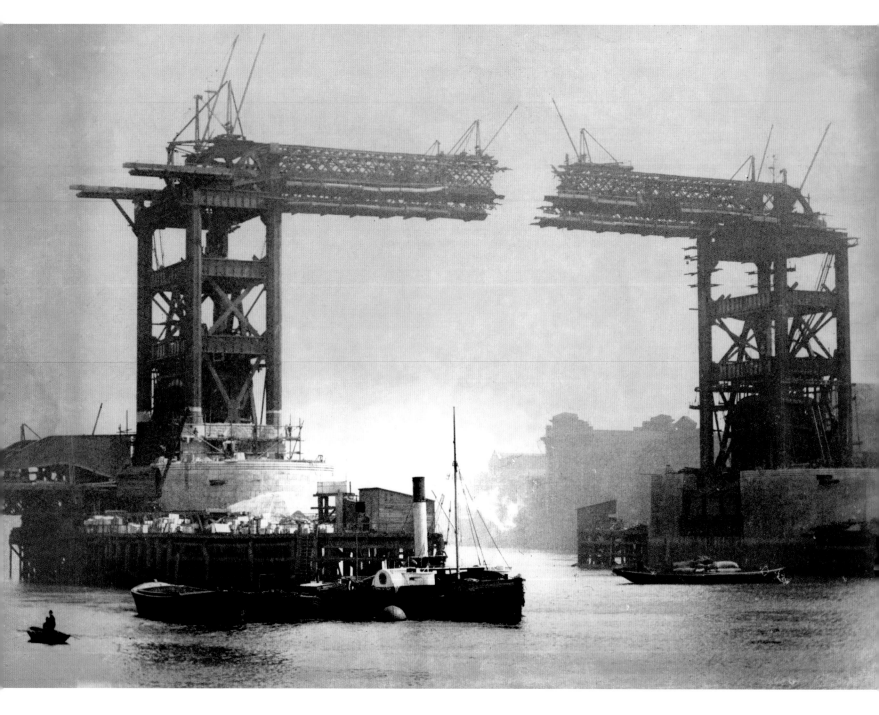

Crossing the great divide

THE RIVER

Above: Tower Bridge, c 1893

The need for a new river crossing was identified as early as 1879. Authorised by an Act of Parliament in 1885, it was designed by the City Corporation architect, Sir Horace Jones and the engineer, John Wolfe Barry as a bascule bridge to allow the passage of large ships into the Pool of London. The Act stipulated a clear span of 200ft, a height of 135ft and the use of the Gothic style to harmonise with the Tower of London. Tower Bridge opened in 1894 and rapidly became a London icon. The new Tower Bridge Approach Road required extensive demolition on the north bank.

The iron frame and upper level walkway can be seen here rising from the great stone bastions sunk into the river.

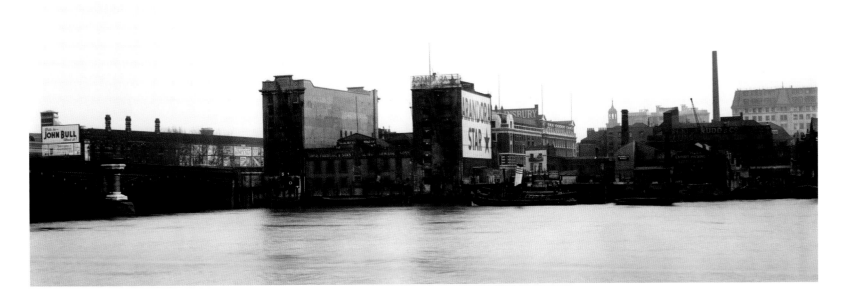

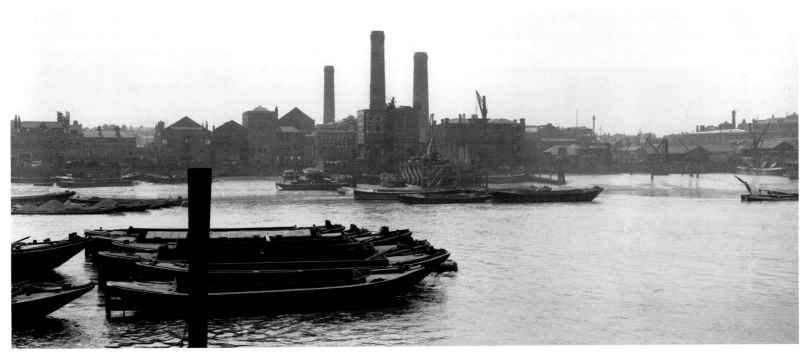

Top: Upper Ground, Blackfriars, c 1912

The whole of the South Bank of the Thames was given over to wharves, warehouses and industry. To the left are the spans of Blackfriars Bridge. The Arandora Star was fated – sunk off the coast of Ireland on 2 July 1940 with heavy loss of life.

Above: Panorama of Bankside from the foreshore near Trig Lane Stairs in the City of London, 21 June 1912

In the centre is the generating station of the City Electric Light Company behind which rise the chimneys of the South Metropolitan Gas Company all of which was swept away for the construction of Bankside Power Station in 1952.

To the left is a short terrace of early 18th century houses; No. 48 to the extreme left is alleged to be the house from which Sir Christopher Wren watched the rebuilding of St Paul's, but there is no evidence for this. Behind lay Moss's Alley and the poisonous warren of courts and yards depicted on pp 256–59. Cardinal Cap Alley still survives next to 48 Bankside.

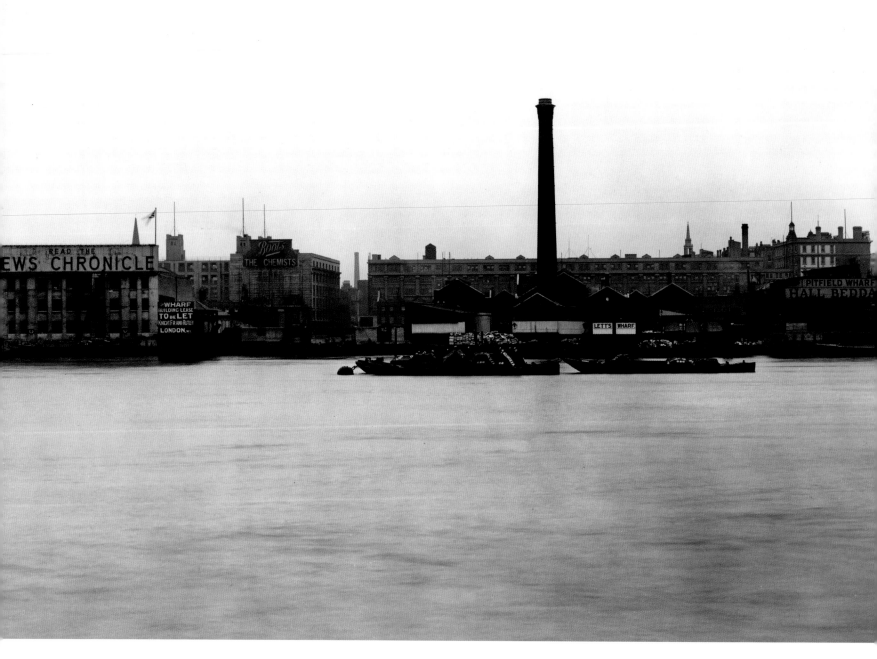

London's backyard

Above: Lett's Wharf, c 1912

In the mid-19th century desperate bands of women sifted rubbish here for anything which could be recycled. Later it became a refuse depot and part of the industrial South Bank. Today it is the site of the National Theatre. In the distance to the right of the chimney is the tower and spire of St John's, Waterloo.

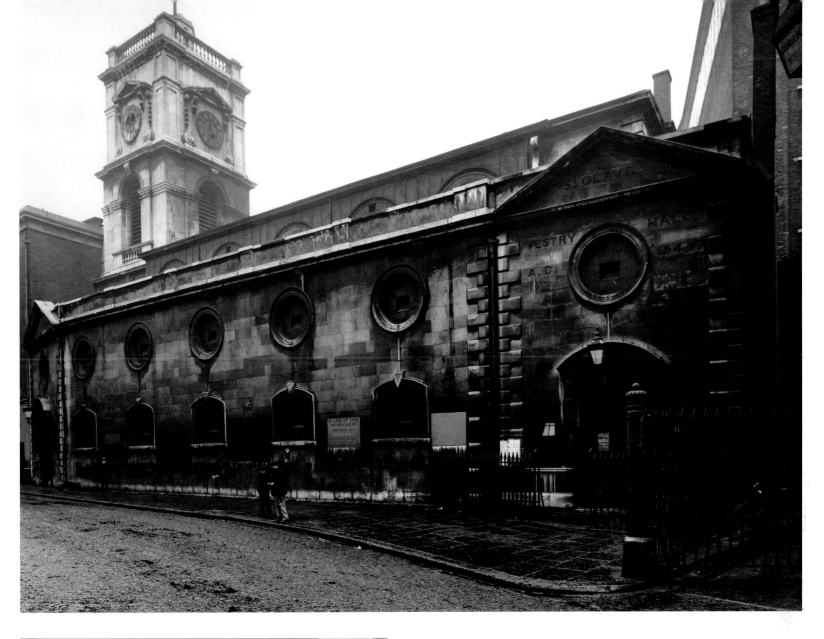

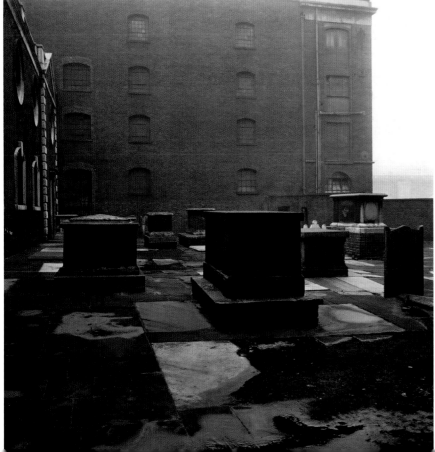

SOUTHWARK

Above: St Olave's Church, Tooley Street, c 1910
Rebuilt in 1740 on the site of a 12th century church, St Olave's stood just south-east of London Bridge. After a catastrophic waterfront fire in August 1843, the church was restored. It survived until 1926 when it was pulled down to make way for St Olaf House, designed by Goodhart-Rendel, one of London's finest Art Deco buildings. The top of the Tower was salvaged for use in Tanner Street Gardens where it still stands as a forlorn remnant.

Left: A melancholic view of St Olave's churchyard which stood between the church and the river. In the background, London Bridge can be seen dimly through the chill river fog.

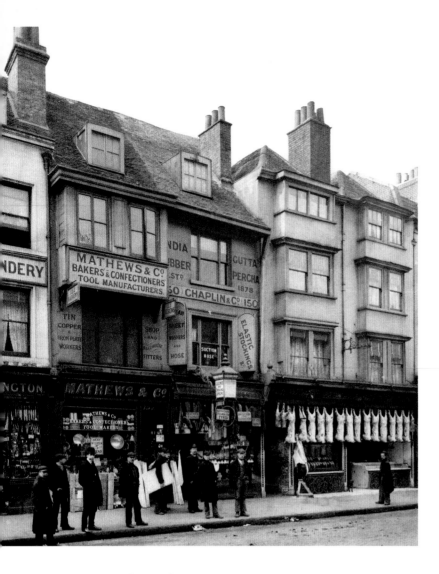

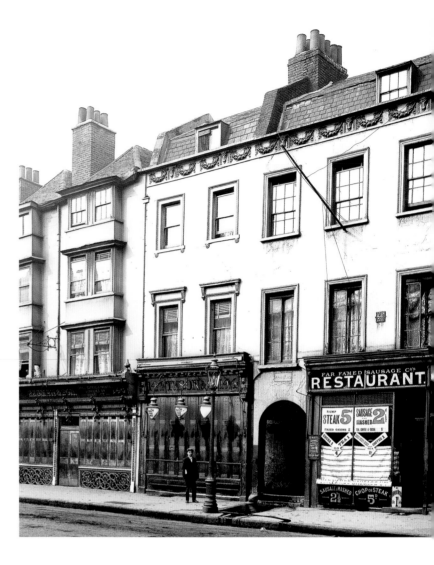

Wretched remains...

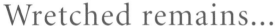

Above left: 146-154 Borough High Street, c 1905
For centuries, Borough High Street was the principal approach to the City of London from the south. It was lined with coaching inns and yards which conferred a very distinctive character.

These 17th century timber-framed houses were typical of the area. Chaplin's was a dealer in India rubber, gutta percha and protective clothing.

Above right: 142-154 Borough High Street, 20 September 1908
Nos. 142-144, with its distinctive parapet frieze of swags and bucrania, was designed by Sir John Soane. Through the central archway was a long, narrow passage lined with terraces and four semi-detached houses built for Francis Adams by Soane in 1785 – hence the inscribed panel over the entrance reading Adams Place. The name was altered later by some wag to Eve's Place.

Opposite top: 309-315 Borough High Street, c 1903
A classic group of 17th century houses with projecting central bays and horizontal sash windows to the gables. The picture eloquently portrays the extraordinary range of details commonly found in the Edwardian high street – elegant signwriting, gilt and glass fascias, applied lettering to shopfronts and spectacular ornamental ironwork. Angled lanterns, which were suspended from fascias and designed to throw light back onto shop window displays, have now vanished from London's streets.

Opposite below left: 189-191 Borough High Street, c 1903
A fine group of 17th century timber-framed vernacular houses on the west side of the street. Many of the goods displayed were beyond the reach of the poorest classes, who were crammed into one of London's most notorious slums in the alleys and yards behind the High Street.

Opposite below right: 199a Borough High Street, 14 September 1908
Borough High Street served the wharves, warehouses and industries clustered along the Thames. Depicted here are the old drying sheds of a vat maker in Layton's Yard, later part of Layton & Young, of Young's brewery. The ancient cobbled road surface is probably part of the Kings Bench Prison, which stood on the site and was demolished in 1758.

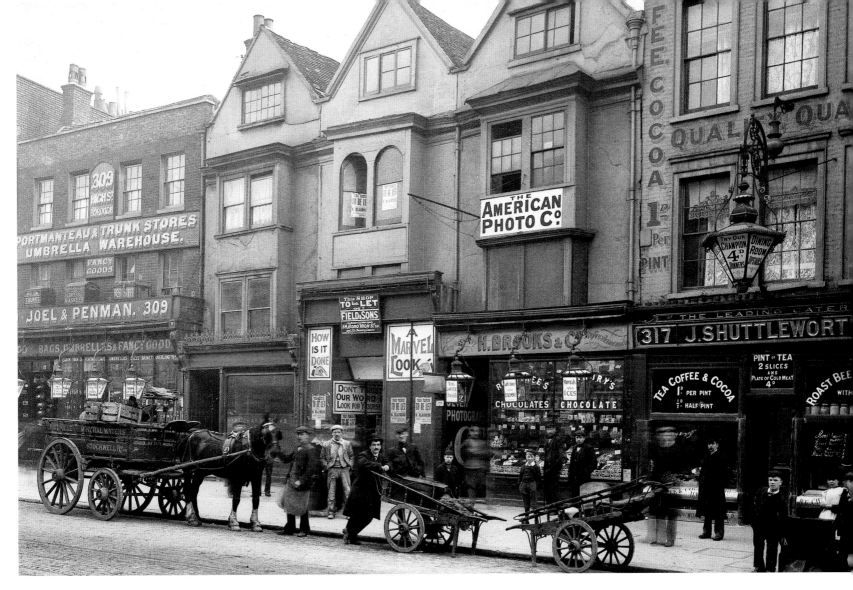

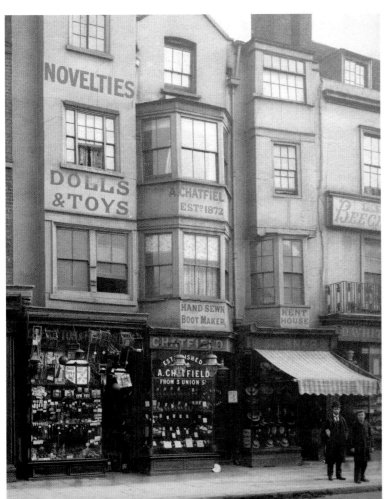

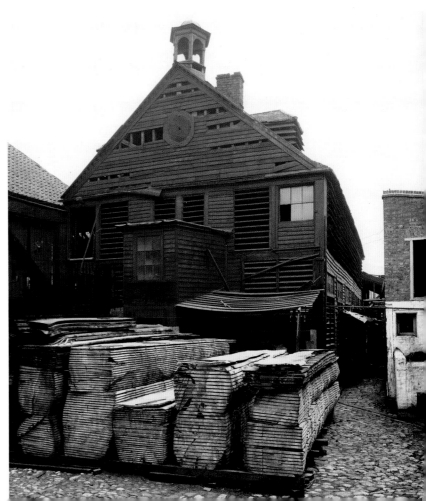

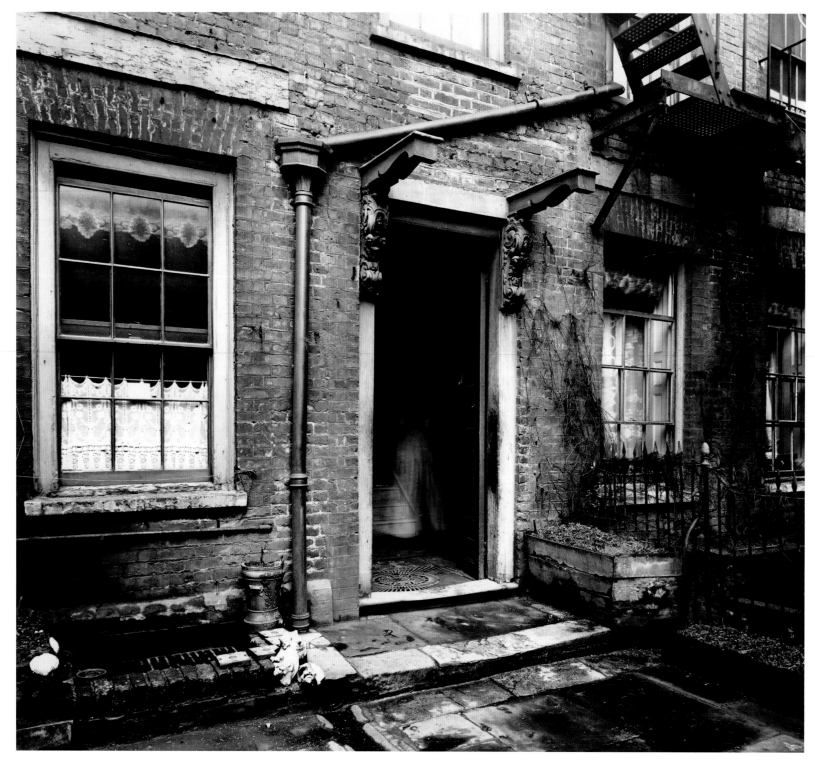

What a strange house was this...

Above: The Old Farm House, Disney Place, 17 February 1910

"There is probably no more picturesque building left standing in London-Over-the-Water than the ancient residence known as the Farm House" (*Daily Chronicle*, 9 January 1914)

The old Farm House was a remarkable survival tucked away at the end of a cul-de-sac and may have been a remnant of a 16th century house built for the Earl of Suffolk. It fell into use as a doss-house and paupers of many parishes were farmed out here – hence the name. For a while it was the lodging of the Welsh tramp poet, W H Davies, who wrote and published *The Soul's Destroyer and other Poems* from here. Dickens knew it well.

The brackets to the elaborate 17th century door canopy are still in place, but its roof has gone. The spectral figure of a young girl can be seen inside the doorway.

Right: The turned and twisted balusters of the once-grand staircase at first floor level.

Below: As a common lodging house, beds were crammed into every room. The first floor east room, shown here, retained its fine original panelling and chimneypiece, crudely whitewashed with a single gas mantle suspended from the ceiling. A chamber pot can be glimpsed beneath the bed.

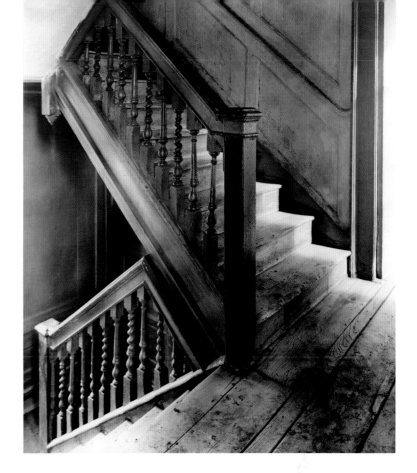

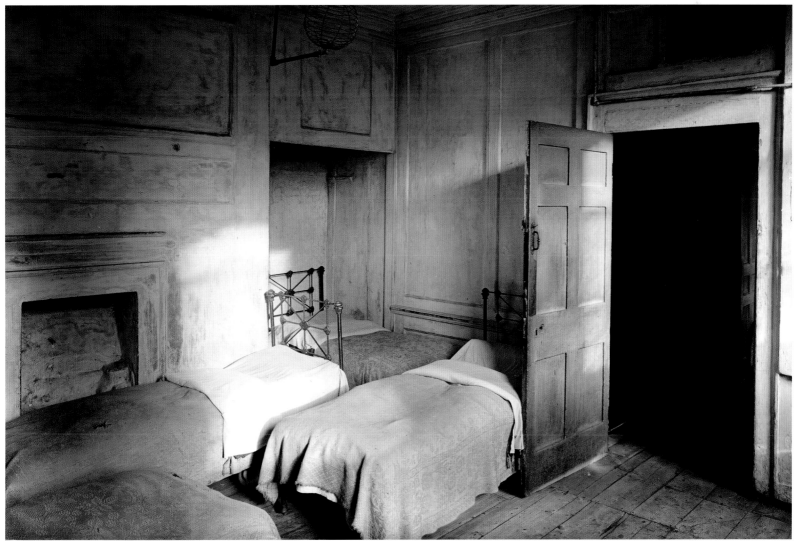

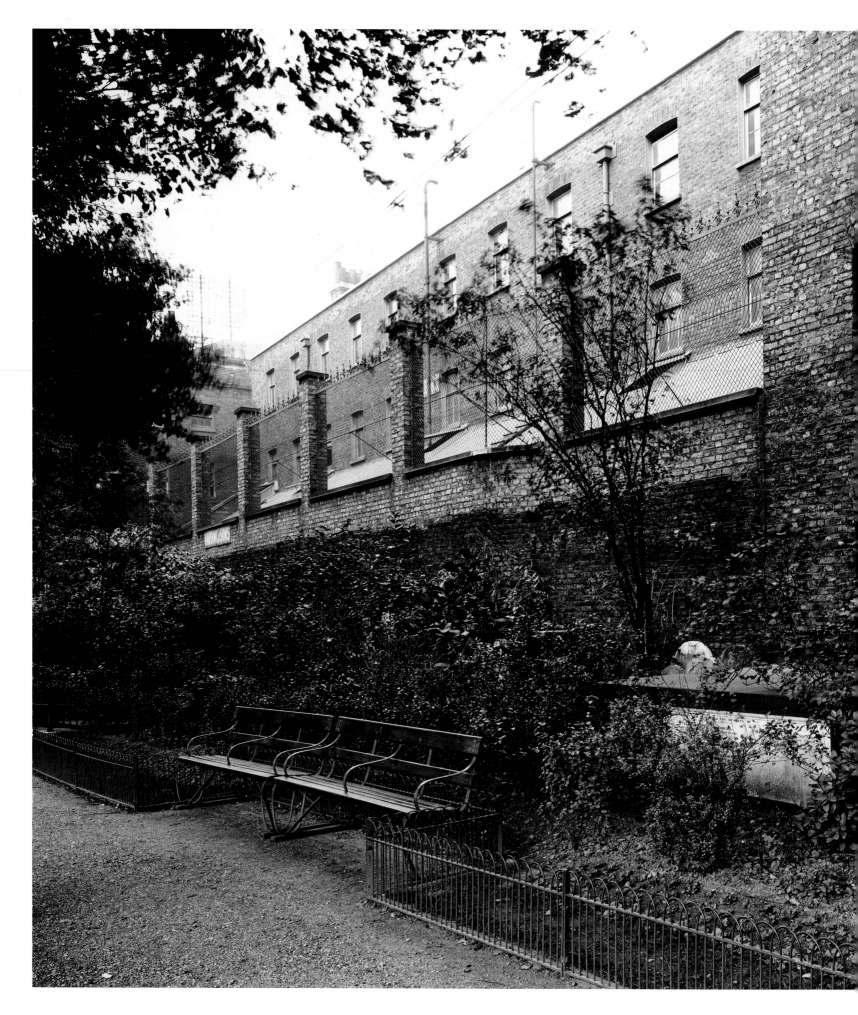

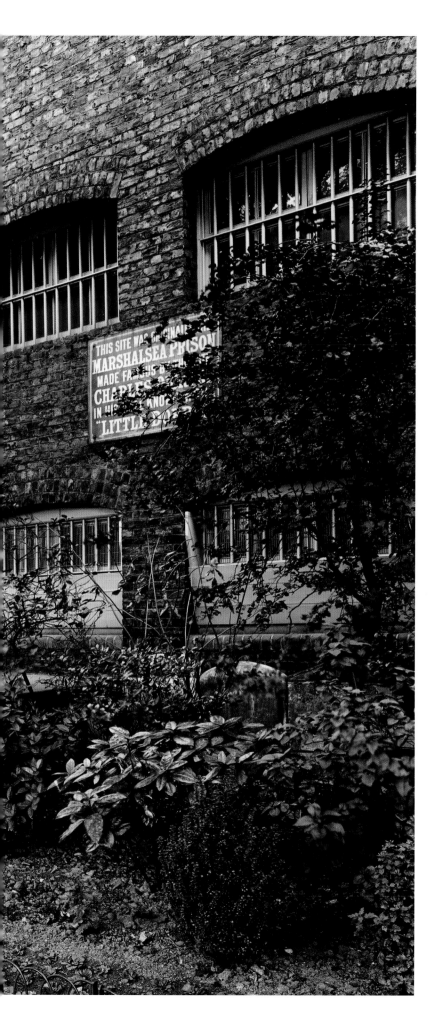

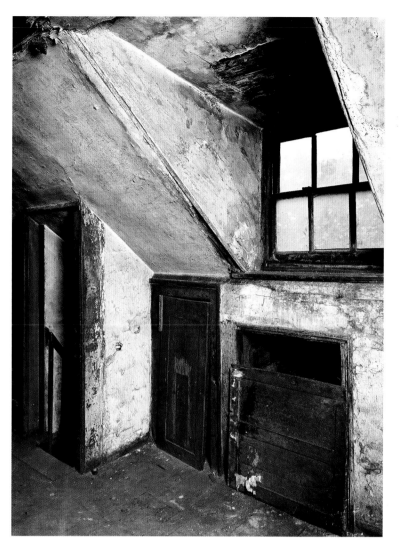

The turnkey's sky parlour – Little Dorrit's bedroom

Opposite: Marshalsea Prison, 14 September 1908
View of the rear of the former Marshalsea Prison from the burial ground behind showing the spiked fence to the old exercise yard. In 1824, Charles Dickens' father was imprisoned for debt in the Marshalsea. In 1842 it was closed and the buildings were used as a factory.

"It was an oblong pile of barrack building, partitioned into squalid houses standing back to back, so that there were no back rooms; environed by a narrow paved yard, hemmed in by high walls, duly spiked at top". (Charles Dickens, *Little Dorrit*)

Above: Little Dorrit's bedroom, 22 September 1908
Dickens frequently based his books on actual places he knew. Much of the early story of Little Dorrit revolved around the Marshalsea. Here, Little Dorrit was born and took lodgings with her godfather in the *"turnkey's sky parlour"* – a bleak garret room – so she could care for her father, brother and sister. This extraordinary photograph shows her home.

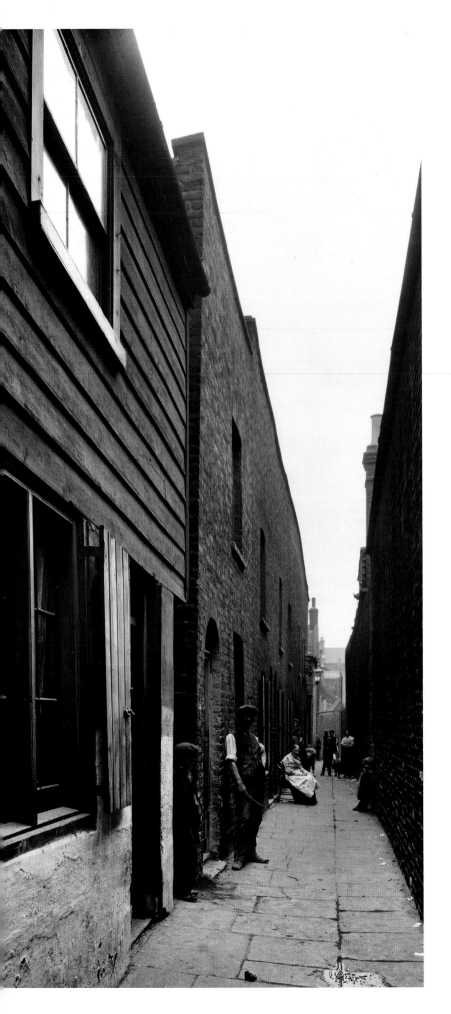

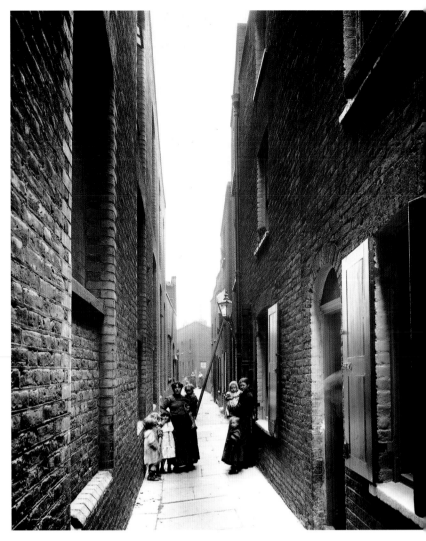

Bankside: views taken on 16 May 1912

In 1902 Charles Booth revealed that the highest concentration of poverty in London – 68% – could be found in the area between Blackfriars and London Bridge. Poisoned by toxic fumes from nearby white lead, gas and engineering works, the squalid maze of dingy streets and sunless alleys behind Bankside contained some of the worst housing in London. All the following images were taken on 16 May 1912.

Left: White Hind Alley

"*The surrounding streets are mean and close; poverty and debauchery lie festering in the crowded alleys …; an air of gloom and dreariness seems … to hang about the scene, and to impart to it a squalid and sickly hue.*" (Charles Dickens, *Pickwick Papers*).

White Hind Alley was a narrow passage lined on one side by mean dwellings and on the other by a high wall to a timber yard which blocked out the light from the houses.

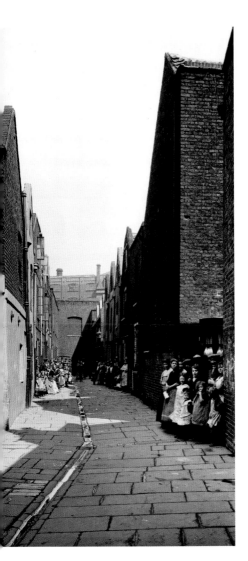
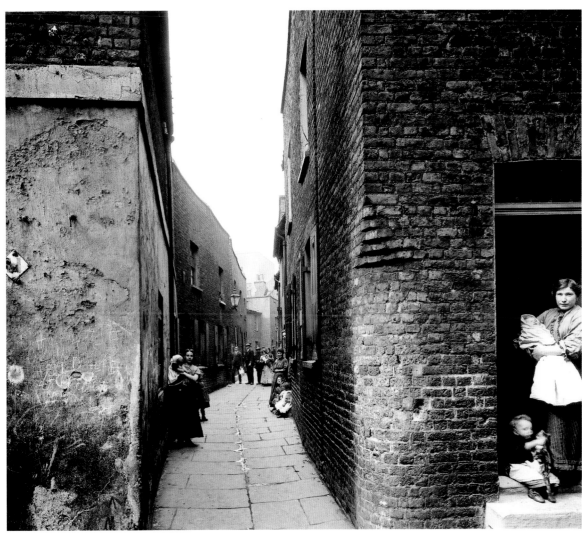

Melancholy streets in a penitential garb of soot...

Opposite right: Moss's Alley

Parts of Moss's Alley were less than 8ft wide, but provided access to a whole nest of small subsidiary courts and yards crammed with families categorised by Booth in the lowest class as semi-criminal, along with occasional labourers and loafers, their children classified as street "arabs".

Above left: Ladd's Court

Ladd's Court viewed from Pitt Place with Moss's Alley running from left to right. The sheer number of people gathered shows the chronic overcrowding. 1,800,000 people in London lived on or below the poverty line with a further 1,000,000 with just one week's wages between subsistence and pauperism. Life was poised precariously between respectability and destitution.

Above right: Moss's Alley

View looking north from the junction with Ladd's Court – a bleak harsh world of hard unremitting grind with the mark of poverty stamped indelibly both on the faces of the people and the houses.

To the left the chalk marks read Chocolate Club Held Here. The child to the right seems intent on throttling a kitten. His mother seems prematurely old, but is probably less than 30.

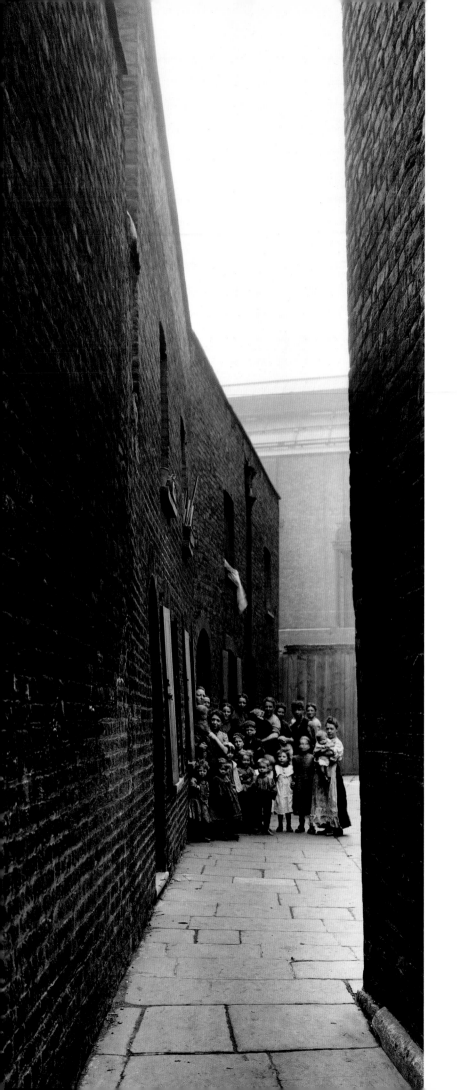

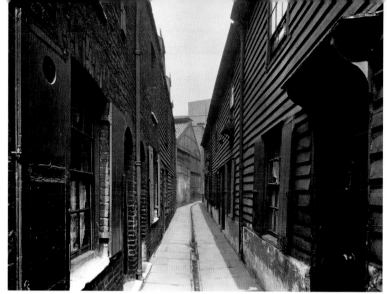

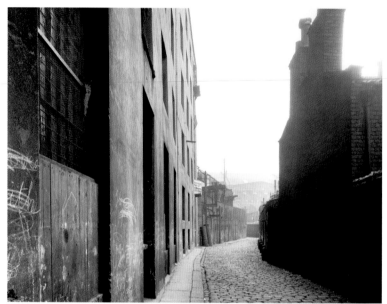

Warren of sunless courts

Left: Taylor's Yard
View from Moss's Alley into Taylor's Yard with the walls of the adjacent saw mills beyond.

Top: Wagstaff Buildings
Wagstaff Buildings was a narrow back alley of dark weatherboarded and brick dwellings sandwiched between an engineering works, which can be seen to the left centre of the picture, and Great Guildford Street.

Above: Cork's Place
Cork's Place (formerly Pleasant Row), which connected with the southern end of Wagstaff Buildings, was lined with industrial works and an iron foundry. To the right is the rear of properties in Zoar Street – another dreary street of two storey early 19th century dwellings.

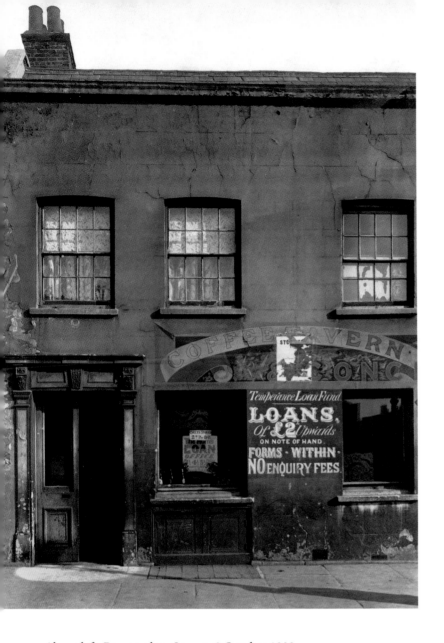

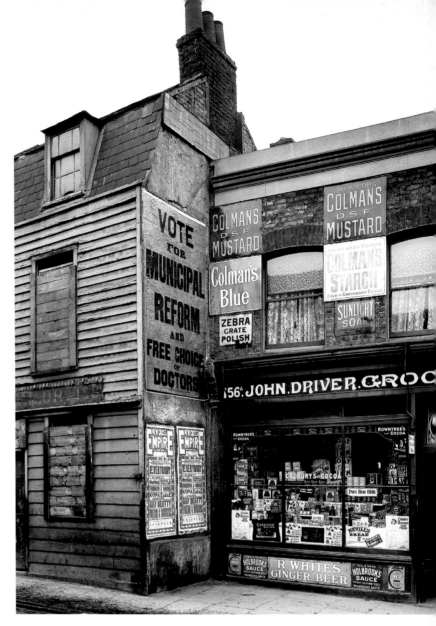

Above left: Bermondsey Square, 9 October 1900
Loan offices and pawnbrokers were common in poor neighbourhoods such as Bermondsey but they provided the only safety net for those out of work or facing destitution.

Above right: 156-162 Long Lane, Bermondsey, 6 February 1913
A splendid display of contemporary posters and advertisements on a mixed group of buildings at the south-west end of Long Lane. No. 158 and the cottages to the left are boarded up awaiting redevelopment together with a large vacant plot at the rear.

Right: Grange Walk, Bermondsey, c 1905
Grange Walk stands on the site of Bermondsey Abbey, of which fragments still remain. The house to the right, which is occupied, has broken front windows – a hallmark of poverty. In the 18th century the brick houses with carved doorcases beyond would have been occupied by prosperous merchants, but as the area declined they fell to multiple occupation.

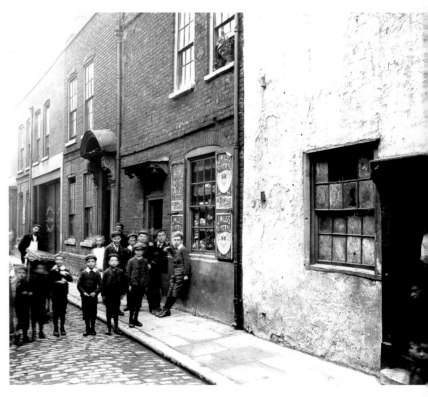

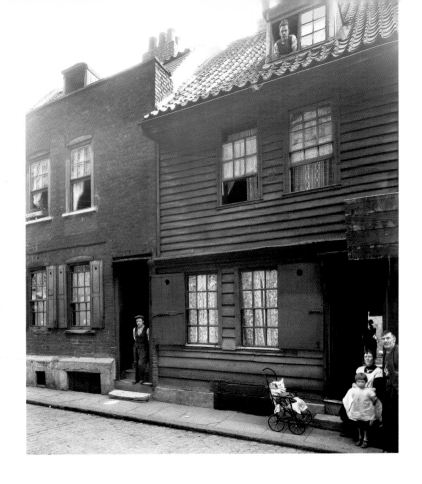

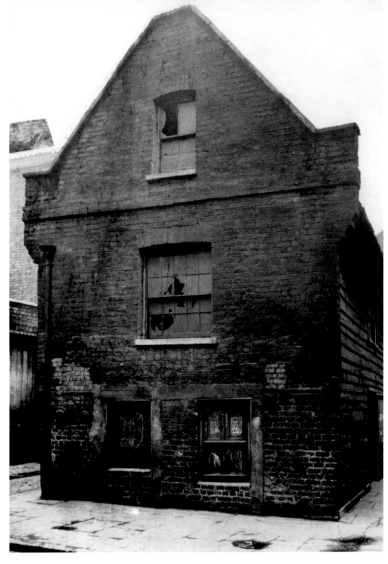

Above left: 24-26 Jacob Street, Bermondsey, c 1910
Timber houses were built in Bermondsey and Southwark using a ready supply of wood from nearby wharves, long after they were proscribed in the Building Act of 1707. These old 18th century houses with massive central chimney stacks were once part of the infamous rookery of Jacob's Island, the setting for Bill Sikes' death in *Oliver Twist*; but by 1910 the area was much changed. The houses seem well cared-for and the occupants relatively respectable.

Above right: New Square, Shad Thames, c 1906
Just west of St Saviour's Dock, New Square was a small enclave of 18th century dockside cottages with weatherboarded frontages, and shared privies at the end of the squalid communal yard.

Right: Brune Place, Newington Butts, Elephant & Castle, 26 November 1911
The cottages at the end of the court are marked with a plaque – Rose Court 1708 – but the remainder are later, 19th century terraces. Those to the left are more generous than most with small front yards for drying washing. The woman in the foreground is heavily pregnant, but all appear to be tired, worn out and depressed.

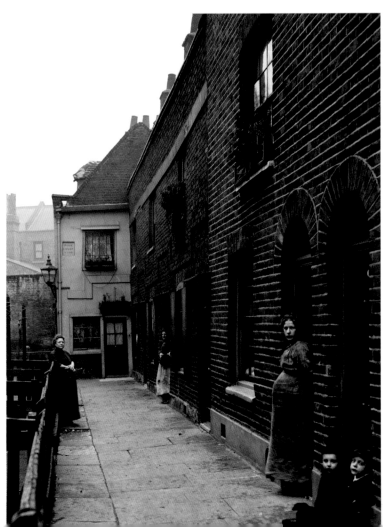

The Dog & Pot

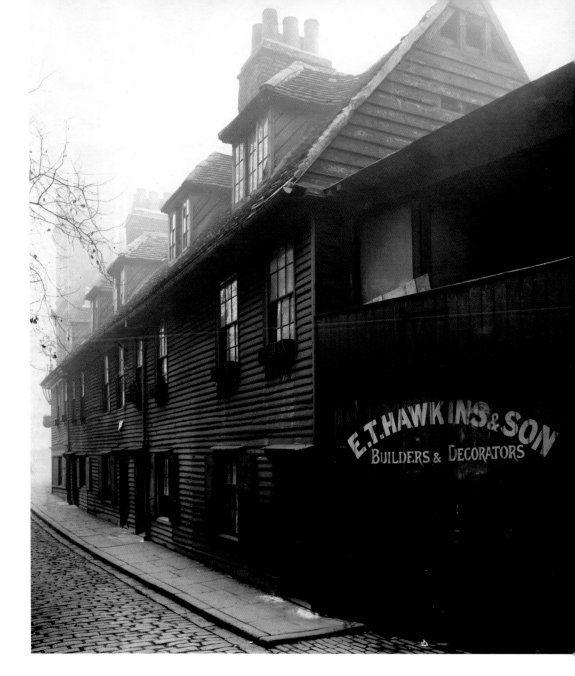

Right above: 72-80 Collingwood Street, Blackfriars, 1908

This short row of timber-framed and weatherboarded tradesmen's cottages stood opposite Christ Church, Southwark, and probably dated from the late 17th century. Each comprised two storeys and an attic with hipped tiled dormer windows and one room to each floor with a small lean-to scullery at the rear. After severe bomb damage they were deemed irreparable and demolished in 1948.

Right below: 196 Blackfriars Road, 25 September 1908

196 Blackfriars Road was a late 18th century building occupied by various firms of ironmongers. The famous wood and brass Dog and Pot sign was used as a trade mark on the firm's coal hole covers and other ironwork. It may have originated from 16th century woodcuts of slovenly housewives, which depicted women wiping a plate with a dog's tail, and the dog licking out a pot. Dickens remarked on *"the likeness of a golden dog licking a golden pot"* when he was lodging in Lant Street, Borough in 1824. The sign is now in the Cuming Museum.

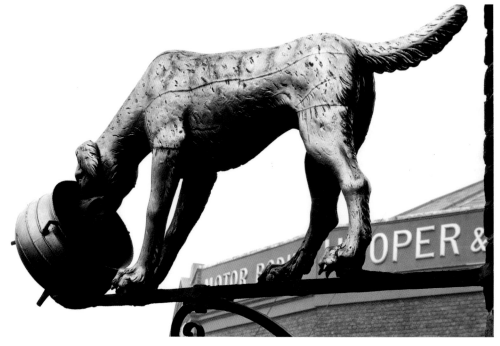

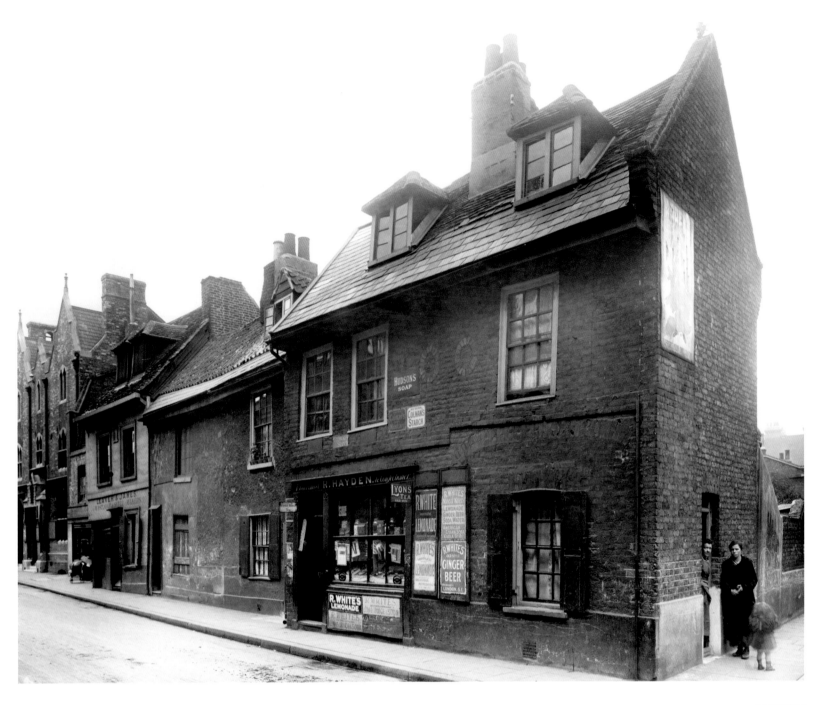

LAMBETH

Above : 20-23 High Street, Lambeth

Lambeth High Street was a busy working neighbourhood coloured by its proximity to the river. Ship chandlers and maritime suppliers were widespread; Leaver and James, mast scull and oar makers, were typical. Compare this view with the later photograph taken in 1923 on p 327.

Right: 49-53 High Street, 9 November 1908

An interesting row of late 17th century artisans' houses with a factory chimney rising behind. Note the huge projecting pedimented hood and simple two panelled door on the first house, the lack of street clutter and the beautifully-laid street surfaces with granite setts and kerbs to the carriageways and tightly-jointed York stone pavement slabs.

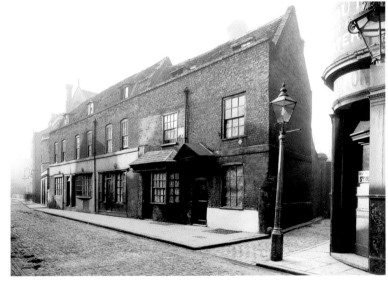

Artisans' quarters

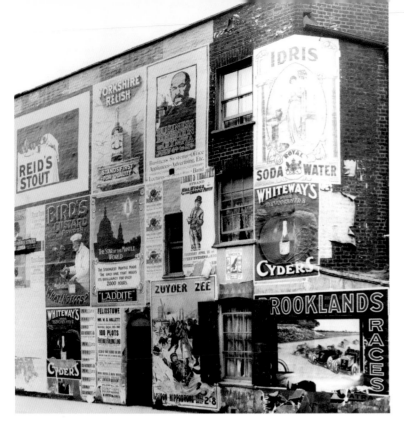

Left: Westminster Bridge Road, 1907
The flank elevation to Gerridge Street is covered in a magnificent array of contemporary posters, which were characteristic of Edwardian London.

Below: 69-79 Nine Elms Lane, 24 August 1908
A short row of six small artisans' houses dating from the early 18th century with large central chimney stacks and pantiled roofs, once typical of inner south London.

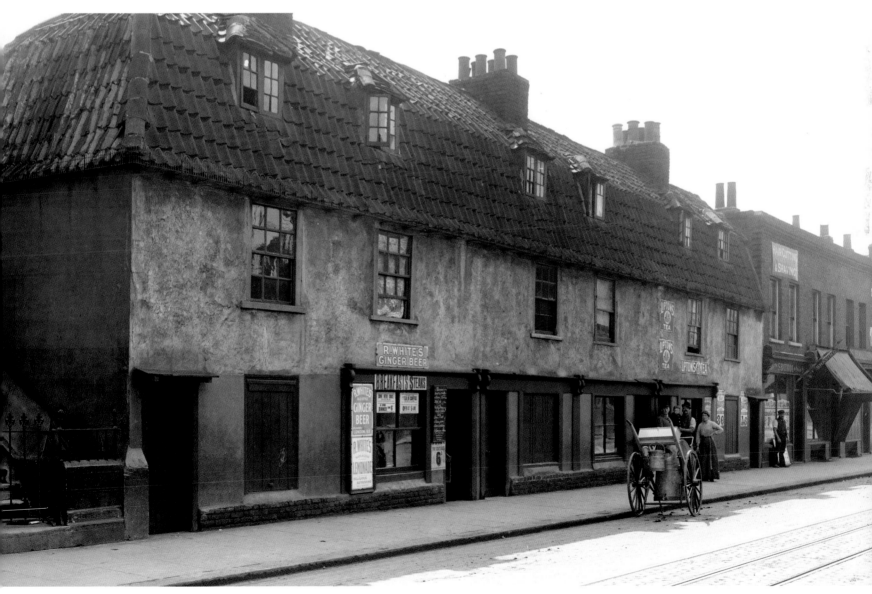

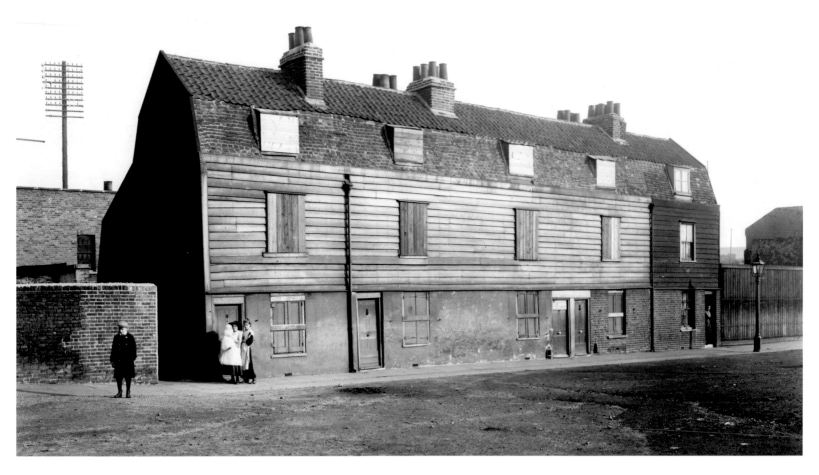

Isolated riverside village

ROTHERHITHE

Above: 1-9 Purnell Place, 8 November 1911

Rotherhithe is effectively a peninsula sandwiched between the Thames and the former Surrey Docks. Rotherhithe Street is the long, sinuous thread which once drew together a host of riverside communities. Purnell Place was a short cul-de-sac, facing open ground, behind the former Stave Dock.

Right: View of the rear elevations showing the massive chimney stacks, weatherboarding and mixture of pantile and tile roofs. The population of Rotherhithe trebled in the 19th century, and these small houses were home to the poorest classes who worked the waterfront and docks.

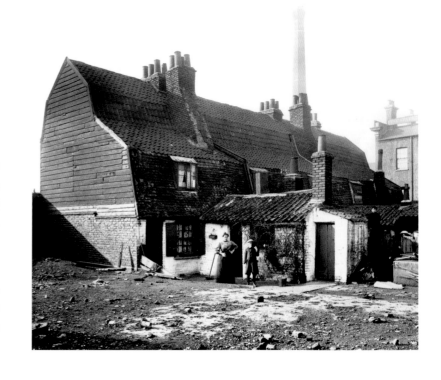

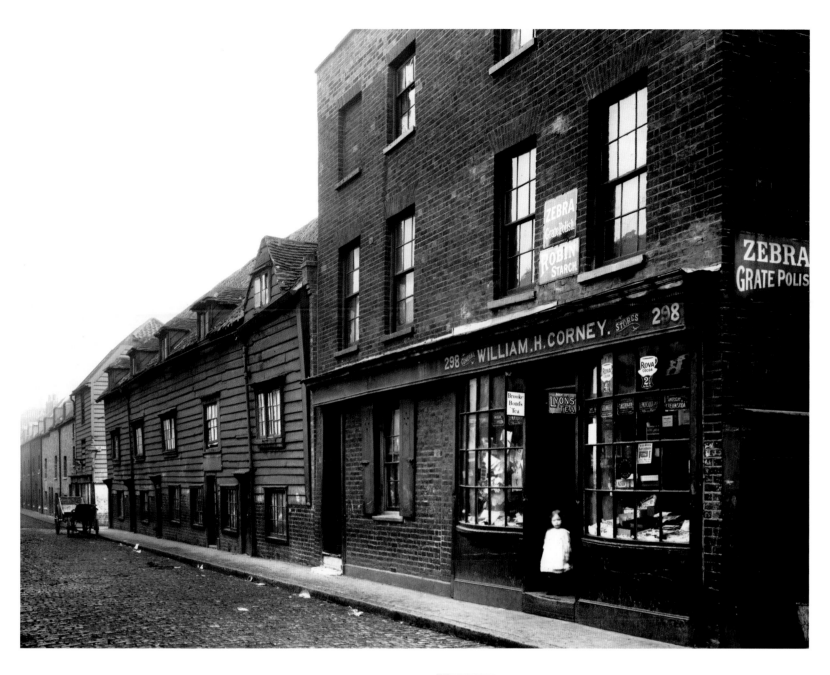

Above: 298-312 Rotherhithe Street, 8 November 1911

An atmospheric view of Rotherhithe Street with St Paul's Lane entering from the right in the middle distance. William Corney's stores has a fine shallow, double-bowed shopfront. Beyond are late 17th century timber-framed houses with weatherboarded walls.

Right: 302-312 Rotherhithe Street, 8 November 1911

A wonderful view of the backs of the houses seen above, which were built as a terrace with weatherboarded, gabled outshots and huge chimney stacks. Beyond is the looming mass of a mid-19th century warehouse at Globe Stairs.

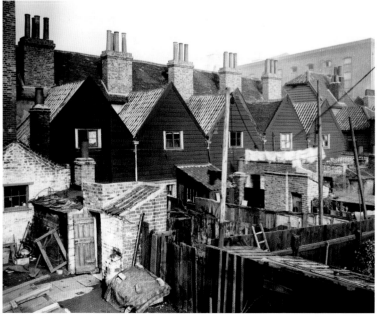

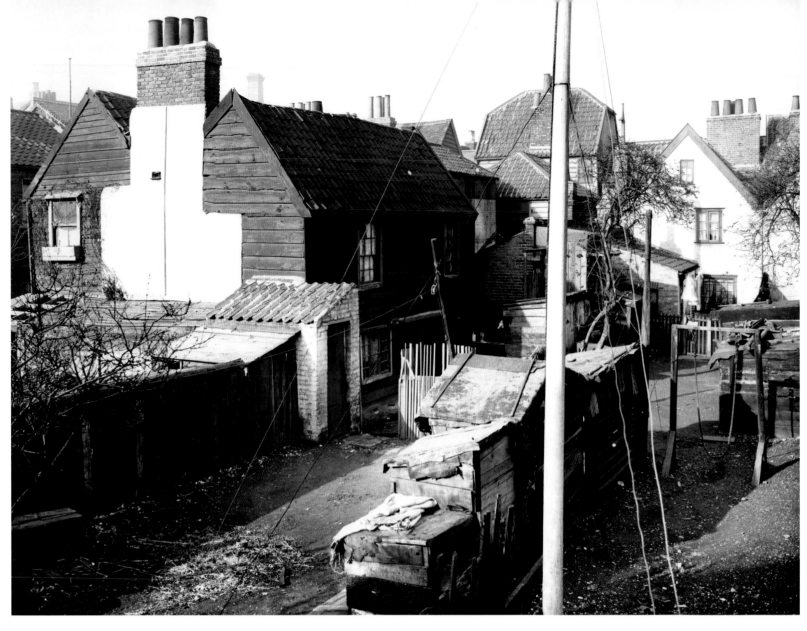

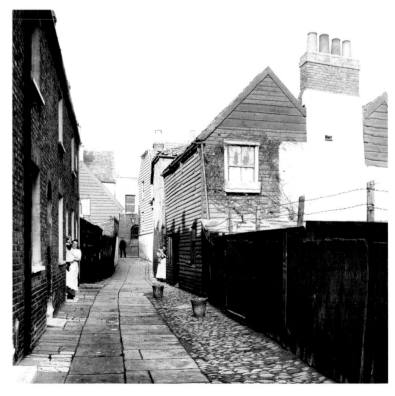

Above: 312 Rotherhithe Street and 2 St Paul's Lane, 8 November 1911
This view demonstrates the remarkable extent to which timber-framed vernacular buildings survived in areas like Rotherhithe well into the 20th century. The panorama of pantiled roofs, stained weatherboarding and ramshackle backyards has more in common with the riverside villages of the Thames estuary than inner London.

Right: 2 St Paul's Lane, 8 November 1911
St Paul's Lane was one of a number of narrow cul-de-sacs that ran off the south side of Rotherhithe Street hard up against the Surrey Docks, but the old 18th century cottages are more redolent of the atmosphere of an Essex fishing village.

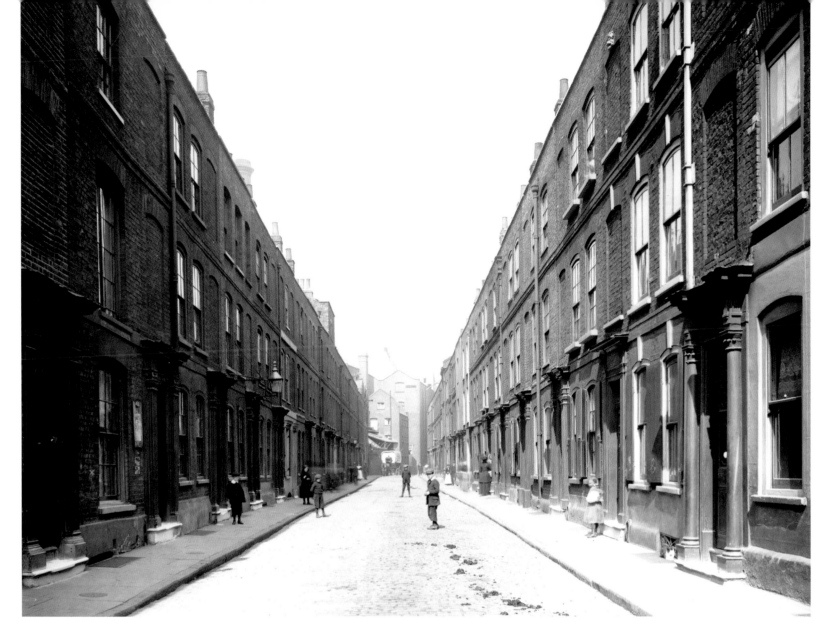

Sea captains and merchants

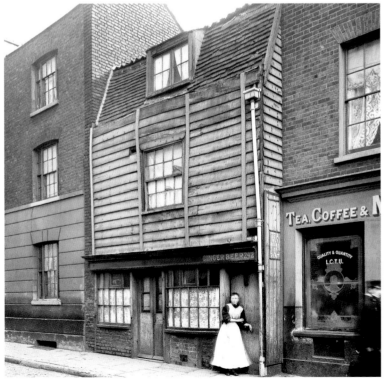

Above: Mayflower Street, Rotherhithe, 16 May 1914

Mayflower Street (formerly Princes Street) was built in 1721-23 as grand houses with a variety of plan forms for sea captains and merchants. Once a gated street, it fell on hard times and by 1914 was in multiple occupation as lodging houses. Much of the street survived the war, but what remained was swept away in the mid-1950s.

Left: 242 Rotherhithe Street, 8 November 1911

An 18th century survivor sandwiched between two later buildings. The house is in poor condition, the windows broken and the weatherboarding held in place by straps.

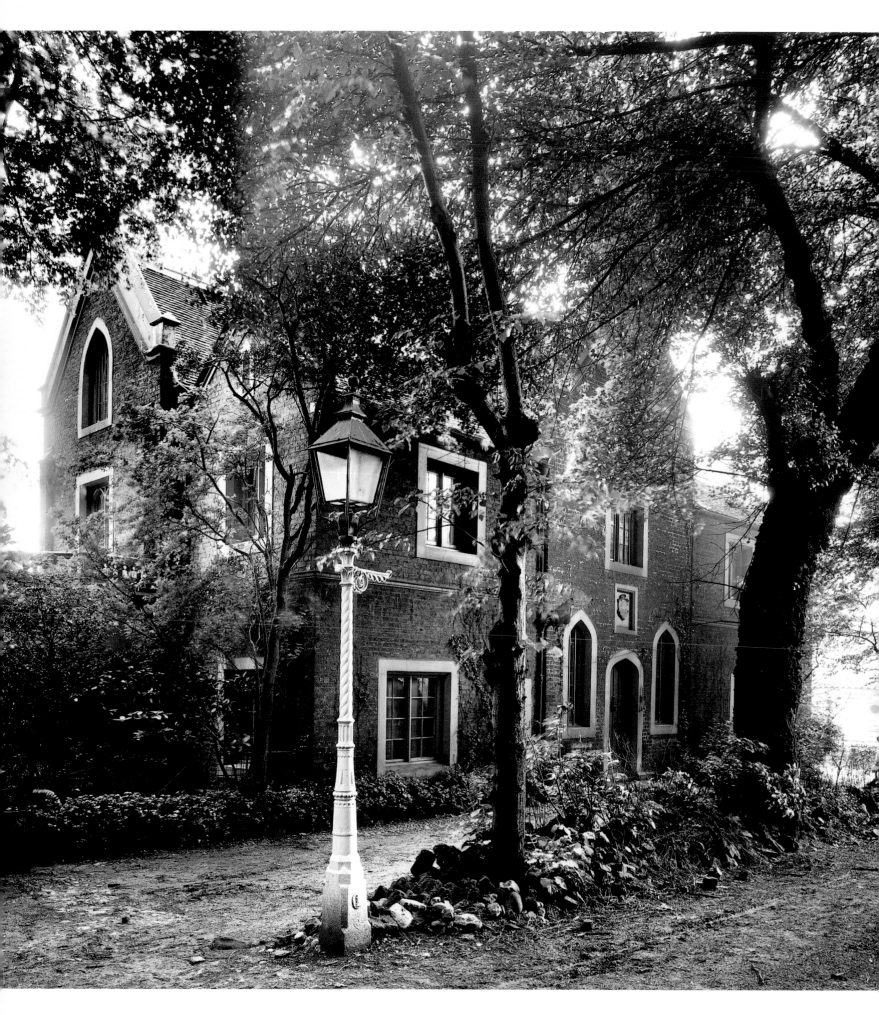

CHAPTER SEVEN

URBAN VILLAGES
Villas and leafy gardens

London is a polycentric city which grew out of a bi-polar centre – the cities of London and Westminster – commerce and court; but the pre-modern suburb attracted a whole series of extra-mural institutions which gravitated towards the outskirts. Here space was not at a premium, and institutions could impose their own rules.

Chelsea, Kensington, Greenwich, Eltham, Kew and Richmond were all moulded by their palaces and hospitals; and Woolwich by its great arsenal and military barracks, so interspersed amongst London's villages were much grander, ancient complexes which generated their own particular dynamics.

A striking feature of London's history is the suburban ideal of 'the retreat'. The city was seen as unnatural. Hatred of the metropolis and the vice and squalor that went with it was a component of early romanticism and radicalism. This was why detached villas and houses in leafy gardens became so fashionable in the inner suburbs for those who could afford them.

Older established villages, particularly to the west of London along the Thames – like Chelsea, Chiswick, Kew and Richmond – retained their social cachet, whilst others elsewhere were beset by changing fortunes – Bromley-by-Bow, for instance, a 16th century royal retreat, was engulfed by the East End and never recovered its fashionable status. Conversely, on the high ground to the north of London Hampstead and Highgate never lost it.

In the late 19th century, as the centrifugal forces driving London's expansion gathered momentum, once-isolated villages were subsumed into the great maw. Sometimes the outlying villas and mansions built by earlier generations remained as islands marooned in a sea of new development, but with rising land values these too succumbed eventually to redevelopment.

Similarly, from 1900 onwards increasingly the fields between the tentacles of ribbon development along the great road corridors leading into the capital were covered by brick and concrete. Old farms, which had once marked the limits of the city were swallowed up by streets and houses for the burgeoning middle classes. Old coaching inns which had once characterised so many older cores were swept away or rebuilt to cater for the needs of new suburban communities. During the Edwardian years alone, over 670,000 people moved into the outer ring as ripples of urban expansion crept remorselessly outwards.

Some of the new communities created were the product of the social idealism which underpinned the emerging town-planning movement. The early garden suburbs at Bedford Park, Brentham, Ealing, and Hampstead, for example, were the product of very English ideals, and attracted the best architects of their day and international acclaim. Elsewhere speculative builder-developers, like the Collins family in Muswell Hill, produced new places of real quality, from which lessons can be learned today.

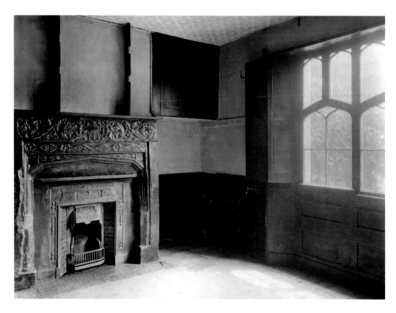

Opposite: Gothic Hall, Highgate Road, 28 June 1909
A haunting view of The Gothic, or Gothic Hall, once the home of Sir James Williams, and at the time of the photograph the residence of the vicar of St Martin's, Gospel Oak, whose wife ran a ladies' school from their home. The site is now part of the grounds of William Ellis School.

Above: View of the school room showing an ancient 16th century chimneypiece.

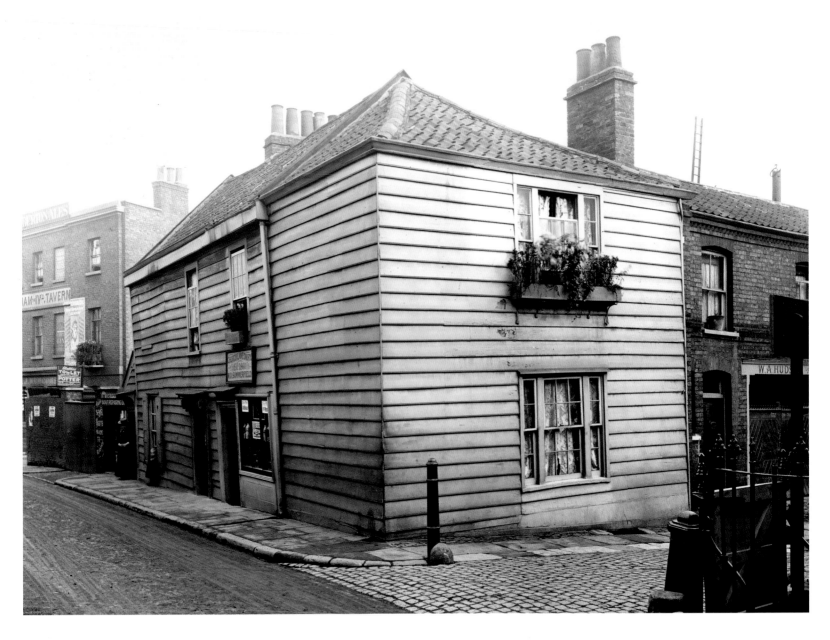

Rural vernacular

HAMPSTEAD

Above: 1, 3 & 5 Perrins Lane, Hampstead, 17 November 1908
18th century weatherboarded cottages with The William IV public house
beyond. The site was redeveloped for modern mews houses in the 1960s.

Right: Romney's House, Holly Bush Hill, 4 February 1908
View from the courtyard showing the weatherboarded artist's studio
which George Romney built in anticipation that "*a new hour of glory was
come*", but his health deteriorated and he only lived there for two years
from 1797. Later it was converted to the Assembly Rooms, where resident
artists and writers met quarterly, before becoming the Constitutional Club.
Today it is once more a private house.

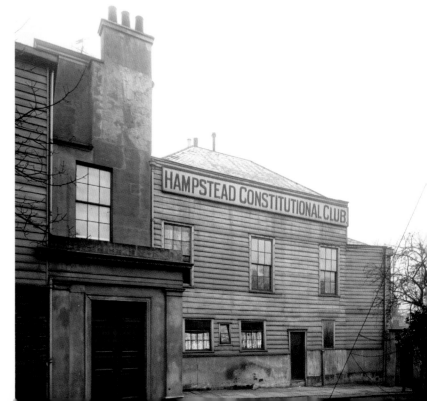

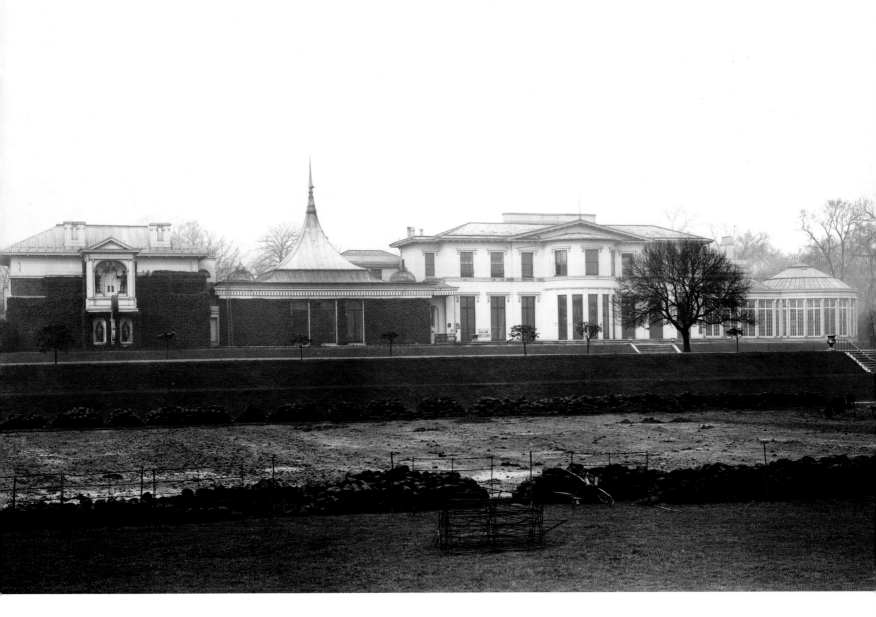

The caliph of Regent's Park

REGENT'S PARK

Above: St Dunstan's House, Outer Circle, Regent's Park, 2 March 1908

St Dunstan's House (formerly Hertford Villa) was the largest of the eight grand villas completed at Regent's Park. Designed by Decimus Burton, Hertford Villa was essentially two houses linked by a magnificent tent room used for receptions by the notorious rake, the third Marquess of Hertford known as the 'Caliph of Regent's Park'. The huge clock to the left with life-size striking figures of Gog and Magog, was rescued by Burton from St Dunstan's Church, Fleet Street, which was demolished in the 1830s. Subsequently they were returned to the rebuilt church.

Later, in 1915, owned by Otto Kahn the financier, the house was used by a blind servicemen's charity founded by Sir John Pearson which gave its name, St Dunstan's, to the charity. Neglected and damaged by fire in the 1930s, it was purchased by Barbara Hutton, the Woolworth heiress, and redeveloped. She donated the new house, Winfield House, designed by Leonard Rome Guthrie, to the US government. It is now the residence of the US Ambassador.

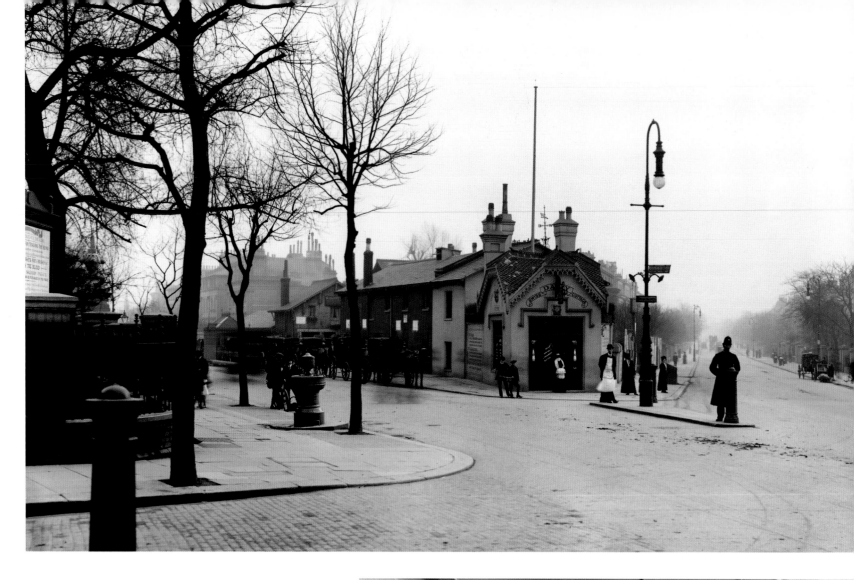

SWISS COTTAGE

Above: The Swiss Cottage, Finchley Road, 28 February 1912
Built as an inn in the 1840s, The Swiss Cottage public house
became a local landmark and gave its name to the entire
district as it developed. The main buildings, which still
survive, can be seen behind the brick cottages in the
foreground. Finchley Road is to the right leading towards St
John's Wood. To the left is Avenue Road with a granite
drinking fountain in the foreground.

Right: View of the kitchen, kitchen maid and cat.

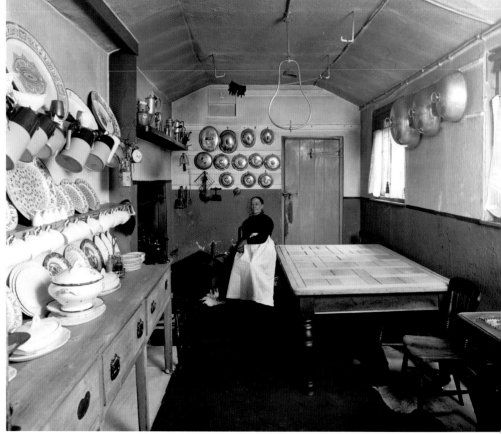

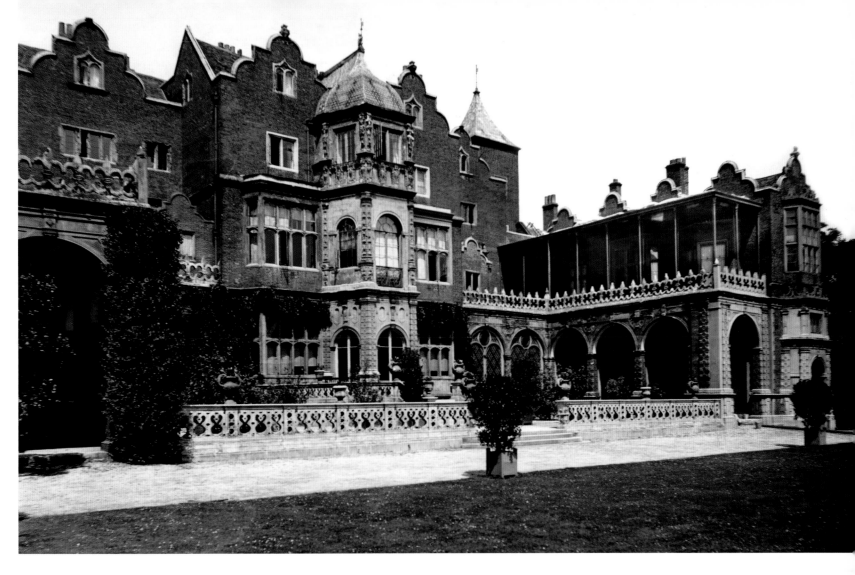

HOLLAND PARK

Above: Holland House, Holland Park, c 1912

Holland House was one of London's grandest Jacobean mansions. From the late 18th to the mid-19th century it belonged to the Fox family – Lords Holland, who embellished both the house and garden. Bombed in 1941, the ruined house was cleared in 1955-57, leaving only a fragmented shell as a backdrop for an open-air theatre, and the east wing, which was converted unsympathetically into a youth hostel.

KENSAL NEW TOWN

Right: 13-20 East Row, Kensal New Town, 6 July 1911

Kensal New Town, a notorious slum, was built in the 1840s, with groups of single storey cottages occupied by poor Irish families. Between Middle Row and East Row was a common used for fairs, markets, dogfights and gipsy camps. From 1880 until the Second World War, Kensal New Town became the laundry centre for the grand houses of the West End. Known as "*Soap Suds Island*" the last of the individual cottages, shown here, were demolished in 1911 for the Emslie Horniman Gardens. Similar cottages in Notting Dale were known as the "*Piggeries*".

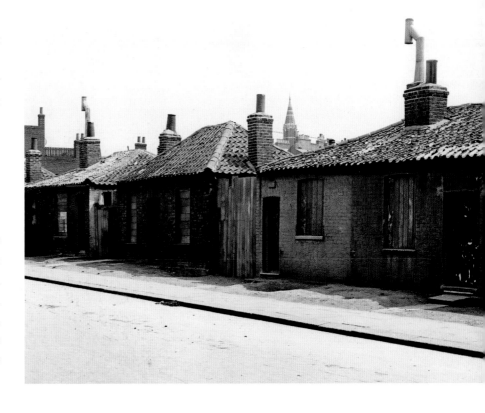

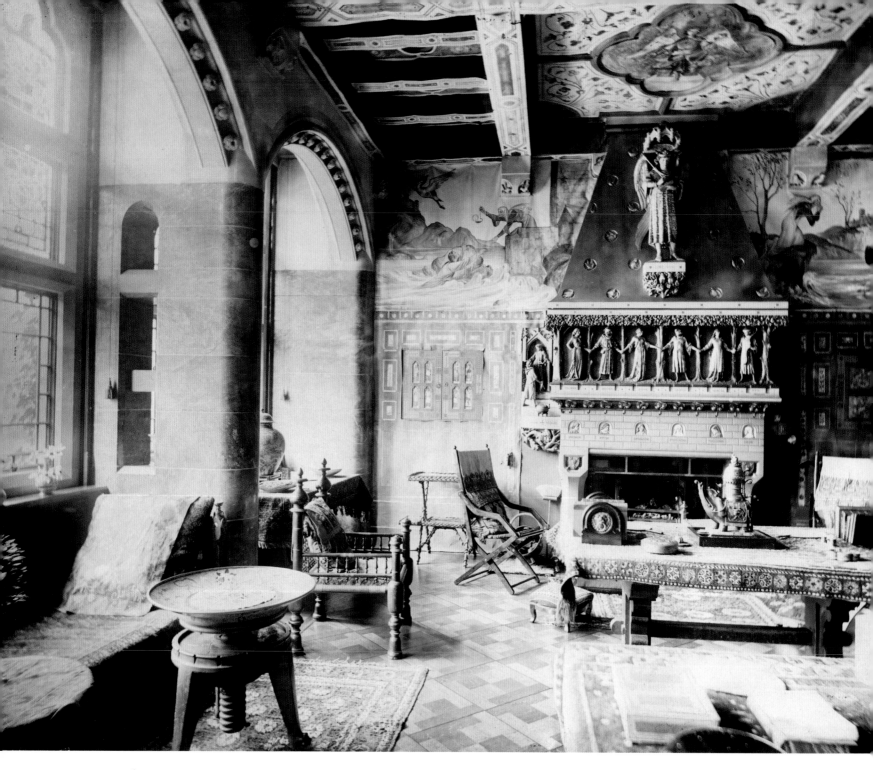

A Gothic extravaganza

KENSINGTON

Tower House, 29 Melbury Road, Kensington, c 1895
Built for his own use by William Burges between 1876-78, Tower House boasts one of the most spectacular interiors in London with superb structural decoration and painted stencilled details in the distinctive High Victorian Gothic style, which Burges perfected at Cardiff Castle and Castell Coch. The house remains in private ownership.

Above: View of the ground floor Drawing Room with its magnificent canopied fireplace. Each room had a particular theme; for the Drawing Room, it was Love. Note the Indian furniture.

Opposite top: View of the guest bedroom showing the original decorative scheme and some of the elaborate French Gothic furniture designed specifically for the room.

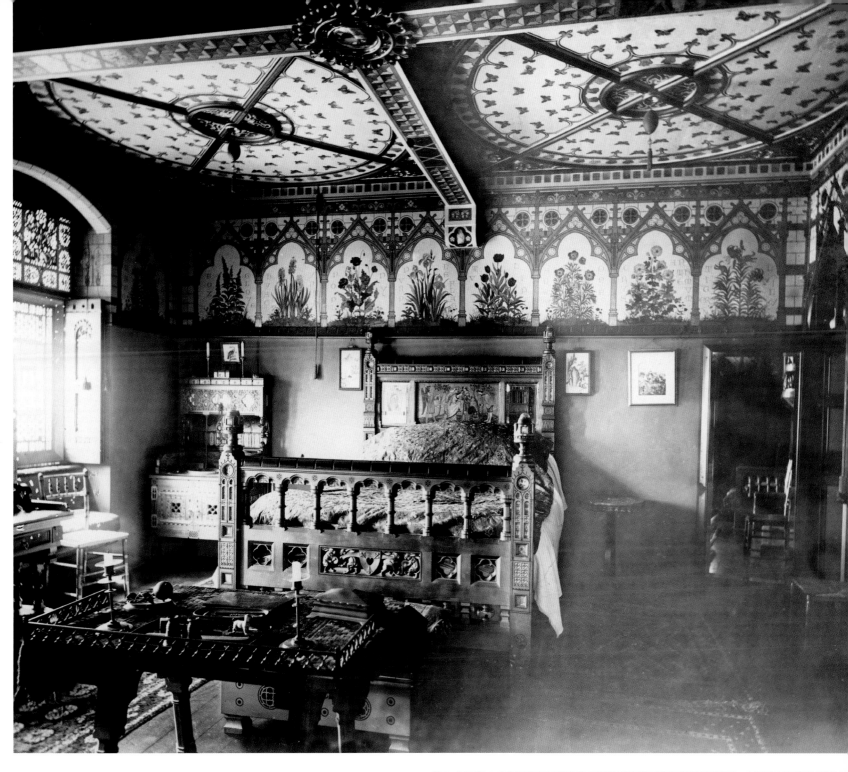

Right: Slaters, Kensington High Street, 1909
The jams and pickles counter at Slaters was typical of many shop interiors
of the period with elaborate Art Nouveau glazing, mirrored counters and
elegant displays of produce.

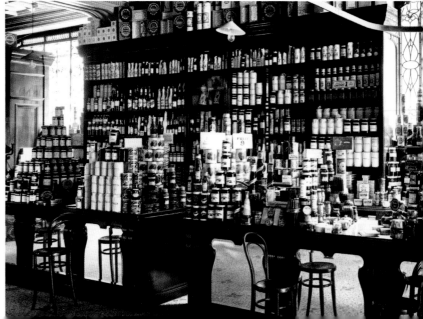

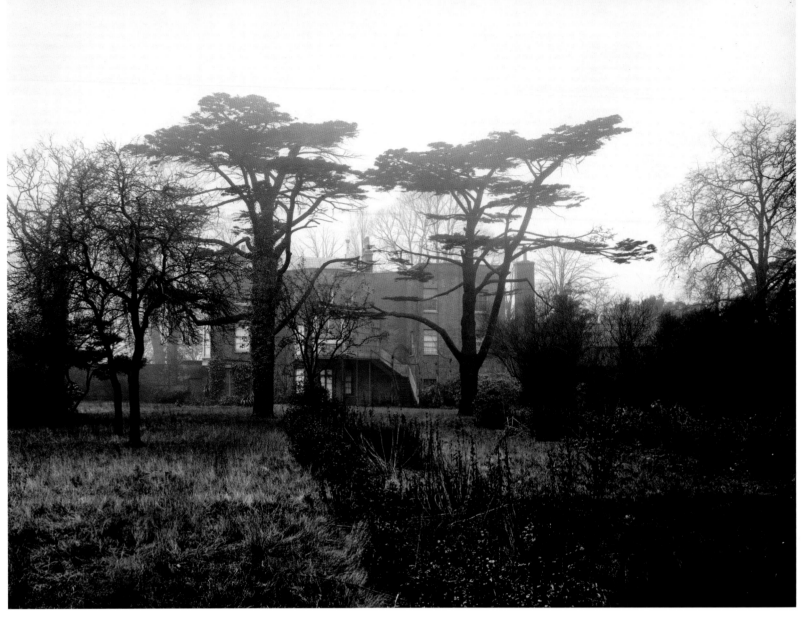

FULHAM

Carnwath House, Fulham, 18 December 1911

Above: View of the east elevation and grounds mid-winter.

"This beautiful villa … commands a fine broad sweep of the river Thames … which flows within a few yards of the pleasure grounds (which) are adorned with some fine cedars of Lebanon and other ornamental trees and shrubs." (*The Beauties of Middlesex,* 1850)

The most easterly of the villas which once lined the riverside at Fulham; from 1842 Carnwath (formerly Lonsdale) House was the home of Sir John and Lady Shelley, and the scene of lavish summer parties, known as "Strawberry Teas", at one of which William Gladstone is reputed to have proposed to his future wife. It was said that more matrimonial matches were made on the lawn here than at any other house in England.

The house was alleged to be the model for Sir Barnet and Lady Skittles' villa at Fulham in *Dombey & Son.*

Right: View showing a large wistaria which grew through the floor of the house and departed through the wall.

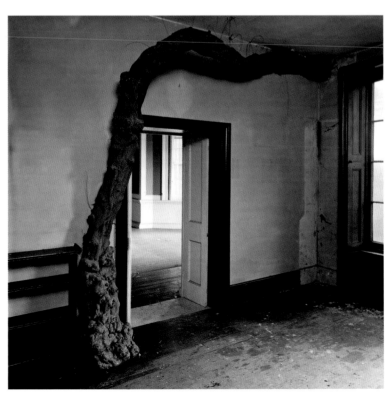

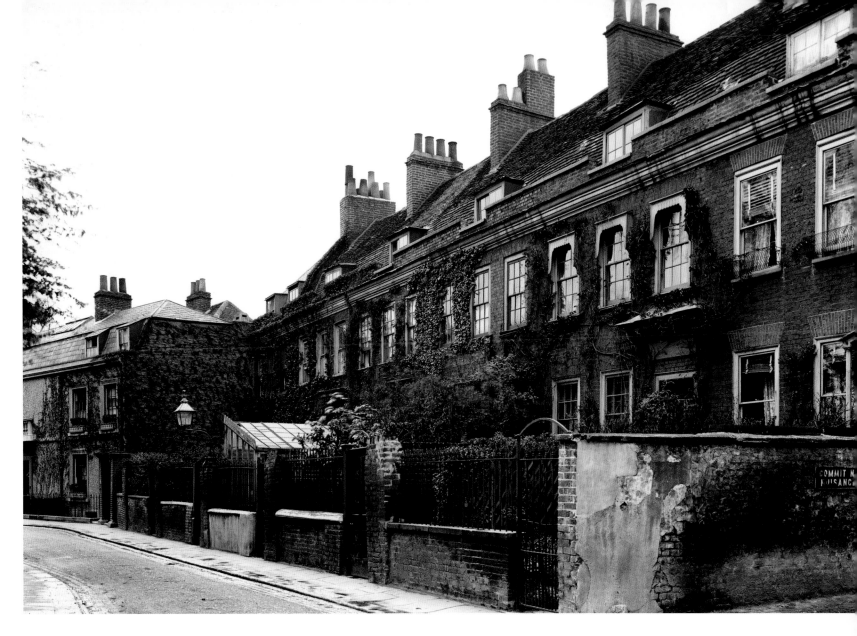

Old urban villages

Above: 1-6 Church Row, Fulham, 6 May 1904

Only Nos. 5 and 6 remain of this splendid group of early 18th century houses in what is now Church Gate. The remainder were demolished in 1905 for a church hall. At No. 1, to the right, "Honest" John Phelps, the Fulham ferryman, lived for over 40 years until 1888. At the rear was a nursery garden.

Right: 98-102 High Street, Fulham, 6 May 1904

A view once redolent of many parts of the inner suburbs: a mixed group of 18th century domestic buildings housing a range of local traders – hair cutting rooms, cobblers, a steam cycle works and sweet shop. *The Fatal Wedding* is showing at the Fulham Theatre.

The entire group was demolished for an extension of the LCC's tramway track from Hammersmith to Putney Bridge in 1909.

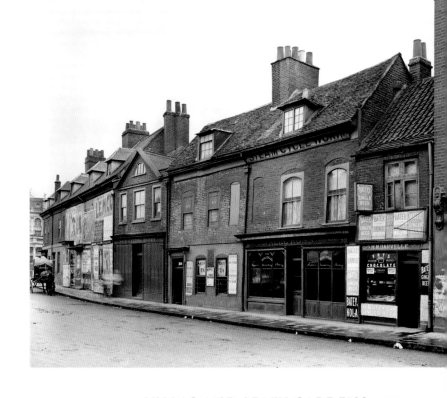

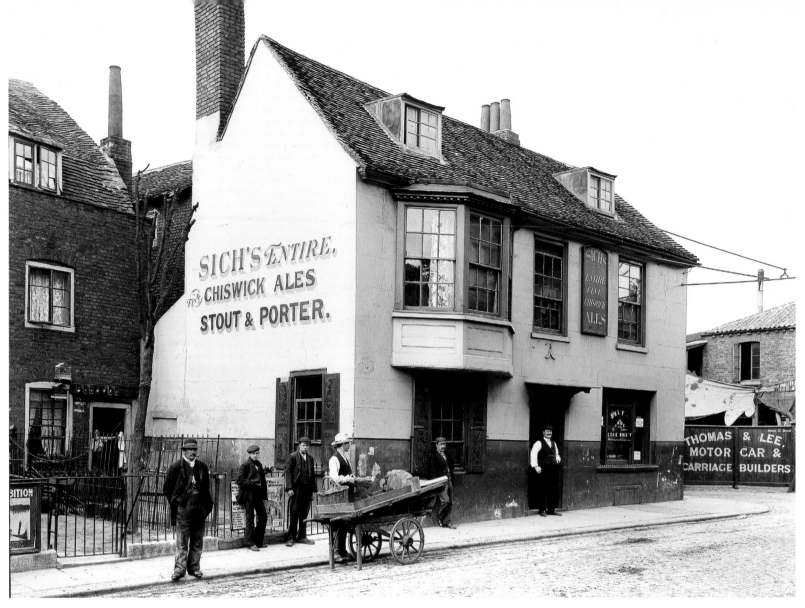

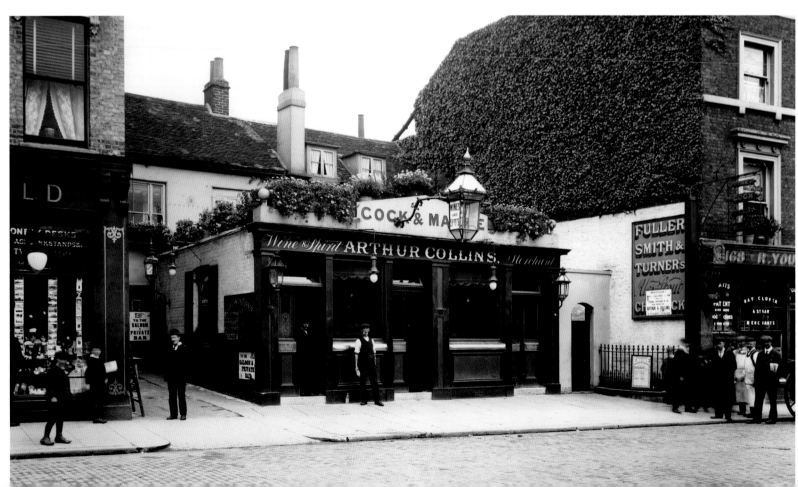

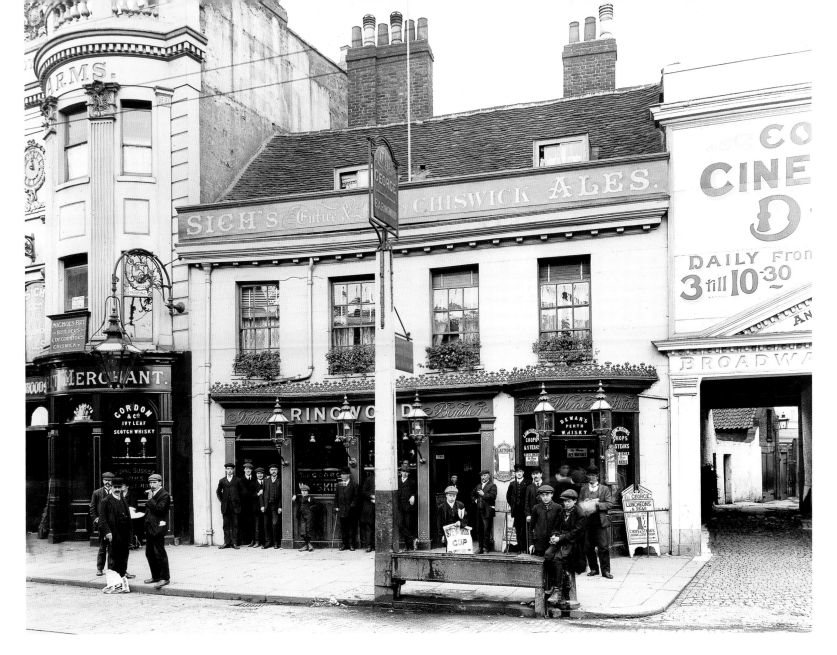

Wayside inns

HAMMERSMITH

Hammersmith was renowned for its large number of coaching inns and taverns, which catered for travellers heading to London from the west.

Opposite top: The Cannon, 80 Queen Street, 13 July 1904
The Cannon public house, at the junction with Bridge Street, was a simple 18th century cottage with a picturesque overhanging bay-window and a steeply-pitched clay tile roof. At the time of the photograph it had survived largely unaltered since it was sketched in 1869. To the left is a pair of houses, remnants of a group of earlier houses that ran down to the river. The group was demolished in 1937 for the Queen's Estate.

Opposite below: The Cock & Magpie, 170 King Street, 26 July 1910
Another early coaching inn with stable yard and garden was The Cock & Magpie PH in King Street, a long, low building set back from the street beneath an ancient tiled roof with a covered skittle ground. It was demolished in 1919 for the Gospel Hall of the Kelly Mission.

Above: The George, The Broadway, 26 July 1910
Originally called The White Horse, behind the later stucco front The George PH was a 17th century tavern and booking office for coaches with extensive stabling and coach houses at the rear. To the left, one of the curved bays of the grand Royal Sussex Arms public house can be seen embellished with a coat of arms, clock and foliated iron brackets to the pendant lanterns.

The buildings were demolished for road widening. A new public house, also called The George, was built immediately behind in 1911.

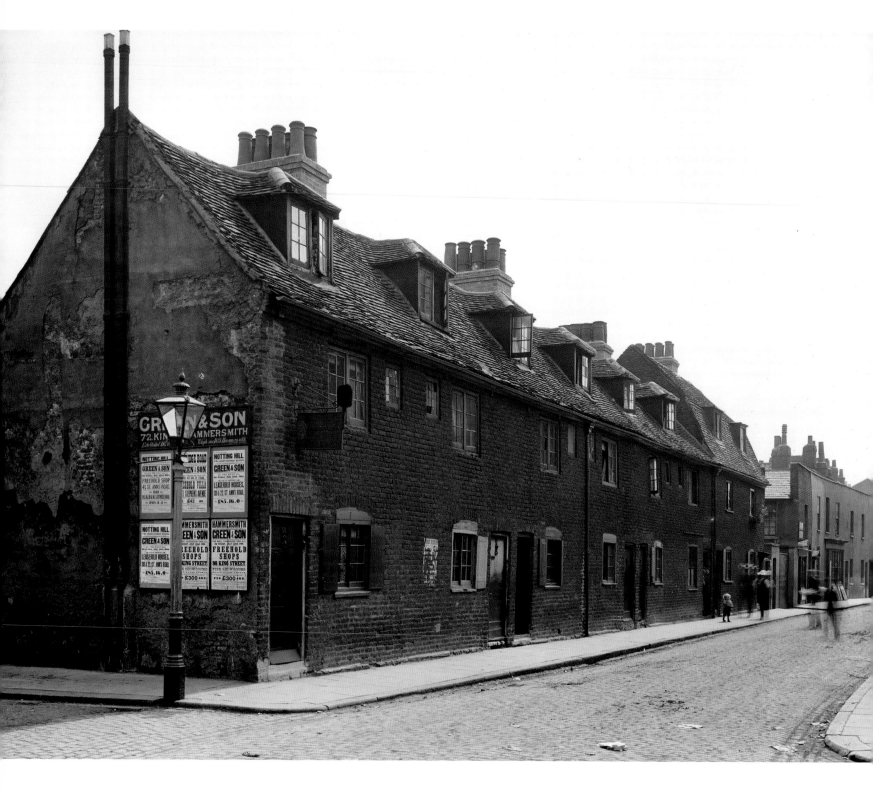

PECKHAM

Above: 65-79 Queen Street, Hammersmith, 21 July 1904
Queen Street (later Queen Caroline Street) was an ancient thoroughfare leading to the river. Nos. 65-79 were a picturesque group of 17th century red brick houses with old wooden casements, some of which retained their original lead glazing. The end house, No. 79, was raised higher with a double-pitched mansard roof. Note the chimney sweep's brush on the projecting sign in the foreground. The buildings were cleared in 1937 for a garage.

Opposite: Ye Olde Bun House, 96 Peckham High Street, c 1895
Once a Peckham landmark, Ye Olde Bun House Refreshment Rooms formed part of a group of modest early 18th century, one-room plan houses. The building was redeveloped in 1898 as 'The Bun House' public house in the conventional red brick style of the period, but the neighbouring early Georgian buildings still survive.

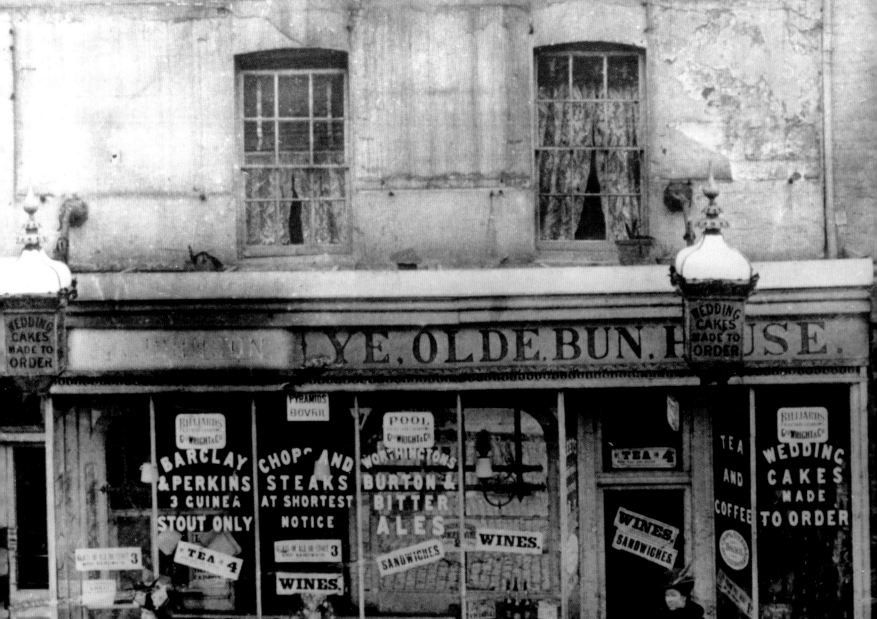

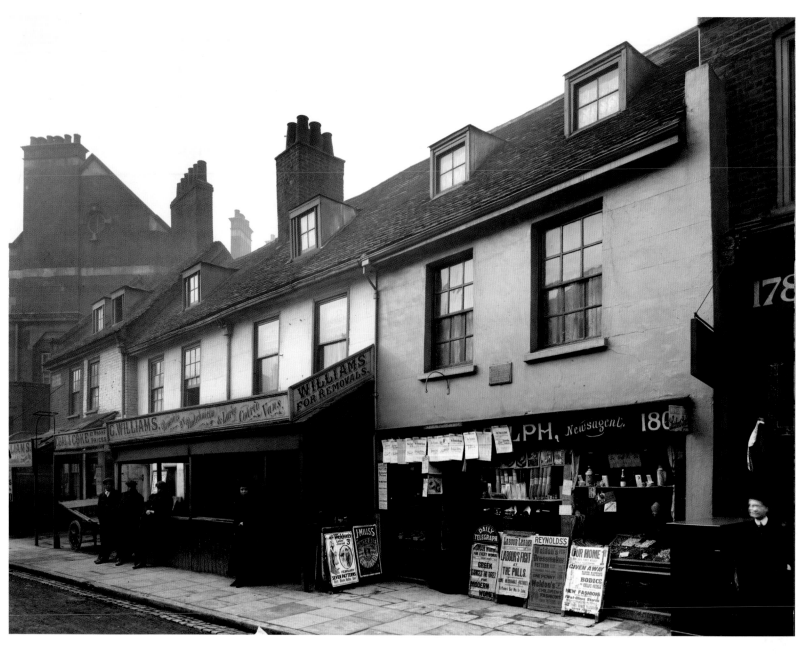

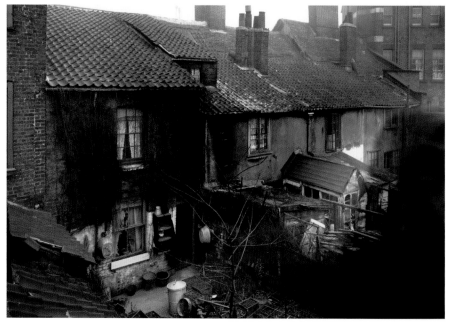

Above: 180 Meeting House Lane, Peckham, 21 January 1910
An interesting row of 17th century cottages. The plaque records
that the house to the right was the original Meeting House of
William Penn, the Quaker and founder of Pennsylvania. In 1947
The Society of Friends denied the statement.

Right: Rear elevations showing pantiled outshots and yards.

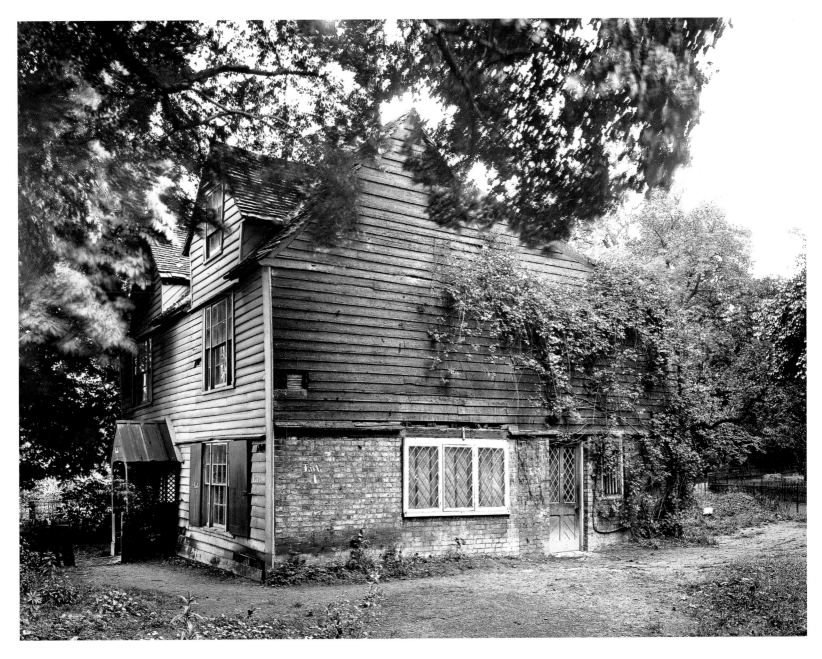

Rural remnants

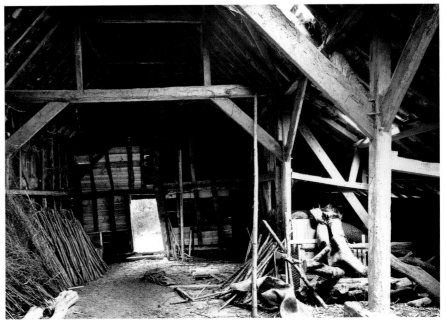

Above: Homestall Farm, Peckham Rye, 11 July 1908
A rustic idyll in the heart of Peckham, enclosed by 150 year old elm trees. Homestall Farm was an old 17th century weatherboarded farmhouse with moss-grown, tiled roofs which was acquired by the LCC in 1894 for an extension to Peckham Rye Park to ease overcrowding in holidays. It was demolished in August 1908.

Right: View of the barn once used by smugglers to store contraband.

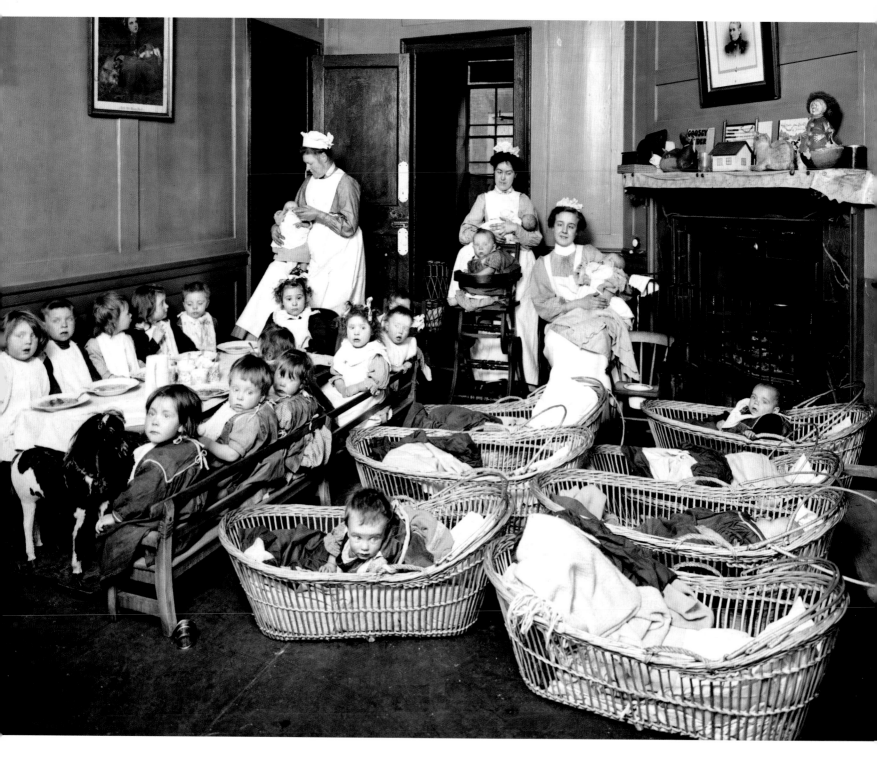

DEPTFORD

Above: 34 Albury Street, Deptford, 30 April 1911
A wonderfully evocative view of the nursery in the ground floor rear room. Note the wooden horse by the table and the copy of Goosey Gander on the mantelpiece.

GREENWICH

Opposite: Pemmell's Court, Church Street, Greenwich, 23 November 1911
View of an unusual range of very narrow, three-storey weatherboarded 18th century houses hidden in a narrow alley between Nos. 13-15 Church Street.

"*These premises were very difficult to find, unknown to either the policemen or postmen, and were only finally discovered by a systematic search up every alley, and court, which at times led to inquisitorial glances and remarks, not always of a complimentary nature.*" (LCC Survey: 2 November 1911)

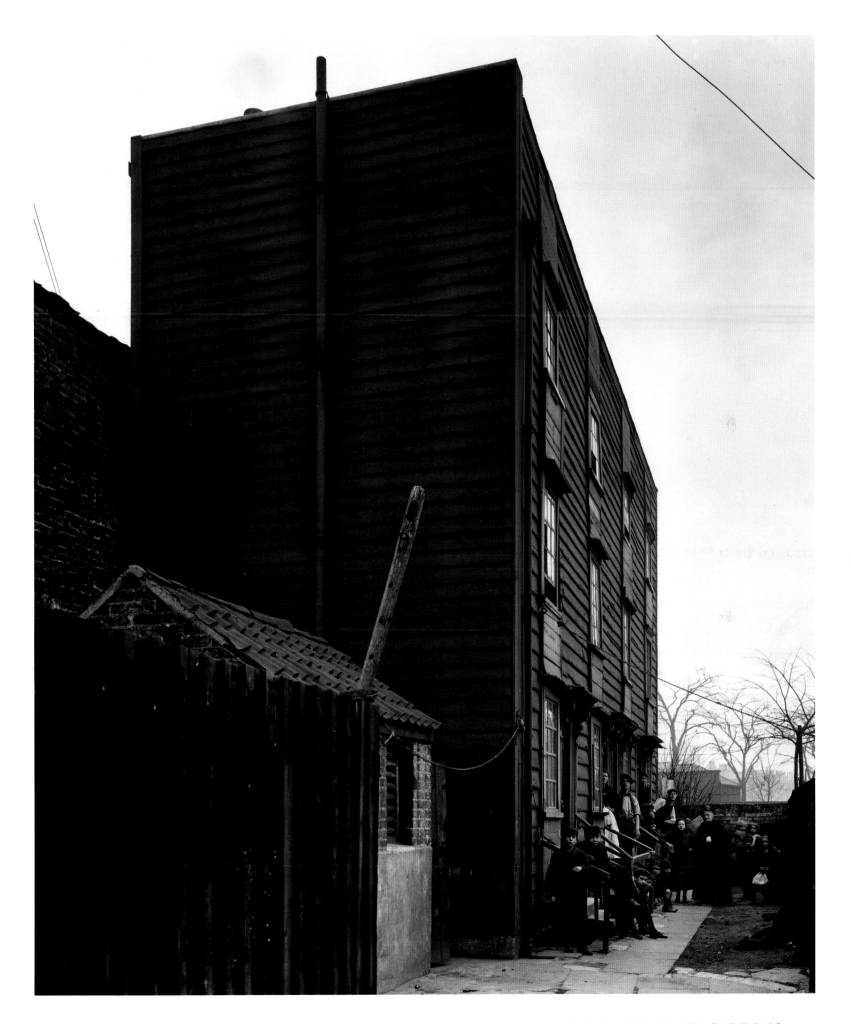

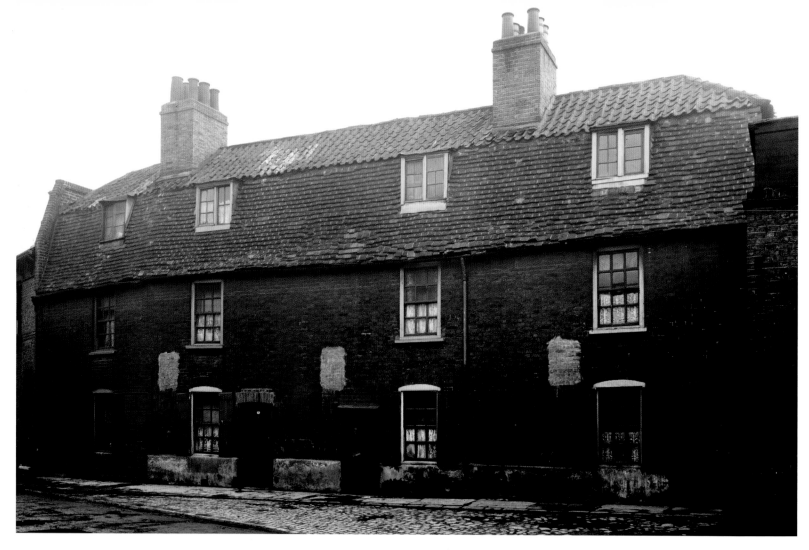

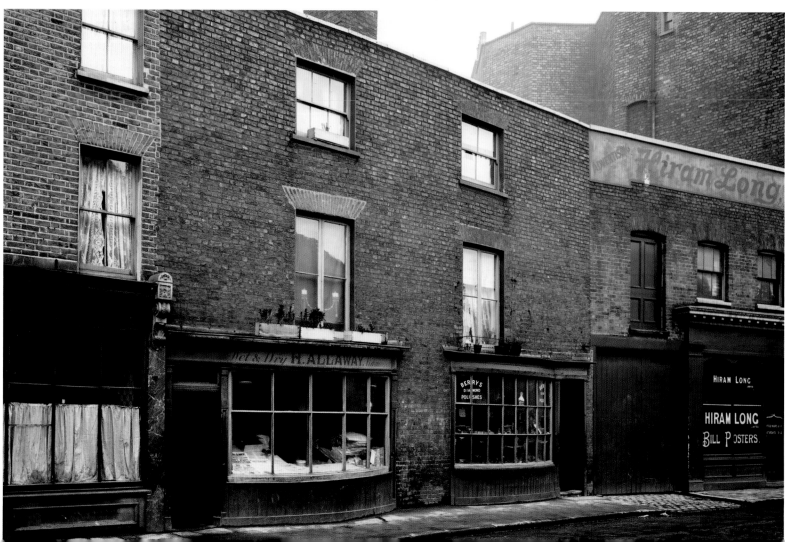

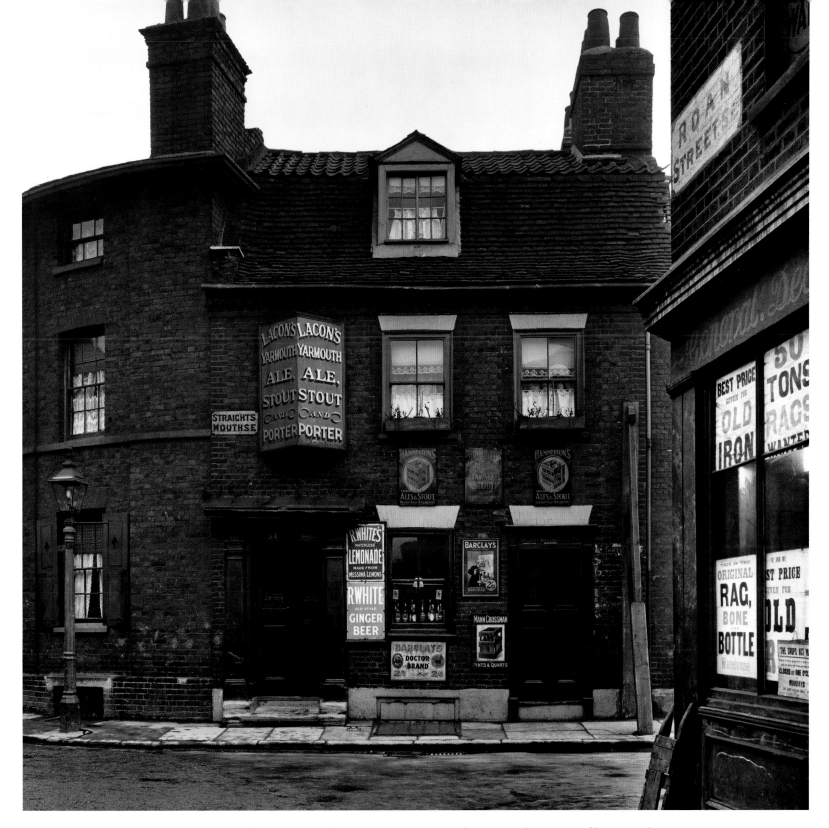

Where Greenwich smiles upon the silver flood

Opposite top: 5-11 Roan Street, Greenwich, 17 January 1913
A late 17th century row of cottages. Note the original thick glazing bars to the sash windows.

Opposite below: 6-8 Roan Street, 17 January 1913
Early 19th century terrace with shallow bowed shopfronts.

Above: The Earl Grey, Straightsmouth, 17 January 1913
A once-fine 18th century merchant's house with an elegant timber doorcase in use as a public house. It was not uncommon for ordinary domestic buildings to be used as public houses.

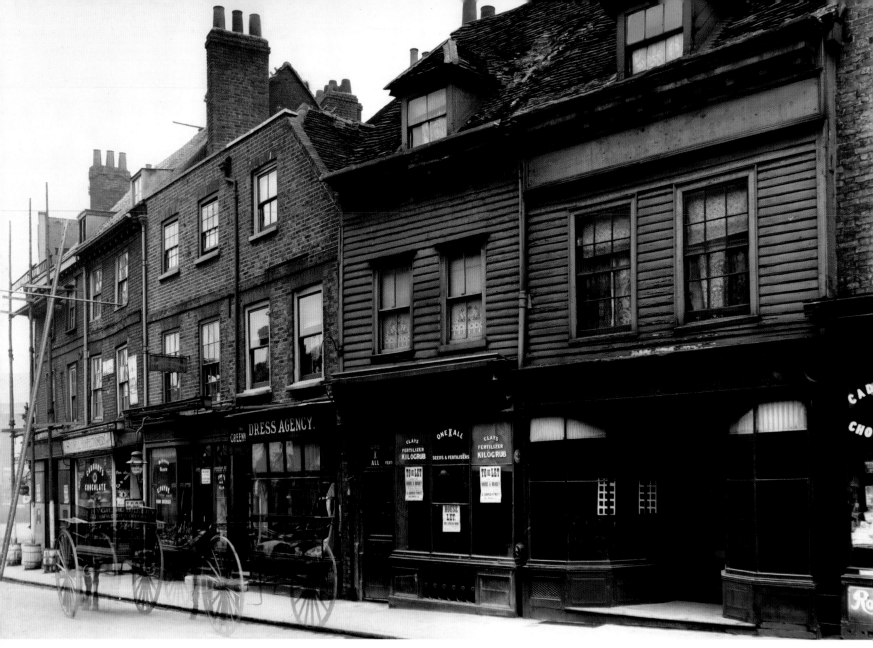

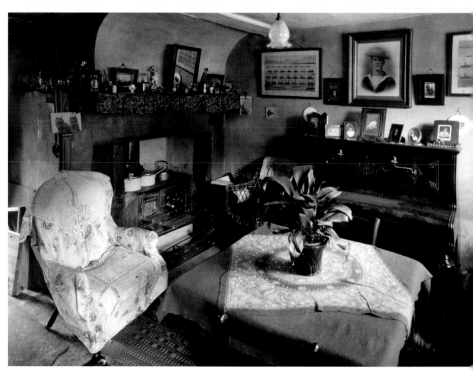

Above: 7-12 Stockwell Street, 1911
The heart of Greenwich and the source of its water supply. The town well was close by and several old wells have been found in the vicinity. A good group of 17th century weatherboarded houses with bracketed timber cornices and steeply-pitched clay tile roofs.

Right: 4 Philipots Almshouses, Philipots Path, c 1910
Philipots Almshouses were built in 1694, and demolished for road widening in 1931. This gives a fascinating glimpse of a ground floor front room. The picture of the Naval Review and framed sailor's portrait highlight the strong maritime links with the nearby Royal Naval Hospital.

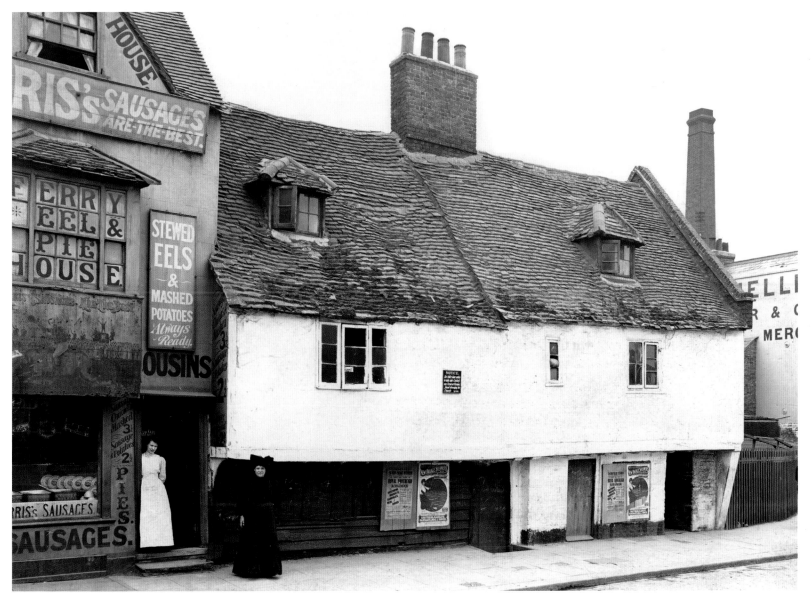

WOOLWICH

Above: 6-7 Nile Street, Woolwich, c 1900

These picturesque timber-framed, 16th century cottages, in what was once called Hog Lane, formed part of a wider group of ancient buildings, which were partly demolished for the Free Ferry in 1887-88.

Right: Ye Olde Kings Arms, Eltham, 20 March 1900

A fine 17th century, twin-gabled public house, which stood opposite the parish church until it was demolished for road widening in the 1920s for a tram route extension.

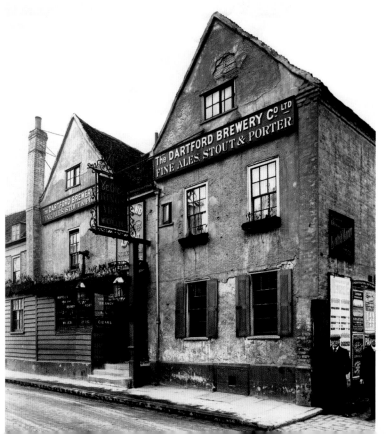

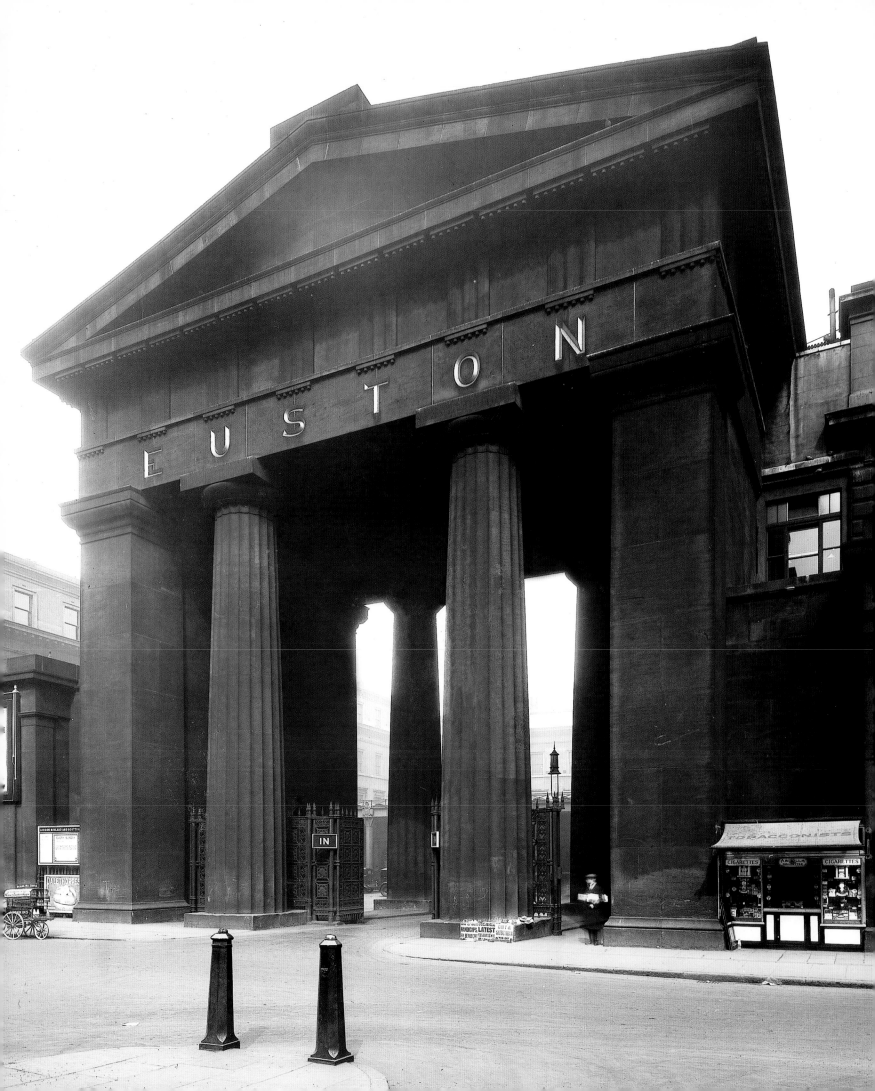

CHAPTER EIGHT

ZENITH 1918-39
Sovereign of Cities

The end of the First World War marked a watershed for London and the dawn of a new age. The population grew by 1.2million in 20 years. Mortality rates fell. Living standards improved and even working class families were able to acquire new luxury commodities, and enjoy new forms of entertainment, like the cinema, radio and gramophone. Increasingly, the chronic poverty which had stalked the Victorian and Edwardian capital was consigned to the past, even if areas of relative deprivation persisted, particularly in the East End, where, in spite of slum clearance and campaigns to improve child health and education, large numbers of London's poor remained trapped.

Rising land values, new transport infrastructure and population growth fuelled the greatest development boom in London's history. Central London was transformed as offices, department stores, hotels, underground stations, cinemas and huge blocks of flats replaced familiar four-storey houses and terraces. Pre-war trends resurfaced with renewed vigour. The redevelopment of Kingsway and Regent Street resumed. The West End consolidated its position as London's great shopping and entertainment centre, whilst many of the old aristocratic mansions of Mayfair gave way to modish new flats and offices. Besieged by developers, London's garden squares were given statutory protection in 1931 in one of the most enlightened pieces of planning legislation ever devised – ensuring a long term future for one of its most distinctive elements and crucial to its sense of place.

The defining characteristic of the inter-war period was the growth of the suburb, driven by the relentless expansion of the transport network. Between 1918-1939 London underwent astonishing spatial expansion. Over

Opposite: Euston Arch, 1934

An heroic monument to Britain's railway age. This huge Greek Doric propylaeum, built in 1838 to the design of Philip Hardwick, rose over 70ft to form a gigantic gateway to Euston, the first mainline terminus in a capital city anywhere in the world. Its demolition in 1962 triggered a public outcry which did much to boost the growth of the conservation movement and popular reaction against the institutional philistinism which characterised the post-war period.

860,000 houses were built in Greater London predominantly in outlying areas for the new middle classes. London's old peripheral villages like Eltham, Carshalton, Stanmore and Enfield were engulfed by a centrifugal tide of low-density development, whilst wholly new suburban communities were built from scratch in a variety of whimsical, and often playful, vernacular and traditional styles. Much derided, London's suburbs remain one of its most notable characteristics – home to over 70% of its population. By 1939 one in five of the people of England and Wales was a Londoner.

Without question, in 1939 London was still the sovereign of cities, the greatest city in the world – its largest port, its largest bank, its largest workshop and the capital of the British Empire. It dominated its hinterland, which embraced the whole of south-east England, but with such a concentration of population, wealth and commerce into just 610 sq miles, it was also shockingly exposed – an unparalleled strategic target wide open to new forms of warfare and, ominously, mass air attack.

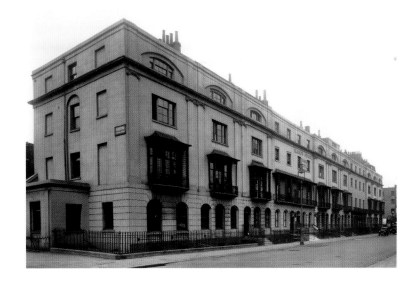

Above: 1-13 Euston Square, c 1937

Euston Station formed the centrepiece of an elegant square of stucco terraces built in 1811 as an extension of Bloomsbury to the south. This terrace stood on the north side at the east end. Only the wreathed lamp column, part of the war memorial, remains.

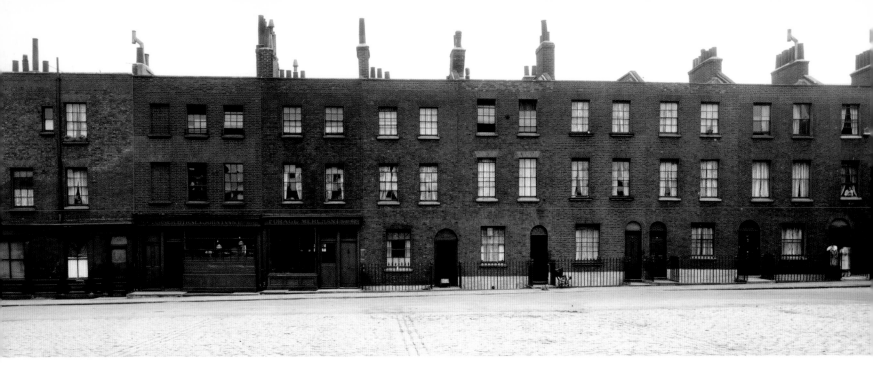

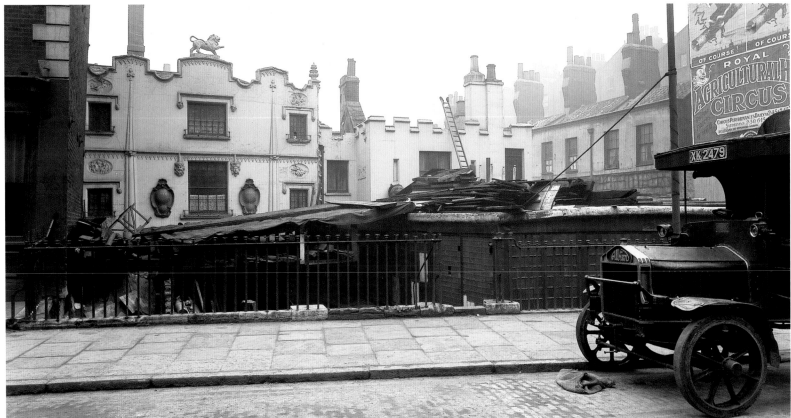

Crossing the River Jordan

SOMERS TOWN

Top: Cumberland Market, Somers Town, c 1930
View of the south side west of Osnaburgh Street. Cumberland Market was a market for hay brought in from the country via the Regent's Canal. The large setted space in the foreground shows its original purpose. The entire area was redeveloped for public housing in the 1930s.

KING'S CROSS

Above: Cromer Street, King's Cross, January 1928
View of the south side at the west end showing a builders' yard eccentrically embellished with items of architectural salvage. To the right is the front of an Albion van.

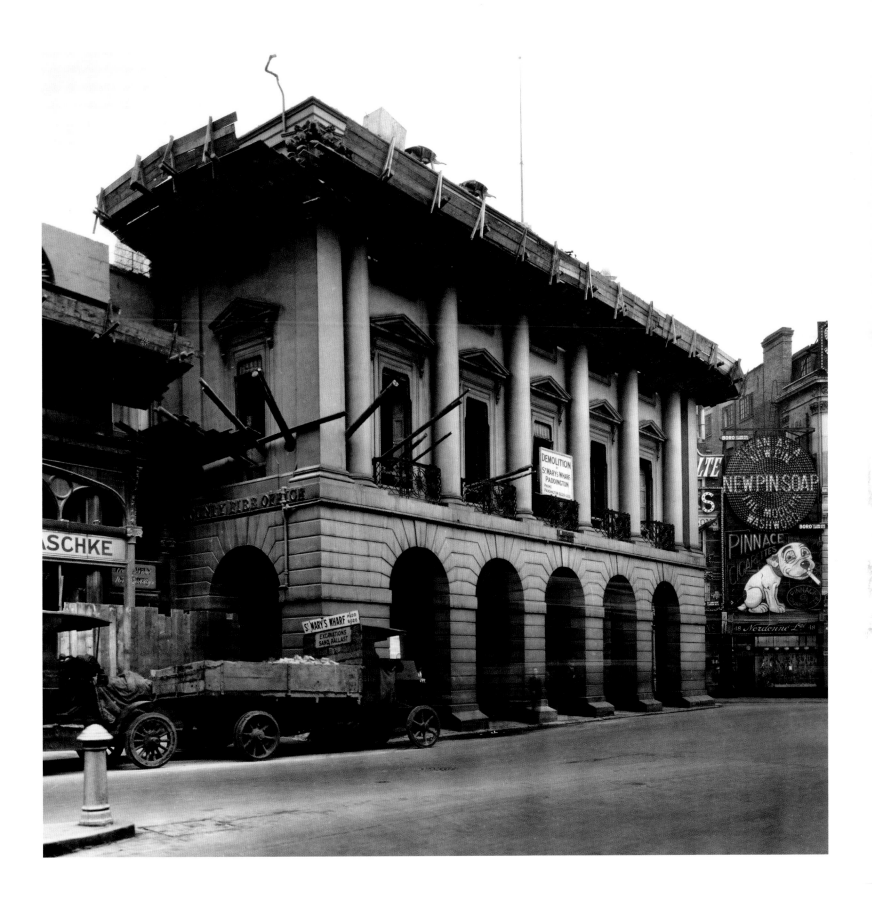

WEST END

Above: Old County Fire Office, Piccadilly Circus, November 1924
Nash's Old County Fire Office in the process of demolition. After much protracted wrangling, it was replaced by a similar handsome arcaded frontage by Sir Reginald Blomfield with massive chimney stacks framing an oval dome designed to terminate the east side of the Quadrant and close the vista from Lower Regent Street.

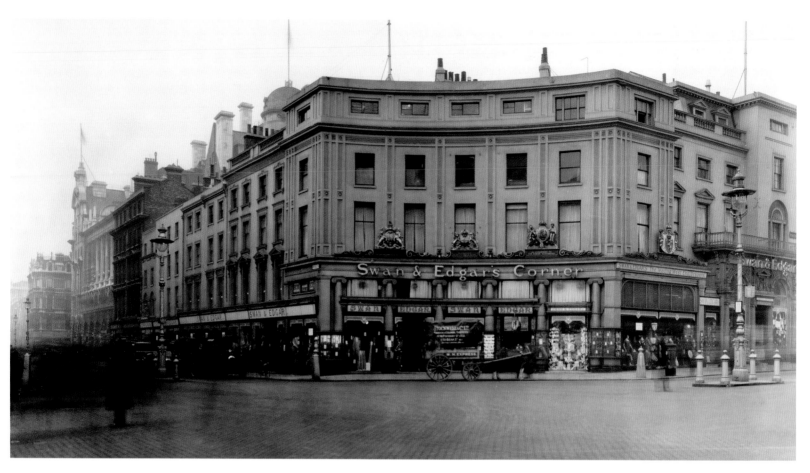

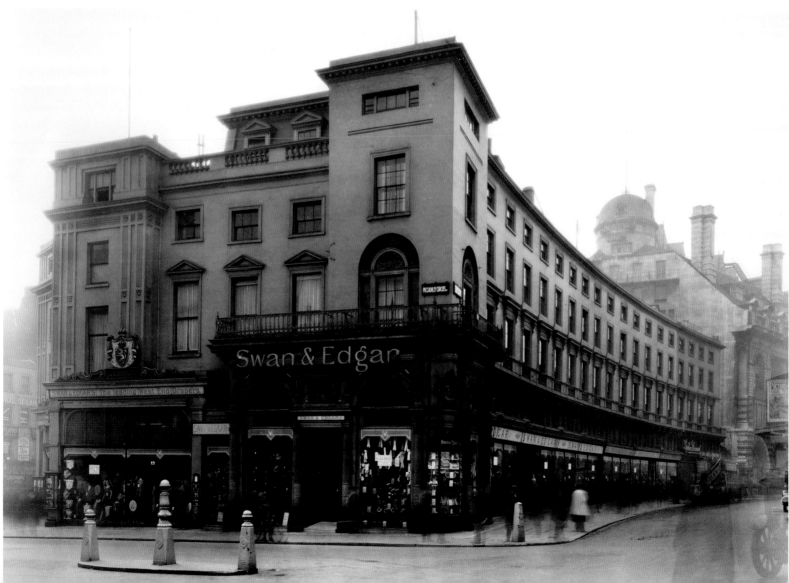

Birth of a new era

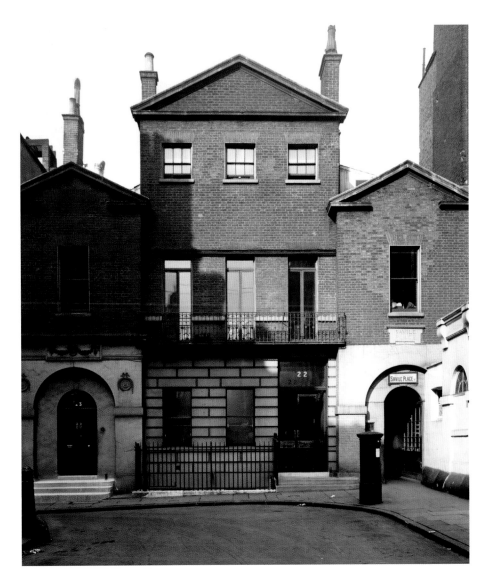

Opposite top: Swan & Edgar, Piccadilly Circus, November 1924
The shallow curve of Swan & Edgar's department store shortly before reconstruction commenced. To the left the step-change in scale generated by Norman Shaw's Piccadilly Hotel can be seen clearly. This dictated the form, bulk and scale of the subsequent redevelopment of the whole area.

Opposite below: View showing the uncomfortable collision of scale between the south-west curve of the Quadrant and the old curve of the Circus. Blomfield's reconstruction created a magnificent new frontage to the west side of the Circus, squaring off the entire junction in a monumental classical composition with huge concave-curved roof pavilions crowned by gilded pineapple finials.

Right above: 22-23 Savile Row, c 1935
Attributed to William Kent, Nos. 22-23 Savile Row were completed in 1735 to close the vista northward from Savile Row. A narrow passage beneath the right hand wing provided access through to Conduit Street beyond. In December 1929 Westminster City Council resolved to extend Savile Row northward. The Council acquired the building for highways purposes, and the building was demolished in 1937: a loss which would be inconceivable today.

Right below: Savile Place, c 1933
In a pale reflection of the Burlington Arcade, which was under construction to the south, in 1818 eight tiny shops were inserted into the walls of Savile Place, reputedly the smallest shops in London. Of the original retailers, a stick shop and cobbler's stall survived until this delightful thoroughfare was demolished in 1937.

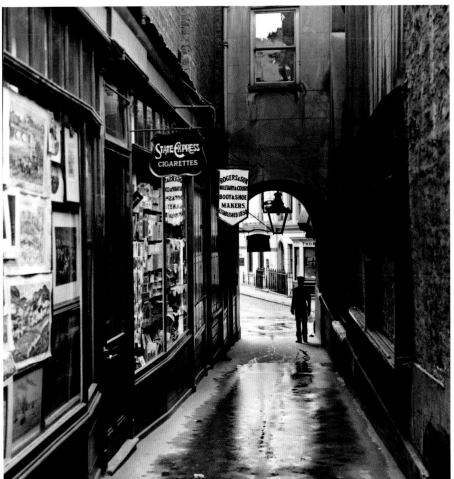

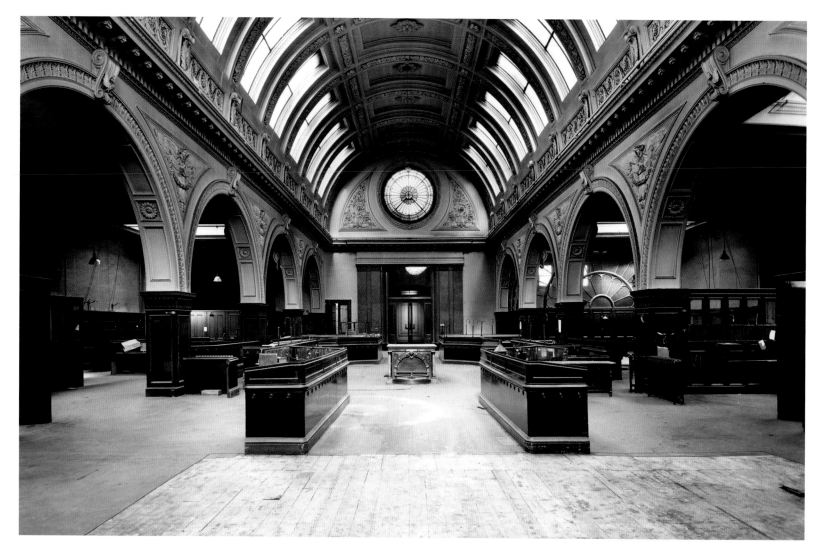

Death of an institution

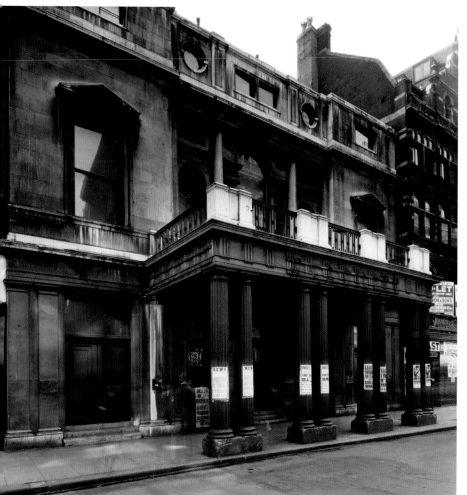

Left: The Pantheon, Oxford Street, 1937
The original Pantheon, designed by James Wyatt, opened in 1772 for concerts and masquerades. Gutted by fire, it was reconstructed as a place of assembly, and in 1811-12 converted to a theatre, which was short-lived owing to restrictions imposed by the Lord Chamberlain. In 1833-34 it was rebuilt as a bazaar by Sydney Smirke, who retained and adapted Wyatt's altered frontage replacing the portico with his own design carried on cast iron Doric columns.

Above: The great barrel-vaulted hall, on the first floor, which was used by W and A Gilbey, the wine merchants, as a showroom and offices from 1867. In 1937 the Georgian Group tried to negotiate the re-erection of the facade, as part of a new country house at Chilgrove, Sussex, but it came to nothing. The building was demolished shortly after for a new Marks & Spencer store in sleek, black moderne style by Robert Lutyens.

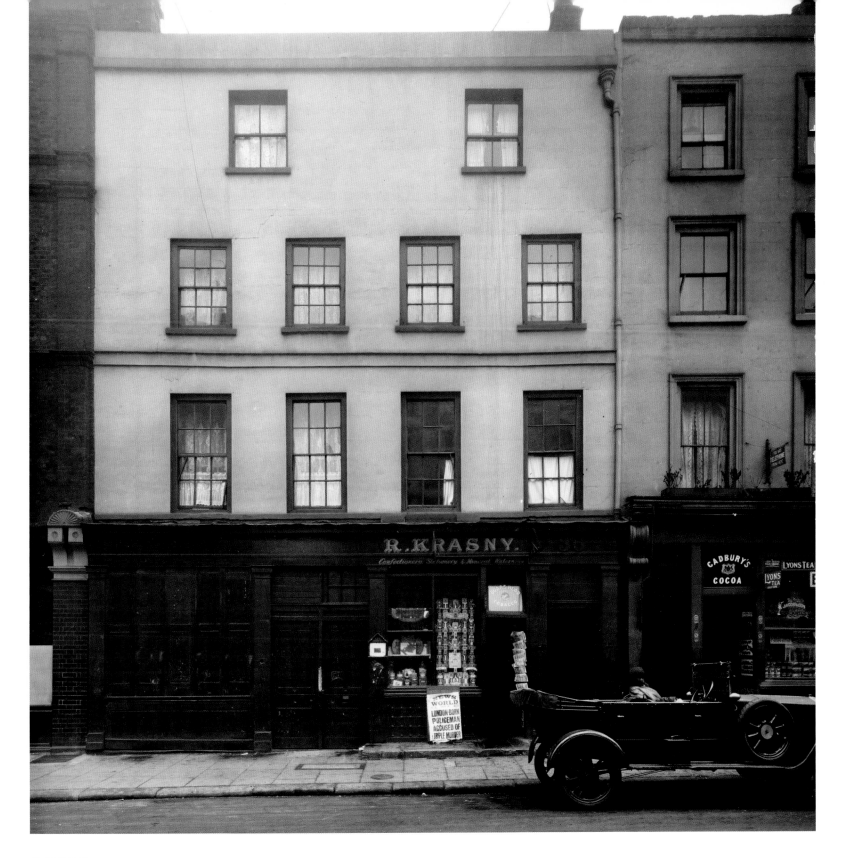

SOHO

Above: 51-53 Broadwick Street, Soho, c 1935

Formerly No. 36, by the 1930s this once-spacious early 18th century
house had been converted into tenements. The original ground floor
rooms and entrance passage were converted into shops, an open passage
inserted at the western end, and another tenement block crammed into
the rear courtyard.

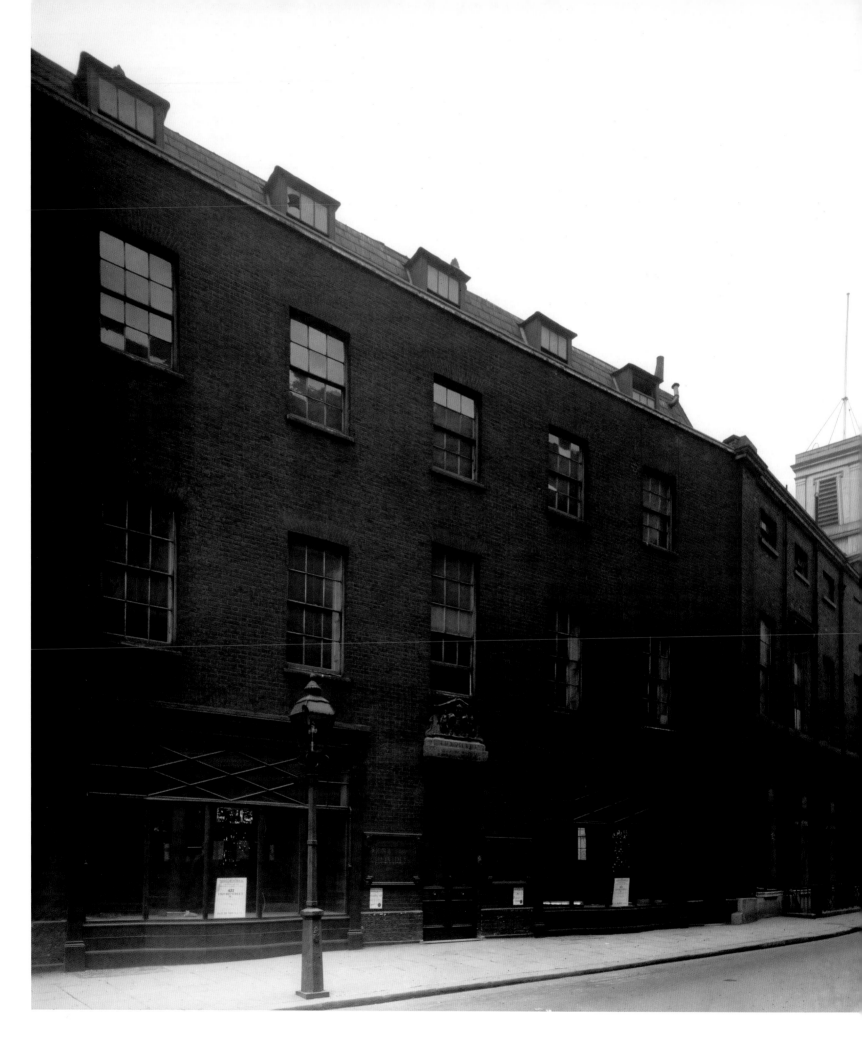

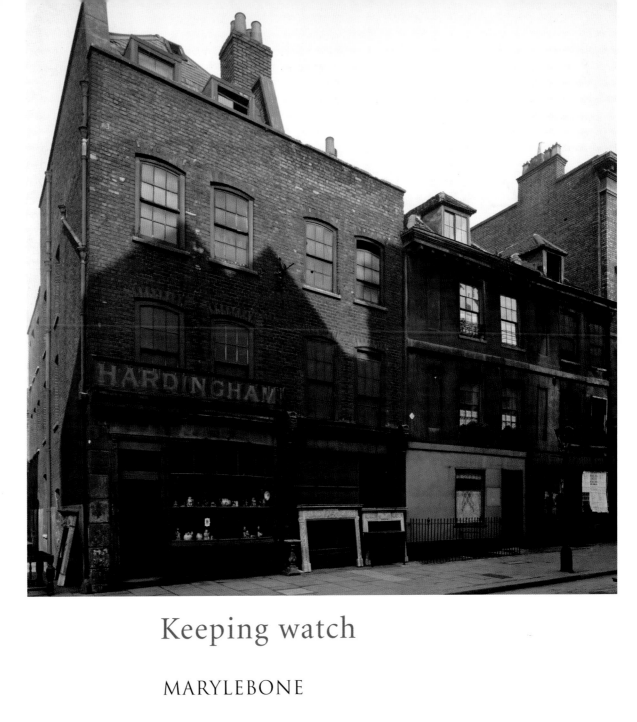

Keeping watch

MARYLEBONE

Opposite: The Old Watch House and Court House, Marylebone Lane, 1935
Built on the site of an old plague pit, the Old Watch House was built in 1804 for five watchmen who made day and night patrols of the parish. The adjoining Court House opened in 1825. Over the door of the Watch House are the arms of the Harley family, dated 1729. With the construction of the new Town Hall in Marylebone Road, the buildings were sold and used briefly as a bookshop, before they were demolished in 1935.

VICTORIA

Above: 29-32 Petty France, Victoria, c 1930
To the right is a pair of late 17th century houses with timber box cornices. To the left is a pair of early 18th century houses. All have fallen on hard times and are indicative of the dilapidated condition of much of central Westminster well into the 20th century. A lucrative trade operated in architectural salvage.

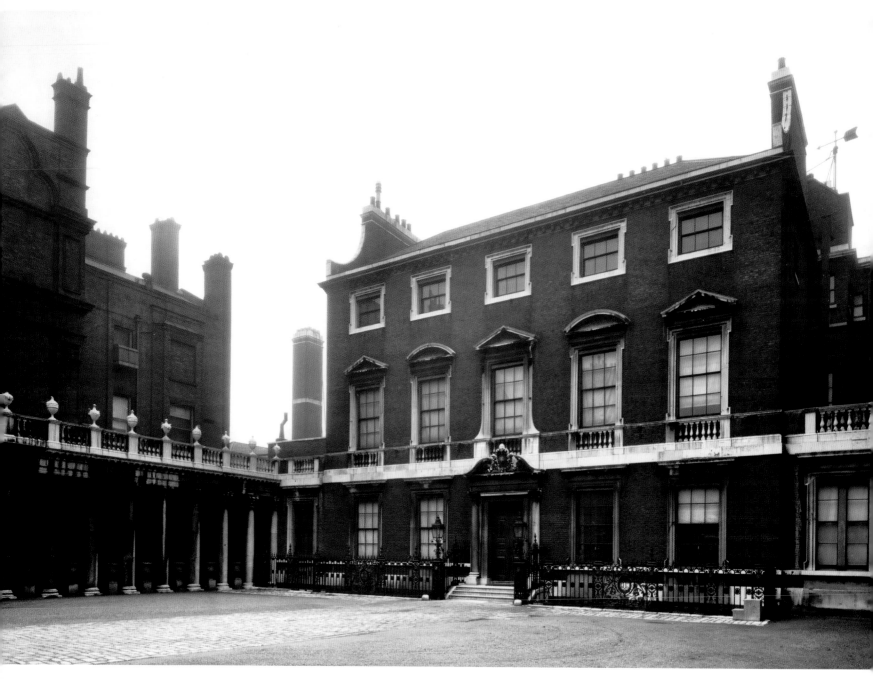

Lost mansions of Mayfair

MAYFAIR

Above: Chesterfield House, South Audley Street, May 1932
Set back from the street behind high walls and a grand arcaded courtyard, Chesterfield House was designed by Isaac Ware for Lord Chesterfield between 1747-52. It was regarded as one of the finest aristocratic town houses in London with a spectacular French rococo interior. From 1894 the house was owned by the brewer, Lord Burton. In 1922 it became the home of the Princess Royal before it was sold and demolished in 1937.

Opposite top: The elaborate French rococo ballroom created out of two of the original rooms by Lord Burton.

Right: The splendid marble staircase and screen was designed by James Gibbs in 1715 for Canons, the great house of the Duke of Chandos at Stanmore, which was demolished in 1748. Adapted and reused by Ware, reputedly the only significant change was to alter the coronet in the balustrade from a Duke's to a Viscount's. The gilt copper lantern came from Houghton Hall. When the house was pulled down in 1937, the staircase was salvaged once again for use in a cinema in Broadstairs where tragically it was destroyed in the war.

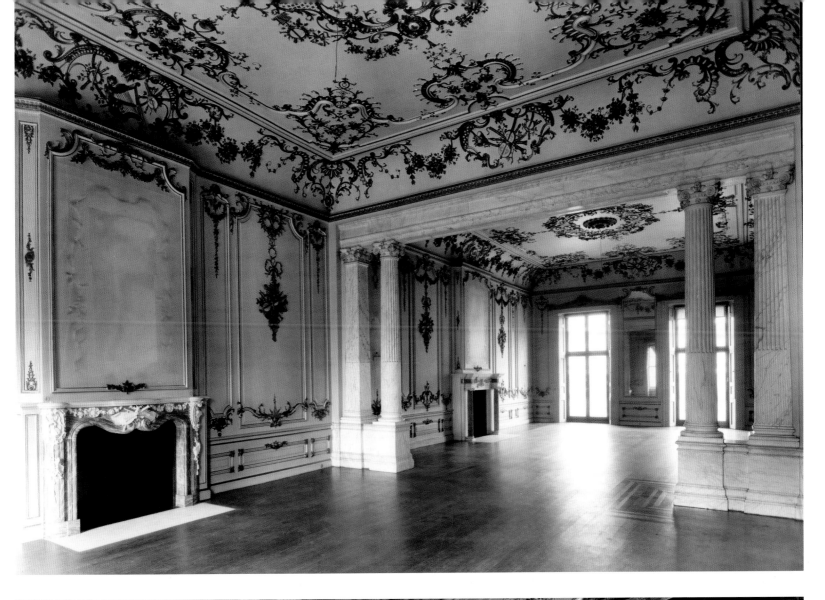

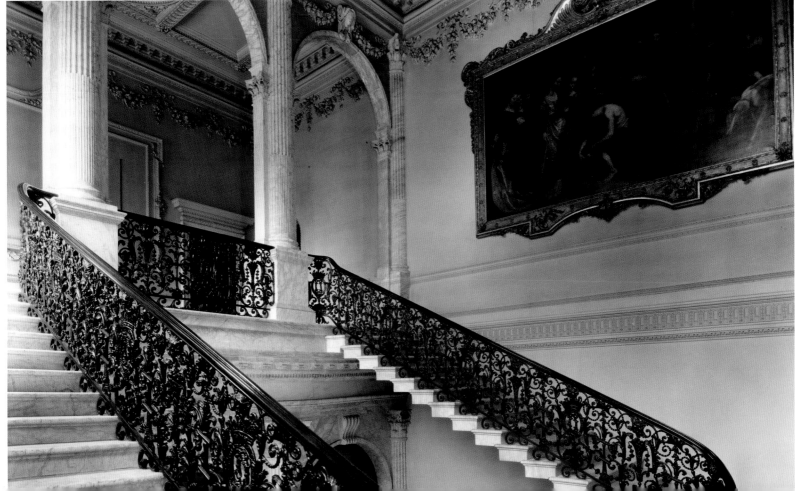

London's finest

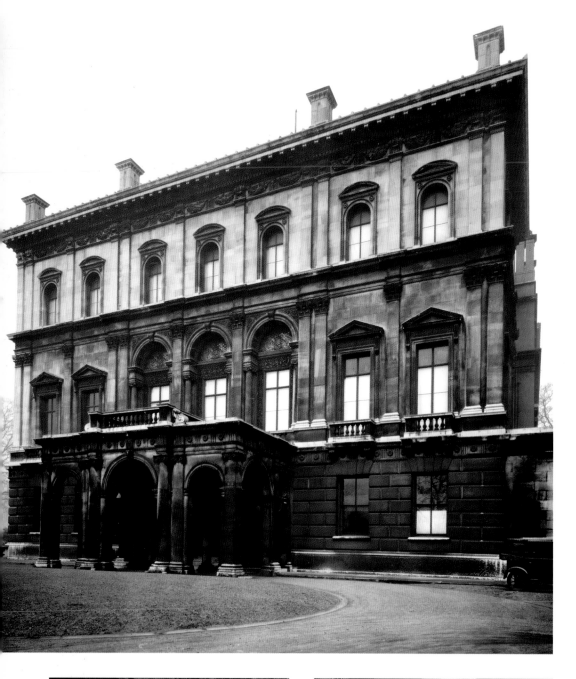

Left: Dorchester House, Park Lane, c 1927
Designed by Lewis Vulliamy, as a massive town house for the millionaire, R S Holford, Dorchester House was regarded as the finest private house in London and the home of its best art collection. It was built between 1851-57 and modelled on the Palazzo della Farnesina in Rome. Later it was occupied by the American ambassador, William Whitelaw Reid, but with rising land values in the post-war period it was pulled down in 1929 to make way for the jazzy new Dorchester Hotel designed by Curtis Green.

Below far left: The spectacular central staircase and balconied hall that rose a full three storeys through the centre of the house flooding it with light. Enriched with different colours of porphyry and marble with columns of Parian ware and decorated vaulted ceilings, it provided a theatrical setting for some of the most lavish balls of the Season.

Below centre: The magnificent Dining Room chimneypiece in Bardiglia marble designed by Alfred Stevens and carried on two immense Carrara marble caryatids with an inner frieze of pietra dura work made of semi-precious stones. Stevens' masterpiece is now in the Walker Art Gallery, Liverpool.

Below right: The sumptuous statuary marble chimneypiece in the West Drawing Room.

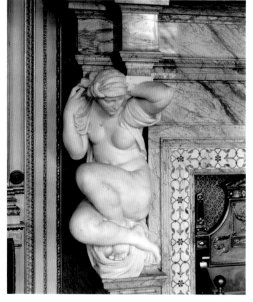

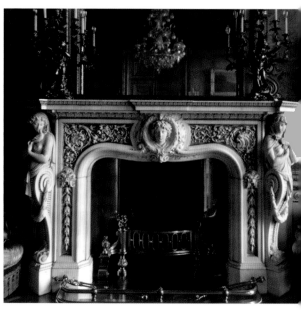

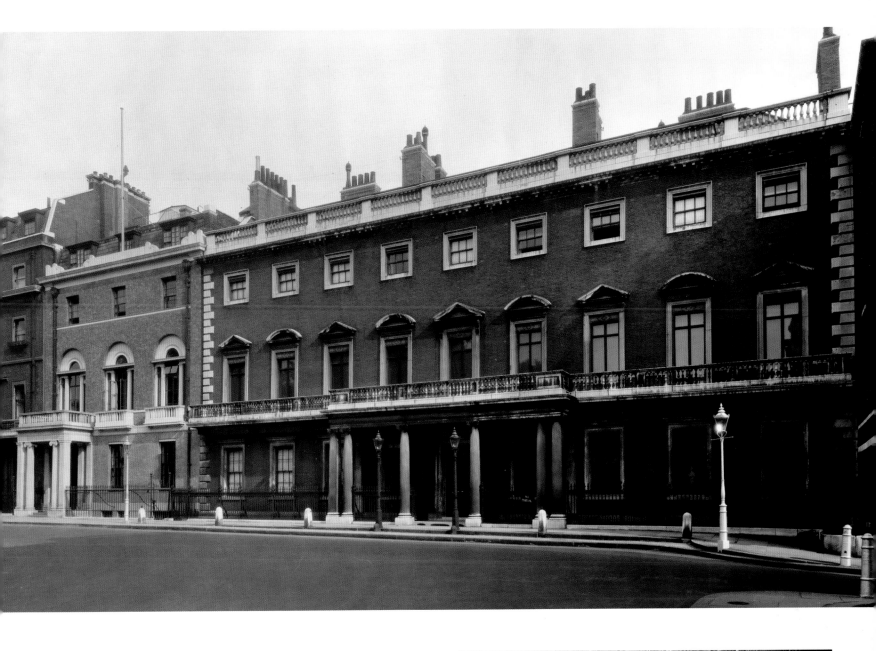

Above: Norfolk House, 31 St James's Square, 1932

Designed by Matthew Brettingham between 1748-52 for the ninth Duke of Norfolk, the Palladian style was inspired by Holkham Hall with a long frontage of nine bays enriched with stone dressings. Together with Chesterfield House, it was renowned for its lavish French rococo interior, one of the earliest in London. Regarded by the LCC as having only limited architectural merit, it was demolished in 1939, although the music room was salvaged and re-erected at the Victoria & Albert Museum.

Right: View of the Salon, or Ballroom which was redecorated in Louis Quinze style in 1845 with papier-mache and carton pierre enrichment and sumptuous gilt-framed mirrors. In the panel over the door is a ducal coronet and scrolled monogram bearing the initials H and C over an N with a gilded plaster ceiling of geometrical circles above. The room is laid out with some of the contents of the house prior to sale.

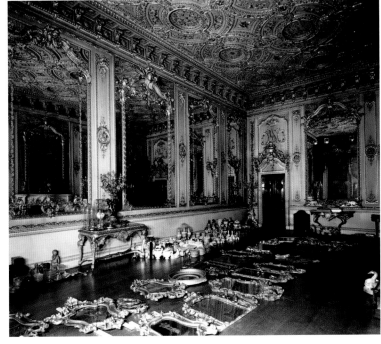

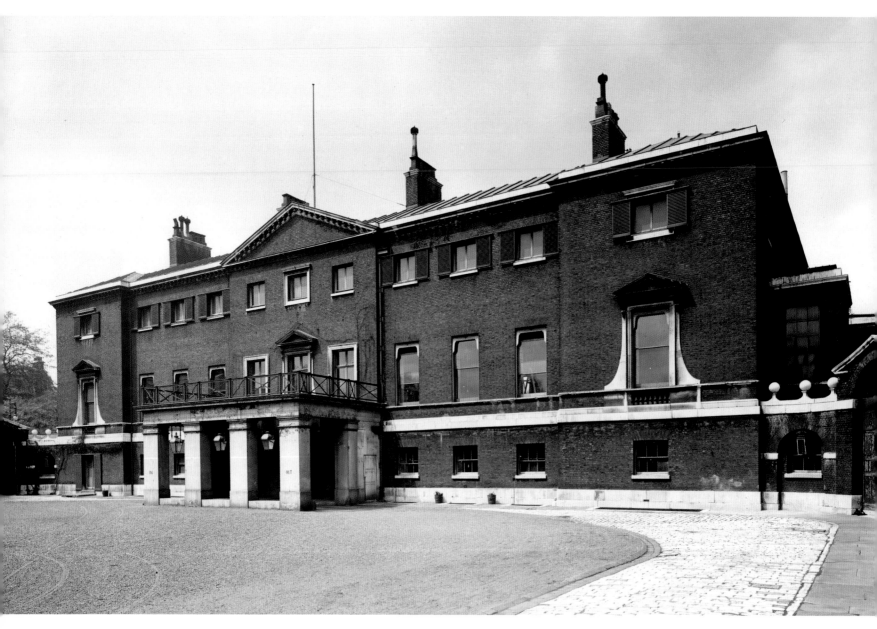

Opulent interiors

Above: Devonshire House, Piccadilly, October 1920
After a disastrous fire in October 1733, the third Duke of Devonshire commissioned William Kent to design a new mansion which stood behind a high wall facing Piccadilly. Much criticised for its external austerity, the interior provided an opulent setting for an extensive art collection including works by Tintoretto, Titian and Rembrandt. The large rear garden was separated from the rear garden of Lansdowne House to the north by Lansdowne Passage.

Right: In 1897 the Piccadilly frontage was embellished with a beautiful set of wrought iron gates and piers from Chiswick House, which until 1838 had adorned the residence of Lord Heathfield at Turnham Green. With the demolition of Devonshire House in 1924 they were moved once again to provide an axial entrance to the tree-lined avenue in Green Park leading from Piccadilly to the Victoria Memorial.

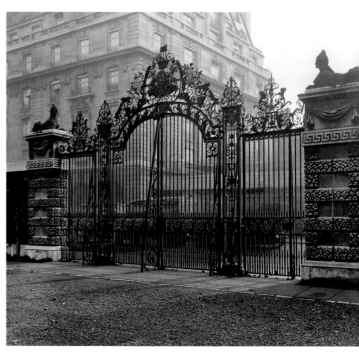

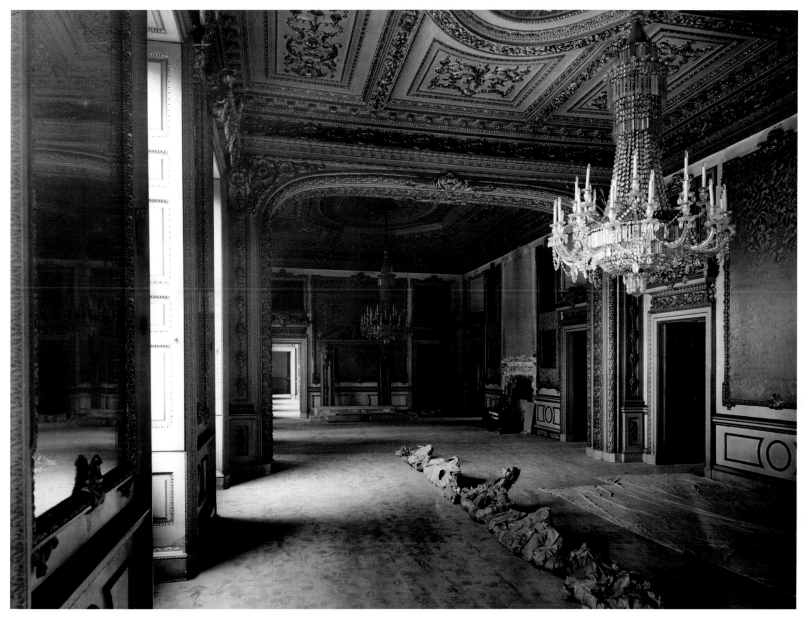

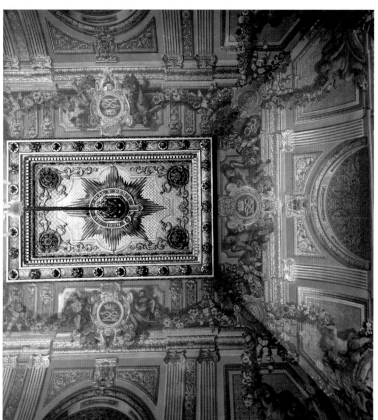

Above: Once the Ballroom was decorated in white and gold and the walls hung with blue and gold brocade as a setting for great canvases by Veronese, Caravaggio, Rubens and Poussin. It is shown here stripped, prior to demolition.

Right: The exquisite ceiling of the Saloon was the pièce de résistance of the entire house – one of Kent's masterpieces – with painted wreaths, festoons of flowers and arabesques embellished with ducal coronets celebrating the power and patronage of the Cavendish family.

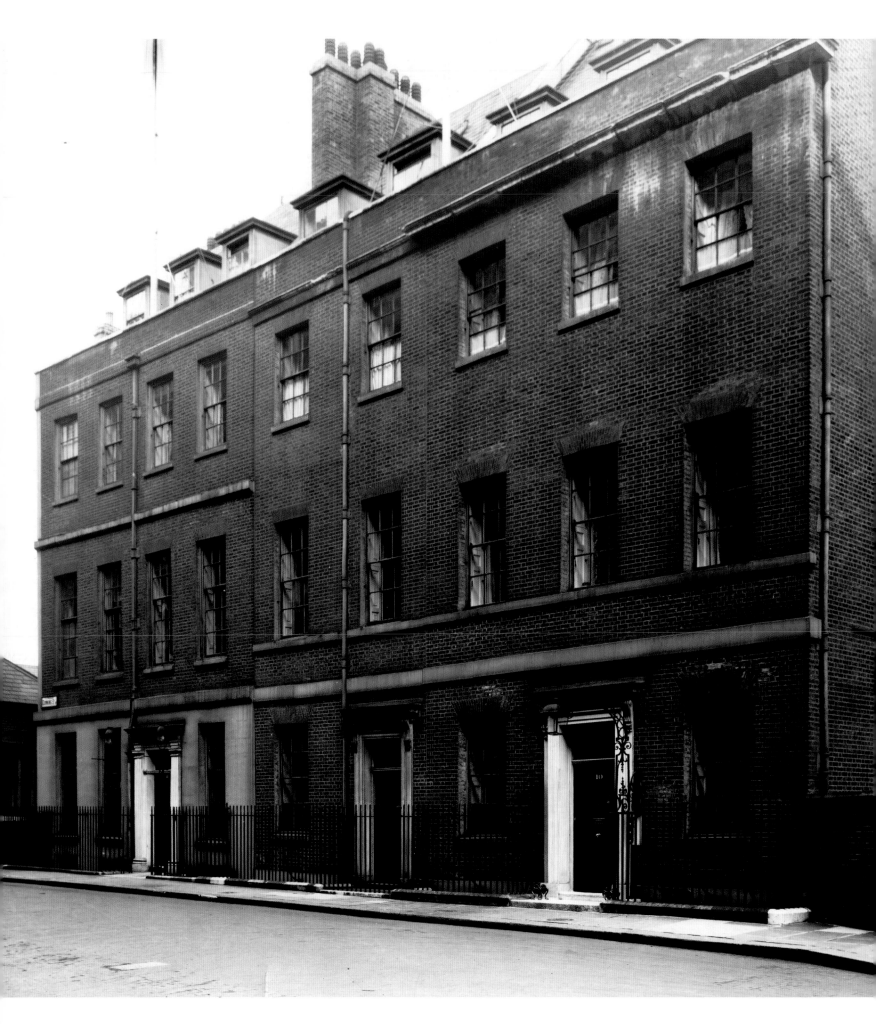

Fulcrum of power

WESTMINSTER

10-11 Downing Street, c 1925

Opposite: Downing Street was developed from 1682. To the right, the facade of No. 10 dates from 1766-74, subsuming an earlier house by William Kent of 1732-35. The two central bays of No. 10A were incorporated into the four bays of No. 11, to the left, in the 1770s. No. 12, the curious single storey 'stump' is all that remains of an earlier house of 1682, which was destroyed by fire in 1879. In 1960-63 the entire complex was remodelled and extended by Raymond Erth.

Left above: View of the Cabinet Room taken during the premiership of Stanley Baldwin, with simple moulded panelled walls, and a plain grey marble chimneypiece. The only touch of opulence is provided by the entrance screen with coupled, fluted Corinthian columns – a room where architecture has not been allowed to distract from affairs of state.

Left below: A wonderful period piece. The basement kitchen occupied a vaulted, double-height space with a huge oak table made from a single 5in thick oak plank. To the right is a massive oak chopping block over 2ft in diameter.

Below: The Prime Minister's bedroom during Stanley Baldwin's occupation. The chimneypiece in statuary marble has detached black columns with Ionic caps and bases framing a frieze and central lion's mask.

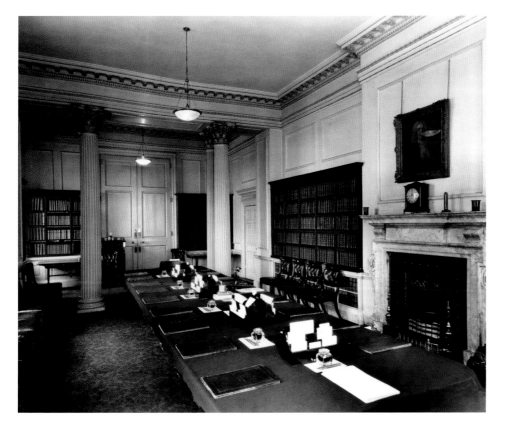

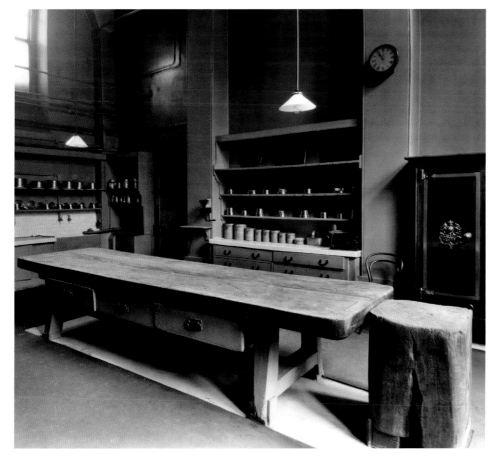

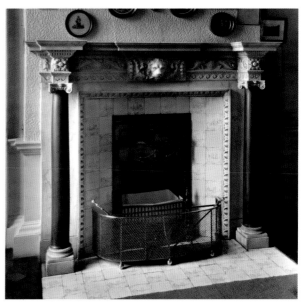

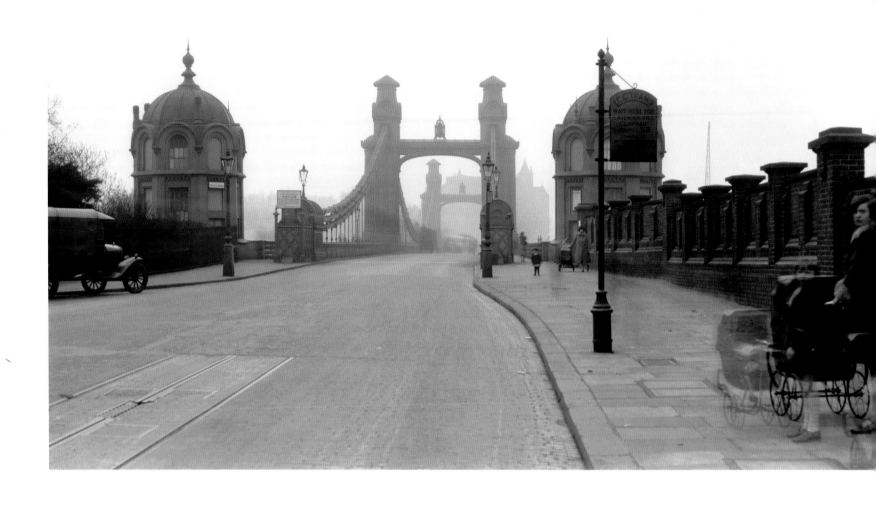

CHELSEA

Above: Chelsea Bridge, c 1930

An evocative period photograph of Chelsea Bridge from the south approach. On the right, note the woman and child with perambulator; to their left is an LCC tram stop for the 32 to Lavender Hill and Clapham: the tram tracks stop abruptly here. At the left of the picture is a delivery van.

KNIGHTSBRIDGE

Right: High Row, 68-92 Knightsbridge, 1931

View of the north side of Knightsbridge immediately to the west of the Hyde Park Hotel which can be seen on the extreme right. These once-grand houses overlooking Hyde Park were bought for redevelopment in the 1930s, but remained empty until their demolition in December 1942. Bowater House was built on the site in 1956-58. The plaque on No. 70 marks the home of Charles Reade, the novelist and playwright who lived there from 1867-82.

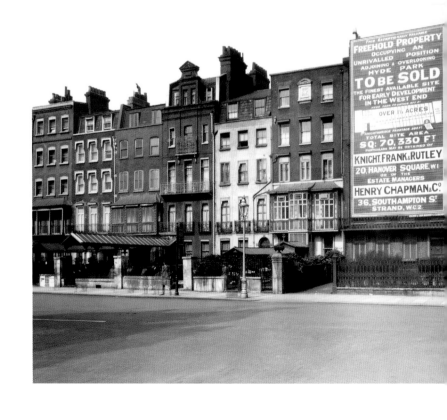

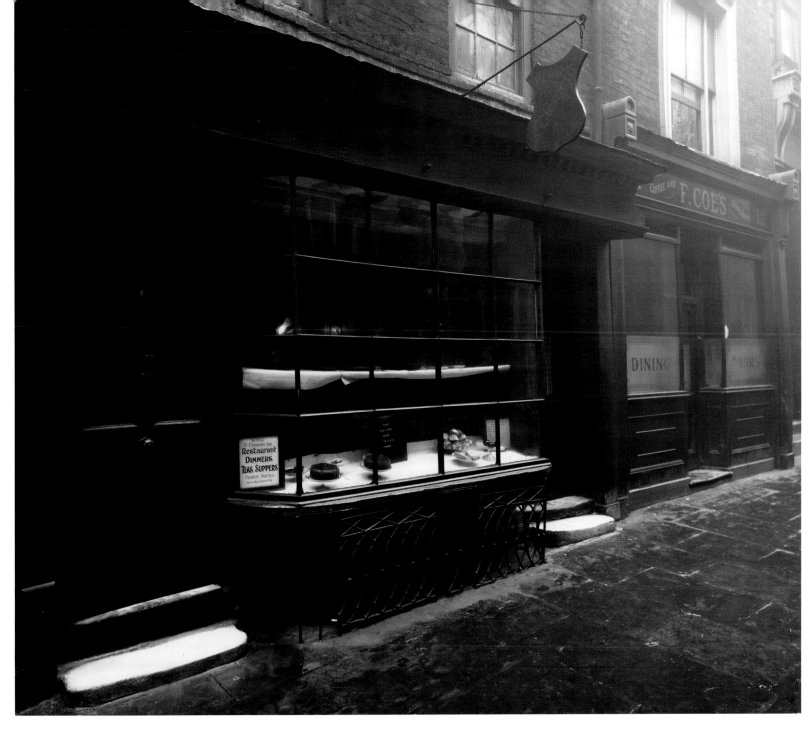

ALDWYCH

**Above & near right: 11 Clements Inn Passage,
7 February 1927**

A superb atmospheric view of Ye Olde St Clements Inn Restaurant, an old 17th century gabled house with a fine 18th century shopfront, which survived the huge Holborn to Strand Improvement scheme, but succumbed to later development.

Far right: 11 Clements Inn Passage, 7 February 1927
View of the ramshackle weatherboarded rear elevation with an old clay tile roof. Note the jug and basin in the rear window.

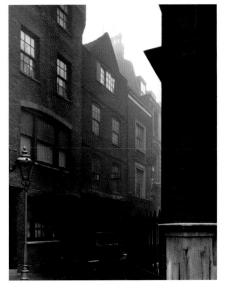

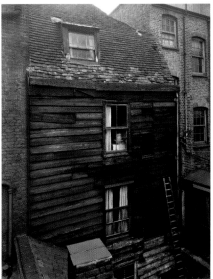

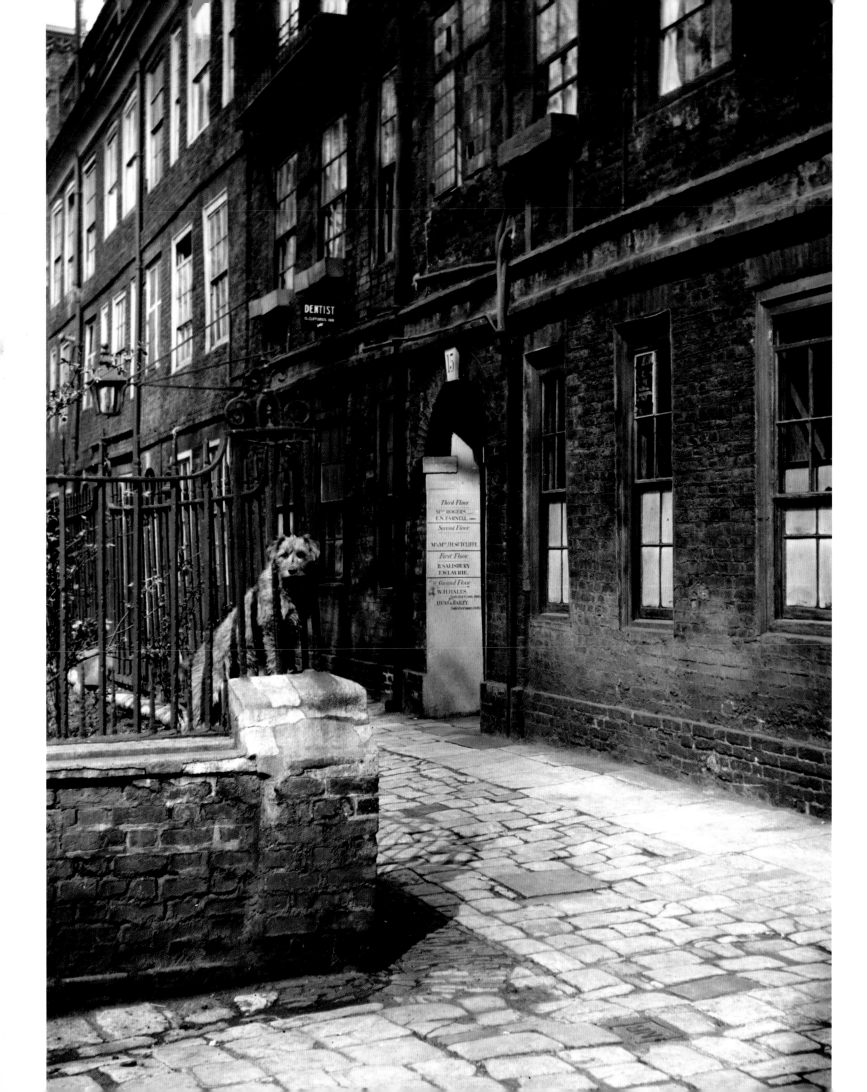

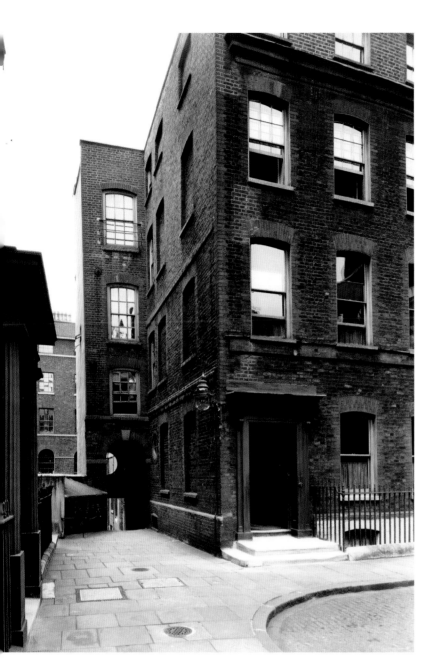

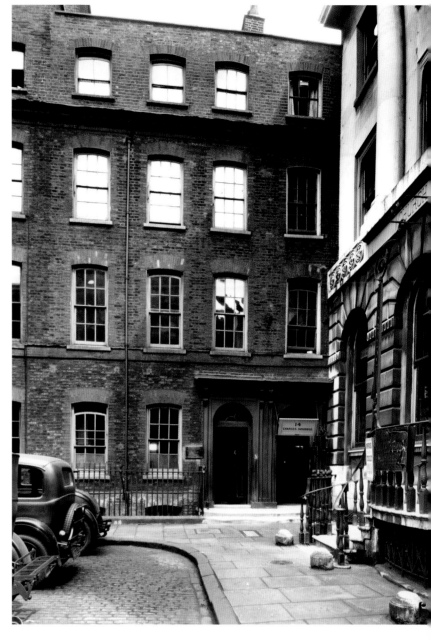

On the eve of destruction

CHANCERY LANE

Opposite: Clifford's Inn, c 1932
View of Clifford's Inn and a local resident. 24 years after it was sold and the images on p108, it remained in occupation until it was pulled down in 1935.

Above: Serjeants Inn, 1932
Serjeants Inn occupied the site immediately west of Clifford's Inn, to which it was connected, with a frontage to Chancery Lane, which had been occupied as early as 1425. As late as 1860 part of the pavement of the inn was flagged in stone taken from old St Paul's, and it retained oil lamps long after the introduction of gas.

Above left: View of the south-west corner. To the left beneath the porch are the offices of the Colonial and Continental Church Society.

Above right: View of north-east side of the square showing some of the elegant early 18th century terraced houses designed by Robert Adam for offices and lawyers' chambers. To the right the grand stone frontage, also by Adam, was used by the Church of England Sunday School Institute.

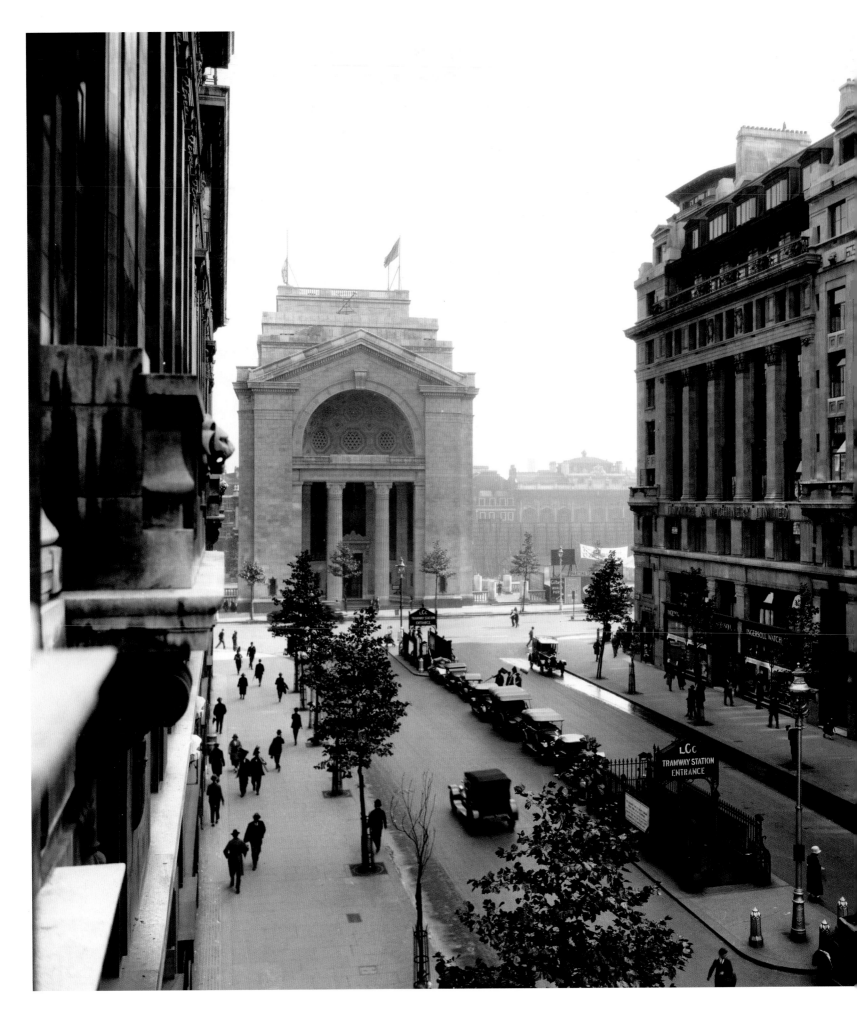

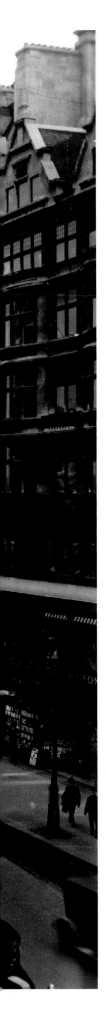

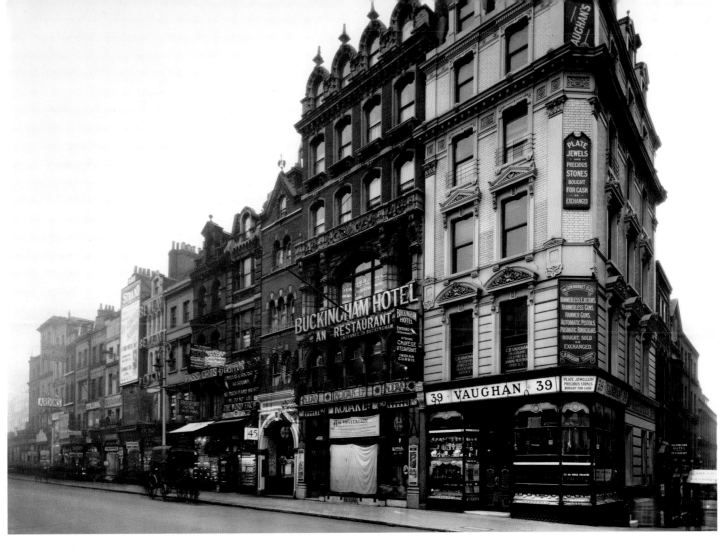

The birth of a new city

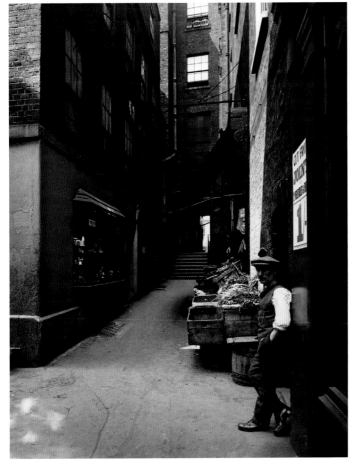

Opposite: Bush House, Aldwych, c 1932

Brave new world. View of Bush House at the centre of the great axial vista south from Kingsway, but prior to the completion of its wings. In the distant haze beyond is the facade of Somerset House. The Holborn to Strand improvements incorporated an underground tramway tunnel, the entrance to which can be seen in the foreground.

STRAND

Above: 39-59 Strand, November 1924

The Strand in its heyday with domestic-scaled buildings of various periods on their original mediaeval plots and a wealth of fascinating detail.

Left: George Court, Strand, c 1935

George Court at the junction with York Place. Note the bird cages in the open window high above the passage entrance.

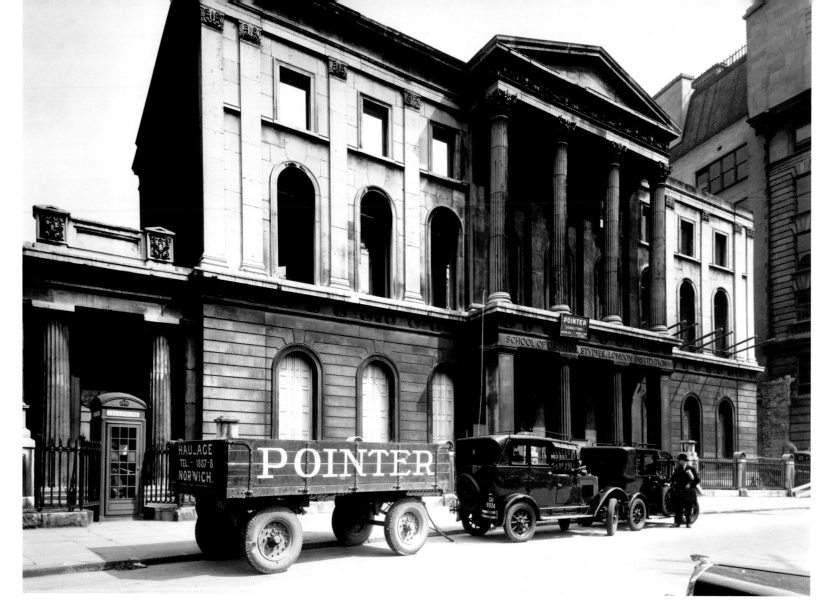

CITY

Above: The London Institution, Finsbury Circus, 1936

View showing demolition works in progress in 1936. Founded in 1806, the London Institution moved to this elegant neo-classical building on the north side of Finsbury Circus in 1819. Designed by William Brooks, it boasted a fine pedimented portico carried on four fluted Corinthian columns over a Greek Doric porch. Intended "for the Advancement of Literature and the Diffusion of Useful Knowledge", it was a lecture hall and later the home of the School of Oriental Studies. Note the careful way in which the K2 telephone kiosk has been sited – framed between the Doric columns of the left-hand bay.

SMITHFIELD

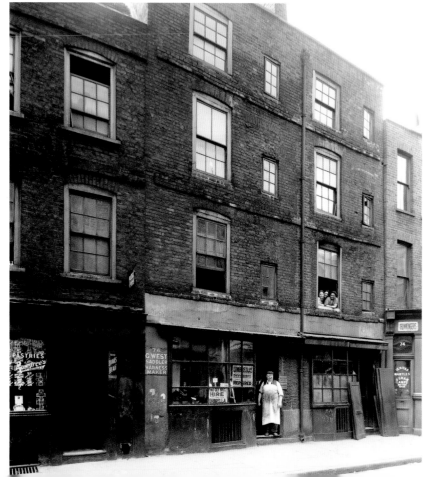

Left: 76 Bartholomew Close, Smithfield, 1927

Early 18th century houses. The small windows denote houses with front staircases – an early plan-form.

CITY

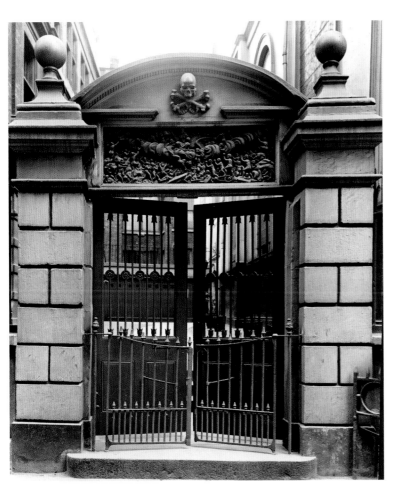

Left: St Stephen's, Coleman Street, 1920

Destroyed in 1666, St Stephen's was rebuilt by Wren between 1674-81. Over the entrance gate was a superb carved Resurrection panel depicting the Last Judgement set in a segmental pediment marked with a skull and crossbones. It was so highly regarded that it was replaced with the plaster-cast replica seen here, the original being removed to the Vestry for safe keeping. Ironically, the original was lost to bombing in 1941, together with a magnificent communion table and other 17th century furnishings, but the replica survived. It is now in the Museum of London. Of the church, not a trace remains.

Below: 15 Cornhill, 10 March 1926

This superb 18th century shopfront with sliding sashes divided by pilasters and spandrels enriched with vases and foliated ribbons was considered of such importance that it was acquired by the Victoria & Albert Museum. The crown under a glass dome in the centre of the window remains a mystery.

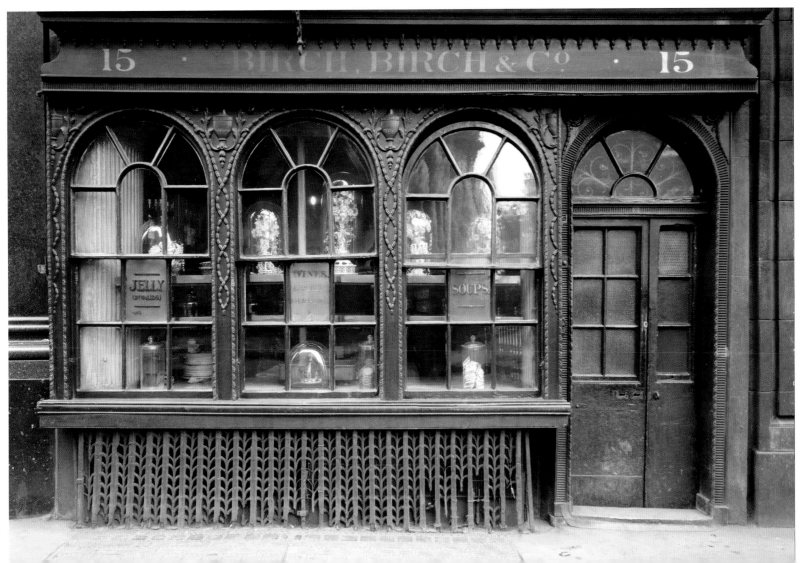

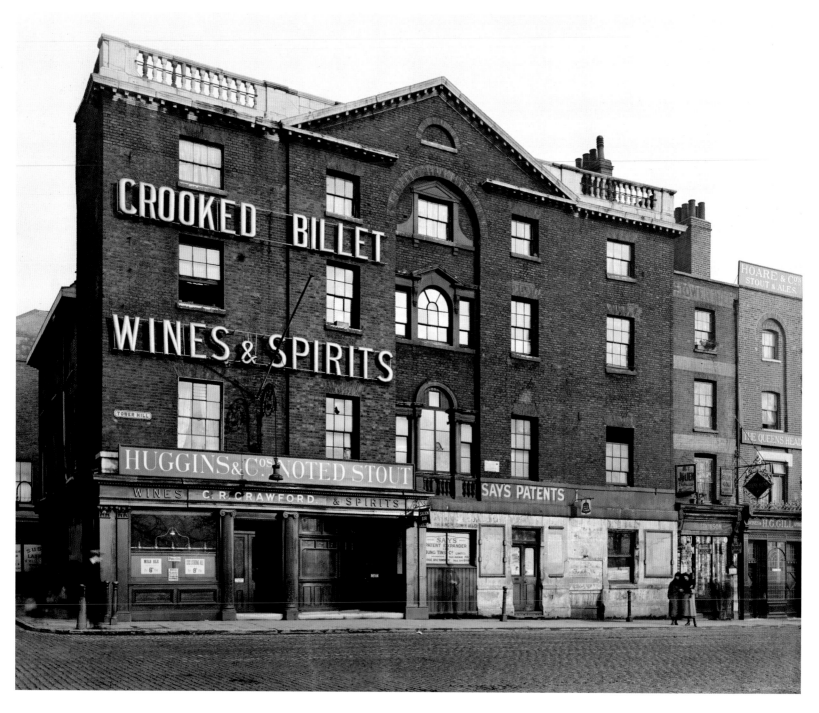

In the shadow of the Tower

TOWER

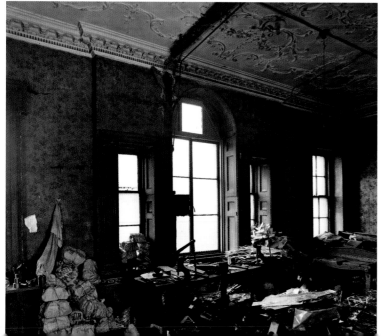

Above: 32-34 Tower Hill, c 1920
This once elegant late 18th century building stood north-east of the Tower with Eastminster (formerly King Street) beyond to the left. The flank elevation and box cornice of No. 1 Eastminster are clearly visible.

Left: The first floor centre room. Its refined Serlian window and delicately-modelled plaster ceiling are in sharp contrast to the mayhem of the tin-making workshop beneath.

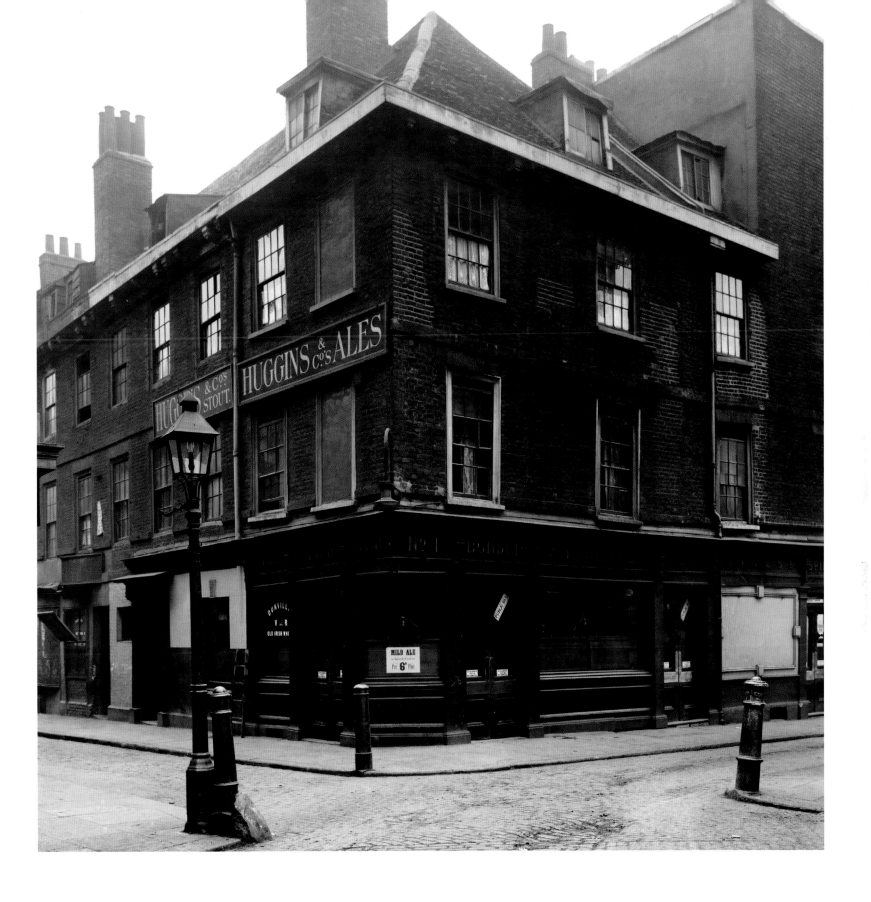

Above: 1-3 Eastminster, Tower Hamlets, 22 November 1920
A remarkable survival of a short row of late 17th century houses retaining
their original bracketed timber box gutters, flush-framed sashes and
steeply-pitched clay tile roofs. The iron bollards mark the boundary
between the City of London and Tower Hamlets.

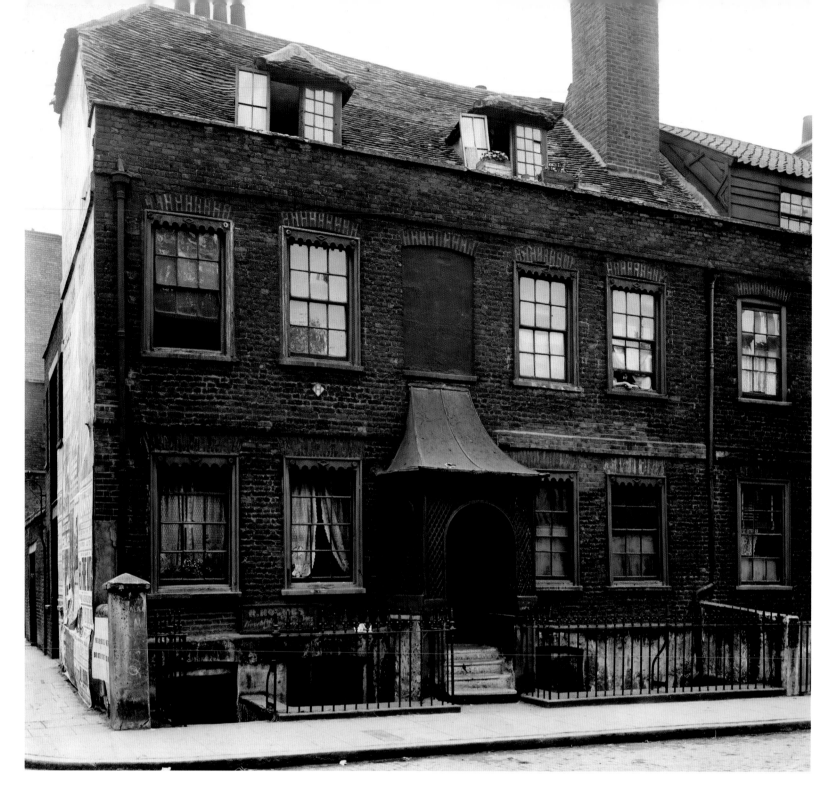

The leading criminal quarter of all England...

SHOREDITCH

Above: 48 Hoxton Square, 1921

View of the south side. Hoxton Square, built in the 1680s, was home to one of the first Dissenters' Academies. By 1902 it was synonymous with poverty, overcrowding and crime, characterised by Charles Booth as "*the leading criminal quarter of London, and indeed of all England*" – the home of the pickpocket, 'whizzer' or 'dip', and gangs of shoplifters or 'hoisters'. It is now one of London's coolest neighbourhoods, a centre for creative industries and nightlife.

Although bombed heavily, some of the original houses survived into the 1970s. Today only a handful remain.

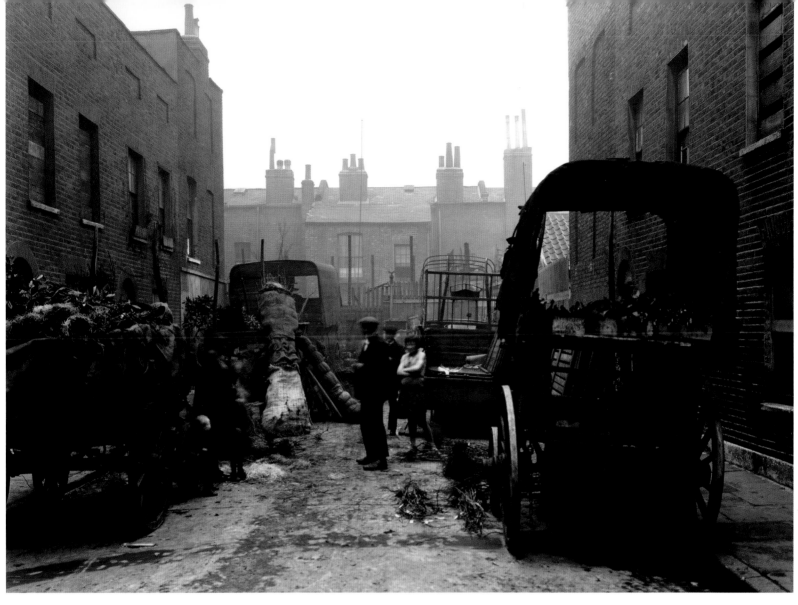

Above: Moneyer Street, Shoreditch, 1931

As early as the 17th century Hoxton was renowned for its market and nursery gardens, and related trades continued well into the 20th century. Columbia Road market is still a mecca for gardeners and enthusiasts.

View showing north end of Moneyer Street, Hoxton, with carts piled high with plants, shrubs and saplings.

Right: Crooked Billet Yard, Kingsland Road, Hackney, 1933

A fascinating view of a short row of 17th century cottages with an external staircase to the first floor entrance beside which a communal privy has been built with a timber modesty screen.

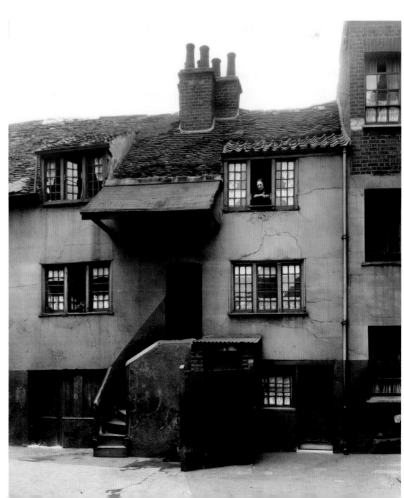

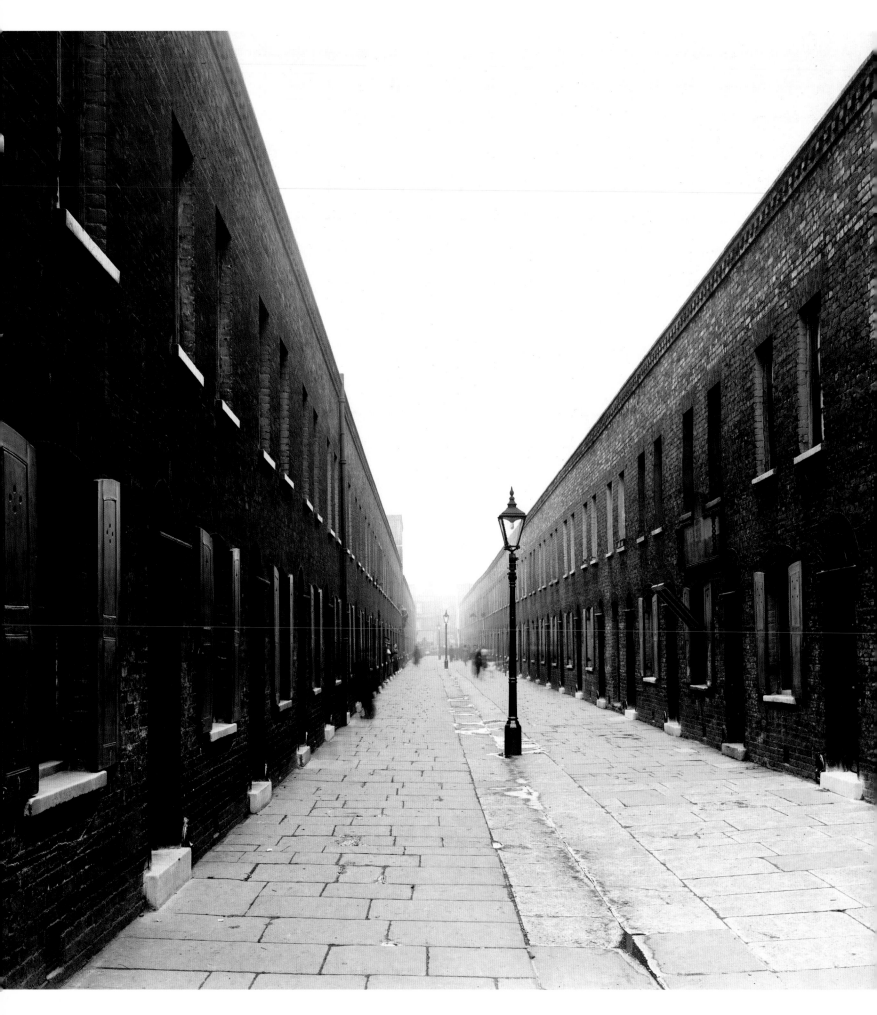

The awful East

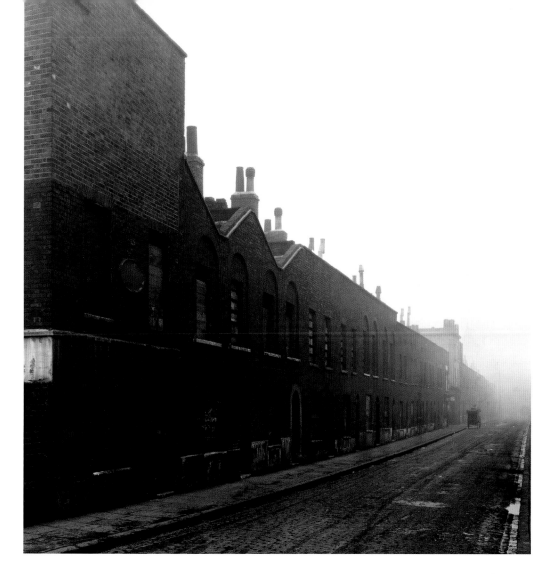

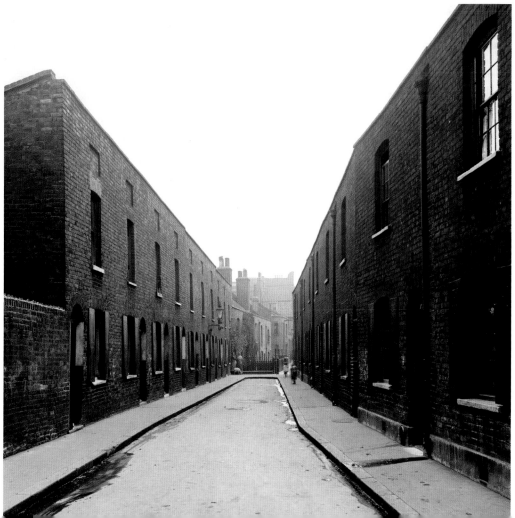

Opposite: Lynedoch Street: Shoreditch, July 1920
The City of Dreadful Monotony. Each house shoulder to shoulder with its neighbour, two storeys high and 18ft wide; street after street of grimy buildings against a slate-coloured sky. Yet beneath the drab exterior lay vibrant working class communities offering each other help and support in times of acute need.

Left above: Provost Street, Shoreditch, 1931
"No more dreary spectacle can be found on this earth than the whole of the awful East ….the colour of life is grey and drab. Everything is helpless, hopeless, unrelieved and dirty ….and the rain, when it falls, is more like grease than water from heaven. The very cobblestones are scummed with grease." (Jack London, *People of the Abyss*)
    View of Provost Street prior to its demolition in 1931.

Left below: Ivy Lane, Shoreditch, July 1920
View looking east. The defining image of the pre-war East End – a limitless sea of repetitive streets with rows of dingy two storey Victorian houses.

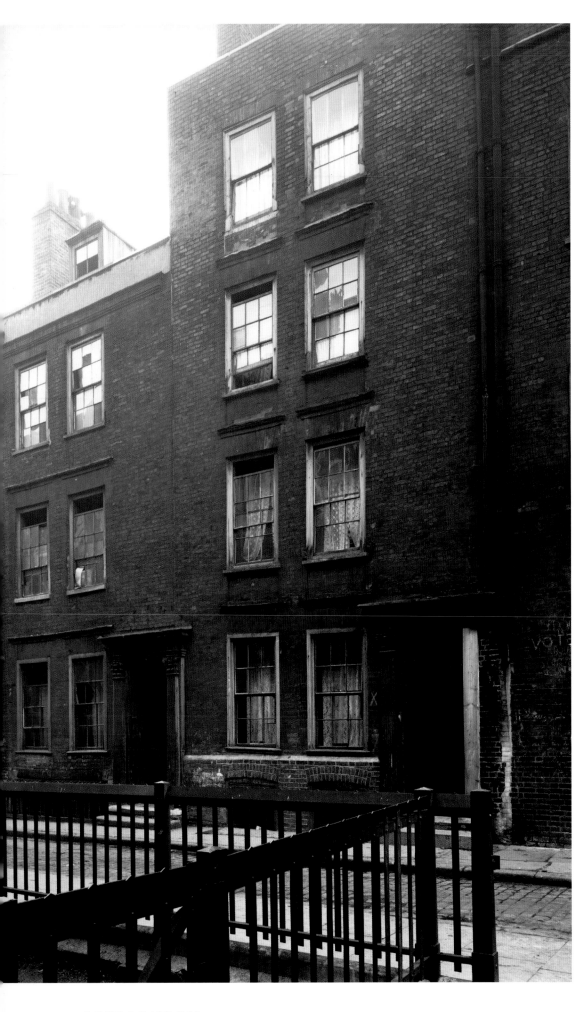
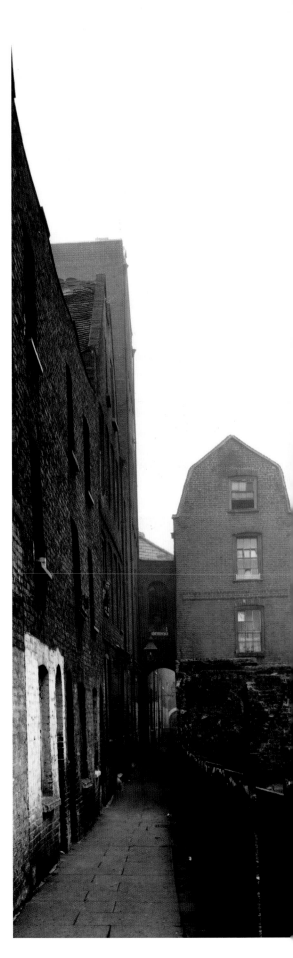

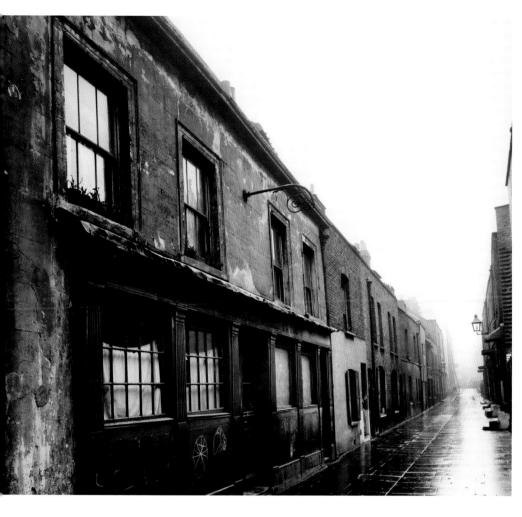

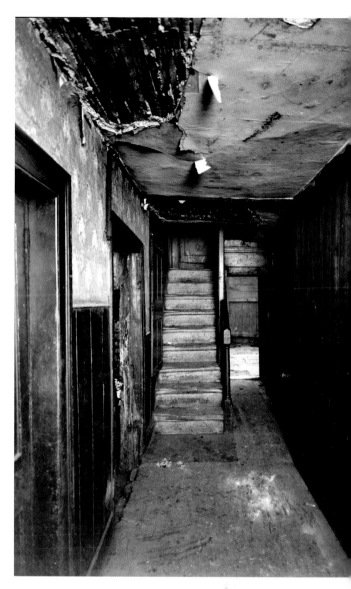

Helpless, hopeless, unrelieved and dirty

WAPPING

Opposite left: 22 Red Lion Street, Wapping, 1928
One of a number of early Georgian buildings close to the river which were once quite grand seamen's houses with doorcases enriched with fluted Corinthian pilasters.

Opposite right: A melancholic view of the narrow passage running behind Red Lion Street. The gabled house to the left is a late 17th century survival. The 18th century building in the background oversailing the passageway was known as The Gatehouse.

Above: 64 Red Lion Street, Wapping, 1928
A bleak, rain-sodden view of the Old George public house depicted a quarter of a century after the picture on p225 when it was still in use. Red Lion Street was slated for demolition in 1929, but a number of the houses are still occupied. Note the ubiquitous chalk marks on the walls.

Right above: View of the disused hall and staircase.

Right below: View of the derelict outhouse and rear yard.

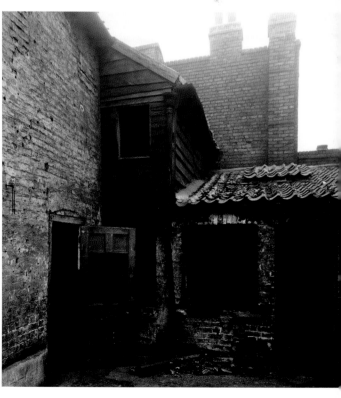

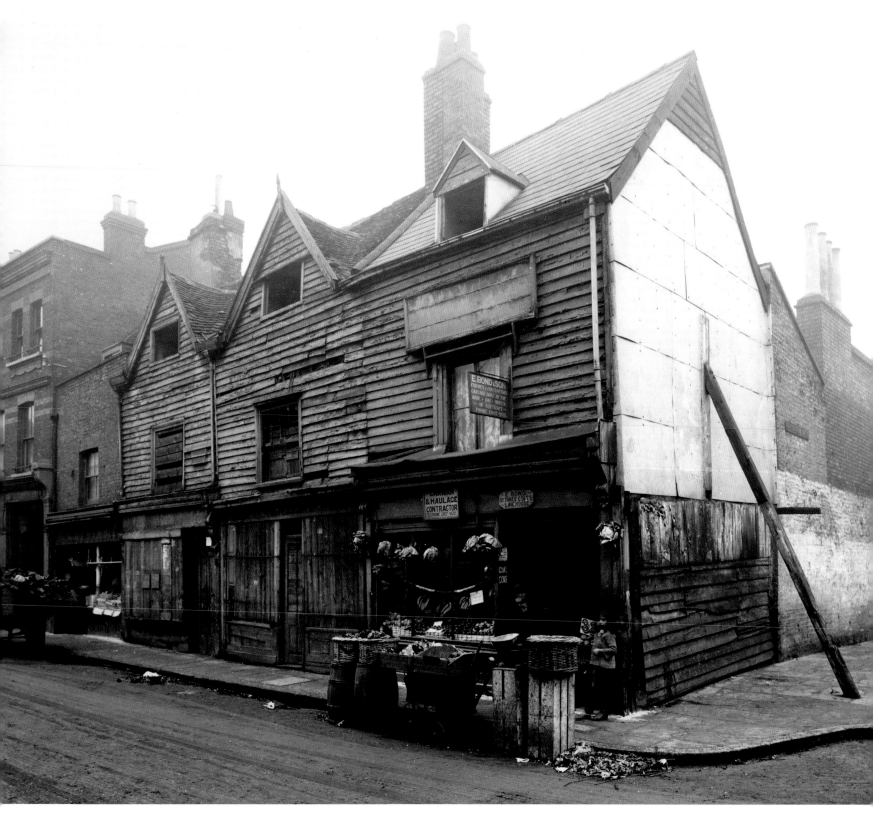

LIMEHOUSE

Above: 91-97 Three Colt Street, Limehouse, c 1923

Three of the five weatherboarded houses shown in the Edwardian photographs on p230 can be seen here in an advanced state of decay, the wooden gable wall supported by a single prop. Two are derelict, but the ground floor of the third is in use as a greengrocers with a pram inventively deployed to support an impromptu market stall.

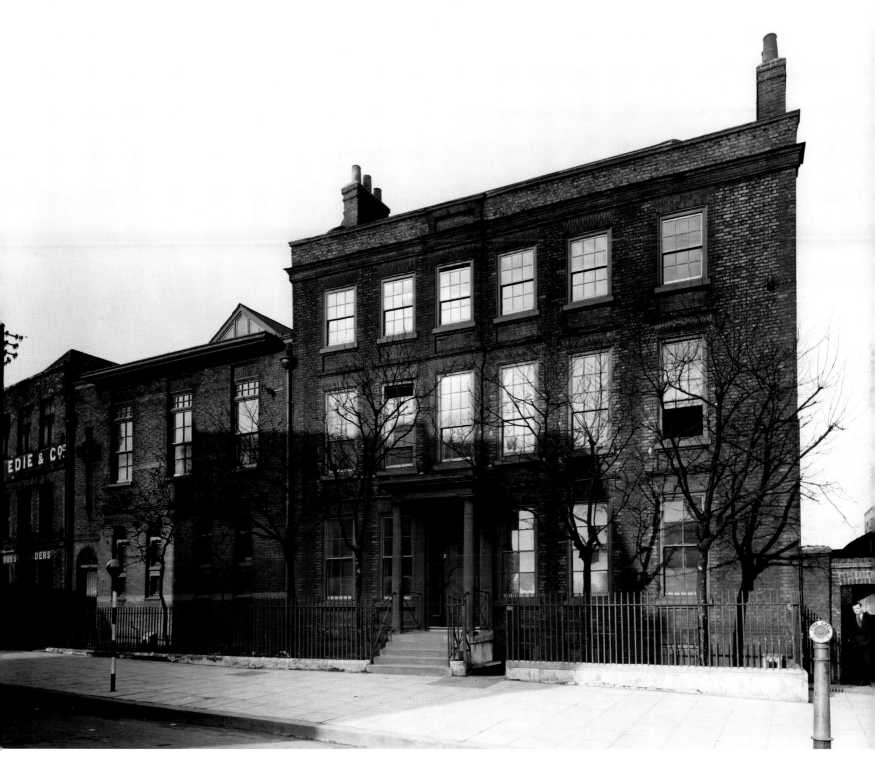

BOW

Above: 97 Bromley High Street, Bromley-by-Bow, 1935
St Mary's Vicarage, Bromley-by-Bow, an exceptionally fine house of around 1720 with a later porch. To the right is a once common fire alarm pillar.

As a place of resort in the 17th and 18th centuries, Bromley-by-Bow once contained some exceptional Georgian houses, but massive damage in the Second World War followed by comprehensive redevelopment and the disastrous construction of the Blackwall Tunnel Northern Approach Road completely severed the neighbourhood and eradicated its identity.

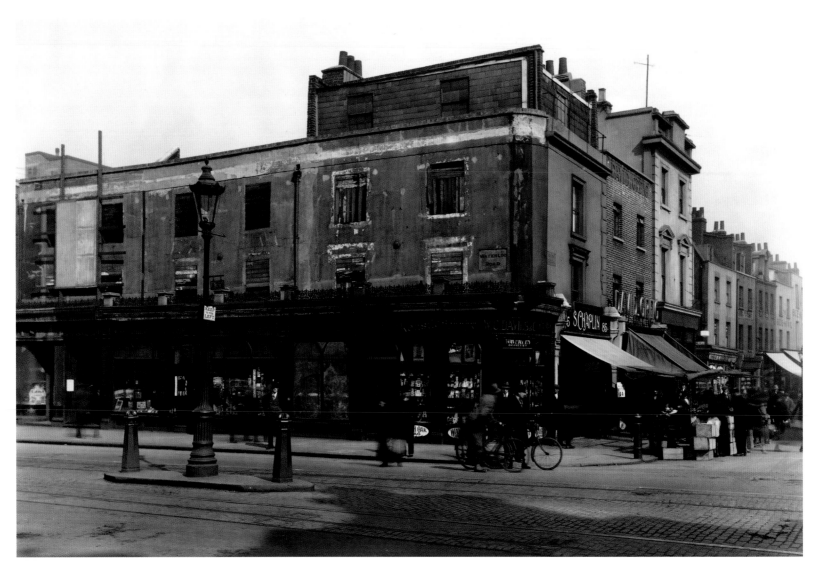

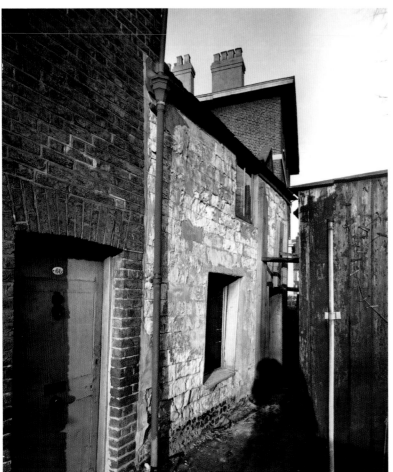

WATERLOO

Above: Waterloo Road, c 1930
Dilapidated stucco buildings at the junction of Waterloo Road and The Cut.

WANDSWORTH

Left: 66 New Park Road, Wandsworth, December 1929
Known as Goods Cottages, this extraordinary dwelling was built of clunch (chalk) on a flint plinth. Although not uncommon in rural areas, clunch was virtually unknown in London.

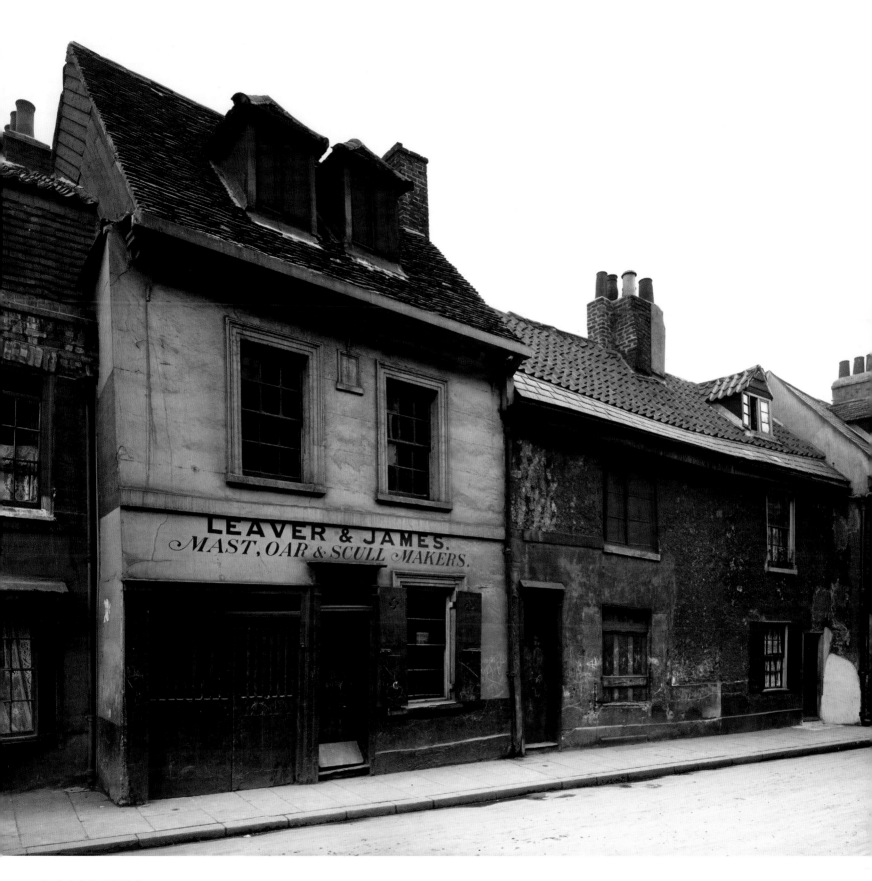

LAMBETH

Above: 20-23 High Street, Lambeth, 1923
By 1923 Lambeth High Street was becoming progressively down-at-heel
and ripe for the comprehensive redevelopment that was soon to eradicate
its distinctive identity as an ancient riverside neighbourhood.

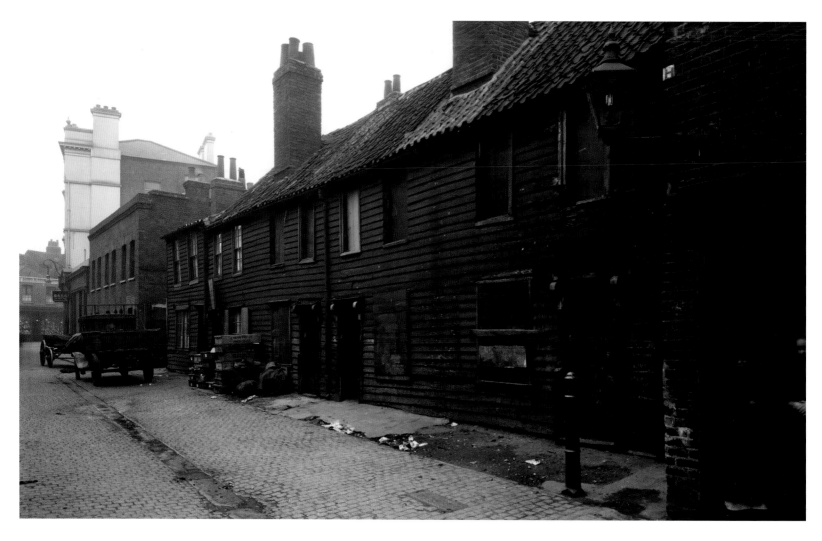

Old vernacular houses in forgotten village cores

PECKHAM

Above: 7-15 Blue Anchor Lane, Peckham, 1928
An old range of 18th century weatherboarded cottages boarded up prior to demolition.

ROTHERHITHE

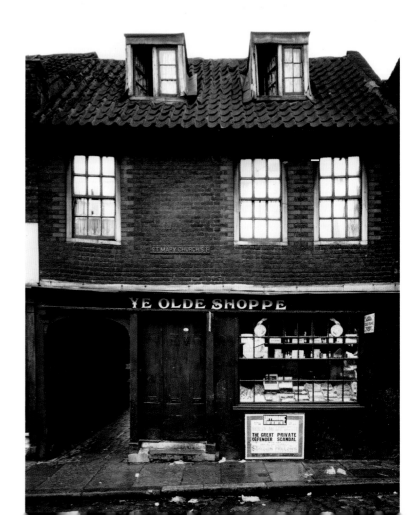

Right: 37 St Mary Church Street, Rotherhithe, December 1934
This early 18th century cottage stood to the west of St Mary's Rotherhithe, at the junction with Elephant Lane, which led through to Elephant Stairs on the river. The weatherboarded passage to the left connected with Princes (later Mayflower Street) which can be seen on p267.

GREENWICH

Right: Three Crowns Inn, 1-3 High Bridge, Greenwich, November 1936
With its twin bay windows and weatherboarded walls, The Three Crowns was typical of many riverside public houses that once lined the lower reaches of the Thames.

Below: 2-10 Pound Place, Eltham, 9 March 1926
17th century cottages with the timber-framing clearly exposed between brick infill panels. The entire group was demolished in 1929.

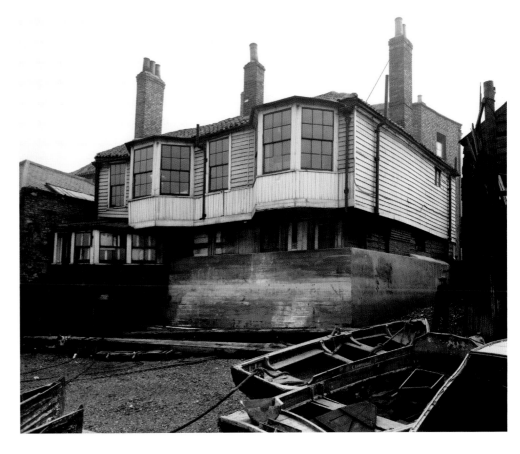

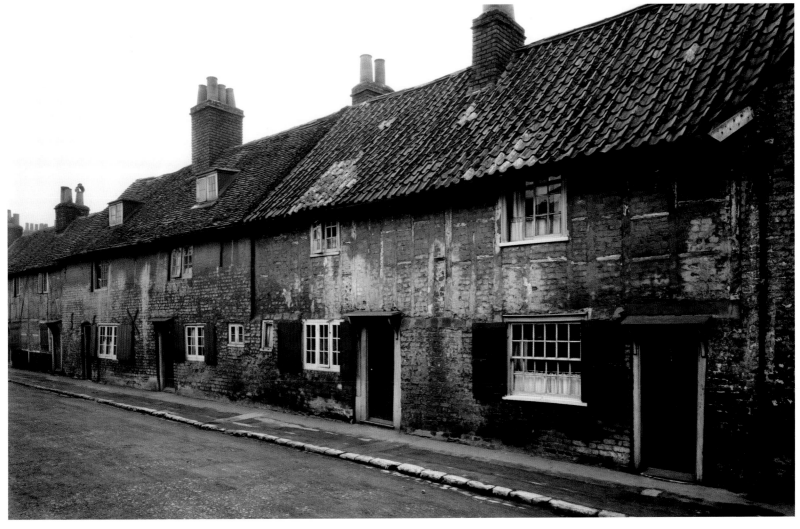

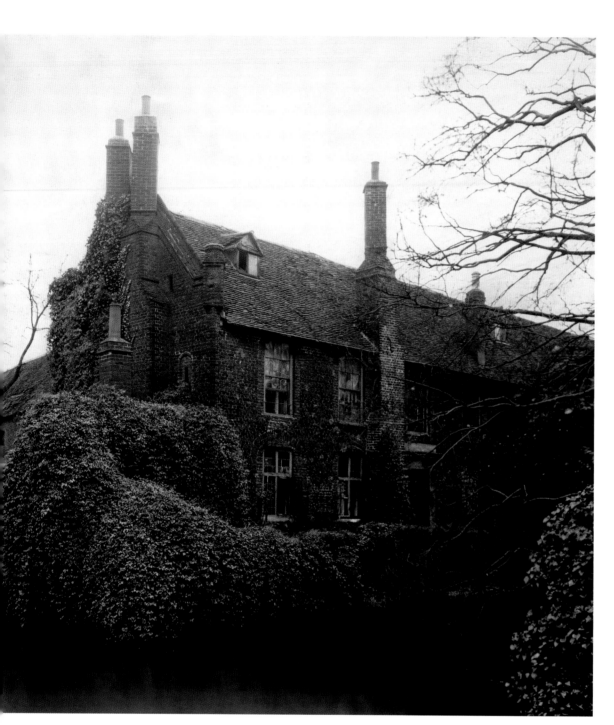

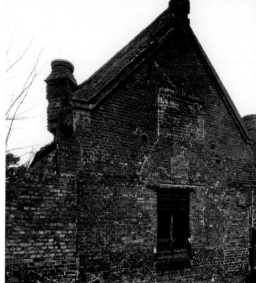

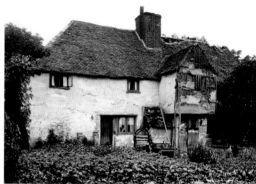

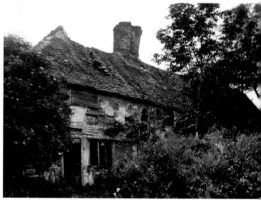

Rare Tudor survival

ELTHAM

Above: Tudor Barn, Well Hall Road, Eltham, 1927
Built in the early 16th century as a moated manor house, and known as the Tudor Barn, this building was one of the outbuildings of the domestic complex of the Well Hall estate of William Roper and Margaret More, Sir Thomas More's daughter. The main house was demolished in 1733, but the Tudor Barn survived. It was bought by Woolwich Borough Council in 1931, and is now a bar and restaurant. The moat and gardens form part of Well Hall Pleasaunce.

Top right: Well Hall Farm – East Gable, 1927
The Tudor brickwork of the great east gable.

Right centre: Well Hall, 1927
The derelict remains of one of the small mediaeval farmhouses which once served the Well Hall estate, prior to its demolition.

Bottom right: Well Hall Cottages, 1927
The ramshackle ruins of a group of cottages in Well Hall Road. The large central clustered brick chimney stack implies Tudor origins. The cottages probably once provided lodgings for servants from William Roper's household.

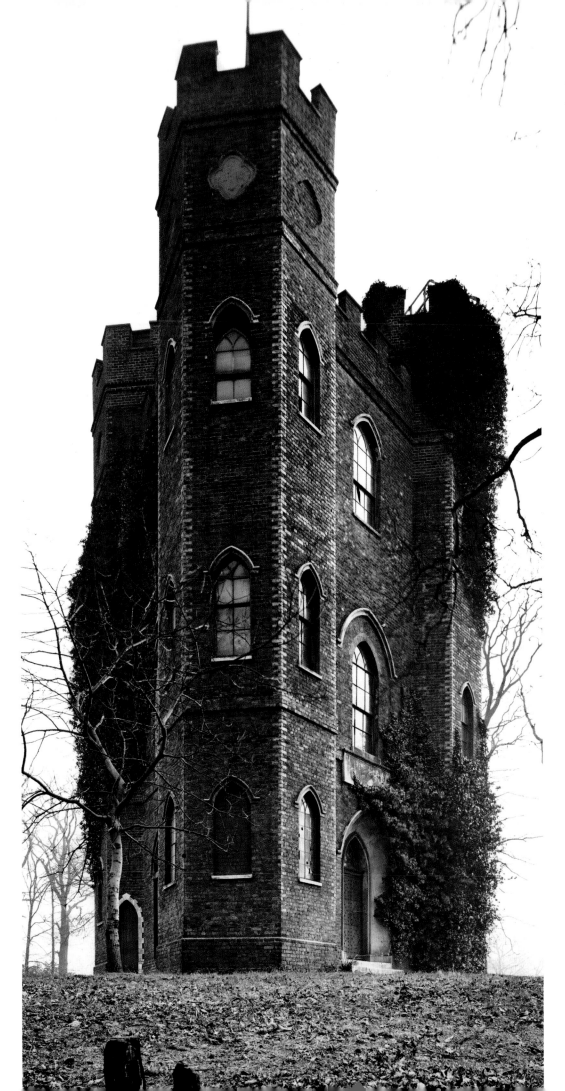

Echoes of Empire

SHOOTER'S HILL

Left: Severndroog Castle, Shooter's Hill, 1922
Severndroog Castle still stands on Shooter's Hill. Designed by Richard Jupp in 1784, it was erected by Lady James of Eltham to commemorate her husband, Commodore Sir William James, who, in April 1755, captured the pirate fortress of Severndroog off the Malabar Coast. Triangular in section with hexagonal corner turrets, inside is a domed plaster ceiling to the first floor.

On a clear day panoramic views can be obtained across London and seven counties.

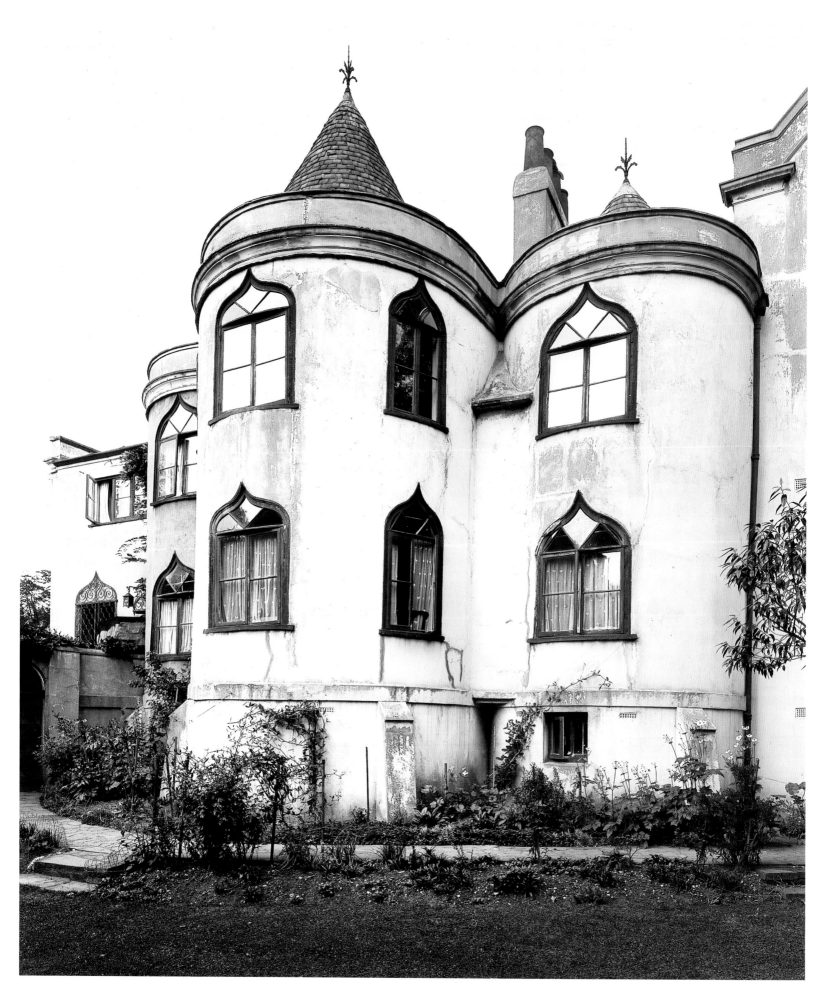

CHAPTER NINE

CATASTROPHE 1940-1945

A city in ruins

Britain and its Empire was the only power to fight two world wars from beginning to end and emerge on the winning side. The death of over 670 Londoners from aerial bombing in the First World War was a profound psychological shock, demonstrating the acute vulnerability of the capital and its economy to mass air attack. On the eve of the Second World War, the authorities feared 58,000 would die in the first raid alone, but this proved wildly alarmist. London's total war casualties amounted to just under 30,000 killed and over 50,000 seriously injured – shocking enough, but nothing like what had been envisaged.

In 1939 London was the greatest city in the world. By 1945 parts resembled a lunar landscape. The City of London was devastated. Whole districts lay in ruins. Countless historic buildings and places were laid waste. 50,000 houses were destroyed or made irreparable in inner London alone, and over 60,000 in outer London. An additional 290,000 houses suffered serious damage, and a further two million or more slight damage. Stepney lost one-third of its entire housing stock, whilst attacks by V1s and V2s thrust many London suburbs into the front line.

The extent of this destruction can be glimpsed in these photographs. A disproportionate number are City churches, but that is the nature of the archive, which concentrated on recording damage to London's architectural set-pieces.

The bombing provided an unprecedented post-war opportunity to eradicate poverty and squalor and to build a brave new world of modern housing and social amenities – aspirations encapsulated in Sir Patrick Abercrombie's Greater London Plan of 1944. But many streets and districts of fine buildings which could have been refurbished were left to rot, adding even greater momentum to the emerging conservation movement.

Opposite: Hunters Lodge, 5 Belsize Lane, Belsize Park, 7 September 1943
The designs for this castellated Gothick cottage ornee were exhibited at the Royal Academy in 1810. Designed by Joseph Parkinson for William Tate, a merchant, the Lodge lost most of its grounds with the development of the immediate area in the 1870s. Reduced in size, it is now known as Belsize Cottage and remains in private occupation.

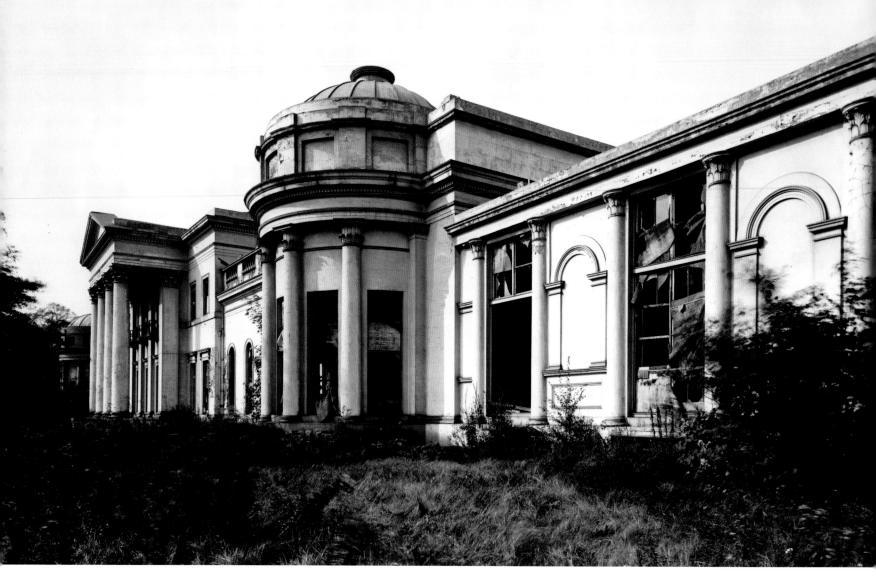

The scars of war

Above: Holford Place, Regent's Park, 10 October 1945
Situated in the north-west corner of Regent's Park, Holford House was the largest of the villas designed by Decimus Burton. It was built in 1832 for James Holford, a wealthy merchant and wine importer, with a majestic central portico and apsidal wings. After his death in 1853 it became Regent's Park Baptist College for the training of ministers. Hit by a V1 in 1944, the site was cleared four years later.

Right: New End Square, Hampstead, 12 June 1942
View looking west showing the bombed-out ruins of the square. In the centre foreground is a street shelter. The houses in the background were all carefully repaired after the war, including the Georgian cottages on the extreme right.

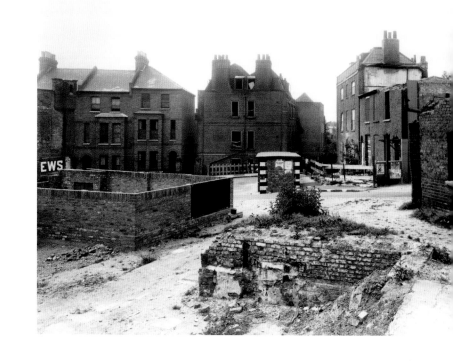

Right: 98 Portland Place, Regent's Park, 10 September 1946

View of the north-east corner of Portland Place at the junction with Park Crescent. By 1946 many of the grand Regent's Park terraces were in a shocking state of disrepair as a result of poor original construction and bomb damage. Following a government committee the Crown Estate embarked on a phased programme of sensitive repair, refurbishment and development. Park Crescent was reconstructed behind the retained original facades between 1960-63.

Below: 10 Carlton House Terrace, St James's, 6 May 1942

View of 10 Carlton House Terrace immediately to the east of Duke of York's Steps. The attic storey has been blown off and the stucco facades are pitted by shrapnel. The opulent Parisian interior of 1905-07 by Blow and Billery survived the war and it is now the home of the British Academy.

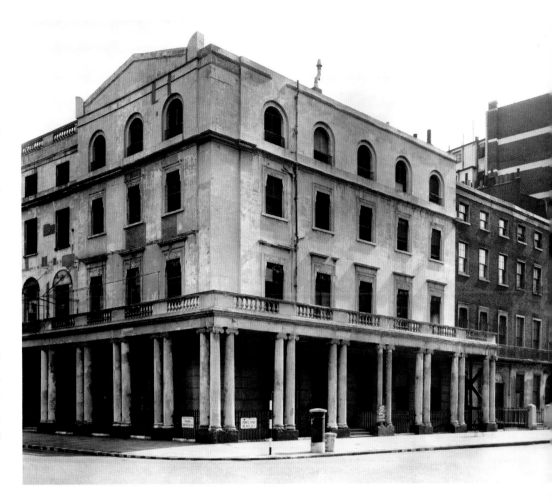

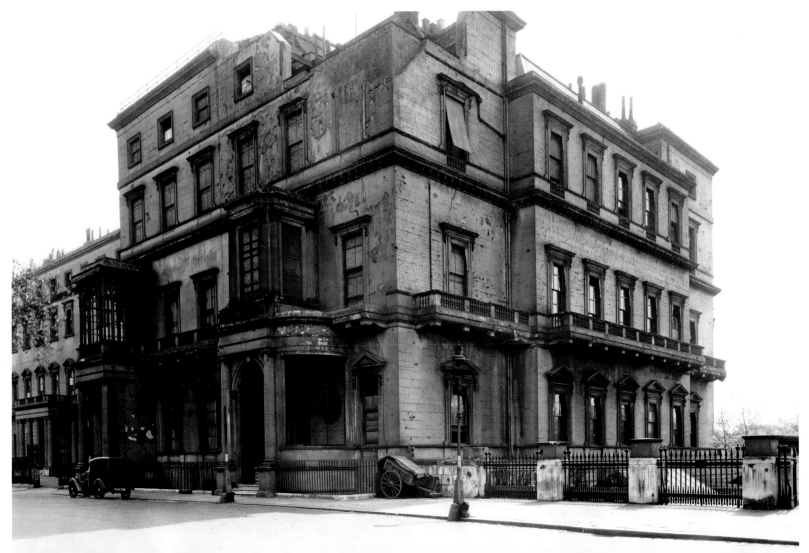

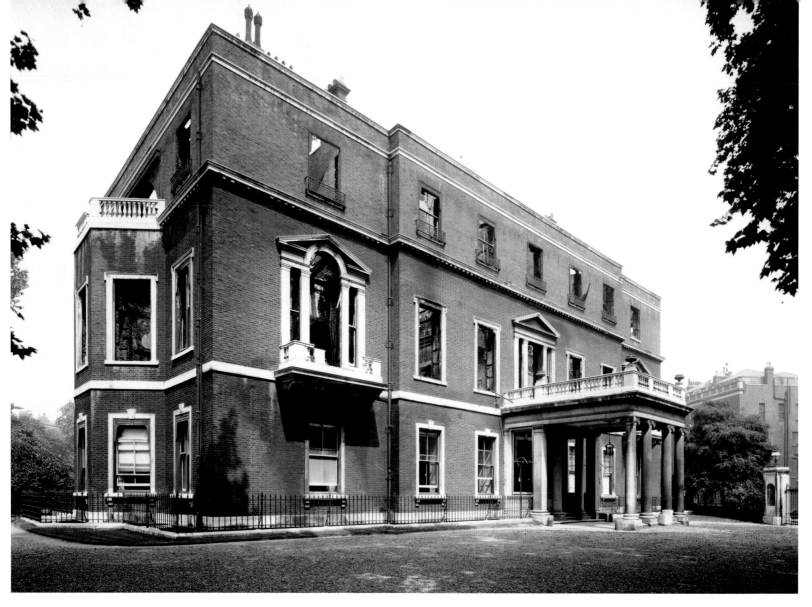

An intellectual salon

Above: Montagu House, 22 Portman Square, 20 June 1941
Montagu House was the salon of the Blue-stocking Club founded by Mrs Elizabeth Montagu, with the object of fostering intellectual debate rather than vacuous social frivolities. Her circle included Horace Walpole, Samuel Johnson and James Boswell. Between 1777-82 she had a mansion built for her to the designs of James Stuart placed diagonally on the north-west corner of the square. One room was decorated entirely with feathers. The house was damaged in May 1941 and, although it could have been saved, it was demolished after the war. The gate piers were dismantled and relocated to Kenwood House.

Right: Montagu House, 22 Portman Square, 9 July 1942
View of the entrance hall and staircase lobby with an Ionic screen in the foreground.

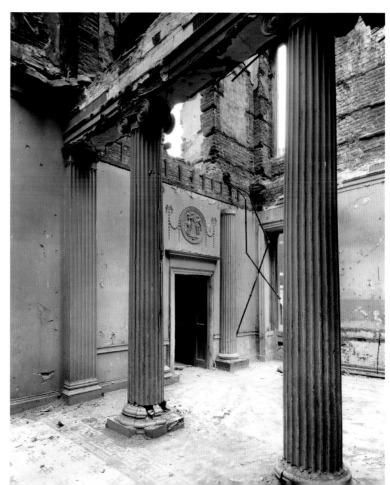

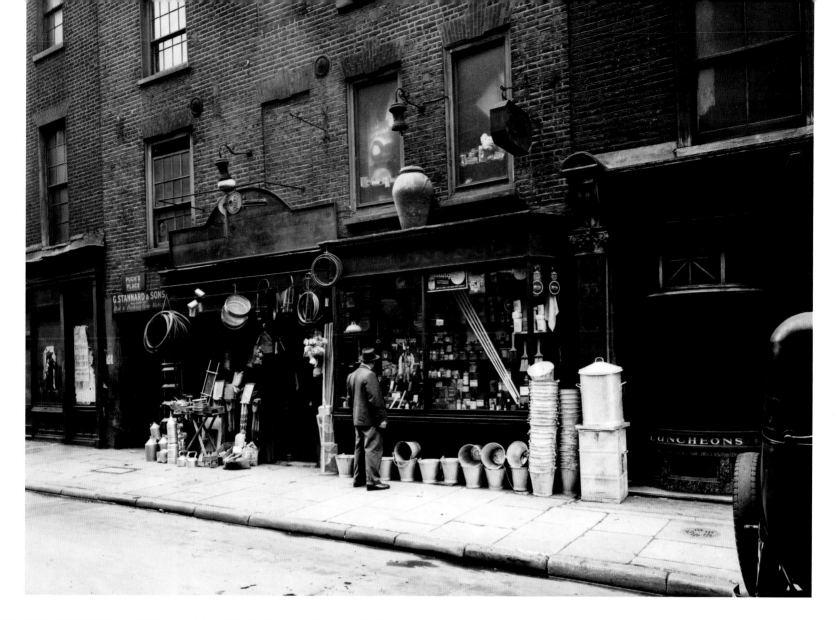

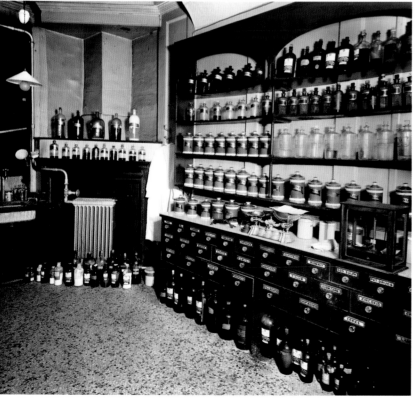

Above: 37-39 Carnaby Street, Soho, 18 October 1944

A remnant of old Soho. Part of a group of late 18th century houses, No. 37 was used by an ironmonger and oilman. Note the oil jar standing on the shop fascia between the first floor windows. At the south end a narrow passage can be seen which led to Pugh's Place, a dingy backland enclave.

Left: 9 Gerrard Street, Soho, 3 September 1946

9 Gerrard Street was built in 1758-59 and was the home of the Linnaean Society from 1805-21. Shortly afterwards the Westminster General Dispensary moved in, where it remained until 1957.

View showing an 18th century panelled interior with traditional chemist's jars.

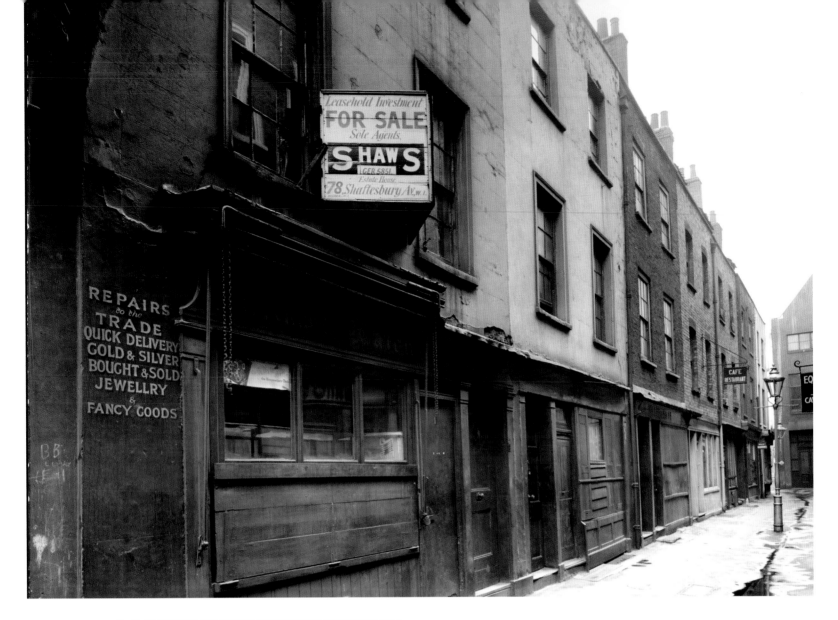

Dark, bleak streets

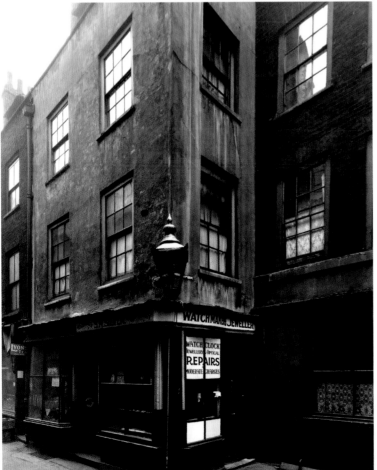

Above: 1-7 St Anne's Court, Soho, 27 February 1949
St Anne's Court links Wardour Street with Dean Street and it still retains
a handful of early 18th century houses on its north side. Nos. 1-7 on the
south side were built in 1735-36 with simple, timber staircases and front
and back rooms divided by panelled partitions. By the 1960s this colourful
thoroughfare was the haunt of prostitutes and clip joints. The entire
terrace was cleared c 1970.

Left: 7 St Anne's Court, Soho, 27 February 1949
View showing the dog-leg corner of the court. Had the terrace survived a
few years longer, almost certainly the houses would have been refurbished
and converted in a similar fashion to those in Meard Street to the south.

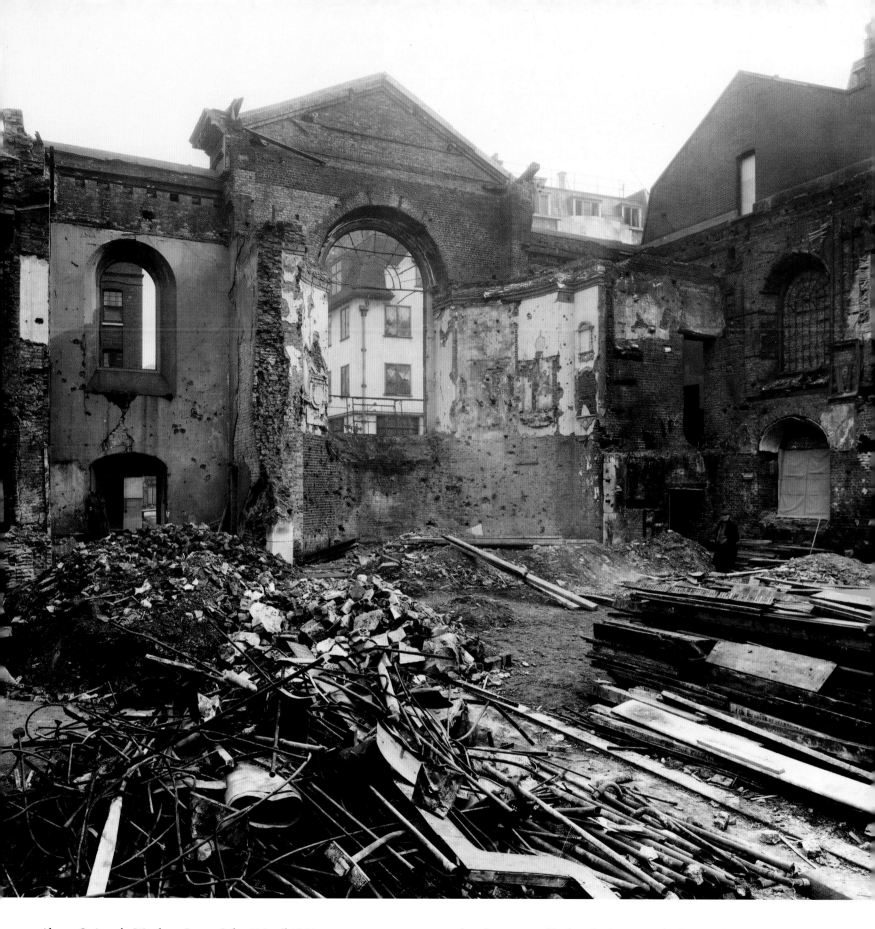

Above: St Anne's, Wardour Street, Soho, 5 April 1941

Both Sir Christopher Wren and William Talman were involved in the original design of the church which was consecrated in March 1685, but its peculiar steeple was added by S P Cockerell in 1801-03. Further remodelling took place in the 1830s under Robert Abraham. In 1940 the church was gutted by bombs, leaving only the steeple and east end walls which can be seen here. In 1956-57 the site was deconsecrated. Eventually it was redeveloped in the 1980s, retaining the tower and steeple. The novelist Dorothy L Sayers was interred under the tower in 1957.

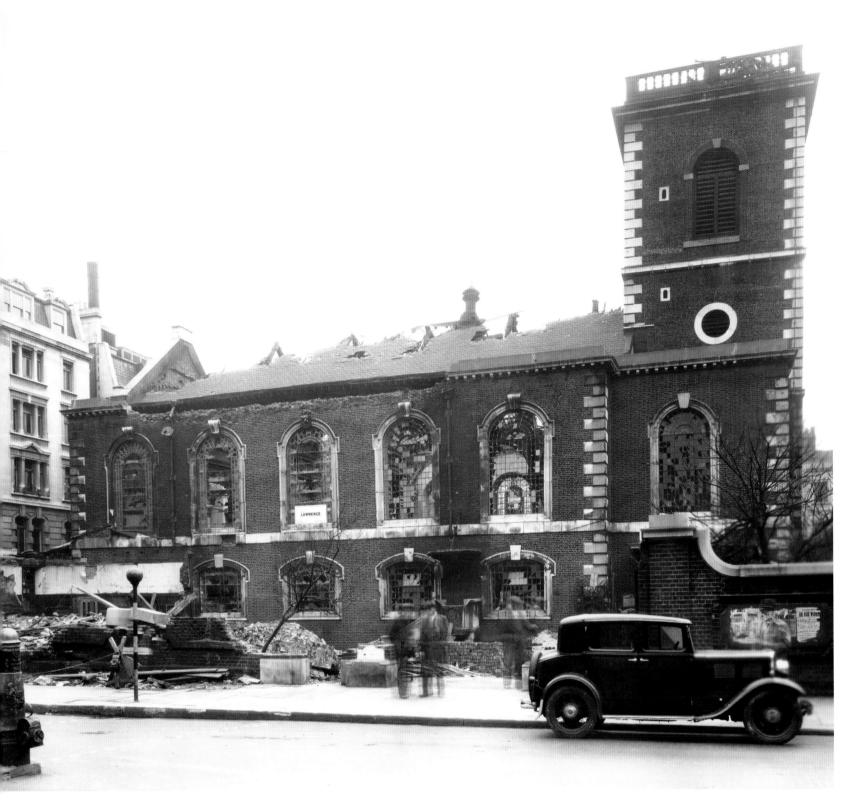

Devastation

Above: St James's, Piccadilly, 1941
Built by Wren between 1676-84 to serve the new development of St James's, then being laid out by Henry Jermyn, Earl of St Albans, on 10 October 1940, the church was damaged severely by high explosives and incendiaries and the Vicarage completely destroyed. After extensive restoration by Sir Albert Richardson, it was rededicated in June 1954 incorporating many original details which survived the bombing, including a Renatus Harris organ from Whitehall Palace and a 17th century reredos by Grinling Gibbons. A new spire designed by Richardson was added in 1968.

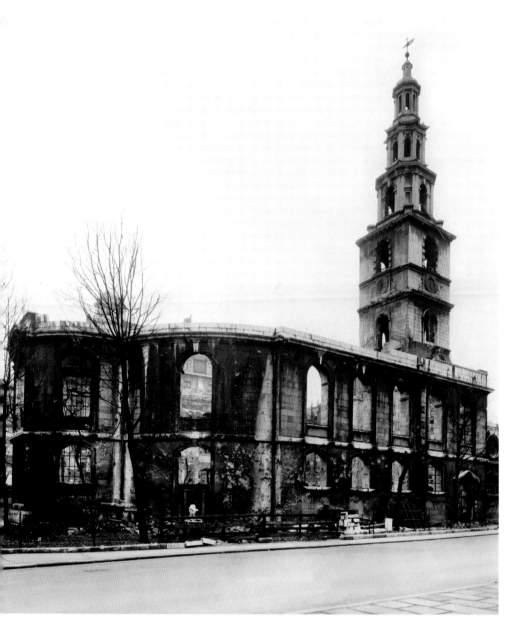

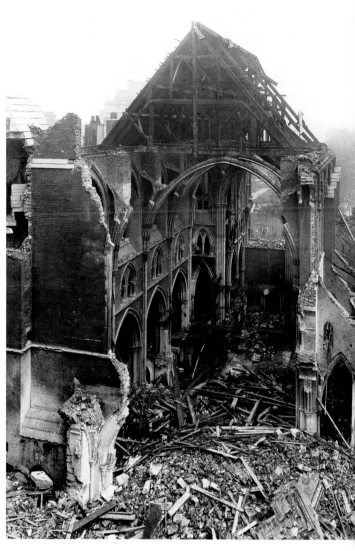

Loss

Above left: St Clement Danes, Strand, 1 March 1942

An historic London landmark, St Clement Danes is an ancient church alleged to have been built by Danish settlers in the 9th century and rebuilt several times since, including by Wren in 1680-82, and James Gibbs, who added the upper tower and spire in 1719-20. In 1941 it was burnt out and left a smouldering ruin, although the bombing unexpectedly revealed the mediaeval crypt under the eastern end of the church. In 1955-58 the interior was restored sensitively by Anthony Lloyd using photographs and drawings of the original plasterwork. The exterior still shows evidence of wartime bomb damage. It is now the RAF church in London with memorials and badges of RAF units lining the walls.

Above right: St John's, Red Lion Square, Holborn, 29 May 1941

Built between 1874-78 to the design of John Loughborough Pearson, St John's was one of London's finest Victorian churches. In May 1941 it suffered severe damage in an air raid, and even worse through the subsequent stripping of the building for scrap. The ruins were cleared in 1960 for the creation of Procter Street, which obliterated the western end of Red Lion Square.

View from the roof of the adjacent School of Arts & Crafts towards Red Lion Square.

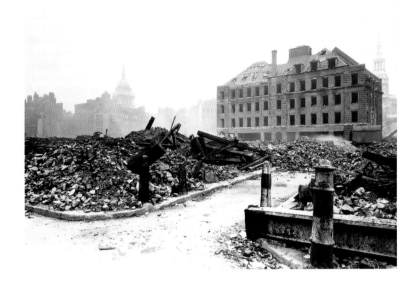

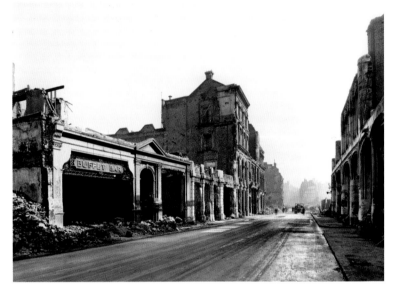

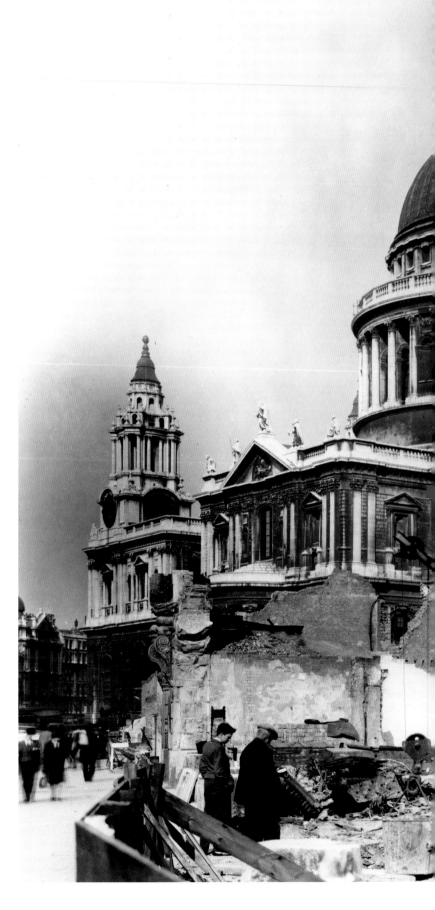

Hope

Top: Paternoster Square area, 7 April 1941

View of the Paternoster Row area from Paternoster Square showing the devastation caused during the catastrophic raid of 29 December 1940 when virtually the entire historic district was levelled.

To the left is the cupola of the Central Criminal Court. To the extreme right is the tower and steeple of Christ Church, Newgate Street, which was burnt out in the same raid.

Above: Fore Street: 10 March 1941

The City in ruins. View from Wood Street looking east along Fore Street towards Moorgate.

Right: St Paul's Cathedral, 15 April 1942

View of St Paul's Cathedral from Friday Street with the ruins of St Augustine's Watling Street in the foreground. The narrow lanes around Old Change seen on p 94 were flattened in the bombing.

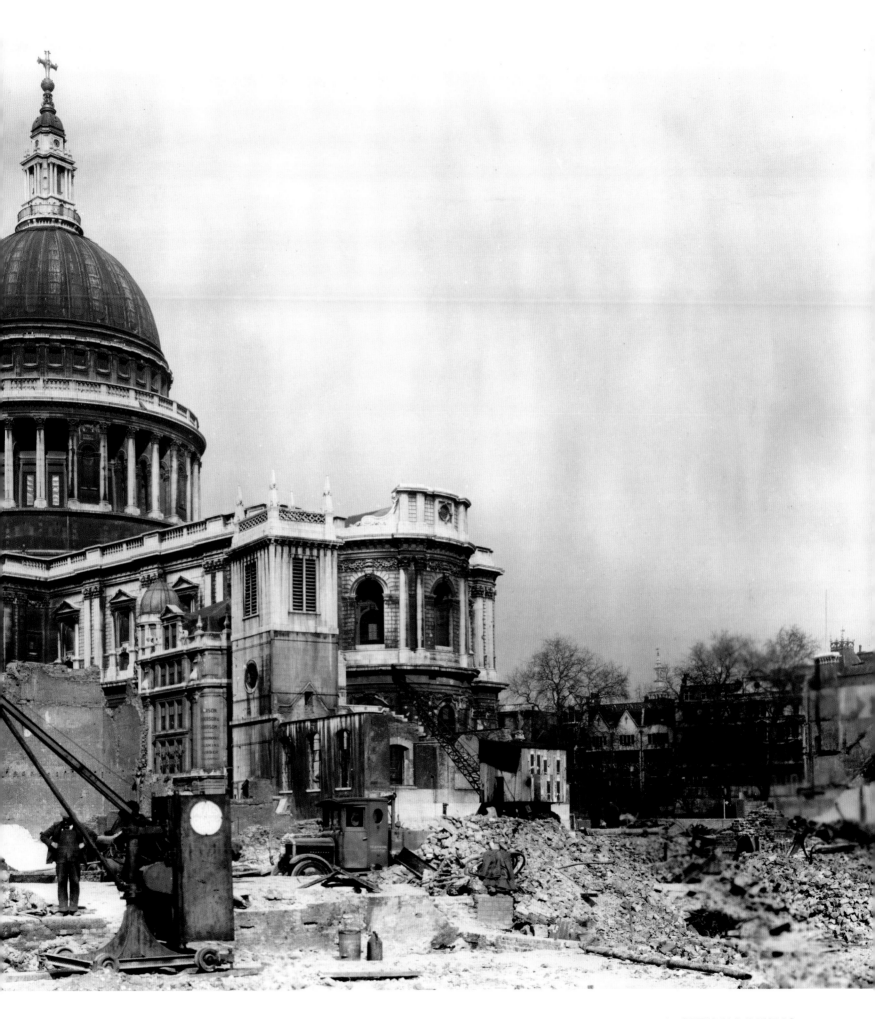

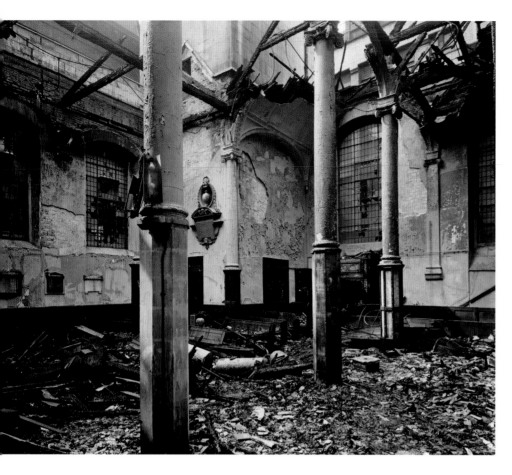

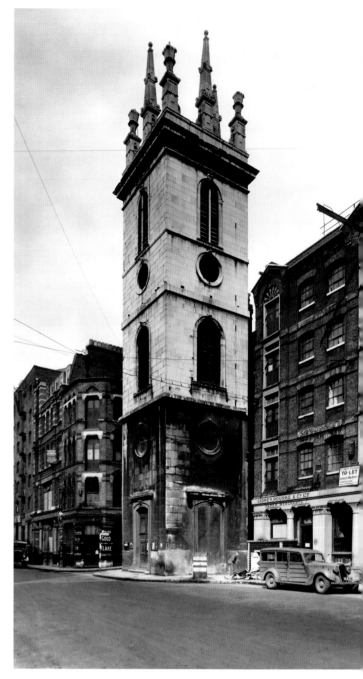

Faith

Above left: St Augustine's, Watling Street, 3 April 1941

The charred ruins of the nave with the tower beyond. It was in this inferno that one of the most touching stories of the Blitz occurred. With remarkable prescience, four times Faith, the church cat (pictured right), carried her kitten from the vicarage three floors down into a recess in the church below. Each time the vicar returned it until finally he relented. Three days later the vicarage and much of the area was devastated by bombing.

The inscription in the church reads:

"*On Monday September 9, 1940, she endured perils and horrors beyond the power of words to tell. Shielding her kitten in a sort of recess she sat through the whole frightful night of bombing and fire, guarding her little kitten.*

"*The roofs and masonry exploded … Floors fell through in front of her. Fire and water and ruin were all around her. Yet she stayed calm and steadfast and waited for help. We rescued her in the early morning, while the place was still burning, and by the mercy of the Almighty God, she and her kitten were not only saved, but unhurt. God be praised and thanked for his goodness and mercy to our little pet.*"

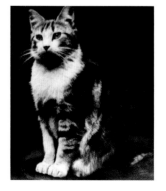

Above right: St Mary Somerset, Upper Thames Street, 3 April 1941

St Mary Somerset was rebuilt by Wren in 1685-94 on the site of its 12th century predecessor. In 1869 the body of the church was demolished, but, as one of Wren's best works, the romantic pinnacled tower was retained. During the Second World War it was used as a rest centre for working women, and in 1956 it was restored as a monument by the City Corporation.

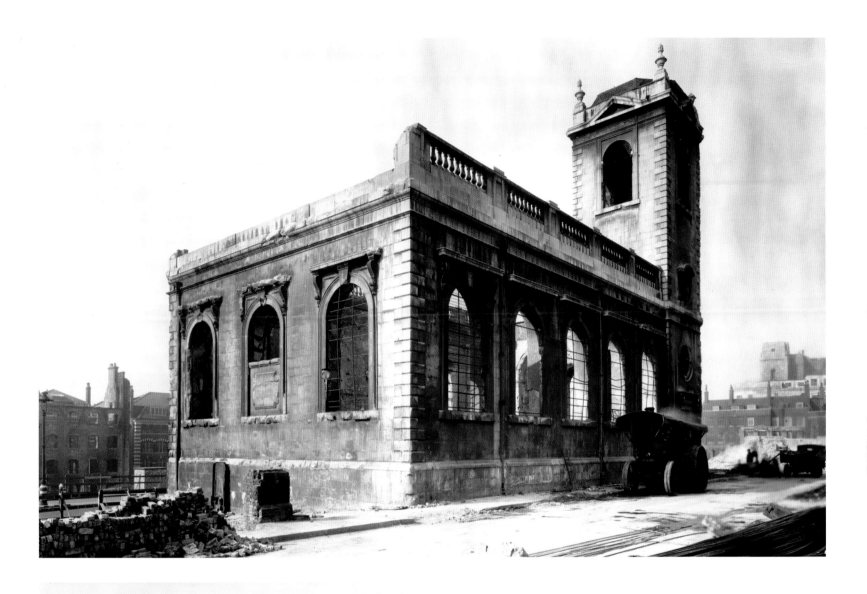

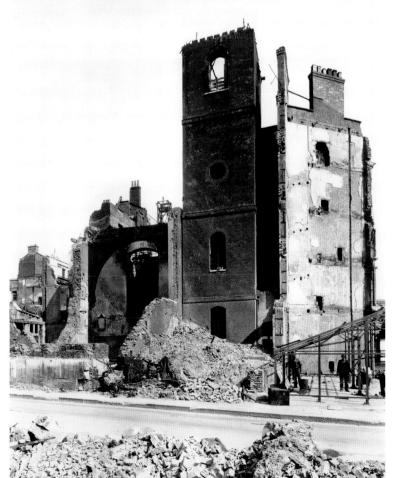

Above: St Nicholas Cole Abbey, 15 April 1942

View looking south-west with the ruins of Queen Victoria Street beyond.

Built by Wren between 1672-78 on the site of an earlier mediaeval church, the building was gutted completely by incendiary bombs in May 1941, which laid waste the surrounding area. It was reconstructed by Arthur Bailey in 1961-62 with a new hexagonal spire closely modelled on the original, but attenuated. Above a small railed gallery and ogee roof is a finial in the shape of a ship taken from the demolished church of St Michael, Queenhithe.

Left: St Mildred's, Bread Street, 15 April 1942

St Mildred's was one of Wren's finest and least altered churches. The poet, Shelley, married Mary Wollstonecraft here in 1816. It retained its original pews, pulpit, altar-rails and reredos, until May 1941 when it was destroyed completely in one of London's worst air raids. Only the tower, seen here, was left standing, but subsequently this too was demolished. Virtually nothing remains to mark the site.

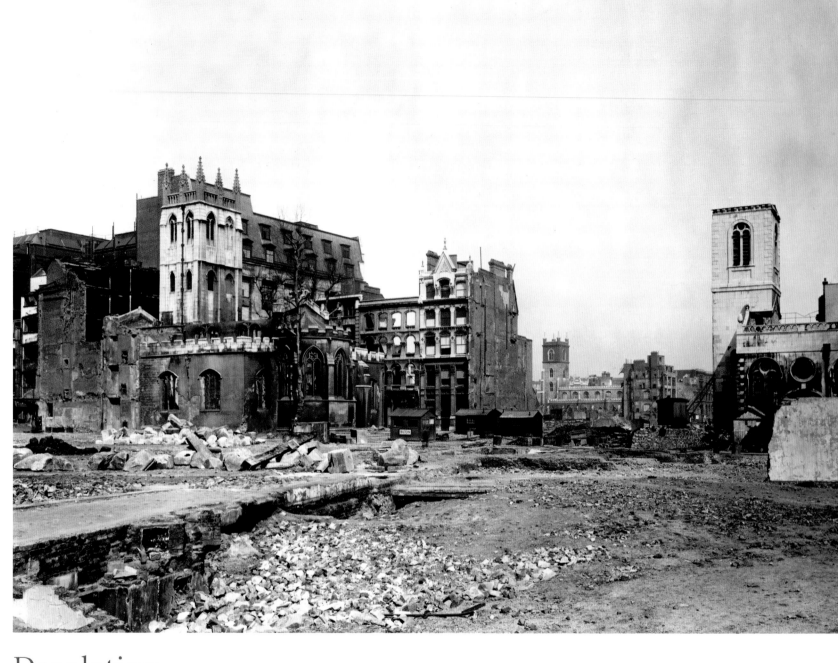

Desolation

Above: Panorama from Milk Street, 16 April 1942
To the left are the ruins of St Alban, Wood Street, by Wren 1682-87, which was destroyed on 29 December 1940. The tower survived and was restored in 1964. Twenty years later it was converted into residential accommodation. In the distance is the tower of St Giles, Cripplegate.

To the right is St Mary, Aldermanbury, also by Wren, which contained the tomb of Judge Jeffreys. The ruins were dismantled and shipped to Fulton, Missouri, where the church was reconstructed painstakingly on the campus of Westminster College as a memorial to Sir Winston Churchill.

Opposite top: St Alban, Wood Street, 20 August 1941
View of the devastated interior of St Alban looking towards the chancel.

Opposite below: St Mary, Aldermanbury, 20 March 1941
View of the gutted shell of the church and the surviving Corinthian columns that divided the nave and aisles.

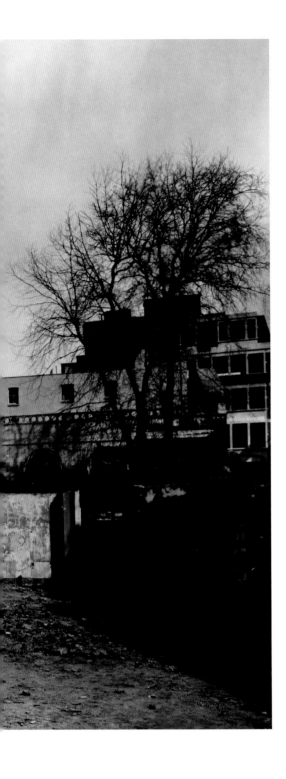

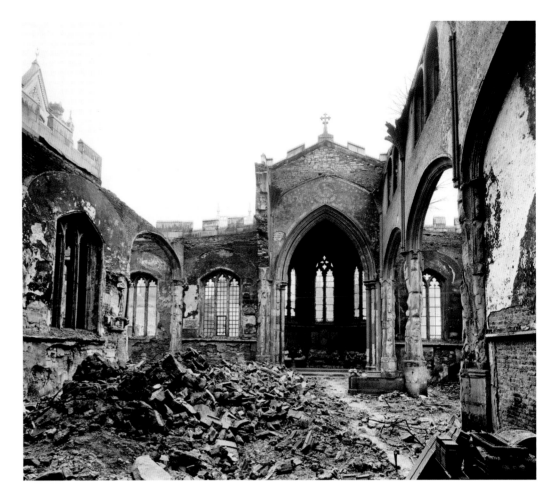

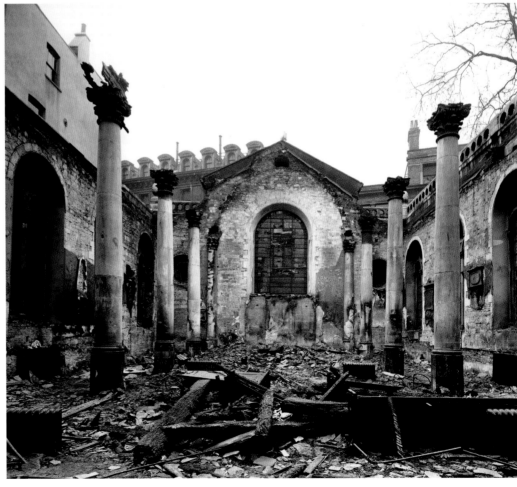

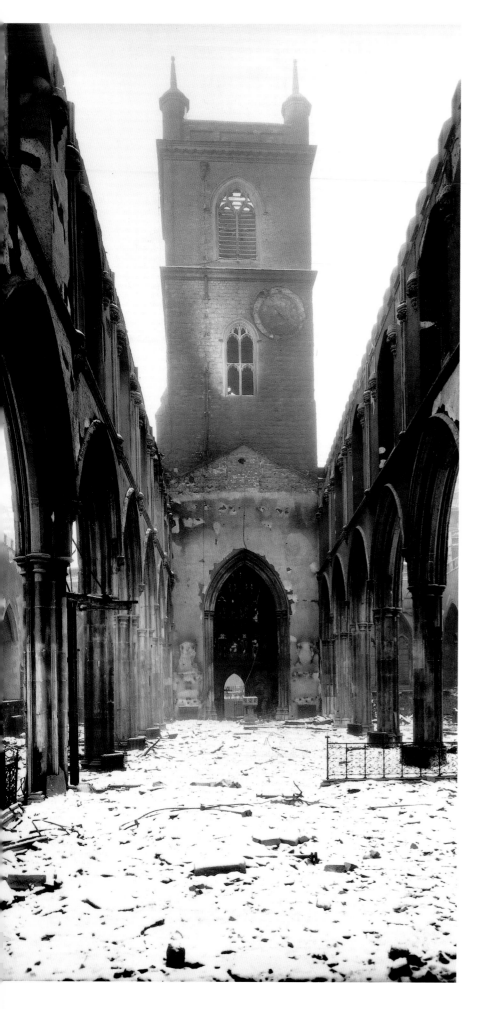

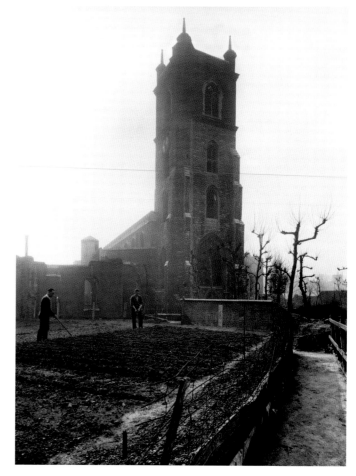

Resurrection

Left: St Giles, Cripplegate, January 1941

St Giles was the first City church to be damaged in the Blitz. Rebuilt following a fire in 1545, it contained several outstanding historic tombs, including those of the explorer, Sir Martin Frobisher (1594), the cartographer, John Speed (1629), and the poet, John Milton (1674). Oliver Cromwell married Elizabeth Bourchier here. The church was restored by Godfrey Allen in 1960, exposing substantial areas of 14th century fabric, and refurnished with fittings salvaged from other churches. The organ case came from St Luke's, Old Street.

A bleak view of the snow-covered nave looking towards the tower.

Above: St Giles, Cripplegate, 16 April 1942

View showing allotments created on the derelict bombsite adjoining the north tower.

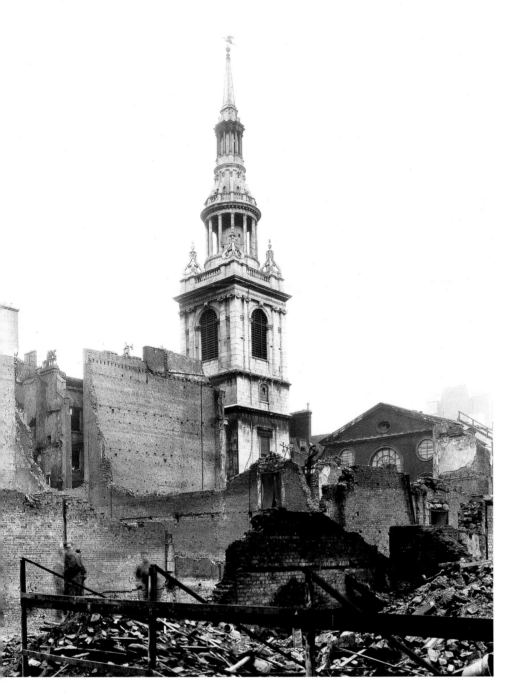

Left above: St Mary-le-Bow, Cheapside, 24 February 1941
Built above an extensive Norman crypt, and modelled on the Basilica of Maxentius in Rome, St Mary-le-Bow is one of Wren's most famous compositions. Capped by a gilded dragon weathervane, the exuberant tower and steeple, completed in 1680, remains a great London landmark. Wrecked by incendiary bombs in May 1941, its sensitive reconstruction took over 8 years from 1956-64, under the watchful eye of Laurence King who recreated Wren's design. The tower, which survived the collapse of the bells in 1941, was dismantled, strengthened and rebuilt as part of the works.

Left below: All Hallows, Barking, Great Tower Street, 28 May 1941
Severely damaged in two separate air raids in December 1940, All Hallows remained ruinous until it was restored in stages by Lord Mottistone of Seely and Paget between 1949-58 with donations from all over the world. The bombing revealed extensive early Anglo-Saxon and Roman remains, including two tessellated pavements in the excavated undercroft. The interior was refurnished with a mixture of salvaged and relocated fittings, including a pulpit (1682) from St Swithin, Cannon Street.

View looking east with the gutted remains of a 19th century warehouse in Tower Hill beyond.

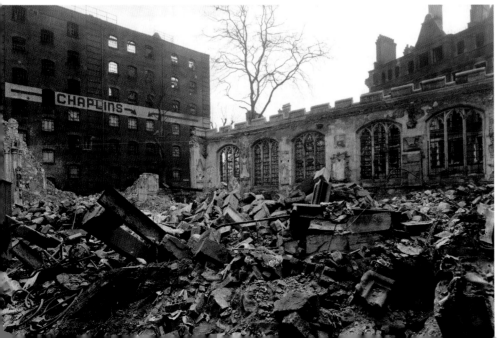

Revelation

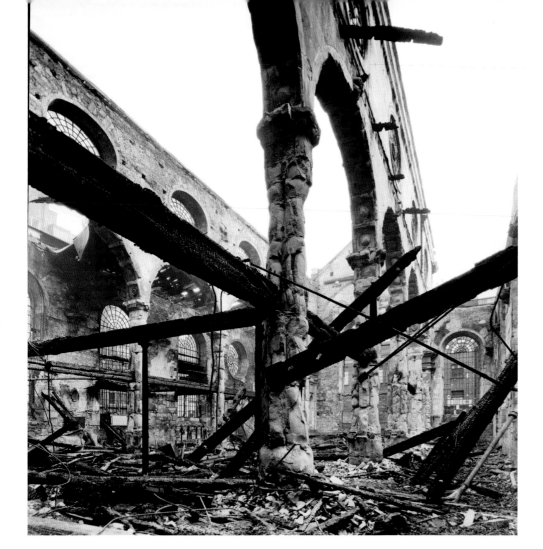

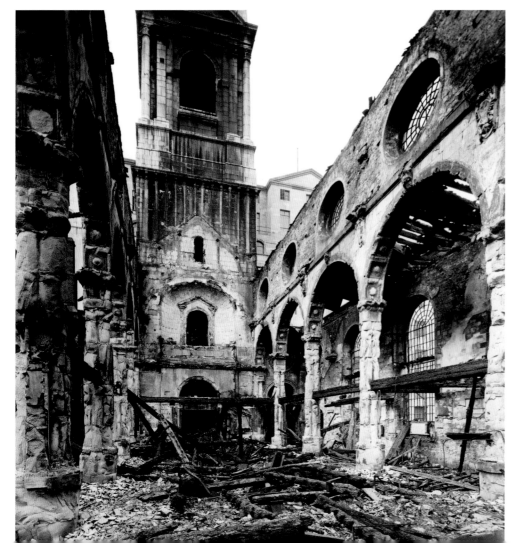

Left above: St Bride's, Fleet Street, 24 February 1941
St Bride's is one of the earliest centres of Christian worship in London. The catastrophic air raid which gutted the church in December 1940 revealed the foundations of seven different churches from the 6th to the 17th centuries, as well as the remains of a Roman villa and the crushed coffin and memorial plaque of the novelist Samuel Richardson, who was buried here in 1761. Wren's distinctive steeple with diminishing octagonal arcades survived the bombing, and the church was reconstructed within its walls by Godrey Allen in 1955-57.

View showing the gutted nave and aisles. The intensity of the heat of the fire has shattered the stonework of the columns.

Left below: View of the nave towards the base of the tower.

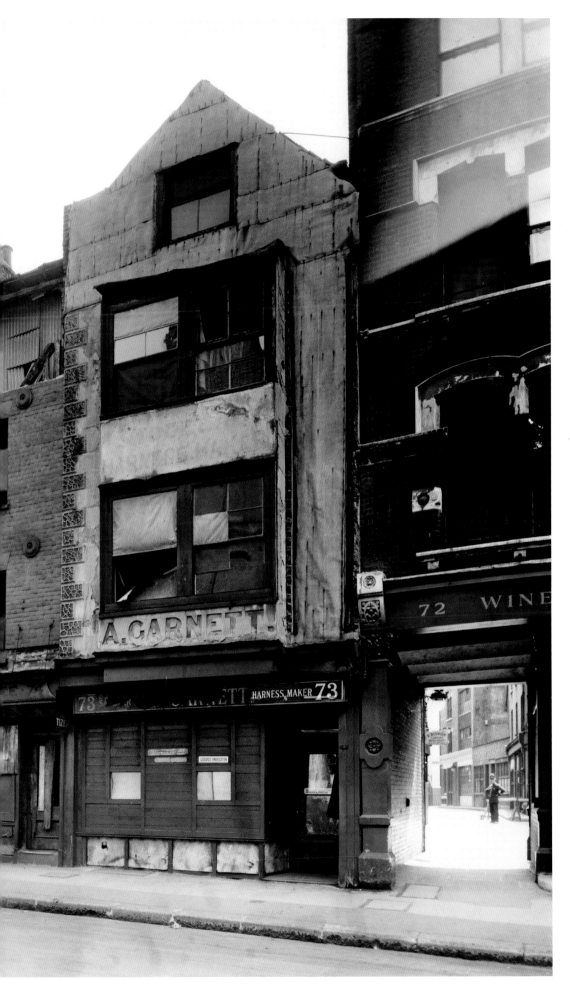

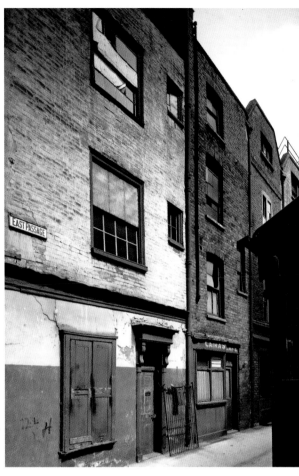

Left: 73-74 Long Lane, Smithfield, 15 August 1945
The battered remains of a pair of 17th century houses covered with temporary sheeting. No. 74 still survives. Note the inquisitive policeman beyond the passageway.

Above: Side elevation to East Passage.

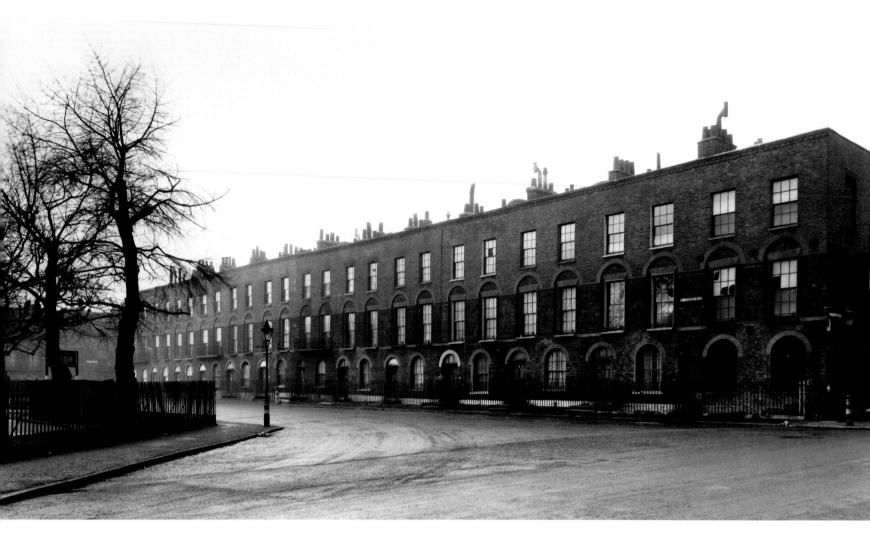

Destructive idealism

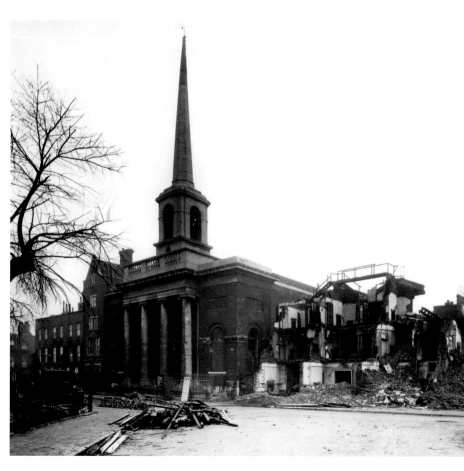

Above: King Square, Finsbury, 2 February 1945
Idealistic post-war planning destroyed more of London's historic neighbourhoods than the Luftwaffe. King Square survived the war, but tragically the buildings were cleared for uninspiring public housing by Finsbury Borough Council in the 1960s.

Right: St Barnabas, King Square, January 1941
Designed by Thomas Hardwick in 1822-26, St Barnabas was the focal point of King Square, its thin needle spire, a local landmark. Although the surrounding buildings were swept away, the church was restored and reopened in 1956.

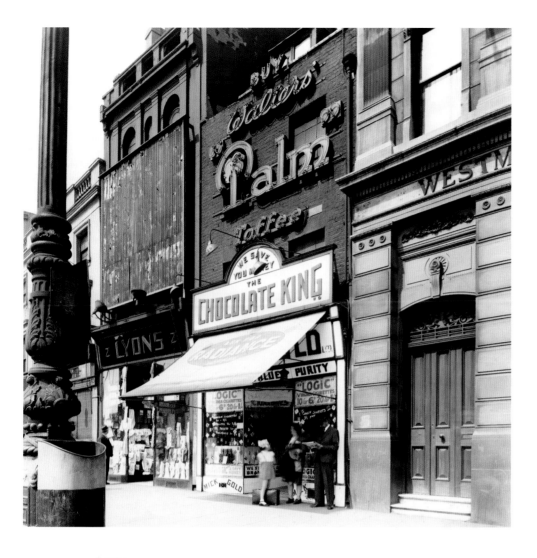

Left: 3 Upper Street, Islington, 30 May 1944
An evocative snapshot of tired wartime London with vitrolite fascias to the shopfronts and dilapidated frontages to the upper floor.

Below: Brooke House, Hackney, 4 April 1941
Brooke House was a remarkable mediaeval house with its first recorded orgins in the 1470s. Later it was owned by Henry Percy, Earl of Northumberland, Thomas Cromwell and various members of the nobility, one of whom, Baron Hunsdon, built the long gallery between 1578-83. From 1759-1940 it was used as a private mental asylum, until October 1940 when it was hit by a high explosive bomb, which destroyed the northern courtyard, seen here, and wrecked the rest of the house. In 1944 it was acquired by the LCC, but after further bomb damage, it was demolished completely in 1954-55: a great loss of a fascinating and historic mediaeval survival.

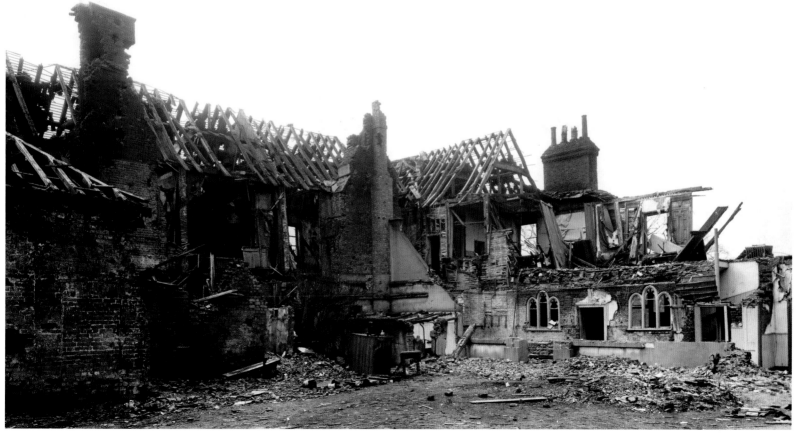

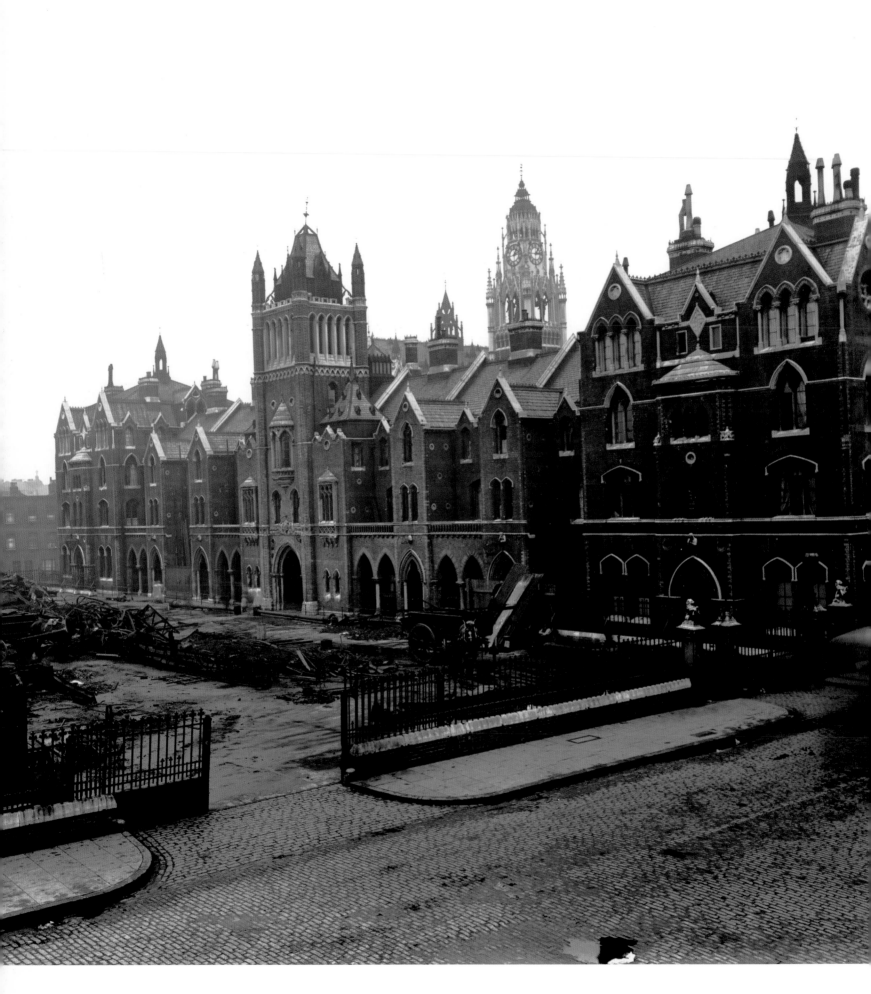

Grievous loss

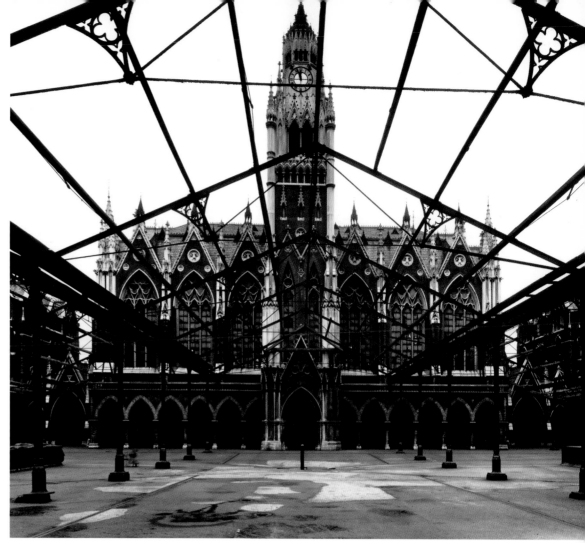

Columbia Market, Shoreditch
24 July 1946
Columbia Market was a white elephant virtually from its inception. It was founded in 1869 by Baroness Burdett Coutts at a cost of over £200,000 in a philanthropic attempt to provide an open food market for the East End, but it was frustrated by a monopoly of local interests and closed in 1885. After acquisition by the LCC in 1915, it was used as workshops until it was finally demolished for public housing in 1958 – one of London's most grievous architectural losses.

Opposite: View of the west range with the magnificent clock tower beyond where the bells rang a hymn tune every 15 minutes.

Right top: View of the magnificent Market Hall and clock tower from the main gate.

Right: View showing the north elevation of the market hall designed by Henry Darbishire in spectacular Flemish Gothic style.

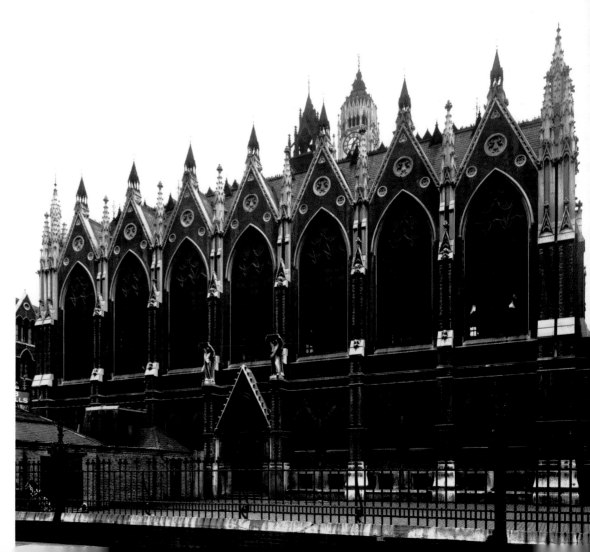

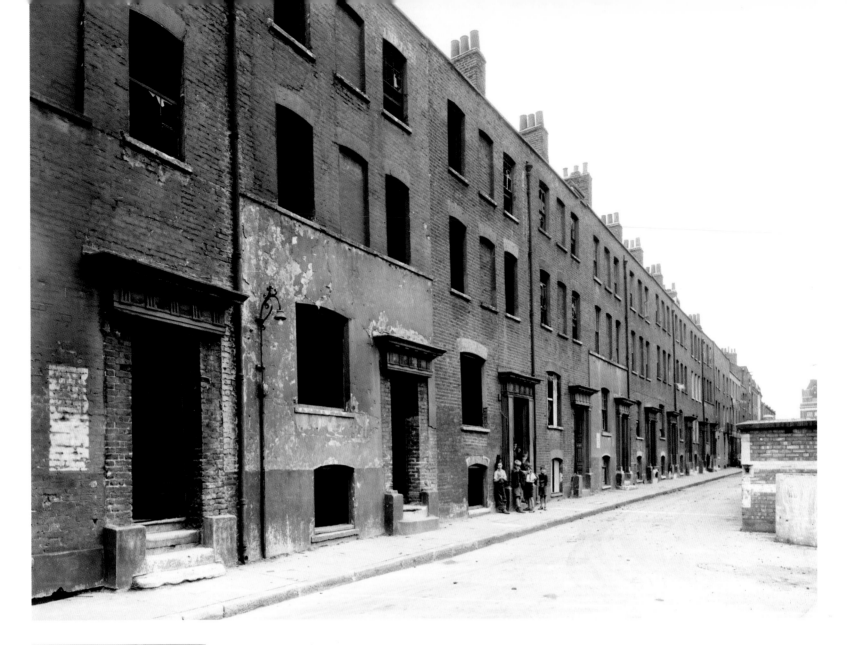

Abandonment

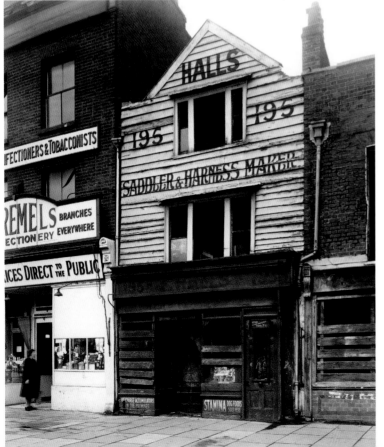

Above: Swedenborg Square, Stepney, 19 August 1945
View of the west side of Swedenborg Square with a street shelter to the right. The pilasters have been removed from the doorcases, prior to demolition.

Left: 195 Mile End Road, 12 November 1944
Demolished shortly after this photograph was taken, No. 195 was a rare surviving weatherboarded timber house of c 1700. A similar larger group at Nos. 169-177 was demolished in 1902 for Stepney Green underground station.

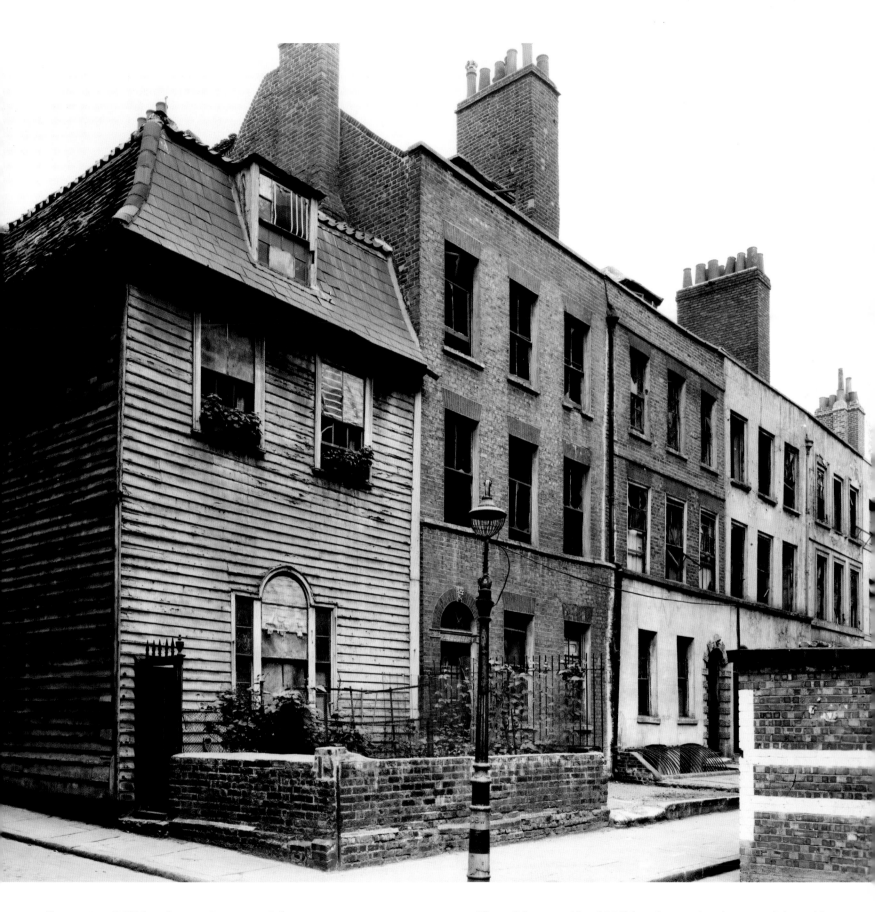

Above: 22-26 Wellclose Square, Stepney, 30 July 1943
Today it is difficult to comprehend the shabbiness of wartime London or the sheer scale of destruction. Many streets of once-fine Georgian houses were abandoned and boarded up after bomb damage.

View of the west side of Wellclose Square showing a surviving mid-18th century timber house with a fashionable Serlian window to the ground floor. Adjacent is a later 18th century derelict terrace with a wartime street shelter marked with white stripes for visibility in the blackout.

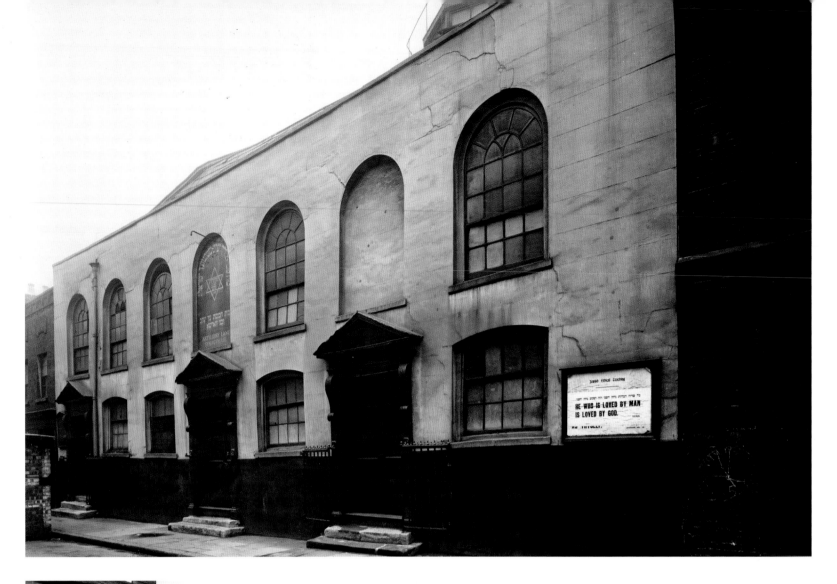

Dereliction

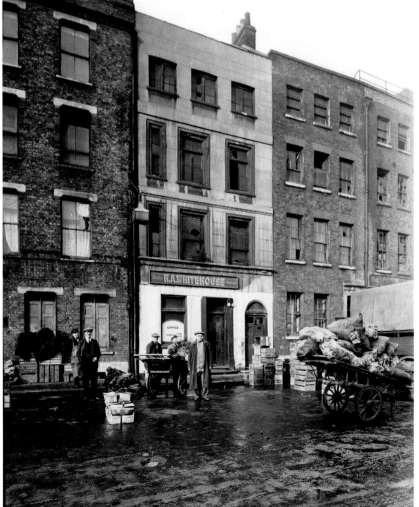

Above: Artillery Lane, Spitalfields, 11 February 1946
The old synagogue in Artillery Lane still survives, but has been converted to offices.

With its pedimented doorcases and simple arched windows, the building was a mid-18th century chapel which was adapted for use as a synagogue from 1896-1948, a common transmutation in the East End as Jewish immigration became a floodtide after the Russian pogroms. The stucco frontage was destroyed shortly after this photograph was taken, but it was later rebuilt in replica. The galleried interior has now gone, but the offset oval dome at roof level survives.

Left: 26 Steward Street, Stepney, 20 November 1944
Business often continued from semi-derelict buildings. In some districts of London it was difficult to find a single house with unbroken windows.

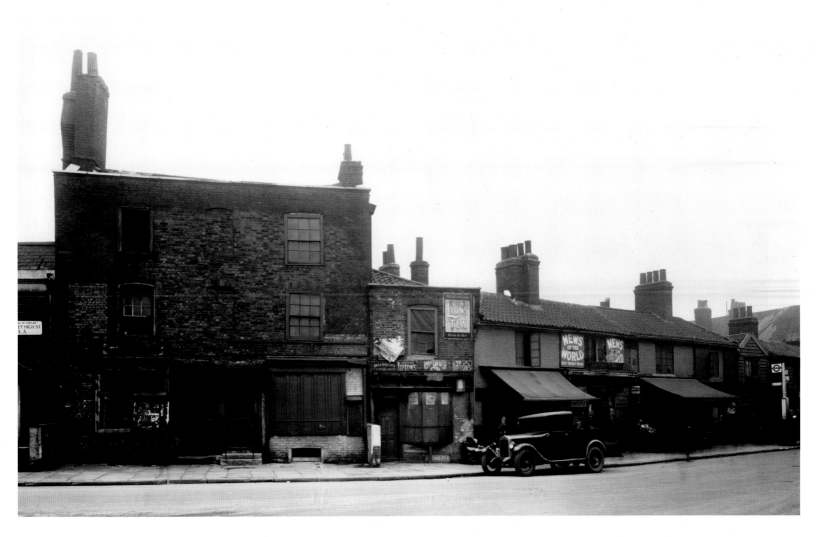

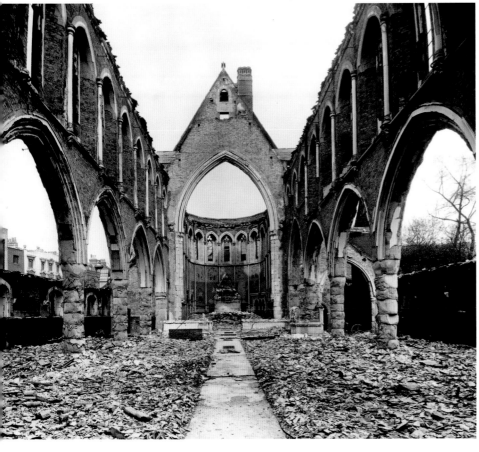

Above: 2-18 High Street, Bromley-by-Bow, 10 February 1943
Bow suffered extensive bomb damage. High Street, Bromley-by-Bow, contained a fascinating group of houses of varied dates. To the left is an early 18th century pair of brick houses next to a single storey building of the same date. To the extreme right is a row of rare 18th century timber houses. What survived the bombing was swept away by post-war comprehensive redevelopment, dispersing the community and eradicating local identity.

Left: St Mary Whitechapel, 9 May 1941
Site of the eponymous "White Chapel", St Mary Matfelon was a 13th century chapel of ease to St Dunstan, Stepney. The church was rebuilt several times, finally by Ernest Lee in 1875-77 in a 13th century style, its slender tower and spire a great East End landmark. After severe war damage, it was demolished in 1952 and its site cleared for Altab Ali Park.

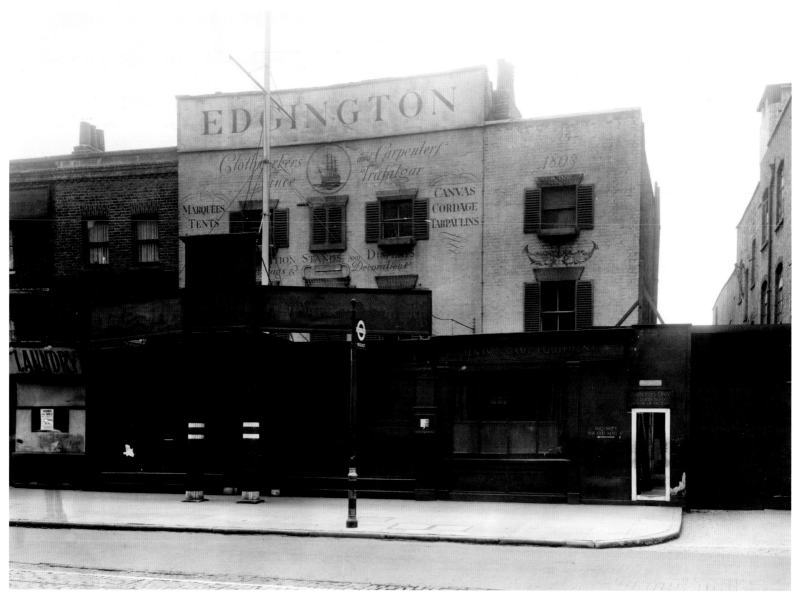

Above: 108 Old Kent Road, Bermondsey, 3 October 1945

Established in 1805, John Edgington & Co Ltd was renowned as a supplier of tents, awnings and sails, including the flags for HMS *Victory*. The huge mural over the entrance was a local landmark. Edgington's supplied tents and marquees for the Great Exhibition and equipped both David Livingstone and Scott of the Antarctic, before producing decoy tanks and shrouds for civilian casualties during the Second World War. On its demolition in 1967, the original shopfront was acquired for display at Woburn Abbey.

Right: 63-66 Grange Walk, Bermondsey, 29 April 1943

View of the rear elevation of a row of timber cottages c 1700. The lath and plaster can be seen clearly beneath the dilapidated weatherboarding. At first floor level are horizontal, sliding "Yorkshire" casements.

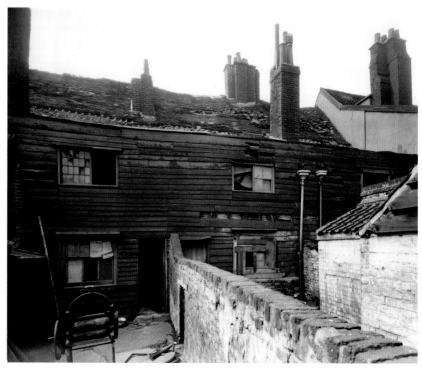

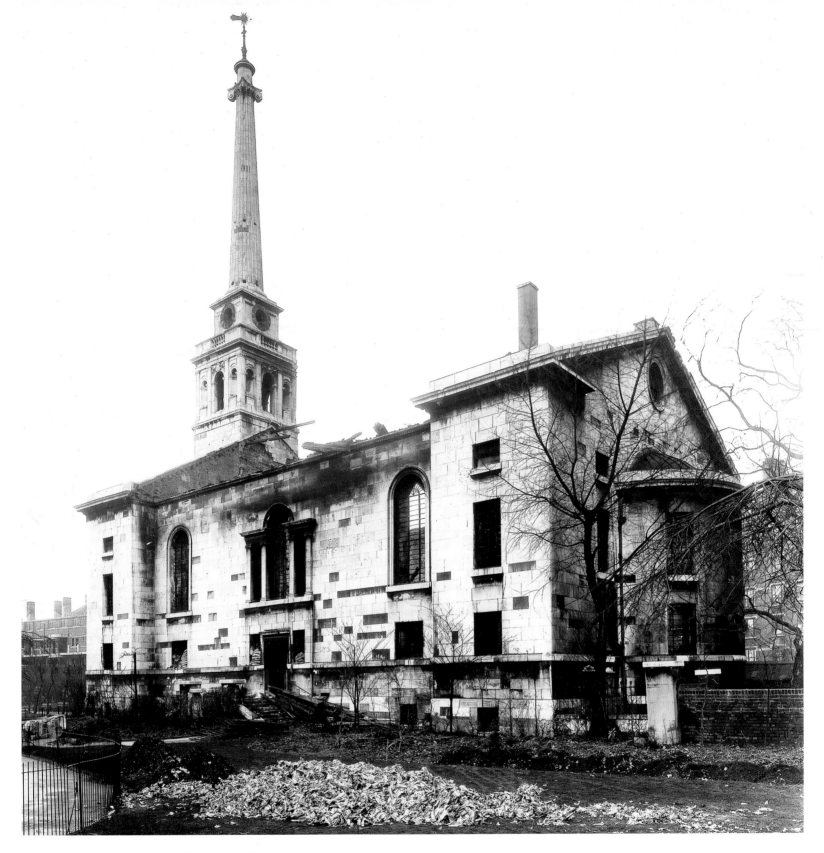

The Louse church

Above: St John's Horsleydown, Bermondsey, December 1940
St John's Horsleydown, just south of Tower Bridge, was one of London's most eccentric landmarks with a huge spire in the form of a fluted Ionic column crowned by a gilded weathervane shaped like a comet. From the ground this resembled a louse, so it was known for many years as the

"Louse Church". Designed by Nicholas Hawksmoor and John James in 1732, it was destroyed by an incendiary bomb in 1940. Sadly, the tower was taken down in 1948. The remaining ruins were cleared in 1972 for the construction of the London City Mission which stands on the crypt of the old church.

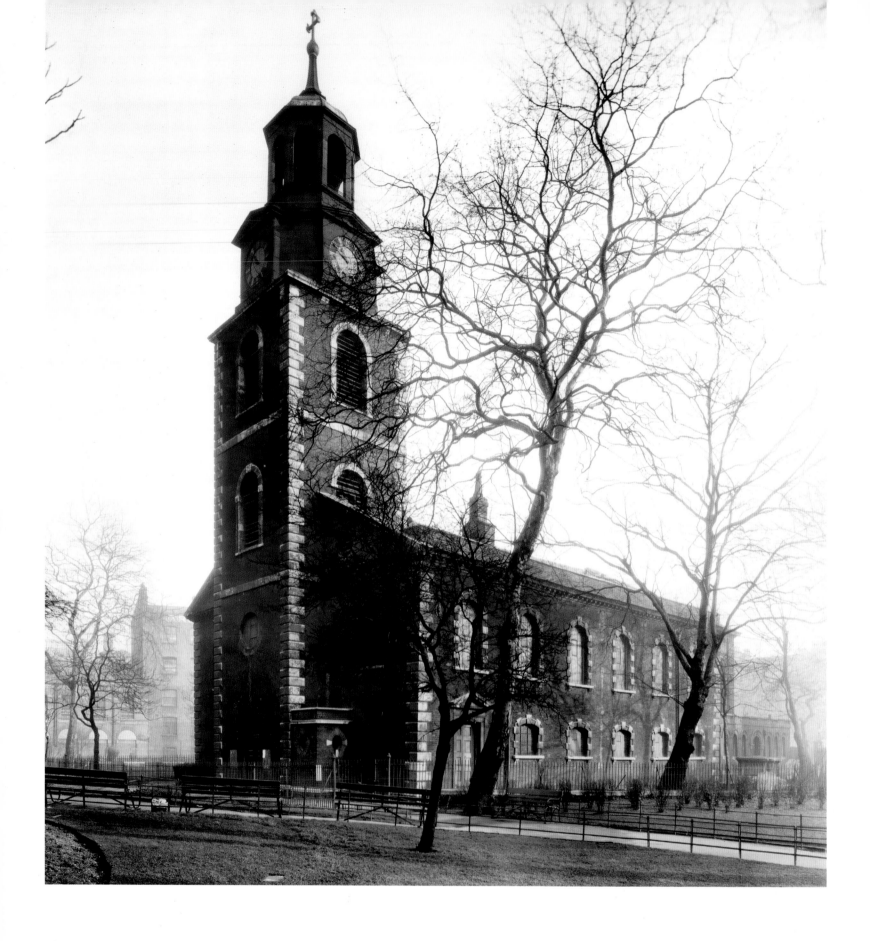

Above: Christ Church, Blackfriars Road, c 1940

Christ Church, Southwark, was rebuilt between 1738-41 on the site of an earlier church founded in 1671. Faced in brick with rusticated stone dressings, the church was plainly detailed with a tower surmounted by an octagonal timber clock turret and cupola. The entire building was consumed by fire following incendiary bombing on 16 April 1941, and later demolished for an unprepossessing post-war church.

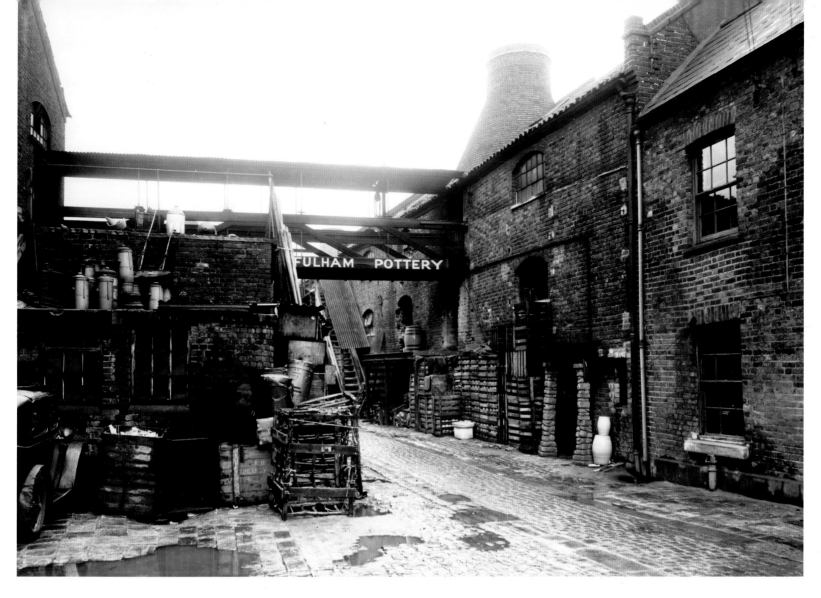

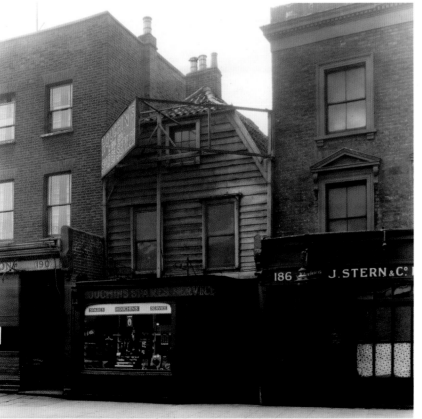

Above: 210 New Kings Road, Fulham, 5 December 1947
Richard Dwight was granted a patent for the manufacture of pottery and ceramics in 1672, and for over 250 years Fulham Pottery was an industrial site at the west end of New Kings Road. The site was redeveloped in 1979-80, but a 19th century bottle kiln with its characteristic domed profile was retained. It can still be seen alongside the new office block.

Left: 188 Peckham High Street, 28 July 1942
Situated only 2 miles from London Bridge, in the 18th century Peckham was a small village and place of resort that developed east-west around a crossroads. A handful of rare, one-room, timber-framed houses still survive, but No. 188 is not among them. It was demolished after the war.

INDEX

FOOTNOTES

1. Rasmussen, Steen Eiler: *London: The Unique City*, p224 (MIT Press, 1983)
2. London, Jack: *The People of the Abyss*, p135 (The Pluto Press, 2001)
3. Booth, Charles: *The Life and Labour of the People in London: Vol 1: Poverty* p.279 (Macmillan 1902)
4. Booth, Charles: *The Life and Labour of the People in London: Vol 1: Poverty* p.279 (Macmillan 1902)
5. *The Standard*: 1894
6. Booth, Charles: *The Streets of London: The Booth Notebooks – South East* p37 (Deptford Forum Publishing 1997)
7. Booth, Charles, *The Life and Labour of the People in London: Vol II: Poverty* p.83 (Macmillan 1902)
8. Booth, Charles, *The Life and Labour of the People in London: Vol II: Poverty* p.83 (Macmillan 1902)
9. Yee, Chiang: *The Silent Traveller in London* p61 (Signal Books 2002)
10. Yee, Chiang: *The Silent Traveller in London* quote p.59 (Signal Books 2002)
11. Booth, Charles: *The Life and Labour of the People in London: Vol 1 Poverty* p.172 (Macmillan 1902)
12. London, Jack: *The People of the Abyss*: p.138 (The Pluto Press 2001)
13. London, Jack: *The People of the Abyss*: p.162/163 (The Pluto Press 2001)
14. Davies, W H: *Autobiography of a Super Tramp*: p.224-225 (A. C. Fifield 1908)
15. Goldsmid, Howard J: *Dottings of a Dosser: Chapt 6 – The Borough* 1886
16. London, Jack: *The People of the Abyss* p.39 (The Pluto Press 2001)
17. London, Jack: *The People of the Abyss* p.31 (The Pluto Press 2001)
18. Booth, Charles: Beatrice Webb in *The Life and Labour of the People in London: Vol 1* p.583 (Macmillan 1889)
19. Ackroyd, Peter: *London: The Biography* p.680 (Chatto & Windus 2000)
20. Dickens, Charles: *The Uncommercial Traveller* p.227 (President Publishing Co, New York 1890)
21. Weightman, Gavin and Humphries, Steve: *The Making of Modern London 1815-1914* p.47 (Sedgewick & Jackson 1983)
22. Ashbee, C R: *Survey of London: Vol 1: Bromley-by-Bow* p.xxxii (P S King & Son, London 1900)
23. Ashbee, C R: *Survey of London: Vol 1: Bromley-by-Bow* p.xxxv (P S King & Son, London 1900)
24. Clunn, Harold: *London Rebuilt 1897-1927* p.11 (John Murray 1927)
25. Rasmussen, Steen Eiler: *London: The Unique City* p.404 (MIT Press 1983)
26. Booth, Charles: *The Life and Labour of the People in London: Vol 1: Poverty* p.227 (Macmillan 1902)
27. Waller, Maureen: *Life in the Debris of War* p.442 (St. Martin's Press 2005)
28. Edinger, George: *The Inn. Yesterday, to-day, to-morrow* GRAYA No. XXVII (27), Easter Term 1948, page 30
29. Rasmussen, Steen Eiler: *London: The Unique City* p.407 (MIT Press 1983)
30. Ashbee, C R: *Survey of London: Vol 1: Bromley-by-Bow* p.xxxvi (P S King & Son, London 1900)

THE PHOTOGRAPHS

With the exception of those listed below, all the photographs in this book were taken from the collection of the former Greater London Council Historic Buildings Division, which subsumed the print collection of its predecessor, the London County Council. On the abolition of the Greater London Council in 1984 the print collection was transferred to the London Region of English Heritage where it remains in daily use for reference purposes. The negatives are held by the London Metropolitan Archives. The illustrations in this book are protected by copyright and may only be reproduced by permission of English Heritage or the London Metropolitan Archives, depending on the source of the image.

English Heritage is also the repository of the National Monuments Record (NMR). This was formed in 1941 as the National Buildings Record for recording historic buildings threatened by enemy action during the Second World War. In 1963 it became part of the Royal Commission on the Historical Monuments of England, which merged with English Heritage in 1999. Based in Swindon, the NMR is the most comprehensive archive of the historic environment in Britain comprising over 10 million photographs, drawings, documents and reports.

The author wishes to thank the following for providing additional illustrations:

NATIONAL MONUMENTS RECORD:
p12 (Shad Thames)
p23 (Westminster Embankment)
p244 (Pool of London)
GUILDHALL LIBRARY:
p25 (Oxford Arms PH)
P27 (Sir Paul Pindar's House)
TOWER HAMLETS LOCAL LIBRARY AND ARCHIVES:
p14 (Cats' Meat Man)
p15 (Knocker-up)
P227 (Frozen Thames)
P228 (East India Dock Road)
IMPERIAL WAR MUSEUM:
p344 (Cat)

ACKNOWLEDGEMENTS

For many years I had hoped that others more qualified than I would take up the task of reviewing and publishing this extraordinary archive of photographs. But it was not to be.

In writing this book I have accumulated vast arrears in debts of gratitude. Many people have helped me with their own insights in to that most elusive of places – Lost London – but particular thanks are due to Greg Hill and Murray Mahon of Transatlantic Press, whose flair for design and detail has been exceeded only by their enthusiasm for the subject matter. John Hudson and Rob Richardson from English Heritage's Publications team worked hard to bring this long-standing project to fruition. I was fortunate to have two such eminent historians as Steven Brindle and Andrew Saint read the introduction and to receive advice on captions from Rory O'Donnell and John Martin Robinson. Patsy Davies offered some fascinating anecdotes and insights into life in Holborn from the 1920s onwards.

Staff at the Guildhall Library and London Metropolitan Archives were as helpful as always in providing me with leads for captions and in directing me to numerous useful sources. Among the unsung riches of London is its treasure trove of local history libraries and archives. Anne Wheelden at Hammersmith & Fulham, Jenny O'Keefe at Greenwich, Stephen Humphrey at Southwark and Malcolm barr-Hamilton at Tower Hamlets all offered invaluable advice and assistance, as did Robert Hodgson at Grays Inn Library. Staff at the National Monuments Record including Katherine Bryson, Lucinda Walker, Emma Whinton-Brown and Alyson Rogers were unfailingly helpful in unearthing material. Vijay Mehta and Steve Hurst of the London Region of English Heritage deserve particular thanks for recognising the value of the archive and for taking on the recataloguing and conservation of the collection.

None of this could have been achieved without the enthusiastic support and commitment of Jane Davies – the only living person with a listed memorial in London – whose passion for London remains a perpetual inspiration.

Finally, the greatest thanks of all must go to Sue Woods of English Heritage, whose organisational and word processing skills imposed clarity and order on an indecipherable manuscript.

BIBLIOGRAPHY

Ackroyd, Peter: *London: The Biography*, Chatto & Windus 2000

Betjeman, John: *Victorian & Edwardian London from Old Photographs*, Batsford 1970

Brindle, Steven with Grady, Damian: *Shot from Above: Aerial Aspects of London*, English Heritage 2007

Booth, Charles: *Life and Labour of the People in London*, Macmillan 1902

Bush, Graham: *Old London: photographed by Henry Dixon and A & J Bool for the Society of Photographing Relics of Old London*, Academy Editions 1975

Chancellor, E Beresford: *The Private Palaces of London*, Kegan Paul 1908

Chancellor, E Beresford: *The West End of Yesterday and Today*, The Architectural Press 1926

Clunn, Harold: *London Rebuilt*, John Murray 1927

Cooper, Nicholas: *The Opulent Eye*, Architectural Press 1976

Davidoff, Leonore: *The Best Circles*, Crown Helm 1973

Davies, Philip: *Troughs and Drinking Fountains*, Chatto & Windus 1989

Dickens, Charles: *The Uncommercial Traveller*, President 1890

Fishman, William J: *The Streets of East London*, Duckworth 1987

Gordon, Charles: *Old Time Aldwych, The Kingsway and Neighbourhood*, 1903

Guillery, Peter: *The Small House in 18th Century London*, English Heritage 2004

Harrison, Fraser: *The Dark Angel: Aspects of Victorian Sexuality*, Sheldon Press 1977

Hibbert, Christopher: *London*, Longmans, Green & Co 1969

Hobhouse, Hermione: *Lost London: A Century of Demolition and Decay*, Macmillan 1971

Howgego, James L: *Victorian & Edwardian City of London from Old Photographs*, Batsford 1977

Information, Ministry of: *What Britain Has Done 1939-45*, pub 1945

London, Jack: *The People of the Abyss*, London, 1903

Mearns, Andrew: *The Bitter Cry of Outcast London*, London 1883

Norman, Philip: *London Vanished and Vanishing*, A&C Black, 1905

Miele, Chris (ed): *From William Morris: Building Conservation and the Arts & Crafts Cult of Authenticity 1877-1939*, Yale University Press 2005

Pevsner, N: *The Buildings of England: London Volumes 1-6*, Yale

Preston, William C: *The Bitter Cry of Outcast London*, James Clarke & Co Ltd, 1883

Pulley, Judy: *Streets of the City*, Capital History 2006

Rasmussen, Steen Eiler: *London: The Unique City*, The MIT Press 1934

Royston Pike, E: *Human Documents of the Industrial Revolution in Britain*, Routledge 1966

Service, Alastair: *London 1900*, Granada 1979

Shelley, Henry: *Inns & Taverns of Old London*, Pitman 1909

Sheppard, Francis: *London 1808-1870: The Infernal Wen*, Secker & Warburg 1971

Stamp, Gavin: *The Changing Metropolis: Earliest Photographs of London 1839-1879*, Viking 1984

Stuart Gray, A: *Edwardian Architecture*, Wordsworth 1985

Summerson, John: *Georgian London*, Barrie & Jenkins 1988

Szreter, Simon and Mooney, Graham: *Urbanisation, mortality and the standard of living debate*, Economic History Review, Vol 51 February 1998

Survey of London: Various volumes

Thurston-Hopkins, R: *This London, Its Taverns, Haunts & Memories*, Cecil Palmer 1927

Walford, Edward: *Old and New London*, Cassell & Co 1897

Waller, Maureen: *Life in the Debris of War*, St Martin's Press 2005

Weightman, Gavin & Humphries, Steve: *The Making of Modern London 1815-1914*, Sidgwick & Jackson 1983

Weinreb, Ben & Hibbert, Christopher: *The London Encyclopaedia*, Macmillan 1983

Wheatley, Henry & Cunningham, Peter: *London Past & Present* (3 vols), John Murray 1891

White, Jerry: *London in the 20th Century*, Vintage Books: 2008

Whitehouse, Roger: *A London Album*, Secker & Warburg 1980

Williams, A E: *Barnado of Stepney*, Allen & Unwin 1943

Winder, Robert: *Bloody Foreigners*, Little, Brown 2004

Yee, Chiang: *The Silent Traveller in London*, 1938

O! London won't be London long,
For 'twill be all pulled down;
And I shall sing a funeral song
O'er that time-honoured town

Attributed to Maginn from *Lost London*,
J. Crowther and E. Beresford Chancellor 1926

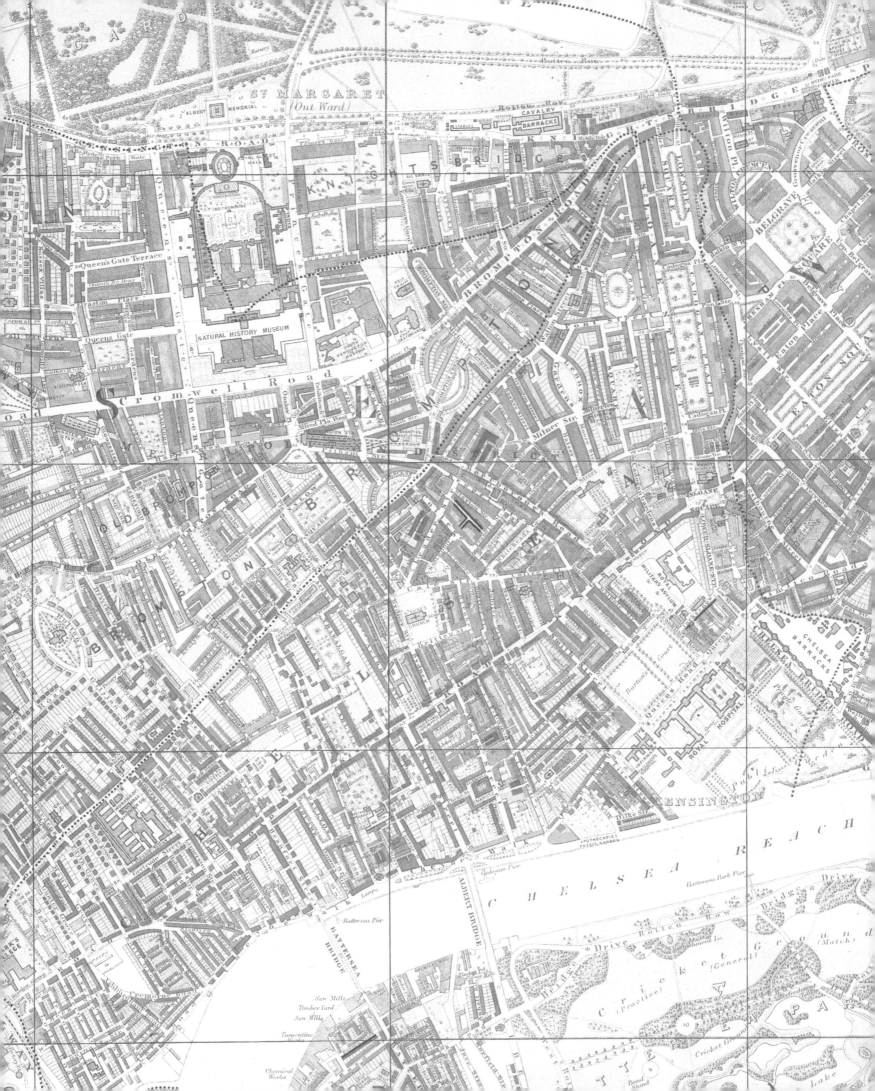